CRUCIFORMITY

CRUCIFORMITY

Paul's Narrative Spirituality of the Cross

Michael J. Gorman

WILLIAM B. EERDMANS PUBLISHING COMPANY
GRAND RAPIDS, MICHIGAN / CAMBRIDGE, U.K.

© 2001 Wm. B. Eerdmans Publishing Co.
All rights reserved

Wm. B. Eerdmans Publishing Co.
255 Jefferson Ave. S.E., Grand Rapids, Michigan 49503 /
P.O. Box 163, Cambridge CB3 9PU U.K.
www.eerdmans.com

Printed in the United States of America

05 04 03 02 01   7 6 5 4 3 2 1

Library of Congress Cataloging-in-Publication Data

Gorman, Michael J., 1955-
Cruciformity: Paul's narrative spirituality of the cross / Michael J. Gorman.
p.   cm.
Includes bibliographical references and index.
ISBN 0-8028-4795-1 (pbk.: alk. paper)
1. Bible. N.T. Epistles of Paul — Theology.
2. Jesus Christ — Crucifixion — Biblical teaching.
3. Paul, the Apostle, Saint — Contributions in theology of the cross.
I. Title.

BT453.G65   2001
227′.06 — dc21

2001023812

Unless otherwise noted, the Scripture quotations in this publication are from the New Revised Standard Version Bible, copyright © 1989 by the Division of Christian Education of the National Council of Churches of Christ in the U.S.A., and used by permission.

To My Family (Nancy, Mark, Amy, Brian) and My Students,

who have taught me much about the apostle Paul,

and about cruciformity

CONTENTS

CONTENTS

ACKNOWLEDGMENTS

I was fortunate to begin the formal study of the apostle Paul with excellent teachers in college, seminary, and graduate school: John Herzog, Bruce Metzger, the late J. Christiaan Beker, Paul Meyer, David Adams, Cullen Story, Betty Edwards, and Martin de Boer. Special thanks are due to Paul Meyer and Martin de Boer, who began and completed, respectively, the supervision of my doctoral dissertation on Paul in the 1980s. Both Martin and Bruce Metzger saw this book in draft form and responded favorably to it.

Two friends and fellow interpreters of Paul, Richard Hays (Duke University Divinity School) and Steve Fowl (Loyola College in Maryland), encouraged me in the writing of the book at different stages, and for that I am very grateful. Richard reacted positively to the thesis of the work when it was little more than a title and outline. Steve, now also my part-time colleague at the Ecumenical Institute of Theology, graciously read and commented carefully on the entire manuscript in draft form, for which I am especially thankful.

Over the last decade, my students at St. Mary's Seminary and University, in both the School of Theology and the Ecumenical Institute of Theology, have inspired me to think about and live with the apostle Paul. I especially acknowledge the following current and former students who reacted with care and interest to this book at various stages as it progressed: Zenaida Bench, Sandra Dagdigian, Steve Gemme, Jason Glover, Joe Jaffa, Betty Kansler, Patrick Keane, Mary Kurek, Jim Lentini, Rob Noland, Mark O'Hern, Jim Poppo, Tom Servatius, Marc Stockton, other members of classes on Paul, and especially Bob Anderson. Also during this time, my research assistants, Rev. Shawn Hill, Karen Wenell (now a Ph.D. student in Glasgow), George Gannon, and especially Bill Garrison, assisted in a variety of ways, for which

ix

ACKNOWLEDGMENTS

I am also very grateful. In addition, several faculty colleagues have been very encouraging, particularly Fr. Paul Zilonka.

Without the assistance of the courteous staff members at St. Mary's Knott Library, especially Mary Cay Reynolds and John Hanson, the research for this book could not have been completed, and thus I express my thanks also to them. My niece, Stacy Feldstein, assisted in proofreading and preparing the indexes, as did my colleague Pat Fosarelli and my friend Karen White.

Finally, I acknowledge with deep gratitude my family. All of my children, Mark, Amy, and Brian, helped with the proofreading and indexing. Above all, however, I remain thankful for the pursuit of cruciform faith, love, power, and hope that I have seen in them and most especially in my wife, Nancy.

Good Friday, 2001

ABBREVIATIONS

BAGD   W. Bauer, W. F. Arndt, F. W. Gingrich, and F. W. Danker. *Greek-English Lexicon of the New Testament and Other Early Christian Literature*. 2nd ed. Chicago: University of Chicago Press, 1979.

HDR   Harvard Dissertations in Religion

JSNTSup   Journal for the Study of the New Testament: Supplement Series

KJV   King James Version

NCB   New Century Bible

NIBC   New International Biblical Commentary

NICNT   New International Commentary on the New Testament

NIV   New International Version

NRSV   New Revised Standard Version

OBT   Overtures to Biblical Theology

RSV   Revised Standard Version

SBLDS   Society of Biblical Literature Dissertation Series

SNTSMS   Society for New Testament Studies Monograph Series

TDNT   G. Kittel and G. Friedrich, eds. *Theological Dictionary of the New Testament*. Translated by G. W. Bromiley. 10 vols. Grand Rapids: Eerdmans, 1964-76.

INTRODUCTION

I n an extraordinarily self-revealing remark, Paul makes the following claim as he writes to the Corinthian church he had founded:

> I decided to know nothing among you except Jesus Christ and him crucified. (1 Cor. 2:2)

The Greek word translated "and" may be better rendered "even" or "that is" in this context, yielding the following translation:

> I decided to know nothing among you except Jesus Christ — that is, Jesus Christ *crucified*. (1 Cor. 2:2)

In context, "to know" means something like "to experience and to announce in word and deed." This is a startling claim from Paul; he seems narrowly focused on Christ's cross, yet he asserts that this narrow vision is *comprehensive*, sufficient both during the time of his original presence among the Corinthians and again, it is implied, during the time of his presence by proxy — his pastoral correspondence.

In his magisterial work of a generation ago, *On Being a Christian*, Hans Küng said this of Paul's cross-centered focus:

> Paul succeeded more clearly than anyone in expressing what is *the ultimately distinguishing feature* of Christianity. . . . The distinguishing feature of Christianity as opposed to the ancient world religions and the modern humanisms . . . is quite literally according to Paul "this Jesus Christ, Jesus Christ *crucified*."

1

Spirituality

It is not indeed as risen, exalted, living, divine, but as crucified, that this Jesus Christ is distinguished unmistakably from the many risen, exalted, living gods and deified founders of religion, from the Caesars, geniuses, and heroes of world history.[1]

It is well known that the idea of a crucified messiah, savior, or deity was ludicrous to Jews and non-Jews alike in antiquity. Paradoxically, however, the early Christians found in the crucified Jesus, now raised and exalted, both the "power of God and the wisdom of God," as Paul put it (1 Cor. 1:24), and a model of humility, self-sacrifice, and suffering worthy of imitation. Paul's spiritual experience was not part of "mainstream" religion, comfortably situated in the center of his social world. He was, rather, well off-center — eccentric (literally, "out of the center"). As Paul himself admitted, identifying with the cross made him and his colleagues into eccentrics, "fools for the sake of Christ" (1 Cor. 4:10). In spite of (or is it because of?) its oddity, the notion of the crucified and exalted Messiah became, in the words of Wayne Meeks, "one of the most powerful symbols that has ever appeared in the history of religions," and "no one seems to have recognized its generative potential so quickly and so comprehensively as Paul and his associates."[2]

The title of this book, *Cruciformity: Paul's Narrative Spirituality of the Cross,* is admittedly somewhat unusual. Some initial definitions of the terms may be helpful before proceeding.

"Spirituality" is a slippery word, one that is both difficult to define with precision and subject to a wide variety of understandings. In many circles today, it is associated with vague feelings of purposefulness or serenity and disassociated from religion, especially from religious community. Even in religious environments, however, "spirituality" is often understood as vague emotion without substantive content, or as an experience that can neither be validated nor challenged.[3]

One standard definition of spirituality in a Christian context is "the lived experience of Christian belief."[4] As a starting point for the understanding of

---

1. Hans Küng, *On Being a Christian* (Garden City, N.Y.: Doubleday, 1976), pp. 409-10; emphasis in the original.

2. Wayne A. Meeks, *The First Urban Christians: The Social World of the Apostle Paul* (New Haven: Yale University Press, 1983), p. 180.

3. For an insightful critique of some of these trends and their proponents, see L. Gregory Jones, "A Thirst for God or Consumer Spirituality? Cultivating Disciplined Practices of Being Engaged by God," *Modern Theology* 13 (1997): 3-28.

4. This is the substance of the "working definition" used in the preparation of Bernard McGinn and John Meyendorff, eds., *Christian Spirituality: Origins to the Twelfth Century* (New

2

spirituality as adopted in this book, we may describe it as the experience of God's love and grace in daily life. This experience includes both receiving love and responding in love. *Spirituality* can also be described, of course, as life in the Spirit. For Christians it can equally be explained as life with and in Christ, in whom the love and grace of God are most fully revealed and experienced. For Christians, spirituality is a relationship with the triune God that impacts their daily life with others. For almost 2000 years, thanks to Paul, it has been described as a life of faith, hope, and love (1 Cor. 13:13). It thus has definable content and shape. Although Paul clearly did not have a "full-blown" Trinitarian theology, we will see that his experience of God can be fairly characterized as Trinitarian.

One other important thing needs to be said about the word "spirituality" in the title: it has been deliberately chosen as an alternative to "theology." Scholars frequently depict Paul as a theologian, which he certainly was, and likely even "the first and greatest Christian theologian."[5] Not only was he a theologian, but, because of the centrality of his experience of the cross to his theology, he was more consistent and systematic in his theological convictions and affirmations than he is often thought to have been. Yet most accounts of Paul the theologian and of Paul's theology pay insufficient attention to his religious experience — his spirituality — and to his fondness for narrating that experience. This inattention to religious experience is a significant blind spot in New Testament scholarship generally, as Luke Johnson has rightly indicated.[6]

With respect to Paul, however, this missing element is particularly odd. Paul's correspondence narrates and interprets the experience of the apostle and the communities to which he writes.[7] There is no "arm-chair theology" pre-

---

York: Crossroad, 1985), p. xv. I am indebted to Dr. Elizabeth Patterson for steering me to this definition.

5. This quotation is from the first sentence of James D. G. Dunn's magisterial work, *The Theology of Paul the Apostle* (Grand Rapids: Eerdmans, 1998), p. 2. By "greatest" Dunn means in part "most influential" (pp. 3-4).

6. Luke Timothy Johnson, *Religious Experience in Earliest Christianity: A Missing Dimension of New Testament Studies* (Minneapolis: Fortress, 1998); and Luke Timothy Johnson with Todd C. Penner, *The New Testament Writings: An Interpretation*, rev. ed. (Minneapolis: Fortress, 1999), pp. 93-104. It should be stressed that James Dunn, quoted above, is among those who *have not* neglected the role of experience in considering Paul as theologian. Indeed, Dunn defines theology so that it is not the antithesis of "religion" or religious experience, but "in a more rounded way, as talk about God and all that is involved in and follows directly from such talk, including not least the interaction between belief and praxis. . . . A theology remote from everyday living would not be a theology of Paul" (*Theology*, p. 9).

7. Reading Paul's letters from this perspective can be dramatically eye-opening. Even a letter such as Romans is fundamentally about experience — that of Paul, his readers, Jews, Gentiles, and the human race.

served in the letters, nor is there primarily "critical reflection on religious experience" — one possible definition of theology. The purpose of Paul's letters generally, and of the various kinds of narratives within them, is not to teach theology but to mold behavior, to affirm or — more often — to alter patterns of living, patterns of experience. The purpose of his letters, in other words, is pastoral or spiritual before it is theological. Today we might speak of his goal as spiritual formation; indeed, Paul himself uses the metaphor of fetal development to describe his ongoing ministry with the Galatians (Gal. 4:19). It is appropriate, therefore, to consider Paul first and foremost as a pastoral or spiritual writer, rather than as a theologian (or ethicist).[8]

The notion of *narrative* spirituality may at first seem odd. The expressions "narrative theology" and "narrative ethics" are commonplace theological terms today, but perhaps not so "narrative spirituality." By it I mean a spirituality that tells a story, a dynamic life with God that corresponds in some way to the divine "story." The importance of narrative for Paul has been increasingly noticed by biblical scholars in recent years.[9] Applying it to his spirituality will seem appropriate once the specific character of Paul's spirituality is understood.

The first and most important word in the title, "cruciformity," is my own term for a concept commonly believed to be central to Paul's theology and ethics: conformity to the crucified Christ.[10] It will be the task of this book to un-

---

8. Raymond Pickett, in *The Cross in Corinth: The Social Significance of the Death of Jesus*, JSNTSup 143 (Sheffield: Sheffield Academic Press, 1997), rightly points out that "[s]cholarship on the death of Jesus in Paul has largely been preoccupied with questions of . . . what Paul *thought* about its significance" (p. 13), whereas Pickett himself appropriately seeks to "move beyond the ideas represented by the symbol of the crucified messiah to a consideration of the social norms and values which it supports" (p. 31).

9. For example, Richard B. Hays, "Crucified with Christ: A Synthesis of the Theology of 1 and 2 Thessalonians, Philemon, Philippians, and Galatians," in Jouette M. Bassler, ed., *Pauline Theology*, vol. 1: *Thessalonians, Philippians, Galatians, Philemon* (Minneapolis: Fortress, 1991), 227-46; Richard B. Hays, *The Faith of Jesus Christ: An Investigation of the Narrative Substructure of Galatians 3:1–4:11*, SBLDS 56 (Chico, Calif.: Scholars Press, 1983); Stephen E. Fowl, *The Story of Christ in the Ethics of Paul: An Analysis of the Function of the Hymnic Material in the Pauline Corpus*, JSNTSup 36 (Sheffield: JSOT Press, 1990); Ben Witherington III, *Paul's Narrative Thought World: The Tapestry of Tragedy and Triumph* (Louisville: Westminster/John Knox, 1994).

10. Until very recently, I believed that I had actually coined this term. I have discovered, however, that my colleague Eric W. Gritsch used the term in two articles more than twenty years ago (see "Defenders of Cruciformity — Detectors of Idolatry: The Case of Sixteenth-Century Restitutionists," *Katallagete* 6 [1977]: 10-14; and "The Church as Institution: From Doctrinal Pluriformity to Magisterial Mutuality," *Journal of Ecumenical Studies* 16 [1979]: 448-56, where the term refers to the Church's condition between Christ's first and second comings). In addition, my student Bill Garrison has found on the Internet that the term is used by at least one

cover what Paul means by conformity to the crucified Christ, showing that this conformity is a dynamic correspondence in daily life to the strange story of Christ crucified as the primary way of experiencing the love and grace of God. Cruciformity is, in other words, Paul's oddly inviting, even compelling, narrative spirituality. It is, as the subtitle says, a spirituality of the cross — the focus of his gospel and life. Paul's mission in life was to seek to "order the lives of Christian congregations by pulling everything into the tremendous gravitational field of the cross."[11]

In contemplating Paul's spirituality of "the cross," finally, we must never forget the meaning of crucifixion during the *pax Romana*.[12] Crucifixion was first-century Rome's most insidious and intimidating instrument of power and political control — "the most miserable [or pitiable] of deaths," "the worst extreme of the tortures inflicted upon slaves," an "accursed thing" or "plague."[13] It was Rome's torturous, violent method of handling those who were perceived to threaten the empire's "peace and security"; everyone in the empire knew of the "terror of the cross."[14] To suffer crucifixion was to suffer the most shameful death possible. Moreover, for Jews a crucified person was a person cursed, since "anyone hung on a tree is under God's curse" (Deut. 21:23). It was therefore an inherently absurd and offensive[15] move on the part of early Christians, Paul included, to make a crucified political criminal and his cross — "the most nonreligious and horrendous feature of the gospel"[16] — the focus of devotion and the paradigm for life in this world. Since this world was indeed the world of the *pax Romana*, centering on the cross was also an inherently anti-imperial posture that unashamedly challenged the priorities and values of the political, social, and religious status quo. The modern interpreter of Paul, who has no firsthand experience of either the horrors or the political function of crucifixion, is obligated to recall this reality deliberately and frequently while reading Paul's letters.

---

church to refer to its emphasis on conformity to Christ, and it has a publication called "Cruciformity." To the best of my knowledge, however, the term has not previously been used in the discussion of Paul, although the adjective "cruciform" is often used.

11. Neil Elliott, *Liberating Paul: The Justice of God and the Politics of the Apostle* (Maryknoll, N.Y.: Orbis, 1994), p. 93.

12. See Martin Hengel, *Crucifixion*, trans. John Bowden (London: SCM, 1977).

13. Josephus, *Jewish War (Bellum Judaicum)* 7.203 (Greek *oiktiston*), and Cicero, *Against Verres (In Verrem)* 2.5.66 and 2.5.62 (Latin *pestem*), respectively. In context Cicero does not mean that Rome would never use crucifixion for anyone other than slaves, but that only the lowest deserved its cruelty (and certainly never a Roman citizen).

14. Cicero, *In Defense of Rabirius (Pro Rabirio)* 5.16.

15. A "stumbling block" and "foolishness" according to 1 Cor. 1:23.

16. J. Christiaan Beker, *Paul the Apostle: The Triumph of God in Life and Thought* (Philadelphia: Fortress, 1980), p. 207.

This book will not be a full treatment of either Paul's theology of the cross or of his "religious experience." For the latter topic, one may begin by consulting part three of James Dunn's superb *Jesus and the Spirit,* which considers the religious experience of Paul and his churches.[17] For the former, readers will profit from Charles Cousar's *A Theology of the Cross: The Death of Jesus in the Pauline Letters.*[18]

The aims of this book, which focuses on the intersection of Paul's experience and the cross, are rather different from the goals of these excellent works. It is intended both for students and others with some familiarity with Paul's letters, on the one hand, as well as more advanced readers, on the other. (Newcomers to the study of Paul may also find it beneficial, though they may wish to avoid the notes.) The first four chapters examine Paul's experience of God — Father, Son, Spirit, and three-in-one. The purpose of these chapters is not to be comprehensive but to show how this experience of God is centered on the cross.[19] The meaning of the cross for Paul as God's act and Christ's act is then examined in chapter five. The bulk of the work is devoted to Paul's experience of the cross as faith (chapters six and seven), love (chapters eight through ten), power (chapter eleven), and hope (chapter twelve). Many of the texts and themes discussed briefly in chapters one through five are explored more fully in chapters six through twelve. Chapter thirteen considers Paul's experience and vision of the Church as a community of cruciformity. A concluding chapter looks at some contemporary challenges to, and some challenges of, cruciformity.[20]

A brief word about the topics considered in chapters six through twelve — cruciform faith, love, power, and hope — is in order. Readers familiar with Paul

---

17. James D. G. Dunn, *Jesus and the Spirit: A Study of the Religious and Charismatic Experience of Jesus and the First Christians as Reflected in the New Testament* (London: SCM, 1975; reprint, Grand Rapids: Eerdmans, 1997), pp. 199-342.

18. Charles B. Cousar, *A Theology of the Cross: The Death of Jesus in the Pauline Letters,* OBT (Minneapolis: Fortress, 1990). For a concise, insightful treatment, see John T. Carroll and Joel B. Green, "'Nothing but Christ and Him Crucified': Paul's Theology of the Cross," in *The Death of Jesus in Early Christianity* (Peabody, Mass.: Hendrickson, 1995), pp. 113-32. This chapter is based, in turn, on Joel B. Green, "Death of Christ," in Gerald F. Hawthorne et al., eds., *Dictionary of Paul and His Letters* (Downers Grove, Ill.: InterVarsity, 1992), pp. 146-63.

19. There are other legitimate approaches to structuring an analysis of Paul's spirituality. One helpful approach looks at Paul's "mysticism" in terms of "the new creation (individual dimension)"; "all of you are one in Christ Jesus (community dimension)"; "for a deeper understanding of him (intellectual dimension)"; "to walk in a new life (ethical dimension)"; and "we will always be with the Lord (eschatological dimension)." See Romano Penna, "Problems and Nature of Pauline Mysticism," in *Paul the Apostle: Wisdom and Folly of the Cross,* trans. Thomas P. Wahl (Collegeville, Minn.: Liturgical, 1996), pp. 235-73.

20. Readers interested only in an overview of Paul's spirituality and its possible contemporary relevance may wish to read the first five and the last two chapters.

will immediately recognize his well-known triad of faith, hope, and love, supplemented with a fourth, power. As chapter five will demonstrate, these topics correspond to narrative patterns about the significance of the cross that appear in Paul's letters.

Quite coincidentally, asking what a biblical text says about faith, love, and hope (in that order) corresponds to an ancient Christian way of reading the Scriptures that flourished in the Middle Ages (from Augustine to Luther) and is enjoying something of a renaissance in the present. This approach asks not merely what a text says but also what it enjoins us to believe (faith), to do (love), and to anticipate (hope).[21] This "coincidence" derives in large measure, of course, from the influence of Paul's triad of faith, hope, and love on the Christian theological and interpretive tradition.

The addition of "power" to faith, love, and hope is appropriate for several reasons. First, power is central to early Christian experience generally and to Paul's spirituality of the cross specifically. Second, the exercise of power is often popularly thought to be in contradiction to love, so the relationship of power to love in Paul needs to be explored (which is why the chapter on power follows the chapters on love). Finally, living after Nietzsche, for whom power was the most important human experience, and living in an age when all relations among people are frequently characterized as power-relations, we simply cannot avoid the topic. To ask a text what it says about power, in addition to faith, hope, and love, seems fitting for both Paul's context and ours.

For Paul, "to know nothing except Jesus Christ — that is, Jesus Christ crucified," is to narrate, in life and words, the story of God's self-revelation in Christ. We attempt in this book, then, to understand Paul's experience of God, mediated by the cross of Christ, as one of cruciform faith, love, power, and hope, and to do so with an eye on how that experience may challenge us today.[22]

---

21. The technical terms for the parts of this fourfold approach to Scripture are the literal, the allegorical (what we are to believe), the tropological or moral (what we are to do), and the anagogical (what we are to hope for). For a brief introduction, see Robert M. Grant with David Tracy, *A Short History of the Interpretation of the Bible*, 2nd ed. (Philadelphia: Fortress, 1984), pp. 83-91, especially pp. 85-86. The actual number (three, four, or more), order, and meaning of the dimensions of this "fourfold" approach varied among theologians and spiritual writers. See Henri de Lubac, *Medieval Exegesis*, vol. 1: *The Four Senses of Scripture*, trans. Mark Sebanc (Grand Rapids: Eerdmans, 1998).

22. The reader should note that I base my analysis on the seven "undisputed" letters of Paul, that is, those concerning which there is no serious scholarly debate about their being written by Paul: Romans, 1 and 2 Corinthians, Galatians, Philippians, 1 Thessalonians, and Philemon. Occasional references to parallel texts in the disputed letters will be made.

CHAPTER 1

THE CRUCIFORM GOD

Paul's Experience of "The Father of Our Lord Jesus Christ"

Knowing God — having an appropriately awe-filled yet intimate relationship, or partnership, with the creator, redeemer of Israel, and sovereign of the universe — is and was the life goal of faithful Jews.[1] It was no less so for Paul. Paul characterizes himself as zealous — both before and after his first experience of Jesus as Messiah — in his pursuit of the means to this knowledge of God and its corresponding life of obedience. The initial and ongoing encounter with Jesus, however, reformulated his understanding of who God is and how God is most fully experienced. That the Messiah, God's Son, was sent by God to be crucified, and then raised by God, meant that somehow *God and the cross were inextricably interrelated.* This connection led Paul to see not only Jesus, but also God the "Father of our Lord Jesus Christ," as defined by the cross. How did this connection occur, and what impact did it have on Paul?

Paul's Knowledge of God

As a faithful Jew, Paul knew God as the one God and creator of all, and as the faithful, merciful God of the covenant. After coming to the conviction that Je-

---

1. Walter Brueggemann notes that the Old Testament witness always portrays the God of Israel (Yahweh) as "Yahweh-in-relation," and that there are four parties "connected" to Yahweh as partners: Israel, all individual human persons, the nations, and creation (*Theology of the Old Testament* [Minneapolis: Fortress, 1997], pp. 408-12). Israel, of course, has a special partnership with God, such that "in a very general way the character and destiny of human persons [especially Jews but also non-Jews] replicates and reiterates the character and destiny of Israel" (p. 451).

sus was God's promised Messiah, Paul of course still related to God as creator:

> For from him [God/the Lord] and through him and to him are all things. To him be the glory forever. Amen. (Rom. 11:36)

Paul alludes to the Jewish shema, or confession of God's oneness (Deut. 6:4), when addressing problems perceived by some in Corinth as idolatrous (1 Cor. 8:7, 10).[2] He does so also when asserting justification by faith for Jews and Gentiles alike, since God, as one, is the God of the Gentiles as well as the Jews (Rom. 3:29-30).[3] Paul continued also to relate to God as covenant-maker and covenant-keeper. Indeed, he did so with renewed vigor, as Romans most clearly demonstrates:

> [3]What if some were unfaithful? Will their faithlessness nullify the faithfulness of God? [4]By no means! Although everyone is a liar, let God be proved true, as it is written, "So that you [God] may be justified in your words, and prevail in your judging." (Rom. 3:3-4)

> [1]I ask, then, has God rejected his people? By no means! I myself am an Israelite, a descendant of Abraham, a member of the tribe of Benjamin. [2]God has not rejected his people whom he foreknew. (Rom. 11:1-2a)

> . . . for the gifts and the calling of God are irrevocable. (Rom. 11:29)

As an apostle of this God, Paul also continued the Jewish tradition, found for instance in some of the psalms, of referring to God with the personal pronoun "my." In the opening prayers of his letters, Paul frequently thanks "my God" for the people to whom he writes (Rom. 1:8; 1 Cor. 1:4; Phil. 1:3; Philem. 4). Paul's sense of personal relationship with God is expressed also in his conviction that "my God may humble me" (2 Cor. 12:21) and that "my God will satisfy every need of yours according to his riches in glory in Christ Jesus" (Phil. 4:19).

Paul can summarize the believer's spiritual experience as "knowing God"

---

2. With other Hellenistic Jews, Paul shares "the fundamental, polemical theme that the diaspora ['dispersed,' or non-Palestinian] synagogue disputed with Hellenism: uncompromising monotheism that stood alone in a world of Roman-Hellenistic religion with its tolerant, syncretistic attitude" (Jürgen Becker, *Paul: Apostle to the Gentiles*, trans. O. C. Dean, Jr. [Louisville: Westminster/John Knox, 1993], p. 43).

3. There is in Paul a heightened awareness of the Jewish conviction of God's impartiality. See Terence L. Donaldson, *Paul and the Gentiles: Remapping the Apostle's Convictional World* (Minneapolis: Fortress, 1997), pp. 88-93. See also Jouette Bassler, *Divine Impartiality: Paul and a Theological Axiom*, SBLDS 59 (Chico, Calif.: Scholars Press, 1982).

(Gal. 4:9a), or better, as "being known by God" (Gal. 4:9b; cf. 1 Cor. 13:12). This language also continues the biblical tradition that speaks of knowing God. For Paul this is clearly an intimate knowledge: his goal is one day to know "even as I have been fully known" (1 Cor. 13:12). Yet for Paul, God is known in Christ; "Christ is determined by God himself as the place where God can be known."[4]

Knowing God Anew in Jesus as "Father"

When Paul encountered Jesus, his Jewish experience of the faithful, righteous, and merciful God of Israel was deepened and broadened.[5] However, one significant change in his knowledge of God occurred. Now, Paul had experienced God in Jesus, and he, like all early Christians, had to find language to articulate both the relationship between God and Jesus and the believers' experience of that relationship. Paul seems to have drawn upon early Christian worship — prayers, hymns, and creeds — to understand and express his new knowledge of God as Father: Father of Jesus Christ the Son, and Father, through "adoption," of all who have faith that Jesus is God's Son and Messiah.

Paul was most likely indebted to his Jewish heritage and to early Christian worship traditions, such as short creeds or confessional statements, in his understanding of Jesus the Messiah as the Son of God. The terminology of "Son of God" itself naturally implied God's fatherhood of the Son. This was derived from, and reinforced by, the biblical and Jewish tradition of referring to the king, and later the Messiah, as God's Son and thus to God as the father of the king/Messiah (see, e.g., Psalm 2). Paul, apparently echoing early Christian acclamations, speaks of God sending his (or, with emphasis, his *own*) Son in Galatians 4:4 and Romans 8:3. Similarly, in Romans 8:32 he speaks of God "not withhold[ing, sparing] his own Son."[6] Some fifteen times in the undisputed Pauline letters Paul refers to Jesus as God's (own) Son (eleven times), the Son of

---

4. Becker, *Paul*, p. 378, referring to 2 Cor. 4:6: "For it is the God who said, 'Let light shine out of darkness,' who has shone in our hearts to give the light of the knowledge of the glory of God in the face of Jesus Christ."

5. Donaldson, *Paul and the Gentiles*, pp. 81-100.

6. It has sometimes been suggested, for theological reasons, that God did not send the Son to be crucified or to die, but only to be obedient, the result of which was his crucifixion. Although on one level this is true, even for Paul, Paul states emphatically that Christ's death was the will and act of God (e.g., in addition to Rom. 8:3-4, 32 and Gal. 4:4-5, see Rom. 3:25; 4:25; 5:8). As we will see, it is crucial for Paul's understanding of the cross that it be an expression of *God's* love and faithfulness as well as Christ's. Otherwise, the cross is neither the divine solution to sin nor the self-revelation of God.

God (three times), or the Son (once).[7] In addition, Paul refers to God as "the God and Father of our/the Lord Jesus [Christ]."[8]

This early Christian identification of Jesus as God's Son and God as Jesus' Father was fueled by Jesus' habit of referring and praying to God as his Father — "Abba," in Jesus' language of Aramaic.[9] The predecessors of Paul, in turn, most likely followed the practice of Jesus in calling God their "Father," too. That Paul twice preserves the Aramaic word "Abba" suggests this continuity from Jesus to the earliest Christians to Paul (Rom. 8:15; Gal. 4:6). Although there was some Jewish precedent for an experience of God as "father" (e.g. Hos. 11:1), biblical and early Jewish sources suggest that this image was not as central to Jewish life and worship as others. Nevertheless, although Israel's experience of God as father is not pervasive in Judaism, the contours of the experience are those of Jesus and Paul: God is the one who provides for his children/heirs, and who is owed honor and obedience.[10]

When Paul speaks of God, especially when referring to God while greeting fellow Christians with an invocation of divine grace and peace, or otherwise praying, he repeatedly uses phrases like "God our Father," "our God and Father," "God the Father," or simply "the Father."[11] In corporate worship, in private prayer, and in invoking God's blessing in written form, Paul experiences God as Father. God is the benevolent Father of all believers and of each community, in contrast to pagan gods and rulers. As Father, God has a family, replacing the gods as the head of a new "race" and the emperor as the community's *pater familias*, or head of the (universal) household.[12] Paul therefore sees himself and all other believers — Gentiles as well as Jews — as God's children.

For Paul, however, possessing this status of "children of God" comes not by

---

7. Rom. 1:3-4, 9; 5:10; 8:3, 29, 32; 1 Cor. 1:9; 2 Cor. 1:19; Gal. 1:16; 2:20; 4:4, 6; 1 Thess. 1:10. See also 1 Cor. 15:28. (God's [own] Son often appears as "his" [own] Son.)

8. Rom. 15:6; 2 Cor. 11:31. "Father" is implied also in Phil. 2:11 ("the Father").

9. For the importance for Jesus of addressing God as Father to express his role of embodying and representing Israel as the son of God, see N. T. Wright, *Jesus and the Victory of God* (Minneapolis: Fortress, 1996), pp. 648-51.

10. See Marianne Meye Thompson, *The Promise of the Father: Jesus and God in the New Testament* (Louisville: Westminster/John Knox, 2000), pp. 35-55, 116-32.

11. "God our Father": Rom. 1:7; 1 Cor. 1:3; 2 Cor. 1:2; Phil. 1:2; "our God and Father": Gal. 1:4; 1 Thess. 1:3; "God the Father": 1 Cor. 8:6; 15:24; Gal. 1:1; Phil. 2:11; 1 Thess. 1:1; "the Father": Rom. 6:4.

12. For a similar perspective, see John L. White, *The Apostle of God: Paul and the Promise of Abraham* (Peabody, Mass.: Hendrickson, 1999), ch. 6 ("God Our Father"), pp. 139-72. It is generally recognized that the empire was perceived as a universal household (Greek *oikoumenē*), modeled on the private household (Greek *oikos*) and governed by a father figure (see, among many, White's discussion, *Apostle of God*, pp. 192-97).

adoption

virtue of creation, and certainly not by unique election or preexistence (as in the case of Jesus), but by special relation to God through faith. The metaphor Paul uses to express this relationship with God, initiated by God, is adoption. It is those adopted by God who may call God "Abba Father," and Paul seems both to do this and to encourage it with delight (Gal. 4:6; Rom. 8:15). In the sending of God's Son, so that Paul and others could enjoy the privileges of being God's children, Paul perceived and experienced the self-giving, life-giving love of God. God had not spared the Son but had given him in love first to be born, but primarily to suffer, die, and be raised on behalf of humanity in the grip of sin. To say that God is our Father, for Paul, is to say above all that God is *for us*, as demonstrated in the giving of his only Son so that that Son could become the first of many "sons" (children) of God (Rom. 8:29). God, that is, is known to be faithful and loving to the entire human race, both Jews and Gentiles.

God for Us

As the Father of our Lord Jesus Christ and as the Father of believers, God for Paul is especially the One who is lovingly "for us" in Christ; indeed, "Christ is 'God for us'":[13]

> [31]If God is for us, who is against us? [32]He who did not withhold his own Son, but gave him up for all of us, will he not with him also give us everything else? (Rom. 8:31b-32)

God is the "God of peace" (Phil. 4:9) — the God who makes peace with us mortal enemies of God (Rom. 5:1-11). Paul knows that "in Christ God was reconciling the world to himself" (2 Cor. 5:19); or, in other words, God's love was and is found in "Christ Jesus our Lord," and nothing "in all creation will be able to separate us" from that love (Rom. 8:39). For Paul, then, God's love is known in Christ's love, specifically in Christ's act of love in death, as Paul says in the same passage: "[I]n all these things we are more than conquerors through him who loved us" (Rom. 8:37), a clear reference, in context, to the Son's death. As Jürgen Becker writes,

> [O]n the basis of the Christ event, Paul infers not only the depth of human lostness . . . but also the depth of divine grace and love. . . . [God] does not wait until he can let the principle of poetic justice rule. Rather, according to

---

13. Becker, *Paul*, p. 399. Brueggemann (*Theology of the Old Testament*, p. 227) reminds us that already in the Old Testament God is essentially Yahweh for Israel, Yahweh *pro nobis*.

Paul, his nature consists in re-creating the unlovely so that under his love they become lovely, in turning enemies into reconciled people, in giving worth to the worthless. This is the self-characterization of the Father of Jesus Christ.[14]

Paul probably would not have expressed his experience of God in the words of 1 John, "God is love" (1 John 4:8, 16), though he had similar sentiments. For Paul love is not primarily God's being but God's *way* of being; it is not primarily God's essence but God's story. It is a story of self-giving love ("his own Son," Rom. 8:3, 32), and it corresponds to the self-giving love of Christ. For Paul, Christ's love is both the sign and the substance of God's love:

> God proves his [literally "his own"][15] love for us in that while we were still sinners Christ died for us. (Rom. 5:8)

Paul, then, would have found his experience of God echoed in the words of the gospel of John:

> For God so loved the world that he gave his only Son, so that everyone who believes in him may not perish but may have eternal life. (John 3:16)

The God whom Paul knows has given the gift of peace and love to his apostle and to all who trust that God's promises are fulfilled in his Son, the Messiah Jesus. Paul's experience of God was personal and transformative. He felt himself "dead to" — unplugged from, so to speak — his former self and life, and thereby alive to and for God:

> For through the law I died to the law, so that I might live to God. I have been crucified with Christ. (Gal. 2:19a)[16]

> So you also must consider yourselves dead to sin and alive to God in Christ Jesus. (Rom. 6:11)

To be "alive to God in Christ Jesus" is to take on a new posture toward God, not one of apathy, rejection, and rebellion, but one of faith, hope, and love.[17]

---

14. Becker, *Paul,* pp. 378-79. Christ is "in such a comprehensive way the crucial loving openness of God toward human beings" (p. 379).

15. The Greek expression is similar to "his own Son" in Rom. 8:3, 32.

16. The phrase "live to God" is a typical Hellenistic expression for devotion to a god. In context, "died to the law" suggests renouncing the law as source of life with God. See the discussion in chapter six.

17. Although Paul usually speaks of the believer's relationship to God as one of faith or —

To continue this relationship with God, Paul urges his fellow Christians (and no doubt also himself) to present themselves and their bodies — the whole of their lives — to this God of mercy who has given them life.

> [P]resent yourselves to God as those who have been brought from death to life. . . . (Rom. 6:13b)

> I appeal to you therefore, brothers and sisters, by the mercies of God, to present your bodies as a living sacrifice, holy and acceptable to God, which is your spiritual worship. (Rom. 12:1)

As Galatians 2:19 (cited above) suggests, however, Paul's relationship to God is intimately linked to his newfound experience of Christ. The uniquely Christian dimension of Paul's experience of God is that he knows God as the Father of Jesus the Son, the Father who sent the Son into the world to accomplish what humans could not accomplish, so that Paul and others could in turn know God as their Father. The act that made this possible was the Son's reconciling death on the cross as an act of obedience and sacrificial love. For that reason, Paul's experience of God was transformed by his encounter with the crucified — and exalted — Christ.

The Father, the Son, and the Cross

Knowing God as the Father who raised and exalted the Son confirmed Paul's understanding of God as all-powerful creator, able even to re-create life out of death. Yet knowing God as the Father of the *crucified* Christ led Paul to another dimension of his experience and understanding of God. Like other ancients, Paul knew the idea, if not the expression, "like father, like son." The necessary similarity of God's children to God, articulated in texts like 1 John 3:9 and 4:7-8 (God's children do not sin, but love), depends on this concept. For Paul, there was a necessary "family resemblance" between the Father and the Son. The Father was like the Son, and vice versa.

If the Christ of Paul's experience was the faithful, obedient Son of God, then he acted in life and especially in death according to the will and character

---

to a lesser degree — hope (see the chapters below on these topics) rather than love, he does occasionally refer to love for God (Rom. 8:28; 1 Cor. 8:3; 2:9, presumably quoting or paraphrasing Scripture or another source; cf. 2 Thess. 3:5). Once he also implies the necessity of love for "the Lord [Jesus]" (1 Cor. 16:22), but for the most part "love" in Paul refers to relations among people, not between people and God or Jesus.

of God. That is to say, the Son's act on the cross was an act of "family resemblance," of conformity to God. If so, Paul would have reasoned from his experience of Christ, God must be a God who by nature wills and does what the Son willed and did. God is, in other words, a God of self-sacrificing and self-giving love whose power and wisdom are found in the weakness and folly of the cross. In a similar vein, Marianne Meye Thompson, alluding to Galatians 5:6, rightly claims that, for Paul, "God's Fatherhood can be summarized as 'faithfulness working through love.'"[18] In subsequent chapters we will argue that this text also encapsulates both Paul's understanding of believers' existence and his view of Christ's death.

For Paul, "Christ — that is, Christ crucified" (1 Cor. 2:2) is the revelation of the love, wisdom, and power of God: "*in* Christ God was reconciling the world to himself" (2 Cor. 5:19); "Christ [crucified] . . . [is] the power of God and the wisdom of God" (1 Cor. 1:24). As such, Christ reveals to Paul a God who is not otherwise known in antiquity.[19] This God is certainly not to be found among Greek or Roman deities, and not even among Paul's fellow Jews. Despite Paul's clarion and legitimate claims of continuity with Israel's experience of God, it is clear that the God he knows in Jesus Christ was not known in the same way by any who preceded him, not even Abraham, who knew God as the One who justifies by faith and raises the dead (Romans 4).[20]

Paul clearly, however, did not believe himself to know a *different* God, but only the same God of Israel, now more fully known and knowable. Yet the difference is tremendously significant. "Confession to [sic] Jesus as the sign of God's decisive act stands God on the head."[21] All claims to knowledge of God

---

18. Thompson, *Promise*, p. 132.

19. While there are ancient myths of dying and rising gods, linked primarily to notions of fertility or the afterlife, none defines divinity in terms of the humiliation of crucifixion.

20. Dieter Georgi, in *Theocracy in Paul's Praxis and Theology* (Minneapolis: Fortress, 1991), notes that Israel was accustomed to "revolutionary revelation" demanding a rethinking of God (p. 21), but none was ever as radical as what had to result from the conviction that God had raised the crucified Jesus. For Paul and the other early followers of Jesus, what happened "is more than a shift in their understanding of themselves and of God. The very essence of the matter is changed: it is God who has been transformed. . . . [T]he crucified one is not only unclean (like any corpse) but accursed. To introduce such a person into the heavenly realm [through exaltation] desecrates heaven itself. The cross of Jesus has transformed heaven as well as earth. Indeed, heaven is no longer heaven. Paul spells out this transformation in his letters" (pp. 20, 22). Similarly, Neil Richardson, in *Paul's Language about God*, JSNTSup 99 (Sheffield: Sheffield Academic Press, 1994), concludes that while Paul's talk of God (especially in 1 Corinthians 1 and 2) has Old Testament parallels, his attribution of folly and weakness to God represents "not only new language about God, but also a new understanding of God" (p. 133).

21. Georgi, *Theocracy*, p. 54.

— and of God's love, wisdom, and power — whether pagan, Jewish, or even (no, especially!) Christian must now pass the test of conformity to the cross of Christ as the revelation of God: "God's stance toward the world is quintessentially demonstrated in the action of Christ [in his death]."[22] If on the cross Christ conformed to God, then God "conforms" to the cross/ *The cross is the interpretive, or hermeneutical, lens through which God is seen; it is the means of grace by which God is known.* As John Carroll and Joel Green write, in Paul we find an

> unyielding affirmation that in the cross we see the character of God; the crucifixion of Jesus is the gauge of God's immeasurable love just as it is the ultimate object lesson for God's unorthodox notion of the exercise of power.[23]

One of the central dimensions of Paul's experience of divine love and power in the crucified Jesus is his discovery that God is the "great subverter of the status quo."[24] Not only is God "stood on the head," but also, consequently, are all human values and visions. The impact of this "discovery" (Paul would say "revelation") on the apostle's life and ministry will unfold in subsequent chapters.

Conclusion: The Cruciform God

Paul's affirmation that the crucified Jesus is now Lord "will strain all our categories [for describing God] to breaking point and beyond. . . . For him, the meaning of the word 'God' includes not only Jesus, but, specifically, the crucified Jesus."[25] This is not to say, however, that for Paul God (the Father) is crucified. In Paul's experience and theology he knows not a "*crucified* God" but a *cruciform* God.[26] In the words of the one-time Archbishop of Canterbury, A. M.

22. Charles B. Cousar, *A Theology of the Cross: The Death of Jesus in the Pauline Letters*, OBT (Minneapolis: Fortress, 1990), p. 186.

23. John T. Carroll and Joel B. Green, "'Nothing but Christ and Him Crucified': Paul's Theology of the Cross," in *The Death of Jesus in Early Christianity* (Peabody, Mass.: Hendrickson, 1995), p. 128.

24. Richardson, *Paul's Language*, pp. 137-38.

25. N. T. Wright, *What Saint Paul Really Said: Was Paul of Tarsus the Real Founder of Christianity?* (Grand Rapids: Eerdmans, 1997), p. 69. Compare Leander E. Keck's comment that for Paul "God made Christ the framework for our understanding of God" ("Biblical Preaching as Divine Wisdom," in John Burke, ed., *A New Look at Preaching* [Wilmington, Del.: Michael Glazier, 1983], p. 153).

26. The well-known phrase "crucified God" comes from the Church Fathers, was used by

Ramsey, "the importance of the confession 'Jesus is Lord' is not only that Jesus is divine but that God is Christlike."[27] Or, as James Dunn writes, Paul's experience of divine power in his experience of Christ is such that "he does not hesitate to characterize the kerygma [proclamation] as the gospel of the *weakness* of God," referring to 1 Corinthians 1:25.[28]

In Paul's experience, God's will and person are known through the cross of Jesus the Messiah and Lord. In other words, cruciformity is the character of God.[29]

Luther, and was popularized in the latter part of the twentieth century by Jürgen Moltmann in *The Crucified God: The Cross of Christ as the Foundation and Criticism of Christian Theology*, trans. R. A. Wilson and John Bowden (New York: Harper & Row, 1974). Cousar is probably correct, however, that Paul is only "a step away" from the notion of a crucified God (*A Theology of the Cross*, p. 50). A provocative book by Richard Bauckham, *God Crucified: Monotheism and Christology in the New Testament* (Grand Rapids: Eerdmans, 1998), argues persuasively that the New Testament writers, including Paul, identified Jesus as "intrinsic to who God is" (p. 42), that is, that the identity (character and personal story [p. 7, n. 5]) of God is revealed in Jesus' lowliness, especially his cross. In ways that are both continuous with and novel to Judaism, Paul experiences "God's sovereignty and glory . . . in the self-humiliation of the one who serves. . . . God's identity appears in the loving service and self-abnegation to death of his Son" (p. 68). While I agree with Bauckham that the "story of Jesus is not a mere illustration of the divine identity; [that] Jesus himself and his story are intrinsic to the divine identity," and that the story of Jesus is "the unique act of God's self-giving" (p. 69), the language of a crucified God may imply that there is no distinction between the Father and the Son. At least for Paul, not to mention later theologians, this distinction is crucial. Thus, speaking of the cruciform rather than the crucified God attempts to preserve Bauckham's legitimate emphasis on divine identity without falling into what later was called "patripassianism" — the suffering of the Father on the cross.

27. A. M. Ramsey, *God, Christ, and the World* (London: SCM, 1969), p. 98.

28. James D. G. Dunn, *Jesus and the Spirit: A Study of the Religious and Charismatic Experience of Jesus and the First Christians as Reflected in the New Testament* (London: SCM, 1975; reprint, Grand Rapids: Eerdmans, 1997), p. 329 (emphasis his).

29. Although this final claim may seem to restrict God's character to one quality, it is rather an attempt to say that for Paul cruciformity encompasses and defines all the divine qualities. These would include faithfulness, love, power, wisdom, and so forth. Fundamentally for Paul, because the cross reveals God, God is known to be cruciform.

18

CHAPTER 2

THE EXALTED CRUCIFIED MESSIAH

"Apprehended by Christ to Be Conformed to Him"

In the previous chapter we discovered that Paul's experience and understanding of God are of a cruciform God, a God revealed and known in the crucified Messiah, Jesus. This crucified Jesus, Paul knew by experience, was also raised and exalted by God. For Paul Jesus now is, and can now be known and experienced as, the living Lord. As such, however, *the living Messiah remains continuous with the crucified Jesus.* In the striking words of the German New Testament theologian Ernst Käsemann, the cross is "the signature of the one who is risen."[1]

This paradox is at the core of Paul's experience of Christ, who, Paul believes, has apprehended him — and all believers — to be conformed to his image.[2] Paul did not share this perspective, of course, in the days prior to his life-changing encounter with the exalted crucified Messiah on the road to Damascus, in pursuit of people already experiencing Jesus as the living Lord. Afterward, however, Paul came to believe that the crucified Jesus was not only the revelation of true divinity but also the paradigm of true humanity. In this chapter we examine in some depth Paul's experience of this Lord, Jesus.

---

1. Ernst Käsemann, "The Saving Significance of the Death of Jesus in Paul," in *Perspectives on Paul*, trans. Margaret Kohl (Philadelphia: Fortress, 1971; reprint, Mifflintown, Pa.: Sigler, 1996), p. 56.

2. It should be noted that "Christ" is not for Paul the last name of Jesus; it retains its meaning "Messiah."

Paul's "Copernican Revolution": Encountering Jesus

In 1 Corinthians Paul claims that just as Christ appeared to the first disciples after his resurrection, so also he appeared to Paul (1 Cor. 15:8). In Galatians, Paul claims that he received his gospel through a "revelation of Jesus Christ" (1:12) and says that God revealed his Son either "to" or "in" him (1:16). In these texts he refers to the experience he had with the crucified but exalted Messiah beginning with this initial encounter in which Paul, according to the book of Acts, who asked Jesus, "Who are you, Lord?" (Acts 9:5; 22:8; 26:15). This transformative experience in Paul's life can be likened to the revolution experienced by the scientific community when Copernicus discerned that the sun, not the earth, was the center of the solar system. Thomas Kuhn, a historian of science, labeled such transformations "scientific revolutions," after which the scientific community is never the same.[3] So too, Paul, the former preacher of Torah and circumcision (Gal. 5:11), the one-time zealous persecutor of the Church (Gal. 1:13-14; 1 Cor. 15:9; Phil. 3:6), became Paul the zealot for Christ. He was never again the same. The Damascus Road was the site of his Copernican revolution.

The interpretation of what precisely happened on the road to Damascus is an extraordinarily difficult enterprise and cannot detain us for long; nor do we have the space to enter into a detailed examination of the connection between this Damascus-road experience and Paul's later experience and theology.[4] Nonetheless, several basic elements of the experience and its consequences seem clear, and they must therefore be mentioned.

According to his letters, Paul's experience of the exalted crucified Jesus began with what some have called a "mystical" encounter in which Jesus appeared to him. A better description might be "apocalyptic" encounter, in the root sense of the Greek word *apokalypsis*, which means "unveiling" or "revelation." It also appears that Paul's ongoing life in Christ was punctuated with additional "mystical" or "apocalyptic" experiences — "visions and revelations of the Lord" he calls them in 2 Corinthians 12:1. The book of Acts agrees with these two general observations, and recent studies of Paul have stressed their importance in the apostle's life.[5] What was the nature and significance of these experiences for Paul?

---

3. For a sustained interpretation of Paul that relies on Thomas Kuhn's model of scientific revolutions, see Terence L. Donaldson, *Paul and the Gentiles: Remapping the Apostle's Convictional World* (Minneapolis: Fortress, 1997), especially pp. 43-47, 293-307.

4. For a collection of essays exploring this issue from several perspectives, see Richard N. Longenecker, ed., *The Road from Damascus: The Impact of Paul's Conversion on His Life, Thought, and Ministry* (Grand Rapids: Eerdmans, 1997).

5. Acts 9:1-19a (parallels in 22:6-16 and 26:12-23) concerns Paul's initial revelation, while 16:6-10; 18:1-11 (especially v. 9); and 22:17-22 narrate subsequent visions. On Paul's Jewish

The key texts in the letters in which he narrates such experiences are the following:

> [8]Last of all, as to one untimely born, he appeared also to me. [9]For I am the least of the apostles, unfit to be called an apostle, because I persecuted the church of God. [10]But by the grace of God I am what I am, and his grace toward me has not been in vain. . . . (1 Cor. 15:8-10a)

> Am I not free? Am I not an apostle? Have I not seen Jesus our Lord? (1 Cor. 9:1)

> [11]For I want you to know, brothers and sisters, that the gospel that was proclaimed by me is not of human origin; [12]for I did not receive it from a human source, nor was I taught it, but I received it through a revelation of Jesus Christ [or, "of Messiah Jesus"]. [13]You have heard, no doubt, of my earlier life in Judaism. I was violently persecuting the church of God and was trying to destroy it. . . . [15]But when God, who had set me apart before I was born and called me through his grace, was pleased [16]to reveal his Son to [or, "in"; NRSV margin] me, so that I might proclaim him among the Gentiles, I did not confer with any human being. . . . (Gal. 1:11-13, 15-16)

> [1]Then after fourteen years I went up again to Jerusalem with Barnabas, taking Titus along with me. [2]I went up in response to a revelation. Then I laid before them (though only in a private meeting with the acknowledged leaders) the gospel that I proclaim among the Gentiles, in order to make sure that I was not running, or had not run, in vain. . . . [7]. . . [W]hen they saw that I had been entrusted with the gospel for the uncircumcised . . . [9]. . . they gave to Barnabas and me the right hand of fellowship, agreeing that we should go to the Gentiles and they to the circumcised. (Gal. 2:1-2, 7, 9)

> [1]It is necessary to boast; nothing is to be gained by it, but I will go on to visions and revelations of the Lord. [2]I know a person in Christ who fourteen years ago was caught up to the third heaven — whether in the body or out of the body I do not know; God knows. [3]And I know that such a person — whether in the

---

mysticism, see especially Alan Segal, *Paul the Convert: The Apostolate and Apostasy of Saul the Pharisee* (New Haven: Yale University Press, 1990), pp. 34-71; Christopher Rowland, *The Open Heaven: A Study of Apocalyptic in Judaism and Early Christianity* (New York: Crossroad, 1982), pp. 374-86; C. R. A. Morray-Jones, "Paradise Revisited (2 Cor. 12:1-12): The Jewish Mystical Background of Paul's Apostolate, Part 1: The Jewish Sources," *Harvard Theological Review* 86 (1993): 177-217; C. R. A. Morray-Jones, "Paradise Revisited (2 Cor. 12:1-12): The Jewish Mystical Background of Paul's Apostolate, Part 2: Paul's Heavenly Ascent and Its Significance," *Harvard Theological Review* 86 (1993): 265-92.

21

body or out of the body I do not know; God knows — [4]was caught up into Paradise and heard things that are not to be told, that no mortal is permitted to repeat. . . . [7]. . . Therefore, to keep me from being too elated, a thorn was given me in the flesh, a messenger of Satan to torment me, to keep me from being too elated. . . . [9]. . . So, I will boast all the more gladly of my weaknesses, so that the power of Christ may dwell in me. (2 Cor. 12:1-4, 7b, 9b)

[18]And all of us, with unveiled faces, seeing the glory of the Lord as though reflected in a mirror, are being transformed into the same image from one degree of glory to another; for this comes from the Lord, the Spirit. . . . 4 [4]In their case the god of this world has blinded the minds of the unbelievers, to keep them from seeing the light of the gospel of the glory of Christ, who is the image of God. . . . [6]For it is the God who said, "Let light shine out of darkness," who has shone in our hearts to give the light of the knowledge of the glory of God in the face of Jesus Christ. (2 Cor. 3:18; 4:4, 6)

We will attempt to make some sense of these texts as witnesses to Paul's initial and ongoing encounter with Jesus.

Paul's Initial Encounter with Jesus

Understanding what happened to Paul is in many respects more difficult to assess than its meaning for him, so we will focus on the meaning. The most obvious significance of Paul's initial encounter with Jesus was its establishment of his apostleship[6] and his gospel: the divine origin of each; the unexpected, grace-filled, and transformational nature of his call; and the focus of his apostolic mission and message on the Gentiles. Paul thus experienced this initial encounter with Jesus as a transformation or conversion, a prophetic call, and a commission.[7] The "revelation" he received years later that led him to go to Jerusalem appears to

6. Indeed, by means of the verb *ōphthē* ("appeared," four times in 1 Cor. 15:5-8), 1 Corinthians 15 stresses the similarity in experience (and hence in apostleship) between the appearance of Christ to Paul and the appearances to the other apostles listed.

7. See further discussion of these three dimensions below under "The Enduring Meaning of the First Encounter." Paul does not explicitly claim in Gal. 1:16 that his commission to preach to the Gentiles occurred precisely at the initial revelation, but only that the purpose of the initial revelation was the commission (which could have come later). However, because the language of Galatians 1 echoes prophetic episodes of call and commission (Isa. 49:1-6; Jer. 1:5), and because the vision/appearance of Jesus described in 1 Corinthians 9 and 15 is so closely connected to Paul's sense of being an apostle, a "sent one," it is virtually certain that he experienced his initial encounter with Jesus as a divine commissioning.

have confirmed all the dimensions of the initial experience and caused him to explain and defend it to the Jerusalem leaders (Gal. 2:1-10).

Yet there is more. The initial encounter with Jesus also revealed to Paul the basic content of his gospel. This is suggested not only by his claim in Galatians 1:11-12 but also by the entire context of the references in Galatians 1–2 and in 1 Corinthians 15. Specifically, what Paul feels the need first to explain in Jerusalem (Gal. 2:1-10), then to defend in Antioch (Gal. 2:11-21), and to "unpack" in Corinth (1 Corinthians 15) is his gospel of the crucified and resurrected Christ (Gal. 2:15-21; 1 Cor. 15:3-6), which makes justification available to Gentiles and Jews alike apart from works of the law, and which guarantees future resurrection to all who are justified.[8]

Yet even to say all this does not fully explain the character of Paul's initial encounter with Jesus. At the deepest level it was, fundamentally, just that and nothing more: an experience of Jesus. In other words, in this experience Paul discovered — Paul would say that God revealed — the identity of Jesus. He is God's Son (Gal. 1:16), the Messiah (1 Cor. 15:3; Gal. 1:12), and Lord (1 Cor. 9:1). He is alive and not dead. Jesus is, to put it in the form of a brief narrative, the crucified Jesus whom God his Father had sent into the world as Messiah and has now exalted to the position of Lord.[9] Henceforth Paul knows no other Jesus (e.g., merely a crucified messianic pretender, cursed by God, or an exalted divine figure unconnected to the crucified Jesus), for that would be to know him "from a human point of view" or "according to the flesh" (2 Cor. 5:16). Paul's initial "mystical" experience, then, is an experience of *the narrative identity* of Jesus. As such, this initial encounter with Jesus provided for Paul the basic framework of what we will call, in subsequent chapters, his "master story."[10]

---

8. 1 Cor. 15:3-6 presents the contours of the gospel as something Paul did in fact receive from humans. The contrast with Gal. 1:12 ("I did not receive it from a human source") is due to the different contexts. In Galatians, on the one hand, Paul must prove the divine origin of his claim about the justification of Gentiles *over against* another apostolic claim (that implied by Cephas's [Peter's] separation from the Gentiles as described in Gal. 2:11-14). In 1 Corinthians, on the other hand, he must prove the logic of believers' resurrection, not in *contrast* to but in *continuity* with Cephas and the other apostles. (It should also be noted, however, that despite his claims to independence from human tradition, even in Galatians Paul likely quotes early Christian formulations of Christ's death in 1:4 and 2:20.)

9. It is clear from Gal. 4:4 (cf. Rom. 8:3-4) that Paul understood the Jesus revealed to him as God's preexistent Son.

10. As we will see, beginning with chapter five, this master story appears most fully in Phil. 2:6-11, which, according to most scholars, is a pre-Pauline hymn. While its poetic quality does in fact suggest that it is a hymn, its similarity (though not exact correspondence) to the narrative identity of Jesus that Paul initially experienced makes Pauline authorship of the hymn quite possible. However, it is also possible that Paul later narrated his initial encounter with Jesus in

mysticism (handwritten marginal note)

Subsequent Revelations

Paul's initial experience of Jesus became also the defining one for him. Whatever subsequent revelations and visions he received — and their frequency and character are a matter of scholarly debate — would confirm and perhaps deepen this first, unique encounter. Thus Paul implicitly connects the revelation that sent him to Jerusalem (Gal. 2:2) with his gospel of the once crucified but now living Jesus (Gal. 2:15-21), and he explicitly connects the famous ascent into heaven (2 Cor. 12:1-10) with his general experience of Christ's power ("resurrection") in the midst of weakness ("crucifixion").

This latter experience — told in the third person ("I know a person in Christ," 2 Cor. 12:2) out of modesty or in typical apocalyptic style — has been the subject of much study and debate.[11] It is almost certainly not to be equated with the Damascus-road experience.[12] In fact, in its general shape, it was not unique in the Judaism of Paul's day, for there are other reports of heavenly ascents in ancient Jewish, as well as Christian, literature. The general term used for the kind of experience that Paul narrates in 2 Corinthians 12 is *merkabah* mysticism, the Hebrew word *merkabah* referring to the chariot-like throne of God described in Ezekiel 1. *Merkabah* mystics, most of whose accounts are later than Paul's, claimed to have visions of the heavenly throne, and particularly of the heavenly glory, of God.[13] It is likely that Paul is describing just such an expe-

---

terms of the narrative identity of Jesus portrayed in a hymn that he had learned from some group of believers.

11. That the experience was in fact Paul's is the common opinion, dating back to Irenaeus in the second century (*Against Heresies* 5.5.1) and held by most commentators today.

12. The attempt of Morray-Jones to equate it with the experience narrated in Acts 22, which occurs appropriately in the temple, is attractive but not convincing ("Paradise Revisited, Part 2," pp. 284-92). In an otherwise fine article, Morray-Jones erroneously reads Paul's insistence that the ascent proves his apostolicity not as one example of many revelations that undergird his apostolic calling (the natural way to read 2 Corinthians 12) but as the "basis of Paul's claim to apostolic authority" (p. 285). On the differences between the experiences narrated in Galatians 1 and 2 Corinthians 12, see William Baird, "Visions, Revelation, and Ministry: Reflections on 2 Cor. 12:1-5 and Gal. 1:11-17," *Journal of Biblical Literature* 104 (1985): 651-62.

13. Other biblical texts associated with this mystical tradition include the famous account of Isaiah's vision of the enthroned Lord, and the prophetic call that accompanied it (Isaiah 6); the vision of the Son of Man in Dan. 7:9-14, and descriptions of God's glory present with Israel, in the temple, or in heaven. In various ways Jewish tradition identified a divine being, or "principal angel," on or near God's throne with the glory of God. Paul would have connected this being with Christ. See Segal, *Paul the Convert*, pp. 40-52 (on *merkabah* mysticism) and pp. 56-58 (Christians' identification of God's glory with Christ). The current consensus of scholarly opinion appears to be that the origins of *merkabah* mysticism do not postdate Paul but are to be found in apocalyptic mystical experiences from his era or earlier.

rience, in which he ascended to "the third heaven" or (perhaps, and then also) to "Paradise" (2 Cor. 12:2, 4), where he "heard things that are not to be told, that no mortal is permitted to repeat."[14] Paul reluctantly relates this experience only in broad strokes, using it as proof of his apostolic status in the face of similar claims from rivals (2 Cor. 11:5, 12; 11:16–12:13).

Although Paul does not relate what he saw or heard, we can speculate with some confidence that whatever he experienced revealed to him, once again, the crucified exalted Jesus as God's Messiah and Son, indeed as the presence of the "glory of God" (2 Cor. 4:6). Paul can even go so far in the context of discussing God's glory as to rename his gospel the "gospel of the glory of Christ" (2 Cor. 4:4). This renaming makes sense, however, only if it has continuity with Paul's gospel as the gospel of the crucified one. What Paul most likely experiences in his heavenly ascent, then, is a confirmation that the crucified Jesus is now the exalted Lord and hence the glory of God.[15] What is important for Paul, who, as a good "mystic," wants to be gradually transformed into that glory (2 Cor. 3:18), is that he return to earth to experience in daily life the very things that will bring about that transformation. Paradoxically, what will cause the transformation or glorification to occur is not a series of further revelations or other experiences of overt power but experiences of weakness (2 Cor. 12:6-10); the transformation into glory through resurrection is in fact accomplished by conformity to Christ's death (Phil. 3:10). In such experiences is the power of Christ realized.[16]

This brings us to the ultimate meaning of Paul's visions and revelations. Recent study suggests that these may have been more numerous and more significant for Paul than previously thought. It would be a mistake to underestimate the so-called "mystical" character of Paul's experience. What mattered most for Paul, however, was not the experiences themselves but the variety of ways in which they confirmed his gospel message and the corresponding cruciform life of weakness and suffering associated with it.

14. See especially Morray-Jones, "Paradise Revisited, Part 2."

15. Compare Phil. 2:9-11. It is quite possible that Paul's experience of heaven was not that different from the experience of John of Patmos, who saw both God on the throne and the Lamb that was crucified or "slaughtered" (Rev. 4–5; 21:22; 22:1, 4), emphasizing the continuity between the crucified and glorified Jesus (see Rev. 5:6, 9, 12; 7:14, 17; 12:11; 13:8; 17:14).

16. Segal (*Paul the Convert*, p. 61) rightly calls the experience narrated in 2 Corinthians 3 a "spiritual metamorphosis," recognizes its connection with Phil. 3:10 (pp. 63-64), and makes the connection between suffering and transformation in Paul's spiritual experience (pp. 65-69). Furthermore, he suggests that the central experience of being "in Christ" and "conformed" to him draws on the Jewish mystical tradition (p. 64), refined by the death of Jesus and the experiences of early Christians such that the way to be "in Christ" is through persecution and difficulty (pp. 68-69).

The Enduring Meaning of the First Encounter

As we have already noted, all of these subsequent "visions and revelations of the Lord" confirmed the life-transforming Damascus-road encounter. In light of Paul's letters, we may draw several major conclusions about the meaning of that first encounter with Jesus for Paul.

First, the Damascus-road experience *took Paul by surprise.* It was an experience of unexpected, undeserved grace (1 Cor. 15:10). There is no evidence that he was experiencing any guilt over his mission of attempting to stop the fledgling Jesus movement. The early "Christians'"[17] near-blasphemous belief in a crucified Messiah raised by God, their hesitation about certain aspects of the Law, and their injudicious openness to Gentiles were sufficient causes for trying to effect their demise. Paul's response to the Damascus-road encounter was surprise (not to mention the shock and suspicion of others) and gratitude. Fumbling for a metaphor, in 1 Cor. 15:8 he calls himself an "abortion" or "miscarriage" (NRSV, "one untimely born"; Greek *ektrōma*), because the "glimpse of the risen Christ had torn him, so to speak, like an aborted fetus, unformed, unprepared, from what he had been to what he became."[18] His gratitude for this surprise led him, it seems abundantly clear, to emphasize grace in everything he said and did and wrote.

Through Christ, he told the Roman believers, "we have obtained access to this grace in which we stand" (Rom. 5:2), namely, the grace of justification, of peace and right relationship with God (cf., e.g., 1 Cor. 1:4). He tells them also that he and they are "under grace" (Rom. 6:14-15), that is, under the benevolent and transformative influence and power of grace. As those who believe that Jesus is the Messiah, Paul and his communities experience the grace of God as "the grace of [our Lord Jesus] Christ" (Gal. 1:6; 1 Thess. 5:28; 2 Cor. 8:9). Paul never tires of invoking the grace of God and of "the Lord Jesus Christ" on his communities, as his greetings and benedictions reveal.

Second, this experience of grace constituted for Paul a *conversion:* not a change of religion (he remained a Jew[19]) but a complete reorientation, what the Hebrew prophets themselves had called *shuv.* The prophets often had unusual

17. The term "Christian" is placed in quotation marks since it is really anachronistic to use it to describe the members of earliest communities focused on Jesus as the living crucified-but-exalted Jewish Messiah.

18. David J. Williams, *Paul's Metaphors: Their Context and Character* (Peabody, Mass.: Hendrickson, 1999), p. 58.

19. His phrase "my earlier life in Judaism" (Gal. 1:13) uses a technical term to refer to his pursuit of a particular form of Judaism, namely, an aggressive, separatist Pharisaism (James D. G. Dunn, *The Theology of Paul the Apostle* [Grand Rapids: Eerdmans, 1998], pp. 346-54).

experiences and changes in direction when they were called. They, however, called the people to ~~turn around~~. Paul had first to do a complete about-face himself, to acknowledge that he had been wrong about Jesus and that this crucified yet exalted Jesus was God's Messiah. As one Jewish scholar of Paul, Alan Segal, writes, no prophet ever needed or had such a radical and complete reorientation:

> Paul was both converted and called. . . . No historical prophet came around on his previous experience as Paul did when called to his task. . . . From the viewpoint of mission Paul is commissioned, but from the viewpoint of religious experience Paul is a convert. Modern studies show that there can be many continuities between a convert's life before conversion and after it. . . . But the primary fact of Paul's personal experience as a Christian is his enormous transformation, his conversion from a persecutor of Christianity to a persecuted advocate of it.[20]

Paul's dramatic change from persecutor to persecuted, from nearly killer to nearly killed, is taken for granted by most people familiar with the story. It should not, however, be underestimated. Paul had been extraordinarily serious about his divine duty to destroy the dangerous messianic movement centered on Jesus and open to Gentiles, which threatened the purity of Israel in its relationship to the God of the covenant. Zeal for Torah would mean opposition to any movement that might pollute Israel, such as the confession of a cursed criminal as Messiah (see Deut. 21:23; Gal. 3:13) or the admission of Gentiles into the covenant on the basis of anything, including faith in the gospel about Jesus, other than circumcision.[21] He was now zealous for Messiah, not Torah.

Paul's complete 180° turn is all the more remarkable when we recognize

---

20. Segal, *Paul the Convert*, p. 6. Segal is arguing against the scholarly tradition, inaugurated by Krister Stendahl, that Paul was "called, not converted" (Krister Stendahl, *Paul Among Jews and Gentiles* [Philadelphia: Fortress, 1976], pp. 7-23). Segal rightly maintains that Paul remained a Jew but was converted from one form (and community) of Judaism to another. Using modern scholarly studies of conversion, Segal concludes that Paul is a convert "in the modern sense of the word" (p. 6). Furthermore, although "Paul himself sometimes uses prophetic language to describe his Christian mission" and "Paul surely found that his new Christian faith was a fulfillment of his hope and outbreak of prophetic spirit," Paul "does not thereafter lose title to the epithet *convert*" (p. 5).

21. Paul stood squarely within a tradition of Jews, some of whom (like the Maccabeans in the second century B.C.) resorted to violence, who were "zealous" for Israel's purity, or distinctiveness. Paul certainly perceived this distinctiveness to be threatened by the earliest Church's implicit or explicit rejection of Torah possession and Torah keeping as the fundamental sign of membership in the covenant community. See Donaldson, *Paul and the Gentiles*, pp. 273-92, and Dunn, *Theology*, pp. 346-54.

that he not only changed from being a persecutor of Christ to being a preacher of Christ, but also forswore all vengeance and violence against enemies (Rom. 12:14-21). Moreover, his zeal to kill, metaphorically and perhaps literally, became a zeal to die, again metaphorically and perhaps literally. Without either psychologizing or oversimplifying, we may safely conclude that something like a life of "cruciformity" — of embracing a daily death (1 Cor. 15:31) — was an inherent and inevitable dimension of Paul's conversion. This was a radical transformation indeed.

Third, Paul experienced this conversion as *a call and a commission,* which he could retell in the language of the prophets like Jeremiah and (Second)[22] Isaiah (speaking perhaps on behalf of Israel):

[15]. . . God, who had set me apart before I was born and called me through his grace, was pleased [16]to reveal his Son to [or, "in"] me, so that I might proclaim him among the Gentiles. . . . (Gal. 1:15-16).

Before I formed you in the womb I knew you, and before you were born I consecrated you; I appointed you a prophet to the nations. (Jer. 1:5)

The Lord called me before I was born, while I was in my mother's womb he named me. (Isa. 49:1b; cf. v. 6)

The name he gave to the grace of this call and commission was "apostleship" — a designation for which he would sometimes have to contend. Through Christ, Paul says of himself and his colleagues, "we have received grace and apostleship [or, "the grace of apostleship"] to bring about the obedience of faith among all the Gentiles for the sake of his name" (Rom. 1:5).[23] Paul the opponent of Gentiles became the champion of Gentiles.

Fourth, Paul experienced his initial encounter with Jesus as *a revelation of the gospel of God's Son and thus of Jesus' true identity.* He received this revelation, not as information to learn, but as a claim to embrace. Or, more precisely, Paul found in the revelation of the crucified Jesus the glory of the God of Israel that was now claiming and embracing him for the sake of the world, especially the Gentile world.[24]

22. Most scholars believe that Isaiah 40–55 was not written by the same hand as chapters 1–39 (Isaiah of Jerusalem, writing in the eighth century B.C.) but by a later, "Second" Isaiah, sometimes called "Deutero-Isaiah" or "Isaiah of the exile" (sixth century).

23. Baird, "Visions," pp. 656-57, outlines the essential elements of a prophetic call narrative and their presence in Galatians 1: divine confrontation, introductory word, commission, objection, reassurance, and sign.

24. As Segal (*Paul the Convert,* p. 157) writes, "Paul's vocation is to make known the identi-

Paul, then, looked back on his Damascus-road experience and associated events as both a traditional prophetic call and a radically new venture. The exalted crucified Jesus, whom God had made Lord, had become *Paul's* Lord, and Paul his apostle and servant. Paul had been "apprehended by Christ" (Phil. 3:12, KJV).[25]

Servant of the Servant-Lord

Throughout the remainder of his life, Paul experienced Christ as a living presence: the crucified, raised, and exalted one was "Lord," a term that for Paul puts the exalted crucified One, in some sense, on a par with God. (It is best not to describe Jesus as the "risen" Lord when referring to Paul's experience of the living Christ, for Paul prefers to speak of Christ as raised and/or exalted by God, more than as "risen.") Paul saw himself as the Lord's apostle, authoritatively commissioned to spread the "gospel of God" (Rom. 1:1; 15:16; 2 Cor. 11:7 ["God's good news"]; 1 Thess. 2:2, 8, 9), which is "the word of the cross" (1 Cor. 1:18, author's translation; NRSV, "the message about the cross"), to the world, particularly the non-Jewish world. Yet he saw himself also as the Lord's *servant* or *slave* (Greek *doulos*), the willingly obedient caretaker of his Lord's people and work. He was a "servant [slave] of Jesus Christ, called to be an apostle" (Rom. 1:1). His life goal was to please his Lord Christ (Gal. 1:10).

Indeed, for Paul there was no greater privilege than to be the servant of Jesus the Lord. The language of servant (or slave) and Lord implied Paul's obedience, which he happily offered to Christ and to God through Christ. Obedience as the slave of *this* Lord meant not obedience to a harsh or capricious lord but obedience to one who had himself taken "the form of a slave" (Phil. 2:7). Paul saw himself as slave to a slave, as servant of the Servant.

---

fication of Jesus Christ as the Glory of God, because others have not been converted in quite so dramatic a fashion and have not seen it as directly as he." My only quarrel with Segal on this point, and throughout his work, is that he does not sufficiently perceive the importance of the continuity between the crucified Jesus and the exalted Christ for Paul's experience. Thus I would alter his text to read "the identification of *the crucified Messiah* Jesus as the Glory of God."

25. See further below. It is unfortunate that most translations do not retain the King James language and fail to convey the vivid metaphor of Paul's having been grasped (Greek *katalambanō*) by Christ. Referring to this text, Raymond E. Brown says that Paul "felt 'taken over' by Christ Jesus" (*An Introduction to the New Testament* [New York: Doubleday, 1997], p. 449).

The words of what appears to be an early Christian poem or hymn, cited by Paul in Philippians 2:6-11,[26] served as a reminder of this continuity between the exalted Lord and the self-emptying, self-humbling slave who was crucified on the cross. So did the early Christian confession "Jesus [Christ] is Lord," which Paul and his churches used (1 Cor. 12:3; Phil. 2:11). It would be "at the name of Jesus" — the human, crucified, and now exalted Jesus — that every knee would one day bow and confess the lordship of this Jesus (Phil. 2:9-11). That the exalted Lord who reigns is one with the suffering Jesus who died means that obedience to the Lord is conformity to Jesus.[27]

Thus Paul sees his life in terms of "slavery," slavery both to Christ and, in conformity to Christ, to others:

> For though I am free with respect to all, I have made myself a slave to all, so that I might win more of them. (1 Cor. 9:19)

> For we do not proclaim ourselves; we proclaim Jesus Christ as Lord and ourselves as your slaves for Jesus' sake. (2 Cor. 4:5)

More concretely, Paul saw Jesus' death as the fullest expression of his slavery; so too, Paul saw manifesting the life-giving death of Jesus as his chief apostolic *modus operandi* and experience of Christ:

> [10][We are] always carrying in the body the death of Jesus, so that the life of Jesus may also be made visible in our bodies. [11]For while we live, we are always being given up to death for Jesus' sake, so that the life of Jesus may be made visible in our mortal flesh. [12]So death is at work in us, but life in you. (2 Cor. 4:10-12)

Paul wanted his life and ministry to tell a story, a story that corresponded to the "story of the cross," to his gospel. His spirituality was therefore a *narrative* spirituality, an experience of re-presenting in living form the word of the cross. This may well be what he had in mind, at least in part, when he wrote the words, "God . . . was pleased to reveal his Son *in* me" (Gal. 1:15-16).[28]

---

26. That Phil. 2:6-11 is an early Christian hymn or hymn fragment is the opinion of most, though not all, New Testament scholars. As indicated in n. 10 above, however, the text's close correspondence to the revelation to Paul of the narrative identity of Jesus suggests that Paul could very well have been the author.

27. See the excellent article by Larry W. Hurtado, "Jesus as Lordly Example in Philippians 2.5-11," in Peter Richardson and John C. Hurd, eds., *From Jesus to Paul*, Francis W. Beare Festschrift (Waterloo: Wilfred Laurier University Press, 1984), pp. 113-26.

28. If the NRSV margin is correct (the Greek preposition is *en*).

As one proof of his being the authorized slave of Jesus the Lord who suffered as a slave, Paul offers the marks on his body:

> From now on, let no one make trouble for me; for I carry the marks of Jesus branded on my body. (Gal. 6:17)

The "marks" (Greek *stigmata*) to which Paul refers have two interrelated meanings. First, the term was used in antiquity for the marks that slave owners branded on slaves. Paul, who bears "the marks of Jesus," identifies himself as Jesus' slave. Second, however, it is highly unlikely that Paul had literally had himself branded or tattooed. Rather, "the marks of Jesus" almost certainly refer to scars on Paul's body — the results of floggings and other forms of persecution.[29] Thus Paul experienced his persecution for the cross of the crucified Lord as appropriate evidence of his slavery to Christ. His body was living proof of his personal story, and as such "his scars are nothing other than the present epiphany of the crucifixion of Jesus."[30]

Paul, then, saw himself as a participant in and continuation of the life-giving death of Jesus his Lord that was narrated in the gospel he preached and the hymns his communities sang. (In later chapters, we will explore this self-understanding in more depth.) However, Paul does not limit participation in Christ's death to himself and other apostles. By implication in many autobiographical passages (which almost always serve as paradigms for the behavior of others), and with explicit language in others, Paul makes it clear that sharing in the death of Christ — not only in its benefits, but in its narrative and substantive character — is for all believers.

Conformity as Cruciformity

We noted above that Paul felt himself to have been "apprehended" by Christ, apprehended, we see now, to be conformed to Christ the Lord, Christ the servant of all. In his letter to the Galatians, Paul describes this experience of being apprehended in language that must have been commonly used in early Chris-

29. Most commentators agree. See, e.g., J. Louis Martyn, *Galatians: A New Translation with Introduction and Commentary,* Anchor Bible 33A (New York: Doubleday, 1997), pp. 568-69, who translates the second half of 6:17: "For I bear in my own body scars that are the marks of Jesus."

30. Martyn, *Galatians,* p. 569. On the topic of the scars and their relation to Paul's ministry, see Basil S. Davis, "The Meaning of *proegraphē* in the Context of Galatians 3.1," *New Testament Studies* 45 (1999): 194-212, esp. 207-10. Davis argues convincingly that Paul's marks would reinforce the public proclamation of the gospel that he claimed to be manifested in his life as "the canvas upon which the crucified Christ was publicly displayed" (p. 208).

tian baptisms: the baptized have "put on Christ," that is, clothed themselves with him — a vivid and intimate metaphor:

> As many of you as were baptized into Christ have clothed yourselves with Christ. (Gal. 3:27)

In another passage on baptism, Paul is even more specific about the nature of this experience:

> Do you not know that all of us who have been baptized into Christ Jesus have been baptized into his death? (Rom. 6:3)

In the immediate context of Romans 6, this death experience refers primarily to a death to sin, separation from the power and manifestations of the former sinful self. Yet "co-crucifixion"[31] with Christ is for Paul also a more general and complete characterization of in-Christ spirituality. In Romans 6, death to sin in baptism leads to life in Christ (6:1-11), and life in Christ is a life of obedience (6:12-23). Obedience, in Romans, is said to be the proper expression of faith (1:5), and it is exemplified in the obedient death of Jesus (5:19). To be baptized into Christ (that is, to be a "Christian"), therefore, is indeed to be baptized into his death in the most comprehensive sense possible.[32] *Paul conceives of identification with and participation in the death of Jesus as the believer's fundamental experience of Christ.* Even "mystical" experiences like visions and revelations are subordinated to and expressive of this fundamental existential reality.

For Paul, this intimate identification with Christ symbolized in baptism is not merely a one-time event but an experience of *ongoing* death, of *ongoing* crucifixion. Paul paradigmatically envisions his entire faith experience with Christ as "co-crucifixion" (Gal. 2:19; Rom. 6:6) or "union" with his death (Rom. 6:5):

> I have been crucified with Christ. (Gal. 2:19c)

> [5][W]e have been united with him in a death like his. . . . [6]We know that our old self was crucified with him. . . . (Rom. 6:5-6a)

---

31. The noun "co-crucifixion" is suggested by the compound verb "co-crucified" used, e.g., by Joseph A. Fitzmyer, *Paul and His Theology: A Brief Sketch,* 2nd ed. (Englewood Cliffs, N.J.: Prentice Hall, 1989), p. 81. As we will see below, the word "with," as a preposition or a prefix ("co-"), is a common way for Paul to express this intimate identification of believers and Christ.

32. This includes even physical death, yet only in a preliminary or proleptic way. Obviously the baptized do not die physically in baptism, but they do acknowledge (1) that their future bodily death will be followed by a future bodily resurrection, and (2) that the death of the old self and life for God in Christ may well result in death by martyrdom.

Cruciformity:

This experience signifies both an identification with Christ and his cross and a death-like separation from other "powers," secular or religious, that might claim Paul's allegiance. These include the "world" (Gal. 6:14), his own "flesh," or the self with respect to its anti-God propensity (Gal. 5:24; so too, as noted above, the "self" in Gal. 2:19c-20a), and the power of sin itself (Rom. 6:1, 6-7, 10-11).[33] As many people have noted, Paul frequently narrates his experience of co-crucifixion in the perfect tense (i.e., "I *have been* crucified . . ."), indicating that it had a clear beginning but is not a one-time experience. Rather, co-crucifixion, or cruciformity, is an ongoing reality, a life-style. Cruciformity is what counts, what matters. In texts about baptism and faith, in paradigmatic autobiographical passages, and (as we will see in later chapters) in hortatory sections of every letter, Paul invites his communities to allow their lives, like his, to tell once again the word of the cross.

In one of the paradigmatic passages, Philippians 3, Paul's experience of Christ is especially well summarized. Paul contrasts his life in relationship to Christ with his prior life:

> [7]Yet whatever gains I had, these I have come to regard as loss because of Christ. [8]More than that, I regard everything as loss because of the surpassing value of knowing Christ Jesus my Lord. For his sake I suffered the loss of all things, and I regard them as rubbish, in order that I may gain Christ [9]and be found in him, not having a righteousness of my own that comes from the law, but one that comes through faith in Christ [or, the faithfulness of Christ], the righteousness of God based on faith. [10]I want to know Christ and the power of his resurrection and the sharing of his sufferings by becoming like him in [literally, "being conformed to"] his death, [11]if somehow I may attain the resurrection from the dead. [12]Not that I have already obtained this or have already reached the goal [been made "perfect"]; but I press on to make it my own, because Christ Jesus has made me his own. (Phil. 3:7-12)

This passage is rich in vocabulary and images that are essential to Paul's perception of himself and his experience of Christ.

Perhaps the most fundamental aspect of this passage from Philippians is the notion of being "apprehended" (so KJV) by Christ (v. 12): that is, Christ "made me [Paul] his own" (NRSV). This is one of Paul's most graphic summaries of the Copernican revolution that he experienced in and after his encounter with the resurrected Christ on the Damascus road. Paul in turn wants to

---

33. As we will see, sin and other "powers" are so personified in Paul that they are often capitalized in English.

grasp that for which he was grasped by Christ (v. 12), that is, to "gain Christ" (v. 8) and eventually, with him, perfection at the resurrection of the dead.

Paul characterizes his ongoing experience of Christ as "knowing Christ Jesus my Lord" (v. 8), which he then defines more concretely as knowing "the power of his resurrection and the sharing [fellowship, *koinōnia*] of his sufferings" (v. 10). Although Paul emphasizes that the resurrection of the dead is future (Phil. 3:11; cf. 1 Corinthians 15), he wants to experience the power of the resurrection in the present. Paradoxically, however, this resurrection power is the power to share in Christ's sufferings by being "conformed" to his death.

Romans 6:1-11 presents a similar pattern of the believer's existence as the outworking of the death and resurrection experience that is baptism. Death and burial with Christ result in a resurrection to newness of life in the present (6:4) and to a resurrection "like his [Christ's]" in the future (6:5).[34] As we saw above, however, the newness of life to which believers are raised is an ongoing experience of death — specifically, death to sin — in order to be alive to God (6:11):

> [4][W]e have been buried with him by baptism into death, so that, just as Christ was raised from the dead by the glory of the Father, so we too might walk in newness of life. [5]For if we have been united with him in a death like his, we will certainly be united with him in a resurrection like his. . . . [11]So you also must consider yourselves dead to sin and alive to God in Christ Jesus.

In a word, then, Paul desires *cruciformity* as a prelude to bodily resurrection. *Cruciformity* will one day be completed by conformity to the glorified Christ, as Paul says later in Philippians 3 and elsewhere:

34. The majority of Pauline interpreters, fearful of finding a "triumphalist" strain in Paul with any notion of present resurrection (or "realized eschatology"), refuse to acknowledge the clear parallel in Rom. 6:4 between Christ's resurrection and believers' newness of life and thus the presence of a present, as well as a future, resurrection of believers. The erroneous assertion that resurrection is only future is, according to G. B. Caird, "a shallow travesty of Paul's argument, which turns from first to last on the style of life which the believer is to live now" because "[t]he old life is dead, crucified with Christ . . . , and a new life lies open, in union with the risen Lord" (G. B. Caird, *New Testament Theology*, completed and edited by L. D. Hurst [Oxford: Clarendon, 1994], pp. 187-88). See also A. J. M. Wedderburn, *Baptism and Resurrection: Studies in Pauline Theology against Its Graeco-Roman Background* (Tübingen: J. C. B. Mohr [Paul Siebeck], 1987), who argues persuasively that the life that emerges from baptism, inasmuch as baptism is a "rite of passage" (pp. 363-71), is indeed a resurrection to new life that anticipates the final resurrected state; it is a "striking, paradoxical combination of realized and not yet fully realized eschatology" (p. 358). As Wedderburn stresses (e.g., pp. 349-50), and we will see throughout this book, this new life has a cruciform character.

He will transform the body of our humiliation that it may be conformed to the body of his glory. . . . (Phil. 3:21; cf. Rom. 8:29; 1 Cor. 15:49; 2 Cor. 3:18)

In 2 Corinthians 3:18, Paul clearly suggests that transformation into glory begins in the present and advances by degrees into the eschatological future:

[A]ll of us, with unveiled faces, seeing the glory of the Lord as though reflected in a mirror, are being transformed into the same image from one degree of glory to another; for this comes from the Lord, the Spirit.

On the surface this appears to contradict the claim that conformity to the cross — cruciformity — is the *modus operandi* of Paul's spirituality in the present. In fact, however, there is no contradiction. No letter stresses cruciformity as the norm of existence in Christ more than 2 Corinthians. Implicitly, Paul's paradoxical point in 2 Corinthians 3:18 is that somehow in the midst of suffering and cruciformity, transformation into the image of the glorified Christ is taking place. (Paul hints at this paradox more explicitly in 2 Corinthians 4:7-12.)

The great Pauline paradox is that one comes to know the power and glory of Christ, the resurrection and life of Christ, through cruciformity. Ernst Käsemann put it this way:

For [Paul], Jesus' glory consists in the fact that he makes his earthly disciples willing and able to take up the cross after him; and the glory of the church and the Christian life is that they are thought worthy to praise the one who was crucified as the power and wisdom of God, to seek salvation in him alone and to turn their existence into the service of God under the token of the cross.[35]

In later chapters, we will explore more precisely what Paul means by this ongoing goal of conformity to the crucified Son of God.

"In Christ and Christ Within"

The Heart of Paul's Experience of Christ

In the text from Philippians 3 cited above, Paul refers to his desire to be found "in" Christ (v. 9). Though the phrase "in him" is not the obvious focus of this passage, the notion of being "in Christ" lies at the heart of Pauline spirituality.

35. Käsemann, "Saving Significance," p. 59.

Much ink has been spilled discussing what Albert Schweitzer called Paul's "in-Christ mysticism."[36] Schweitzer eloquently argued that this, not "righteousness/justification by faith," was the center of Paul's theology and experience:

> The doctrine of righteousness by faith is therefore a subsidiary crater, which has formed within the rim of the main crater — the mystical doctrine of redemption through being-in-Christ.[37]

In 1977 E. P. Sanders once again challenged the dominant interpretation of Paul by suggesting that "participation in Christ," not justification by faith, was the center of Paul's theology.[38] This personal, if not "mystical" (an elusive adjective), experience of being in Christ is certainly the heart of Paul's experience, and perhaps also of his theology. Yet it is important to understand how Paul understood and described his experience.

The phrase "in Christ [Jesus]" occurs more than fifty times in the undisputed Pauline letters, while the phrases "in the Lord [Jesus/Jesus Christ]" and "in Christ Jesus our Lord" together appear a total of nearly forty times.[39] Some of these texts refer to what God has done "in Christ,"[40] but the vast majority refer to existence in Christ. The language is not so much mystical as it is spatial: to live within a "sphere" of influence. The precise meaning of the phrase varies from context to context, but to be "in Christ" principally means to be under the influence of Christ's power, especially the power to be conformed to him and his cross, by participation in the life of a community that acknowledges his lordship.

This communal dimension of Paul's in-Christ spirituality is very important.[41] Spirituality for Paul is not private but communal; this fact is much more

---

36. Albert Schweitzer, *The Mysticism of the Apostle Paul* (London: Black, 1931).

37. Schweitzer, *Mysticism*, p. 225.

38. E. P. Sanders, *Paul and Palestinian Judaism* (Philadelphia: Fortress, 1977), pp. 431-523. Some of the most significant lines in Sanders's argument are the following: "The participatory union is not a figure of speech for something else; it is, as many scholars have insisted, real" (p. 455); "That Paul, in thinking of the significance of Christ's death, was thinking more in terms of a *change of lordship* which guarantees future salvation than in terms of the expiation of past transgressions, is readily seen by reviewing the passages concerning the Christian's *death with Christ. It is these passages which reveal the true significance of Christ's death in Paul's thought*" (p. 466; emphasis in the original); "[Paul] is not primarily concerned with juristic categories, although he works with them. The real bite of his theology lies in the participatory categories, *even though he himself did not distinguish them in this way*" (p. 502; emphasis in the original).

39. Also, the phrase "in him" occurs twice in the undisputed letters. Altogether, then, the "in [Christ/the Lord]" phraseology occurs almost 100 times.

40. For example, "in Christ God [or God in Christ] was reconciling the world to himself" (2 Cor. 5:19).

41. See esp. ch. 13.

evident in Greek than in English translation, since nearly all of Paul's pronouns of address ("you," etc.) are plural pronouns in the Greek text. Being "in Christ" refers to the experience not merely of the individual but of the community, into which the person of faith is baptized and in which he or she coexists with others:

> There is therefore now no condemnation for those who are in Christ Jesus. (Rom. 8:1)

> Are you [plural] not my work in the Lord? (1 Cor. 9:1d)

> [A]ll of you are one in Christ Jesus. . . . (Gal. 3:28)

> [I]n Christ Jesus neither circumcision nor uncircumcision counts for anything; the only thing that counts is faith working through love. (Gal. 5:6)

As we will see below, Paul's "in Christ" language can be used as a reminder that a church does not merely exist in itself, as a human community, but as a community in Christ:

> Have this mindset in your community, which is indeed a community in Christ. (Phil. 2:5; author's translation)[42]

To say that Paul's spirituality is not private does not mean, however, that his spirituality is impersonal. As we saw earlier, Paul speaks of "knowing Christ Jesus *my* Lord" (Phil. 3:8). He says that he "rejoice[s] in the Lord" (Phil. 4:10). Moreover, he describes his relationship with Christ not only as one of being in Christ but also as one of Christ being in him:

> [I]t is no longer I who live, but it is Christ who lives in me. (Gal. 2:20a; cf. Rom. 8:10)

Here, as Richard Hays writes, "Paul is provocatively denying his own role as the acting 'subject' of his own life and claiming that he has been supplanted in this capacity by Christ."[43]

Even this aspect of a relationship with Christ, however, is not merely an in-

---

42. More literally, "in you [all], which is also in Christ." For a defense of this translation, see the excursus below.

43. Richard B. Hays, *The Faith of Jesus Christ: An Investigation of the Narrative Substructure of Galatians 3:1–4:11*, SBLDS 56 (Chico, Calif.: Scholars Press, 1983), p. 168. Hays continues, remarking on the meaning of 2:20b: "'the faith of the Son of God' is now the governing power in Paul's existence." The meaning of the second half of this text will be discussed in the chapters on faith.

embryological,
symbiosis, or
interpenetration.

Christ-intimacy

reciprocal or
mutual
indwelling

dividual experience. In Galatians 4:19, for example, Paul describes his ministry in embryological terms as participating in the process of Christ's being "formed" within the Galatian community. Similarly, he admonishes the Corinthians as a community to examine themselves to discern whether Christ is truly "in" — that is, "within" or "among" — them corporately:

> Examine yourselves to see whether you [plural] are living in the faith. Test yourselves. Do you not realize that Jesus Christ is in you [plural; therefore "in your fellowship"]? — unless, indeed, you [plural] fail to meet the test! (2 Cor. 13:5)[44]

This relationship of believers in Christ and Christ in believers is sometimes referred to as "symbiosis" or "interpenetration."[45] A vivid description was offered by Adolf Deissmann in the early part of the twentieth century, who compared Paul's "Christ-intimacy" to the air we breathe:

> Just as the air of life, which we breathe, is "in" us and fills us, and yet we at the same time live in this air and breathe it, so it is also with the Christ-intimacy of the Apostle Paul: Christ in him, he in Christ.[46]

Another way to describe this relationship is as the *reciprocal* or *mutual indwelling* of Christ and believers: the Christ in whom believers live also lives in them, both individually and corporately. As James Dunn succinctly puts it, this is for Paul and his communities "something like a mystical sense of the divine presence of Christ *within and without.*"[47] Yet this "mystical sense" yields not an emotional experience but a narrative of reciprocity. Just as believers have been baptized into Christ's story, so also his story is relived in and among the baptized.

Interestingly, Paul suggests that the relationship of mutual indwelling between Christ and the believer has a precedent. For those outside of Christ, sin both dwells in them (Rom. 7:17, 20) and is the sphere in which, and under the power of which, they dwell (Rom. 7:14; cf. 3:9). For Paul, the presence and power of Christ have replaced sin as the power that lives within him and the

---

44. The phrase translated "in you" is the same as that used in Phil. 2:5 *(en hymin)* and should also be rendered "in your midst" or "in your community."

45. "Symbiosis": Fitzmyer, *Paul and His Theology,* p. 84; "interpenetration": Ben Witherington III, *Paul's Narrative Thought World: The Tapestry of Tragedy and Triumph* (Louisville: Westminster/John Knox, 1994), p. 277.

46. Adolf Deissmann, *Paul: A Study in Social and Religious History* (New York: Harper, 1957; orig. 1912, rev. 1926), p. 140.

47. Dunn, *Theology,* p. 401; emphasis added.

power within which he lives. Those outside of Christ are "in the flesh," the sphere governed by sin, a location from which they cannot please God (Rom. 8:8).

Paul can also describe his experience of the indwelling Christ as "the power" of Christ "dwell[ing] in me" (2 Cor. 12:9) or "the love of Christ compel[ling] us" (2 Cor. 5:14; NRSV "urges us on" is too weak). In these passages about the presence, power, or love of Christ within, as we shall see in detail in later chapters, Paul connects Christ's present indwelling to his past death on the cross, and Christ's indwelling power to Paul's own weakness. The indwelling Christ is the loving Christ, the one whose love found its definitive expression in his self-giving death on the cross (Gal. 2:20). These connections together echo Phil. 3:10, cited above, in which Paul's experience of the power of Christ's resurrection is linked to his suffering and his conformity to Christ's death.

Conformity and Indwelling: Individual and Corporate

Two texts that demonstrate the centrality and vitality of Paul's spirituality of mutual indwelling are Galatians 2:20 and Philippians 2:5:

> [I]t is no longer I who live, but it is Christ who lives in me. And the life I now live in the flesh I live by faith in [or, "by the faithfulness of"][48] the Son of God, who loved me and gave himself for me. (Gal. 2:20)

> Let the same mind be in you that was in Christ Jesus. . . . (Phil. 2:5, NRSV)

As suggested above, and as will be argued in the excursus below, the better translation of this verse is as follows:

> Have this mindset in your community, which is indeed a community in Christ. . . .

These two texts, Galatians 2:20 and Philippians 2:5, have several things in common. First, each is part of the "hub" of its particular letter. Galatians 2:20 occurs in the thesis paragraph of Galatians, 2:15-21. Philippians 2:5 introduces the Christ-hymn that Paul cites as the centerpiece of that letter, and it connects the hymn to the moral exhortations given in context.

Second, each of these texts uses the preposition "in" with respect to Christ,

---

48. For this translation, which is to be preferred, see the discussion in chapter six.

though in different ways. According to Galatians 2:20, Christ is "in me," that is, in Paul. Speaking both autobiographically and paradigmatically, Paul claims that his normal, everyday life is somehow enabled by another, namely, Christ, such that the hyberbolic statement "I no longer live" makes sense. Christ is within Paul and, indeed, within every individual believer; this is a personal spirituality of being indwelt by Christ. According to Philippians 2:5, as I have suggested in the alternative translation above, the community is in Christ; this is a corporate spirituality of dwelling in Christ.

Because Philippians 2:5 is a notoriously difficult translation problem, and because the translation significantly affects our understanding of Pauline spirituality, a close analysis of this verse, its traditional translations, and the alternative offered here is presented in the following excursus. Readers may choose to follow the argument of the excursus or accept its conclusion and continue reading after the excursus (p. 43).

EXCURSUS

Philippians 2:5 is a significant Pauline text because it forms a bridge between an exhortation (1:27–2:4, especially 2:1-4) and a poetic text (believed by most scholars to be a pre-Pauline hymn or hymn fragment) about Christ that somehow functions as the basis for the exhortation. The interpretation of 2:5 affects the interpretation of the connection between hymn and exhortation, between Christology and spirituality. Does Paul exhort the Philippians to adopt a mindset that Christ had, or does he tell them to maintain a mindset that they already have "in Christ"? Does he promote the imitation of the suffering, dying Jesus, or does he promote obedience to Christ the Lord? Or, somehow, does he do both?[49]

The verse, including the first word of verse 6, reads as follows in the Greek text and in a wooden translation of the Greek:

touto phroneite	*en hymin*	*ho kai*		*en Christō Iēsou, hos . . .*
This think	in yourselves	which also	[verb missing]	in Christ Jesus, who . . .
	["you" plural]			

The chief difficulties in the translation of verse 5 are two, and they are related. First, to what do the words "this" (Greek *touto*) and "which" (Greek *ho*) refer?

---

49. The literature on this verse, as on 2:6-11, is vast. For a balanced approach to the entire problem, see Hurtado, "Jesus as Lordly Example."

Second, what verb is to be supplied after "which also" (Greek *ho kai*) in order to make sense of the text? We will begin with the second issue, which affects the first.

The verb missing after the word translated "also" has traditionally been understood as either (a) a form of the verb "to be," usually "was," or (b) another occurrence of the verb translated "think," this time making a statement rather than an exhortation. The two basic translations are as follows:

a Think this in yourselves which also *was* in Christ Jesus, who. . . .
b Think this in yourselves which also *you think* in Christ Jesus, who. . . .

In actual translations, these two options emerge in such ways as the following:

a Let the same mind be in you that *was* in Christ Jesus, who. . . . (NRSV and most translators and interpreters)
b Let the same mind be in you that *you have* in Christ Jesus, who. . . . (NRSV margin and some translators and interpreters)

Those (the majority) who support translation "a" normally understand "this" and "which" to look ahead to the hymn and believe that the hymn depicts the "thinking" or "mind" that was "in" Christ, that is, Christ's attitude of humility. Because of similarities between the "mind" of Christ described in the hymn and the behavior enjoined for believers in 2:1-4, the word "this" may also refer backward to the content of 2:1-4. This interpretation often sees the connection between exhortation *(phroneite)* and hymn as the imitation of Christ.

Those who prefer translation "b" emphasize (rightly) that the Pauline phrase "in Christ" is a standard term for the community that lives in the sphere of Christ's lordship, not for some inward attitude Christ had. They tend to take "this" and "which" not as references ahead to Jesus' mindset but as general references to the Christian mindset, or as references to the "attitude" articulated in 2:1-4. Verse 5, identifying a mindset the readers already have in Christ, means something like "become what you are" or "live out the attitude that you in fact have in the realm of Christ, the one who was humbled but is now your exalted Lord." The connection between exhortation and hymn in this view is obedience within Christ's lordship (see 2:12). Critics of this interpretation, however, point out (rightly) the awkward if not nonsensical translation that emerges when the indicative verb "you have" is supplied.

A different translation from "a" and "b," which combines some insights of "a" (Jesus as example) and "b" ("in Christ" as a reference to the community in him and under his lordship) is possible but has seldom been suggested.[50] This translation takes "in Christ" as a reference to the community (option "b"), and thus it does not take the word "which" to refer back to "this" as a reference to the "attitude" that was supposedly "in" Christ.[51] Rather, and what is completely new, the word "which" is understood in conjunction with the following word, translated "also," and with the missing verb. Together they produce, with emphasis, something like the Greek equivalent of the Latin phrase *id est* ("i.e.") or the English "that is." The resulting phrase, "which also [is]" (Greek *ho kai* [*estin*]), functions like an equal sign for the two linguistic elements on either side.[52]

The Greek phrase *ho kai* ("which also") was, in fact, used in public inscriptions to identify a person's "alternative name" or "nickname" and to link the person's formal name to this informal name (Latin *signum*). Thus the phrase *ho kai* meant something like "[who is] also called" or, as we say in English, "a.k.a."[53] "Which also" should be interpreted, therefore, as a phrase linking and equating "in you [plural]," meaning *among* you," with "in Christ."[54] The phrases are parallel:

en hymin	"in [among] you"
ho kai	which also [is]
en Christō	"in Christ"

The resulting (wooden) translation is:

'50. The only other interpreter of whom I am aware who follows this line of interpretation is G. B. Caird in his commentary on Philippians (*Paul's Letters from Prison in the Revised Standard Version*, NCB [Oxford: Oxford University Press, 1976], pp. 118-19). Gordon D. Fee (*Paul's Letter to the Philippians*, NICNT [Grand Rapids: Eerdmans, 1995], p. 201, n. 33) rejects it prematurely. For a more thorough discussion of this translation, see Michael J. Gorman, "The Self, the Lord, and the Other: The Significance of Reflexive Pronoun Constructions in the Letters of Paul, with a Comparison to the 'Discourses' of Epictetus," Ph.D. diss., Princeton Theological Seminary, 1989, pp. 690-98, esp. pp. 694-98.

51. It is preferable, but not necessary, to understand the word "this" to refer backward, to the mindset or way of perceiving and acting described in 2:1-4 (so, e.g., Caird). However, it could also refer ahead to the narrative of Christ, in whom believers live, as an embodiment of the mindset described in 2:1-4. In either case, however, the word "which" is not to be connected with "this."

52. Caird (*Paul's Letters*, pp. 118-19) specifically interprets the Greek *ho kai* as the "equivalent of the Latin *id est* [i.e.]" and translates the text as follows: "'this is the disposition which must govern your common life, i.e. your life in Christ Jesus, because he. . . .'"

53. See Jerome Murphy O'Connor, *Paul: A Critical Life* (Oxford/New York: Oxford University Press, 1997), p. 43 and the citations there. The Latin equivalent in inscriptions was *qui et*.

54. As noted above, this Greek phrase is the same one *(en hymin)* Paul uses in 2 Cor. 13:5 and is similar to the gospel text that is correctly translated to say that the kingdom of God is "among" — not "within" — you: Luke 17:21 *(entos hymōn).*

Think this way in [*en*] **yourselves**, which also is in [*en*] Christ, who. . . .

A better translation, as suggested above, would be:

Have this mindset **in your community**, which is indeed a **community in Christ**, who. . . .

The emphasis in the text is on the reality that life "within you (all)" is life "within" Christ. For this reason, there must be a correspondence between Christ and believers, between his story and theirs, between the hymnic narrative of Christ (presented in vv. 6-11) and the "attitude" or way of thinking and life of the Philippian community.

Thus the "in Christ" language of this verse is thoroughly consistent with its most common usage elsewhere in Paul: a reference to corporate life in union with Christ and within his sphere of influence and lordship. (Indeed, there is no Pauline text in which Paul speaks of some thing or attitude being "in" Christ.) The verses that are "bridged" by 2:5, that is, 2:1-4 and 2:6-11, define the character of life — the spirituality — of the in-Christ community as a correspondence to the one within whom they live.

Third, then (returning to our points of commonality in Gal. 2:20 and Phil. 2:5), in each of these texts Paul connects the spiritual-moral life to Christology (convictions about Christ) — not only *his* Christology, but that of the broader community of churches. Galatians 2:20, most scholars believe, adapts a traditional creedal "formula" in the words "the Son of God who . . . gave himself for me," while Philippians 2:5, as we have noted, may introduce a pre-Pauline hymn text.

More specifically, in each text it is the crucified and now resurrected or exalted Christ who indwells or is indwelt. Paul claims in Galatians 2:20 that it is no longer he who lives "but it is Christ who lives in me." Since clearly the dead cannot "live" in anyone, there is an implicit reference here to Jesus as the living Lord, raised from the dead, exalted, and able in some sense to be present in the life of Paul. Nonetheless — and this is absolutely crucial — this living Christ is the same Son of God who "loved me and gave himself for me." As noted at the beginning of this chapter, the cross is the "signature" of the risen Lord.[55] That

55. Käsemann, "Saving Significance," p. 25. Käsemann also appropriately notes that Christ "would have no name by which he could be called were it not the name of the crucified" (p. 56). Thus, he continues, "it is only the one who was crucified who is risen, and the lordship of the one who is risen marches with the present service of the one who was crucified" (p. 57); and "Je-

is, the indwelling Christ is the crucified Son of God, and the life he now lives in "me" — in and through my life — corresponds to the life of self-giving love he exemplified in his death by crucifixion.[56]

In Philippians 2, Paul seeks to describe and encourage the appropriate kind of "mind," thinking, or attitude for the ("Christian") community, for those "in Christ" (2:5). This "mind" is really a life-style of love and humility, as the preceding verses indicate (1:27–2:4, especially 2:1-4).[57] We will examine these verses carefully in a later chapter. For now we simply note that Paul grounds this life-style of unity through humility and love in the following hymn-text, where Christ is presented as a humble servant, not merely as an example but as the defining presence within which the community lives. Or, to put it once again in narrative terms, *the narrative of the crucified and exalted Christ is the normative life-narrative within which the community's own life-narrative takes place and by which it is shaped.* Only living in the presence of the exalted Christ, and perceiving the meaning of his death, makes this possible. What the exalted Christ, properly perceived, makes possible is a life conformed to his own story of self-humbling and self-giving, even to the point of death. Those who live in this Messiah will cultivate the vision of life articulated in Philippians 2:1-4 because it was first embodied in him.

---

sus remains the one who was crucified; and it is only as the one who was crucified that he remains Jesus" (p. 59).

56. In an otherwise excellent article, Victor Paul Furnish ("'He Gave Himself [Was Given] Up . . .': Paul's Use of a Christological Assertion," in Abraham J. Malherbe and Wayne A. Meeks, eds., *The Future of Christology: Essays in Honor of Leander E. Keck* [Minneapolis: Fortress, 1993], pp. 109-21, esp. 113-15, 119-21) — trying to rescue Paul from the temptation to "moralize" — fails to note the clear correspondence in Galatians between Christ's act of love for our justification and his ongoing activity of love in the community's experience, whereby Christ's "act of utterly selfless love" (p. 115) becomes the community's mandate and norm. Furnish claims that Paul does not use the traditional self-giving texts "either to heroize Jesus' death or to moralize about it. In every instance it is only its soteriological [salvific] significance, even if variously understood, that Paul has in view" (p. 121). Furnish's conclusion is especially surprising and misdirected since he himself links Paul's words about Christ's self-giving to the themes of freedom and crucifixion of the old self, which are clearly moral topics.

57. Stephen Fowl has rightly emphasized in personal conversation that the activity indicated by the Greek words *phroneō* and *phronēsis* is not a purely mental event but a perceptual skill, a way of seeing that results in a corresponding way of living.

"In" Christ as "with" Christ, "according to" Christ, and "for" Christ

We have seen that for Paul, to be in Christ is to live a life of cruciformity, to be shaped by his presence and his story, not only from without but also from within, because it is true also that "Christ lives in me." As noted briefly earlier, the intimacy of this Pauline experience often finds expression in phrases and words that are translated into English using the word "with." In the Greek text, some of these are expressions using the preposition "with" (Greek *syn*), while others are words having the preposition as a prefix meaning "with" or "co-." These passages express intimate identification with Christ. A list of these texts follows, with the English rendition of prepositions italicized and of prefixed words boldfaced:

"we have been **buried with him** [*synetaphēmen*] by baptism into [his] death, so that, just as Christ was raised from the dead by the glory of the Father, so we too might walk in newness of life" (Rom. 6:4)

"I **have been crucified wit**h [*synestaurōmai*] Christ" (Gal. 2:19c)

"our old self was **crucified with him** [*synestaurōthē*]" (Rom. 6:6)

"I want to know Christ and the power of his resurrection and the sharing of his sufferings by **becoming like him** [*symmorphizomenos*, "co-formed"] in his death" (Phil. 3:10)

"if we have been **united with him** [*symphytoi*] in a death like his, we will certainly [be united with him] in a resurrection [like his]" (Rom. 6:5; the words in brackets occur in the NRSV but are only implied in the Greek text)

"if we have died *with* Christ [*apethanomen syn Christō*], we believe that we will also **live with** him [*syzēsomen*]" (Rom. 6:8)

"if children [of God], then heirs, heirs of God and **joint heirs** [*synklēronomoi*] with Christ — if, in fact, we **suffer with him** [*sympaschomen*] so that we may also **be glorified with him** [*syndoxasthōmen*]" (Rom. 8:17)

"those whom he foreknew he also predestined to be **conformed** [*symmorphous*] **to** the image of his Son" (Rom. 8:29)

"the Lord Jesus Christ . . . will transform the body of our humiliation that it may be **conformed** [*symmorphon*] to the body of his glory" (Phil. 3:20-21) "the one who raised the Lord Jesus will raise us also *with* [*syn*] Jesus, and will bring us with you into his presence" (2 Cor. 4:14)

"my desire is to depart [die] and be *with* [*syn*] Christ" (Phil. 1:23)

"then . . . we will be *with* [*syn*] the Lord forever" (1 Thess. 4:17; cf. v. 14)

"[the Lord Jesus Christ] died for us, so that whether we are awake or asleep [alive or dead] we may live [or perhaps "come to life"] *with* him [*syn autọ*]" (1 Thess. 5:10)

"we are weak in him, but in dealing with you we will live *with* [*syn*] him by the power of God" (2 Cor. 13:4)

The list of highlighted words and phrases suggests clearly that Paul envisions life in Christ as life *with* Christ, from baptism to death and resurrection, from inception to glorious and eternal "conclusion." In fact, the highlighted terms correspond very closely to early creedal texts that have been preserved in the New Testament, including 1 Corinthians 15:3-7. That is, this series of "with" and "co-" phrases tells the story of Christ and of believers. Paul's spirituality is, as we have already noted, a *narrative* spirituality. The believer's life is life with Christ, corresponding to all the key moments of Christ's story, and participating in each of them individually and the entire life of Christ as a whole. English expressions containing the word "with" simply do not do justice to much of Paul's language, experience, or thinking in this regard. The prefix "co-" does a better job; Paul says that we have been co-buried and co-crucified with Christ, that we have been co-formed with his death and will be co-formed with his resurrection in glory, that if we co-suffer with Christ we are co-heirs with him and will be co-glorified with him.

The focus of this participation is on suffering and death with Christ in the present, and on resurrection and glory in the future. According to Romans 6:4, however, as we noted above, the resurrection begins already by means of a new life, a life — as Paul implies in Romans 6 and says explicitly elsewhere — of conformity to Christ's death. The language of Romans 6:5, though it focuses on future resurrection, suggests, by using the perfect tense ("we have been united with him in a death like his"), that union with Christ's death is not a one-time past event but an ongoing reality.[58] Present resurrection, then, is resurrection to "death," to cruciformity. What the present and future, cruciformity and glory,

58. See Robert C. Tannehill's classic study, *Dying and Rising with Christ: A Study in Pauline Theology* (Berlin: Alfred Töpelmann, 1966), pp. 38-39. As Tannehill suggests, there is also an echo of Phil. 3:10 in the Greek text of Rom. 6:5.

have in common, is that they both take place with Christ, in his presence. Whether dead or alive, Paul and his communities are <u>*with* Christ</u>, as 1 Thessalonians 5:10 puts it.

This last text (1 Thess. 5:10) leads us briefly to two other prepositions, "for," which is expressed in Greek not with a preposition but by means of the "case," or meaning-bearing form, of nouns,[59] and "according to" or "in accordance with" (Greek *kata*). To live *in* Christ and *with* Christ is ultimately also to live *for* Christ. Paul expresses this thought concretely only twice, but the phrases are central to his thinking and experience:

> [7]We do not live to ourselves, and we do not die to ourselves. [8]If we live, we live to [i.e., for the sake of] the Lord, and if we die, we die to [for the sake of] the Lord. . . . [9]For to this end Christ died and lived again, so that he might be Lord of both the dead and the living. (Rom. 14:7-9)

> [Christ] died for all, so that those who live might no longer live for themselves, but for him who died and was raised for them. (2 Cor. 5:15)

We will return briefly to these texts in later chapters. For now we note that Paul connects both the *motive* for and the *goal* of spirituality to the death and resurrection of Jesus, just as elsewhere he connects the *form* of spirituality to Jesus' death and resurrection. That is to say, the cross and resurrection both motivate and shape daily life. The appropriate life "for" or "toward" Christ is the cruciform life.

Life "for" Christ, however, is simultaneously life "for" others. This has to be the case because the cross and resurrection were for others. This will be the subject especially of the chapters on cruciform love. For now we simply note that in Romans 14 and 15 Paul spells out the practical consequences for community life of living for Christ, and he does this most emphatically by appealing to the example of Christ:

> [1]We who are strong ought to put up with the failings of the weak, and not to please ourselves. [2]Each of us must please our neighbor for the good purpose of building up the neighbor. [3]For Christ did not please himself; but, as it is written, "The insults of those who insult you have fallen on me." . . . [5]May the God of steadfastness and encouragement grant you to live in harmony with one another, in accordance with *(kata)* Christ Jesus, [6]so that together you may with one voice glorify the God and Father of our Lord Jesus Christ. (Rom. 15:1-3, 5-6)

---

59. "For" can be expressed in Greek with the dative case.

To live "à la" Christ is Paul's experience and vision. It is this vision of unity, especially between Jews and Gentiles, within congregations and ultimately throughout the whole world, that drives him to live and preach the word of the cross.

Conclusion: Cruciformity and the "Imitation" of Christ

It is here, in the context of conformity, indwelling, and living "with," "for," and "according to" Christ, that we should conclude by briefly considering the traditional notion of Paul's "imitation" of Christ. For many centuries the imitation of Christ motif has been a central part of Christian spirituality, though its meaning has hardly been static. Some Pauline scholars, however, have argued that Paul himself had no concept of imitating Christ. For Paul, they argue, Christ is to be obeyed as Lord, not imitated. One of their objections, as noted above in the discussion of Philippians 2:5, is that Paul's "in Christ" language indicates a relational "sphere" in which one lives under the domain of a lord; Christ is not a distant object to be copied or even a heroic person (divine or otherwise) to be emulated.

This is a classic case of "either-or" interpretations that should be "both-and." Paul does speak of himself as an imitator of Christ, and he does understand himself — and other faithful believers — to be similar in certain fundamental ways to Christ the Lord. Paul's being an imitator of Christ is not so much something he does but something that has happened to him.[60] It is the result of being in Christ and of Christ being in him; it is the result of an influence, a power, that operates in and on Paul. "Imitation," especially if understood as a process of human effort, is not the best word to describe this experience. As Robert Tannehill has said, for Paul being imitators of Christ "is less a matter of conscious imitation than the result of the power of the gospel working itself out in the lives of believers so that a certain pattern results."[61]

The process of "imitation" is therefore better called Christ's *formation* in believers (Gal. 4:19), and the result, believers' *conformity* to Christ, especially to his cross (Phil. 3:10). Cruciformity, I therefore suggest, is a term more appropriate for what has often been referred to as the "imitation" of Christ. Cruciformity is an ongoing pattern of living in Christ and of dying with him

60. It is interesting, and possibly significant in this regard, that Paul admonishes his congregations to "become imitators" of him (1 Thess. 1:6; 1 Cor. 4:16) and of him as an imitator of Christ (1 Cor. 11:1), but he seldom or never uses the verb "imitate" (only 2 Thess. 3:7, 9, if authentic). Nor does he ever directly say to imitate Christ.

61. Tannehill, *Dying and Rising*, p. 103.

48

Cruciformity

that produces a Christ-like (cruciform) person. Cruciform existence is what being Christ's servant, indwelling him and being indwelt by him, living with and for and "according to" him, is all about, for both individuals and communities.

For Paul, cruciformity cannot be attributed to human effort. There is a power at work within him and within his communities that somehow, he claims, produces Christ-like qualities. This power enables the exalted crucified Christ to take shape in and among those who belong to him and live in him. It enables the narrative of the cross to be retold and relived. This power is, for Paul, the Spirit of God, who is also the Spirit of Christ. In the next chapter we examine Paul's experience of the Spirit, the Spirit of cruciformity.[62]

---

62. For a provocative treatment of Paul's *merkabah* experiences and his entire life as one of being possessed by the Spirit, see John Ashton, *The Religion of Paul the Apostle* (New Haven and London: Yale University Press, 2000), which appeared too late for use throughout this book. Although some will balk at Ashton's comparison of Paul to a shaman, he rightly stresses Paul's religious experience. My chief quarrel with Ashton is that he does not sufficiently stress the cruciform character of Paul's Spirit-possession.

CHAPTER 3

THE SPIRIT OF CRUCIFORMITY

Paul's Experience of the Spirit of God, the Spirit of Christ

The Spirit of God is usually associated with power: the power of creation, of moral and spiritual transformation, and ultimately of new creation. For Paul, too, the Spirit was powerful, but power had been redefined in his experience by the "word of the cross . . . [which is] the power of God" (1 Cor. 1:18, author's translation). In this chapter we briefly explore Paul's experience of the Spirit in light of, and in connection with, his experience of the crucified and exalted Jesus.[1]

An Uncharismatic Charismatic

The word "charismatic" has two uses. In general usage it refers to someone who is dynamic and magnetic in personality or leadership style. In religious circles, it refers to someone who is possessed by the Spirit of God and manifests certain spiritual experiences and gifts. Paul was a charismatic believer, but a very unusual, indeed an uncharismatic, charismatic.

On the one hand, Paul considered himself to have had numerous spiritual gifts and experiences that are often termed "charismatic." His Spirit-inspired gifts, he testifies, included not only that of apostleship but also glossolalia

1. The most thorough work on Paul and the Spirit is Gordon D. Fee, *God's Empowering Presence: The Holy Spirit in the Letters of Paul* (Peabody, Mass.: Hendrickson, 1994). See also his abridgment of this work, *Paul, the Spirit, and the People of God* (Peabody, Mass.: Hendrickson, 1996). For a brief but important overview, see Paul W. Meyer, "The Holy Spirit in the Pauline Letters," *Interpretation* 33 (1979): 3-18. See also now John Ashton, *The Religion of Paul the Apostle* (New Haven and London: Yale University Press, 2000).

uncharismatic
Paul is

(speaking in tongues: 1 Cor. 14:18) and, it would seem, the ability occasionally to perform "signs and wonders" (Rom. 15:19; 2 Cor. 12:12), including the power to heal and even exorcise evil spirits (Acts 19:11-13; 28:7-10; cf. Gal. 3:5).[2] In defense of his own apostleship, he maintains that

> [t]he signs of a true apostle were performed among you with utmost patience, signs and wonders and mighty works. (2 Cor. 12:12)

Moreover, as we saw in the last chapter, Paul received at least one "revelation of Jesus Christ" (Gal. 1:12; cf. 1:16), and he had other visionary or revelatory experiences, including the one he described as a voyage to heaven (2 Cor. 12:1-7a). *are* Paul forbids the hindrance of charismatic gifts in corporate worship, though he provides certain criteria for their use (1 Corinthians 14; 1 Thess. 5:19-21). He not only reports his possession of such gifts, he can even boast of his own charismatic experience to demonstrate either the appropriateness of expressing the gifts (1 Cor. 14:18) or, as noted in the previous chapter, the value of them as confirmation of his apostleship (2 Cor. 12:12).

On the other hand, however, Paul was quite uncharismatic. He shunned rhetorical eloquence (at least in person: 1 Cor. 2:1-5), and he was roundly criticized for his weak, uncharismatic presence (2 Cor. 10:10; cf. also 1 Cor. 4:3-5). Thus Paul experienced both the ecstasy of charismatic (that is, Spirit-inspired) experience and the embarrassment, at one level, of uncharismatic (that is, unbecoming, unimpressive) presence.

These two uses of "charismatic," one referring to religiosity, the other to personality, may at first seem unrelated. Yet in Paul's day, Spirit and power — including personal and rhetorical power — were interconnected.[3] Nevertheless, although Paul can (hesitantly) boast of his charismatic experience, he boasts even more of his weakness, and he does so *in the same context:*

> [5]. . . [O]n my own behalf I will not boast, except of my weaknesses. . . . [9]. . . I will boast all the more gladly of my weaknesses, so that the power of Christ

---

2. On these matters the book of Acts and Paul's letters agree, even if they receive less emphasis in the letters. According to Acts 20:7-12, Paul may also have raised the dead on at least one occasion.

3. Raymond Pickett (*The Cross in Corinth: The Social Significance of the Death of Jesus*, JSNTSup 143 [Sheffield: Sheffield Academic Press, 1997], p. 56) finds evidence that "in Greco-Roman society rhetorical skill could be regarded as proof of the speaker's possession of the Spirit." Pickett's book argues that at Corinth the display of manifestations of the Spirit was understood as power, and also that the culturally powerful were assumed to be spiritually powerful as well. See also Wayne Meeks, *The Moral World of the First Christians* (Philadelphia: Westminster, 1986), pp. 119-22.

may dwell in me. . . . [10][F]or whenever I am weak, then I am strong. (2 Cor. 12:5b, 9, 10b)

Understanding Paul's experience of the Spirit enables us to comprehend this paradox. *The distinctive feature of Paul's experience of the Spirit, and his resulting understanding of the essence of this Spirit, is the paradoxical symbiosis (union) of power and weakness, of power and cruciformity.* The charismatic Spirit is also the cruciform Spirit.

The Presence and Power of the Spirit

The presence and power of the Spirit is a fundamental dimension of the experience of Paul and his communities. "For Paul the Spirit, as an experience and living reality, was the absolutely crucial matter for Christian life, from beginning to end."[4] Paul everywhere assumes, and occasionally states, that all believers have the Spirit, and that without the Spirit there is no Christian believer, no Christian community (e.g., 1 Cor. 12:1-13; Rom. 8:9, 14). By the Spirit, people are "baptized into one body" and "drink" of one Spirit (1 Cor. 12:13). "In the Spirit of our God," as well as "in the name of our Lord Jesus Christ," believers were "washed . . . sanctified . . . justified" (1 Cor. 6:11). The reception and ongoing experience of the Spirit, no less than justification, is an act of God's grace appropriated by faith:

> [2]. . . Did you receive the Spirit by doing the works of the law or by believing what you heard? . . . [5]Well then, does God supply you with the Spirit and work miracles among you by your doing the works of the law, or by your believing what you heard? (Gal. 3:2b, 5)

Paul's experience and understanding of the Spirit derive at least in part from his being steeped in the Hebrew Scriptures. Of particular importance is the connection he makes between the Spirit and the human heart: God has "sent" (Gal. 4:6) or "poured out" (Rom. 5:5) the Spirit into the hearts (Greek *kardiai*) of those who respond to the gospel in faith. The Spirit-heart connection is significant in two ways. First of all, it is the (especially Gentile) human heart *(kardia)* that has been darkened by failure to acknowledge God as God (Rom. 1:21, 24; NRSV has "mind" in v. 21), and it is the (especially Jewish) human heart that has become "hard and impenitent" (Rom. 2:5) and is thus in need of "circumcision" (Rom. 2:29). The heart, then, is the "seat" of the funda-

---

4. Fee, *God's Empowering Presence*, p. 1.

52

mental human problem and the appropriate "target" for repair. Logically, then, it is in and from the heart that human response to the gospel occurs, both faith (Rom. 10:9-10) and obedience (Rom. 6:17).

These texts, and others, point to the second significant dimension of Paul's heart-Spirit link, namely, his understanding of the Spirit's presence as the fulfillment of Hebrew biblical injunctions to "circumcise the heart" (Deut. 10:16; Jer. 4:4)[5] and prophetic promises to take away Israel's hard and stony heart and replace it with a new spirit and heart, a heart of flesh (Ezek. 11:19; 18:31; 36:26). The "Israel of God" (Gal. 6:16), the community of Jews and Gentiles who have received Jesus as God's Messiah, has also received the promised Spirit, the Spirit's heart circumcision, and the law written on their hearts by the Spirit (2 Cor. 3:3; cf. Jer. 31:31-34).[6] This Spirit, then, has powerfully renewed and reconstituted God's people and now lives among them.

The Ministry of the Spirit

Romans 8 is of particular importance in understanding Paul's experience of the Spirit, the Spirit's role or "ministry" in the believer and the believing community. Several key verses may be cited:

> [3]God has done what the law, weakened by the flesh, could not do: by sending his own Son in the likeness of sinful flesh, and to deal with sin, he condemned sin in the flesh, [4]so that the just requirement of the law might be fulfilled in us, who walk not according to the flesh but according to the Spirit. . . . [8][T]hose who are in the flesh cannot please God. [9]But you are not in the flesh: you are in the Spirit, since the Spirit of God dwells in you. Anyone who does not have the Spirit of Christ does not belong to him. [10]But if Christ is in you, though the body is dead because of sin, the Spirit is life because of righteousness. [11]If the Spirit of him who raised Jesus from the dead dwells in you, he who raised Christ from the dead will give life to your mortal bodies also through his Spirit that dwells in you. (8:3-4, 8-11)

In this passage Paul narrates his understanding of the Spirit's role in his own life as well as that of all believers ("us," v. 4; "you," vv. 9-11; "anyone," v. 9); we can safely infer that Paul's description of the Romans' experience of

---

5. In Jer. 9:26 Israel, and in Ezek. 44:7-9 "foreigners," are described as people of uncircumcised heart.

6. The precise meaning of the term "Israel of God" in Paul has been debated, but the understanding I have offered here seems inevitable, at least for the letter to the Galatians.

the Spirit derives from his own experience. We also see here the interrelationship of God (the Father), the Son (Christ), and the Spirit in Paul's theology and spiritual experience; we will have more to say about this in the next chapter.

With respect to the Spirit per se, Paul characterizes the experience of being in Christ as "walking . . . according to the Spirit" (v. 4). Later, he says that believers are "led" or "guided" by the Spirit (v. 14; cf. Gal. 5:25). This language echoes many passages of the Hebrew Scriptures in which God's people are called to live out their lives as a journey in the way of the Lord, guided by the law of the Lord (e.g., Ps. 119:1). Paul, believing that the unstoppable human propensity to sin ("the flesh") had disabled the Law and prevented the doing of God's will, finds in the gift of the Spirit the power to fulfill the "just requirement of the law" (v. 4). Thus, to live "according to" the Spirit is not merely to have an external norm, but a power within, a power that acts to override, indeed to replace, the power of "the flesh," the power of sin (Rom. 7:17, 20).

Gordon Fee has recently written of Paul's understanding and experience of the Spirit as "God's empowering presence."[7] While this is certainly an accurate descriptive phrase (e.g., "the Spirit of him who raised Jesus from the dead," v. 11; "Spirit of God," v. 14), it is not sufficient, for Paul's experience of the Spirit is closely linked to his experience of Christ. As Fee himself notes, the Spirit of God is also the Spirit of Christ (Rom. 8:9; Gal. 4:4; Phil. 1:19).[8] Furthermore, Paul speaks not only of being in Christ and Christ being within, as we saw in the last chapter, but also, in Romans 8 in analogous fashion, of being in the Spirit and of the Spirit being within:

> [Y]ou are in the Spirit, since the Spirit of God dwells in you. (v. 9; cf. two occurrences in v. 11)

Thus the mutual indwelling of Christ and believers finds a parallel in the mutual indwelling of the Spirit and believers. In fact, within this very passage, Paul apparently effortlessly shifts gears and includes a reference to "Christ . . . in you" (v. 10).[9]

The multifaceted experience of the Spirit within and surrounding believers can be summarized for Paul in one word, "life":

---

7. See n. 1 above. Fee's book is a superb study, and I do not mean to imply otherwise by questioning the adequacy of the title.

8. Fee, *God's Empowering Presence*, pp. 837-38.

9. The Spirit is also said to be "in you" (plural, referring to the community) in 1 Cor. 3:16, where the image of the temple of God/the Holy Spirit is used. In 1 Cor. 6:19, the indwelling of the Spirit in individuals is implied by the use of similar "temple" imagery.

The Spirit is life...

> [I]f Christ is in you, though the body is dead because of sin, the Spirit is life because of righteousness. (v. 10)

In the present, the Spirit powerfully brings life out of sin and death; in the future, the same Spirit will give life to the dead in parallel to the raising of Jesus (v. 11). In other words, the Spirit is life because the Spirit *transforms* death into life. The Spirit of life is the transforming Spirit. As James Dunn writes, Paul experiences both

> the power of the Spirit as *the power of life beyond death* . . . a power which is superior to the forces of corruption and death . . . [and] the power of the Spirit as *the power of life out of death* . . . a power which enables him . . . to crucify himself in his fleshness (Rom. 8.13; Gal. 5.24) even while living "in the flesh."[10]

Because the Spirit forges a link between believers' present and future experience, Paul refers to the Spirit as the "down payment" or "first installment" (NRSV; Greek *arrabōn*) of future life with God (2 Cor. 1:22).

Paul refers metaphorically to the transformation in the present that is effected by the Spirit as the Spirit's "fruit" (Gal. 5:22). Though Paul can list nine aspects of this "fruit,"[11] it is clear that love — understood as service to the neighbor — and freedom are, paradoxically, the chief work of the Spirit. The freedom of the Spirit is in fact the freedom to love, to become servants of one another:

> [13]For you were called to freedom, brothers and sisters; only do not use your freedom as an opportunity for self-indulgence [literally, "the flesh"], but through love become slaves to one another. [14]For the whole law is summed up in a single commandment, "You shall love your neighbor as yourself." (Gal. 5:13-14)

Thus the transforming work of the Spirit relates Paul (and every believer) to others as their "slave." To live otherwise is to return to "the flesh." Although the flesh, with its "passions and desires," has been "crucified" in Paul's experience of Christ and the Spirit (Gal. 5:24), and although he can describe the experience of being in the Spirit as no longer being "in [i.e., under the power of] the

---

10. James D. G. Dunn, *Jesus and the Spirit: A Study of the Religious and Charismatic Experience of Jesus and the First Christians as Reflected in the New Testament* (London: SCM, 1975; reprint, Grand Rapids: Eerdmans, 1997), pp. 337-38 (emphasis his).

11. In the NRSV they are love, joy, peace, patience, kindness, generosity, faithfulness (Greek *pistis*), gentleness, and self-control.

flesh" (Rom. 8:9), it is clear that Paul believes that believers can allow their freedom in the Spirit to become "an opportunity for the flesh" (Gal. 5:13; NRSV: "for self-indulgence"), the desires of which are not to be gratified (5:16). In Dunn's words, "life *in* the flesh[12] can very easily and quickly (and unconsciously) become life *according to* the flesh."[13]

Paul's experience of the Spirit also relates him intimately to God as the Father. The Spirit of God is a "Spirit of adoption" (Rom. 8:15; I have deliberately capitalized the "s" in "Spirit"). As noted in chapter one, the early Christian's address to God as "Abba! Father" — derived no doubt from the practice of Jesus himself — is the work of the Spirit to assure believers of their identity as "children of God" (Rom. 8:14-16). Paul here clearly refers to all believers, including himself ("we" throughout vv. 16-17), not merely to Gentiles, as adopted children of God.

Paul does not, however, sentimentalize the Spirit. To be sure, the Spirit relates Paul and all believers to God in an intimate way and helps them in their weakness and inability to pray (Rom. 8:26). Yet the Spirit who does this, and who confirms believers' identity as children of God and thus as "heirs of God and joint heirs with Christ" (Rom. 8:17), does so, so to speak, with a condition — two conditions, to be precise. First, in the present the Spirit works within the believing community to effect a kind of death experience:

> [12]So then, brothers and sisters, we are debtors, not to the flesh, to live according to the flesh — [13]for if you live according to the flesh, you will die; but *if* by the Spirit you put to death the deeds of the body [i.e., the body dominated by the flesh], you will live. (Rom. 8:12-13; emphasis added)

As Robert Tannehill has noted, here

> the Spirit has an *active killing function.* Through the Spirit what took place decisively in the death of Christ continually takes place: the believer dies to the old life "according to the flesh." . . . The believer is still part of an untransformed world and through the body is subject to the attack of the old powers. In the face of such attacks, the believer's past death with Christ must be maintained and affirmed in the present. Thus the believer's existence continues to be characterized by dying with Christ.[14]

12. That is, in the body, understanding "flesh" as a neutral term, as Paul sometimes uses it.

13. Dunn, *Jesus and the Spirit,* p. 336 (emphasis his).

14. Robert C. Tannehill, *Dying and Rising with Christ: A Study in Pauline Theology* (Berlin: Alfred Töpelmann, 1966), p. 80 (emphasis his). The notion of the Spirit's having "an active killing function" does not mean that believers are passive; rather, the Spirit is the enabler ("by the Spirit") of the dying process that believers choose and desire to undergo ("you put to

Moreover, writes Paul, noting the second condition,

> [16]it is that very Spirit bearing witness with our spirit that we are children of God, [17]and if children, then heirs, heirs of God and joint-heirs with Christ — *if, in fact,* we suffer with him [Christ] so that we may also be glorified with him. (Rom. 8:16-17; emphasis added)

In Paul's experience and understanding, the Spirit creates hope for the future (see also Gal. 5:5), but the Spirit does so on the two conditions indicated above, as the presence of the word "if" in each text quoted indicates: *if* we put to death the deeds of the body, and *if* we suffer with Christ. The Spirit propels people to put to death the flesh — and thereby to serve and love others — and to suffer with Christ in the present. *The Spirit, in other words, links Paul to the cross, and via the cross to Christ in suffering and to others in love.* The Spirit is the Spirit of cruciformity. The Spirit marks and "seals" people as God's own children, God's own "possession" (2 Cor. 1:22, 5:5), but only inasmuch as they are marked by conformity to the death of Christ.

The Spirit of Cruciformity

It is commonly acknowledged that Paul connects his experience of the moral life ("fruit," Gal. 5:22), service ("gifts," 1 Corinthians 12; Rom. 12:3-8), God's love (Rom. 5:5), unity (1 Corinthians 12), and hope (Romans 8) — to name the most customary topics — with his experience of the Spirit. Far less commonly recognized or fully explored is the connection between *cross* and Spirit.[15] Fundamentally, however, Paul's experience of the Spirit is one of being conformed to Christ and his cross: that is, for Paul the Spirit is the Spirit of cruciformity.

---

death"). The active responsibility of the believer is rightly stressed also by John M. G. Barclay, *Obeying the Truth: Paul's Ethics in Galatians* (Minneapolis: Fortress, 1991), p. 117, in commenting on Gal. 5:24 ("those who belong to Christ Jesus have crucified the flesh with its passions and desires").

15. A major exception is Charles H. Cosgrove, *The Cross and the Spirit: A Study in the Argument and Theology of Galatians* (Macon, Ga.: Mercer University Press, 1988), esp. pp. 169-94. The interpretation of Galatians, which we will consider momentarily, is a good test case for the connection between cross and Spirit. See also Richard B. Hays, "Christology and Ethics in Galatians: The Law of Christ," *Catholic Biblical Quarterly* 49 (1987): 268-90. Unlike Cosgrove and Hays, Barclay, in his otherwise excellent work *Obeying the Truth*, draws little or no connection between cross and Spirit (there is a brief hint on p. 133), other than insisting on the importance for Paul of the "crucifixion" of the flesh (e.g., pp. 117, 205-6, 213).

This connection of cross and Spirit, mentioned briefly but very explicitly in Romans 8, appears in broader but less explicit strokes in Paul's other letters. In Galatians, for example, Paul speaks of the indwelling Christ as the one who "loved me by giving himself for me" (Gal. 2:20; author's translation). This is the language of self-giving love, of sacrificial service and even slavery, as similar language in Philippians 2 suggests. One might reasonably conclude, therefore, that a person in whom such a Messiah and Son of God lives would be, or would become, a person of self-giving, self-sacrificing love.

Paul does not, however, explicitly draw that conclusion. What he does do is to make the connection clear in three steps:

1. he identifies the Son of God's death as self-giving love (2:20);
2. he then identifies the Spirit sent by God as the Spirit of the Son (4:6); and
3. he describes life in the Spirit as a life of love and service to others:

> [D]o not use your freedom as an opportunity for self-indulgence [literally, "the flesh"], but through love become slaves to one another. (Gal. 5:13b)

> The fruit of the Spirit is love. (Gal. 5:22)

In other words, the past "work" of God's Son, embodied on the cross, has become the present work of the *Spirit* of God's Son, embodied in the believer and in the community. The fact that immediately following Paul's discussion of Christ's love, death, and indwelling (2:19-20) he reminds the Galatians that they have received the Spirit (3:1-5) reinforces this connection. The believers' experience is a reception of both the Son and the Spirit sent by the Father (Gal. 4:4-6), and both the Son and the Spirit produce love — cruciform love — in those who receive them.

This work of love is not the only dimension of experiencing the Spirit to which Paul refers in Galatians. The Galatians, Paul says, "received" and "began with" the Spirit and have continued to experience the Spirit, especially the Spirit's "mighty works" or "miracles," in their community (3:2-5).[16] Thus to experience the Spirit is to experience power. Paradoxically, however, even here the Spirit is linked to the cross. Paul implies that the Galatians received the Spirit — a reference to their "conversion" or initiation into the faith and the commu-

16. Greek *dynameis;* Cosgrove (*Cross and Spirit,* pp. 174-75) translates "mighty works"; J. Louis Martyn (*Galatians: A New Translation with Introduction and Commentary,* Anchor Bible 33A [New York: Doubleday, 1997], pp. 281, 285), "wonders"; and NRSV, "miracles." The working of *dynameis* by the Spirit is common to the Pauline experience and expectation for all believers as well as apostles (see also Rom. 15:19; 1 Cor. 12:10, 28-29; 2 Cor. 12:12).

Charismatic Spirit = Cruciform Spirit ? (handwritten)

nity — by responding to Paul's "public portrayal" of Jesus Christ crucified (3:1). The power of the Spirit is inseparable from the power of the cross. Indeed, the preaching of the cross unleashes the power of the Spirit.

From the beginning, then, the Galatians should have understood the connection between the response of faith to the message of the Crucified and the gift of the Spirit. Paul's task (in part) in Galatians is to show that the connection of cross and Spirit expresses itself not only in miraculous power but also in cruciform love.

Similarly, Paul finds it necessary to connect cross and Spirit in his letters to the Corinthians, where he insists that the Spirit's power is bankrupt without the Spirit's cruciformity. In both 1 and 2 Corinthians, this symbiosis of power and cruciformity becomes the criterion for judging all supposed experiences of God's Spirit.[17]

In 1 Corinthians Paul makes the combination of cruciformity and power the test for all claims to possession of the Spirit. According to the letter, especially chapter 14, charismatic gifts such as glossolalia have become indicators of spirituality, power, and status at Corinth. Into this situation Paul introduces love as the *modus operandi* for the exercise of all spiritual gifts (1 Corinthians 13). Without love, spiritual gifts are worthless (13:1-3). Love does not seek its own interests (13:5) but edifies others, and so must the exercise of charismatic gifts in public worship (14:1-5).

The reader of 1 Corinthians knows that this understanding of love as the *modus operandi* of a true experience of the Spirit's power is related to Paul's earlier exhortation to the Corinthians to "be imitators of me, as I am of Christ" (11:1). By Christ, Paul of course means "Jesus Christ — that is, Jesus Christ crucified" (2:2). The exhortation in 11:1 concludes a section of 1 Corinthians (8:1–11:1, Paul's response to divisions over the appropriateness of eating meat offered to pagan idols) that begins by contrasting knowledge and love: "Knowledge puffs up, but love builds up" (8:1). In the middle of this section, Paul offers himself as an example of denying one's "rights" (Greek *exousia*, power, in 9:4, 5, 6, 12, 18) for the edification, or love, of others. He summarizes his own example as "not seeking my own advantage but that of many" (10:33). That is what he means by the "imitation" of Christ (11:1, the next verse).

As in Galatians, so also in 1 Corinthians Paul makes several moves to show that the charismatic Spirit is also the cruciform Spirit. First, Paul identifies Christ as Christ crucified (2:2). Second, he urges people to be imitators of this crucified Christ by imitating himself, as Christ's apostle (11:1). Third, he characterizes his ministry as the renunciation of power, rights, and self-interest for

17. See also Fee, *God's Empowering Presence*, pp. 269-71, 365-66.

the good of others (ch. 9; 10:33). Fourth, he makes this self-denying, others-regarding edification the hallmark of love (8:1; 13:5). Fifth, by placing the "love chapter" (ch. 13) in the middle of a discussion of the Spirit's gifts (chs. 12–14), he makes love the work of the Spirit (not surprisingly, in light of Gal. 5:22). *Thus the criterion of the Spirit's activity is cruciformity, understood as Christ-like love in the edification of others rather than oneself.*

In 2 Corinthians Paul again unites power and cruciformity in the Spirit. The so-called "super-apostles" (11:5) who were disrupting the Corinthian community no doubt excelled in powerful rhetoric (11:5-6) and charismatic experiences, especially visions (12:1-13). These people apparently took pride in such powers, as did their Corinthian followers, and thus Paul feels forced (12:11) to boast a bit about his own charismatic experiences and powers that authenticate his apostolic call (12:12).

What the "super-apostles" lack, from Paul's perspective, is any symbiosis of power and cross in their experience of the Spirit. For Paul, the point of apostolic pride is his self-debasing, not self-exalting (11:7); his weakness, not his power (11:21–12:13, especially 11:30; 12:9). His boast is his suffering for Christ, in which he is truly strong by the power of Christ (12:9). Because the super-apostles' claims to spirituality and apostolicity lack this focus on the weakness and self-debasing associated in Paul's experience with the cross, their claims are completely illegitimate in Paul's eyes; they preach a different Jesus, a different Spirit, a different gospel (11:4). As in Galatians and 1 Corinthians, so too in 2 Corinthians, the charismatic Spirit is the cruciform Spirit. A similar emphasis can also be found in Romans 5 and 8, which are important texts in Paul's treatment of the Spirit, as we have already seen.[18]

For Paul, then, the Spirit of power is the Spirit of weakness, the Spirit of the cross. Paul's distinctive experience of the Spirit, and his articulation of that experience, lie in being "*related . . . to the figure of Jesus Christ* — in Paul's terms, to the pattern of death and resurrection that is central to his credo."[19] James Dunn, reflecting on contemporary as well as ancient Christian experience, says it well:

> As soon as a charismatic experience becomes an experience only of the exalted Christ and not also of the crucified Jesus, it loses its distinctive Christian character.[20]

18. See also Meyer, "Holy Spirit," pp. 5-10.

19. Meyer, "Holy Spirit," p. 5 (emphasis his). Meyer adds (p. 13): "Paul's Christology everywhere provides the context for his *pneuma*tology [theology of the Spirit]."

20. Dunn, *Jesus and the Spirit,* p. 331.

Thus, according to Paul, we know and experience the Spirit only as we know and experience the Spirit as the Spirit of the cross.[21]

Conclusion: The Spirit of Cruciform Community

In this chapter we have considered the paradoxical character of Paul's experience of the Spirit as the symbiosis of power and cruciformity. This symbiosis is not limited to individual experience (such as Paul's) but is the defining character of the Spirit-filled community as a whole. Just as life in Christ is personal but not private, so also is life in the Spirit. The Spirit *forms* the Christ-centered community and is *found* in that community. The Spirit "in our hearts," as Paul is fond of saying, is also the Spirit in our assembly, our *koinōnia* (see, e.g., 1 Corinthians 12, 14; Phil. 2:1).

Indeed, the charismatic criterion of cruciformity — especially the need for edifying love — is grounded in part in Paul's conviction that the Spirit dwells in our midst, not just in our hearts. The Spirit of cruciformity is the Spirit of Christian community, and it is by means of cruciformity that the Spirit produces unity. That is the explicit or implicit foundation of every call to unity found in the Pauline epistles. A portion of the letter to the Philippians provides only one example of this ever-present theme:

> [1]If then there is any encouragement in Christ, any consolation from love, any sharing (Greek *koinōnia*) in the Spirit, any compassion and sympathy, [2]make my joy complete: be of the same mind, having the same love, being in full accord and of one mind. [3]Do nothing from selfish ambition or conceit, but in humility regard others as better than yourselves. [4]Let each of you look not to your own interests, but to the interests of others. (Phil. 2:1-4)

Paul continues with the "bridge" verse (v. 5) discussed in the previous chapter, and with the hymn contained in verses 6-11, in which the cruciform Lord

---

21. Compare Cosgrove's characterization of the basic concern of Galatians, which can be generalized for all of Paul: *"participation in Christ's cross"* as *"the sole condition for ongoing life in the Spirit"* as well as the sole condition for starting that life (*Cross and Spirit*, p. 172 [emphasis his]; cf. pp. 179-81). J. Louis Martyn says that the important question of how we know (epistemology) is answered by Paul with the Spirit connected to the cross: "knowing by the Spirit can occur only in the form of knowing by the power of the cross," for "until the parousia [second coming], the cross is and remains the epistemological crisis, and thus the norm by which one knows that the Spirit is none other than the Spirit of the crucified Christ" ("Epistemology at the Turn of the Ages," in *Theological Issues in the Letters of Paul* [Edinburgh: T&T Clark; Nashville: Abingdon, 1997], p. 108).

Christ is set forth in narrative as the paradigm of the Spirit's activity in the Philippian church. Their story in the Spirit is to be shaped by the story of Christ that they sing in worship.[22]

We will return to many of these themes and texts, in more detail, in the chapters on cruciform love and cruciform power. First, however, in the next chapter, we examine the "trinitarian" implications of Paul's insistence that God is cruciform, that the crucified Jesus is the exalted Lord, and that the Spirit of God and of Christ is the Spirit of cruciformity.

22. Life in the Church, the "new-creation community," is "[t]o know by the power of the cross . . . to know and to serve the neighbor in need" (Martyn, "Epistemology," p. 109).

CHAPTER 4

THE TRIUNE GOD OF CRUCIFORM LOVE

Paul's Experience of the Trinity

So far we have attempted to discern something of Paul's experience of God the Father, the exalted crucified Jesus, and the charismatic yet cruciform Spirit. However, Paul hardly experienced these three as separate "divine realities." His encounter with each "person" — for lack of a better term — was inextricably interrelated to his encounter with the other two. In this chapter we will see that Paul's experience of Father, Son, and Spirit as an engagement with one God was discerned in his own experience and that of the believing communities he knew, and that this experience was grounded in the common participation of the three "persons" in the event of the cross and resurrection. Paul's personal involvement with the reality and power of the cross — his cruciformity — reflects and reveals an *experiential* or *narrative* Trinity that leads inevitably to the theological conclusion that God is one yet three.[1]

Trinity in Paul?

Most interpreters of Paul have been very hesitant to ascribe anything resembling Trinitarian thought to the apostle. Paradoxically, on the whole they have been more willing to speak of Paul's *theology* proper (i.e., his "doctrine" of God), approximating an understanding of God as the "crucified God." Thus it seems that hesitation about Trinitarian language is in reality hesitation about *Christological* language in Paul, an unwillingness to associate Christ with God

---

1. The Trinity as the "experienced" reality of God is normally referred to as the "economic" Trinity.

(rather than God with the cross and thus with humanity), since Paul does not explicitly call Christ "God."[2]

Typical in attitude, if idiosyncratic in expression, is J. Christiaan Beker's position on the Trinity in Paul:

> Paul has only an incipient doctrine of the Trinity. . . . Christ is never called "God" — not even in Rom. 9:5b — but remains . . . subordinate to the Father. . . . We must . . . not read later Trinitarian developments into Paul. . . . *Christ and the Spirit function as apocalyptic heavenly "assistants" of God — not unlike Irenaeus's concept of Christ and the Spirit as God's hands.*[3]

There is, however, evidence of change taking place. Recently, biblical theologian Ulrich Mauser has written of a "dynamic unity" of Father, Son, and Spirit in Paul in which "Paul manifests not a trace of uncertainty that his synopsis of the act of God, of Christ, and of the Spirit might contradict the clarity of the affirmation that God is one."[4] Mauser draws on a number of Pauline passages (most of which, and more, are discussed below) to conclude that the distinctive activities of Father, Son, and Spirit also constitute "a unity of divine will, insight, and act," a "triune activity."[5] Mauser even hints that God, Christ, and the Spirit may exist for Paul as one, not only in activity, but in "being and act."[6] Moreover, Gordon Fee affirms that Paul has "a Trinitarian faith, even if he did not use the language of a later time"; and Fee carefully speaks of three "persons" when analyzing Paul's view of the Spirit as God's personal presence.[7]

Space does not permit a full analysis of intimations of the Trinity in Paul's

---

2. The possible exception is Rom. 9:5, but the interpretation of this text is notoriously difficult. The ascription of the title "Lord" to Jesus is also, in the view of many, an exception, especially in light of the parallel between Phil. 2:9-11 and Isa. 45:23. See the discussion below.

3. J. Christiaan Beker, *Paul the Apostle: The Triumph of God in Life and Thought* (Philadelphia: Fortress, 1980), p. 200 (emphasis added). (Irenaeus was the late-second-century theologian and bishop of Lyon.) Even Beker admits, however, that "[w]e can say that Paul is moving toward a fuller Trinitarian conception; for example, God's love for the world in the cross of Christ (Rom. 5:6, 8) moves toward the idea of a 'crucified God.' Yet because Paul does not have a full Trinitarian scheme, it would be inappropriate to incorporate suffering into the being of God or to equate God's compassion for the world with the finality of the cross of Christ as 'the crucified God'" (p. 200). In this last remark, Beker shows more hesitation than some others about speaking of a "crucified God" in Paul's understanding.

4. Ulrich W. Mauser, "One God and Trinitarian Language in the Letters of Paul," *Horizons in Biblical Theology* 20 (1998): 102-3 (main quote), 107 ("dynamic unity").

5. Mauser, "One God," pp. 107, 108.

6. Mauser, "One God," p. 103.

7. Gordon D. Fee, *God's Empowering Presence: The Holy Spirit in the Letters of Paul* (Peabody, Mass.: Hendrickson, 1994), p. 829.

Trinity

letters. Rather, we will look briefly at a few texts suggesting that for Paul there is one Lord in three, and then explore how Paul (and his communities) experienced and expressed this three-in-oneness.

One Lord in Three

As noted at the beginning of chapter one, Paul consistently reaffirms his Jewish conviction that there is but one God. Paul's experience of the one God as "Father," described in chapter one, is, however, closely related to his experience of the Son and the Spirit. As Romans 8 indicates, Paul's ability to cry "Abba! Father!" is the work of the Spirit assuring him, and all believers, that they are children — and thus heirs — of God and joint heirs with Christ (Rom. 8:14-17).

The early Christian — and Pauline — affirmation "Jesus is Lord" could have posed a threat to the claim of remaining monotheistic:

> . . . [10]at the name of Jesus every knee should bend, in heaven and on earth and under the earth, [11]and every tongue should confess that Jesus Christ is Lord. . . . (Phil. 2:10-11)

This text is a Christian interpretation of Isaiah 45:21-23, one of the most powerful affirmations of Yahweh's sovereignty, salvation, and sole divinity:[8]

> [21]. . . There is no other god besides me, a righteous God and a Savior; there is no one besides me. [22]Turn to me and be saved, all the ends of the earth! For I am God, and there is no other. [23]By myself I have sworn, from my mouth has gone forth in righteousness a word that shall not return: "To me every knee shall bow, every tongue shall swear."

This strong monotheistic affirmation, when applied to Jesus, seems to necessitate the ascription of divine status to Jesus (as does Phil. 2:6, according to many interpreters: "did not regard [this/his] equality with God as something to be exploited"),[9] challenging Yahweh's sole divinity. In fact, however, the Philippians hymn itself claims that it was God (i.e., Yahweh) who "highly exalted" Jesus to this position (Phil. 2:9) and that this super-exaltation and universal acclamation are all "to the glory of God the Father" (Phil. 2:11; cf. 1:11). Therefore, for

---

8. The early Christian interpretation of this text in Philippians includes granting Jesus not only the title "Lord" but also the title "Savior" (Phil. 3:20).

9. There are, however, other (though problematic) ways to interpret this apparent ascription of deity to Jesus that make him more of a "vice-regent" without full divine status.

Paul the application of Isaiah 45:23 to Jesus does not negate or infringe upon Israel's monotheism.

That the affirmation "Jesus is Lord" is simultaneously an affirmation of this unity within God is suggested also by the following:

> I want you to understand that no one speaking by the Spirit of God ever says "Let Jesus be cursed!" and no one can say "Jesus is Lord" except by the Holy Spirit. (1 Cor. 12:3)

In this text Paul acknowledges that the confession "*Jesus* is Lord" is the will and work of *God,* whose *Spirit* enables the confession. Thus Paul sees no compromise of his Jewish monotheism in proclaiming

> one God, the Father, from whom are all things and for whom we exist, and one Lord, Jesus Christ, through whom are all things and through him we exist. (1 Cor. 8:6)

Christ is for Paul "the image of God" (2 Cor. 4:4), in whom God "has shone in our hearts to give the light of the knowledge of the glory of God in the face of Jesus Christ" (2 Cor. 4:6).

Clearly, then, God's "glory" — God's *shekinah* or presence — is the commonality between God the Father and Christ the Son. Paul complicates things just a bit by introducing the Spirit into this discussion, who is, as we saw in the previous chapter, the Spirit "of God" and "of Christ." In the same context of 2 Corinthians, Paul asserts that "the Lord is the Spirit" (3:17-18).[10] Paul's somewhat confusing language should not be forced into saying more than it does. Paul is not so much making tight theological arguments as he is reflecting on the common experience of his communities, in which there is intimate association between Father, Son, and Spirit in the process of transformation into the image of God in Christ (3:18).[11]

Paul's chief interest in affirmations that imply a Trinitarian God is not speculation but transformation. As we have seen in previous chapters, Paul and his communities experienced God as Father, Son, and Spirit. As we will see below, he and they also experienced the three as one. This does not mean, however, that Paul confused the roles of Father, Son, and Spirit. The Father did not die on the cross; nor did the Spirit. And the Son does not send himself, of

---

10. For interpretive options, see the commentaries and Fee, *God's Empowering Presence,* pp. 311-14.

11. On this entire difficult passage (2 Cor. 3:16-18), see the sane discussion in Victor Paul Furnish, *II Corinthians,* Anchor Bible 32A (Garden City, N.Y.: Doubleday, 1984), pp. 210-16, 234-52.

course, nor the Spirit. Yet Paul is absolutely certain that to know and experience one of these "persons" is also to know and experience each of the others and the "whole" — the one God. His interest in the "Trinity" is first of all in the unity and continuity of the believer's experience as an experience of the grace and love of the one and only God, revealed climactically on the cross of Christ and discovered in the life of the Spirit-led community.[12]

Three-in-One in Spiritual Experience

Paul's affirmations of one Lord who is yet three, affirmations that were at least in part given to him by the tradition,[13] not created by him, find parallels in his descriptions of essential elements of the spiritual experience of Paul himself and his communities: baptism, confession (of faith), life in God, prayer, and the moral life (specifically, sexuality).

The experience of *baptism* in the Pauline communities was clearly Christocentric and, specifically, cross-centered. It was a baptism "into Christ [Jesus]" (Gal. 3:27; Rom. 6:3) and "into his death" (Rom. 6:3), producing a union with him (Rom. 6:5) that could be described as being "clothed" with Christ (Gal. 3:27). Baptism was also an incorporation into the one body of Christ (1 Cor. 12:12-13; cf. Gal. 3:28).

Yet baptism for Paul was not Christomonistic — not focused on Christ alone:

> For in [or, "by"] the one **Spirit** we were all baptized into one body — Jews or Greeks, slaves or free — and we were all made to drink of one **Spirit**. (1 Cor. 12:13)

> [Y]ou were washed, you were sanctified, you were justified in the name of the **Lord Jesus Christ** and in the **Spirit** of our **God.** (1 Cor. 6:11b)

In these texts, baptism is clearly associated with the presence and/or infusion of the Spirit, who is the Spirit of *God*. Moreover, the three passive verbs used in 1 Corinthians 6:11b ("washed . . . sanctified . . . justified") imply the activity of God. Thus baptism, the community's "rite of initiation," is, according to Paul, an experience of God (the Father), the Lord Jesus Christ, and the Spirit of God.

---

12. Compare Fee, *God's Empowering Presence*, p. 827: "At the heart of [Paul's letters] lies the mystery of the Trinity, but it does so in a presuppositional, experiential way, not by reflective theologizing. By that I mean that Paul expresses his experience of God in a fundamentally Trinitarian way, but never grapples with the theological issues that this experience raises" (cf. p. 839).

13. For example, the confession "Jesus is Lord" and the hymn (assuming it is pre-Pauline) in Philippians 2.

Furthermore, the most basic *confession of faith* of the baptized individual and community, "Jesus is Lord" (1 Cor. 12:3; Phil. 2:11), is itself an act of relating not only to Jesus but to God [the Father], who wills the confession, and the Spirit, who empowers it:

> Therefore I want you to understand that no one speaking by the **Spirit of God** ever says "Let **Jesus** be accursed!" and no one can say "**Jesus** is **Lord**" except by the **Holy Spirit.** (1 Cor. 12:3)

It is no wonder, as earlier chapters have suggested, that Paul experienced the new life as one of "dwelling" in and with Christ the Son, the Spirit of God/ the Spirit of Christ, and God the Father. In his earliest preserved letter, 1 Thessalonians, Paul narrates the founding and ongoing existence of the Thessalonian church as a relationship with the Father, Son, and Spirit. In 1 Thessalonians 1:1-10, the Father is named seven times, the Lord (Jesus) six times,[14] and the Spirit twice. The Thessalonians entered *into* "God the Father and the Lord Jesus Christ" by virtue of the Spirit's power, where they now remain, despite persecution, by virtue of the same Spirit:

> [1] . . . To the church of the Thessalonians in **God the Father** and the **Lord Jesus Christ.** . . . [2]We always give thanks to **God** for all of you . . . [3]remembering before our **God and Father** your work of faith and labor of love and steadfastness of hope in our **Lord Jesus Christ.** [4]For we know, brothers and sisters beloved by **God,** that he has chosen you, [5]because our message of the gospel came to you . . . in power and in the **Holy Spirit.** . . . [6]And you became imitators of us and of the **Lord,** for in spite of persecution you received the word with joy inspired by the **Holy Spirit.** . . . [8]For the word of the **Lord** has sounded forth from you . . . in every place your faith in **God** has become known. . . . [9] . . . [Y]ou turned to **God** from idols, to serve a living and true **God,** [10]and to wait for his **Son** from heaven, whom he raised from the dead — **Jesus,** who rescues us from the wrath that is coming. (1 Thess. 1:1-10)

So, too, in Romans 8, perhaps Paul's most passionate description of the believer's experience, life in Christ is also life in the Spirit as well as life as the children of God, who is "Abba! Father!":

> [9] . . . you are in the **Spirit,** since the **Spirit of God** dwells in you. . . . [10][I]f **Christ** is in you . . . the **Spirit** is life because of righteousness. [11]If the **Spirit of him who raised Jesus** from the dead dwells in you, **he who raised Christ**

---

14. Counting references to the "Lord" as references to Jesus.

from the dead will give life to your mortal bodies also through his **Spirit** that dwells in you. . . . [14]For all who are led by the **Spirit of God** are children of **God**. . . . [15]. . . [Y]ou have received a spirit of adoption. When we cry, "**Abba! Father!**" [16]it is that very **Spirit** bearing witness with our spirit that we are children of **God**. . . . (Rom. 8:9-16)

Similarly (though more concisely), Paul informs the Romans that their life is one in relation to God (the Father), Christ, and the Spirit:

[17]. . . the kingdom of **God** is not food or drink but righteousness and peace and joy in the **Holy Spirit**. [15]The one who thus serves **Christ** is acceptable to God and has human approval. (Rom. 14:17-18)

It is especially significant that in this text Paul equates life "in the Holy Spirit" with service to Christ and acceptability to God. This coincides with Romans 8 and other texts that demonstrate the overlap in terminology between Christ and the Spirit, both of whom live in believers, and in whom, in turn, believers also live.[15] This is reaffirmed, with emphasis on the experience of the Spirit, by the following claim in 2 Corinthians:

[21][I]t is **God** who establishes us with you in **Christ** and has anointed us, [22]by putting his seal on us and giving us his **Spirit** in our hearts as a first install-ment. (2 Cor. 1:21-22)

Similarly, Paul describes the Thessalonians' spiritual life as a relationship of *prayer* with God, the Lord, and the Spirit:

[16]Rejoice always, [17]pray without ceasing, [18]give thanks in all circumstances; for this is the will of **God** in **Christ Jesus** for you. [19]Do not quench the **Spirit**. (1 Thess. 5:16-19)[16]

Prayer is commonly recognized not only as a fundamental means of experienc-ing God, but also as a manifestation of one's understanding of God. The an-cient Christian Church coined the phrase *lex orandi, lex credendi,* roughly translated "the rule of faith is the rule of prayer," or "prayer reveals the prayers' true theology." If this is true, then Paul's benediction, or prayer wish, at the con-clusion of 2 Corinthians is significant:

---

15. See chapter two on Paul's experience of Christ.

16. Compare 2 Thess. 2:13: "But we must always give thanks to **God** for you, brothers and sisters beloved by the **Lord**, because **God** chose you as the first fruits for salvation through sanc-tification by the **Spirit** and through belief in the truth."

The grace of the **Lord Jesus Christ**, the love of **God**, and the communion of the **Holy Spirit** be with all of you. (13:13)

Paul's request of the Roman community in Romans 15:30 is also important:

I appeal to you, brothers and sisters, by our **Lord Jesus Christ** and by the love of the **Spirit,** to join me in earnest prayer to **God** on my behalf.

Furthermore, Paul addresses the sensitive issue of believers' _sexual life,_ as an aspect of their relationship with God, in Trinitarian terms. In 1 Corinthians 6, he speaks of believers having union with Christ (vv. 15-17), being the temple of the Holy Spirit (v. 19), and glorifying God in their bodies (v. 20).

These texts indicate the interrelated role of the "Spirit," "Jesus Christ," and "God" in Paul's spiritual life, both in general and in certain specifics. This experience of God as three-in-one begins in the response of faith and baptism, wherein a person begins a participation in the cross of Christ, on the one hand, and simultaneously enters "into" the sphere and life of God, of the Lord Jesus, and of the Spirit, on the other. Clearly this is one and the same experiential reality viewed from different perspectives.

As earlier chapters have shown, and as we will see again below, the cross itself, including participation in it, is related to the activity of Father, Son, and Spirit. For Paul, to be a baptized person, and to be part of a praying, living community focused on Jesus as God's Messiah, is to experience God as community, as a triad — a tri-unity — of love and grace. Both Paul and his converts experienced God intimately as Trinity.

Trinity in Ministry

Also Trinitarian in nature are Paul's experience and spirituality of ministry. He speaks of being

a minister of **Christ Jesus** to the Gentiles in the priestly service of the gospel of **God**, so that the offering of the Gentiles may be acceptable, sanctified by the **Holy Spirit**. (Rom. 15:16)

In the same context, Paul can refer to his ministry as "the grace given me by **God**" (v. 15), "what **Christ** has accomplished through me" (v. 18), and as "the power of the **Spirit of God**" (v. 19). The results of his ministry — the communities he has founded — Paul understands in similar Trinitarian terms:

[Y]ou show that you are a letter of **Christ**, prepared by us, written not with ink but with the **Spirit** of the living **God**. . . . (2 Cor. 3:3)

The fundamental experience of spiritual giftedness, or the ministry of the entire community, is the work of the same divine Triad:

[4]Now there are varieties of gifts, but the same **Spirit**; [5]and there are varieties of services, but the same **Lord**; [6]and there are varieties of activities, but it is the same **God** who activates all of them in everyone. (1 Cor. 12:4-6)

As Richard Hays notes, this passage demonstrates that, although Paul did not have "an explicit doctrine" of the Trinity, "he *experienced* God as Trinity."[17]

The texts we have discussed so far in this chapter all point to the Trinitarian character, or structure, of Paul's spiritual and ministerial experience. To be sure, Paul does not always portray the believer's experience as "trinitarian" but sometimes as "binitarian." He often speaks, for instance, of grace and peace proceeding from "God the Father and the Lord Jesus Christ" (1 Thess. 1:1).[18] He can also speak monolithically of the "grace of our Lord Jesus Christ" (Gal. 6:18). However, just as this text does not deny God the Father as a source of grace, neither do the binitarian prayers for grace deny the role of the Spirit with God the Father and the Lord Jesus. In fact, as we saw in the previous chapter, Paul's ease in speaking of the Spirit as the Spirit of God as well as the Spirit of Christ demonstrates how closely he associates the Spirit with both God the Father and the Lord Jesus, and how difficult it is for him to distinguish them and their present activities from one another.

At this point, we must make an important distinction between Paul's *experience* of Father, Son, and Spirit as three-yet-one, as Trinity, and the *basis* of that experience. For Paul, the basis of all experience is the revelation of God, especially God's revelation in the cross of Christ, confirmed by the resurrection. That basis, too, is Trinitarian in character.

17. Richard B. Hays, *First Corinthians,* Interpretation (Louisville: Westminster/John Knox, 1997), p. 210 (emphasis his).

18. Compare, in or near salutations, Rom. 1:7b; 1 Cor. 1:3; Gal. 1:3; Phil. 1:2. Other "binitarian" texts exist, too, such as 1 Cor. 8:6, in which Paul appears to interpret the Jewish *shema* (Deut. 6:4) and its affirmation of the one "Lord God" as a reference to two-in-one, the Lord (Jesus Christ) and God (the Father).

Trinity and Cross

A significant text in Galatians further demonstrates Paul's understanding of the interconnected role of Father, Son, and Spirit in salvation history and in his own spiritual experience:

> 4But when the fullness of time had come, **God** sent his **Son**, born of a woman, born under the law, 5in order to redeem those who were under the law, so that we might receive adoption as children. 6And because you are children, **God** has sent the **Spirit of his Son** into our [or, "your"] hearts, crying, "**Abba! Father!**" (Gal. 4:4-6)

In this passage Paul twice speaks of God "sending." First, in the fullness of time and in order to accomplish our redemption and adoption, God sent his Son (4:4-5). Then, in order to make the accomplished adoption known in experience, God sent the "Spirit of his Son into our hearts," the Spirit who cries out to the Father "Abba! Father!" (4:6). In this passage, the continuity between Son and Spirit is emphasized. The Spirit is the Spirit of the Son; as such, the Spirit almost vicariously prays *as* the Son and *for* the newly adopted children, "Abba!" The Spirit makes experiential ("in our hearts, crying") that which the Son accomplished, namely, the reality of being adopted children of God the Father.

Even more fully than what we noted above, in this text Paul's experience of God as *Father* is simultaneously an experience of the *Spirit* of God's *Son*. This is because the "work" of the Spirit is to make real and effective the "work" of Christ on the cross, which in turn was the "work" of God the Father. That is, the cross — understood as both apocalyptic event and personally experienced reality — is the united activity of Father, Son, and Spirit.

Perhaps the most telling revelation of the Trinitarian character of Paul's experience of God occurs in Romans 5. Romans 5:1-11 begins and ends on the "binitarian" note of peace and reconciliation with God "through our Lord Jesus Christ" (vv. 1, 11). In the middle of the passage, however, Paul refers also to the experience of God's love "poured into our hearts through the Holy Spirit that has been given to us" (v. 5; cf. 15:30). The proof or demonstration of this divine love, however, is the death of Christ:

> God proves his love for us in that while we were still sinners Christ died for us. (v. 8)

For Paul, then, the love of God that was revealed in history through Christ's one-time act is experienced in human lives through the Spirit's ongoing action.

divine love

As Paul Meyer puts it, for Paul the believer's "experience of the Spirit and . . . of the demonstration of God's love in the death of his Son . . . are here scarcely distinguishable sides of one and the same reality."[19] *This Trinitarian interconnection of love manifested in the cross is at the root of Paul's references to the Spirit as both the Spirit of God and the Spirit of Christ.*

Romans 5:1-11 is critical for understanding Paul's spirituality. This is true not only because of the text's focus on the Trinitarian love of God, Christ, and the Spirit, but also because Christ's death is said to be the concrete expression of this divine love (v. 8) and thus the source of the community's experience of grace (v. 2) and peace (v. 1).

The following question therefore arises: In other passages where Paul speaks of grace and peace, should we not assume that he is referring to the grace and peace that people experience in receiving the unmerited love of God revealed in the death of Christ? The answer to that question is unquestionably "yes." For Paul, "grace and peace" are benefits of God's act in Christ's death, communicated by the Spirit.

Conclusion: The Experience of Cross, Love, and Trinity

The cross, to summarize, is the source and focus of Paul's Trinitarian spirituality, because in it the possibility of experiencing God's love, grace, and peace is made real. In the cross, according to Paul, we learn that God is *pro nobis* — for us; in some unfathomable way, Christ's death for us both *demonstrates* and *defines* divine love. This divine love is the love of the Father who sends in love, the Son who dies in love, and the Spirit who produces the fruit of love in those hearts he inhabits.

To be sure, the cross ultimately bears this meaning only because God raised the crucified Jesus and because, therefore, he is a living Lord whose Spirit can be sent into human hearts and communities. Paul assumes this in Romans 5 and Galatians 4, and says so in Romans 8, in a text quoted above:

> If the Spirit of him who raised Jesus from the dead dwells in you, he who raised Christ from the dead will give life to your mortal bodies also through his Spirit that dwells in you. (Rom. 8:11)

19. Paul W. Meyer, "The Holy Spirit in the Pauline Letters," *Interpretation* 33 (1979): 6. Luke Timothy Johnson (*Reading Romans: A Literary and Theological Commentary* [New York: Crossroad, 1997], p. 82) notes the effect of Paul's attributing love to God, Christ, and the Spirit on the later doctrine of the Trinity.

In the same chapter Paul affirms at both its inception and its conclusion that the sending of the Son to die on the cross is the demonstration of God's loving concern (Rom. 8:3, 32, 39). Paul cannot, and does not, separate the cross from the resurrection, however. Without the resurrection, death *can* separate us from the love of God (contrary to Rom. 8:38-39) and makes the indwelling of the Spirit of Christ nonsense.

Thus Christ's death, Christ's resurrection, and the presence of the Spirit of Christ/of God are at once distinct yet unified. They are distinct parts of one story, discrete acts in the divine drama. There are three chief characters in this drama. Yet, when the "audience" — the human, especially the believing, community — experiences the drama, they experience it as one ongoing act of divine love with one main divine character known in three distinct but inseparable characters. In the cross, which is the love of God in Christ, experienced by the presence of the Spirit and guaranteed by the resurrection, the divine drama finds its climax. Paul's Trinity is experienced and narrated as the mysterious key to the divine drama of salvation.

Does this imply that the Father, Son, and Spirit are also of one "essence," one in "being"? To use this language is probably to go "beyond what is written," to borrow an enigmatic Pauline phrase (1 Cor. 4:6).[20] Nevertheless, it is absolutely crucial for Paul — and for us — to keep the Father, Son, and Spirit united as one in relation to the cross. Otherwise, the cross becomes a place only for the outpouring of divine wrath on an innocent but passive "son"; the "spirit" of these two can hardly be one. Rather, for Paul the cross is the demonstration of God's love and of the Son's love, both of which become real by the action of their one Spirit.

To a fuller exploration of Paul's understanding of Christ's death on the cross, then, we now turn.

---

20. See also Fee, *God's Empowering Presence*, pp. 827, 839. As previously noted, in the words of the later theological tradition Paul primarily describes the "economic" (or experienced) Trinity rather than the "immanent" (or ontological) Trinity. Similarly, James D. G. Dunn (*The Theology of Paul the Apostle* [Grand Rapids: Eerdmans, 1998], p. 264, with a helpful diagram) concludes that "early Christian experience may have played a significant part in the development of a trinitarian conception of God," for "the believers in Paul's churches experienced worship as a double relationship — to God as Father and to Jesus as Lord — and attributed this experience to the Spirit." Dunn's tentativeness ("may have played") seems to me unnecessary, but his emphasis on worship is correct. He does not, however, note the centrality of the cross in this interrelational experience.

CHAPTER 5

THE WORD OF THE CROSS

Narratives of the Cross, Patterns of Cruciformity

In the first four chapters we have seen how the cross of Christ is at the center of Paul's experience of God the Father, Christ, and the Spirit, both "individually," so to speak (Paul relating to each "person"), and "corporately," as the triune God (Paul relating to the three "persons" in unity). We have not, however, systematically considered the full breadth of meaning of the cross for Paul. In this chapter we will examine what Paul says about Christ's death on the cross, as an act of God and an act of Christ himself, focusing on how Paul narrates that death to give it significance.

As James Dunn notes, Paul's theology of the cross is "somewhat enigmatic":[1]

> Paul never felt it necessary to expound his theology of Christ crucified in any detail. All his references are either creedal or kerygmatic formulae or brief allusions . . . because it was not a matter of unclarity or controversy between Paul and his readers. Formulaic or allusive references were sufficient to recall a central theme in their shared faith.[2]

What we will discover in this chapter is that in these "creedal or kerygmatic [preaching] formulae" and "brief allusions" Paul tells the story of Christ's death in several recognizable narrative patterns. Nearly all of these patterns corre-

---

1. James D. G. Dunn, *The Theology of Paul the Apostle* (Grand Rapids: Eerdmans, 1998), p. 211.

2. Dunn, *Theology*, p. 212. The most detail, it would seem, can be found in Paul's interpretation of Christ's death with respect to Adam (e.g., Rom. 5:12-21), a theme that is central to Dunn's interpretation of Paul.

spond, in turn, to patterns of spirituality, to patterns of cruciform existence. That is, Paul's chief way of "expounding" his theology of Christ crucified was to show the correspondence between Christ's death and the believing community's life.[3] Paul, then, ultimately focuses on the *spirituality* of the cross. The patterns of correspondence are seldom explicit in the traditional formulations; rather, they are the product of Paul's experience and reflection.[4] These various patterns of cruciformity will become the focus of most of the remainder of this book.

The Scope of Texts to Be Considered

Some interpreters of Paul (e.g., J. Christiaan Beker)[5] have distinguished between Pauline texts that refer to Christ's death without mentioning the cross and those that speak of the cross explicitly. In fact, most of Paul's references to Christ's death do not name the cross per se. Surprisingly, Paul uses the verb "crucify" of himself almost as often as he uses it of Christ, including his references to being "co-crucified" with Christ.[6] While the specific role of the words

3. Jürgen Becker (*Paul: Apostle to the Gentiles*, trans. O. C. Dean, Jr. [Louisville: Westminster/John Knox, 1993], p. 401) aptly remarks that Paul's "terse traditional statements" about the death of Jesus in verses here and there do not normally lead to extended expositions of Jesus' death, but when Paul speaks of living "under the transforming power of the gospel," he occupies not verses but entire chapters.

4. Compare Raymond Pickett, *The Cross in Corinth: The Social Significance of the Death of Jesus*, JSNTSup 143 (Sheffield: Sheffield Academic Press, 1997), p. 129: "Paul's contingent application of the symbol of Christ's death resulted in new shades of meaning which the symbol did not possess apart from the given context. The interpretation of the death of Jesus which he inherited from the early church was constantly being expanded as he elaborated on its significance for the community." Similarly, Ernst Käsemann ("The Saving Significance of the Death of Jesus in Paul," in *Perspectives on Paul*, trans. Margaret Kohl [Philadelphia: Fortress, 1971; reprint, Mifflintown, Pa.: Sigler, 1996], p. 59) concludes that "[P]auline theology therefore circles round in ever new attempts to bring out the saving significance of the cross," by which he means the significance of the cross for Christian life. Paul W. Meyer ("The Holy Spirit in the Pauline Letters," *Interpretation* 33 [1979]: 5) enunciates an important principle for the recognition of "recurring patterns" in Paul's letters: we must respect the "integrity" of every text in its context yet "not hesitate to group passages from different contexts together, for these will suggest characteristic features of Paul's understanding that remain his own as he moves from one context to another and that transcend each immediate context for writing."

5. J. Christiaan Beker, *Paul the Apostle* (Philadelphia: Fortress, 1980), p. 198.

6. "Crucify" of Christ: 1 Cor. 1:23; 2:2, 8; 2 Cor. 13:4; Gal. 3:1; of Paul (or believers including Paul): 1 Cor. 1:13 (was Paul crucified for them?); Gal. 5:24 (those who belong to Christ have crucified the flesh); 6:14 (the world crucified to Paul and Paul to the world); "co-crucify": Rom. 6:6 (believers' old selves were crucified with Christ); Gal. 2:19 (Paul is crucified with Christ). In-

"cross" and "crucify" is important, it is far more important to recognize that when Paul thinks and speaks of Christ's death he always has the mode of that death — crucifixion — in mind.[7] Thus in this chapter we will consider all references to Christ's death as references to his death on a cross.[8]

As noted above, many of the texts we will examine are believed by most scholars to be "traditional" texts, that is, items from the theological wordbook of early Christianity incorporated into short confessions of faith, summaries of the gospel, and hymns. Whatever their origin, however, the texts in Paul's letters are now his; he has owned them and often given them his own interpretation, especially with respect to their meaning for believers' existence.[9]

We will begin with a list of texts, arranged in canonical order, that refer explicitly or implicitly to Christ's death with Christ as the subject of the sentence, fulfilling the linguistic role of "actor" and the narrative role of protagonist. We will then look at explicit and implicit references to Christ's death in which God is the subject/actor/protagonist. Finally, we will consider the (relatively few) texts in which both God and Christ are named as the subject/actor/protagonist. The bulk of the chapter will consist of a brief analysis and synthesis of these texts, showing the patterns that are present. The chapter concludes with suggestions about patterns of cruciformity that correspond to the crucified Christ as narrated in these texts.

Narrative Texts with Christ as Subject/Actor/Protagonist

Romans 3:21-22
[21]But now, apart from law, the righteousness of God has been disclosed . . . [22]. . . through the faithfulness of [NRSV margin; NRSV has "faith in"][10] Jesus Christ for all who believe.

---

deed, in Romans, the only explicit reference to Christ crucified is Rom. 6:6, and even that is in connection with believers' co-crucifixion ("our old self was crucified with him").

7. This would explain the line "even death on a cross" (Phil. 2:8c), which most scholars believe is Paul's addition to a preexisting early Christian hymn that he cites in Phil. 2:6-11.

8. On this matter, Charles B. Cousar (*A Theology of the Cross: The Death of Jesus in the Pauline Letters*, OBT [Minneapolis: Fortress, 1990], p. 24) wisely says, "While one can appreciate the peculiar power of the statements using crucifixion language, they are to be seen alongside and in tandem with other statements of Jesus' death, not in isolation from them or from their contexts."

9. Even Dunn (*Theology*, p. 21, n. 19) admits, for example, that although Paul does not really develop his theology of the cross, "Paul's theology of suffering in 2 Corinthians (particularly his own suffering as an apostle) is in effect an extended theology of the cross."

10. As we will suggest below, and argue in the next chapter, the preferred translation for this and parallel passages is not "faith in Christ" but "faithfulness of Christ."

Romans 3:26	[God] justifies the one who has the faith of Jesus [NRSV margin; NRSV has "faith in"].
Romans 5:15	. . . much more surely have the grace of God and the free gift in the grace of the one man, Jesus Christ, abounded for the many.
Romans 5:18-19	[18][J]ust as one man's trespass led to condemnation for all, so one man's act of righteousness leads to justification and life for all. [19]For just as by the one man's disobedience the many were made sinners, so by the one man's obedience the many will be made righteous.
Romans 6:6, 8	[6]We know that the old self was crucified with him so that the body of sin might be destroyed, and we might no longer be enslaved to sin. . . . [8]But if we have died with Christ, we believe that we will also live with him.
Romans 6:10	The death he died, he died to sin, once for all; but the life he lives, he lives to God.
Romans 8:17	. . . if, in fact, we suffer with him so that we may also be glorified with him.
Romans 14:9	For to this end Christ died and lived again, so that he might be Lord of both the dead and the living.
Romans 15:3	. . . Christ did not please himself; but, as it is written, "The insults of those who insult you have fallen on me."
1 Corinthians 1:13	[W]as Paul crucified for you?[11]
1 Corinthians 8:11	. . . those weak believers for whom Christ died. . . .
2 Corinthians 1:5	[J]ust as the sufferings of Christ are abundant for us, so also our consolation is abundant through Christ.
2 Corinthians 4:10	. . . always carrying in the body the death [or "dying"] of Jesus. . . .
2 Corinthians 5:14-15	[14]For the love of Christ urges us on, because we are convinced that one has died for all; therefore all have died; [15]and he died for all, so that those who live might no longer live for themselves, but for him who died and was raised for them.

11. That is, "Paul was not crucified for you, was he? Christ was!"

2 Corinthians 8:9	For you know the generous act [Greek "grace," *charis*] of our Lord Jesus Christ, that though he was rich, yet for your sakes he became poor, so that by his poverty you might become rich.
2 Corinthians 13:4	For he [Christ] was crucified in weakness, but lives by the power of God.
Galatians 1:4	[the Lord Jesus Christ] gave himself for our sins to set us free from the present evil age, according to the will of our God and Father. . . .
Galatians 2:16	. . . we know that a person is justified not by the works of the law but through the faith of [NRSV margin; NRSV has "faith in"] Jesus Christ. And we have come to believe in Christ Jesus, so that we might be justified by the faith of Christ [NRSV margin; NRSV has "faith in"], and not by doing the works of the law. . . .
Galatians 2:19-21	[19]. . . I have been crucified with Christ; [20]and it is no longer I who live, but Christ who lives in me. And the life I now live in the flesh I live by the faith of [NRSV margin; NRSV has "by faith in"] the Son of God, who loved me and gave himself for me. [21]I do not nullify the grace of God; for if justification comes through the law, then Christ died for nothing.
Galatians 3:22	But the scripture has imprisoned all things under the power of sin, so that what was promised through the faith of Jesus Christ [NRSV margin; NRSV has "through faith in Jesus Christ"] might be given to those who believe.
Philippians 2:6-8	[6][Christ Jesus], though he was in the form of God, did not regard equality with God as something to be exploited, [7]but emptied himself, taking the form of a slave, being born in human likeness. And being found in human form, [8]he humbled himself and became obedient to the point of death — even death on a cross.[12]
Philippians 3:9-11	[9]. . . [a righteousness] that comes through the faith of

12. See below, under God as actor, for 2:9.

Christ [NRSV margin; NRSV has "faith in"]. . . . [10]I want to know Christ and the power of his resurrection and the sharing [*koinōnia*] of his sufferings by becoming like him in his death, [11]if somehow I may attain the resurrection from the dead.

1 Thessalonians 1:6	And you became imitators of us and of the Lord, for in spite of persecution you received the word with joy inspired by the Holy Spirit.
1 Thessalonians 5:9-10	[9][O]ur Lord Jesus Christ . . . [10]died for us, so that whether we are awake or asleep we might live with him.

Narrative Texts with God as Subject/Actor/Protagonist[13]

Romans 1:4	[Jesus Christ, God's Son] . . . was declared to be Son of God with power according to the spirit of holiness by resurrection from the dead. . . .
Romans 3:24-26	[24][T]hey are now justified by his grace as a gift, through the redemption that is in Christ Jesus, [25]whom God put forward as a sacrifice of atonement by his blood, effective through faith. He did this to show his righteousness, because in his divine forbearance he had passed over the sins previously committed; [26]it was to prove at the present time that he himself is righteous and that he justifies the one who has the faith of Jesus [NRSV margin; NRSV has "who has faith in Jesus"].
Romans 4:25	[Jesus our Lord] was handed over to death [by God] for our trespasses and was raised for our justification.
Romans 6:4	. . . Christ was raised from the dead by the glory of the Father. . . .
Romans 6:9	We know that Christ, being raised [by God] from the dead, will never die again; death no longer has dominion over him.
Romans 8:3	[God] . . . sending his own son in the likeness of sinful

---

13. These include texts with passive verbs in which the actual agent is clearly God.

	flesh, and to deal with sin [or "as a sin offering," NRSV margin], he condemned sin in the flesh.
Romans 8:11	If the Spirit of him who raised Jesus from the dead dwells in you, he who raised Christ from the dead. . . .
Romans 8:32	He who did not withhold his own Son, but gave him up for all of us, will he not also with him give us everything else?
1 Corinthians 6:19-20	[19]Or do you not know that . . . you are not your own? [20]For you were bought [by God] with a price. . . .
2 Corinthians 5:18-19	[18]All this is from God, who reconciled us to himself through Christ. . . . [19]that is, in Christ God was reconciling the world to himself, not counting their trespasses against them. . . .
2 Corinthians 5:21	For our sake he [God] made him to be sin who knew no sin, so that in him we might become the righteousness of God.
Galatians 1:1	. . . God the Father, who raised him from the dead. . . .
Philippians 2:9	Therefore God also highly exalted him. . . .

Narrative Texts with Both God and Christ as Subject/Actor/Protagonist

Romans 5:6-10	[6]For while we were still weak, at the right time Christ died for the ungodly. . . . [8]God proves his love for us in that while we still were sinners Christ died for us. . . . [9]. . . [W]e have been justified by his blood. . . . [10]. . . [W]hile we were still enemies, we were reconciled to God through the death of his Son.
Romans 8:34	. . . Christ Jesus who died, yes, who was raised [by God], who is at the right hand of God, who indeed intercedes for us.
1 Corinthians 15:3-4	[3]. . . that Christ died for our sins in accordance with the scriptures, [4]and that he was buried, and that he was raised [by God] on the third day in accordance with the scriptures. . . .

Polyvalent — death of X on the cross

Narrative Patterns

Even a cursory reading of these texts reveals that for Paul the death of Christ on the cross is multidimensional, indeed polyvalent. Various interpretations of that death appear, constituting a "dazzling array of colors in the mural of Paul's theology of the cross,"[14] no doubt often linked to the rhetorical purpose for mentioning the death in the first place.

In the midst of this diversity of meanings for Christ's death, several themes or narrative patterns are discernible. These patterns are not mutually exclusive but are often intermingled. However, more than a dozen distinct patterns may be discerned as Paul narrates Christ's death in ways that reveal its polyvalence.[15]

Corresponding to many of these narrative patterns are distinct _syntactical_ patterns, that is, patterns of vocabulary and grammar. The existence of these syntactical patterns assists us in observing and categorizing the narrative patterns.

The narrative patterns of Christ's death, described here briefly (with notes about their syntactical patterns, where appropriate), include the following:

1. _Obedience/Righteousness/Faith(fulness)._ Christ's death was an act of obedience, righteousness, and faith(fulness): that is, a response to the will of God. This is stated most unambiguously in passages like Philippians 2:8 ("obedient to the point of death"), Romans 5:18-19 ("one man's act of

---

14. John T. Carroll and Joel B. Green, "'Nothing but Christ and Him Crucified': Paul's Theology of the Cross," in _The Death of Jesus in Early Christianity_ (Peabody, Mass.: Hendrickson, 1995), p. 114. Compare the comment of Richard Hays that the cross is a "complex symbol in Paul's thought-world, encoding a rich variety of meanings" (_The Moral Vision of the New Testament: A Contemporary Introduction to New Testament Ethics_ [San Francisco: HarperCollins, 1996], p. 27), and of Pickett that it is "a symbol with a surplus of meaning" (_The Cross in Corinth_, p. 1). For a concise survey of the twentieth century's major interpretations of the significance of Christ's death for Paul, see Pickett, _The Cross in Corinth_, pp. 1-24.

15. Attempts to simplify this polyvalence to one primary theme may be insightful in what they affirm but are problematic in what they deny. For example, according to John S. Pobee (_Persecution and Martyrdom in the Theology of Paul_, JSNTSup 6 [Sheffield: JSOT Press, 1985], pp. 47-73), the Pauline language of self-giving and sacrifice derives from the tradition of martyrdom and thus reveals that Paul primarily understands Jesus' death as a martyrdom involving voluntary obedience to God, sacrifice for the sins of the people, and cosmic victory: "In short, Jesus was a martyr" (p. 59). With respect to the texts about Christ's self-giving and later exaltation, Pobee (pp. 47-53, 81-82) denies any connection to the suffering servant hymn (Isa. 52:13–53:12), which for most interpreters is critical to understanding Paul. It is more likely that some of the same biblical images (including that of the suffering servant) were employed both in the Jewish theology of martyrdom and in the Christian theology of Christ's death than that Paul (or other early Christians) took Christ's death simply as a martyrdom.

righteousness . . . one man's obedience), and Galatians 1:4 ("according to the will of our God and Father"). Recent scholarship suggests also that Christ's death is depicted as his act of "faith" or "faithfulness" *(pistis)* in seven passages where the Greek grammar is ambiguous: Romans 3:22, 26; Galatians 2:16 (twice); 2:20; 3:22; Philippians 3:9. Traditionally the ambiguities have been rendered "faith *in* Christ," but the arguments for translating these phrases as "faith[fulness] *of* Christ" are persuasive to many, including this writer. If "faith of Christ" is the correct translation, then Paul says that Christ's faithful death embodies the righteousness of God (Romans) and constitutes the objective basis of justification (Galatians and Philippians).[16]

2. *Love.* According to Paul, Christ died as a demonstration of his (and God's) love. To express this most directly, Paul constructs sentences in which the verb "love" precedes a reference to Christ's death. Paul does this with reference to Christ in Galatians 2:20 ("loved me and gave himself for me") and with reference to God in Romans 5:8 ("God proves his love for us in that while we still were sinners Christ died for us"). He also does so implicitly in 2 Corinthians 5:14 ("the love of Christ controls us").

For several reasons, the Galatians 2:20 text may be better translated as "the Son of God who loved me by giving himself for me," rather than "loved me and gave himself for me."[17] This translation suggests that Christ's death was the mode of his loving. A similar thought about God is conveyed if we read Romans 5:8 as "God shows," rather than "God proves," his love.[18]

3. *Grace.* For Paul, Christ's death is an act of unmerited generosity on the part of both Christ and God. 2 Corinthians 8:9 identifies Christ's act as his *charis*, that is, his "grace," and Romans 5:15 identifies the grace of Jesus in his obedient death also as the grace and free gift *(dōrea)* of God. Romans 5:6-10, though missing the word "grace," embodies its meaning, and the references to the sending or giving of God's own Son suggest grace by the extravagance of the gift. Grace, as God's gift (see also #6 below), implies love, too.

---

16. This issue will be examined fully in the next chapter.

17. "Loved me and gave himself for me" is an example of what grammarians call "hendiadys" — literally "one through two," or two separate grammatical items (in this case linked by "and") referring to one actual thing or event. Paul is clearly not referring to two separate "events," an act of loving and a separate act of dying.

18. "Demonstrates" is the translation of James D. G. Dunn, *Romans,* Word Biblical Commentary 38A, 38B, 2 vols. (Waco, Tex.: Word, 1988), 1:256; "shows forth" is the rendering of Joseph A. Fitzmyer, *Romans: A New Translation with Introduction and Commentary,* Anchor Bible 33 (New York: Doubleday, 1993), pp. 393, 400.

4. *Sacrifice.* Several Pauline texts indicate that Christ died (as a sacrifice) for sins, at both his own and his Father's initiative. The semantic pattern of these texts generally consists of relatively simple sentences in which it is said that Christ died or gave himself for sins, or in which God is said to have handed Christ over as a sacrifice for the forgiveness of sins. This interpretation of Christ's death is found especially in Pauline citations of early tradition, such as 1 Corinthians 15:3 and Galatians 1:4 (where the verb is not "died" but "gave himself"). God's initiative is stressed in Romans 3:25; 4:25; 8:3 (where the sacrificial motif is only implicit). Romans 5:9 ("justified by his blood") is ambiguous with respect to initiative.

5. *Altruism/Substitution.* Numerous passages in Paul exchange the semantics of "for sins" to "for X person(s)." That is, Christ died "for" people — not only for sins — which at the very least means for their benefit, again at his own initiative as well as his Father's. Substitution per se may or may not be involved in these texts, though some sense of representation and "interchange" (see #10 below) is certainly at work.[19] In any case, Paul's emphasis is on the altruistic motive and effect of the act.

This narrative pattern with Christ as the actor occurs in 1 Thessalonians 5:9-10 ("for us"); 2 Corinthians 5:14-15 ("for all"); 1 Corinthians 8:11 (for "weak believers [brothers/sisters]"); Galatians 2:20 ("for me"); 2 Corinthians 8:9 ("for your sakes"); and, implicitly, 1 Corinthians 1:13 ("for you").

With God taking the initiative this pattern of altruism is found in 2 Corinthians 5:21 ("for our sake"), Romans 5:6 ("for the ungodly"), and 5:8 ("for us [sinners]"). The two texts in Romans 5 indicate the close similarity between this pattern and the pattern of sacrifice expressed in Romans 5:9.

6. *Self-giving/giving.* Christ's death was an act of self-surrender or self-giving that was also a divine gift. The vocabulary of Christ's self-giving and of God's giving his Son over to death seems clearly to have predated Paul. The Christocentric forms of this pre-Pauline pattern, in which the verb is often a form of the verb "give" *(didōmi)* or "hand over" *(paradidōmi)* and the object of the verb is a reflexive pronoun (e.g., "himself"), are sometimes called "surrender formulae." Reflexive constructions express self-initiated,

---

19. See especially Dunn's treatment of this question in *Theology,* pp. 208-23, where substitution, as "only half the story" of sacrifice (p. 223), is linked not only to sacrifice but also to representation and participation. Becker *(Paul,* p. 409) is probably correct to find elements of a theology of replacement or substitutionary death in 1 Thess. 5:10; 1 Cor. 1:13; 8:11; Rom. 5:8.

self-involving acts. Two instances of this pattern occur in Galatians: the Lord Jesus Christ "gave himself for our sins to set us free" (1:4); "the Son of God loved me by giving himself for me" (2:20). These are clearly examples of a pattern of *self*-surrender. Similar in tone are the texts in Philippians 2:7, 8 ("emptied himself . . . humbled himself"), which also form part of a larger pattern (see #7).

In Romans Paul also says that God sent his own Son (8:3), not "with-hold[ing]" him but giving him up "for all of us" (8:32). Romans 4:25 has a passive verb — "was handed over" — but the implied actor is most likely God. In these texts the pattern is one of divine surrender of the Son.

In all of these passages, Christ's self-giving and God's giving are interpreted, either implicitly or explicitly, as acts of love.

7. *Voluntary self-humbling/abasement*. Another narrative pattern that Paul commonly expresses in reflexive constructions tells of Christ's death as an act of self-abasement or condescension, a voluntary "descent" in status. Some of these texts may also predate Paul.

In this pattern the privileges of the original, higher status are acknowledged but renounced. Semantically, this is achieved most directly by using a participle (for example, "being") that functions to express an "in-spite-of condition." This "concessive" function of the participle is usually translated into English with the adverb "although."

The clearest example of this pattern is the hymn text (as most scholars see it) Paul quotes in Philippians 2:6-11. The gist of this text is that although Christ had equality with God (*status;* literally, "[though] being in the form of God . . ."), he did not exploit it for his own advantage (*renunciation*) but rather enslaved and humbled himself (*abasement*) even to the point of dying on the cross. Because of the importance of Philippians 2:6-11, a more thorough analysis of this passage appears below.

Strong echoes of this pattern are heard also in 2 Corinthians 8:9: although Christ was rich (*status;* literally, "[though] being"), he became poor (*renunciation, abasement*), a metaphor for Christ's "incarnation" (to borrow a later word) and especially death. Another echo, though not quite as full, is heard in Romans 15:3: "Christ did not please himself" but (to paraphrase Paul's scriptural quotation) accepted the consequences of sin on behalf of others.

As in the texts about self-giving, these texts also occur in discussions about love.

8. *Culmination of a story that includes "incarnation" and suffering*. Although Paul does not frequently associate the verb or noun "suffer[ing]" with Christ, he does do so in Romans 8:17; 2 Corinthians 1:5; Philippians 3:10;

and, by implication, 1 Thessalonians 1:6. In each of these texts, Christ's sufferings are mentioned as something in which Paul and (sometimes) others now share. Furthermore, both Philippians 2:6-11 and 2 Corinthians 8:9 indicate that for Paul the death of Christ is the culmination of a story, a process that is more than the death itself. "The cross" is an icon for Paul of the full story of Christ's becoming human, suffering (1 Thess. 1:6: "imitators of . . . the Lord," referring to persecution), and dying. Thus he can refer to the "dying" *(nekrōsis)* of Jesus as a prototype and paradigm of apostolic suffering (2 Cor. 4:10).[20]

Death on the cross, however, is itself a culmination of the story of Christ only in a preliminary way. As other texts indicate, the story's real conclusion is in resurrection and exaltation (see #13 below).

9. *Paradoxical power and wisdom.* Much of Paul's understanding of the cross is paradoxical. The greatest paradox of all in Paul's description of the cross is his claim that its weakness is in fact power, its folly, true wisdom (1 Cor. 1:24-25; 2 Cor. 13:4).

10. *Interchange.* Christ's death effected an interchange of "character" between himself and believers: wealth for poverty (2 Cor. 8:9) and righteousness for sin (2 Cor. 5:21). In a word, he for us. This interchange effects transformation of those who benefit from the interchange.[21]

11. *Apocalyptic victory and liberation for new life and transformation.* Christ's death ended the reign of certain alien and hostile powers, thereby effecting liberation from them and from this age (Gal. 1:4) and inaugurating the new age or new creation. The powers whose reign has ended include especially sin and death (Rom. 6:9-10) but also the (old) self (Rom. 6:6; 2 Cor. 5:15; 1 Cor. 6:19). The victory transfers those who believe into the sphere of Christ's lordship (2 Cor. 5:14-15; Rom. 14:9; 1 Thess. 5:9-10), which was in fact the purpose for the death. Paradoxically, Christ's death brings life; its purpose and effect are not restricted to the forgiveness of sins (sacrifice) but include a fundamental renewing and reorienting of life.

12. *Reconciliation and justification.* These two Pauline experiences and interpretations of the cross are often associated with the "benefits" of Christ's

---

20. It should be noted that there has been considerable debate about the meaning of the *nekrōsis* of Jesus. Is it synonymous with *thanatos* and does it mean the event of death? Or does it have a different sense, either of the state caused by the event of death ("deadness") or, as suggested here, the process of "dying"? While the context favors the interpretation offered here, the existential implications for Paul are not seriously affected by the nuance of meaning.

21. See Morna D. Hooker, "Interchange in Christ," pp. 13-25, and "Interchange and Atonement," pp. 26-41, in *From Adam to Christ: Essays on Paul* (New York/Cambridge: Cambridge University Press, 1990).

death or said to be two (of many) metaphors to interpret that death.[22] Whatever their precise role in Paul's theology, it is clear that for him the cross is a kind of power in that it effects a right relationship with God when met with faith. These narrative patterns are found primarily in Galatians (2:15-16) and Romans (3:22; 4:25 [associated with the resurrection]; 5:18-19).

13. *Prelude to resurrection/exaltation.* Christ's death is not the conclusion of his life story but rather the first act of a drama that culminates in God's resurrection and exaltation of him. This also implies continuity between the crucified and the exalted Jesus. Death and resurrection were joined early in Christian tradition and its liturgical vocabulary, as 1 Corinthians 15:3-4; Romans 1:4; and Romans 4:25 (traditional formulae cited by Paul) indicate. Paul echoes this tradition again in such texts as Galatians 1:1 and Romans 6:4, 9 and 8:17 ("raised/raised him from the dead"), as well as Romans 8:34 ("who died, yes who was raised, who is at the right hand of God . . .") and 6:10.

Philippians 2:9-11 completes the story of humiliation narrated in 2:6-8 with a concluding exaltation by God. The two parts together yield a complete story corresponding to the pattern of exaltation following humiliation that permeates Hebrew wisdom literature and finds graphic expression in Isaiah's fourth servant song (Isa. 52:13–53:12).

Galatians 2:20 demonstrates the importance of the continuity of the resurrected/exalted Christ with the crucified One. The (resurrected and thus living) indwelling Christ is identical with the Son of God "who loved me by giving himself for me."

Without diminishing the significance of the cross, we can say that for Paul it was a prologue or prelude to resurrection and exaltation, as long as we understand this prelude to be essential and definitive rather than merely introductory. Without the resurrection and exaltation, the cross is only human weakness and folly. Paul therefore stresses the indivisibility of cross and resurrection even while granting pride of place to the polyvalent cross.

This brief synopsis of Paul's patterns of narrating the cross suggests not only that the cross is, for Paul, a multidimensional reality and symbol, but also that the narrative patterns often coalesce in particular passages. Romans 3:21-26; Romans 6:1-11; Romans 8; 2 Corinthians 5:14-21; Galatians 2:15-21; and

22. So Joseph A. Fitzmyer, *Paul and His Theology: A Brief Sketch,* 2nd ed. (Englewood Cliffs, N.J.: Prentice Hall, 1989), pp. 55-71.

Philippians 2:6-11 are passages that contain multiple images or clusters of narrative patterns. These passages are extraordinarily important in any discussion of Paul's theology and experience, and they will appear repeatedly in the chapters that follow.

Of all the narratives of the cross in Paul's letters, including the clusters mentioned above, one in particular seems to be foundational in nature, both by reason of the comprehensive scope of its narrative and by reason of its pervasive echoes throughout Paul's writings. This narrative is contained in Philippians 2:6-11, which, ironically, is possibly not Paul's original work but his adaptation of an early hymn. Nonetheless, in this text, in parallels to it,[23] and in the contexts in which it and the parallels occur, we find nearly all the patterns and images of the cross noted above: obedience, love, grace, sacrifice, altruism, grace, self-giving, voluntary self-humbling, culmination of a story of incarnation and suffering, liberation for new life, and prelude to exaltation/resurrection. This hymnic narrative found in Philippians 2:6-11 may therefore be accurately described as *Paul's master story of the cross.*

Paul's Master Story

Philippians 2:6-11 may well have received more scholarly attention in the modern period than any other Pauline passage.[24] As noted above, most scholars believe that its vocabulary, style, and structure suggest that it is a very early Christian hymn, perhaps even dating from the first years of the Church's existence. These features also suggest that the hymn predates Paul, though Paul has clearly owned the text for himself, perhaps altering it a bit (e.g., adding the line "even death on a cross"), and using it in Philippians as the centerpiece of the letter and its message.

Because of its complexity, richness, and universally recognized importance to Paul, many aspects of this text have been vigorously debated. In this context, we can only attempt to read this text with an eye to its narrative structure(s) as Paul's foundational "word of the cross," or master story. This story is presented

---

23. Parallels include especially the following: Gal. 1:4; 2:20; 2 Cor. 8:9.

24. For a comprehensive introduction to the debate, see Ralph P. Martin, *A Hymn of Christ: Philippians 2:5-11 in Recent Interpretation and in the Setting of Early Christian Worship,* 3rd ed. (Downers Grove, Ill.: InterVarsity, 1997; earlier editions [1967, 1983] went under the title *Carmen Christi*). For a very insightful and persuasive interpretation of the text in context, see Larry W. Hurtado, "Jesus as Lordly Example in Philippians 2.5-11," in Peter Richardson and John C. Hurd, eds., *From Jesus to Paul,* Francis W. Beare Festschrift (Waterloo: Wilfred Laurier University Press, 1984).

below in the NRSV version and in the author's own translation. My translation, using boldface and italicized print, attempts to provide readers of English with a sense of the verbal parallelisms and nuances that occur in the Greek text:[25]

NRSV	Author's translation
[6][T]hough he [Christ Jesus] was in the form of God,	[6][T]hough *being* in the form of God,
[he] did not regard equality with God as something to be exploited,	[Christ Jesus] **did not consider his equality with God as something to be exploited for his own advantage,**
[7]but emptied himself,	[7]but **emptied himself**
taking the form of a slave,	*by taking* the form of a slave,
being born in human likeness.	*that is, by being born* in the likeness of human beings.
And being found in human form,	And *being found* in human form,
[8]he humbled himself	[8]he **humbled himself**
and became obedient	*by becoming obedient*
to the point of death —	to death —
even death on a cross.	even death on a cross.
[9]Therefore God also highly exalted him	[9]Therefore God has **highly exalted** him
and gave him the name that is above every name,	and **bestowed** on him the title that is above every title,
[10]so that at the name of Jesus	[10]that at the name of Jesus
every knee should bend,	every knee should **bend,**
in heaven and on earth and under the earth,	in heaven and on earth and under the earth,

25. Specifically: (1) I use English verb forms that correspond more closely to the Greek text. For example, Greek participles appear consistently as English participles (English words ending in "-ing"). (2) Participles are italicized, while main (finite) verbs are boldfaced. (3) Precise interpretations of key participial phrases are provided. (4) Indentations are used to show key syntactical relationships, especially the relationship of participial phrases to the main verbs with which they are connected.

[11]and every tongue should confess that	[11]and every tongue **acclaim** that
Jesus Christ is Lord,	Jesus Christ is Lord,
to the glory of God the Father.	to the glory of God the Father.

As noted above, most scholars agree that Philippians 2:6-11 is a pre-Pauline hymn (or an excerpt from such a hymn) that Paul quotes and perhaps modifies with the addition of lines such as "even death on a cross" (v. 8c). Its poetic form and vocabulary suggest to some a hymnic contrast between the first and second Adam, and to others the preexistent Wisdom of God that comes to earth. While both of these motifs are no doubt present, for many others (including the present writer) the poetic structure and idiom suggest above all an interpretation of the fourth (suffering) servant hymn found in Isaiah 52:13–53:12 in light of God's exaltation of the crucified Messiah Jesus.[26]

Within the text of Philippians 2:6-11, five significant structural or narrative patterns are discernible. First, the entire passage is arranged as a basic pattern of reversal, of humiliation (vv. 6-8) followed by exaltation (vv. 9-11). This pattern reflects the common Scriptural motif of God's exalting the humble, a motif that also forms the basic structure of the fourth servant hymn (Isa. 52:13–53:12), in which God vindicates the servant following suffering and death. This vindication is first announced as the theme of the servant hymn and then played out in the narrative of the hymn itself:

> [13]See, my servant shall prosper; he shall be exalted and lifted up, and shall be very high. [14]Just as there were many who were astonished at him — so marred was his appearance, beyond human semblance, and his form beyond that of mortals — [15]so he shall startle many nations. . . . (Isa. 52:13-15a)

> [11]. . . The righteous one, my servant, shall make many righteous, and he shall bear their iniquities. [12]Therefore I will allot him a portion with the great, and he shall divide the spoil with the strong; because he poured himself out to death, and was numbered with the transgressors; yet he bore the sin of many, and made intercession for the transgressors. (Isa. 53:11b-12)

Four additional patterns may be discerned in verses 6-8 of Philippians, as noted above. First, these three verses as a unit express a pattern of voluntary self-humbling, the first half of the humiliation/exaltation schema. This pattern involves the possession of *status* ("though being in the form of God," v. 6a); *renunciation,* or refusal to exploit the status for selfish gain ("did not consider his

---

26. This text from Isaiah will be discussed in more detail in chs. 8 and 12.

equality with God as something to be exploited for his own advantage," v. 6b); and *abasement,* or voluntary self-humbling ("emptied himself by taking the form of a slave . . . humbled himself . . . ," vv. 7-8a). We may abbreviate this pattern and express it as a kind of formula as follows:

Although [x], not [y] but [z].

That is,

Although [*status*], not [*selfishness*] but [*self-abasement/slavery*].

Or, more fully,

Although [*equal with God*], not [*selfish exploitation*] but [*self-emptying slavery in incarnation and self-humbling obedience in death*].

Second, within the third element of this formula, "z," yet another pattern emerges and is expressed twice, the actual pattern of self-giving and self-humbling. Verses 7 and 8 use two self-involving verbal phrases ("reflexive constructions," grammatically speaking) to express this: "emptied himself" and "humbled himself." In these expressions the text refers poetically to the "kenotic" (self-emptying) nature of Christ's incarnation and death. The metaphorical nature of these phrases, especially the former, requires an explanatory comment, which the text provides in participial phrases, three for "emptied himself" ("taking the form of a slave . . . being born in the likeness of human beings . . . being found in human form") and one for "humbled himself" ("becoming obedient to death"). Third, the entire sequence of vv. 6-8 expresses not merely a single act of *kenosis* but depicts Christ's death as the culmination of a series of related events.

Finally, the explanatory phrase attached to the verb "humbled himself" presents still another narrative pattern of the cross within this hymn, namely, the pattern of obedience — meaning, of course, obedience to God — specifically obedience "to [the point of] death — even death on a cross."

We see, then, that the very structure of this pre-Pauline hymn contains several of the most basic and common narrative patterns of the cross in Paul's letters: (#13) prelude to resurrection/exaltation; (#7) voluntary self-humbling/abasement; (#6) self-giving/giving; (#8) the culmination of a story that includes "incarnation" and suffering; and (#1) obedience/righteousness/faith[fulness]. Interestingly, however, there is no explicit statement in these verses about the cross as a means of salvation or a paradigm for conduct.[27]

27. That is, the hymn has no explicit soteriology (teaching on how salvation is accomplished) or ethics.

Christ's relationship is portrayed vis-à-vis God alone, as God's obedient servant. Nothing specific is said about this polyvalent kenosis and death having life-giving power or being *for* us, either for our benefit or for our imitation. Yet these basic interpretations of the hymn are precisely the ones that Paul will make as he uses it in Philippians[28] and alludes to it — or at least to its narrative patterns — elsewhere in his letters. Thus he reads the master story in Philippians also as a narrative of love (#2), grace (#3), altruism (#5), and weakness that is power (#9).

Indeed, the patterns of the cross found in this hymn echo throughout Philippians and the entire Pauline corpus. Both in Philippians and elsewhere, Paul takes these patterns, and often the vocabulary associated with them, and interprets them in a variety of ways. For Paul, this hymn, like Christ's cross, is extraordinarily polyvalent. Although Paul may not have fully developed a *theology* of the cross (as Dunn reminds us), he did fully develop a *spirituality* of the cross.

Specifically, as we will see in subsequent chapters, the patterns of the cross narrated in this hymn are reflected in — and seem in fact to have shaped — his understanding of faith, hope, power, and especially love, though none of these terms appears in the text of the hymn. Paul not only sees Jesus in this foundational hymnic text, he sees also himself and every believing individual and community. *For Paul, to be in Christ is to be a living exegesis of this narrative of Christ, a new performance of the original drama of exaltation following humiliation, of humiliation as the voluntary renunciation of rights and selfish gain in order to serve and obey.* Paul's spirituality of cruciformity is a narrative spirituality, and the master narrative that shapes his spirituality is Philippians 2:6-11.

Conclusions: Patterns of Cruciformity and the Story of God

Anyone familiar with the letters of Paul will recognize that Paul's multidimensional, polyvalent approach to narrating the cross of Christ, in Philippians 2:6-11 and elsewhere, corresponds in large measure to his way of characterizing existence in Christ in accordance with the cross. The life of conformity to the cross — cruciformity — that Paul seeks to embody and transmit is as multifac-

---

28. In Philippians, for example, the themes of humility and love (1:27–2:4), as well as obedience (2:12) and divine power (2:13), occur in the immediate context. Throughout the rest of the letter, altruistic, self-giving love and humility are shown to be exemplified in Paul, Epaphroditus, Timothy, and (it is hoped) Euodia and Syntyche. Moreover, Paul describes in detail the correspondence between Christ's suffering and exaltation and that of believers (3:2-21).

eted as the cross itself. For Paul, then, patterns of the cross narrative become patterns of cruciformity.[29] Christ's love, freedom, self-giving, humility, and so on become for Paul the standard for life in Christ, embodied in all of life's contingencies.

As one would expect, certain narratives of the cross lend themselves more naturally and more frequently to corresponding ways of describing life in Christ. In the chapters that follow, we will therefore pay closest attention to the narrative patterns that have most fundamentally shaped Paul's narrative of the spiritual life. Nonetheless, each of the narrative patterns described above does have some impact on Paul's spirituality.

It would be possible to explore these patterns of cruciformity in several ways. One option would be to proceed on a text-by-text basis, but this would result in detailed analysis still begging for extensive synthesis at the end. Another possibility would be to examine each letter, but as a fundamental organizing principle that would again require significant synthetic work at the end, in order to discern patterns. A third option, and the one employed here, is basically synthetic: to begin by identifying some commonalities among the many patterns noted above and to proceed by analyzing them as they give birth to patterns of cruciformity in Paul's corpus of letters.

Following this procedure, from the thirteen patterns of narrating the cross discussed in this chapter, we may identify four fundamental patterns of cruciformity in Paul's letters.

1. The first, taken from the first cross-narrative pattern (#1), is cruciformity as faithful obedience, or cruciform *faith*.
2. The second, synthesizing the next several patterns (#2-8), is cruciformity as voluntary self-emptying and self-giving regard for others, or cruciform *love*.
3. The third, corresponding to patterns #9-12, is cruciformity as — paradoxically — life-giving suffering and transformative potency in weakness, or cruciform *power*.
4. The fourth, found in the last narrative pattern (#13), the pattern of reversal, is cruciformity as requisite prelude to resurrection and exaltation, or cruciform *hope*.

---

29. Wayne A. Meeks also notes the importance of a variety of patterns of correspondence, which he calls "patterns of life" or "homologies" between the crucified Messiah and the life of the believing communities. He notes, for example, patterns of theodicy, behavior, hope, and power (*The First Urban Christians: The Social World of the Apostle Paul* [New Haven: Yale University Press, 1983], pp. 180-83; cf. 146-47).

Paul's story of the cross, then, is a story of faith, love, power, and hope. This story Paul tells in a set of patterns that correspond to each of these dimensions of the master story. Understood as a story of faith, it is narrated in patterns of compliance; as a story of love, in patterns of relinquishment; as a story of power, in patterns of paradox; and as a story of hope, in patterns of reversal. Corresponding to these four basic patterns of the cross are four basic patterns of cruciformity.

Each of these four basic patterns — cruciform faith, love, power, and hope — will be the subject of one or more of the following seven chapters. In each chapter or group of chapters we will first examine the narratives of the cross that generate the particular pattern of cruciformity, and then carefully explore cruciformity as Paul experiences it and envisions it. In every instance there is a close connection between the story of Christ, the story of Paul, and the story of the communities to which he writes.[30] Before we move on to the exploration of this multidimensional story of the cross in the world, however, we must briefly place the story of the cross in the framework of an even larger story.

In this and earlier chapters we have seen repeatedly that the story of the cross has not only Christ but God as central character. The cross is the revelation of the love, power, wisdom, and even weakness and folly of God. The cross reveals not only the faithfulness of Jesus but also the faithfulness of God. The crucifixion and exaltation of Jesus bring glory to God. The cross, in other words, is not an independent story but part of God's universal and cosmic story.[31]

The cross links ethnic Israel to the Israel of God (with Gentiles "grafted on," according to Romans 9–11), the first Adam to the second Adam, and the creation of the cosmos to its redemption. This is why the "word of the cross" is "the gospel of God," and the "gospel of God" is "the word of the cross." Paul's narratives of the cross summon his hearers and readers to take their part in this divine drama and story by conforming to the cross in faith, love, power, and hope.[32] Within this context, we may proceed to examine each of these dimensions of cruciformity in turn.

30. "True apostleship may involve tasks which are different from the tasks of all other members of the church. But its absolutely decisive criterion does not divide the apostle from other Christians. It is the discipleship of the one who was crucified" (Käsemann, "Saving Significance," p. 58).

31. On this larger story see especially the work of N. T. Wright, *The New Testament and the People of God* (Minneapolis: Fortress, 1992), pp. 403-9, an important perspective to be worked out more fully in a forthcoming volume on Paul; see also Ben Witherington III, *Paul's Narrative Thought World: The Tapestry of Tragedy and Triumph* (Louisville: Westminster/John Knox, 1994).

32. Becker (*Paul,* pp. 374-75) comments that Paul is one who "thinks and lives out of his experience of the gospel" and whose "basic idea" is that "God calls through the gospel and human beings answer in faith, love, and hope."

CHAPTER 6

CRUCIFORM FAITH (I)

Paul, the "Fundamental Option," and the Faith of Jesus Christ

Cruciformity, the previous chapter suggested, is manifested as faith, love, power, and hope. In this and the following chapter we consider Paul's experience and understanding of faith. Even a cursory reading of Paul's letters suggests that "faith" is central to his experience and theology; whatever else people may know about Paul, they frequently associate him with justification by *faith*.

It is clear that for Paul faith is certainly not mere intellectual assent to a set of creedal affirmations, though that is part of faith. Neither does faith simply mean "trust," however much trust is essential to faith. Nor does faith refer only to an initial experience, though faith, in the Pauline sense, often has a clear starting point. Even if "justification by faith" is Paul's watchword and is understood as initiation into Christ (and both points are debated), Paul never intends for believers to stop having faith.

The difficulty in understanding Paul on faith is complicated by the linguistic fact that "faith" (the root *pist-*) in Greek can be both noun and verb, whereas in English we have the related noun and verb "belief" and "believe" but no corresponding verb for "faith." Moreover, the Greek noun "faith" *(pistis)* can mean not only "belief" but also "faithfulness." So what then is faith for Paul? In this chapter, we examine faith as an *initial and ongoing cruciformity, grounded in the faithfulness of Jesus the Messiah*. In the next chapter, we will consider more carefully the character of faith, and specifically what "justification by faith" might mean in connection with cruciformity.

Faith as Narrative Posture:
The Right Ordering of the "Fundamental Option"

Like many of the items in Paul's vocabulary, "faith" is a polyvalent term. Essentially, faith is Paul's shorthand for the appropriate human response to the gospel of God, the word of the cross:

> [F]aith comes from what is heard, and what is heard comes through the word of Christ. (Rom. 10:17)

> For the word of the Lord has sounded forth from you not only in Macedonia and Achaia, but in every place your faith in God has become known. . . . (1 Thess. 1:8)

Paul saw his own mission as bringing about the "obedience of faith," especially among the Gentiles (Rom. 1:5; 16:26; cf. Gal. 5:7). Faith, then, is the appropriate "posture" before God in light of the gospel. As one commentator on Paul has said, "Faith is that response to God's initiative that opens the gates of the self to God's transforming power."[1] For this reason, some interpreters of Paul have understood faith in Paul's lexicon to mean obedience (e.g., Rudolf Bultmann, Luke Johnson), fidelity or faithfulness (Richard Hays), submission or commitment (Joseph Fitzmyer), or even "conversion" (Alan Segal).[2] There is a large measure of truth in each of these understandings.

The Fundamental Option

One other helpful, but largely unexploited, way to describe a person's basic orientation of faith toward God in the Pauline sense is the phrase "fundamental

1. Sam K. Williams, *Galatians,* Abingdon New Testament Commentaries (Nashville: Abingdon, 1997), p. 143.

2. Obedience: Rudolf Bultmann, *Theology of the New Testament,* 2 vols., trans. Kendrick Grobel (New York: Charles Scribner's Sons, 1951, 1955), 1:314; Luke Timothy Johnson, *Reading Romans: A Literary and Theological Commentary* (New York: Crossroad, 1997), pp. 54, 60, passim. Fidelity/faithfulness: Richard B. Hays, *The Faith of Jesus Christ: An Investigation of the Narrative Substructure of Galatians 3:1–4:11,* SBLDS 56 (Chico, Calif.: Scholars Press, 1983), pp. 248-51, passim; Richard B. Hays, "Christology and Ethics in Galatians: The Law of Christ," *Catholic Biblical Quarterly* 49 (1987): 279-80. Submission/commitment: Joseph A. Fitzmyer, *Paul and His Theology: A Brief Sketch,* 2nd ed. (Englewood Cliffs, N.J.: Prentice Hall, 1989), pp. 84-85. Conversion: Alan Segal, *Paul the Convert: The Apostolate and Apostasy of Saul the Pharisee* (New Haven: Yale University Press, 1990), p. 121 ("radical reorientation and commitment," the "paradigm" being "Paul's own conversion"). It should be noted that Hays includes obedience as well as trust within the scope of his interpretation of faith as faithfulness.

option." This phrase, used primarily in Roman Catholic ethics, is a succinct way of referring to Paul's notion that human beings are basically oriented either toward or away from God. For Paul, the fundamental option, rightly ordered, issues in a person's right relationship with God, what we might call his or her appropriate posture before God.

The concept of "fundamental option," though an integral part of contemporary Catholic moral theology, is not normally used in the fields of biblical studies, non-Catholic ethics, or spirituality. Even in Roman Catholic theological circles, the term itself is subject to various interpretations. I do not intend to reflect the nuances of this discussion, nor do I claim as a Protestant to use the term precisely as any particular Roman Catholic moral theologian uses it. Yet the term itself is a very helpful one.

One highly influential participant in the discussion of fundamental option, Joseph Fuchs, employs a variety of interrelated phrases that illuminate the concept, and it will be useful to review his perspective briefly.[3] For Fuchs, the fundamental option is a basic decision to accept or refuse the love and grace of God offered in Christ.[4] It is a person's "free and basic self-commitment, consisting ultimately of the gift or refusal of the self in love to God."[5] Referring to Romans 1:18-31, Fuchs finds his perspective echoed in Paul's distinction between sins (plural) and sin (singular), the latter expressing the "single sin of culpable godlessness":

> [T]he many sins of all kinds are really and ultimately more than they indicate in their specific classification: they express a person's fundamental free disposition . . . as a whole in face of the God of salvation, a total disposition therefore, that is present at the deepest level of the many individual sins.
>
> Sin (in the singular) which is present in all sins (in the plural) as their fundamental reality is the self-sufficient refusal to accept the love of the God of our salvation that is offered to us.[6]

The proper decision and expression of the fundamental option is a "total act" of "total surrender of the self" to God and to the demand God makes upon

---

3. Joseph Fuchs, "Basic Freedom and Morality," in Ronald P. Hamel and Kenneth R. Himes, eds., *Introduction to Christian Ethics: A Reader* (New York: Paulist, 1989), pp. 187-98. Fuchs normally employs the term "basic freedom" for the basic intention that is "activated" by the fundamental option. This chapter was taken from Fuchs's book *Human Values and Christian Morality* (Dublin: Gill and Macmillan, 1970).

4. Fuchs, "Basic Freedom and Morality," pp. 195-96, passim.

5. Fuchs, "Basic Freedom and Morality," p. 188.

6. Fuchs, "Basic Freedom and Morality," pp. 191, 196.

us as persons.[7] It is "placing ourselves as persons unreservedly at the disposal of him who has the greatest claim on us, because he — who is God — created us as persons."[8] The person so "activated in basic freedom" will seek to

> integrate with his [or her] basic intention every part of his [or her] being and life. Thus grace makes its way from the centre of a [person] into all areas of life, into the many acts of free choice and beyond these into the formation of the world.[9]

This fundamental option, or expression of basic freedom (i.e., free self-commitment),[10] when rightly ordered toward God, may be referred to as the "love of God."[11] Love of God, then, is the (appropriate) "basic intention"; it is "total surrender" to "self-commitment in loving God," which constitutes "the really fundamental relationship to God."[12] This "required self-surrender" can occur, however, only

> in overcoming the egoism of human concupiscence and in abandonment to God as Father, *after the example of his Son-become-man,* that is, . . . it is *possible only in grace.* Were it to be otherwise, salvation would lie within a [person's] own power.[13]

Commenting on Paul himself, J. Louis Martyn stresses even more forcefully the necessity of grace for the freedom to surrender to and trust in God:

> When we trust God, Paul would say, we signal that we ourselves have been invaded by God's presuppositionless grace, and we confess that the locus of God's invasion is especially our will! Far from presupposing freedom of the will (cf. Hos 5:4), Paul speaks of the freeing of the will for the glad service of God and neighbor.[14]

---

7. Fuchs, "Basic Freedom and Morality," p. 189.

8. Fuchs, "Basic Freedom and Morality," p. 188.

9. Fuchs, "Basic Freedom and Morality," p. 197. We will hear echoes of this point in the discussion of Paul.

10. For Fuchs, the act of acceptance or refusal of God's grace constitutes the activation of "basic freedom," one's free and self-determined orientation toward God, which is then worked out in daily life as a series of free choices.

11. Fuchs, "Basic Freedom and Morality," p. 188.

12. Fuchs, "Basic Freedom and Morality," pp. 193-94.

13. Fuchs, "Basic Freedom and Morality," p. 195 (emphasis added).

14. J. Louis Martyn, *Galatians: A New Translation with Introduction and Commentary,* Anchor Bible 33A (New York: Doubleday, 1997), p. 271, n. 173.

In other words, the required self-surrender of the person to God requires a grace, a power, from outside the person. As we will see below, Paul would say, more specifically, that because human beings are under the power of sin (e.g., Rom. 3:9), they need an act of God to liberate them from their wrong-headed orientation away from God that will lead them to "abandonment to God as Father." Paradoxically, Fuchs contends, it is in self-surrender to God (and others) in love that a person finds self-realization.[15]

Faith in Israel

This concept of the fundamental option rightly ordered, understood as "self-commitment in loving God," is reminiscent of the biblical call for total commitment to YHWH. Israel was to "have no other gods" and to forswear the construction or worship of idols (Exod. 20:3-6; Deut. 5:6-8). The Lord's steadfast love, or compassionate faithfulness, required Israel's response of absolute and undying love and faithfulness within the bonds of a covenant that could be compared to marriage (e.g., Hosea). Thus Israel has always proclaimed the oneness of God, not merely as a theological affirmation but as a call to unswerving devotion, as the opening of the creed called the *shema* ("Hear!") makes clear:

> [4]Hear, O Israel: The Lord is our God, the Lord alone [or, "The Lord is our God, the Lord is one"]. [5]You shall love the Lord your God with all your heart, and with all your soul, and with all your might. (Deut. 6:4-5)

For Israel, according to the Old Testament witness, love for God was a total, complex response to God's initiative. It had both an affective and an ethical (one might even say "political") dimension, the former consisting of self-abandonment, devotion, and trust, the latter of "hearing," loyalty, and obedience.[16]

---

15. Fuchs, "Basic Freedom and Morality," pp. 188, 195, passim. We will, again, hear echoes of this point in Paul.

16. On the dimensions of love for God, see Walter Brueggemann, *Theology of the Old Testament: Testimony, Dispute, Advocacy* (Minneapolis: Fortress, 1997), pp. 419-20. Brueggemann uses the terms "affective" and "political" for the twofold character of Israel's love for God (*The Covenanted Self: Explorations in Law and Covenant*, ed. Patrick Miller [Minneapolis: Fortress, 1999], p. 65). He also argues that Israel's "fundamental testimony" is that God commands (*Theology*, pp. 181-86) and that Yahweh's "primal command . . . is the exclusive claim of loyalty" (p. 183). Thus Israel's first task is to *obey Yahweh* (pp. 417, 454-56, passim), that is, to *love Yahweh* (p. 420). Thus this obedience must not be understood either as an unhappy duty (but rather a deep desire as part of communion with God; see pp. 420-21) or as uncritical assent (but rather inclusive of self-assertion and questioning).

While the Psalms especially express the affective dimension, another text from Deuteronomy explains the ethical or political implications of love for God:

> [1]If prophets . . . [2][or others] say, "Let us follow other gods" (whom you have not known) "and let us serve them," [3]you must not heed the words of those prophets . . . for the Lord your God is testing you, to know whether you indeed love the Lord your God with all your heart and soul. [4]The Lord your God you shall follow, him alone you shall fear, his commandments you shall keep, his voice you shall obey, him you shall serve, and to him you shall hold fast. (Deut. 13:1-4)

The love of God is, therefore, a "political idiom," a "pledge to the policies of Yahweh"; to love God "means to refuse every other ultimate love or loyalty."[17] In sum, love for God means *faith* ("trust") and *faithfulness*.

Jewish tradition, as reflected in the teaching of Jesus and elsewhere, understood this command to love God, together with the injunction to love one's neighbor, as the epitome of the Law.[18] Israel's sins and unfaithfulness, as described by the prophets, can be summarized as varied transgressions of these two fundamental commandments. Or, more simply, Israel has failed to keep covenant with God because love for the loving God of Israel always leads to love of neighbor. While the two aspects of the covenant — love of God and love of neighbor — are not synonymous, they are inseparable.[19]

Fundamental Option and Faith in Paul

Both Fuchs's notion of the rightly ordered fundamental option and Israel's tradition of understanding human faithfulness as complete love for God have many echoes in Paul's thought and experience. As we noted in chapter one, however, Paul only occasionally speaks of humans' *love* of God. The love of God, understood in the twofold sense of "trust" and "faithfulness" noted above, could also be described as "faith." For whatever reason, this became Paul's pre-

---

17. Brueggemann, *Covenanted Self,* pp. 65, 50.

18. For the teaching of Jesus, see Mark 12:28-34; Matt. 22:36-40; Luke 10:25-28.

19. The famous text from Micah (6:8) illustrates this inseparability very nicely: "He has told you, O mortal, what is good; and what does the Lord require of you, but to do justice, and to love kindness, and to walk humbly with your God?" Brueggemann, on at least one occasion, refers to the "remarkable equation of love of God with love of neighbor" as "what is most characteristic and distinctive in the life and vocation" of Israel as Yahweh's partner (*Theology,* p. 424). However, he more appropriately speaks of love of God and neighbor (or communion with Yahweh and justice) as components of an undivided life, a life of integrity (pp. 428-30).

ferred way of referring to the comprehensive and uncompromising response to God that he knew from his Jewish heritage. For Paul, the key term for the fundamental option, rightly ordered, is not love but *faith*. Faith is humanity's appropriate posture before God. It is devotion, total commitment, faithfulness. Furthermore, as we will see as we explore Paul's spirituality more carefully, it always issues in love for others.

The right ordering of the fundamental option, or the appropriate human posture before God, as Paul sees it, is not defined merely by his own experience or that of his predecessors (such as Abraham) or his contemporaries (such as the Thessalonian or Corinthian believers). In this chapter we will see that recent interpreters of Paul have noted that he attributes "faith" not only to believers but also to Jesus. Jesus' "fundamental stance," as a true human being and as God's Messiah, was a posture of faithful obedience to God, expressed supremely in his death. (Fuchs's reference to abandonment to God "after the example of his Son-become-man," noted above, is again parallel to Paul's position.) As Sam K. Williams writes, "Christian faith is Christ-faith, that relationship to God which Christ exemplified, that *life-stance* which he actualized and which, because he lived and died, now characterizes the personal existence of everyone who lives in him."[20]

Therein lie the radical experience and perspective of Paul: making a connection between faith and death, between believing and dying. Corresponding to the obedient faithfulness of Christ, which was expressed in death, the believer's faith — the cornerstone of the believer's experience — is, from beginning to end, a liberating, life-giving "death," a response to God that Paul calls "the obedience of faith" (Rom. 1:5; 16:26). This faith is somehow, as we will see, analogous to Christ's total commitment or "faith." *The appropriate fundamental stance for human beings, then, is also faith, understood as an initial and ongoing experience of cruciformity.*[21]

---

20. Sam K. Williams, "Again *Pistis Christou*," *Catholic Biblical Quarterly* 49 (1987): 446.

21. Robert C. Tannehill (*Dying and Rising with Christ: A Study in Pauline Theology* [Berlin: Alfred Töpelmann, 1966], p. 6) similarly notes that there are "two kinds of dying with Christ" texts in Paul, those that refer to "a decisive, past event" and those that refer to "a present experience," the former being the basis, and the latter the structure, of the new life. Charles H. Cosgrove (*The Cross and the Spirit: A Study in the Argument and Theology of Galatians* [Macon, Ga.: Mercer University Press, 1988], p. 179), working with Galatians, refers to these as "cosmic" and "existential" crucifixion with Christ, respectively. Tannehill (*Dying and Rising with Christ*, pp. 123-27) links this twofold experience to faith as the death of the old self; Cosgrove (*Cross and Spirit*, pp. 176-77) makes the connection with faith more implicitly. However, both unfortunately narrowly restrict the present crucifixion with Christ primarily to suffering (Cosgrove, *Cross and Spirit*, p. 184, passim; Tannehill devotes some attention to "ethical action" [*Dying and Rising with Christ*, pp. 77-83] but focuses on suffering [*Dying and Rising with Christ*, pp. 84-123]).

The word "stance," "life-stance" (Williams), or "posture" might imply a static position, but such "calm" is far from Paul's experience of faith. For Paul, this posture toward God is a dynamic one, always soliciting action rather than inaction. Yet, as we will see, this action, though not fully predictable, is ordered; it has a pattern and tells a story. We may therefore say that for Paul faith is the appropriate *narrative* posture toward God. It is a dynamic posture, one that involves movement and action. It is, as we will see, faith as faithfulness, as obedience through cruciformity.

In the rest of this chapter we will look first at Paul's understanding of Jesus' fundamental narrative posture, embodied on the cross, and its intended effect on others. We will then consider, in the next chapter, the faith of believers, that is, the Pauline narrative posture (or the fundamental option, rightly ordered), as cruciformity.

The Word of the Cross

The Cross As Apocalyptic Event of Liberation

To understand Paul's interpretation of Christ's obedient and faithful death fully, we must first understand his view of the human condition. Although it is probably the case that his view of the human problem was defined (or at least refined) by his experience of the solution, namely, Jesus Christ, nevertheless we must start with Paul's analysis of the human predicament.

Paul lived in an apocalyptic age and held certain central apocalyptic convictions. In apocalyptic thought, the present age is characterized by evil and injustice in anticipation of the age to come, the age of righteousness and peace. Paul inherits this mindset and radicalizes it. Fundamentally, he believes that human beings are under the power of an interlocking directorate[22] of anti-human and anti-God realities and forces. As the following list of texts indicates, these forces are named by Paul as sin, death, the world, this age, idols and cosmic powers, Satan ("the god of this age"), the flesh, and even the self.[23] More-

---

22. I borrow from the striking phrase "interlocking directorate of death," coined by Daniel Berrigan in the 1970s to refer to the culture's network of death and killing that, he said, stretches from the Pentagon to the abortion clinic.

23. There is much scholarly debate about the meaning(s) for Paul of the Greek word *sarx*, usually translated "flesh." Most scholars agree that Paul uses the word to mean different things, sometimes with a neutral connotation (e.g., human being, the normal sphere of human existence) but often with a negative connotation (e.g., in opposition to the spirit or the Spirit). There is, indeed, a "spectrum" of meaning of *sarx* for Paul, who probably did not have an "inte-

over, sin, perhaps the most immediately powerful of these forces, has hijacked the holy, just, and good Law into its service:[24]

[W]e have already charged that all, both Jews and Greeks, are under the power of sin. . . . (Rom. 3:9b)

[S]in exercised dominion in death. . . . (Rom. 5:21)

. . . having once been slaves of sin. . . . (Rom. 6:17a; cf. 6:20a)

Formerly, when you did not know God, you were enslaved to beings that by nature are not gods. (Gal. 4:8)

In their case the god of this world has blinded the minds of the unbelievers, to keep them from seeing the light of the gospel of the glory of Christ, who is the image of God. (2 Cor. 4:4)

---

grated concept of *sarx*" (James D. G. Dunn, *The Theology of Paul the Apostle* [Grand Rapids: Eerdmans, 1998], p. 70). One scholar, John M. G. Barclay, tries to solve the problem by finding one basic meaning, "the merely human," in all of Paul's uses of the term "the flesh" (*Obeying the Truth: Paul's Ethics in Galatians* [Minneapolis: Fortress, 1991], pp. 202-15, esp. p. 209), a revision of an older view that is also generally followed by the Revised English Bible (REB) translation. The majority of scholars, however, do not adopt this unilateral approach but rather focus on the flesh in its "negative" sense(s) in Paul. Among the significant interpretations of this negative connotation for *sarx* are two major kinds, anthropological (or psychological) and apocalyptic, that is, an aspect of the human person and a power to which the person succumbs. Proponents of an apocalyptic force or power — the flesh as a cosmic anti-God power (like sin) — include Martyn (*Galatians*, pp. 289-94, 485-86, 492-95: the flesh attacks, and can even dwell within, a community) and, before him, Bultmann, though Bultmann stressed the "mythological" character of the language of "powers" (*Theology of the New Testament*, 1:197-200, 245). Proponents of the anthropological view offer several variations on the theme: (a) an anthropological *dimension:* the flesh as a person's "sinful nature" (e.g., the NIV); (b) an anthropological *component:* the flesh as an aspect of a person's constituency (like spirit or soul); (c) an internal anthropological *force or power:* the flesh as the anti-God impulse or inclination that characterizes, in part, every human being (similar to the Jewish view of the "evil impulse"); and (d) an anthropological *perspective:* the flesh as human nature viewed in its natural self-centeredness, hostility to God, and/or weakness and insufficiency (e.g., Paul W. Meyer, "The Holy Spirit in the Pauline Letters," *Interpretation* 33 [1979]: 12; Dunn, *Theology,* p. 70: "the weakness of a humanity constituted as flesh and always vulnerable to the manipulations of its desires and needs as flesh"). Further nuances of these interpretations exist, too. As for me, I find a combination of the two basic approaches to be most satisfactory in defining *sarx* used negatively in Paul: "the self under the power of sin and controlled by its anti-God impulses." Alternatively, it may mean the natural anti-God power within each human being and within which each human being lives. In either case, some aspects of the anthropological and the apocalyptic interpretations need to be merged.

24. For further discussion of the powers, see chapter eleven on Paul and power.

While we were living in the flesh, our sinful passions, aroused by the law, were at work in our members to bear fruit for death. (Rom. 7:5)

[11][S]in, seizing an opportunity in the commandment [against covetousness], deceived me and through it killed me. . . . [13]Did what is good [the law], then, bring death to me? By no means! It was sin, working death in me through what is good. . . . (Rom. 7:11, 13a)

[14]For we know that the law is spiritual; but I am of the flesh, sold into slavery under sin. . . . [17]. . . [I]t is no longer I that do it [what I do not want], but sin that dwells within me. (Rom. 7:14, 17)

And he died for all, so that those who live might live no longer for themselves, but for him who died and was raised for them. (2 Cor. 5:15)[25]

This interlocking directorate of hostile powers of this age has rendered the human race spiritually and morally dysfunctional. Manifestations of this dysfunction are many, as Paul enumerates in Romans 1–3, but at root there are two: disordered relations with God and disordered relations with other humans. In the early chapters of Romans, Paul segments Gentiles and Jews. The fundamental Gentile problems (1:18-32) are idolatry (improperly relating to God) and immorality (improperly relating to self and others), while for Jews the problems are pride and hard-heartedness (improperly relating to God; Rom. 2:5, 25-29) and hypocrisy (improperly relating to self and others; Rom. 2:1-4, 17-24). The two problems are interrelated, indeed inseparable (e.g., Rom. 1:24-25; 2:23-24). Both Gentiles and Jews, then, are disobedient to the summons of God found in nature or the Law. Each fails to love God with heart, mind, and soul and neighbor as self. In a nutshell, human beings fail in both aspects of the covenant. They lack what Paul calls *faith* and *love*.

No matter who they are, no matter what they do, human beings cannot break free from the grip of the disabling powers and their ever-growing effects. Human beings, then, are in a "no-exit" situation (J. Christiaan Beker[26]), from which escape is necessary but impossible to achieve on their own power. What Paul needs to find for the human race, then, is a solution that will deal not only with "sins" (plural) but with sin, and that will reconcile not only people to God but also people to one another.

The good news, according to Paul, is that

25. The language and structure of this text imply two different "owners" and thus two different "slaveries," depending on one's relationship to Christ.

26. A favorite expression used by J. Christiaan Beker in classes and seminars; its location in print has escaped me.

[3]God has done what the law, weakened by the flesh, could not do: by sending his own Son in the likeness of sinful flesh, and to deal with sin, he condemned sin in the flesh, [4]so that the just requirement of the law might be fulfilled in us, who walk not according to the flesh but according to the Spirit. (Rom. 8:3-4)

That solution, in a word, is the cross of Christ, which is (as we will see in detail in this and subsequent chapters) *simultaneously Jesus' faithfulness to God and his loving service to others* — "the faith of the Son of God, who loved me by giving himself for me" (Gal. 2:20b, author's translation). Those who now have the Spirit (of God's Son, Gal. 4:6) share in this solution and thus are enabled to relate properly to God and to others. They are able to exhibit faith and love.

The cross of Christ inaugurates the new age by liberating those who respond in faith from the powers of the present age:

[The Lord Jesus Christ] . . . gave himself for our sins to set us free from the present evil age, according to the will of our God and Father. . . . (Gal. 1:4)[27]

Christ was sent in "the fullness of time" (Gal. 4:4); the reference is not to some imaginary "perfect timing" due to the existence of the *pax Romana* and its benefits, but to the time of God, the eschatological (end-times) moment promised by the prophets but hitherto not experienced. For Paul, the time of Christ is the time when "the ends of the ages have come" on us (1 Cor. 10:11). More accurately translated, this text refers to the "overlap" of the ages, when the promised age to come has reached back into the present evil age. This overlapping of the present and the future was inaugurated by the death of Christ, which can therefore be termed an eschatological or apocalyptic event.

The most basic power from which Christ's death liberates is sin. His death was "to sin," meaning with respect to sin, permanently ending the power of sin over those who respond in faith:

The death he died, he died to sin, once for all; but the life he lives, he lives to God. (Rom. 6:10)

Similar to Romans 8:3-4, 2 Corinthians 5:21 says that people in Christ can now "become" the righteousness they were not:

27. See also Gal. 4:1-11, 31; 5:1, 13, in which Paul specifies believers' liberation from death, slavery, the flesh, and even the Law. Martyn (*Galatians*, p. 490) notes that Paul speaks of the "enslaving Law" at least twenty-five times in Galatians. In Romans, however, perhaps to clarify his words in Galatians, Paul affirms both believers' liberation from the Law (6:15; 7:1-6) and the goodness of the Law, blaming sin for co-opting the Law for evil ends (e.g., Rom. 7:7-13).

For our sake he [God] made him to be sin who knew no sin, so that in him we might become the righteousness of God.

In the sphere of Christ's power, humans are liberated from sin so that the formerly impossible is now possible. They are no longer covenantally dysfunctional.

One of the powers from which Christ's death liberates is the power of the self.[28] Paul believes that humans outside Christ are enslaved to themselves, living a life improperly oriented toward themselves rather than toward God and others. Christ liberates them from themselves so that they can live for him; they exchange one "lord" (self) for another, proper lord:

[H]e died for all, so that those who live might no longer live for themselves, but for him who died and was raised for them. (2 Cor. 5:15)

So too in 1 Corinthians 6:19-20, Paul borrows the language of liberation from slavery to emphasize the effects of Christ's death, referred to as the "price" of the redemption:

[19][D]o you not know that . . . you are not your own? [20]For you were bought with a price; therefore glorify God in your body.

That "you are not your own" is true only because God has redeemed "you" from being your own — that is, your own "owner" or "master." Believers have been redeemed from slavery to themselves in order to belong to their rightful owner.[29] Those who were *once* their own are *no longer* their own. So also in Galatians 2:19-20, Paul narrates his experience of liberation from both the self and the Law:

[19][T]hrough the law I died to the law, so that I might live to God. I have been crucified with Christ; [20]and it is no longer I who live, but it is Christ who lives in me. . . .[30]

---

28. I do not mean to imply that Paul had a modern notion of selfhood. However, as a study of the use of reflexive constructions in ancient writers reveals, the meaning of appropriate self-involving actions and appropriate disposal of the self (even as a form of enslavement to others or to self) was a significant concern in antiquity. For this subject in the writings of Paul and the *Discourses of Epictetus,* see Michael J. Gorman, "The Self, the Lord, and the Other: The Significance of Reflexive Pronoun Constructions in the Letters of Paul, with a Comparison to the 'Discourses' of Epictetus," Ph.D. diss., Princeton Theological Seminary, 1989.

29. See Hans Conzelmann, *1 Corinthians,* Hermeneia (Philadelphia: Fortress, 1975), p. 113.

30. The phrase "died to the law" is a difficult one. Barclay (*Obeying the Truth,* pp. 80-81, n. 14) is probably right in suggesting the background of the Jewish principle that a dead person

Similarly, according to Romans 6:6, the "old self" or "old person" (Greek *palaios anthrōpos*) has died.

For Paul, then, the cross marks the beginning of the divinely promised "new creation" (Gal. 6:15; 2 Cor. 5:17). The cross of Christ is simultaneously *God's* apocalyptic act and *Christ's* human, suffering-servant act intended to redeem or liberate humanity from the interlocking directorate of powers that enslaves us. The new creation is inaugurated by God but also by a representative human, Jesus the Messiah. To the character of his fully human act — one of obedience and faithfulness to God — we now turn.

The Cross as Christ's Obedience

Only two times in his letters does Paul refer to the obedience of Christ, but the significance of these two occurrences is weighty. We will consider each one and then reflect on the overall significance of Christ's obedience for Paul.

Philippians 2

The first text referring to Christ's obedience is possibly not even original to Paul, appearing in Philippians 2:8 as part of a hymn text he likely quotes but clearly owns:

> [7]. . . And being found in human form, [8]he humbled himself and became obedient to the point of death — even death on a cross. (Phil. 2:7d-8)

As suggested in the previous chapter, a better translation of this text would understand "became obedient" (expressed in Greek with a participle) as the specific way in which Christ humbled himself:

> . . . he humbled himself *by* [or perhaps *in*] *becoming obedient*. . . .

The phrase "by [in] becoming obedient . . ." explains "humbled himself," just as "[by] taking the form of a slave, being born in human likeness" explains the enigmatic phrase "emptied himself" in verse 7.

The obedience of Christ, then, is the concrete manifestation of his self-

---

is no longer obligated to the Law, as well as the likely connection with Gal. 3:13, where Christ is cursed by the Law for hanging on a tree. Together, these suggest that by identifying with the crucified and cursed-by-the-Law Messiah ("through the law"), believers end their relationship of slavery to the law ("died to the law").

humbling. It is an obedience that expresses itself in death, even death by cruci-fixion. Though the text of verse 8 suggests that this obedient death was the cul-mination of an entire human life of service and obedience, it focuses on the death as the ultimate and preeminent form of that obedience.

Since clearly the one whom Christ obeyed is God (the Father), the hymn portrays Christ's crucifixion, paradoxically, as both the will of God and the free act of Christ. The voluntary character of the obedience is stressed not only in the phrase "he humbled himself" but also throughout the hymn text, where Christ's free initiative is described in phrases such as "did not regard equality with God as something to be exploited" (v. 6) and "emptied himself" (v. 7). God's response to this voluntary obedience to death is exaltation to lordship, completing the humiliation-exaltation, or obedience-vindication, schema that is so prominent in the Bible.[31]

Thus Christ's death by crucifixion is for Paul a voluntary act of obedience, the culmination of a human life lived as the servant of God. Obedience as God's servant (despite possessing equality with God!) was, for Paul, Christ's "life-stance" before God, his "narrative posture." The image of servant, as suggested in the previous chapter, probably derives from Isaiah 52:13–53:12. Yet it is also possible that Paul (or the hymn) intends an allusion to Adam and thus to Christ as the contrast, or anti-type, to Adam. Adam, of course, was disobedient to God's command and may well have tried to exploit for selfish gain his being made in the image of God.[32] Whether or not Paul intends such an allusion here, he makes the Adam-Christ contrast clear in his other reference to Christ's obe-dience, Romans 5:19.[33]

Romans 5

In Romans 5:12-21 Paul contrasts the effects on the human race of the one rep-resentative "trespass" and act of "disobedience" of Adam with the effects of the

---

31. See the discussion in chapter twelve.

32. According to Gen. 3:5, Adam is tempted to "be like God," and of course he succumbs, disobeying God.

33. Among those arguing for an allusion to Adam here are Dunn (e.g., *Theology*, pp. 281-87) and N. T. Wright (*The Climax of the Covenant: Christ and the Law in Pauline Theology* [Ed-inburgh: T&T Clark, 1991; Minneapolis: Fortress, 1993], pp. 90-98). Paul's "Adam christology works by antithetic parallelism" (Dunn, *Theology*, p. 285, n. 90). Wright argues correctly (against Dunn's earlier work, for instance) that the presence of an "Adam-christology" does not rule out simultaneous allusions to the suffering servant or an affirmation of Christ's preexistence. In his *Theology*, Dunn appears more open to seeing Christ's preexistence in the text.

one representative act of "grace," "righteousness," and "obedience" of Christ. Through Adam's trespass came the power of sin and, from sin, death (v. 12). Many (meaning "all," v. 12) "were made" sinners (v. 19), as Adam's sin was ratified by every other human being (v. 12), sin becoming the human norm. Death's arrival is described as its *reign* ("exercised dominion," vv. 14, 17). Under death's reign, of course, "many died" as a result of the one trespass (v. 15), which also brought judgment leading to condemnation for all (vv. 16, 18).

The thesis of this section of Romans, however, is that "the free gift is not like the trespass" (v. 15). This free gift is the grace of God demonstrated in "the grace of the one man, Jesus Christ" (v. 15). This grace "abounded for the many" (v. 15), bringing grace (v. 17), justification (v. 16), and righteousness (v. 17) to those who receive it. They "exercise dominion in life" (v. 17), implying that they are liberated from the dominion of sin and death inaugurated by the first Adam.

That this "grace" is Christ's death is made certain in verses 18-19, where Paul speaks of "one act": "one man's act of righteousness [that] leads to justification and life for all" (v. 18), and "one man's obedience [by which] the many will be made righteous" (v. 19). The death was one act of righteousness to undo the one trespass and all its effects, one act of obedience to undo the one act of disobedience and all its consequences.

This one act of obedience to God, claims Paul, was cosmic, even apocalyptic, in scope and effect. By means of this obedient death, death's reign is ended and life begins. Sin is no longer the norm for those who receive the grace effected by this death; the righteousness of One leads to the righteousness of many. That is also to say, implicitly, that the *obedience* of One leads to the *obedience* of many. Thus the gift of Christ's obedient death restores (believing) humanity to a proper relationship with God ("justification," v. 16), whereby those who respond are now able to become righteous and obey. Christ's death is simultaneously an act of obedience to God and, as such, a gift of grace to humanity. His obedience permits ours.

This one act of obedience, moreover, Paul also characterizes as an act of faith. (To anticipate our conclusion, then, Christ's faith permits ours.) In light of Paul's phrase "the obedience of faith," this is not surprising. Indeed, one major New Testament scholar has called Romans 5:15-21 Paul's exposition of "the faith of Jesus Christ" previously mentioned and described very compactly in Romans 3:21-26.[34] We turn now to examine the cross of Jesus as his "faith."

---

34. Luke T. Johnson, "Romans 3:21-26 and the Faith of Jesus," *Catholic Biblical Quarterly* 44 (1982): 87-89, and his *Reading Romans*, pp. 78, 90-93.

The Cross as the Demonstration of Christ's Faith

In recent years, students of Paul have been struck by the existence of a Pauline phrase suggesting that Paul saw Jesus's death not only as an act of obedience but also as an act of faith or faithfulness. The Greek phrase in question, which occurs seven times in Paul's letters, is *hē pistis [Iēsou] Christou* — literally "the faith of [Jesus] Christ," or "the faith of [Jesus] the Messiah" — or a variant thereof. This phrase has traditionally been translated as "faith in [Jesus] Christ." (See Gal. 2:16 [twice]; 2:20 [faith of the Son of God]; 3:22; Rom. 3:22, 26; Phil. 3:9.[35]) This traditional translation is actually a possible rendition of the Greek genitive case used in the phrase *(Christou),* but whether it is the best translation — or whether it conveys Paul's intention — is a matter of debate.

Space does not permit a review of the scholarly debate over "faith of Christ" versus "faith in Christ."[36] Some of the key arguments for the newer translation, "faith of Christ," are:

1. it expresses the most natural translation of the Greek phrase;[37]
2. it makes God (rather than God and Christ) the consistent object of faith for Paul;[38]
3. it is parallel in form and content to "the faith of Abraham" in Romans 4:12, 16;
4. it can be given coherent sense, as a reference to Christ's faith or faithfulness (the Greek word *pistis* can mean either) expressed in death, in the overall structure of Paul's experience and theology, making the most fundamental

---

35. See the texts printed in chapter five and below.

36. The debate is sometimes described in grammatical terms as the subjective (Christ's faith) versus objective (faith in Christ) construal of the Greek genitive, and in theological terms as the Christological (Christ's faith) versus anthropological (human faith in Christ) interpretation. For a strong summary of the "faith of Christ" interpretation, with full bibliography, see Richard B. Hays, "*PISTIS CHRISTOU* and Pauline Theology: What Is at Stake?" in E. Elizabeth Johnson and David B. Hay, eds., *Pauline Theology,* vol. 4: *Looking Back, Pressing On* (Atlanta: Scholars Press, 1997), pp. 35-60. See also Martyn, *Galatians,* pp. 263-75, esp. pp. 269-75. For the traditional interpretation, see James D. G. Dunn, "Once More, *PISTIS CHRISTOU,*" in E. Elizabeth Johnson and David B. Hay, eds., *Pauline Theology,* vol. 4: *Looking Back, Pressing On* (Atlanta: Scholars Press, 1997), pp. 61-81.

37. While this is debated (e.g., by Dunn, "Once More," pp. 63-67), two articles by G. Howard are particularly convincing: "On the Faith of Christ," *Harvard Theological Review* 60 (1967): 459-65, and "The Faith of Christ," *Expository Times* 85 (1974): 212-15.

38. The only exceptions in the undisputed Pauline letters would be Gal. 2:16 and Phil. 1:29 (see also Col. 2:5), but these texts involve the use of "believe into," which has to do with faith effecting transfer of allegiance and social location ("into Christ") rather than the object of faith.

basis of salvation not anthropocentric (our faith) but theo- and Christocentric (Christ's faith);[39] and

5. it grounds Paul's emphasis on the inseparability of faith and love in the one faithful and loving act of Christ on the cross.

Indeed, Paul's experience of Christ and of faith, and his narration of that experience, will be understood quite differently from traditional interpretations by those many interpreters of Paul, including the present writer, who find the "faith of Christ" translation compelling. The "stakes" are quite high in this debate. Richard Hays argues that significant aspects of one's understanding of Paul depend on how one interprets the "faith of Christ/faith in Christ" texts.[40] On the whole, at least in this country, a major shift has occurred in scholarship, and the acceptance of "faith of Christ" is widespread and ever-increasing.[41] This is because, to apply to all of Paul's letters what Leander Keck said of Romans, "in every case, construing [*pistis Iēsou*, faith of/in Jesus] as the fidelity of Jesus not only removes unwarranted awkwardness from Paul's statements but clarifies the key point — the role of Jesus in salvation."[42]

The seven texts in the undisputed Pauline letters that contain the phrase "the faith of Christ" (or a close variant) are the following, listed in the translations of the NRSV and the NRSV margin, with the phrases in question boldfaced:

39. This point is reflected in the terminology now sometimes used to distinguish the two interpretations of *pistis Christou* characterized in n. 36 as either "anthropological" ("faith in Christ") or "Christological" ("faith of Christ").

40. Hays, *"PISTIS,"* pp. 55-57. For Hays' initial and still insightful explorations of the importance of "the faith of Christ" for understanding Paul, see his *Faith of Jesus Christ,* pp. 247-66.

41. The claim that the arguments for this change are "decisive," resulting in a nearly universally accepted paradigm shift in the interpretation of Paul (so Stanley K. Stowers, *A Rereading of Romans: Justice, Jews and Gentiles* [New Haven: Yale University Press, 1994], p. 194), is probably overstated. In private conversation in November 1997, James Dunn indicated that the acceptance of "faith of Christ" is largely a North American phenomenon, but this is changing. The Protestant Dunn and the (American) Roman Catholic Joseph Fitzmyer are two prominent Pauline scholars who remain unconvinced. Nonetheless, it seems likely to me that the next edition of the RSV-NRSV tradition of English Bible translations, or perhaps another new translation, will opt for "faith of Christ" in the not-too-distant future. Already, a new electronic translation, the NET Bible or New English Translation, has rendered the phrases in question as the "faith of Christ." See www.bible.org for this translation of the New Testament.

42. Leander Keck, "'Jesus' in Romans," *Journal of Biblical Literature* 108 (1989): 454.

Faith in Christ (NRSV) | Faith of Christ (NRSV margin)

Galatians 2:15-16, 19-21

[15]We ourselves are Jews by birth and not Gentile sinners; [16]yet we know that a person is justified not by the works of the law but through **faith in Jesus Christ**. And we have come to believe in Christ Jesus, so that we might be justified by **faith in Christ**, and not by doing the works of the law, because no one will be justified by the works of the law.

[19]. . . I have been crucified with Christ; [20]and it is no longer I who live, but it is Christ who lives in me. And the life I now live in the flesh I live by **faith in the Son of God**, who loved me and gave himself for me. [21]I do not nullify the grace of God; for if justification comes through the law, then Christ died for nothing.

Galatians 3:21-22

[21]. . . [I]f a law had been given that could make alive, then righteousness would indeed come through the law. [22]But the scripture has imprisoned all things under the power of sin, so that what was promised through **faith in Jesus Christ** might be given to those who believe.

Romans 3:21-22, 26

[21]But now, apart from law, the righteousness of God has been disclosed, and is attested by the law and the prophets, [22]the righteousness of God through **faith in Jesus Christ** for all who believe. . . . [26]it was to prove at the present time that he [God] himself is righteous and that he justifies the one who has **faith in Jesus**.

Galatians 2:15-16, 19-21

[15]We ourselves are Jews by birth and not Gentile sinners; [16]yet we know that a person is justified not by the works of the law but through **the faith of Jesus Christ**. And we have come to believe in Christ Jesus, so that we might be justified by **the faith of Christ**, and not by doing the works of the law, because no one will be justified by the works of the law.

[19]. . . I have been crucified with Christ; [20]and it is no longer I who live, but it is Christ who lives in me. And the life I now live in the flesh I live by **the faith of the Son of God**, who loved me and gave himself for me. [21]I do not nullify the grace of God; for if justification comes through the law, then Christ died for nothing.

Galatians 3:21-22

[21]. . . [I]f a law had been given that could make alive, then righteousness would indeed come through the law. [22]But the scripture has imprisoned all things under the power of sin, so that what was promised through **the faith of Jesus Christ** might be given to those who believe.

Romans 3:21-22, 26

[21]But now, apart from law, the righteousness of God has been disclosed, and is attested by the law and the prophets, [22]the righteousness of God through **the faith of Jesus Christ** for all who believe. . . . [26]it was to prove at the present time that he [God] himself is righteous and that he justifies the one who has **the faith of Jesus**.

Philippians 3:8-9	Philippians 3:8-9
[8]. . . I regard everything as loss because of the surpassing value of knowing Christ Jesus my Lord. For his sake I have suffered the loss of all things, and I regard them as rubbish, in order that I may gain Christ [9]and be found in him, not having a righteousness of my own that comes from the law, but one that comes through **faith in Christ**, the righteousness from God based on faith.	[8]. . . I regard everything as loss because of the surpassing value of knowing Christ Jesus my Lord. For his sake I have suffered the loss of all things, and I regard them as rubbish, in order that I may gain Christ [9]and be found in him, not having a righteousness of my own that comes from the law, but one that comes through **the faith of Christ**, the righteousness from God based on faith.

Of particular note is that each of these texts appears in a discussion of the basis of justification, and in each discussion the role of human faith is emphasized *apart* from the phrase that the NRSV translates "faith in" Christ and the NRSV margin translates as the "faith of" Christ. That is, Paul in no way diminishes the significance of the faith of believers by stressing the faith of Jesus.[43] In fact, through the preaching of the gospel, "Christ's faith elicits our faith."[44] (As we have already seen, and will continue to see in the next chapter, Paul does *define* faith and its role differently from our most common understandings of faith.) What precisely, then, is "the faith of Jesus Christ"?

Galatians

In Galatians, the issue addressed in the two passages where "faith of Christ" language occurs (2:16, 20; 3:22) is the means of justification or righteousness (Greek *dikaiosynē*). Traditional interpretations suggest that Paul pits justification by "[doing the] works of the law" (2:16), abbreviated to "through the law" (2:21; 3:21), over against faith in Jesus Christ. However, there is a clear parallelism between 2:16 and 2:21 that suggests a different pair of antithetical possibilities for the basis of justification:

---

43. See Gal. 2:16; 3:22; Rom. 3:22, 26. Even Philippians 3, which does not speak of faith, insists on the believer's active knowing of Jesus (3:8, 10).

44. Martyn, *Galatians*, p. 277. Martyn may, however, minimize human responsibility in his emphasis on faith as God's freeing of the human will (pp. 276-77).

Rejected Basis of Justification: The Law/Works of the Law	Affirmed Basis of Justification: The Faith/Death of Christ
2:16	**2:16**
[W]e know that a person is justified not by **the works of the law**	but through **the faith of Jesus Christ**.
	And we have come to believe in [literally, "into"][45] Christ Jesus, so that we might be justified by **the faith of Christ**,
and not by **doing the works of the law,** because no one will be justified by **the works of the law.**	
2:21	**2:21**
I do not nullify the grace of God; for if justification comes through **the law,**	then **Christ died** for nothing.

Whereas 2:16 by itself does not provide a clear interpretation of precisely what Paul affirms as the alternative to doing the works of the law, 2:21 makes a clear statement: it is the death of Christ, a death that would have been without purpose or meaning if justification were possible through the law.

That Christ's death is synonymous with Christ's faith is evident not only from this parallelism but from 2:20, which interprets Christ's faith as his self-giving death:

> [19]. . . I have been crucified with Christ; [20]and it is no longer I who live, but it is Christ who lives in me. And the life I now live in the flesh I live by **the faith of the Son of God,** who loved me and gave himself [or, better, "by giving himself"] for me. (Gal. 2:19b-20)[46]

Though the word "death" or "died" is absent from the last part of 2:20, the meaning of the Son's loving act of self-giving is clearly his death, as the end of 2:19 ("crucified with Christ") suggests and 2:21 ("Christ died") makes explicit: "his faith *is* his sacrificial act."[47] This death is the *objective* basis of justification, but it must still be met with faith (2:16), which is related to, and perhaps synon-

---

45. The Greek construction is not the same as the one ("faith of" or "faith in") debated. Rather, there is a verb and a preposition clearly indicating an act of faith that "moved" the speaker into Christ (Greek *hēmeis eis Christon Iēsoun episteusamen*).

46. For arguments in support of "the faith of the Son of God" in this verse, see Hays, *Faith of Jesus Christ*, pp. 167-69. For the translation "by giving himself," see chapter five (p. 83, n. 17).

47. Martyn, *Galatians*, p. 259.

ymous with, crucifixion with Christ (2:19). The response of faith (or co-crucifixion, or perhaps even "co-faith"), one might say, is then the *subjective* basis of justification, as we will see in the next chapter.

Galatians 3:21-22 reinforces the contrast between the two possible means of justification and affirms that only the faith of Jesus Christ brings justification:[48]

> [21]. . . [I]f a law had been given that could make alive, then righteousness would indeed come through the law. [22]But the scripture has imprisoned all things under the power of sin, so that what was promised through **the faith of Jesus Christ** might be given to those who believe.

No specific explanation of "the faith of Jesus Christ" is offered here; readers are expected to carry forward the understanding of the phrase put forth in 2:15-21, the letter's thesis.[49] Furthermore, they are to understand from the context of Galatians 3 and 4 that this faith of Christ is effective because it redeems people from the curse of the very law by which some seek justification.[50] Once again, however, as in 2:15-21, the necessity of human faith to match Christ's faith ("given to those who believe") is stressed.

Thus in Galatians, "the faith of Christ" is his loving, self-giving death, which is somehow for Paul both the means of justification and the means of present life for those who believe. This fundamental understanding of the faith of Christ reappears in Romans and Philippians.

Romans

In Romans 3, Paul again contrasts "the law" and "the faith of Jesus Christ" as antithetical options for the basis of justification and defines the faith of Jesus as his redemptive death:

> [21]But now, apart from law, the righteousness of God has been disclosed, and is attested by the law and the prophets, [22]the righteousness of God through **the faith of Jesus Christ** for all who believe. For there is no distinction, [23]since all have sinned and fall short of the glory of God; [24]they are now justified by his grace as a gift, through the redemption that is in Christ Jesus,

48. The most compelling examination of this text is Hays, *Faith of Jesus Christ,* pp. 157-67.

49. That 2:15-21 is the thesis of Galatians has been persuasively argued by Hans Dieter Betz, *Galatians,* Hermeneia (Philadelphia: Fortress, 1979), and many following his lead.

50. Further references to Christ's death surround 3:21-22: 3:1 ("crucified"), 3:13-14 ("Christ redeemed us from the curse of the law"), and 4:5 ("to redeem those who were under the law"). The faithful death of Jesus is the ground of, and legitimation for, the experience of Gentiles receiving the blessing of the Spirit. See Hays, *Faith of Jesus Christ,* pp. 193-212, 225-35.

[25]whom God put forward as a sacrifice of atonement by his blood, effective though faith. He did this to show his righteousness, because in his divine forbearance he had passed over the sins previously committed; [26]it was to prove at the present time that he [God] himself is righteous and that he justifies the one who has **the faith of Jesus.**

This passage (3:21-26) is one of the most complex in all of Paul's letters, but its fundamental affirmations are nonetheless clear:

1. God's means of justification is not the law but the faith of Jesus Christ.
2. The faith of Jesus Christ is manifested in his death, which effects justification, redemption, and atonement.
3. The righteousness that comes through the faith of Jesus comes ultimately from God. Indeed, the faithful act of Jesus is also the demonstration of the faithfulness of God.[51]
4. The faithfulness of God demonstrated in the faith of Jesus must be met by the human response of faith for the death to be effective.
5. Although justification is not by means of the law but by means of Jesus' faith met by human faith, the law and prophets bear witness to this means of justification.
6. Implicitly, this justification by means of God's faithfulness, revealed in the faith of Jesus, is available to all people, apart from their relationship to "the works of the [Jewish] law" — whatever precisely they may be.[52]

In summary, as Richard Hays comments, Romans 3:21-26 is Paul's way of saying that

> God has solved the problem of human unrighteousness and Israel's faithlessness by putting forward as a sacrifice the one perfectly faithful human being, Jesus. Though others rebelled and refused to give glory to God, he remained faithful. His death is an act of *pistis* [faith]: human *pistis* — the counter-

---

51. Here a primary theme of the letter to the Romans appears, namely, the integrity of God — God's faithfulness to the covenant, God's righteous character. Paul claims that in the death of Jesus, God is shown to be both faithful and righteous by providing redemption from sin. Thus it is clear that the faith, or faithfulness, of Jesus is his atoning death. Yet that death, Christ's faithfulness to God, is also God's faithfulness to Israel and, through Israel, to all the world. See the quote from Hays below.

52. Compare 3:28: "For we hold that a person is justified by faith apart from works prescribed by the law." The debate about this phrase is ongoing, but most interpreters understand it to mean "boundary markers" such as circumcision and food and calendar customs required by the Law.

weight of Israel's *apistia* ("unfaithfulness") — because it is an act of perfect obedience through which many will be made righteous vicariously (5:19), and divine *pistis* [faith/faithfulness] because it affirms God's unbreakable love . . . (5:8). . . . Christ's death is — mysteriously — an act of divine love and faithkeeping (cf. 15:8).[53]

Although Romans 3:21-26 contains the only two explicit references to "the faith of Christ" in Romans,[54] it is possible that Paul alludes to the faith of Christ in the thesis of Romans (1:16-17), and it is likely that Paul wants his readers to understand the description of Christ's obedience (5:12-21) as an "exegesis" of the phrase "the faith of Christ."[55]

Once one understands that Romans 3:21-26 speaks of the faithfulness of God revealed in the faith(fulness) of Christ, which is meant to engender human faith leading to justification, the text of Romans 1:16-17, traditionally and correctly understood as the thesis of Romans, seems to summarize those claims succinctly:

> [16]For I am not ashamed of the gospel; it is the power of God for salvation to everyone who has faith, to the Jew first and also to the Greek. [17]For in it the righteousness of God is revealed through faith for faith [Greek *ek pisteōs eis pistin*, literally, "from faith toward faith"]; as it is written, "The one who is righteous will live by faith." (Rom. 1:16-17)

In particular, 3:21-26 suggests that 1:17a should be understood to define the righteousness of God that the gospel reveals as the faithfulness of God (God's covenant fidelity) that is revealed in the faithful death of Jesus and for the purpose of evoking a response of covenant faithfulness from both Jews and Gentiles.[56] Preserving the sense of the Greek prepositions, which

53. Hays, "*PISTIS*," p. 45; cf. *Faith of Jesus Christ*, pp. 170-74.

54. Sam K. Williams, *Jesus' Death as Saving Event*, HDR 2 (Missoula: Scholars Press, 1975), pp. 47-51 (echoed by Hays, "*PISTIS*," p. 46), argues that Rom. 3:25 contains yet a third reference to the faith of Jesus ("through [the] faith"), but this reference is more likely to God's faithfulness (so Dunn, "Once More," p. 76, n. 66) — although not to the traditional referent of the human faith response.

55. See Hays and Johnson, as cited earlier on this point.

56. Similarly, Johnson, *Reading Romans*, p. 59: "Jesus' human faith is the means of the revelation of God's righteousness." Some have even suggested that the first mention of faith in v. 17, as well as the Scriptural quotation in v. 17, are references directly to the faith of Jesus the righteous. See, e.g., Richard B. Hays, "'The Righteous One' as Eschatological Deliverer: A Case Study in Paul's Apocalyptic Hermeneutics," in Joel Marcus and Marion L. Soards, eds., *Apocalyptic and the New Testament: Essays in Honor of J. Louis Martyn*, JSNTSup 2 (Sheffield: Sheffield Academic Press, 1989), pp. 191-216.

indicate the origin and goal of faith,[57] we may paraphrase Romans 1:17a as follows:

> The gospel proclaims that God's righteousness both *originates in* fidelity — God's fidelity, revealed in Christ's fidelity — and *engenders* fidelity — ours.

The faith of Jesus receives further amplification not only in 3:21-26 but especially in 5:12-21, where, as noted above, Paul's equation of faith and obedience elsewhere suggests that his description of Christ's obedience is likewise a sketch of Christ's faith:

> For just as by the one man's disobedience the many were made sinners, so by the one man's obedience the many will be made righteous. (Rom. 5:19)

The context clearly identifies Adam and Christ as the two persons contrasted, and their historic, defining actions as sin, transgression, trespass, and disobedience, on the one hand, versus free gift, grace, act of righteousness, and obedience, on the other. Though Paul does not here specifically use the word "faithlessness" or "faith," it is clear throughout Romans 5:12-21 that Christ's one act is his obedient death that reveals the grace of God and effects justification. Grace and justification come, according to 3:21-26, through the faith (Romans 5 uses the synonym "obedience") of Christ.[58]

In Romans, then, Christ's faith is, as in Galatians, the means of justification that must be met with human faith. The accent is placed, however, on the faithfulness of God manifested in the faithful death of Jesus.[59]

Philippians

Philippians continues the antithesis between the faith of Jesus and the law as the basis for righteousness, and it also retains the necessity of human faith. The emphasis on God's faithfulness is not present, however, as it was in Romans:

> [8]. . . I regard everything as loss because of the surpassing value of knowing Christ Jesus my Lord. For his sake I have suffered the loss of all things, and I regard them as rubbish, in order that I may gain Christ [9]and be found in him,

---

57. Greek *ek* and *eis,* as noted above.

58. It should be noted that if the "faith of Jesus" were understood as "faith in Jesus," then the means of justification according to Rom. 3:21-26 (human faith in Christ and his death) and according to Rom. 5:12-21 (Christ's death) would be different.

59. This emphasis is not entirely lacking in Galatians, which does speak of God's initiative in the redemptive death of Christ (Gal. 1:4; 4:4-5).

not having a righteousness of my own that comes from the law, but one that comes through [Greek *dia*] **the faith of Christ**, the righteousness from God based on [Greek *epi*] faith. (Phil. 3:8b-9)

It is from the immediate and larger contexts that we know that Paul again speaks of the cross of Christ as the basis of righteousness, and therefore as the content of Christ's faith. In 3:10 Paul notes that the goal of his life is to be conformed to the death of Christ in order to be raised with him. He then invites the Philippians to imitate him, and others who live like him, rather than those who live as "enemies of the cross of Christ" (3:17-18).

Looking outside chapter 3 of Philippians, we cannot help but consider the earlier hymn text of 2:6-11 as an amplification of what Paul means by "the faith of Christ."[60] Indeed Philippians 2:6-11 interprets this term for this letter, just as Romans 5:12-21 explained it for Romans. What marked Christ, according to the hymn, was his obedience — his faithfulness to God, even to the point of death (2:8). It is this obedience to God — and not human keeping of laws or ethnic boundary markers — that is the basis of justification now and resurrection in the future.

Conclusion: The Faith of Jesus Christ

In summary regarding "the faith of Jesus Christ," we may say several things. First of all, the faith of Christ, rather than the law or the works of the law, is the basis and instrument of justification and righteousness; this is stressed in all the passages. Second, the faith of Christ is manifested in his death, his act of self-giving obedience to God and self-giving love for humanity. Third, the faith, or faithfulness, of Christ is the manifestation of the faithfulness of God, as God takes the initiative to fulfill the covenant with Israel and extend it, as promised, to the Gentiles. Fourth, Christ's faith must be shared by those who wish to be justified. As J. Louis Martyn puts it, believers' "trust in God has been awakened, kindled by God's trustworthy deed in Christ."[61]

One of James Dunn's major objections to the interpretation presented in this chapter is the ambiguity of the term "faith of Christ," a question that, he contends, is too seldom asked:

60. So also Frank J. Matera, in a discussion of 2:6-11 in his chapter on Paul's Christology as "The Climax of Israel's Story," in *New Testament Christology* (Louisville: Westminster/John Knox, 1999), pp. 125-31: "this text may be viewed as another example of what Paul means by the faith of Jesus" (p. 131).

61. Martyn, *Galatians*, p. 272, n. 173.

What does "the faith of Christ" mean? To what does it refer? The answer is hardly clear. The ministry of Jesus as a whole? The death of Christ in particular? The continuing ministry of the exalted Christ in heaven?[62]

Drawing on the arguments offered in this chapter, we may say in summary that *the "faith" of Christ is his "narrative posture" of faithfulness or obedience toward God, the right ordering of his "fundamental option," which led him to, and which was particularly manifested in, the cross.* Dieter Georgi rightly suggests that the "faith" of Christ means fundamentally Christ's "trust or (even better) *loyalty*."[63] The term "the faith of Christ," in all its precise formulations, is a "summary allusion" to the story of "Jesus' fidelity in carrying out his mission" vis-à-vis God and us,[64] the focus and epitome being the cross. Jesus embodied the faith to which Israel was called. Depending on the context, Paul can use the term to stress Christ's faith also as God's (Romans), the self-giving and loving narrative pattern of the crucifixion (Galatians), or, most fully, the self-denying, self-humbling, self-emptying narrative pattern of both "incarnation" and cross (Philippians).

We see, then, that Paul experiences the grace of God in Christ's death as a fully divine and fully human action. In Christ's death, God is faithful to us, and Christ is faithful to God. Christ's faithful act thereby, as we will see in detail below, becomes the prototype of humanity's appropriate dynamic, narrative posture before this faithful God. So what does this mean for believers? To anticipate the next chapter, as Christ was obedient and faithful in dying as the representative righteous human being, so also now those who wish to benefit from God's grace must "have" or "share in" the faith of Jesus. God, Paul says, justifies those who share this faith (Rom. 3:26); they can therefore be described as being "co-crucified" with Christ (Gal. 2:19).[65] The justified, in turn, continue to live "by the faith of the Son of God," whose faithfulness to God expressed itself in self-giving love (Gal. 2:20).

In light of these aspects of Paul's narrative of the cross, we need to consider more fully, in the next chapter, what Paul means by "faith" as it characterizes believers throughout their life in Christ. This reexamination will assist us in

---

62. Dunn, "Once More," p. 70.

63. Dieter Georgi, *Theocracy in Paul's Praxis and Theology* (Minneapolis: Fortress, 1991), p. 36, n. 9 (emphasis added). "Deliverance from the prison and slavery of sin and law is accomplished through Jesus as a revelation of loyalty" (p. 43).

64. Hays, "*PISTIS*," p. 37. Martyn (*Galatians*, p. 259) claims that in Galatians 2 Christ's "faith *is* that sacrificial act" of love on the cross.

65. Hays ("*PISTIS*," p. 54) points out a consistent Pauline pattern of Christ's faith followed by human faith in Rom. 1:17; 3:22; Gal. 2:16; 3:22.

seeing the implications of the thesis that Christ's obedient death is also his act of faith, and that believers' faith is a sharing in the faith of Christ that was expressed on the cross. Faith, in other words, is cruciform from start to finish.

CHAPTER 7

CRUCIFORM FAITH (II)

The Character and Cost of Faith

In simplest terms, as we noted at the beginning of the previous chapter, faith is the appropriate response to hearing the gospel (Romans 10). Faith is "the decisive and most distinctive note of Paul's spirituality."[1] More specifically, as the last chapter suggested, faith is an initial and ongoing cruciformity grounded in the cross (the faith) of Christ. In this chapter we seek to explore more fully the character of that faith: what it is, what it does, and what justification "by faith" means if faith is essentially a form of cruciformity. In addition, we examine the possible consequences — the cost — of cruciform faith.

Faith as Initiation

To be sure, for Paul faith continues throughout life in Christ and thus defines a believer's total existence. Yet faith is first of all the means of *beginning* life in Christ, life in the Spirit (Gal. 3:1-5). Faith, in this most basic sense, is the response of conversion or initiation into the messianic faith and community. It is a term pregnant with meaning, and Paul employs numerous metaphors, as well as alternative terms, to interpret faith to his churches.

As shorthand for conversion-initiation, "faith" is closely associated with baptism in Paul's mind, as texts like 1 Corinthians 6:11 and Galatians 3:22-29 demonstrate. We turn first to 1 Corinthians:

---

1. W. K. Grossouw, *Spirituality of the New Testament,* trans. Martin W. Schoenberg (St. Louis/London: Herder, 1961), p. 135.

[Y]ou were washed, you were sanctified, you were justified in the name of the Lord Jesus Christ and in the Spirit of our God. (1 Cor. 6:11b)

Although neither the word "faith" nor the word "baptism" (or "baptize") explicitly appears in this text, the conjunction of "washed . . . sanctified . . . justified" with "in the name of the Lord Jesus . . ." suggests the presence of faith ("justified") among the Corinthians as evidenced in the confession of Jesus and in baptism ("washed") in his name, and concurrent with the reception of the Spirit.[2]

Similarly, Galatians 3:22-29 describes the role of faith — the term occurs seven times in these verses — in the new dispensation inaugurated by the death of Christ. Those who believe (3:22) are justified by faith (3:24), becoming children of God (3:26) and heirs of Abraham (3:29) and thus recipients of the Spirit (cf. 3:1-18; 4:1-7). Faith and baptism appear together as dimensions of initiation into Christ:

> [26][I]n Christ Jesus you are all children of God through faith. [27]As many of you as were baptized into Christ have clothed yourselves with Christ. (Gal. 3:26-27)

Since space does not permit a thorough investigation of this relationship between faith and baptism, we will simply note two things. First, for Paul private belief and public confession of it — including baptism — go hand in hand.[3] Both are needed for salvation. That is, conversion-initiation is both personal and public; faith brings a person into a relationship with God in Christ, and also with other believers. Baptism makes public and communal that which is first of all private and individual, but cannot remain so.[4]

Second, baptism is a parabolic enactment of faith, a symbolic narrative.[5] It expresses both the primary content of the faith — Jesus' death, burial, and resurrection (compare Rom. 6:1-11 and 1 Cor. 15:3-4) — and the nature of faith as a sharing in, not merely an affirmation of, the narrative of Jesus. What Paul says of baptism, therefore, he would say also of faith. For instance, according to

---

2. The phrase "in the name of the Lord Jesus Christ and in the Spirit of our God" clearly modifies all three verbs.

3. In addition to the texts cited above, see the similarities between Romans 6 and Rom. 10:5-13.

4. In baptism, people "leave one world, cross a boundary, and enter another world," comments Jerome H. Neyrey in *Paul, In Other Words: A Cultural Reading of His Letters* (Louisville: Westminster/John Knox, 1990), p. 88. See also Wayne A. Meeks, *The First Urban Christians: The Social World of the Apostle Paul* (New Haven: Yale University Press, 1983), pp. 150-57.

5. Meeks, *First Urban Christians*, pp. 150-57.

Galatians 3:27, people are "baptized into Christ," but according to Galatians 2:16, people "believe into Christ."[6] Indeed, it is probably the case that Paul's primary concern is faith, understood as participation in the story of Jesus, with baptism as a demonstration of the reality of faith that has no meaning apart from faith or apart from the story of Jesus. Whatever is said of baptism, therefore, can likely also be said of faith.[7]

These close connections between baptism and faith suggest that we may legitimately look at various metaphors and terms of conversion-initiation, especially texts about baptism, to understand Paul's experience of faith. What, then, can we learn about this experience?

First of all, as noted above, faith is the appropriate response to the gospel (Rom. 10:17). As such, faith has a significant *cognitive* dimension; it affirms the content of the gospel as true. For instance, Paul reminds the Corinthians of the various faith affirmations that he received and passed on to them (1 Cor. 15:3-7). Most basic of all for Paul and his churches was the confession "Jesus is Lord," which entailed for Gentiles rejection of idols (e.g., 1 Thess. 1:10) and for Jews a new understanding of the one God of Israel that will allow them to ascribe to the crucified and exalted Jesus that which their Scriptures ascribed to God alone:

---

6. Translations, unfortunately, do not usually maintain the parallel Greek expressions found in Gal. 2:16 and 3:27, where the same preposition *(eis)* indicates movement from outside to inside Christ, by means of faith or baptism. The phrase in Gal. 2:16 is usually translated "we have believed [NRSV, "come to believe"] in Christ." Discussion of the translation "believe into" may be found in Sam K. Williams, *Galatians,* Abingdon New Testament Commentaries (Nashville: Abingdon, 1997), p. 70; and Sam K. Williams, *Jesus' Death as Saving Event,* HDR 2 (Missoula: Scholars Press, 1975), p. 433.

7. On the primacy of faith, see Hans Dieter Betz, *Galatians,* Hermeneia (Philadelphia: Fortress, 1979), p. 123, followed by David Seeley, *The Noble Death: Graeco-Roman Martyrology and Paul's Concept of Salvation* (Sheffield: JSOT Press, 1989), pp. 48-49. Betz contends that Gal. 2:19, referring to crucifixion with Christ, "may contain the theological principle by which Paul interprets the ritual of baptism in Romans 6." See also James D. G. Dunn, *The Theology of Paul the Apostle* (Grand Rapids: Eerdmans, 1998), pp. 442-59, who rightly stresses that for Paul and his converts the initial experience of the Spirit was more important than the ritual of baptism (esp. pp. 452-55), and that the Pauline image of baptism into Christ's death likely emerged not merely from the experience of baptism, but from the gospel tradition of Jesus describing his death as a baptism (Mark 10:38-39 and parallels; pp. 451-52). A. J. M. Wedderburn (*Baptism and Resurrection: Studies in Pauline Theology against Its Graeco-Roman Background* [Tübingen: J. C. B. Mohr (Paul Siebeck)], p. 49) and others rightly follow Robert C. Tannehill (*Dying and Rising with Christ: A Study in Pauline Theology* [Berlin: Alfred Töpelmann, 1966], p. 13) in stressing the "subordinate place" of baptism for Paul, even in Romans 6. What really matters is dying with Christ in reality, not in the ritual.

By myself I have sworn, from my mouth has gone forth in righteousness a word that shall not return: "To me every knee shall bow, every tongue shall swear." (Isa. 45:23; cf. Phil. 2:9-11)

As we shall see in subsequent chapters, the confession of Jesus as Lord also entailed, for Jews and Gentiles alike, the renunciation of Caesar as Lord.

This cognitive or theological rearrangement required by the gospel is only the beginning of an appropriate response. Faith, second, is complete *trust and confidence* — what Paul, living in a culture of honor and shame, calls "pride" — in God alone and in no one and nothing else. It is abandonment of all other gods and of all other grounds for assurance before God, especially the shaky ground of self-confidence. Paul describes his own experience of abandoning self-assurance as no longer having "confidence in the flesh":

> 3. . . [W]e worship in the Spirit of God and boast in Christ Jesus and have no confidence in the flesh — 4even though I, too, have reason for confidence in the flesh. (Phil. 3:3-4)

Even more graphically, he says that believers "have crucified the flesh with its passions and desires" (Gal. 5:24).

Paul blends the cognitive (affirmation) and emotive, experiential, or spiritual (trust) dimensions of faith in several ways. The focus of faith, for example, is the God who raises the dead. To believe in this kind of God is to go contrary to natural impulses, as Abraham reminds Paul (Romans 4). To believe in this God is to have confidence that God brings life out of death. Paradoxically, however, the God who brings life out of death does so by means of death — Christ's death and the believers'.

The Effects of Faith

In Paul's theology and experience, this initial act of faith is the response to God's action that triggers the planned effects of that work of God in believers. More specifically, faith actualizes all the intended outcomes of Christ's death. Faith *liberates* and *enslaves;* it *incorporates* and *inaugurates.* It liberates from the interlocking directorate of hostile powers that enslave human beings in order to make them servants of God; it incorporates people into Christ; and it inaugurates in them a new life of faithfulness made possible by the Spirit. All of this is an experience of cruciformity. Faith, for Paul, is a death experience, a death that creates life.

Liberation and Reenslavement

As a death experience, faith terminates certain relationships and realities. 1 Corinthians 6:11 suggests that those who have experienced washing, sanctification, and justification — those, that is, who have responded to the gospel with faith (probably expressed publicly in baptism) — have been liberated and transformed. They have left behind the ways of idolatry, immorality, and injustice that characterize the world in rebellion against God (Rom. 1:18-32). In other words, they have had the experience that Paul has had when he writes that "the world has been crucified to me and I to the world" (Gal. 6:14).

This crucifixion to the world is one way in which Paul expresses the death that has occurred in those who have faith, namely, death to sin. The "world" is the sphere in which sin reigns. This death with respect to sin is expressed definitively in the initial act of faith and in baptism, parallel to the once-for-all death of Christ to sin:

> [2]. . . How can we who died to sin go on living in it? [3]Do you not know that all of us who have been baptized into Christ Jesus were baptized into his death. . . . [6]We know that our old self was crucified with him so that the body of sin might be destroyed, and we might no longer be enslaved to sin. [7]For whoever has died is freed from sin. . . . [10]The death he [Christ] died, he died to sin, once for all; but the life he lives, he lives to God. [11]So you also must consider yourselves dead to sin and alive to God in Christ Jesus. (Rom. 6:2b-3, 6-7, 10-11)

This death or crucifixion to sin and the world includes also death to the self ("our old self was crucified"); that is, to what Paul also calls, or at least associates with, the "flesh" — the self under the power of sin and controlled by its anti-God impulses:[8]

> And those who belong to Christ Jesus have crucified the flesh with its passions and desires. (Gal. 5:24)

Paul says that he himself has been crucified with Christ and no longer lives (Gal. 2:19-20). That is, he no longer lives for himself and the desires inspired by the flesh, just as he no longer lives for sin or the world. Rather, he lives for God, he lives for Christ.[9]

---

8. See n. 23 on the flesh in chapter six.

9. The act of crucifixion even involves death with respect to the Law (Gal. 2:19; Rom. 7:4, 6), though the precise meaning of this death is debated.

Baptism (and the faith it expresses) is a kind of "imaginative reenactment" — "a coalescence of the literal and the imaginative" — of Christ's death and resurrection.[10] The believer, of course, does not literally die, but "Paul seems to think that the act of 'dying with Christ' ritually creates virtually the same sort of disjunction customarily associated with literal death."[11] Faith, then, is indeed a death experience, freeing those who die and enter into a new sphere of life from the reign of powers associated with the predeath existence. It produces therefore much more than an "imaginative" death; it effects a real liberation from sin and associated powers and realities.[12]

This experience of liberation through sharing in Christ's dying to sin and rising to new life toward God is often referred to as a *transfer* of dominions, from a sphere of existence ruled by sin, death, and unrighteousness, to one ruled by righteousness and life. This is a transfer from a malevolent to a benevolent lord. It is necessary because, in Paul's worldview, human beings always live under the sway and control of one power or another, either God or that which is opposed to God.[13] (As we have seen, the latter power is really a set of powers.)

Faith, then, effects a *liberation* from all the evil powers, but it also effects a new "enslavement" (to pursue the necessary but imperfect analogy, Paul says [Rom. 6:15-23]) to God, to Christ, to righteousness. Faith in the gospel, expressed in baptism, transfers a person from the realm and reign of sin, death, the self, the flesh, the Law, and unrighteousness into the realm and reign of the true Lord. In describing and interpreting this experience in these terms, Paul stands firmly in the tradition of Israel and its experience of the Exodus. As Brueggemann reminds us, the Exodus "was not a contextless emancipation. Rather, it was an exchange of overlords." Israel becomes Yahweh's servant (see Lev. 25:42), and "Yahweh is the new 'owner' of Israel."[14]

Just as Paul affirms the early Christian depiction of Jesus as God's servant or slave, God's *doulos*, so also he sees himself as Christ's slave, his *doulos*. This

10. Both terms are from Seeley, *Noble Death,* pp. 102 and 101, respectively.

11. Seeley, *Noble Death,* p. 148.

12. This is a weakness of Seeley's discussion: an imaginative reenactment alone could be understood as something less than the powerful, transformative experience that Paul and those to whom he writes have known.

13. For classic discussions of the experience of transfer of dominions, see Victor Paul Furnish, *Theology and Ethics in Paul* (Nashville: Abingdon, 1968), pp. 115-18, and E. P. Sanders, *Paul and Palestinian Judaism* (Philadelphia: Fortress, 1977), pp. 463-72. See further below under "Incorporation and Inauguration."

14. Walter Brueggemann, *Theology of the Old Testament: Testimony, Dispute, Advocacy* (Minneapolis: Fortress, 1997), p. 182.

self-understanding is so fundamental to Paul that he uses it to identify himself at the beginning of several letters (Rom. 1:1; Phil. 1:1; Gal. 1:10): "slave of Christ (Jesus)."[15] Furthermore, Paul gladly stresses his status of "servant" or "minister" (2 Cor. 11:23; Greek *diakonos*) in the face of rivals who call his position into question. Similar terms are appropriate also for his colleagues (e.g., Timothy, Phil. 1:1; Apollos, 1 Cor. 3:5; 4:1). Not unexpectedly, moreover, Paul understands himself and his coworkers also as *God's* "servants" or "ministers" (2 Cor. 6:4; Greek *diakonos*), and specifically as "ministers" of a new covenant (2 Cor. 3:6) and of righteousness (2 Cor. 11:15).

As for all believers, Paul does not frequently apply the term "slave" to them, but he affirms its reality in other ways. The Corinthian correspondence contains perhaps the most important texts, though they are often overlooked:

> [19][D]o you not know that your body is a temple of the Holy Spirit within you, which you have from God, and that you are not your own? [20]For you were bought with a price; therefore glorify God in your body. (1 Cor. 6:19-20)

> [Christ] died for all, so that [Greek *hina*] those who live might no longer live for themselves, but for him who died and was raised for them. (2 Cor. 5:15)

In these texts Paul assumes that human beings apart from Christ belong to and live for themselves; that is, they live with themselves as the benchmark and goal of their existence, in a kind of slavery "under the direction of their own ambitions."[16] The experience of faith, triggered by the apocalyptic event of the cross, reorients people, bringing them "into" Christ from outside (2 Cor. 5:17) and causing them to orient their lives away from self and toward the Christ in whom they live. God has redeemed them — the language of 1 Corinthians 6:20 is that of the slave market — by means of Christ's death.[17] They are no longer "master of their own fate" but have become the slave of another. This shift from life-for-self to life-for-Christ is not an optional addition to believers' experience; it is rather the *essence* of that experience, for it was the very reason (Greek

---

15. Similar terms of Paul's self-designation are *diakonos,* "servant" (e.g., 1 Cor. 3:5), and *hypēretēs,* "steward" (1 Cor. 4:1).

16. Victor Paul Furnish's translation in *II Corinthians,* Anchor Bible 32A (Garden City, N.Y.: Doubleday, 1984), p. 311. The phrase "live for" or "live to" oneself was a common idiom for the selfish life (see Michael J. Gorman, "The Self, the Lord, and the Other: The Significance of Reflexive Pronoun Constructions in the Letters of Paul, with a Comparison to the 'Discourses' of Epictetus," Ph.D. diss., Princeton Theological Seminary, 1989, pp. 495-502; BAGD s.v. *zaō* 3b). It is also important to note the phrase "no longer" in 2 Cor. 5:15.

17. Hans Conzelmann, *1 Corinthians,* Hermeneia (Philadelphia: Fortress, 1975), p. 113.

hina) for Christ's death, according to 2 Corinthians 5:15. Thus Paul can summarize the meaning of believing existence as "serv[ing] the Lord" (Rom. 12:11), that is, "serv[ing] Christ" (Rom. 14:18). To do so, he uses the verb related to the noun *doulos, douleuō*.[18]

As we will see in the section below on daily cruciformity, Paul exploits this image to the fullest in Romans 6, where he reminds his readers, in language echoing 2 Corinthians 5:15, that

> our old self was crucified with him so that [Greek *hina*] the body of sin might be destroyed, and we might no longer be enslaved to sin. (Rom. 6:6)

Thus believers are "dead to sin and alive to God in Christ Jesus" (Rom. 6:11) that is, "enslaved to God" (Rom. 6:22). If Gentiles, they have turned from idols to "serve (Greek *douleuō*) a living and true God" (1 Thess. 1:9). Therefore, they are daily to offer themselves fully, expressed by the use of their (bodily) "members," to God their new lord (Rom. 6:13, 16, 19). We find the change of lords expressed also in the language of the flesh and the Spirit in Galatians 5 and Romans 8 to be guided by the Spirit is to be under a power that is stronger than the inner or outer impulses of the flesh (Gal. 5:16-17). The children of God are liberated from all past slaveries and their related fears, but only as they are led in Christ by the Spirit (Rom. 8:9-17). This is the kind of slavery that liberates and empowers. True freedom, in Paul's experience, is belonging to the right master. This paradox is perhaps expressed most succinctly in 1 Corinthians 7, which suggests that each believer is both the Lord's freed person and the Lord's slave:

> [22][W]hoever was called in the Lord as a slave is a freed person belonging to the Lord, just as whoever was free when called is a slave of Christ.[23]You were bought with a price. . . . (1 Cor. 7:22-23a)[19]

18. See also Rom. 16:18, about those who do not serve the Lord Jesus Christ. It is interesting to note that in Rom. 12:9-13 Paul refers explicitly to both love (vv. 9-10, and implied in v. 13) and hope (v. 12), suggesting that the missing element — faith — is precisely the subject of v. 11: "Do not lag in zeal, be ardent in spirit, serve the Lord." (If correct, this reading would resolve the textual question, as many editions note, of whether Paul wrote "serve the Lord" (using the Greek *kyrios*) or "serve in the time [remaining]" (using the Greek *kairos*). For the essential connection between leaving behind preoccupation with the self and devoting oneself to both Christ and others, see Troels Engberg-Pedersen, *Paul and the Stoics* (Louisville: Westminster/John Knox, 2000).

19. The context of this passage is Paul's relativizing of marriage and singleness, as well as other social institutions and states, including slavery, in the light of the eschatological time in which the Church exists. Although there is dispute about Paul's understanding of the social institution of slavery, it is clear that he experienced and understood faith as an experience of being "bought with a price," as in 6:20, that yielded both freedom and slavery in Christ.

Incorporation and Inauguration

Faith, therefore, is a liberation that is also an *incorporation,* specifically an incorporation into Christ the new lord, and into his body. Paul can refer to this, as we have seen, as believing "into" Christ (Gal. 2:16); the image suggests a movement from outside Christ to inside Christ (note "in Christ" in Gal. 2:17). Paul understands both faith (Gal. 2:16) and baptism (Gal. 3:27) as the experience of transfer, of movement from one realm of existence, both existentially, or "spiritually," and sociologically, into another. As we have seen, this incorporation into Christ is simultaneously a crucifixion to "the world" that is left behind (Gal. 6:14).[20]

Paul can also speak of "put[ting] on the Lord Jesus Christ" (Gal. 3:27; Rom. 13:14) and, as noted above, of being baptized into Christ (Gal. 3:27). Not far away is the idea that baptism into Christ is baptism into his death (Romans 6), which means that being in Christ is somehow also being within his death, being under the ongoing influence of his death. This results in death to sin, as noted above, but also in other aspects of a perpetual mode of dying, of being crucified. Thus faith is an *inauguration* into a community and into a life of dying, or cruciformity.

The most significant of these other dimensions inaugurated by faith is cruciform love for others, for what matters in Christ is not circumcision or lack thereof but "faith working through love" (Gal. 5:6). The sense of this very important phrase, to which we will return in subsequent chapters, is "faith operating effectively through love," "faith working practically through love," or even "faith expressing itself in love."[21] This quintessential formulation of Paul's spirituality focuses on the inseparability of faith and love, a love that has the character of cruciform service. (The next three chapters will explore the meaning of this kind of love in detail.) The text suggests that faith inaugurates the life of

20. A helpful understanding of "the world" for Paul is provided by Charles Talbert, though offered in commenting on a different writer (John): "humanity mobilized in defiance of the divine purpose" (*Reading John: A Literary and Theological Commentary on the Fourth Gospel and the Johannine Epistles* [New York: Crossroad, 1992], p. 102).

21. The first rendering is from James D. G. Dunn, *A Commentary on the Epistle to the Galatians,* Black's New Testament Commentaries (London: A&C Black, 1993), p. 270. The second is from Bruce W. Longenecker, *The Triumph of Abraham's God: The Transformation of Identity in Galatians* (Nashville: Abingdon, 1998), pp. 73, 82, 161. Nearly all commentators today understand the form of the Greek verb *energeō* ("working," "operating") that appears in this verse to be middle, not passive, such that whatever the translation, (a) faith and love are inseparable, (b) faith is the presupposition of love, not the other way around (i.e., love does not give rise to faith), and (c) love is the means (note the Greek preposition *dia,* "through") by which faith is expressed. We prefer the translation "faith expressing itself in love."

love because it is a power, a force that operates on and in individuals and communities.[22]

In his classic work *Paul and Palestinian Judaism*, E. P. Sanders summarizes the meaning of faith for Paul as liberation, reenslavement, incorporation, and inauguration in the term "participation." He argues against an understanding of Paul's experience that highlights only the acceptance of atonement for past sins. Rather, Sanders contends rightly,

> the prime significance which the death of Christ has for Paul is . . . that, by *sharing* in Christ's death, one dies to the *power* of sin or to the old aeon, with the result that one belongs to God. The *transfer* is not only from the uncleanness of idolatry and sexual immorality to cleanness and holiness, but from one lordship to another. The transfer takes place by *participation* in Christ's death.[23]

Faith, then, for Paul is first of all cruciform participation with Christ that liberates participants from the hostile powers that rule human existence and brings them into the powerful sphere of Christ's benevolent lordship and community. For Paul, however, faith does not end when life in Christ begins.

"The Obedience of Faith": Faith as Daily Cruciformity

A phrase like "faith expressing itself in love" (Gal. 5:6) demonstrates how erroneous it would be to think that Paul understands faith only as an initial act of conversion-initiation. As J. A. Ziesler remarks, "As faith is indivisible, there is no distinction of that faith which is a response to God's action in Christ (i.e. justifying faith) from that which is the Christian's continuing life."[24] Baptism is a symbolic narrative not only of incorporation into Christ but also of ongoing life in Christ. Although a once-for-all death to sin occurs in baptism, as Christ died only once, this death must be constantly reactualized. Referring to his own ministry, Paul says that he "die[s] every day" (1 Cor. 15:31; cf. 2 Cor. 11:28). So

---

22. So also Betz, *Galatians*, p. 263, n. 97, and Dunn, *Galatians*, p. 271.

23. Sanders, *Paul and Palestinian Judaism*, pp. 467-68. Sanders bases his conclusion especially on an examination of Rom. 6:3-11; 7:4; Gal. 2:19-20; 5:24; 6:14; Phil. 3:10-11. Sanders, however, asserts that resurrection for Paul is only future (e.g., p. 468), when the baptismal act itself, as well as Paul's interpretation of it, suggests a present resurrection to new life — a life of cruciformity — as well as a future bodily resurrection.

24. J. A. Ziesler, *The Meaning of Righteousness in Paul: A Linguistic and Theological Enquiry*, SNTSMS 20 (Cambridge: Cambridge University Press, 1972), p. 165.

too, believers die daily to sin and self, constantly in need of re-presenting themselves to God and to righteousness:

> ¹¹So you must also consider yourselves dead to sin and alive to God in Christ Jesus. . . . ¹³No longer present your members to sin as instruments of wickedness, but present yourselves to God as those who have been brought from death to life, and present your members to God as instruments of righteousness. . . . ¹⁹ . . . [J]ust as you once presented your members as slaves to impurity and to greater and greater iniquity, so now present your members as slaves to righteousness for sanctification. (Rom. 6:11, 13, 19b)

The phrases "no longer" (v. 13) and "once . . . now" (v. 19b) suggest that one habitual action of self-presentation is to be replaced by another in persons who have moved from death to life. Sanctification — growth in holiness, or dedication to God — replaces "greater and greater iniquity." This growth is achieved, according to Paul, by means of regular self-offering to God. This is for believers, as it was for Christ, a dynamic and ongoing narrative posture before God.

This dynamic narrative posture before God is, in fact, the primary subject of Romans 6. Because baptism is the initial subject of Romans 6, readers of Paul often mistakenly think that it is the main topic of the chapter. It is clear, however, that although Paul begins with the initial experience of baptism as dying to sin (the emphasis of 6:1-11, as noted above), his focus is on the structure and contours of the new life (6:12-23, with hints already in 6:1-11).[25] Those who have died to sin in baptism and now live to God in Christ Jesus (Rom. 6:11) embrace a logical ("therefore," Rom. 6:12) corollary: they now offer themselves in obedience not to their passions but to their newfound lord.

Elsewhere, Paul captures this ongoing dimension of faith graphically in the grammatical construction with which he expresses his own cruciformity. "*I have been* crucified with Christ" (Gal. 2:19; Greek perfect tense) he writes, not "I *was* crucified with Christ" (Greek aorist, a more "simple" past tense). The perfect tense can often be translated as a present tense: "I *am* crucified with Christ." The sense of this text is that this crucifixion had a starting point but has no ending point, at least not this side of the eschaton. So also Paul says that "the world *has been* crucified to me, and I to the world" (Gal. 6:14). The daily life of Paul, and of believers, is one of reaffirming and reactualizing the separation from former ways (whether pagan or ethnic Jewish) that faith in the gospel inaugurated and baptism expressed. It is the ongoing expression of their "funda-

---

25. This is also how I would take Tannehill's overall reading of Romans 6 in *Dying and Rising* (pp. 21-39, 77-83), even though he claims (p. 39) that Romans 6 itself focuses on the past event while keeping past and present experience together.

mental option" rightly ordered, their narrative posture of dynamic faith toward God.[26]

This constant, or comprehensive, dimension of faith is rooted in the faith(fulness) of Jesus. Although Paul focuses on Jesus' voluntary death as the one-time, representative act of faith, he also sees that death as the culmination of a life of servant-like obedience to God, as we noted in examining Philippians 2. To share in Christ's faith is to share in his obedience. Indeed, whereas Romans 5 reveals that Christ's death as his obedience, or faith, is the basis of salvation, Romans 6 reveals that heartfelt obedience to this teaching (6:17) means accepting Christ's death not merely as the *source* of salvation but as the *pattern* of faith/obedience:[27]

> But thanks be to God that you, having once been slaves of sin, have become obedient from the heart to the form of teaching to which you were entrusted. (Rom. 6:17)

Paul summarizes this interrelationship between faith and obedience in the phrase he coined to describe the goal of his preaching: the "obedience of faith" (Rom. 1:5; 16:26). Obedience is not an option for Paul, not even a good supplement to faith. "One is not freed from sin and then, perhaps, also put under a new Lord."[28] The gospel is not merely to be *believed*, but *obeyed*; obedience and faith are essentially synonymous, as Romans 10 demonstrates:

> [14]But how are they to call on one in whom they have not **believed**? And how are they to **believe** in one of whom they have never heard? . . . [16]But not all have **obeyed** the good news; for Isaiah says, "Lord, who has believed our message?" (Rom. 10:14a-b, 16a [emphasis added])[29]

---

26. "[I]n faith one places oneself in an all-inclusive, lifelong relationship with God, which involves one's final and lasting determination: one's salvation" (Jürgen Becker, *Paul: Apostle to the Gentiles,* trans. O. C. Dean, Jr. [Louisville: Westminster/John Knox, 1993], p. 412). Furthermore, Becker observes, Paul modifies the baptismal tradition and "does not let the repetition of death and life describe the unique baptismal act but indicates the life of a Christian as a whole" (p. 419).

27. Similarly, though in more traditional language that has a tendency to separate "justification" from "sanctification," James R. Edwards (*Romans,* NIBC [Peabody: Hendrickson, 1992], p. 157) notes that "Christ's death is not only the means of our salvation, it is the pattern of our sanctification."

28. Tannehill, *Dying and Rising,* p. 82, where he adds that one "is saved *because*" (emphasis his) one has a new Lord and is thus rescued from the old when, and only when, incorporated into the new.

29. The section of Romans 10 in which these verses appear concludes with v. 21, which speaks of Israel as a "disobedient and contentious people."

This new obedience to the gospel replaces the old obedience to one's passions,[30] but the "obedience of faith" can be achieved only when one knows the will of the one to be obeyed, namely, God. For Paul, the will of God is known in essence in the obedient death of Jesus. In concrete and specific ways, however, God's will is known only when one offers oneself and one's body daily as a living sacrifice to one's rightful Lord:

> [1]I appeal to you therefore, brothers and sisters, by the mercies of God, to present your bodies as a living sacrifice, holy and acceptable to God, which is your spiritual [or, "reasonable"] worship. [2]Do not be conformed to this world [or, "age"], but be transformed by the renewing of your minds, so that you may discern what is the will of God — what is good and acceptable and perfect. (Rom. 12:1-2)[31]

When this self-offering occurs, the results are nonconformity to this age — what Paul elsewhere calls "death" or "crucifixion" to the world — and transformation of the mind — what he elsewhere calls having the mind of Christ (Phil. 2:5; 1 Cor. 2:16), that is, conformity to Christ crucified, or "cruciformity." This transformation of the mind is the fruit only of a stance toward God that welcomes the divine power of the cross to effect change.[32]

The Cruciform Faith of Jesus and of Believers: Galatians

We have already noted that believers are called to share the obedience of Jesus in order to share his faith. This faith, we have suggested, is rooted in the faith(fulness) of Jesus and connected to the experience of co-crucifixion with

---

30. So also Gal. 2:14; 5:7, which employ the phrases "acting consistently with the truth of the gospel" and "obeying the truth," respectively. See John M. G. Barclay, *Obeying the Truth: Paul's Ethics in Galatians* (Minneapolis: Fortress, 1991), pp. 92, 236.

31. See also 1 Thess. 1:9, which describes the Thessalonian believers' turning "to God from idols, to serve a living and true God," and which in context is clearly a description of their "faith" (1:3, 8).

32. That Paul depends on the grace and power of God, not on the self's own power, for sanctification is abundantly clear throughout his writings. Grossouw (*Spirituality of the New Testament*, pp. 105-6) wisely notes that Paul is realistic about human weakness, and not merely by acknowledging that all humans are somewhat weak, morally speaking, for it "goes much, much deeper; it is not a psychological, but a religious-existential understanding of oneself as basically powerless (and as being supported by God's merciful grace at the very roots of one's being). This understanding is a source of great spiritual power. . . . It frees us from all paralyzing nervousness, and opens the way to love."

him. We must now examine in detail one text that spells out the interconnection between faith and cruciformity: Galatians 2:15-21.

By nearly all accounts, Galatians 2:15-21 contains the proposition or thesis of the letter. Paul's challenge in this letter is to refute the claims of certain teachers, who have arrived at the Galatian church in his absence, that Gentile believers must be circumcised and (most likely) adopt other Jewish practices. In 2:15-21 Paul re-presents and clarifies the essence of his message, asserting and defining faith — the Greek is *pistis* — as the basis of "justification." This is a term in Paul's lexicon that needs to be defined before we look at Galatians 2:15-21, where the word occurs five times, in more detail.

Perhaps no topic or phrase is more closely associated with the apostle Paul than "justification by faith." In recent years, interpreters of Paul have reexamined and even hotly debated the meaning of this phrase and its place in Paul's experience and theology. A full review of the topic or the debates is of course impossible here, but we must engage in a brief analysis of what Paul means by "justification," a term about which there is much confusion.

In both Hebrew and Greek, the terms justification, justice, and righteousness are all related to the same root. In each language, this root word is part of at least three interrelated lexical clusters from Paul's Jewish environment: the language of divine and human virtue, the language of covenant, and the language of apocalyptic judgment. In biblical theology, God is a righteous and just God who has created a people from whom corresponding righteousness and justice are expected. The righteous character of God is supposed to be embodied in the righteous character of the people, expressed in such ways as care for the widow and the orphan.[33] Those who are truly righteous will be acquitted and vindicated on the day of judgment. However, the covenant relationship of the Righteous One with the righteous ones suffers from the faithlessness and sin of the people and is in need of repair and restoration. On the one hand, then, justification is the language of restoring and maintaining right covenant relations in the present; on the other, justification is the language of acquittal and acceptance on the apocalyptic day of judgment.[34] In both cases, right relationship with and acceptance by God include the right treatment of other people, for those who are in a right relationship with God will express the righteous character of God through the righteous treatment of others.

Paul has all three of these lexical clusters (virtue, covenant, vindication) in

---

33. See Brueggemann, *Theology of the Old Testament*, pp. 421-24, 460-64.

34. See N. T. Wright, *What St. Paul Really Said: Was Paul of Tarsus the Real Founder of Christianity?* (Grand Rapids: Eerdmans, 1997), pp. 95-133, for a lucid exposition of "justification," and Paul Achtemeier, *Romans*, Interpretation (Atlanta: John Knox, 1985), pp. 61-66, for a parallel discussion of "righteousness" in covenantal terms.

mind when he speaks of the experience of justification. Justification is "right-wising"; that is, establishing right covenant relations with God. This proper relationship with God, furthermore, assures acquittal or vindication by God at the judgment. Paul himself refers to both of these aspects of justification in Romans 5, where he "unpacks" the experience of justification as present reconciliation with God that guarantees future salvation from the wrath of God:

> [1]Therefore, since we are justified by faith, we have peace with God through our Lord Jesus Christ, [2]through whom we have obtained access to this grace in which we stand; and we boast in our hope of sharing the glory of God.... [9]Much more surely then, now that we have been justified by his blood, will we be saved through him from the wrath of God. [10]For if while we were enemies, we were reconciled to God through the death of his Son, much more surely, having been reconciled, will we be saved by his life. [11]But more than that, we even boast in God through our Lord Jesus Christ, through whom we have now received reconciliation. (Rom. 5:1-2, 9-11)

Yet justification also means the performance of just or righteous deeds, specifically, the "just requirement" of the law that the law itself could not effect in people. This just or righteous activity is now made possible by the work of the Spirit in the justified:

> [3]For God has done what the law, weakened by the flesh, could not do: by sending his own Son in the likeness of sinful flesh, and to deal with sin, he condemned sin in the flesh, [4]so that the just requirement of the law might be fulfilled in us, who walk not according to the flesh but according to the Spirit. (Rom. 8:3-4; cf. Gal. 6:16-26)

Justification, then, may be described as (1) right relations with God (covenant) issuing in (2) right (even "godly") relations with others (virtue) and (3) acquittal on the day of judgment (vindication). In other words, justification, righteousness, and their related terms in English refer to *covenant faithfulness with respect to God and neighbor,* and *ultimate divine approval.*[35]

In Galatians 2:15-21 Paul clearly and repeatedly states that justification is not on the basis of (literally, "out of") "works of the law" (2:16) or "through the law" (2:21). Scholars are divided on the meaning of these "works of the law." Are they the moral deeds required by the law, as parallel phrases from the

---

35. For a similar interpretation, in addition to Wright (previous note), see Richard B. Hays, "Justification," in David Noel Freedman, ed., *Anchor Bible Dictionary* (New York: Doubleday, 1992), 3:1129-33, esp. 1130-32.

Qumran (Dead Sea) Scrolls would suggest, or are they the ethnic "boundary markers" such as circumcision and dietary and calendar laws?[36] Whatever they are, either or both, observing them is not the basis for justification. Rather, that basis is *pistis,* or "faith." Yet the meaning of "faith" in this passage requires careful analysis.

Traditionally, the faith spoken of in Galatians 2:15-21 has been understood as human faith, specifically faith in Jesus Christ. As we saw in the previous chapter, however, many interpreters of Paul today believe that some of the phrases traditionally thought to describe the believer's response of faith actually refer to the faith of Jesus.

As noted in chapter six, the substance of Galatians 2:15-21 begins and ends on the same note, in verses that are parallel to one another (vv. 16, 21): the means of establishing right relations with God is not the (works of the) law but rather the one faithful deed of Jesus Christ. The faith or faithfulness of Jesus consists in his death. *The faith of Jesus is thus the objective basis of justification.*

This act of faith on the part of Jesus does not, however, bring about justification in people without a response on their part. That response is faith, specifically faith "toward" or "into" *(eis)* Christ Jesus (v. 16). The "movement" toward Christ suggested by the pronoun *eis* is confirmed by the phrase "in our effort to be justified in [*en*] Christ" (v. 17). Those who respond in trust or faith to the faith of Christ are moved into Christ, into the sphere of his life. In that sphere, and there alone, is justification to be found. Simultaneously, those who move into Christ find that Christ has moved into them, so to speak. Paul says that "Christ lives in me" and that what sustains and empowers him in this life is the very faith of the Son of God (v. 20). Paul's act of faith has enabled him to share in the faith of Jesus, the faith that expressed itself in self-giving love.

Justification by (Cruciform) Faith

This experience of faith in response to the faith of Jesus is most graphically captured by Paul in the metaphor of death. Once again, as in vv. 16a and 21 (with reference to Jesus' faith), Paul's parallelism clarifies what he means by faith (author's translations):

> . . . even we *placed our faith in the direction of Christ* Jesus, *so that* [Greek *hina*] we might be *justified* on the basis of the faith of Christ. . . . (v. 16)

36. Among the many discussions, see Dunn, *Theology,* pp. 354-66.

For I, through the law, *died with respect to the law, so that* [*hina*] I might *live with respect to God.* (v. 19)

I have been *crucified with Christ.* So no longer do I live, but *Christ lives in me.* (vv. 19c-20a)

In these verses, the purpose clauses of verses 16 and 19 — introduced by "so that" — stand out and suggest that "faith" and "death to the law" are parallel to each other, as are "justified" and "live with respect to God." Faith, then, is a death to the law that enables life to God. Furthermore, the language of "death with respect to the law" (v. 19) finds parallel language in "crucified with Christ" (v. 20a), as does the phrase "live with respect to God" (v. 19) have a parallel in the phrase "Christ lives in me" (v. 20a).

In other words, here in Galatians 2, as in Romans 6, faith is a death experience that, paradoxically, engenders life — life to God, life in Christ (v. 17), Christ's life within (v. 20). Faith is a separation from the law ("I died to the law") and the self ("It is no longer I who live"), and an identification with the cross of Christ ("I have been crucified"). It is an experience of participation in the death of Christ in order to experience the life of Christ: in the words of A. J. M. Wedderburn, the believer's experience is a matter of both "life through death" and "life in death."[37] Death is not merely the path to life, it is the *destination.*[38] As such, faith is an initial and ongoing participation in the faith (i.e., faithful death) of Jesus. As we noted earlier, this is the force of the perfect tense: "I have been crucified with Christ." In Paul's experience and theology, this is the nature of the response of faith. *It is this kind of faith, and only this kind of faith, that truly embraces the grace of God (v. 21) and results in justification.* Justification is by cruciform faith.

What does this mean concretely in Paul's experience? Faith *begins* by acknowledging the faith of Jesus and dying with him by no longer relying on the law and the self for right relations with God. Faith *continues* by daily relying on Christ as the energizing force for all of life, and by allowing the faith of the Son

---

37. Wedderburn, *Baptism and Resurrection,* pp. 381-92. Wedderburn is speaking of baptism, and does not specifically call this experience "faith," but his emphasis is not on the rite per se but on its *"structure and existential effects"* (p. 381 [emphasis his]) as an event of total transformation.

38. Wedderburn, *Baptism and Resurrection,* p. 392. Wedderburn (p. 350) also notes that the use of the perfect tense to describe the believer's death with Christ ("I have been crucified") means that "for Paul the Christian crucified with Christ still hangs on his cross; this vivid language shows that it is incumbent upon the Christian to be conformed to Christ in his death until that time when they [*sic*] can take the form of his risen state. . . . [D]eath continues on into the present."

of God, expressed in his self-giving, loving death, to reexpress itself in the life of the believer (v. 20b). The Christ who lives in Paul (and by extension in all believers) is the paradigm of faith, and of faith expressed in love.

It is no accident that Paul's summary of believers' existence in Galatians 5:6 — "**faith** expressing itself in **love**," or "**faith** working through **love**" (NRSV) — is a deliberate echo of Galatians 2:20b: "I live by the **faith** of the Son of God, who **loved** me by giving himself for me." It is the powerful presence of this paradigmatic person in Paul's life that enables him to live the life of faith before God and, as we shall see in the next chapters, of love for others.

Galatians 2:15-21, then, defines the life of faith, both as initial experience and as ongoing reality.[39] Paradoxically, this life is a death, a crucifixion, so that the Crucified One may live in the crucified one; the crucified but living Christ lives in and through the crucified but living believer. Also paradoxically, this life of faith, of trust, is first of all a life of *distrust*, distrust of the self or the law (or anything else, for that matter) as the basis for justification. This death to the law and the self is an essential aspect of crucifixion with Christ. Most importantly, crucifixion with Christ is not a *supplement* to faith, it is the *essence* of faith.

Sharing the Faith of Jesus and the Faith of Abraham: Romans

This understanding of justifying faith as cruciform faith is echoed in Romans 3:21-26. This passage, like Galatians 2:15-21, contains a summary of the letter in which it is found, a thesis statement of sorts. As noted in chapter six, the passage refers to the "faith of Jesus Christ" (v. 22), namely, his atoning death. This death is thus the *objective* basis of justification, to which a *subjective* response is necessary. The "righteousness of God" is for "all who believe" (v. 22); it is made "effective through faith" (v. 25).

The nature of this faith is not spelled out in the detail of Galatians 2:15-21, but if the NRSV margin is correct, it is nonetheless defined as "having," or perhaps "sharing in," the faith of Jesus (v. 26). The Greek phrase in question, "the one out of the faith of Jesus" *(ton ek pisteōs Iēsou),* further identifies who it is whom God justifies. The phrase is difficult to translate, and most versions of the Bible are content to render it something like "the one who has faith in Jesus" (so NRSV). This phrase, however, is grammatically parallel to a similar phrase

---

39. Barclay (*Obeying the Truth,* p. 237) writes: faith is "not just an entry requirement" but "the fundamental determinant of all Christian behaviour." I agree with Barclay, even though he rejects the "faith of Christ" reading of Galatians.

in Rom. 4:16, where the NRSV translates the text as "those who share the faith of Abraham," such people being the recipients of God's promise.[40] In view of the consistent sense we have found in translating these phrases as "the faith *of* Jesus," we should do so also here: God justifies the one who "lives out of," or "shares," the faith of Jesus. There is, Paul contends, a "faith of Jesus Christ" like the faith of "our father" Abraham (Rom. 4:12, 16), and like the faith of Abraham, the faith of Jesus can be — indeed must be — shared.

Summary: Christ's Faith and Ours

For Paul, to share the faith of Abraham is to believe that God can bring life out of death to fulfill a promise (4:16-22).[41] In fact, it is to "have faith in" the God who *has* fulfilled all promises by handing Jesus over to death and then raising him from the dead for our justification (4:24-25). Thus, while Abraham displays both the necessity and character of faith, Jesus demonstrates even more. His death is both the promise fulfilled and faith fully expressed. Those who share the faith of Abraham must do so by sharing the faith of Jesus. To enter into relationship with this God is to identify fully, both cognitively and existentially (in *head* and in *heart*), with the cross and resurrection of Jesus. The details of this full identification Paul leaves for his discussion of baptism in Romans 6, where the narrative language of dying and being raised with Christ explains what Paul means by sharing in the faith of Abraham and the faith of Jesus.

For Paul, to summarize, faith is a response to and sharing in Christ's faith — meaning his faithfulness, or covenant fidelity, expressed in his death. As Bruce Longenecker argues in reference to Galatians 2, faith for Paul *is* participation:

> Paul's "faith" language in these verses [Gal. 2:16-21] is fundamentally a language of participation. For just as he speaks of being crucified with the cruci-

---

40. Richard B. Hays ("*PISTIS CHRISTOU* and Pauline Theology: What Is at Stake?" in E. Elizabeth Johnson and David B. Hay, eds., *Pauline Theology*, vol. 4: *Looking Back, Pressing On* [Atlanta: Scholars Press, 1997], p. 47) says that the parallelism between 3:26 and 4:16 is a "fatal embarrassment for all interpreters" who deny that Paul speaks of Jesus' faith, a faith for others to share, in 3:26. See also Luke Timothy Johnson, *Reading Romans: A Literary and Theological Commentary* (New York: Crossroad, 1997), pp. 60-61. Brendan Byrne (*Romans*, Sacra Pagina [Collegeville, Minn.: Liturgical, 1996], p. 134) is among those who reject this interpretation, however.

41. The character of faith as trust in God's promise is also highlighted in Galatians 3.

fied one, of dying with the one who died in order to live with the one who lives, and of "sonship" arising out of participation in the "sonship" of Jesus, so he can talk of participation in the faithfulness of Christ *(pistis Christou)* through faith *(pistis)*.[42]

By faith, people are justified — restored to a right covenant relationship with God. However, it is not merely the case that this covenant relationship with God is "based on and emerges from" Jesus' own faith;[43] the response that inaugurates and maintains the relationship, and thus also the relationship itself, substantially *corresponds* to Jesus' faith. *That is, the believer's faith conforms to Christ's faith. Specifically, the believer's faith is cruciform faith because Christ's faith(fulness) was expressed on the cross.*

It is this conviction that underlies Paul's frequent switching of metaphors, especially in Galatians and Romans, between so-called "juridical" ("justification by faith") and "participationist" ("dying and rising with Christ") models of spiritual experience.[44] In reality, "justification by faith," because it is by means of *cruciform* faith, and "dying and rising with Christ," are synonymous. *Justification is experienced only by participation in Christ's death, only by cruciform faith.*[45] As Morna Hooker writes, "Justification is a matter of participation; so, too, is believing. . . . Even the believer's instant response — his faith — is a sharing in the obedient, faithful response of Christ himself."[46]

---

42. Bruce W. Longenecker, "Contours of Covenant Theology in the Post-Conversion Paul," in Richard W. Longenecker, ed., *The Road from Damascus: The Impact of Paul's Conversion on His Life, Thought, and Ministry* (Grand Rapids: Eerdmans, 1997), p. 135.

43. Longenecker, "Contours," p. 135. I obviously do not disagree with Longenecker's basic understanding of the relationship between Christ's faith and that of believers; I only wish also to stress the continuity in the *content* of faith from Jesus to believers.

44. The "juridical" approach to understanding Paul focuses on his use of legal or forensic ("juridical") metaphors like justification to describe believers' association with the benefits of Christ's death, while the "participationist" approach focuses on metaphors that suggest participation in the event, like dying and rising with Christ. For a helpful chart comparing these two approaches, see Bart D. Ehrman, *The New Testament: A Historical Introduction to the Early Christian Writings,* 2nd ed. (New York: Oxford University Press, 2000), p. 328.

45. For similar conclusions see Hays, *"PISTIS CHRISTOU,"* pp. 49-50, and the bibliography there, as well as his *The Faith of Jesus Christ: An Investigation of the Narrative Substructure of Galatians 3:1–4:11,* SBLDS 56 (Chico, Calif.: Scholars Press, 1983), pp. 250-54.

46. Morna D. Hooker, *"PISTIS CHRISTOU,"* in *From Adam to Christ: Essays on Paul* (New York/Cambridge: Cambridge University Press, 1990), p. 185.

Objections to "Justification by Cruciform Faith"

None of the foregoing discussion results in a denial of justification by faith (or, better, *by* grace *through* faith) as central to Paul's experience and belief. For Paul, however, the only kind of faith that justifies is faith that abandons every other possible basis for justification — whether the Law (understood as moral precepts or as boundary markers), the self, or whatever. Paul's metaphorical language for this abandonment is the language of death, specifically the language of crucifixion. Justification, then, is by cruciform faith, an obedient, Christ-like trust in and covenant faithfulness to God, and a separation from all else. It is cruciform, then, in two principal ways: because it conforms to Christ's faith as expressed on the cross, and because it is the experience of being crucified with respect to the powers that promise freedom and life but deliver slavery and death. Furthermore, as we will explore in subsequent chapters, faith is cruciform because it expresses itself in cruciform love, just as Christ's faith toward God issued in his loving act of self-giving for humanity on the cross.

Objections to this interpretation of faith in Paul's experience and theology might include three particular criticisms: (1) that this interpretation confuses justification and sanctification, turning justification into moral transformation rather than judicial pronouncement; (2) that it makes faith a "work," mutating it from a simple, heartfelt response into an exacting effort; and (3) that it depends too heavily on a retranslation of "faith in Christ" into "the faith of Christ." We will deal at some length with the first objection and then briefly with each of the other two.

(1) In some theological traditions, a clear distinction between justification and sanctification is made, the former being normally understood as the declaration of God the Father as judge, the latter as the work of God the Holy Spirit. While this distinction may be helpful in suggesting that forgiveness of past sins and a "clean slate" are necessary prerequisites for receiving the Spirit who effects moral transformation, it creates the very un-Pauline problem of making the new moral life supplemental or ancillary to the supposedly real problem of a private transaction, sometimes even characterized as a "legal fiction," between God and the believer.[47]

Within these theological traditions, the difficulty with justification by "faith alone" — understood as faith rather than human "works" or effort — is sometimes recognized and addressed by saying, "Justification is by faith alone, but not by faith that is alone." Or, again, "Works do not justify, but they are the evidence of justification." To these and similar claims, Paul might say, "Justifica-

---

47. See, e.g., Edwards, *Romans*, p. 43, commenting on Rom. 1:16-17.

tion is not merely a declaration but a restoration to covenant faithfulness, and that is an inherently moral enterprise, as the Greek and Hebrew terms make clear but the English terms obscure." To be sure, this justification is a gift, an unmerited act of sheer divine grace, but from start to finish the gift demands and offers complete identification with the cross of Christ, not only as the *basis* of a right relationship with God, but as the very *shape* of that relationship.

The neat distinction between justification and sanctification is often buttressed by a popular but mistaken reading of Romans 5–8. These chapters are frequently given a sequential or serial reading, in which the normal progression of Christian experience is supposedly narrated. In this interpretation, chapter 5 discusses justification (as God's declaration), chapter 6 deals with sanctification, chapter 7 portrays the Christian's inner struggle between the flesh and the Spirit, and chapter 8 proclaims the present and future victory of the Spirit in the believer's life.[48]

This reading is undermined, however, by several factors, including the difficulty of taking chapter 7 as a narrative of Christian experience. Most interpreters today understand Romans 7 as Paul's Christian reflection on the pre-Christian predicament, especially the pre-Christian Jewish struggle to do the Law while under the power of sin.[49]

A more appropriate way of reading Romans 5–8 understands these chapters not as a sequence of justification and its consequences but as a brief summary of justification (5:1-11) followed by a series of *fundamentally synonymous* perspectives on the contrast between life *before* and life *after* the faithful act of Jesus and the resulting justification of those who share his faith. The justified, according to these chapters, are also the *liberated*, especially from sin, death, the flesh, and the Law.

Romans 5:12-21 describes the contrast in the salvation-history terms of life in Adam, under the reign of sin, death, and the Law, and life in Christ, under the reign of righteousness. Romans 6:1–7:6 contains three closely related pairs of contrasts. It uses (a) the sacramental language of baptism, (b) the metaphorical language of slavery, and (c) the metaphorical language of the death of a spouse to describe the contrast, respectively, in terms of (a) life before and after dying with Christ, (b) life as slavery under one lord (sin) and then another (God, righteousness), and (c) life as an unbreakable relationship with sin until an event of death permits commitment to Another. Finally, Romans 7:7–8:39

---

48. This is basically the reading of Edwards, *Romans,* though most contemporary commentators reject it.

49. See, among many others, Paul J. Achtemeier, *Romans,* Interpretation (Atlanta: John Knox, 1985), pp. 119-24. An exception to the rule is Edwards, *Romans,* pp. 184-96.

contrasts life in the flesh, under the power of sin, with life in the Spirit, liberated for life as God's children. The latter part of chapter 8 concludes the entire set of contrasts by returning to the themes of 5:1-11 and proclaiming the ultimate victory of the justified because of God's love in Christ.

On this reading of Romans 5–8, which recognizes the vital role of contrasting pairs in the structure of Paul's presentation, "sanctification" and life in the Spirit are not supplements to justification but perspectives on, even synonyms for, the experience of being justified. The faith that "triggers" justification simultaneously triggers death to — and thus liberation from — sin, the flesh, the Law, and (ultimately) death itself. For Paul, identification with the death of Christ by faith means that Christ has become "for us wisdom from God, and righteousness and sanctification and redemption" (1 Cor. 1:30) — a single gift that can be viewed through many lenses and expressed simultaneously in many metaphors.

(2) In Romans 10 (and perhaps elsewhere) Paul seems to make a statement that faith is a relatively simple, unencumbered thing, the assent of a sincere heart to the offer of grace:

> [9][I]f you confess with your lips that Jesus is Lord and believe in your heart that God raised him from the dead, you will be saved. [10]For one believes with the heart and so is justified, and one confesses with the mouth and so is saved. (Rom. 10:9-10)

In reading this text, it is important to remember its context: Paul is celebrating the wonderful, universal grace of God in Jesus, available to all, Jew and Gentile alike, as promised in the Hebrew Scriptures. Paul is not so much defining faith, or even salvation, here as he is declaring its universal availability. Nonetheless, the text still defines a simplistic understanding of faith. The belief and confession that are required maintain that the crucified Jesus has been raised by God and exalted to the position of Lord.

To make such a confession is to place oneself under the lordship of this Jesus, to make a deliberate move from the sphere of any other lord (whether pagan idol, Roman emperor, or anything else) into the sphere of this crucified Lord. He is the divinely approved focus of acclamation and worship, the rightful Lord of the entire cosmos and every human being on earth. To make the confession "Jesus is Lord" is also implicitly to make the confession "And I am the servant of this exalted crucified Lord." It is to change from a posture of disobedience[50] to obedience. It is to have the heart remade, as the Hebrew

---

50. Note Rom. 10:21, where Paul quotes the Lord from Isa. 65:2: "All day long I have held out my hands to a disobedient and contrary people [Israel]."

prophets had promised, so that it is softened and compliant to the will of God found in Messiah Jesus. The confession "Jesus is Lord," Luke Johnson rightly contends, is a "*performative* statement — that is, a statement that finds its sense not only as a declaration about reality but as a declaration concerning how the speaker really lives."[51] This, then, is a confession with consequences, consequences that faith understood merely as assent to a divine promise or declaration (of forgiveness, for instance) would not necessarily include.

Then is such a faith, such a confession, a "work"? By no means, as Paul would say, if by "work" one means a human deed or badge that merits divine favor. Justification is a gift, but as Dietrich Bonhoeffer said, it is a costly gift.[52] Faith is the confession that Jesus is Lord and that I am his servant, and the conviction that God's offer and demand are one gift to bring about the restoration of covenant faithfulness in disobedient, faithless Israel and in ungodly humanity at large.

One more point on this topic must be made. The kind of faith Paul knows is covenantal, or relational, and is therefore both dynamic and constant. If it ceases to exist — that is, if an initial experience of faith aborts — justification has not occurred. Once again, this claim does not betray the simplicity of Paul's call to faith; it merely articulates the nature of faith for Paul. As Luke Johnson concludes with respect to New Testament spirituality generally, "since faith is a response to the living Lord who presses upon us at every moment, there is no time at which we can quit without betraying the entire process in which we have been engaged."[53] Or again, as Calvin put it in his commentary on Romans 5:

> [Paul means that] faith is not a changeable persuasion, only for one day; but that it is immutable, and that it sinks deep into the heart, so that it endures through life. It is then not he, who by a sudden impulse is led to believe, that has faith, and is to be reckoned among the faithful; but he who constantly, and, so to speak, with a firm and fixed foot, abides in that station appointed him by God, as to cleave always to Christ.[54]

(3) While it is true that the interpretation of faith in Paul offered in this chapter is clarified and strengthened by reading the Greek phrase *pistis*

---

51. Luke Timothy Johnson, *Living Jesus: Learning the Heart of the Gospel* (New York: HarperSanFrancisco, 1999), pp. 5-6 (emphasis in the original).

52. Dietrich Bonhoeffer, *The Cost of Discipleship*, rev. ed., trans. R. H. Fuller (New York: Macmillan, 1959), esp. ch. 1, pp. 45-60. See also the discussion of Bonhoeffer in ch. 14.

53. Johnson, *Living Jesus*, p. 195.

54. John Calvin, *Romans*, quoted in Edwards, *Romans*, p. 143.

Christou as "the faith of Christ," it does not depend solely on that reading.[55] Throughout Paul's letters, as we have seen in this and the previous chapter, the death of Jesus is portrayed as an act that liberates those who respond to it with faith. This liberation is never portrayed as some supplemental or "post-conversion" experience, but rather as essential to the purpose of Christ's death and to any response of faith to that death. The phrase "the faith of Christ," when seen as something that is paradigmatic for believers, and in which they participate, simply makes explicit what other texts already suggest: that the only appropriate response to the cross is to identify fully with the One who died and with his death.

The Cost of Cruciform Faith

It should come as no surprise that Paul sometimes associates faith with trouble and danger. After all, his master story is one of obedience to the point of death, even death on a cross (Phil. 2:8). The life of obedient faith, of identifying with the One who died such a death, is a costly one, as Jesus, Paul, and some, if not all, of Paul's communities knew well.

The Cost for Paul

Paul, of course, knew much suffering, which he interpreted as a sharing in Christ's afflictions: "the sufferings [Greek *ta pathēmata*] of Christ are abundant for us" (2 Cor. 1:5). Writing to the Philippians while imprisoned for Christ, he stressed his desire to

> know Christ and the power of his resurrection and the sharing of his sufferings [Greek *pathēmatōn*] by becoming like him in his death. (Phil. 3:10)

"Becoming like him in his death" is a polyvalent expression for Paul, referring to the cruciform shape of his existence. Yet the sufferings and death to which he refers are not mere metaphors for an interior life of self-discipline. Paul's safety and life are constantly — and willingly — at risk, for he is not an enemy but a friend of Christ's cross (Phil. 3:18; cf. Gal. 6:12). To become like Christ in his death is the ultimate form of obedience, and hence of faith; the suffering and death may indeed be literal, as Paul tells the Philippians:

55. Indeed, my interpretation of faith is very similar to those of Tannehill and Barclay, for instance, neither of whom follows the "faith of Christ" reading.

> But even if I am being poured out as a libation over the sacrifice and the offering of your faith, I am glad and rejoice with all of you. (Phil. 2:17)

Sharing the gospel, the word of the cross, frequently brought emphatically negative, as well as positive, reactions, as it did in both Philippi and Thessalonica:

> [T]hough we had already suffered and been shamefully mistreated at Philippi, as you know, we had courage in our God to declare to you the gospel of God in spite of great opposition [Greek *en pollō agōni*]. (1 Thess. 2:2)

In preaching a crucified Messiah and Lord, Paul naturally offended both Jew and Gentile, the former unable to associate messianic status with crucifixion, the latter unable to associate imperial or divine status with the cross (cf. 1 Cor. 1:18-25). If the faith Paul preached was deemed offensive by many, their negative reactions could have been displayed in a variety of ways, from verbal to social to physical harassment. No matter the opposition, no matter the cost, Paul was "not ashamed of the gospel," for it is the power of God that saves both Jew and Gentile (Rom. 1:16).

For Paul the high cost of faith was part and parcel of his identity as an obedient "slave" (e.g., Rom. 1:1) of Jesus Christ. In the ancient world slaves were often "branded" with the identifying marks, known as *stigmata*, of their owner. Paul understands himself and his suffering in light of this practice:

> From now on let no one make trouble for me; for I carry the marks [Greek *stigmata*] of Jesus branded on my body. (Gal. 6:17)

Paul carried on his body reminders — to himself and to all — of the consequences of cruciform faith: scars from the flogging, lashing, beating, and stoning (2 Cor. 11:23-25). The so-called "catalogs of suffering" in Paul's letters, as well as numerous narratives in Acts, document the variety, frequency, and extent of Paul's suffering. While this suffering is linked closely to his understanding of obedient faith, we will see in later chapters, where we examine those catalogs in some detail, that it is also closely associated with his experience of love, power, and hope. Thus for Paul the obedience of faith that issues in suffering cannot be disconnected from other dimensions of his experience of "slavery" to Christ, his experience of the cross.

The Cost for the Philippians and Thessalonians

If suffering is constitutive of true faith, then Paul would not want the communities he founded to be surprised by their own afflictions for the gospel. He reminds his communities that persecution is the believer's lot, and that one of his pastoral goals is to work "so that no one would be shaken by these persecutions [Greek *thlipsesin*]" (1 Thess. 3:3a) for which believers are "destined":

> [3]. . . Indeed, you yourselves know that this [persecutions] is what we are destined for. [4]In fact, when we were with you, we told you beforehand that we were to suffer persecution [Greek *thlibesthai*]; so it turned out, as you know. (1 Thess. 3:3b-4)

Indeed, Paul avers, suffering for one's faith is even an experience of grace:

> [A]ll of you share in God's grace with me, both in my imprisonment and in the defense and confirmation of the gospel. . . . (Phil. 1:7b)

> [29][H]e has graciously granted you the privilege not only of believing in Christ,[56] but of suffering for him [Greek *hyper autou paschein*] as well — [30]since you are having the same struggle [Greek *agōna*] that you saw I had and now hear that I still have. (Phil. 1:29-30)

The Philippian believers were clearly under attack from outside forces (in addition to having internal dissension). These forces, called "dogs" and "evil workers" by Paul in 3:2, are difficult to identify with precision, but they advocate circumcision and are thus among the "enemies of the cross" in Paul's view (3:18).[57] Because the issue giving rise to the attack is supposedly "doctrinal" in nature, readers of Philippians too often assume that the threat to the Philippians is not physical in nature. This is neither necessary nor logical. The entire letter focuses on the physical dangers, the real costs, associated with the cross, whether in Christ's story or Paul's. The Philippians therefore are not going to be exempt from suffering for their faith. Following the example of Christ and of Paul, however, they should know both that suffering can result in good — in salvation, for instance, and in the spread of the gospel (Phil. 1:12-14) — and that it can be endured with joy (Phil. 1:25).

Like the Philippians, the Thessalonian believers were also severely afflicted.

---

56. Better, "entering into Christ by faith [Greek *eis auton pisteuein*]."

57. For a helpful survey of the options, see Peter O'Brien, *The Epistle to the Philippians* (Grand Rapids: Eerdmans, 1991), pp. 26-35. The antithesis between crucifixion and circumcision in Paul's mind and experience is the focus of the entire letter to the Galatians.

From the moment they believed, or "received the word with joy" (1 Thess. 1:6), their faith was tested by persecution, as both Acts 17 and 1 Thessalonians report. Paul reminds them:

> [6]And you became imitators of us and of the Lord, for in spite of persecution [Greek *en thlipsei pollē*, literally, "in much affliction"] you received the word with joy inspired by the Holy Spirit, [7]so that you became an example to all the believers in Macedonia and in Achaia. [8]For the word of the Lord has sounded forth from you not only in Macedonia and Achaia, but in every place your faith in God has become known, so that we have no need to speak about it. (1 Thess. 1:6-8)

In spite of this suffering, the Thessalonians' faith — which is the focus of the first and third chapters of Paul's first letter to them[58] — endured, engendered joy, and even spread like wildfire throughout Macedonia. Though Paul had feared that the afflictions might shake their faith, he is comforted and overjoyed at their stability and their resistance to "the tempter" (1 Thess. 3:5-10). Their faith and joy in the midst of persecution may well have been an inspiration to the Philippians — or vice versa.

In lauding them for their enduring faith, Paul connects their experience to his own and to that of Jesus; the Thessalonians "became imitators of us and of the Lord," suggesting that the suffering associated with faith is to be expected.[59] The ongoing experience of affliction (1 Thess. 3:3-4)[60] is normal. The precise nature of this persecution is not named, though it certainly would have included harassment and ostracism, and perhaps also physical attack and even killing. When these believers express concern about the fate of their dead brothers and sisters at the coming of Jesus (1 Thess. 4:13-18), they are more likely to be concerned about those who have been martyred than about those who have died of old age, since the time that elapsed between Paul's visit and letter was not great.[61]

---

58. Faith (Greek *pistis*) appears in 1 Thess. 1:3, 8; 3:2, 5, 6, 7, 10.

59. 1 Thess. 2:14-16 offers a similar insight, though some scholars believe that the vocabulary and tone of these verses differ markedly from the rest of the letter and from Paul generally. They argue (though not convincingly) that 2:14-16 is a later addition to the original letter (an interpolation). See the commentaries for the issues and proposed solutions.

60. Compare 2 Thess. 1:4, 6; 2 Cor. 8:1-2.

61. For the issues, see John M. G. Barclay, "Conflict in Thessalonica," *Catholic Biblical Quarterly* 55 (1993): 512-30, esp. 512-16.

The Cost for the Corinthians, Galatians, and Romans

Not only the Philippians and Thessalonians, but also the Corinthians, Galatians, and even the Romans shared in the sufferings of Christ and his apostle. In his first letter to the Corinthians, Paul uses sarcasm to chide the Corinthians — or at least the spiritually and socio-economically elite at Corinth — for their comfortable, painless, even exalted life-style in contrast to Paul's own:

> [8]Already you have all you want! Already you have become rich! Quite apart from us you have become kings! Indeed, I wish that you had become kings, so that we might be kings with you! [9]For I think that God has exhibited us apostles as last of all, as though sentenced to death. . . . [11]To the present hour we are hungry and thirsty, we are poorly clothed and beaten and homeless. (1 Cor. 4:8-9, 11)

In 2 Corinthians, however, Paul comforts and challenges the Corinthians, who have now experienced some affliction:

> [6]If we are being afflicted [Greek *thlibometha*], it is for your consolation and salvation; if we are being consoled, it is for your consolation, which you experience when you patiently endure the same sufferings [Greek *pathēmatōn*] that we are also suffering [Greek *paschomen*]. [7]Our hope for you is unshaken; for we know that as you share in our sufferings [Greek *pathēmatōn*], so also you share in our consolation. (2 Cor. 1:6-7)

While the context suggests that at least one facet of the Corinthians' sharing in Paul's suffering is their prayerful concern for him (2 Cor. 1:8-11), the text itself does not limit the suffering to that concern. Rather, it states that the Corinthians themselves suffer and must therefore remain firm in the faith (cf. 1:24).

With a series of questions Paul also challenges the Galatians, who in his view are abandoning the gospel of the cross by flirting with Gentile circumcision:

> [1]You foolish Galatians! Who has bewitched you? It was before your eyes that Jesus Christ was publicly exhibited as crucified! [2]The only thing I want to learn from you is this: Did you receive the Spirit by doing the works of the law or by believing what you heard? [3]Are you so foolish? Having started with the Spirit, are you now ending with the flesh? [4]Did you experience [Greek *epathete;* literally, "did you suffer"] so much for nothing? — if it really was for nothing. [5]Well, then, does God supply you with the Spirit and work miracles among you by your doing works of the law, or by your believing what you heard? (Gal. 3:1-5)

Here Paul rehearses the Galatians' initial and ongoing experience of the Spirit and of faith ("believing" in reference to the past, v. 2, and the present, v. 5). Part of their experience is, literally, suffering (Greek *epathete*, v. 4), though the NRSV and many commentators interpret the word as a generic reference to spiritual "experience," pointing to the references to the Spirit in the immediate context.[62] However, for Paul, as we saw in chapter 3 and as Galatians makes clear, suffering and the experience of the Spirit are not antithetical experiences. Indeed, they can be closely connected. The larger context of the letter, moreover, suggests that suffering and persecution are the fate of those who have an exclusive focus on the cross — which explains at least in part the Galatians' desire to embrace circumcision:

> But my friends, why am I still being persecuted [Greek *diōkomai*] if I am still preaching circumcision? In that case the offense of the cross has been removed. (Gal. 5:11)

> It is those who want to make a good showing in the flesh that try to compel you to be circumcised — only that they may not be persecuted [Greek *diōkōntai*] for the cross of Christ. (Gal. 6:12)

Supplementing the message of the cross alone and faith alone, by demanding Gentile circumcision, may relieve a person or community of persecution, but it also cuts one off from Christ, in Paul's view (5:2-4).

Finally, Paul also reminds the Roman believers, whom he has largely not met in person, that the faith that yields justification also brings suffering, and yet that suffering is a source of joy and hope:

> [1]Therefore since we are justified by faith, we have peace with God through our Lord Jesus Christ, [2]through whom we have obtained access to this grace in which we stand; and we boast in our hope of sharing the glory of God. [3]And not only that, but we also boast in our sufferings [Greek *thlipsesin*], knowing that suffering [Greek *thlipsis*] produces endurance, [4]and endurance

---

62. Charles H. Cosgrove (*The Cross and the Spirit: A Study in the Argument and Theology of Galatians* [Macon, Ga.: Mercer University Press, 1988], pp. 185-87) rightly takes the text to refer to the experience of the Spirit in the midst of suffering. J. Louis Martyn (*Galatians: A New Translation with Introduction and Commentary*, Anchor Bible 33A [New York: Doubleday, 1997], p. 285), Frank Matera (*Galatians*, Sacra Pagina [Collegeville, Minn.: Michael Glazier, 1992], p. 113), and Ben Witherington III (*Grace in Galatia: A Commentary on Paul's Letter to the Galatians* [Grand Rapids: Eerdmans, 1998], pp. 214-15) take it as a general reference to the experience of the Spirit.

produces character, and character produces hope, [5]and hope does not disappoint us. . . . (Rom. 5:1-5a)[63]

Summary: The Cost of Faith

For Paul and the communities to which he writes, then, cruciform faith is *costly*. It cost Jesus his life, it yields relentless suffering and persecution for the apostle, and it frequently brings affliction to believing communities. "This is what we are destined for" (1 Thess. 3:3). The Second Letter to Timothy, though perhaps written by a "disciple" of Paul, summarizes Paul's perspective and experience:

> Indeed, all who want to live a godly life in Christ Jesus will be persecuted [Greek *diōchthēsontai*]. (2 Tim. 3:12)

The only appropriate response to such persecution for one's faith is more faith; it is patient endurance (Greek *hypomonē;* e.g., Rom. 5:3-4; 2 Cor. 1:6; 1 Thess. 1:3; 2 Thess. 1:4; 3:5). No doubt Paul would ground that endurance, as he grounds faith more generally, in Christ. Indeed, that is what 2 Thessalonians, whether by Paul or not, explicitly does:

> May the Lord direct your hearts to the love of God and to the steadfastness [Greek *hypomonēn*] of Christ. (2 Thess. 3:5)

Conclusion: Cruciform Faith

In the history of the interpretation of Paul, various aspects of his thinking have been proposed as the center of his theology. Among the most prominent of these proposals are (1) justification by faith, the traditional interpretation since the Reformation; (2) participation in Christ's death and resurrection, a twentieth-century alternative argued at the beginning of the century by Albert Schweitzer and in the latter part of the century preeminently by E. P. Sanders;[64] and (3) more recently, theocentric apocalypticism as a supplement, if not alternative, to both (argued, e.g., by J. Christiaan Beker[65]). These may be referred to

---

63. Paul says much more about suffering in Romans 8, which will receive careful examination especially in chapter twelve on cruciform hope.

64. Albert Schweitzer, *The Mysticism of the Apostle Paul* (London: Black, 1931); and Sanders, *Paul and Palestinian Judaism.*

65. J. Christiaan Beker, *Paul the Apostle: The Triumph of God in Life and Thought* (Philadelphia: Fortress, 1980).

as the juridical, participationist, and apocalyptic understandings of the Pauline center, and they are normally thought to be in some tension with one another.

Our exploration of Paul's experience and understanding of faith suggests that these three "models" are in fact closely related dimensions of the central Pauline reality: cruciformity. In particular, in this chapter we have discovered that faith is cruciformity in five chief respects:

1. Faith is renunciation of — that is, death or crucifixion with respect to — any other possible basis for justification. Any boasting, other than in God, or in the cross, is absurd.
2. Faith is liberation from the hostile powers that enslave humans, including those about which humans may be tempted to boast.
3. Faith is conformity to Jesus' faith, his narrative posture of faithful obedience and trust before God.
4. Faith is an initial and ongoing experience of each of the above dimensions; cruciform faith liberates people from the powers of this age, and it inaugurates and maintains the restored covenant relationship with God.
5. Faith, like Jesus' faithfulness, can be costly.

Faith, then, is the dynamic response to God's initiative in Christ, the fundamental narrative posture of the person and community that recognizes the apocalyptic revelation of the righteousness of God in the obedient faithfulness of Jesus. It is a response that is both "participationist" in character and "apocalyptic" in effect: "If anyone is in Christ, there is a new creation" (2 Cor. 5:17).

It is clear from his letters that the goal of Paul's endeavors is the creation of communities that embody the obedience of faith and thus constitute the new creation, the "Israel of God" (Gal. 6:16). In essence, this obedient faith is the self-offering, or complete presentation of the self, to God, as both Romans 6 and 12 state so eloquently:

> [P]resent yourselves to God as those who have been brought from death to life, and present your members to God as instruments of righteousness. (Rom. 6:13b)

> I appeal to you therefore, brothers and sisters, by the mercies of God, to present your bodies as a living sacrifice, holy and acceptable to God, which is your spiritual worship. (Rom. 12:1)

Faith is the narrative posture of obedient self-offering to God. In this regard, faith truly is sharing the faith of Jesus (Rom. 3:26). As Richard Hays says re-

153

garding faith in Galatians 3 and 4, "righteousness and life are gifts of grace in which Christians participate because of Christ's *pistis,* and . . . *pistis* is consequently the distinguishing mark of the life given to those who live 'in' him."[66]

The "fundamental option," rightly ordered, is the life story of self-giving to God, of faith understood as faithfulness, as covenant fidelity.[67] It is "worship in everyday life,"[68] not by means of sacrificing animals but through self-giving first to God and then to others (see 2 Cor. 8:5). This fundamental posture of cruciform faith before God finds expression in relationships with other people. Cruciform faith becomes cruciform love, the subject of the next chapters.

66. Hays, *Faith of Jesus Christ,* p. 235.

67. Joseph A. Fitzmyer's helpful discussion of faith (*Paul and His Theology: A Brief Sketch,* 2nd ed. [Englewood Cliffs, N.J.: Prentice Hall, 1989], pp. 84-85) is marred by his claim that Paul's notion of faith "far transcends the OT idea of fidelity" in its demand for total commitment, rejection of reliance on the self, and so forth (p. 85). While Fitzmyer is right to affirm the radical character of faith according to Paul, it is difficult to imagine a more radical demand on the human person than the covenantal requirement of total allegiance to, and love of, God with the entire self — heart, soul, body, strength, and so forth.

68. See Ernst Käsemann, "Worship in Everyday Life: A Note on Romans 12," in *New Testament Questions of Today* (London: SCM, 1969), pp. 188-95.

CHAPTER 8

CRUCIFORM LOVE (1)

The Pattern of the Crucified Messiah

P aul was nothing if not someone overwhelmed by the love of God. He experienced this divine love, according to his letters, in Christ and by the working of the Spirit. As Raymond Brown notes:

> In the revelation [on the road to Damascus] Paul, who already knew the love shown by the God of his Israelite ancestors, discovered a love that went beyond his previous imagination. He felt "taken over" by Christ Jesus (Phil 3:12). With awe Paul exclaims: "The Son of God loved me and gave himself for me" (Gal 2:20). What he avows in Rom 8:35-37 must have been uttered many times in the travails [he experienced] . . . : "Who will separate us from the love of Christ? Will anguish or persecution or famine or nakedness or peril or the sword? . . . In all these things we are conquerors because of him who loved us." This love became the driving factor of Paul's life when he came to understand how encompassing it was: "The love of Christ impels us once we come to the conviction that one died for all" (II Cor 5:14).[1]

This love of Christ was in fact, as we saw in chapter four, an experience of the love of the triune God. Divine love experienced had to become divine love expressed. As we noted in the previous two chapters on faith, Paul's understanding of the human condition means that people have disordered relationships with both God and other people. Paul's solution to this comprehensive relational disorder is amazingly simple: "faith expressing itself in [or, "working through"] love" (Gal. 5:6). This phrase, indicating the *sine qua non* of Paul's

---

1. Raymond E. Brown, *An Introduction to the New Testament* (New York: Doubleday, 1997), p. 449.

spirituality, incorporates both the "vertical" and "horizontal" (faith and love) dimensions of an appropriate response to the gospel of God's love in Christ mediated by the Spirit.

In this and the following two chapters we explore the narrative and cruciform experience of love that is central to Paul's spirituality. To begin, in this chapter we consider first the fundamental meaning of love for Paul and then its grounding in the story of Christ crucified. In the next chapters, we will explore the meaning of cruciform love as expressed concretely in the life of Paul (apostolic cruciform love, chapter nine) and in the life of his communities (the narrative shape of the faithful community, chapter ten).

The Centrality of Love

Perhaps the best-known and best-loved of all Pauline texts is his brief but poignant poem or meditation on love contained in 1 Corinthians 13. In these verses, which are probably to be understood as an "encomium," or ancient text in praise of a virtue, Paul proclaims the necessity (vv. 1-3), character (vv. 4-7), and endurance (vv. 8-13) of love (Greek *agapē*). In the immediate context of 1 Corinthians, which addresses the diversity of spiritual gifts (ch. 12) and their proper exercise when the church is assembled (ch. 14), love is set forth as the *modus operandi* for the use of all spiritual gifts. In the larger context of the entire letter, which addresses issues of division, pride, selfishness, and related ills (many of which are echoed in the center section of 1 Corinthians 13),[2] love is held up as the appropriate mode of existence for all of life and as the antithesis of Corinthian behavior generally.

Love, then, is at the core of Paul's understanding of the experience of individuals and communities in Christ. It is the defining characteristic of the individual in relation to others and of the community as a whole; it is what "counts" (Gal. 5:6), as it puts faith, one's fundamental posture toward God, into action toward others. Thus Paul counsels his churches to "pursue" love (1 Cor. 14:1); he prays that their love will "overflow" (Phil. 1:9), that the Lord will make them "increase and abound in love for one another and for all," just as he abounds in love for them (1 Thess. 3:12). Love is not something to have in small measure, but great; and though it is focused on the members of the community, it is not limited to them ("and for all," 1 Thess. 3:12).[3] Indeed, Paul imagina-

---

2. See the parallels discussed in Richard B. Hays, *First Corinthians,* Interpretation (Louisville: Westminster/John Knox, 1997), pp. 226-28.

3. Compare Gal. 6:10: "[W]henever we have an opportunity, let us work for the good of all, and especially for those of the family of faith."

tively expresses the centrality of love in Romans 13:8 as the one legitimate debt for those in Christ:

> Owe no one anything, except to love one another, for the one who loves another has fulfilled the law. (Rom. 13:8)

This text points to another essential element of Paul's basic understanding of love: that it is the fulfillment of the Law. He says this again clearly in Galatians 5:14, after exhorting the Galatians, "through love," to "become slaves to one another":

> For the whole law is summed up [better, "fulfilled" or "completed"; Greek *peplērōtai*] in a single commandment, "You shall love your neighbor as yourself." (Gal. 5:14)

Love, then, is absolutely essential because it fulfills the will of God expressed in the Law and, as we shall see more fully below, embodied in Christ.[4]

The notion of love's fulfilling the Law, however, does not for Paul mean that love is merely a human effort to obey a "summary" of the Law (rather than the whole of it). While Paul urges his communities to pursue love, he also believes that love is first of all the work of the triune God, Father, Son, and Spirit. Thus he says that the Thessalonians have been "taught by God to love one another" (1 Thess. 4:9), that "the love of Christ urges [them] on" or "controls [them]" (2 Cor. 5:14), and, in a text almost as well-known as 1 Corinthians 13, that "the fruit of the Spirit is love" (Gal. 5:22; cf. Rom. 15:30).

Love, then, is the evidence (and, by implication, the test) of the presence of Christ by his Spirit in a person or community. Without it, spiritual gifts (such as speaking in tongues or prophecy), and even faith itself, are without value. "Love" is a term with many meanings, both ancient and modern. What does Paul mean by the word "love"? As we might expect, Paul's notion of love is peculiar, linked to his understanding of the cross as the expression of God's love in Christ. Yet Paul does not always say this explicitly, so we must begin with an examination of the basic character of love as presented in key Pauline texts.

---

4. For a lucid discussion of believers' fulfilling (Greek *plēroun*) rather than doing or performing (Greek *poiein*) the law, see Bruce W. Longenecker, *The Triumph of Abraham's God: The Transformation of Identity in Galatians* (Nashville: Abingdon, 1998), pp. 83-88.

The Basic Character of Love

In 1 Corinthians 13, Paul presents a catena, or chain, of texts, seven affirmations and eight negations, about the character of love:

> [4]Love is patient; love is kind; love is not envious or boastful or arrogant [5]or rude. It does not insist on its own way; it is not irritable or resentful; [6]it does not rejoice in wrongdoing, but rejoices in the truth. [7]It bears all things, believes all things, hopes all things, endures all things. (1 Cor. 13:4-7)

In the Corinthian context, each of these affirmations and negations is significant and on the mark as a standard against which to measure the Corinthians' problematic behavior. There is one of the eight negations, however, that seems to be of particular importance to Paul in 1 Corinthians — "does not insist on its own way" (v. 5).

The Greek expression behind the NRSV translation "does not insist on its own way" contains the verb "to seek" and an abbreviated idiomatic phrase, "one's own X" (Greek *zētein ta heautou*).[5] Thus, for example, the King James rendition was "seeketh not her own." The precise missing element in the idiomatic phrase "one's own X" must be supplied from the context, though the Greek idiom normally refers to one's own (proper or improper) interests or welfare.[6]

What Paul means by "seeking one's own X" in 1 Corinthians 13:5 is clarified by his use of parallel phrases earlier in 1 Corinthians:

> . . . I try to please everyone in everything I do, not seeking my own advantage [Greek *mē zētōn to emautou symphoron*], but that of many, so that they may be saved. (1 Cor. 10:33)

> [23]"All things are lawful," but not all things are beneficial [Greek *sympherei*]. "All things are lawful," but not all things build up [Greek *oikodomei*]. [24]Do not seek your own advantage [*to heautou zēteitō*][7] but that of the other. (1 Cor. 10:23-24)

---

5. The actual phrase in 1 Cor. 13:5 is the feminine form of the idiom *(zētein ta heautēs)* due to the feminine subject "love" *(hē agapē)*.

6. See Michael J. Gorman, "The Self, the Lord, and the Other: The Significance of Reflexive Pronoun Constructions in the Letters of Paul, with a Comparison to the 'Discourses' of Epictetus," Ph.D. diss., Princeton Theological Seminary, 1989, pp. 603-4, 613-17; BAGD s.v. *symphoron*.

7. As in 1 Cor. 13:5, the Greek phrase is abbreviated to "seek one's own X," but from the context the missing word to be supplied is clearly something like "benefit" or "edification" (thus NRSV "advantage").

In these two texts from the end of 1 Corinthians 10, Paul both explicitly (v. 33) and implicitly (v. 24) indicates that for him the phrase "to seek one's own X" means to seek one's own advantage, interest, benefit (all possible translations of *symphoron* and related words), or edification (*oikodomia* and related words). Love, then, according to 1 Corinthians 13:5 (in light of 1 Corinthians 10) does not seek its own interest or edification but seeks, instead (implicitly), the interest and edification of others. That love does not "insist on its own way" (NRSV) is true, if understood in this broader sense of not seeking self-benefit and self-edification. As such, it is a principle or maxim with "many-sided possibilities of application."[8]

That the positive side of "not seeking one's own advantage/edification" is "seeking the advantage/edification of others" is made clear in another description of love in 1 Corinthians. The texts from 1 Corinthians 10 cited above conclude a rather long and complex discussion (1 Cor. 8:1–11:1) of the propriety of eating meat offered to idols, whether in a pagan temple or in a private home. In addressing this matter, Paul especially urges concern for the effect of such behavior on others, not only in the concluding lines cited above (1 Cor. 10:23-24, 33) but also in the opening words:

> Now concerning food sacrificed to idols: we know that "all of us possess knowledge." Knowledge puffs up, but love builds up [Greek *oikodomei*]. (1 Cor. 8:1)[9]

Here Paul contrasts knowledge, and the rights supposedly associated with such knowledge, with love. The knowledge in question is that meat is meat, created by the one true God, and that eating it is not a matter of grave consequence to those who (rightly) believe that the pagan gods to whom it is offered do not even exist (1 Cor. 8:4-6). Insistence on the right to eat such meat, when it might cause someone with a weaker conscience to return to idolatry, is for Paul unconscionable and unloving (8:7-13 in light of 8:1). Such an attitude toward knowledge and rights is arrogant and self-centered, and therefore unloving, as 1 Corinthians 13 also says. Love "builds up" (8:1; Greek *oikodomei*), that is, builds up others, showing concern for them.

Returning to 1 Corinthians 13 in its context, we see the same principle at work. If love "does not seek its own advantage/edification" (the meaning of 13:5), in concrete terms this means that a loving person does not publicly speak

---

8. Hans Conzelmann, *1 Corinthians*, Hermeneia (Philadelphia: Fortress, 1975), p. 176, esp. n. 10.

9. The words of the text in quotes are almost certainly a "slogan" of a group (the elite?) within the Corinthian community.

in tongues without an interpreter (1 Corinthians 14) because "[t]hose who speak in a tongue build up themselves [Greek *heauton oikodomei*], but those who prophesy build up [*oikodomei*] the church" (14:4). The loving thing to do in church is to prophesy, to pray in tongues only with an interpreter, or to pray for the gift of interpretation oneself (14:13). However, to pray in tongues in church without interpretation is to engage in the same kind of self-centered behavior as those who insist on eating meat offered to idols without concern "that this liberty . . . [might] become a stumbling block to the weak . . . believers for whom Christ died" (8:9-11).

Love, then, has for Paul an essential two-dimensional character, as summarized in 1 Corinthians 13:5 and 1 Corinthians 8:1. *Negatively*, it does not seek its own advantage or edification. It is characterized by status- and rights-renunciation. *Positively*, it seeks the good, the advantage, the edification of others. It is characterized by regard for them. Love, according to the apostle, is the dynamic, creative endeavor of finding ways to pursue the welfare of others rather than one's own interests. It is not self-centered but others-oriented. As we will see below, this means that love is characterized by self-giving for the good of others.

Although we have looked at only two "definitions" of love in Paul's writings, both from 1 Corinthians, this fundamental understanding of love as "seeking the good not of the self but of others" permeates all of Paul's letters. For example, in the introduction to the well-known Philippians hymn (Phil. 2:6-11) discussed in previous chapters, Paul issues a call to unity grounded in humility, compassion, sympathy, and love (2:1-3). He explains this unity-creating love concretely as follows in v. 4:

> Let each of you look not to your own interests [Greek *ta heautōn*], but to the interests of others [*ta heterōn*].

The idiom "one's own X" appears here once again, as in 1 Corinthians, in connection with love. Here Paul is very explicit, uniting both the negative (not self-interest) and positive (but rather others' interest) in one text. He makes it clear that love looks out, not for the self, but for the other.[10]

---

10. This verse poses many problems for the translator. The presence of the Greek word *kai* ("and," "also," "even") after the word "but" and before the phrase "the interests of others" has led some interpreters to suggest that Paul exhorts his readers to look out for others' interests *in addition* to their own: "Let each of you look not only to his own interests, but *also* [Greek *kai*] to the interests of others" (e.g., RSV). In the context, however, and in light of Paul's statements elsewhere, this reading seems contradictory and highly unlikely. Grammatically speaking, the Greek word *kai* here probably functions as a particle, not to qualify the "but" (Greek *alla*) that

Furthermore, as we noted above, in Galatians Paul prefaces his remarks about love as the summary and fulfillment of the law with the following exhortation:

> For you were called to freedom, brothers and sisters; only do not use your freedom as an opportunity for self-indulgence, but through love become slaves to one another. (Gal. 5:13)

To twentieth-century ears Paul's "become slaves" may seem harsh, and has sometimes been translated "become servants." In either case, however, the phrase reveals the paradoxical character of love according to Paul; it consists in the freedom of becoming slaves, of serving others rather than indulging the self. It reveals also the Christological character of love, for the connection of freedom and slavery with love, as well as the goal of seeking others' good rather than one's own, is an echo of a number of Pauline texts about Christ and his death. To these texts we now turn.

The Word of the Cross and the Love of Christ

When Paul writes to the Corinthians that "[I am] not seeking my own advantage, but that of many" (1 Cor. 10:33), he follows this claim immediately with a corresponding claim and exhortation:

> Be imitators of me, as I am of Christ. (1 Cor. 11:1)

Has Paul betrayed his own counsel against arrogance? What precisely does he mean?[11]

In the context of 1 Corinthians Paul is pointing to his own behavior (narrated in chapter 9, to which we will return in the next chapter) as behavior that

---

precedes it ("also"), but rather to strengthen it ("indeed," "rather"). This interpretation is confirmed by the absence of the word "only" (Greek *monon*; see Gorman, "The Self, the Lord, and the Other," pp. 614-20). Some Greek manuscripts do not have the Greek particle *kai*, perhaps because certain scribes and interpreters concluded that Paul could not have meant "also." (It is also theoretically possible, but unlikely in light of the manuscript evidence, that a scribe added *kai*.) The NRSV translators ("look not to your own interests, but to the interests of others") apparently followed either the semantic logic offered above or concluded that the Greek particle *kai* had been added by scribes to Paul's original text without *kai*. The RSV, however, had assumed that *kai* was original and meant "also." The NIV has the same mistranslation.

11. The specific issue of what the "imitation" of Christ (and Paul) means for Paul (conformity to the crucified Christ) was discussed in a preliminary way in chapter two and will be considered again below.

seeks to edify others rather than self and thus to embody his own principles that "love does not seek its own benefit" (1 Cor. 13:5, author's translation) and "love builds up" (1 Cor. 8:1). By claiming to be an imitator of Christ in this regard, Paul implies (a) that Christ acted similarly, (b) that this way of Christ was an expression of love, and (c) that this love is paradigmatic not only for Paul but for all who belong to Christ.

As we have seen in previous chapters, Paul also speaks more explicitly about Christ's love, specifically of the cross as the expression of Christ's love. Indeed, Paul never speaks of Christ's love without mentioning or alluding to the cross in the same breath. The following texts make this connection between the cross and Christ's love explicit:

> [19]. . . I have been crucified with Christ; [20]and it is no longer I who live, but Christ who lives in me. And the life I now live in the flesh I live by the faith of the Son of God [NRSV margin], who loved me by giving himself for me. [21]I do not nullify the grace of God; for if justification comes through the law, then Christ died for nothing.[12] (Gal. 2:19-21)

> [34]Who is to condemn? It is Christ Jesus, who died, yes, who was raised, who is at the right hand of God, who indeed intercedes for us. [35]Who will separate us from the love of Christ? . . . [37][I]n all these things [sufferings] we are more than conquerors through him who loved us. (Rom. 8:34-35a, 37)

> [14]For the love of Christ urges us on, because we are convinced that one has died for all; therefore all have died. [15]And he died for all, so that those who live might no longer live for themselves, but for him who died and was raised for them. (2 Cor. 5:14-15)

In Galatians 2:20, as we have already seen, Paul defines Christ's death on the cross as both an act of faith (or faithfulness) toward God and an act of self-giving love for "me" — that is, for Paul speaking representatively. Christ's love thus consists in the giving of himself. Here Paul echoes and amplifies a phrase he wrote earlier in Galatians:

> [The Lord Jesus Christ] . . . gave himself for our sins to set us free from the present evil age, according to the will of our God and Father. (Gal. 1:4)

It is widely believed that Galatians 1:4 cites an early Christian text (perhaps from a creed or brief confessional statement) that is sometimes called a "self-

---

12. For the preferred reading from the NRSV margin, and for the alternate rendering "by giving himself," see the discussion in chapter six.

surrender formula."[13] Its antiquity, and probable pre-Pauline formulation, are revealed by the phrase "for our sins," suggesting an early understanding of Christ's death as an atonement for sins.[14] Paul certainly agrees with this statement and its theology, but Galatians 2:20 more fully divulges Paul's own experience of the cross. "For sins" in 1:4 becomes "for me" in 2:20. The cross is Christ's loving gift of himself for "me," for us, for all. His death for sins was not anything other than an act of love, a voluntary gift of the self.

This perspective is reinforced by the text cited above from Romans 8. The last section of this chapter is a meditation on the meaning of Christ's death as an act of both God's love and Christ's love for us in the face of persecution and other forms of suffering. Just prior to 8:34-37, Paul has reminded the Romans that God cannot be "against us" but only for us, since God "did not withhold his own Son, but gave him up for all of us" (8:32). The love of God is the love of Christ, embodied in the cross. From the Father's perspective it is the selfless giving expressed in sacrificing one's own dear Son; from the Son's perspective it is the selfless giving of oneself. This is "the love of God in Christ Jesus our Lord" (8:39), from which nothing whatsoever can separate Paul or his believing readers and hearers.

For Paul, however, the love of Christ expressed on the cross is not merely a past, one-time event but also an ongoing reality. Christ's love can be experienced now, even and especially in the midst of persecution or other hardships. Its character remains the same: action "for us," most specifically in intercession for us (Rom. 8:34). Christ's present activity of intercession is a natural continuation of the love expressed in death and vindicated by God in the resurrection. That is to say, Christ in love sought, and continues to seek, the edification of others.

The continuing reality, character, and power of this love are experienced by Paul not only as a recipient of Christ's love but as its conduit. As 2 Corinthians 5:14 indicates, the living force of Christ's love "controls" or "constrains" Paul. His missionary and reconciling activities are motivated and governed, he claims, by Christ's love. Paul's apostleship "is a response to the eschatological rule of love instituted by Christ's death."[15] This ongoing love, as in Romans 8, is continuous in character with the past expression of love on the cross — "he died for all" — which in turn echoes the self-surrender formula in Galatians 2:20 — "he gave himself for me." Christ now loves through others.

13. See, e.g., J. Louis Martyn, *Galatians: A New Translation with Introduction and Commentary,* Anchor Bible 33A (New York: Doubleday, 1997), pp. 88-91, 94-96.

14. Paul himself is much more prone to speak about sin (singular) than sins.

15. Raymond Pickett, *The Cross in Corinth: The Social Significance of the Death of Jesus,* JSNTSup 143 (Sheffield: Sheffield Academic Press, 1997), p. 145.

Paul's "Master Story" as a Story of Love

When Paul writes to the Philippians that he "long[s] for all of [them] with the compassion of Christ Jesus" (Phil. 1:8), he again refers to an ongoing awareness of Christ's love as a present reality that shapes his own apostolic relationships. But once again this love or "compassion" (Greek *en splanchnois*) is also implicitly connected, in context, to Christ's love displayed on the cross. In the preface to the Christ hymn, the word "compassion" reappears, together with both love *(agapē)* and the significant idiom "one's own X" *(ta heautōn):*

> ¹If then there is any encouragement in Christ, any consolation from love [*agapēs*], any sharing in the Spirit, any compassion [*splanchna*, as in 1:8] and sympathy, ²make my joy complete: be of the same mind, having the same love [*agapēn*], being in full accord and of one mind. ³Do nothing from selfish ambition or conceit, but in humility regard others as better than yourselves. ⁴Let each of you look not to your own interests, but to the interests of others. Let the same mind be in you that was in Christ Jesus [or, better, "Have this mind in your community, which is indeed a community in Christ Jesus"], who. . . . (Phil. 2:1-5)

Since this passage clearly points forward to Christ's activity that is narrated in the hymn, or Paul's "master story" (see ch. five), we may rightly infer that Paul interprets that activity as constituting both an expression and a paradigm of the humility and love called for in vv. 1-5. In other words, the "affection" of Christ (1:8, Greek *en splanchnois*) that Paul has is the same affection (Greek *splanchna*)[16] and love that he urges the Philippians to have "in Christ" (2:1), which affection in turn is found originally and paradigmatically in Christ's "incarnation" and death (2:6-11, the hymn itself).

It must be noted, however, that Christ's actions narrated in Philippians 2:6-11 are never explicitly described in ethical (or even soteriological) terms within the hymn itself.[17] The narrative is simply that, oriented toward God ("humbled himself," "became obedient") if toward anyone. There is no "for us," no explicit "emptied himself *as an act of love*" or "humbled himself as an example for us." It

16. NRSV has "compassion" instead of affection, although the Greek echoes the reference to Christ in 1:8.

17. This was discussed in chapter two and has been noted by numerous interpreters, emphatically so by Ralph P. Martin, *A Hymn of Christ: Philippians 2:5-11 in Recent Interpretation and in the Setting of Early Christian Worship*, 3rd ed. (Downers Grove, Ill.: InterVarsity, 1997), but often with erroneous conclusions about its (supposedly nonethical) meaning for Paul. The absence of ethical or soteriological interest in the hymn itself does not negate its use for such interests, as most interpreters now stress.

is Paul who characterizes the actions narrated in the hymn as deeds of humility and love by placing the hymn in its context. Once that move is made however, Paul thereby connects the various activities narrated in the hymn with love, thereby explaining what he means by the "affection" or love of Christ. Just as Paul understands that the phrase "gave himself for our sins" (Gal. 1:4) means "loved me by giving himself for me" (Gal. 2:20), so also he understands that the text "emptied himself . . . humbled himself" (Phil. 2:7-8) means that Christ loved with a love that "does not seek [one's] own interests" (Phil. 2:4, author's translation). Thus Paul's reading, or exegesis, of the community's hymn is evident from the context in which he places it.[18]

That Paul wants his readers to draw this conclusion — that the hymn is really about the love of Christ — becomes even clearer when we examine the content of the first half of the hymn (Phil. 2:6-8) and the parallels between it and 2:1-5, the hymn's hortatory preface.

As we saw in chapter five on the cross, Philippians 2:6-11 contains several significant narrative patterns, two of which are found in verses 6-8 (author's translation):

[6][A]lthough[19] being in the form of God,

---

18. As we will see in chapters nine and ten, the broader context of the letter affirms this conclusion inasmuch as Paul, Timothy, and Epaphroditus are presented as examples of seeking the interests of others.

19. The word "although" does not actually appear in the text but is an interpretation of the Greek participle *hyparchōn*, "being" or "existing." There are actually three main possible meanings for this participle: (1) concessive force: "although being/although he was" (most interpreters); (2) temporal or circumstantial force: "while [when] being/while [when] he was" (e.g., Gordon D. Fee, *Paul's Letter to the Philippians,* The New International Commentary on the New Testament [Grand Rapids: Eerdmans, 1995], p. 202, n. 40); and (3) causal force: "because he was" (e.g., Peter O'Brien, *The Epistle to the Philippians* [Grand Rapids: Eerdmans, 1991], p. 211; N. T. Wright, *The Climax of the Covenant: Christ and the Law in Pauline Theology* [Edinburgh: T&T Clark, 1991; Minneapolis: Fortress, 1993], p. 83 n. 110; C. F. D. Moule, "Further Reflexions on Philippians 2:5-11," in W. W. Gasque and R. P. Martin, eds., *Apostolic History and the Gospel: Biblical and Historical Essays Presented to F. F. Bruce on His 60th Birthday* [Exeter: Paternoster, 1970], pp. 264-76). For a discussion of the grammar, see the commentaries and other literature. The translation "although" has seldom been questioned, but the third alternative, "because," is especially provocative. It would make a very blunt affirmation about the meaning of divinity for Paul (see chapter one and the note below). Despite the attraction of this translation, however, it is not likely to be correct, since the whole pattern of Paul's interpretation of this hymn here and in parallels throughout his letters depends on the renunciation of something *although* one has the right to use it. However, there is some truth to the causal reading of the participle. On this reading, the text suggests that contrary to our expectations of deity ("equality with God"), Christ challenges our understanding of deity by becoming a servant. In retrospect, in contemplating this revolution in the understanding of God, therefore, the reader is in fact invited to

[he] did not consider his equality with God as something to be exploited
for his own advantage,[20]
⁷but emptied himself,
    by taking the form of a slave,
    by being born in the likeness of human beings.

    And being found in human form,
⁸he humbled himself
    by becoming obedient to death
     — even death on a cross.

It is helpful to list the key affirmations that Paul makes about Christ in these
three verses:

1. he was "in the form" of God, which meant he possessed equality with God;
2. he did not consider this equality as something to use for his own advantage;[21]

---

confess that *because* Christ was in fact God in this radically self-giving way, he did indeed refuse self-advantage and emptied himself. In the process, God is recharacterized fundamentally as self-emptying ("kenotic") or cruciform. Nevertheless, because the emphasis in the hymn is on the unexpected character of Christ's act, we should render the participle "although" rather than "because."

20. According to most recent interpreters, this is the most likely meaning of the Greek word used here, *harpagmos*. See, among others, Stephen E. Fowl, *The Story of Christ in the Ethics of Paul: An Analysis of the Function of the Hymnic Material in the Pauline Corpus,* JSNTSup 36 (Sheffield: JSOT Press, 1990), pp. 54-57, as well as his "Christology and Ethics in Philippians 2:5-11," in Ralph P. Martin and Brian J. Dodd, eds., *Where Christology Began: Essays on Philippians 2* (Louisville: Westminster/John Knox, 1998), pp. 142-43. The definitive studies of *harpagmos,* upon which this interpretation is based, are Roy W. Hoover, "The *Harpagmos* Enigma: A Philological Solution," *Harvard Theological Review* 56 (1971): 95-119, and N. T. Wright, "*harpagmos* and the Meaning of Philippians 2:5-11," *Journal of Theological Studies* n.s. 37 (1986): 321-52, updated in "Jesus Christ Is Lord: Philippians 2:5-11," in his *Climax of the Covenant,* pp. 56-98 (esp. 62-90).

21. It must be noted that these first two affirmations have been the subject of especially heated debate. My interpretation is based not only on the term *harpagmos* but also many other philological, grammatical, and literary factors. These other factors only confirm Hoover's philological study of *harpagmos,* which concludes that the term always refers to "something already present and at one's disposal" and that "the question . . . is not whether one possesses something, but whether or not one chooses to exploit something" ("*Harpagmos* Enigma," p. 118). With respect to the logic of the passage and its use in Paul's reflection, L. D. Hurst rightly concludes that "within the context of Paul's ethics it would seem to make more sense to say that the Christ of the hymn *already possessed* the right to be treated as equal with God, but freely surrendered the right for the sake of a greater principle — God's purpose of love in the

3. instead of using his equality with God for his own advantage, he did two similar things, in sequence: he "emptied himself" and he "humbled himself";
4. his self-emptying consisted of taking the "form of a slave," that is, being born as a human rather than retaining his status of equality with ("being in the form of") God;
5. after emptying himself, that is, while in this "form" of slave/human being (in contrast to God), in similar fashion he "humbled himself";
6. his self-humbling consisted of becoming obedient to God to the point of dying, even dying by crucifixion.

As noted in chapter five, in these verses we find (1) a pattern of voluntary renunciation rather than exploitation of status and, within that pattern, (2) a pattern of self-humbling. Building on the discussion of these patterns in that chapter, we may present them as follows:

(1) Although [*x*], not [*y*] but [*z*]

or

(1) Although [*status*], not [*selfishness*] but [*self-abasement/slavery*]

and

(2) [*z*] = [*a and b*]

or

(2) [*self-abasement/slavery*] = [*self-emptying and self-humbling*]

What Paul narrates, using language that moves back and forth between the metaphorical and the literal, is a radical two-act drama of self-denial and self-humbling. The culmination of this drama is Christ's crucifixion, which Paul here describes, as we noted in chapter five, as his obedience: "became obedient to [the point of] death — even death on a cross." From Paul's perspective, this obedience was also Christ's "faith," as we likewise saw in chapter six.

---

incarnation. The voluntary laying down of rights already possessed, in other words, is central to Paul's ethical appeal elsewhere, and there is no reason to abandon this principle in our understanding of the hymn of Philippians 2" ("Christ, Adam, and Preexistence Revisited," in Martin and Dodd, *Where Christology Began*, p. 90 [emphasis in the original]). Recent scholarship suggests that the Greek phrase rendered "equality with God" was a status normally attributed only to the emperor.

In Galatians 2:20, it will be recalled, Paul explicitly describes Christ's death as both an act of faith and an act of love. The structural and material parallels between verses 6-8 and verses 3-4 of Philippians 2 demonstrate that once again Paul understands Christ's faith/obedience toward God also as his love for others. The key word in the structure of Philippians 2:6-8 is the word "but" (Greek *alla*) at the beginning of verse 7, which functions as the hinge for the entire passage:

> [A]lthough being in the form of God ([x]) . . . [he] did not consider his equality with God as something to be exploited for his own advantage ([y])
> *but*
> he emptied himself . . . he humbled himself. . . . ([z])

The resulting structure indicates the radical contrast between what Christ could have done by virtue of his status and what, instead, he did do. Specifically, Christ refused to use his status for selfish gain but rather descended in status from deity to humanity/slavery. In so doing, he emptied and humbled himself to the extreme point of an obedient death by crucifixion.

Similarly, the word "but" (Greek *alla*) is the hinge for both verse 3 and verse 4 of the preface.

v. 3
Do nothing from selfish ambition or conceit,
but
in humility regard others as better than yourselves.

v. 4
Let each of you look not to your own interests,
but
to the interests of others.

In these two more-or-less synonymous exhortations, Paul urges the Philippians to love: to have humble regard for others rather than self. The verses are clearly structured in form and content in parallel to the first half of the hymn (vv. 6-8). These clear parallels between the explicit exhortation to Paul's particular understanding of love (vv. 3-4, defining the word "love" named in vv. 1-2) and the Christ narrative (vv. 6-8) mean that Paul understands the actions of Christ narrated in verses 6-8 not only as Christ's obedience but also as his love.

Christ's love, then, is understood by Paul to be the fundamental content of the first half of the hymn text cited in Philippians 2:6-11. *Paul's "master story" is a story of love.* Furthermore, Paul understands this love of Christ to have consisted of refusing to exploit status for selfish gain, freely renouncing such status, and preferring others over self by emptying himself in "incarnation" (to use a later theological term) and by humbling himself in death.[22] Although the hymn does not make these things explicit in itself, Paul's use of it does, and his use makes it clear that he sees the hymn's narrative as both a story of Christ's love, especially in his crucifixion, and a paradigmatic story about love to be followed by those in Christ. That will be the subject of the next chapter.

Echoes of the Master Story of Love

Once we understand that Philippians 2:6-8 unfolds the shape and meaning of Christ's love, we can look also at two additional texts where love is not explicitly mentioned but certainly implied: 2 Corinthians 8:9 and Romans 15:1-3.

2 Corinthians 8 and 9 contain Paul's appeal to the Corinthians to participate in the relief offering for the church in Jerusalem. The dominant theme of these two chapters is that giving is an act of divine "grace" (Greek *charis*), a word that appears seven times in the two chapters, and that such grace always appears in overflowing measure.[23] In chapter 8 Paul urges the Corinthians to "abound in this grace [of giving]" (8:7, author's translation)[24] by appealing to two examples of gracious giving: "the grace of God that has been granted to the churches of Macedonia" (8:1-5), and "the grace of our Lord Jesus Christ" (8:9, RSV; also NRSV margin). The appeal culminates in chapter 9 with another reference to God's gracious gift, implying both material abundance and especially the Son and his salvific death: "the surpassing grace of God that he has given you. Thanks be to God for his indescribable gift!" (9:14b-15).

Paul clearly sees God's generous gifts of abundance and salvation as gifts of love, though he uses the word "love" only once in the two chapters. He tells the Corinthians that his request is a test of "the genuineness of [their] love" (*agapēs,* 8:8). What immediately follows this verse is a brief narrative of the paradigmatic act of love, the "grace" or "generous act" *(charis)* of "our Lord Jesus Christ," in 8:9. Here Paul employs a pattern that echoes Philippians 2:6-8:

22. Wright is correct to argue that the hymn also portrays Jesus as "the revelation, in action, of the love of God" and that the "real theological emphasis of the hymn, therefore, is not simply a new view of Jesus. It is a new understanding of God. . . . [I]ncarnation and even crucifixion are to be seen as *appropriate* vehicles for the dynamic self-revelation of God" (*Climax of the Covenant,* pp. 83-84). In the context, however, Paul stresses the Christological dimension.

23. Words for "abundant" and "surpassing" appear some ten times in the two chapters.

24. The NRSV's "excel also in this generous undertaking" (margin "grace") is not as vivid or as close to the Greek text.

For you know the generous act of our Lord Jesus Christ,
> that though he was rich,
>> yet for your sakes he became poor,
>> so that by his poverty
> you might become rich.

Like Philippians 2:6-8, 2 Corinthians contains not one but several Pauline patterns of narrating Christ's acts, and it fills them with vivid metaphor. First, like Philippians 2:6-8, the entire verse has the structure of "although [x] . . . [z]"; that is, it is built around the idea of renunciation of status. Christ renounced wealth for poverty. The phrase "though he was rich" is parallel to "though he was in the form of God" (Phil. 2:6),[25] while "became poor" is reminiscent of "emptied himself" and "humbled himself" (Phil. 2:7-8). The metaphor of self-impoverishment may be deliberately vague in order to be a comprehensive reference to Christ's "incarnation" and death, but it certainly includes the latter.[26]

That there is a reference to Christ's death is confirmed by another narrative pattern in the text. Unlike Philippians 2, 2 Corinthians 8:9 explicitly defines the act as being others-oriented, that is, "for your sakes." This phrase is reminiscent of references to Christ's loving death in 2 Corinthians 5:14 ("for all") and Galatians 2:20 ("for me").[27]

Once again, then, we have a narrative pattern — or rather a set of narrative patterns — that present Christ's death as his act of love, specifically his act of renouncing status, and thus refraining from any act of selfishness or self-interest,[28] for the benefit of others. 2 Corinthians 8:9 tells the story of Christ in the language of the fundamental two-dimensional character of love (it does not seek its own interest, it seeks the interest of others) we discovered at the beginning of this chapter. As we shall see in the next chapter, Paul claims to be con-

---

25. In both texts the English word "[al]though" represents a Greek participle of a verb meaning "to be" or "to exist" (*hyparchōn* in Phil. 2:6 and *ōn* in 2 Cor. 8:9) used "concessively" to express contrast with the main verb of the sentence.

26. Another pattern here, though absent from Philippians 2, is the notion of "exchange"; that is, the Corinthians received the wealth that Christ gave up. Morna D. Hooker ("Interchange in Christ," in *From Adam to Christ: Essays on Paul* [New York/Cambridge: Cambridge University Press, 1990]) has shown that such patterns of "interchange in Christ" refer to Christ's death.

27. Although the Greek preposition used in the phrase differs from the other verses and may carry a less sacrificial or substitutionary sense, the effect of expressing altruistic action is fundamentally the same.

28. Although, in contrast to Phil. 2:6-8, 2 Cor. 8:9 has no explicit phrase narrating what Christ did *not* do, the idea is clearly implicit that he did not exploit his wealth for his own advantage.

formed to this narrative of self-impoverishment and self-giving, and he urges the Corinthians to do the same. Indeed, this reality of the grace-filled Christ story becomes for Paul the foundation "upon which all the specific imperatives of the Christian life are ultimately based."[29]

Yet another text in which Christ's death is narrated in similar terms and presented implicitly as an act of love is Romans 15:3:

> Christ did not please himself; but, as it is written, "The insults of those who insult you have fallen on me."

In the latter part of this verse Paul cites a portion of Psalm 69 (v. 9) understood to represent the attitude and prayer of Jesus at his death. This psalm functions in all of the gospel passion narratives and was apparently commonly read in the early churches as a psalm pointing to Jesus' death. The structure of the verse, therefore, is parallel to part of Philippians 2, namely "not [x] but [y]." Christ's death is interpreted as an act not of his pleasing himself but, rather, of his acting with respect to God for the benefit of others. The citation of Psalm 69:9 also echoes texts such as 2 Corinthians 5:14 and Galatians 1:4, in which Christ's death is presented as beneficial for others by being a death for their sins.

Romans 15:3 presents Christ paradigmatically (see also v. 5, "in accordance with Christ Jesus") in the context of an exhortation to have concern for edifying one's neighbor rather than pleasing oneself, and to do so as a means to unity. Specifically, in Romans 15:1-3, which concludes a description and analysis of a situation of conflict provided in chapter 14, Paul calls for the "strong" (those who have no dietary scruples) not to judge but to accept the "weak" (those with such scruples) and perhaps even to modify their diets for the good of the weaker members of the community.[30] Furthermore, Paul calls on all — Gentiles and Jews, strong and weak — to

> [7][w]elcome one another . . . just as Christ has welcomed you . . . [8][f]or I tell you that Christ has become a servant [Greek *diakonon*] of the circumcised. . . . (Rom. 15:7-8a)

The word "love" does not appear in these verses or in 15:3 itself. However, the context and vocabulary indicate beyond any doubt that Paul understands Christ's act, and the corresponding exhortations, in terms of love. Love is the

29. Victor Paul Furnish, *II Corinthians,* Anchor Bible 32A (Garden City, N.Y.: Doubleday, 1984), p. 417.

30. So Richard B. Hays, *The Moral Vision of the New Testament: A Contemporary Introduction to New Testament Ethics* (San Francisco: HarperCollins, 1996), p. 28.

dominant theme of the entire hortatory section of Romans (chs. 12–15) and of chapter 14 in particular. "Let love be genuine" (12:9), Paul writes, and "Owe [Greek *opheilete*] no one anything, except to love one another; for the one who loves another has fulfilled the law" (13:8; cf. vv. 9-10). Moreover, in 15:1-2, immediately preceding the claim that "Christ did not please himself," there are numerous echoes of the language of love from Paul's letters generally and from Romans 12–14 in particular — the language of "debt/owing," "pleasing," "neighbor," and "edification":[31]

> [1]We who are strong ought [literally, "have a debt," Greek *opheilomen*] to put up with the failings of the weak, and not to please ourselves. [2]Each of us must please our neighbor for the good purpose of building up [Greek *oikodomēn*] the neighbor. (Rom. 15:1-2)

Clearly, then, in Romans 15:3 Paul interprets Christ's death as an act of love, love being once again understood as a choice for others rather than self, as a "bearing" of others' burdens and in so doing as a "pleasing" of others rather than oneself. It is thus an act of hospitality and service. For Christ, of course, the "burdens" borne are specifically "the insults of those who insult you," that is, those who insult or sin against God.[32] Elsewhere, as we have seen (e.g., Gal. 1:4; 1 Cor. 15:3), these burdens that Christ endured are referred to simply as our "sins," for which Christ died. In Romans 15, Christ's dying is a paradigmatic act of burden-bearing and others-pleasing love that can engender a host of analogous acts by Paul and his communities. As we shall see in the next chapters, this is true of all the texts and patterns of the cross as Christ's love.

The Narrative Pattern ("Law") of the Crucified Messiah

So far in this chapter we have looked carefully at several narrative patterns of the cross that, in Paul's interpretation and use of them, proclaim Christ's death,

---

31. Indeed, it has been pointed out that Romans 14–15 is reminiscent of (if not borrowed from) 1 Cor. 8:1–11:1 as a whole. Furthermore, other vocabulary items used in the context are associated with love elsewhere in Paul's letters. For example, the phrase "bear[ing] the weaknesses of the not-strong" (v. 1, author's translation) uses the same verb *(bastazein)* as "bearing one another's burdens" in Gal. 6:2, by which believers fulfill the law of Christ — probably a reference to the law of self-enslaving love. Also, as we saw in Phil. 2:1-4, for Paul the pleasing of others rather than self is an act of love in that it builds unity in the community; the call to live "in harmony" in Rom. 15:5 uses the same Greek idiom as Phil. 2:2 *(to auto phronein)*. See further discussion in chapter ten.

32. So all commentators.

either explicitly or implicitly, as his act of love. For the most part, these narrative patterns are not coined by Paul but are traditional, taken from preexisting liturgical texts and generally cited as descriptions of love — that is, cruciform love — in the context of communal exhortation or spiritual reflection.

Three general patterns of the cross understood as an act of love have emerged in this discussion, ranging from the simple to the complex. These patterns overlap greatly in meaning, and sometimes in form. Their differences are worthy of note for two reasons. First, they show Paul's creativity in adapting diverse traditions and formulas for one fundamental purpose: to express the love of the crucified Christ. Second, as we will see in the next chapter, Paul employs or echoes now one and now another of these patterns in his exhortations to love.

1. The first, and simplest, pattern we may call the pattern of *sacrificial love,* expressed in phrases such as "Christ Jesus, who died" (Rom. 8:34) or "Christ died for all/us" (e.g., 2 Cor. 5:14).[33] This pattern depicts Christ's love as a costly act to benefit others.[34]

2. The second we may call the pattern of *self-giving love,* expressed in reflexive phrases such as "he gave himself" (Gal. 2:20; cf. Gal. 1:4), "he emptied himself" (Phil. 2:7), and "he humbled himself" (Phil. 2:8). This pattern portrays Christ's love as a fully self-involving act to benefit others.[35]

3. The third, and most complex, pattern we may describe as *status-renouncing love,* which is formulated most fully in the pattern "although [x], not [y] but [z]" (Phil. 2:6-8), but also in abbreviated form as "though [x], [z]" (2 Cor. 8:9) and "not [y] but [z]" (Rom. 15:3). This pattern expresses Christ's love as a deliberate abandoning of status and self-interest and a freely chosen act of concern for others. This third pattern may contain and combine elements of the other two (e.g., Phil. 2:6-8).[36]

The act narrated in these patterns is primarily Christ's death on the cross, but a corollary of this act of cruciform love is Christ's becoming human (his "incarnation"), which is narrated once explicitly (Phil. 2:6-7) and may be implied one other time (2 Cor. 8:9).

33. See also 1 Cor. 15:3, "Christ died for our sins," though in the context Paul does not interpret the text in terms of love, and Rom. 5:8, "Christ died for us," which is understood explicitly as the manifestation of God's love but also, implicitly, as Christ's act of love.

34. This pattern is discussed as numbers 4 and 5, "sacrifice," and "altruism/substitution," in chapter five.

35. This pattern is discussed as part of number 6, "self-giving/giving," in chapter five.

36. This pattern is discussed as number 7, "voluntary self-humbling/abasement," in chapter five.

As suggested above, that Paul adopts or adapts traditional patterns to narrate the event of Christ's cross (and "incarnation") is not remarkable in itself. What *is* remarkable, however, is that he consistently understands these patterns as descriptive of love, first as Christ's love and then, as we will see in the next chapters, as believers' love, whether apostolic or ordinary, in its polyvalent manifestations. Furthermore, the existence of these distinct yet similar patterns suggests that Paul has a fundamental understanding of Christ as the embodiment of status-renouncing, self-giving, others-oriented love.

It should not be unexpected, then, that Paul himself would recognize and even name the pattern he so clearly articulates in his letters. In two instances, in fact, he refers to a "law" (Greek *nomos*) of Christ: Galatians 6:2 and 1 Corinthians 9:21:

> Bear one another's burdens, and in this way you will fulfill the law of Christ. (Gal. 6:2)

> To those outside the law I became as one outside the law (though I am not free from God's law but am under Christ's law) so that I might win those outside the law. (1 Cor. 9:21)

There has been an enormous amount of debate on the meaning of these two references to the "law" of Christ, particularly with respect to Galatians 6:2.[37] In light of this chapter's analysis of Paul's patterns of narrating the cross as an act of self-giving, others-regarding love, a specific interpretation of "the law of Christ" suggests itself. That is, "the law of Christ" is Paul's shorthand for the paradigmatic pattern(s) of cruciform love that are expressed in Christ's "incarnation" and, especially, death for us. As Luke Johnson has suggested, the best translation of "the law of Christ" is probably something like "the pattern of the Messiah."[38] More specifically, the "law of Christ" is *the narrative pattern of self-giving, others-regarding love of the crucified Messiah Jesus* — the only Messiah Paul knows (1 Cor. 2:2).[39] This "law," then, is the master story, ex-

---

37. For four basic interpretive options, see John M. G. Barclay, *Obeying the Truth: Paul's Ethics in Galatians* (Minneapolis: Fortress, 1991), pp. 126-34. In my estimation, Barclay himself does not fully see the importance of the connection between the law of Christ and the cross of Christ.

38. For example, in a paper read at the annual meeting of the Society of Biblical Literature, fall 1997, and in his *Living Jesus: Learning the Heart of the Gospel* (New York: HarperSanFrancisco, 1999), p. 111.

39. The primary arguments for this interpretation of "the law of Christ" depend on an analysis of the two occurrences of the phrase in their contexts, which we will do in the discussion of these texts in the next chapter. However, something like the suggestion of Luke Johnson,

pressed most fully in Philippians 2, which will also become the community's "rule of life."[40]

(Cruciform) Faith Being Expressed through (Cruciform) Love

This narrative pattern, or law, of Christ's self-giving, others-regarding love is Paul's way of expressing Christ's fundamental attitude toward and action on behalf of the human race. It focuses, in other words, not on Christ's relationship to his "God and Father" but to people. Nonetheless, as we saw in chapter six, the cross was indeed a manifestation of Christ's relationship to his Father, such that the cross expressed both his obedience and his faith toward God. *In other words, the cross was simultaneously Christ's act of faith and his deed of love; it united the "vertical" and "horizontal" dimensions of covenant.*

This is expressed most clearly and succinctly in Galatians 2:20:

> I live by the faithfulness of the Son of God, who loved me by giving himself for me.[41]

Christ's faith toward God resulted in love toward us, Paul asserts. Thus the narrative pattern of the crucified Messiah Jesus is a pattern of faith as well as love,

---

and as expanded here, may be found (with various nuances) in Richard B. Hays, "Christology and Ethics in Galatians: The Law of Christ," *Catholic Biblical Quarterly* 49 (1987): 268-90; Hays, *Moral Vision;* Longenecker, *Triumph of Abraham's God;* and Barclay, *Obeying the Truth,* pp. 131-35. Hays ("Christology and Ethics," p. 276) speaks of the law of Christ as "a regulative principle or structure of existence." Longenecker, in particular (*Triumph of Abraham's God,* pp. 83-88), wants to maintain a link between the "law" of Christ fulfilled by believers and the "law" of Moses. Others (less often now than in the past) wish to connect the "law of Christ" to all or some of the teachings of the historical Jesus. Although Paul did clearly know and draw upon some of the traditions of Jesus' teachings, the phrase "the law of Christ" is not used in the context of such sayings.

40. Reminiscent of Hays interpreting "the law of Christ," but commenting on Philippians 2, G. B. Caird (*Paul's Letters from Prison in the Revised Standard Version,* NCB [Oxford: Clarendon, 1994], p. 123) contends that the example of Jesus' "self-forgetful love" furnishes "the rule for the common life of the church."

41. Although this text most explicitly interprets Christ's death as both faith and love, it is not the only such text. For example, the hymn in Phil. 2:6-11 presents Christ's death as his ultimate act of obedience (faith) and is then interpreted by Paul, as we have just seen, as the paradigm of love. Similarly, Rom. 5:12-21 presents Christ's death as his act of obedience and faith, while Rom. 5:1-11 and Romans 8 speak of it as an act of love, either of the Father or both the Father and the Son.

of faith expressing itself in love. Each "virtue" or dimension of the act (faith, love) is an expression of cruciformity, of yielding voluntarily to another, a simultaneous manifestation of the appropriate fundamental posture toward God (faith) and the corresponding appropriate relation toward others (love). We must therefore refine our description of the "law of Christ" to be *the narrative pattern of faith expressing itself in self-giving, others-regarding love of the crucified Messiah Jesus.*

That is, in one unified act of faith and love, Christ fulfilled both tablets of the Law, both of its essential commands: love of God, or "faith," and love of neighbor, or "love." In so doing, Christ really is for Paul the opposite, or "antitype," of Adam (Rom. 5:12-21) and of all other human beings (Rom. 1:18–3:20), whose condition is one of lacking both faith and love. *Because the Scriptures of Israel link love of God and neighbor as the essence of a life of integrity and covenant fulfillment,*[42] *Jesus' faithful, loving death on the cross is for Paul the quintessential Jewish, and therefore the quintessential human, act.* It expresses the essence of covenant keeping in one deed, and in so doing fulfills the Law.

Paul's twinning of the Son's faith and love has a remarkable parallel in Galatians 5:6, where Paul writes:

[I]n Christ Jesus neither circumcision nor uncircumcision counts for anything; the only thing that counts is faith working through love.

The essence of the believer's life, claims the apostle, is faith working through love. Because faith and love define the cross, faith and love also define life "crucified with Christ" (Gal. 2:19). What the believer's faith and love have in common is participation in the narrative pattern of faith and love of the crucified Jesus. What they have in common, in other words, is cruciformity. Faith is cruciformity vis-à-vis God, while love is cruciformity vis-à-vis other people.[43]

In Paul's experience of Christ, he came to see that the Son's fundamental option came to its most complete expression in an act of faith that was simultaneously an act of love. Thus in Paul's spirituality, the appropriate exercise of the fundamental *option,* which is a cruciform posture toward God, must become the exercise of the fundamental *virtue,* which is a cruciform posture toward others. Indeed, the two are inseparable, just as they were for Christ. To be in Christ, to live shaped by his narrative pattern of faith expressing itself in love, is

42. Walter Brueggemann, *Theology of the Old Testament: Testimony, Dispute, Advocacy* (Minneapolis: Fortress, 1997), p. 429, passim.

43. For the connection between Gal. 5:6 and 2:20, see Hays, "Christology and Ethics"; Martyn, *Galatians,* p. 474; Frank J. Matera, *Galatians,* Sacra Pagina (Collegeville, Minn.: Liturgical, 1992), pp. 183, 189.

to embrace a singular yet two-sided spirituality. The only thing that counted, and that counts, "in Christ," is "faith working through love." As James Dunn observes, this phrase "is almost a single concept, faith-through-love, love-energized-faith."[44]

Love, then, is no more an "option" for believers than it was for Jesus. Belief and love, or "ethics," are not independent realities for Paul, the latter being a kind of "supplement" to the former. No, cruciformity is a seamless garment. To put it in traditional language, there is for Paul no "justification" without "sanctification." Faith does not exist apart from love, for the Christ in whom believers live, and who lives in them, expressed his faith toward God by loving others. That is part and parcel of the "law of Christ," the pattern of the crucified Messiah Jesus.

Conclusion: Law of Christ

The concern of this chapter has been Paul's fundamental understanding of love as denial of self-interest (negatively) and regard for others' edification (positively) as grounded in the love of the crucified Christ. The "patterns" of love depicted in key Pauline texts were found to be parallel to patterns of narrating the cross: self-sacrificing, self-giving, status-renouncing. Moreover, we discovered that the cross is the unified expression of both the faith and the love of the Messiah, which results in an overarching pattern, or "law," of faith expressing itself in love.

Paul's goal in narrating the cross is not primarily to express his convictions about Christ, though the narratives do indeed accomplish that. Rather, his chief aim is to form individuals and especially communities according to these narrative patterns. That is, his goal is formative, not informative; it is spiritual and behavioral, not theological (narrowly understood as convictional). Throughout this chapter we have already seen hints that Paul's ultimate concern in narrating the love of Christ is to interpret his own life as a manifestation of that kind of love, on the one hand, and to urge his communities to embody it as well, on the other. In the next two chapters we consider how Paul understands the "law of Christ" — the narrative pattern of love of the faithful, crucified Messiah Jesus — to be operative in his own life (chapter nine) and in the life of the communities to which he writes (chapter ten).

44. James D. G. Dunn, *A Commentary on the Epistle to the Galatians,* Black's New Testament Commentaries (London: A&C Black, 1993), p. 272, where he adds that in Gal. 5:6 "Paul comes as close as he ever does to James."

CHAPTER 9

CRUCIFORM LOVE (II)

Apostolic Cruciformity

In the previous chapter we discovered that Paul's understanding and experience of love were fundamentally two-dimensional: that is, denying self-interest and seeking instead the good of the other. Paul interprets and presents the cross, in various patterns, as the actualization of divine love in Christ's self-giving, others-regarding love. This is the "law of Christ," the narrative pattern of the crucified Messiah Jesus. The cross is always and fundamentally for Paul the embodiment of love, specifically faith expressing itself in love.

Those who have experienced this kind of love poured into their hearts by the Holy Spirit, Paul suggests, feel both compelled and empowered to express analogous embodiments of cruciform love to others. He calls on others to imitate him, as he was an imitator of Christ (1 Cor. 11:1). In this chapter we explore Paul's self-understanding and experience of being an imitator of Christ, an apostle conformed to Christ crucified. What did it mean for him to extend the story of the cruciform love of Christ through his apostolic ministry? After addressing that question in this chapter, in the next chapter we will explore the ways in which Paul urges the communities to which he writes to actualize similar cruciform love.

Driven by Love

Paul is universally admired (or at least acknowledged) for his unfailing zeal despite incredible hardship and opposition, as both his letters and the book of Acts testify. How are we to explain Paul the "driven missionary," this person willing to

178

suffer so much and "subject himself to all this 'grief'"?[1] As we noted in the previous chapter, Raymond Brown calls the love of Christ "the driving factor of Paul's life."[2] As Paul himself says, "the love of Christ urges us on" (2 Cor. 5:14).

His missionary activity was the natural extension of this experience of love:

> [T]he mission to the Gentiles who would otherwise not hear is not for Paul an abstract conclusion, but an inevitable translation into action of the overflowing love that he had experienced. . . . The hardships encountered in the mission became for Paul more than means to be endured toward an end. If the love of God was manifested in the self-giving of Christ, how could the love of Christ be shown to others except in the same way?[3]

That Paul suffered is well known; that he did so, at least from his own perspective, out of love, is not always recognized. Yet Brown is right to underline Paul's experience of God's love in Christ and his claim to be motivated and shaped by that compelling love. When Paul the prisoner for Christ expresses his sentiments to the Philippians, he tells them, "I long for all of you with the compassion of Christ Jesus" (Phil. 1:8). In the same context, he distinguishes between those who preach Christ "from envy and rivalry . . . out of selfish ambition" and those who do so "from goodwill . . . out of love" (Phil. 1:15-17). It is clear that Paul places certain preachers (perhaps his critics or rivals) in the former category (yet still rejoices that "Christ is proclaimed in every way, whether out of false motives or true," 1:18), but himself and his colleagues (several of whom he lauds in Philippians) in the latter. The Philippians are called, indeed, "my beloved" (Greek *agapētoi mou*, 2:12).

To the Thessalonians, whom he also addresses as "beloved" (*agapētoi*, 1 Thess. 2:8), Paul describes his love as that of a nursing mother and caring father (1 Thess. 2:8-12). Answering accusations about his integrity, Paul claims that his love, and that of his colleagues, is profound and personal:

> So deeply do we care for you that we are determined to share with you not only the gospel of God but also our own selves, because you have become very dear [Greek *agapētoi*] to us. (1 Thess. 2:8)

> And may the Lord make you increase and abound in love for one another and for all, just as we abound in love for you. (1 Thess. 3:12)[4]

1. Raymond E. Brown, *An Introduction to the New Testament* (New York: Doubleday, 1997), pp. 447-48.
2. Brown, *Introduction to the New Testament*, p. 450.
3. Brown, *Introduction to the New Testament*, p. 450.
4. Compare 1 Thess. 2:17-20; 3:9-10.

While it is true that Paul acknowledges all believers as God's beloved (e.g., Rom. 1:7) and thus also as his beloved — even the Romans, whom he had never met (Rom. 12:19) — Paul's expressions of love should not be understood as mere formalities but rather as an essential dimension of his experience of apostleship. In fact, when Paul is accused of preaching for any other reason, he rises quickly to defend his integrity and especially his love. Nowhere is this clearer than in his relationship with the Corinthians.

In 1 Corinthians Paul addresses the Corinthian believers as his beloved (10:14), his beloved children (4:14), and his beloved brothers and sisters (15:58), to whom he writes, "My love be with all of you in Christ Jesus" (16:24), to conclude the letter. Paul's love is greater than the chaos at Corinth that he addresses throughout the letter. So, too, in 2 Corinthians (whether this is one letter or several) Paul again addresses the Corinthians as his beloved (7:1; 12:19). It is clear, however, that as the relationship between Paul and the Corinthians deteriorated, as 2 Corinthians 10–13 suggests, Paul felt strongly the need to prove that what he was about was love:

> I will most gladly spend and be spent for you. If I love you more, am I to be loved less? (2 Cor. 12:15; cf. 2 Cor. 11:11)

> Everything we do, beloved, is for the sake of building you up [Greek *oikodomēs*]. (2 Cor. 12:19c)

Here Paul clearly applies to himself the standard of love enunciated for the Corinthians in 1 Corinthians 8:1; 10:23; 14:1-5: love gives of the self to edify others.

Paul claims in 2 Corinthians 12:19 that "everything" he did was done out of love. Yet what did this claim of love mean concretely for Paul? Above all this love issued in five fundamental, concrete, and interrelated dimensions of his ministry:

1. renouncing the use of apostolic rights, especially the right to financial support from those to whom he preached, and refusing to burden anyone financially but rather supporting himself with manual labor;
2. adapting to the needs of others more generally as a form of self-enslavement;[5]
3. preaching, teaching, and other forms of "pastoral care";

---

5. "Self-enslavement" is used here to mean not slavery to oneself but the giving up of self to another that can be described (despite the harshness of the image to modern sensitivities) as the enslavement of the self to the other.

4. suffering, physically and psychologically, for the sake of his people and his churches; and

5. choosing life over death, for the sake of those to whom he ministers.

Each of these behaviors represented, for Paul, his embodiment of the narrative pattern of cruciform love found paradigmatically in Christ. This "all-encompassing love of Christ" was the "goal to which he had devoted every waking hour."[6]

These aspects of Paul's ministry are mentioned in various texts throughout his letters, but they are seldom presented in any systematic way. Perhaps Paul's most sustained systematic reflection on his own experience of cruciform ministry appears in 1 Corinthians 9, where we begin our exploration and focus on the first two dimensions of his cruciformity listed above.

Paul and the Narrative Pattern of the Crucified Messiah

1 Corinthians 9 is a passage with multiple functions in the letter, in Paul's overall relationship with the Corinthians, and in Paul's fundamental perception and experience of his own apostolic ministry. For these reasons, we will look at it in some detail. In this chapter of 1 Corinthians Paul defends his apostolic rights, defends his right to *renounce* those rights, and offers himself to the Corinthians as an example of the renunciation of personal rights for the benefit of others.[7] The chapter reaches its climax in verse 19, where Paul claims, "Though I am free, I have made myself a slave [Greek *emauton edoulōsa,* "enslaved myself"] to all." This claim must be understood in both its literary (1 Cor. 8:1–11:1) and historical contexts, which are closely interconnected.

1 Corinthians 8:1–11:1 contains Paul's response to the issue of eating meat that had come from animals offered to idols, concerning which the Corinthians had written after the church had split into two groups over the issue.[8] The group that freely ate such meat Paul refers to as "you who possess knowledge,"

---

6. Brown, *Introduction to the New Testament,* p. 450.

7. For an excellent treatment of this purpose of 1 Corinthians 9, see W. L. Willis, "Apostolic Apologia? The Form and Function of 1 Corinthians 9," *Journal for the Study of the New Testament* 24 (1985): 33-48.

8. It is generally agreed that there existed at Corinth two main groups: (1) those who had no reluctance to eat such meat, on the basis of their knowledge (8:1) that there is but one God and idols do not really exist (8:4); and (2) those who felt eating meat offered to idols was wrong, because they had been previously accustomed to worshipping idols and would view eating meat offered to idols as precisely that — an offering to idols (8:7, 10). There is, however, disagreement over the location(s) of the meat eating that Paul has in mind, especially in 1 Corinthians 8, where he describes the problems.

the group that would not as "the weak" (8:9-10). Paul sides in part with the knowledgeable ones, for they do know the truth, at least partially. Yet while Paul affirms certain tenets of the knowledgeable ones' theology ("idols do not truly exist, since there is but one God," v. 6), he challenges their ethics, specifically their view of freedom and the exercise of rights as the fundamental moral principle and pattern of Christian existence.[9]

Paul says that an act that could hurt fellow "believers" (NRSV; literally, "brother [or sister]") is (a) sin against one(s) for whom Christ died and (b) sin against Christ (8:11-12). An act that might be permissible in isolation can be deadly in the context of the community. In so condemning this kind of act, Paul institutes a new motive for concern for fellow believers, namely, the fact that Christ died for them. This new motive then leads to a new direction or pattern of life in which the effect of an act on another — and therefore on Christ — is central. Thus, Paul seeks to replace the ethic of freedom and rights, which is grounded in knowledge, with an ethic of love expressed in concern for (8:9, 13) and the building up of (8:1) others, which is grounded in Christ's death. The misguided ethic is one of *concern for self and independence from the needs of others;* the new ethic is one of *orientation away from self and toward others.* So radical is this ethic of concern for others that one ought to be willing to forgo one's rights completely for the sake of the other — which Paul himself would do (8:13). Such is love as Paul understood it.[10]

Having introduced the pattern of love that renounces rights and edifies the other as the basic pattern for life in the Corinthian community, in chapter 9 Paul builds on the claim of 8:13, offering himself as a model of this pattern. He can do so, however, only by simultaneously establishing that he had rights and that his renunciation of these rights was a *good* rather than a *bad* thing. Paul says that although he himself, like the knowledgeable ones, is free — independent of all people and obliged to none (9:1, 19) — he has freely "enslaved himself" in order "to win more of them" (9:19).

When Paul speaks of his self-enslavement (that is, the enslavement of himself), he is referring to two things.[11] First, described in the preceding verses, is

9. Only later (10:1-22) will Paul challenge the act of eating meat offered to idols at a pagan temple from a theological (as opposed to ethical) perspective. See also Richard B. Hays, *First Corinthians,* Interpretation (Louisville: Westminster/John Knox, 1997), p. 159.

10. See further discussion of this passage in the following chapter.

11. According to Dale B. Martin, *Slavery as Salvation: The Metaphor of Slavery in Pauline Christianity* (New Haven and London: Yale University Press, 1990), pp. 86-116, there existed in the first century two models of leadership. The more conservative model was one of benevolent patriarchy ("kind but superior father-king"), while the other, "populist" model was of self-enslavement to the people and identification with the lower class.

his decision to renounce certain apostolic rights, especially the right to financial support, and instead to preach the gospel "free of charge" (9:18) by supporting himself with his tent making. Second, and described in the succeeding verses, is his decision to adapt himself to the peculiar needs of his audience, whether those "under" or "outside" the Law (i.e., Jewish or Gentile, 9:20-23), or the "weak" (9:22a); he became "all things to all people" (9:22b). In this context Paul claims that becoming like those "outside" the Law did not mean being "free from God's law but . . . under Christ's law" (9:21). For Paul, enslaving himself to all and being under Christ's law were, as we will see, synonymous. We will first consider Paul's self-enslavement by tent making and then, in the next section, through adaptability more generally.

Tent making was normally done by slaves or freedmen recently released from slavery; the artisans worked hard but usually remained poor, and their social status was very low.[12] For Paul, who as an educated Roman citizen came from a significantly higher social class, the decision to work as a tent maker was an act of self-enslavement — deliberate socioeconomic self-abasement, self-humiliation, and status renunciation.[13] Some at Corinth, particularly the few but influential wise, powerful, and noble (1:26), would have viewed Paul as a slave engaged in the most humiliating work and worthy of no respect.[14] Cicero, for instance, speaks representatively for the elite by referring to "craftsmen, petty shopkeepers, and all that filth of the cities," claiming that "the work of the artisan is degrading" and that "[t]he very wages of a laborer are the badges of slavery."[15] Paul's willingness to accept this stigma, even to make it part of his "ground for boasting" (9:15b) and "reward" or pay (9:18), demonstrates how his tent making was a "constitutive part" of his apostolic self-understanding.[16] It was part of his strategy of "gaining" or "winning" people to the gospel.[17]

Paul's tent making was not just a matter of renouncing rights, but also of

12. See Ronald F. Hock, *The Social Context of Paul's Ministry: Tentmaking and Apostleship* (Philadelphia: Fortress, 1980), esp. pp. 34-37.

13. My colleague Dante Beretta, a classicist, is right to point out that although Paul could have been born into a relatively high social class, he could also have reached it by his own efforts, especially efforts at education.

14. Hock, *Social Context*, pp. 36, 57-58.

15. Cicero, *Pro Flacco (In Defense of Flaccus)* 18 and *De officiis (On Duty)* 1.50, cited in Ramsay MacMullen, *Roman Social Relations: 50 B.C. to A.D. 284* (New Haven: Yale University Press, 1974), pp. 114-15. MacMullen explains the rationale for this disdain: "Since the better part of man was mental and spiritual, whoever depended on mere physical powers for his living lived that much lower" (p. 114).

16. Hock, *Social Context*, p. 62.

17. The Greek verb "to gain" *(kerdainō)* appears once in each of four consecutive verses (vv. 19-22).

accommodating himself to others, a strategy of flexibility or adaptability, about which we will have more to say below. Although the social stigma of humiliating himself by assuming the position of a slave was vitally important to Paul, and the strategy of accommodating himself probably effective, 1 Corinthians 9 makes it clear that Paul viewed his self-enslavement and self-accommodation as much more than effective strategy. The language of these verses is replete with theological and spiritual significance for him.[18]

First, Paul emphasizes to the Corinthians that he has *voluntarily* renounced (9:15) the rights (*exousiai*, 9:4-6, 12, 18; cf. 8:9) owing to his status as an apostle (9:1-12a). Paul insists that he has in no way made use of his biblically sanctioned right to financial support, or any other apostolic right (9:12b, 15a, 18b).[19] Verse 19 is deliberately worded to stress the voluntary character of this renunciation, emphasizing Paul's freedom and initiative ("though I am free . . . I have made myself a slave").[20] Although Paul preaches the gospel under compulsion, he preaches it *without charge* of his own free will (9:17-18). For Paul, then, his ministry is both an act of freedom and an act of obedience — as was Christ's death.

Second, Paul's self-enslaving means self-sacrificial giving for the benefit of others. This concern for others is expressed in the series of six purpose (Greek *hina*) clauses, or rationales for his activity, in 9:20-23. His goal is to "gain" not wages but converts — that is, to "save" (9:22) others, both Jews and Gentiles. His concern and corresponding action are rooted in the gospel, in which he himself shares only to the extent that he shares it with others (v. 23). As Dale Martin writes,

18. According to Martin (*Slavery as Salvation,* pp. 76-77, passim), Paul's slavery would have been seen by the upper class as a descent in status but by the lower class as an ascent, as a place of high status by virtue of being Christ's slave representative or steward. While this may be true, the point of Paul's appeal to his slavery is to get the more upper-class, or higher-status, Corinthians to descend voluntarily by forgoing the exercise of rights (as Martin rightly argues, pp. 77-85). Neither is it clear, as Martin argues, that Paul is primarily interested in modeling leadership (pp. 125-26), though the intended audience of his message of self-enslaving love certainly includes leaders.

19. Paul piles up evidence for the right to financial support from a variety of sources (9:7-14), including Scripture and (probably) common Christian custom.

20. Martin (*Slavery as Salvation,* pp. 133-34) suggests that the translation of the Greek participial phrase in this verse with the words "though I am free" is misleading. Paul saw himself not as still being free and paradoxically a slave (an enslaved free person, or a free slave), he argues, but as one who has made the move from free to slave status. His interpretation might be rendered, "When I was a free man, I became enslaved [and stopped being a free man]. . . ." While it is true that Paul stresses his downward mobility, it would be wrong to suggest that Paul thinks he forsakes his freedom — only his rights. Most commentators rightly translate this participle with concessive force ("though/although").

The point of 1 Corinthians 9 is that Paul takes on manual labor *because* of (not in spite of) his view that it is demeaning; he takes it on in order to gain the weak. . . . He lowers himself in order to gain those who are themselves of lower status.[21]

Third, Paul views his self-enslaving for the benefit of others as an act of love. When he explicitly offers himself as an example to the Corinthians in 1 Corinthians 10:32–11:1, he summarizes his ministry (seeking not to offend [i.e., positively, to benefit] Gentiles, Jews, and the church of God, 10:32-33) in terms of the maxim that he has given to the Corinthians: "not seeking my own advantage but that of many" (10:33; cf. 10:24). As we have seen, according to 13:5, such denial of self-interest is a fundamental characteristic of love. In Paul's ministry this involved self-accommodation to both Jews and Gentiles (9:20-22); that is, to all (9:23). Thus Paul's self-enslavement so that others might be saved was a manifestation of self-accommodating, nondiscriminating (universal) love.

Fourth, Paul sees his self-enslaving as being "under Christ's law" (9:21, NRSV; Greek *ōn . . . ennomos Christou,* from *en* "in" and *nomos* "law"). This phrase is difficult to translate precisely; James Dunn and Ben Witherington attempt to catch both the form and content of the idiom with the rendering "in-lawed to Christ."[22] Perhaps the preposition "in" is best captured with a phrase that catches Paul's "in Christ" metaphor or idiom: "being within," "being enveloped by," or "being shaped by" Christ's "law." The phrase appears almost parenthetically as Paul tries to prevent any misunderstanding of his claim to have become "without law" *(anomos)* to those without the law (Gentiles). He emphasizes that he does *not* mean that he acted inconsistently with the law or will of God but rather consistently with the "law" of Christ. He was, we might say colloquially, thoroughly "into" the law of Christ.

The parenthetical placement of this phrase should not, however, be permitted to hide the phrase's centrality to Paul's discussion of his self-enslaving for others. The action of Christ is the norm or standard for Paul's actions; as he will say in 11:1, he is a *mimētēs* — an imitator — of Christ. Since according to

---

21. Martin, *Slavery as Salvation,* p. 124 (emphasis in the original).

22. James D. G. Dunn, *The Theology of Paul the Apostle* (Grand Rapids: Eerdmans, 1998), p. 668, and Ben Witherington III, *Paul's Narrative Thought World: The Tapestry of Tragedy and Triumph* (Louisville: Westminster/John Knox, 1994), p. 240. BAGD, s.v. *ennomos,* suggests "subject to the law of Christ" or, possibly, "true to the law of Christ" or "according to the judgment of Christ." Whatever the translation, the term suggests conformity to a pattern — or narrative — embodied in Christ (so also Hays, *First Corinthians,* pp. 154-55). See also the brief discussion at the end of the previous chapter.

10:24–11:1 Paul imitated Christ in that he did not seek his own interest but, in love, sought the welfare of others, the "law" of Christ to which Paul conformed must be the law or principle of "not seeking one's own." In other words, the law of Christ is the principle of rights-renouncing, others-oriented love. Being under the law of Christ for Paul means having his ministry shaped by Christ's paradigmatic status-denying, others-regarding love. Since this love is known and preached by Paul in narrative form, Christ's "law" is more a "pattern" than a law or even a principle. Paul's ministry, his being "into" the law of Christ, is therefore his being shaped by the narrative pattern of Christ's cruciform love, as the last chapter suggested.

This meaning of Christ's law as the pattern of cruciform love becomes clear when one sees that Paul narrates his own act of Christ-like love in his self-enslavement as a parallel of Christ's self-renouncing, others-regarding incarnation and death. The structure of 1 Corinthians 9:19 is strikingly parallel to the first half of the hymn in Philippians 2. In 1 Corinthians 9:19, Paul employs a version of the "although [x] not [y] but [z]" pattern of Philippians 2:6-8:

Philippians 2:6-8	1 Corinthians 9:19
[x]: [Christ Jesus,] **though** he was in the form of God,	[x]: For **though** I am free with respect to all,
[y]: did not regard equality with God as something to be exploited,	[y]: [implied in context (9:12b, 15a, 18b): I did not exercise my rights that derive from that freedom, but]
[z]: but emptied himself, taking the form of a **slave**, being born in human likeness. And being found in human form, he humbled himself and became obedient to the point of death — even death on a cross.	[z]: I have made myself a **slave** to all, so that I might win more of them.

The similarity in vocabulary, syntax, and movement of each of the brief "narratives" is clear, so much so that one is nearly forced to conclude that the *parallels are not accidental.*[23] Paul views his own refusal to accept financial support as a

---

23. This is not to deny the existence of differences in the two texts. Most important, perhaps, is the fact that the slavery of Christ in Philippians 2 is first of all slavery (obedience) to God, whereas Paul's own slavery in 1 Corinthians 9 is to others. However, this difference should not be exaggerated. In the context of Philippians 2, as we saw in the previous chapter, Paul interprets Christ's act of slavery or obedience toward God as an act of love toward human

manifestation of the status-rejecting, self-enslaving death of his Lord. His brief autobiographical narrative is thus a *restatement* of his Christ narrative. Other echoes of this Christ narrative appear throughout chapter 9:[24]

Philippians 2:6-8	1 Corinthians 9
[*x*]: [Christ Jesus,] though he was in the form of God,	[*x*] If others share this rightful claim on you, do not we still more? (v. 12a) In the same way, the Lord commanded that those who proclaim the gospel should get their living by the gospel. (v. 14)
[*y*]: did **not** regard equality with God as something to be exploited,	[*y*] Nevertheless, we have **not** made use of this right. . . . (v. 12b) But I have made **no** use of any of these rights, nor am I writing this so that they may be applied in my case. (v. 15a)
[*z*]: but emptied himself, taking the form of a slave, being born [literally, "**becoming**"] in human likeness. And being found in human form, he humbled himself and **became** obedient to the point of death — even death on a cross.	[*z*] . . . but we endure anything rather than put an obstacle in the way of the gospel of Christ. (v. 12c) To the Jews I **became** as a Jew. . . . To those outside the law I **became** as one outside the law. . . . To the weak I **became** weak. . . . (vv. 20-22)

Paul's self-enslaving, others-regarding love is clearly an ongoing process, not a one-time act. It thus constitutes, as Hans Conzelmann notes, Paul's fundamental "self-understanding"[25] and mode of existence; it is his *modus operandi,* his "m.o." This self-enslaving is focused on his refusal of financial support, but it is not *limited* to that specific activity. It is the constant pattern of his life and ministry; Paul views this ongoing activity as one changeless yet dynamic and even polyvalent mode of existence. Just as Paul portrays Christ in

---

beings. Moreover, it is equally clear that Paul's "slavery" to other people is the corollary, or even the flip side, of his "slavery" to God. This surface difference, then, actually serves to highlight the deeper and most fundamental similarity: that "slavery" to God and "slavery" to others are inseparable. Or, in the language for which we have been arguing, cruciform faith must always be joined with cruciform love.

24. As we shall see, this is only the first of many similar parallel patterns in Paul's letters.

25. Hans Conzelmann, *1 Corinthians,* Hermeneia (Philadelphia: Fortress, 1975), p. 160.

brief narratives of self-enslavement, he portrays himself in a narrative of ongoing enslavement to all. Paul is not only the slave of Christ but also the slave of others.

Paradoxically, as we noted above, Paul's self-enslavement is a concrete expression of his freedom. Paul boldly affirms that he is free (9:1, 19). Whether this refers specifically to his spiritual, apostolic, social, or financial freedom — or is purposely vague and implies all of them — Paul never renounces his freedom, only his rights (cf. 9:12b). Precisely as he becomes a slave, both literally and figuratively, Paul not only maintains his freedom but exercises it to the fullest by conforming to the Lord in whom he has found freedom. Like Christ (Phil. 2:8), Paul obeys, but — also like Christ — he obeys freely. In so doing he can preach, with integrity, "the obedience of faith" to others.[26]

Paul sets forth his own pattern of life as the pattern for others to imitate in its essential character of status-renouncing, self-giving love. This is implicit in the juxtaposition of chapters 8 and 9 of 1 Corinthians and explicit in 1 Corinthians 10:24–11:1. The pattern Paul presents can now be summarized according to the status-renouncing ("although [x] not [y] but [z]") pattern, which he finds in Christ and in his own ministry, and which he commends to meat-eating Corinthian believers:

[x]: *possessing knowledge* (9:7-12a, 13-14; cf. 8:1a, 2, 4-6) *of one's status/freedom/rights* (9:1-6; cf. 8:8-9a);

[y]: *not using but renouncing rights* (9:12b, 15-18; cf. 8:13);

[z]: *self-enslaving to and loving of others* (9:19-23; cf. 8:7, 9-12)

Paul makes it clear, however, that the only reason for his being an example to the Corinthians is that his life is an imitation of Christ's, the paradigm of love (11:1).

Cruciform Adaptability

Paul's tent making, we have suggested, was in part an expression of his flexibility or adaptability. We have already noted that Paul experienced this adaptabil-

---

26. It must also be said that Paul's self-enslavement is, paradoxically, an expression of his authority. See especially Martin, *Slavery as Salvation,* pp. 117-35. Martin, however, incorrectly argues that "Paul's slavery to Christ in 1 Corinthians 9:16-18 does not represent self-abasement" (p. 117), when in fact Paul's slavery is the exercise of both authority and self-abasement, freedom and slavery, power and love. As Martin himself admits, the claim of no self-abasement "needs to be qualified" (p. 84) because as Christ's slave Paul gives up the right to be paid (pp. 84-85).

ity in ministry as a mode of cruciformity. He "enslaved himself to all" in order to "win" all — or at least as many as possible from all ethnic and socioeconomic groups, specifically Jews and Gentiles and "the weak" (1 Cor. 9:19-23). What specifically did this apostolic adaptability entail and mean?[27]

Let us begin with what it did *not* mean. Clearly for Paul his adaptability did not mean that he led a "chameleon-like" existence, that he was erratic, unpredictable, or inconsistent in his conduct.[28] Just as clearly, however, for some people his behavior was indefensible — which is precisely why he had to compose the self-defense contained in 1 Corinthians 9. Furthermore, although Paul certainly nuanced his preaching and pastoral instructions to reach each specific group or community, his adaptability does not refer to his gospel.[29] For him, the gospel of Christ crucified, resurrected, exalted, and returning was nonnegotiable; it was not only what he preached, but who he was. His flexibility had to embody, not in any way contradict, that gospel.

The bare facts suggested by the text are that Paul behaved like a Jew when ministering to Jews, like a Gentile when ministering to Gentiles, and like "the weak" when ministering to them:

> [20]To the Jews I became as a Jew, in order to win Jews. To those under the law I became as one under the law (though I myself am not under the law) so that I might win those under the law. [21]To those outside the law I became as one outside the law (though I am not free from God's law but am under Christ's law) so that I might win those outside the law. [22]To the weak I became weak, so that I might win the weak. I have become all things to all people, that I might by all means save some. [23]I do it all for the sake of the gospel, so that I may share in its blessings. (1 Cor. 9:20-23)

We can assume, therefore, that Paul followed the Jewish calendar and dietary laws when evangelizing Jews or working with Jewish communities of believers or groups of believers within his churches.[30] How often he did this, we do not

---

27. To a reader of Acts, there are episodes illustrative of the principle of flexibility (16:1-5; 21:17-26). To a reader of the letter to the Galatians, however, where Paul is inflexible on the issue of circumcision and apparently holds the Law in low esteem, Paul may at first glance appear to be exaggerating his case. In fact, however, Galatians proves his point; Paul will not allow the peculiarities of Jewish ritual and custom to be transferred onto the Gentiles who have been baptized into Christ.

28. Among many discussions, see the classic article by Henry Chadwick, "'All Things to All Men' (1 Cor. 9.22)," *New Testament Studies* 1 (1954-55): 261-75.

29. "He will adapt his behavior (not his message!) in whatever way necessary" to win people to the gospel (Hays, *First Corinthians*, p. 153).

30. This is not to say that Paul preached Torah as the Jewish means to salvation, only that

189

know, but he more often worked with Gentiles. In their presence he ignored such Jewish requirements so that they would not think that believing in Christ meant adapting Jewish customs. As for the weak (which may refer to weakness with respect to faith [1 Corinthians 8], socioeconomic status [1 Cor. 1:26-27], or both), Paul would have abandoned any prerogatives of conscience or class that would have been a barrier to their reception of the gospel message. Most likely, he is referring here especially to the working with his hands that gained him access to other laborers.

If Paul had followed the typical sophistic model of the teachers of his day, he would have sought a rich patron to house and support him, and to provide a suitable place for him to teach. He probably would have also charged for his teaching, an indication of its value, as well as a means of income. Had the apostle chosen this path, he would have clearly gained more contact, influence, and status among the wealthy of Corinth and other cities. However, he would have lost contact, effectiveness, and respect among the working class and the poorer levels of society.[31] Paul chose another path, a "downwardly mobile" option of identifying and working with those of lower status.

In sum, then, "Paul's slavery to Christ is expressed in the form of submitting himself in various ways to the cultural structures and limitations of the people he hopes to reach with the gospel."[32] Yet more important than the "what" of Paul's adaptability is the "why." What is explicitly stated in the parallel phrases of 9:20-21, and implied in yet another parallel phrase in 9:22, is that Paul's adaptability is a voluntary "movement" into a group of people by one who is not part of that group: "though I myself am not under the law . . . though I am not free from God's law but am under Christ's law . . . [though I myself am not weak]."[33] The pattern of adaptability is thus "although I was not bound to conform to the group, I did so anyhow for the sake of the gospel." This pattern is once again a direct echo of the pattern of Christ's love narrated

---

he was willing to submit to certain Jewish boundary markers in order to preach the crucified Messiah to his fellow Jews and not offend them on nonessential matters (see Gal. 5:6 and Romans 14).

31. See Hock, *Social Context,* pp. 50-55; Martin, *Slavery as Salvation,* p. 124; Graham Tomlin, *The Power of the Cross: Theology and the Death of Christ in Paul, Luther and Pascal* (Carlisle, U.K.: Paternoster, 1999), pp. 84-85.

32. Hays, *First Corinthians,* p. 153.

33. It is clear from 1 Corinthians 8 and Romans 14 that Paul did not consider himself part of the believing "weak" (probably those who followed Jewish calendar and dietary laws), and if "weak" meant also lower class (e.g., 1 Cor. 1:26-27), Paul was clearly not from that group but from the "upper 1-2 percent of well-educated people in his day" (Witherington, *Paul's Narrative Thought World,* p. 216), though how he attained that status, and what his "status of origin" was, are difficult historical questions.

in Philippians 2 and elsewhere: "though he was in the form of God" (Phil. 2:6); "though he was rich" (2 Cor. 8:9).[34] In other words, Paul's adaptability expresses his conformity to Christ. *The consistent element in his flexibility is the cruciform character of his actions,* whether among Jews, Gentiles, or the weak.

Paul can alter his behaviors because he does not believe that any of them — keeping Jewish dietary laws or not, for example — are essential to covenant life with God in Christ. These behaviors are what the Stoics termed *adiaphora* — nonessential matters.[35] Yet the apostle makes it clear that although the nature of the specific behaviors makes it possible for him to adapt or reject them depending on the audience, he must in some way follow the pattern of status renunciation if he wants to share in the blessings of the gospel (1 Cor. 9:23). That is, the specifics of cruciform adaptability are flexible (and, one might say, negotiable), but the general, cruciform pattern itself is consistent and required — at least for those who want a share in Christ's life now and later. Thus Paul's adaptability is not merely part of an "evangelistic strategy," for the gospel has an "inner dynamic" that requires Paul to "take the same self-lowering path taken by the Christ who was crucified."[36] In particular, as Paul's emphasis on accommodating to the "weak" demonstrates, cruciformity requires a "preferential option for the poor" and a kind of "downward mobility," to put Paul's words into contemporary idiom.[37]

Apostolic adaptability, then, entails a voluntary yet necessary — necessary in the sense of required and compelled by the paradigm of Christ's love — accommodation to the ethnic, religious, and socioeconomic sensitivities of others. It is not static but flexible; yet especially in Paul's communities, Paul's specific example of identifying with both Jews and Gentiles gave him the authority to urge others to do the same, in accord with the pattern of the one who gave himself for all (see Rom. 14:1–15:13, discussed in the next chapter).

Pastoral Care as Cruciform Love

In examining 1 Corinthians 9 we saw that for Paul apostolic cruciform love was both specific to his calling and capable of generalization for imitation by oth-

---

34. As noted in chapter eight, in all of these texts the Greek contains a "concessive" participle, translated "[al]though."

35. Paul restates this Stoic principle in very Christocentric terms in Rom. 14:1–15:13, urging the Roman believers to accept their differences and welcome one another.

36. Tomlin, *Power of the Cross,* p. 95. Tomlin appropriately notes Martin's apt comment that Paul's self-lowering is therefore "soteriologically significant" (*Slavery as Salvation,* p. 129).

37. See Hays, *First Corinthians,* p. 157.

ers. Such is the case with three other instances, two of which have already been mentioned in passing, in which he renounces his own rights or interest in the interest of others' welfare. Paul's action in particular situations is peculiar to his apostolic ministry but also worthy (from his perspective) of imitation.

1 Thessalonians

Paul's first letter to the Thessalonians begins with a thanksgiving that quickly becomes an apostolic apology, not unlike 1 Corinthians 9, based on the reality of the Thessalonians' response to the gospel and the integrity and very personal nature of the apostolic team's ministry (1:4–2:12, the thanksgiving resuming at 2:13). In chapter 2 Paul appears to be defending himself against charges by some of "deceit or impure motives or trickery" (2:3) as well as using "words of flattery" and having a "pretext for greed" (2:5). To describe his team's ministry to the Thessalonians, Paul draws upon the images of maternal and paternal relationships with children as well as the language of self-sacrifice. In using all of these images, as in the image of slavery in 1 Corinthians 9, Paul retells the narrative of his own (that is, his team's) ministry with the Thessalonians in parallel to the narrative of Christ. These parallels may be set out as follows:

Philippians 2:6-8	1 Thessalonians 2:5-12
[*x*]: [Christ Jesus,] **though** he was in the form of God,	[*x*]: . . . **though** we might have made demands as apostles of Christ (v. 7a)
[*y*]: did **not** regard equality with God as something to be **exploited**,	[*y*]: . . . we **never** came with words of flattery or with a **pretext for greed**; nor did we seek praise from mortals. . . . (vv. 5b-6) [implied in v. 7a: "we did not make demands/throw our weight around"] . . . our labor and toil . . . ; we worked night and day, so that we might **not** burden any of you. . . . (v. 9a-b)
[*z*]: **but** emptied **himself**, taking the form of a slave, being born [literally, "becoming"] in human likeness. And	[*z*]: **But** we were gentle among you like a nurse, tenderly caring for **her own** children. (v. 7b)

being found in human form, he humbled **himself** and became obedient to the point of death — even death on a cross.

. . . We are [or, "were"] determined to share with you not only the gospel of God but also **our own selves.** . . . (v. 8a)

. . . our labor and toil . . . ; we worked night and day, so that we might **not burden** any of you. . . . (v. 9a-b)

. . . we dealt with each one of you like a father with his children, urging and encouraging you. . . . (vv. 11-12a)

The first image (1 Thess. 2:7-8) is that of a nursing mother (or perhaps a [wet-]nurse nursing her *own* children; so NRSV) who is gentle with and cherishes each of her precious children. The image is in deliberate contradistinction to the description of how Paul and his companions could have been as apostles — "we might have made demands" (2:7) or, more literally, "we might have thrown our weight around" (Greek *dynamenoi en barei einai*). That is, they could have exercised their authority in a demanding and even harsh way, as some itinerant Cynics were known to do.[38] The Thessalonians, however, were as dear to Paul and his companions as are children to their loving mother in their most intimate moment — nursing. The image is reinforced with the references to deep caring and love in verse 8. This affection was demonstrated both in Paul's general self-giving (2:8b) and in his nonburdensome self-support (2:9).[39] In these matters, Paul, like Christ, renounced status and rights, refusing to use them for selfish gain or to place a burden on people — though he could have thrown around his apostolic weight. Instead, he chose the option of weakness (as his culture saw it) and love as the embodiment of his gospel in himself.[40]

Included in the imagery of Paul's relationship to the Thessalonians as that of a mother to her children is the following sentence, which was quoted in part above:

38. Abraham Malherbe, "Gentle as a Nurse," in *Paul and the Popular Philosophers* (Minneapolis: Fortress, 1989), pp. 35-48.

39. The Greek verb translated "burden" in 2:9 *(epibarēsai)* echoes the idiom in 2:7 translated "make demands" *(dynamenoi en barei einai),* both having a form of the word "weight" (root *bar-*) in them.

40. For the importance of Paul's embodying the gospel in himself in his work with the Thessalonians — that is, early in his ministry — see Jerry L. Sumney, "Paul's 'Weakness': An Integral Part of his Conception of Apostleship," *Journal for the Study of the New Testament* 52 (1993): 71-91, with special reference to 1 Thessalonians 2 on pp. 87-89.

So deeply do we constantly care [or, "did we care"] for you that we are [or, "were"] determined to share with you [Greek *metadounai*] not only the gospel of God but also our own selves [Greek *tas heautōn psychas*], because you have become very dear [Greek *agapētoi*] to us. (1 Thess. 2:8)

The maternal imagery in this text and its context is significant. The motherly affection that causes a woman to impart to her children their necessary sustenance and, more importantly, her whole self is analogous to the love that led Paul and his co-laborers to impart to the Thessalonians not only their "spiritual sustenance" — the gospel of God — but also their very selves.

The phrase "our own selves" (or, "our own souls/lives") continues the emotion-laden, personal language of the section. The context makes it clear, however, that the phrase means emotional involvement coupled with unrestrained sacrificial service, evidenced in working "night and day" so as not to burden the Thessalonians financially (2:9) and even in the act of preaching itself, which required boldness from God in the face of previous suffering and of opposition in Thessalonica (2:2; cf. 1:5-6; 3:3-4).

The expression "to share with you . . . our own selves" (Greek *metadounai . . . tas heautōn psychas*) is parallel to the pattern of Christ narratives that refer to Christ's death as self-giving or self-surrendering (Greek [*para*]*didonai heauton*).[41] The terminology and context of 2:8 suggest that Paul has adapted a Christological formula about Christ's self-giving death to the pastoral situation of interpreting his ministry to the Thessalonians.[42] When Paul says that he and

---

41. For example, Gal. 1:4; 2:20. Although the verbal prefix *meta-* with the Greek verb *didonai* is unexpected and does not appear in any of the "surrender formulae" preserved in the NT, this is probably a deliberate adaptation to the pastoral and emotive context. Likewise, Paul's use of the phrase "our own selves" *(tas heautōn psychas),* rather than the reflexive pronoun that he normally has in self-surrender formulae, is an appropriate adaptation to the purpose of the letter. The noun "self" or "life/soul" *(psychē),* rather than the reflexive pronoun, does occur in surrender formulae outside of Paul's letters: John 10:11; Mark 10:45; 1 John 3:16.

42. Two contextual factors further demonstrate that Paul is alluding to a Christological narrative pattern in 1 Thess. 2:8. First, as in Gal. 2:20 (cf. Rom. 15:1-3; Phil. 2:1-8), Paul's connection of love to self-giving appears (cf. *agapētoi*). Second, there is at least one, and perhaps another, reference to the Thessalonians' having become "imitators" of Paul and of the Lord by receiving the word in much affliction and suffering (1 Thess. 1:6; 2:14-15, if authentic). In 1:6 Paul depicts his suffering in ministry as something parallel to Jesus' suffering. In 2:8-10 he describes his ministry among the Thessalonians as one of self-giving and self-sacrifice (in pastoral care and in self-support). If Paul explicitly refers to his ministry as something akin to Jesus' sufferings (1:6), then it is likely that a description of his ministry, in the same general context, as self-sacrifice (2:8) would be an allusion to Christ's self-sacrifice. For an interpretation that highlights some of these parallels, see F. F. Bruce, *1 & 2 Thessalonians,* Word Biblical Commentary 45 (Waco, Tex.: Word, 1982), pp. 28-33.

his co-workers "shared themselves" with the Thessalonians in love, he is saying that their ministry had the shape of cruciform love in imitation of their Lord.

The maternal and sacrificial images are followed by a description in paternal terms. The point now is a relationship of instruction. Paul and his companions trained each of the Thessalonians in how to live in a manner worthy of God, just as a father would give moral education to his children. They did so without burdening them financially (2:9), which would be inappropriate for a father, and by "urging and encouraging" (2:12) rather than demanding. Once again, Paul says that he had decided not to throw his weight around but to treat the Thessalonians with Christ-like love.

2 Corinthians

The issue of Paul's refusal of support is raised not only in 1 Corinthians and 1 Thessalonians but also in 2 Corinthians. His refusal became especially acute when the people Paul sarcastically calls "super apostles" tried to convince the Corinthians that Paul and his gospel were inferior to them and their gospel, in part because they demonstrated greater eloquence and signs of power than did Paul, and in part because Paul refused money (2 Corinthians 10–13). This was a certain sign, so they apparently argued, of the lesser value of his message.

Immediately in responding to these charges Paul first of all associates himself with Christ:

> [1]I myself, Paul, appeal to you by the meekness and gentleness of Christ — I who am humble when face to face with you, but bold toward you when I am away. . . . [5]. . . [W]e take every thought captive to obey Christ. (2 Cor. 10:1, 5)

When he actually discusses his own refusal to take money (11:7-15) he again appeals to his similarity with Christ. He describes his refusal as an act of self-humbling ("humbling myself," 11:7; Greek *emauton tapeinōn*), once again an echo of the Christ narrative preserved especially in Philippians. Paul says also that he did not wish to burden anyone — and that he will continue to refuse to be a financial burden (11:9; cf. 1 Thess. 2:9).

Paul's obstinacy in this matter apparently led some to call it unloving or even sinful (11:7, 11), but Paul stands firm. Indeed, it is this refusal to be a financial burden that manifests his love for the Corinthians (11:11) — that is to say, Paul's understanding and experience of Christ-like cruciform love.

Philemon

In addition to the renunciation of rights as an expression of love for the Thessalonians and for the Corinthians, as we saw above, Paul also follows this course of action — with great rhetorical power and effect — in his briefest and very self-revelatory letter to Philemon. In this short letter of only twenty-five verses, Paul expresses his deep apostolic affection for the two main "characters" of the letter, employing the noun "love" three times in the letter (vv. 5, 7, 9), and referring to both Philemon the master and Onesimus the slave as "beloved" (vv. 1, 16).

The letter to Philemon has been subject to intense scholarly scrutiny in recent years, and the older interpretation — that Paul is trying to persuade Philemon to welcome and forgive his runaway slave Onesimus, who had stolen from his master, had met and been converted by Paul in prison, and wished to return to his master without being subject to cruel punishment — has been questioned.[43] Some newer readings of the letter point to the Roman practice of allowing slaves to seek out third-party help, often from a mutual friend, to settle disputes with their masters. Thus the runaway Onesimus guilty of theft may be a figment of our imagination; the nature of his wrong (v. 18) is unclear. Also, the specific goal of Paul's letter is debated. While some older readings suggested simply that Paul wanted Philemon not to treat Onesimus harshly for his crime, some contemporary interpretations understand Paul's goal to be Onesimus's release from slavery. Other readings stress Paul's (almost selfish?) desire to have Onesimus released to be his "useful" missionary assistant as the chief goal of the letter (cf. vv. 12-14).[44]

In any reading of the text, however, two things are clear. First, Paul is the "spiritual father" of both Onesimus, the new convert (v. 10) and potential "useful" servant in the gospel, and Philemon (v. 19), Paul's current "beloved fellow-worker" (v. 1 [NRSV, "dear friend and co-worker"]; cf. v. 17). That Philemon and Onesimus are now fellow believers, and spiritual sons of the same father, makes them both "brothers" (cf. v. 16). The complexity of rela-

---

43. In addition to the many recent commentaries, see the brilliant work of Norman R. Petersen, *Rediscovering Paul: Philemon and the Sociology of Paul's Narrative World* (Philadelphia: Fortress, 1985).

44. "Onesimus" means "useful," and there is a play on words with his name throughout the letter (especially vv. 11, 20). On the issues of the "occasion" of Philemon, the discussion of James D. G. Dunn, *The Epistles to the Colossians and Philemon: A Commentary on the Greek Text* (Grand Rapids: Eerdmans, 1996), pp. 301-7, is particularly lucid. Dunn is among those who reject the "fugitive slave" interpretation for the view that Onesimus sought out Paul as a third-party mediator.

tionships triggered by the conversion of Onesimus is astounding.[45] Second, Paul wants (and is confident of) Onesimus's obedience (v. 21) without ordering him to comply (v. 8). It is this tension between apostolic authority and individual freedom that creates the plot, conflict, and rhetoric of this letter's narrative (cf. especially vv. 8, 14).

One might argue that Paul attempts to manipulate Philemon into compliance by both heaping up praise (vv. 1-7) and inflicting feelings of guilt (vv. 17-19), not to mention possibly using peer pressure (by presenting the matter to the entire church, v. 2) and even a subtle threat (vv. 21-22). Yet Paul, at least, sees the issue at hand as one of love, specifically rights-renouncing and others-oriented cruciform love. First of all, he portrays his own dealings with Philemon as a form of rights-renouncing love, and then he urges Philemon to respond with the same kind of love, as he has done in the past.[46]

Paul narrates his own action vis-à-vis Philemon in the now-familiar pattern of rights-renouncing cruciform love, parallel to Philippians 2:

Philippians 2:6-8	Philemon 8-10, 14
[x]: [Christ Jesus,] **though** he was in the form of God,	[x]: [8]For this reason, **though** I am bold enough in Christ to command you to do your duty,
[y]: did **not** regard equality with God as something to be **exploited,**	[y]: [9]**yet** because of love I **encourage/appeal to** [Greek *parakalō*] you — and I, Paul, do this as an old man, and now also as a prisoner of Christ Jesus. [author's translation]
[z]: **but** emptied **himself,** taking the form of a slave, being born [literally, "becoming"] in human likeness. And being found in human form, he humbled **himself** and became obedient to the point of death — even death on a cross.	[z]: [10]I am appealing to you [or, "encouraging you," Greek *parakalō*] for my child, Onesimus, whose father I have become during my imprisonment. . . . [14]but **I preferred to do nothing without your consent,** in order that your good deed might be voluntary and not something forced.

45. See Petersen, *Rediscovering Paul,* pp. 22-24.

46. See the next chapter for a discussion of the response of love Paul expects from Philemon.

The pattern is clear: although Paul has the apostolic[47] right to force Philemon's acquiescence to his wish (whatever precisely it may be), he is voluntarily choosing to renounce the use of that power and choosing instead to appeal on the basis of Philemon's love (cf. vv. 5, 7) and freedom (v. 14).[48] Even the language itself is parallel to Philippians 2.

In the text set out above, I have offered my own translation of the first half of Philemon 9 *(y)* since the NRSV can erroneously be read to mean that the appeal, rather than the *decision* to appeal, is grounded in love: "I would rather appeal to you on the basis of love." Paul has already made that point by connecting ("for this reason") his decision to Philemon's love (vv. 7-8), but in verse 9 the point is that Paul's *decision* is a decision of love.[49] The NRSV phrase "on the basis of love" is better translated "because of love" and actually appears at the very beginning of the verse, not in the middle, indicating the reason for the shift from the use of apostolic boldness or authority to the use of everyday Christian encouragement, or *paraklēsis,* Paul's common term for Christians' mutual moral and spiritual responsibility. In effect, Paul has relinquished his role as apostle and chosen to become for the moment an ordinary believer, exercising the responsibilities of brother rather than apostle. To label this simply a rhetorical device or a thinly masked exercise of power is completely to miss the parallels Paul draws between himself and Christ.

Love, then, is both the motivation for the decision and the content of the decision, inasmuch as it is parallel to the self-emptying of Christ. Once again, Paul has — ironically — exercised his apostolic authority by *not* exercising it, but rather by imitating the cruciform love of Christ. Even more ironically, in so doing he exercises in truth the authority of his office. As noted above, Paul desperately wants Philemon to respond with love, both to him and to Onesimus. For Paul, the two responses are inseparable, even one response (vv. 17, 20).

To reinforce this desire, Paul takes yet another step and offers to absorb the

---

47. This must surely be the force of Paul's "I am bold enough in Christ."

48. Arguing, as some do, that Paul's refusal to exercise authority is only a rhetorical device is a failure to recognize the Christological roots and significance of Paul's decision. See, for example, Chris Frilingos, "'For My Child, Onesimus': Paul and Domestic Power in Philemon," *Journal of Biblical Literature* 119 (2000): 91-104, here p. 100. While Frilingos is right that Paul exercises a kind of paternal "gentle compulsion" (pp. 103-4) toward Philemon, he underestimates the (paradoxical, tension-creating) role of Paul's humility and brotherly equality with Philemon.

49. The Greek phrase *dia tēn agapēn* ("because of love") precedes the main verbal phrase *mallon parakalō* and, especially in connection with *mallon,* indicates the reason for the transition from wielding authority to engaging in *paraklēsis.* Dunn (*Colossians and Philemon,* p. 326), with most commentators, disagrees and thinks the "love" is the same love (Philemon's) of which Paul has already spoken.

costs of any wrongs Onesimus may have done, any debts he may owe: "If he has wronged you in any way, or owes you anything, charge that to my account" (v. 18). Again Paul is offering to act in imitation of Christ, absorbing the injuries of another (cf. Rom. 15:1-3), hopeful that Philemon will follow his example. (In v. 19b Paul also unambiguously reminds Philemon that he owes Paul a great debt, his very self/soul/salvation!)

For Paul, then, his apostolic ministry of care for converts in this instance — as in the others we have examined — is both motivated and shaped by the cruciform love of Christ, whatever additional rhetorical strategies he brings to the situation. He offers himself, thereby, as a narrative continuation of the cross of his Lord, and he invites others to join in the story that his ministry continues to unfold. That is the essence of pastoral ministry, in his estimation.

Suffering Love

Paul is popularly — and rightly — known as the apostle who suffered dearly for his convictions. Paul himself, on several occasions and as a point of pride, recalls and lists for his readers the physical and psychological pain he has endured for the sake of the gospel and his communities. What readers of Paul do not always recognize, however, is that for Paul *suffering is a manifestation of love*.[50] For those who confess the love of God in the death of Jesus, two existential corollaries automatically follow: suffering for others is inevitable, and suffering for others must be motivated by love in order to be worthwhile. Paul not only believes this but attempts to live by it and to interpret his experience (and then by extension the life of his communities) in light of it. As we examine the texts in which Paul recounts and interprets his experience of suffering, we find four key elements of Paul's experience and its meaning for him:

1. suffering allows Paul to identify with and express to others the self-sacrificial, nonretaliatory love of God in Christ — that is, in Christ's death;
2. suffering is, for Paul, a chief source of his identity and honor as an apostle;
3. Paul is willing to sacrifice everything, even his physical life or his salvation, for the sake of others; and

---

50. Jerome H. Neyrey, *Paul, in Other Words: A Cultural Reading of His Letters* (Louisville: Westminster/John Knox, 1990), pp. 167-80, mistakenly asserts, with little support from the text, that Paul understands suffering as "the attack of Satan and Evil Powers on God's holy people" (p. 168). While this is occasionally the case (2 Cor. 12:7 and perhaps 2 Cor. 11:29), Paul's suffering is primarily related to his experience of Christ's love and power, not evil powers.

4. even, and especially, in suffering, Paul experiences the love of God in Christ by means of the Spirit.

We turn now to the texts in which Paul recounts and reflects upon this suffering, giving special attention to the first two elements noted above.

Suffering as Apostolic Love and Identity

As noted above, Paul provides his readers, especially the Corinthians, with several lists, or "catalogs," of his own sufferings. In 1 Corinthians 4 we first find the following general self-description of apostolic ministry, set in contrast to the understanding of a believer's existence (and probably apostolic ministry) held by many of the Corinthians:

> [8]Already you have all you want! Already you have become rich! Quite apart from us you have become kings! Indeed, I wish that you had become kings, so that we might be kings with you! [9]For I think that God has exhibited us apostles as last of all, as though sentenced to death, because we have become a spectacle to the world, to angels and to mortals. [10]We are fools for the sake of Christ, but you are wise in Christ. We are weak, but you are strong. You are held in honor, but we in disrepute. [11]To the present hour we are hungry and thirsty, we are poorly clothed and beaten and homeless, [12]and we grow weary from the work of our own hands. When reviled, we bless; when persecuted, we endure; [13]when slandered, we speak kindly. We have become like the rubbish of the world, the dregs of all things, to this very day. (1 Cor. 4:8-13)

In this passage Paul is contrasting the often miserable experience of himself and his fellow ministers with the claims to exalted experience made by certain Corinthians, especially perhaps certain leaders. In addition to stark generalizations in which "[e]choes of crucifixion abound"[51] — "last of all," "sentenced to death" and a "spectacle to the world,"[52] "rubbish of the world," and "dregs of all things" — Paul notes the specific sufferings of public disgrace and psychological pain ("fools," "disrepute," "reviled," "slandered"), physical deprivation ("weak," "hungry and thirsty," "poorly clothed and . . . homeless"), fatigue from

---

51. Tomlin, *Power of the Cross*, p. 94.

52. Together these two phrases should probably be rendered "like men condemned to death in the arena," referring metaphorically to combat with wild beasts or gladiators in the Roman amphitheater (John S. Pobee, *Persecution and Martyrdom in the Theology of Paul*, JSNTSup 6 [Sheffield: JSOT Press, 1985], pp. 1-2).

physical labor ("weary from the work of our own hands"[53]), and physical pain ("beaten," "persecuted"). These same categories reappear in other catalogs.[54]

What is especially striking in this eloquent, rhetorically powerful text is the echo of the beatitudes and Jesus' teachings about enemy love preserved in the "Sermon on the Mount" in Matthew's gospel and the "Sermon on the Plain" in Luke's:[55]

> [3]Blessed are the poor in spirit, for theirs is the kingdom of heaven. [4]Blessed are those who mourn, for they will be comforted. [5]Blessed are the meek, for they will inherit the earth. [6]Blessed are those who hunger and thirst for righteousness, for they will be filled. [7]Blessed are the merciful, for they will receive mercy. . . . [10]Blessed are those who are persecuted for righteousness' sake, for theirs is the kingdom of heaven. [11]Blessed are you when people revile you and persecute you and utter all kinds of evil against you falsely on my account. [12]Rejoice and be glad, for your reward is great in heaven, for in the same way they persecuted the prophets who were before you. (Matt. 5:3-7, 10-12)

> [43]You have heard that it was said, "You shall love your neighbor and hate your enemy." [44]But I say to you, Love your enemies and pray for those who persecute you. (Matt. 5:43-44)

> [28][B]less those who curse you, pray for those who abuse you. . . . [32]If you love those who love you, what credit is that to you? For even sinners love those who love them. . . . [36]Be merciful, just as your Father is merciful. (Luke 6:28, 32, 36)

Paul again echoes these texts in his admonition to nonretaliatory love in Romans 12:9-21:

> [9]Let love be genuine; hate what is evil, hold fast to what is good; [10]love one another with mutual affection. . . . [14]Bless those who persecute you; bless and do not curse them. . . . [19]Beloved, never avenge yourselves. . . . (Rom. 12:9-10a, 14, 19a)

Paul's citation of these teachings of Jesus demonstrates implicitly in 1 Corinthians 4, and explicitly in Romans 12, that he understands suffering for the gospel, without retaliation, to be an expression of love for enemies. These may

53. Compare 1 Thess. 2:9; 1 Cor. 9:6-7, 13-14, 18; 2 Cor. 11:7-11; 2 Thess. 3:8.
54. See the chart of Paul's sufferings in ch. 11, pp. 286-87.
55. Material from the putative "Q" source.

be enemies of the gospel in general or opponents of his ministry in particular. Paul knows that to be a "steward" of the divine "mysteries" (1 Cor. 4:1) of the God who loved enemies in the cross (Rom. 5:6-8), and of the Lord who taught enemy love in his ministry on earth (Matthew 5; Luke 6), requires no less love. Furthermore, he is convinced that in such suffering for the sake of the gospel, he is expressing his love also for the "beloved children" (1 Cor. 4:14) whom he has spiritually fathered, and whom he loves so dearly that he feels compelled to discipline them with the truth of the gospel of the cross.

Additional catalogs and descriptions of suffering in the Corinthian correspondence are found in 2 Corinthians 1:3-11; 4:7-12; 6:3-10; 11:23-29; 12:10. This letter contains Paul's most comprehensive explanation and defense of his ministry, and in it suffering clearly figures prominently. In some of these texts, Paul's focus is on suffering primarily as power and as ground of hope, and they will be considered carefully in those later chapters. Nonetheless, suffering as cruciform love is never far from Paul's mind.

2 Corinthians is a challenging and complicated composition, addressing distinct yet related topics. Scholars have often divided the letter into two or more letters, distinguishing among the tone and contents of chapters 1–7 (often minus 6:14–7:1, which many believe to be an interpolation), chapters 8–9 (sometimes seen as two letters), and chapters 10–13.[56] For our purposes, which focus on texts from chapters 1–7 and 10–13, we may simply note that Paul's tone is generally conciliatory and explanatory in chapters 1–7, where reconciliation with God and with the Corinthians is the preeminent theme, while it is critical and defensive in chapters 10–13. In the latter chapters, Paul is dealing head-on with people he considers to be "super-" (11:5) or "false" (11:13) apostles, Satanic messengers of darkness posing as angels of light (13:14). With a rhetorical "pull-out-all-the-stops" approach, he lambasts his opponents' refusal, as he sees it, to embrace and embody the one gospel of the cross. In both sections of 2 Corinthians, Paul emphasizes that he is motivated by love.

In the more conciliatory section, chapters 1–7, Paul clearly expresses his affection for the Corinthians and describes his suffering as a form of his love that redounds to their benefit. The letter opens with Paul's claim that apostolic affliction is accompanied by divine consolation, and that both are ultimately for the Corinthians' good:

> [3]Blessed be the God and Father of our Lord Jesus Christ, the Father of mercies and the God of all consolation, [4]who consoles us in all our affliction, so that

---

56. For these issues, see the introduction to any commentary on 2 Corinthians, such as Victor Paul Furnish, *II Corinthians*, Anchor Bible 32A (Garden City, N.Y.: Doubleday, 1984).

we may be able to console those who are in any affliction with the consolation with which we ourselves are consoled by God. ⁵For just as the sufferings of Christ are abundant for us, so also our consolation is abundant through Christ. ⁶If we are being afflicted, it is **for** [Greek *hyper*] **your consolation** and salvation; if we are being consoled, it is **for** [*hyper*] **your consolation**, which you experience when you patiently endure the same sufferings that we are also suffering. ⁷Our hope for you is unshaken; for we know that as you share in our sufferings, so also you share in our consolation. (2 Cor. 1:3-7)

This claim sets the tone for the entire letter (or at least chapters 1–7) by trying to assure the Corinthians that *whatever* Paul has done in the course of his ministry, but especially his suffering, he has done it for them, as he stresses again in chapter 4:

> ⁷But we have this treasure in clay jars, so that it may be made clear that this extraordinary power belongs to God and does not come from us. ⁸We are afflicted in every way, but not crushed; perplexed, but not driven to despair; ⁹persecuted, but not forsaken; struck down, but not destroyed; ¹⁰always carrying in the body the death of Jesus, so that the life of Jesus may also be made visible in our bodies. ¹¹For while we live, we are always being given up to death for Jesus' sake, so that the life of Jesus may be made visible in our mortal flesh. ¹²So death is at work in us, but life in you. ¹³But just as we have the same spirit of faith that is in accordance with scripture — "I believed, and so I spoke" — we also believe, and so we speak, ¹⁴because we know that the one who raised the Lord Jesus will raise us also with Jesus, and will bring us with you into his presence. ¹⁵Yes, **everything is for your sake**, so that grace, as it extends to more and more people, may increase thanksgiving, to the glory of God. (2 Cor. 4:7-15 [emphasis added])

Paul, in other words, does not suffer for his own benefit but for the benefit of others, here specifically the Corinthians. In so doing, he and his colleagues "carry in the body" the life-giving death of Jesus, which was itself a death for others — "for [*hyper*] all" — motivated by love and carried out for the benefit of all (2 Cor. 4:15). To suffer for the gospel of the cross is to extend the life-giving, loving death of Jesus on that cross to those who do not yet know its benefits.

It is within this context that Paul can try to effect reconciliation with the Corinthians on several fronts. Paul's postponed visit (1:15–2:4) was not the result of vacillation or unfaithfulness, but of love, to "spare" the Corinthians "another painful visit" (1:23; 2:1) by substituting a letter written "out of much distress and anguish of heart and with many tears, not to cause you pain, but to let you know the abundant love that I have for you" (2:4). Whatever else we perceive in this text, we cannot miss the emotional pain that Paul has experienced in his attempt to love the Corinthians as he feels he ought.[57]

Again and again in 2 Corinthians 1–7 Paul refuses to "proclaim" (4:5) or even "commend" himself (3:1-6; 5:12; 6:4), even while commending himself as an apostle of integrity and cruciformity (1:12; 4:2). The language of affection is meant to prepare the readers for the ultimate call to reconciliation in 5:11–6:13.[58] Enveloping Paul's message of God's reconciling activity in the loving death of Jesus (5:14b-6:2) is an equally potent reminder that Paul's ministry is part of that ongoing divine reconciliation (5:11-14a; 6:3-13). Though perceived as "beside ourselves" (5:13), Paul and his colleagues are "ambassadors for Christ" (5:20) inasmuch as their ministry bears the marks of suffering love. For that reason, reconciliation with this apostolic ministry is essential to complete reconciliation with God. Paul's emotions spill onto the page as he relates to the Corinthians the narrative of his cruciform love for them:

> [3]We are putting no obstacle in anyone's way, so that no fault may be found with our ministry, [4]but as servants of God we have commended ourselves in every way: through great endurance, in afflictions, hardships, calamities, [5]beatings, imprisonments, riots, labors, sleepless nights, hunger; [6]by purity, knowledge, patience, kindness, holiness of spirit, **genuine** [*anypokritō*][59] **love**, [7]truthful speech, and the power of God; with the weapons of righteousness for the right hand and for the left; [8]in honor and dishonor, in ill repute and good repute. We are treated as impostors, and yet are true; [9]as unknown, and yet are well known; as dying, and see — we are alive; as punished, and yet not killed; [10]as sorrowful, yet always rejoicing; as poor, yet making many rich; as having nothing, and yet possessing everything. [11]We have spoken frankly to you Corinthians; **our heart is wide open to you**. [12]There is no restriction in our affections, but only in yours. [13]In return — I speak as to children — open wide your hearts also. (2 Cor. 6:3-13 [emphasis added])

Similarly, in 2 Corinthians 10–13, where he writes more defensively, Paul urges the Corinthians to accept his suffering not only as a sign of divine power but also as a manifestation of love. He begins these chapters with a claim to be

57. As we will see in the next chapter, the theme of love continues in 2 Cor. 2:1-5, where Paul attempts to get the congregation to reconcile with an offender.

58. In a brilliant rhetorical move, language of the "heart" allows Paul both to express love and to receive a commendation: "You yourselves are our letter, written on our hearts, to be known and read by all . . . a letter of Christ, prepared by us, written . . . not on tablets of stone but on tablets of human hearts" (3:2-3).

59. As in Rom. 12:9.

acting "by the meekness and gentleness of Christ" (10:1), even if that, ironically, means "punish[ing] every disobedience when your obedience is complete" (10:6). This "gentle authority," given by Christ, is further explained as given to Paul "for building you up [Greek *eis oikodomēn*] and not for tearing you down" (10:8), language that is crucial to Paul's understanding of love. So, too, near the conclusion of these chapters Paul reminds his readers that they are his "beloved," and that everything he does "is for the sake of building you up [*oikodomēs*]" (12:19; cf. 13:10). For Paul, in other words, all apostolic activity must be edifying, working out for the welfare of others, whether in the form of apostolic correction or other apostolic ministry, since all ministry springs from the "edifying" or loving reality of the crucified Messiah.

Thus Paul suggests not only that his defense of his own ministry is edifying or loving — that is, essentially cruciform — and thus properly apostolic, but, more importantly, that his normal apostolic ministry is fundamentally driven by cruciform love. This applies both to his refusal of financial support — which some saw in a very poor light — and, by extension, to his other forms of suffering:

> ⁷Did I commit a sin by humbling myself so that you might be exalted, because I proclaimed God's good news to you free of charge? ⁸I robbed other churches by accepting support from them in order to serve you. ⁹And when I was with you and was in need, I did not burden anyone, for my needs were supplied by the friends who came from Macedonia. So I refrained and will continue to refrain from burdening you in any way. ¹⁰As the truth of Christ is in me, this boast of mine will not be silenced in the regions of Achaia. ¹¹And why? **Because I do not love you? God knows I do!** (11:7-11 [emphasis added])

> ¹⁴Here I am, ready to come to you this third time. And I will not be a burden, because I do not want what is yours but you; for children ought not to lay up for their parents, but parents for their children. ¹⁵I will most gladly spend and be spent for you [literally, "for your souls," Greek *hyper tōn psychōn hymōn*]. **If I love you more, am I to be loved less?** (12:14-15 [emphasis added])

"To spend and be spent for you/your souls" functions as a motto of Paul's apostolic existence. Its referent is not, however, merely the spending of money, but rather the spending of self in manual labor and in physical and psychological suffering for the Corinthians: "weaknesses, insults, hardships, persecutions, and calamities for the sake of Christ [Greek *hyper Christou*]" (12:10). For Paul, suffering for others (12:15) is ultimately suffering for Christ (12:10) — who suffered for others.

Paul relates similar experiences in his letter to the Romans, in which he quotes the Septuagint text of Psalm 43:23 (44:22):

For your sake we are being killed all day long; we are accounted as sheep to be slaughtered. (Rom. 8:36)

The language is remarkably cruciform and thus appropriate, echoing both the tradition of Jesus' loving death ("for your sake") and the suffering servant hymn ("reckoned as sheep for the slaughter"; cf. Isa. 53:4, 7). Paul and his colleagues thereby experience suffering as a participation in the love of Christ, the servant who suffers and dies for his people.[60]

It is for this reason that Paul's ministry is an extension of Christ's; inasmuch as Paul and other ministers suffer for others, for the gospel of Christ, they are "ministers of Christ" (2 Cor. 11:23).[61] About this Paul will boast — that he in his sufferings embraces and embodies the suffering love of God in Christ, which is the power of God. Thus his most thorough catalog of sufferings appears in the form of a boast about participating in this authentic ministry of Christ:

[21]To my shame, I must say, we were too weak for that! But whatever anyone dares to boast of — I am speaking as a fool — I also dare to boast of that. [22]Are they Hebrews? So am I. Are they Israelites? So am I. Are they descendants of Abraham? So am I. [23]Are they ministers of Christ? I am talking like a madman — I am a better one: with far greater labors, far more imprisonments, with countless floggings, and often near death. [24]Five times I have received from the Jews the forty lashes minus one. [25]Three times I was beaten with rods. Once I received a stoning. Three times I was shipwrecked; for a night and a day I was adrift at sea; [26]on frequent journeys, in danger from rivers, danger from bandits, danger from my own people, danger from Gentiles, danger in the city, danger in the wilderness, danger at sea, danger from false brothers and sisters; [27]in toil and hardship, through many a sleepless night, hungry and thirsty, often without food, cold and naked. [28]And, besides other things, I am under daily pressure because of my anxiety for all the churches. [29]Who is weak, and I am not weak? Who is made to stumble, and I am not indignant? [30]If I must boast, I will boast of the things that show my weakness. (2 Cor. 11:21-30)

60. See Luke Timothy Johnson, *Reading Romans: A Literary and Theological Commentary* (New York: Crossroad, 1997), pp. 136-37.

61. According to Dieter Georgi, in the text of this verse (printed below), "one catches a glimpse of the face of Jesus himself" (*Theocracy in Paul's Praxis and Theology* [Minneapolis: Fortress, 1991], p. 64).

This text, which clearly links weakness to true apostolicity, will be explored more thoroughly in chapter 11 on power, to which weakness is linked in 12:9-10. For now we simply note again that, for Paul, cruciformity in suffering love is the focus of his pride and honor as an apostle.

Willing to Make the Ultimate Sacrifice: Choosing Death over Life

We have already noted the emotional price that Paul says his love for others cost him (2 Cor. 11:28). The depth of this feeling and commitment is expressed most forcefully in a text conveying Paul's love, not for believing communities, but for unbelieving Israel:

> [1]I am speaking the truth in Christ — I am not lying; my conscience confirms it by the Holy Spirit — [2]I have great sorrow and unceasing anguish in my heart. [3]For I could wish that I myself were accursed and cut off from Christ for the sake of my own people, my kindred according to the flesh. (Rom. 9:1-3)

Here Paul begins his famous essay on the faithlessness of Israel and the faithfulness of God by expressing his willingness to sacrifice himself for the sake of his fellow — but unbelieving — Jews.[62] Paul is prepared to surrender his attachment to Christ, and thus his gift of salvation and eternal life, for the sake of his people. This is Paul's echoing of the pattern of self-sacrificial love that he has experienced in Christ.[63] Whether deliberate or instinctual, we cannot determine, but sincere and painful it clearly was.

---

62. There has been some debate about the grammar and hence the meaning of the phrase in v. 3 translated "For I could wish." Whether or not Paul thought his wish attainable, the context suggests that it is a real, heartfelt desire (so also James D. G. Dunn, *Romans,* Word Biblical Commentary 38A, 38B, 2 vols. [Waco, Tex.: Word, 1988], 2:524) in the present, not the past (so also Joseph A. Fitzmyer, *Romans: A New Translation with Introduction and Commentary,* Anchor Bible 33 [New York: Doubleday, 1993], p. 544).

63. As Richard Hays points out, Paul's willingness to sacrifice himself expressed in these verses also has connections to the Akedah tradition of Abraham (and God) not sparing his beloved son (*Echoes of Scripture in the Letters of Paul* [New Haven: Yale University Press, 1989], p. 62). Paul's language in Rom. 9:3, in fact, is reminiscent of Rom. 8:32: the phrase "for the sake of [Greek *hyper*] my own people" echoes "[God] gave him [the Son] up for [*hyper*] all of us." However, the difference — willingness to sacrifice self, versus one's beloved son — means that Paul's interest is more in Paul's resemblance to Christ, not God. The text therefore reminds us also of 2 Cor. 5:14-15: Christ "died for [*hyper*] all."

Suffering Love and the Experience of God's Love in Christ

Paul's "fascination" with suffering, as we have repeatedly seen, is rooted in his conviction that God's love has been made real and human in an act of self-giving suffering for others. Paul believes with all his heart that the cross is the ultimate icon of both Christ's love and God's. Thus for Paul, unlike so many others who have suffered, suffering does not represent God's abandonment or absence. What sustains Paul is his certainty that God in Christ is present with him and for him as he suffers for others, just as God was present in the death of Christ. Paul addresses this most succinctly and powerfully at the conclusion of Romans 8.

Romans 8:31-39 is "one of the most stunning pieces of rhetorical art in the New Testament."[64] In it Paul pours out his soul about the depths of his suffering and yet about the absolute certainty of God's presence in the midst of the current pain, as well as God's final victory in the future:

> [31]What then are we to say about these things? If God is for us, who is against us? [32]He who **did not withhold his own Son**, but gave him up for all of us, will he not with him also give us everything else? [33]Who will bring any charge against God's elect? It is God who justifies. [34]Who is to condemn? It is Christ Jesus, who died, yes, who was raised, who is at the right hand of God, who indeed intercedes for us. [35]Who will **separate us from the love of Christ**? Will hardship, or distress, or persecution, or famine, or nakedness, or peril, or sword? [36]As it is written, "For your sake we are being killed all day long; we are accounted as sheep to be slaughtered." [37]No, in all these things we are more than conquerors through him who **loved** us. [38]For I am convinced that neither death, nor life, nor angels, nor rulers, nor things present, nor things to come, nor powers, [39]nor height, nor depth, nor anything else in all creation, will be able to **separate us from the love of God in Christ Jesus our Lord.** (Rom. 8:31-39 [emphasis added])

Clearly Paul is convinced that the faithfulness of God, the love of God expressed on the cross, remains reliable. The past is God's promise about both the present and the future. If nothing whatsoever can separate the apostle from "the love of God in Christ Jesus our Lord," then neither can anything stop him from sharing that love with others. Rather than feeling unloved by God in the thick of sufferings, Paul feels loved by the One who gave and the One who died. As such a beloved child and servant of God, Paul labors to let others know that

---

64. Johnson, *Reading Romans,* p. 133. We will have more to say about this passage in the discussion of cruciform hope in ch. 12.

suffering for the good of another can be an experience, not of God's absence and disfavor, but of God's presence and love.

Choosing Life over Death

Paul loved his communities, but he also knew that a final victory awaited him and all believers after this current time of suffering. Few readers of Paul's letters recognize the attraction that death would have had to him, particularly during or after especially trying times of being persecuted for preaching his gospel. In 2 Corinthians, for example, in which Paul repeatedly recalls his many experiences of suffering for Christ and the churches, he says this after cataloguing his sufferings and meditating on their purpose (4:7-15):

> [16]So we do not lose heart. Even though our outer nature is wasting away, our inner nature is being renewed day by day. . . . 5[1]For we know that if the earthly tent we live in is destroyed, we have a building from God, a house not made with hands, eternal in the heavens. [2]For in this tent we groan, longing to be clothed with our heavenly dwelling. . . . [6]. . . [E]ven though we know that while we are at home in the body we are away from the Lord. . . . [8]. . . [W]e would rather be away from the body and at home with the Lord. (2 Cor. 4:16; 5:1-2, 6, 8 [emphasis added])

So too in his letter to the Philippians, written while a prisoner "for Christ" (1:13), Paul expresses the superiority of death as he contemplates his future fate:

> [20]It is my eager expectation and hope that I will not be put to shame in any way, but that by my speaking with all boldness, Christ will be exalted now as always in my body, whether by life or by death. [21]For to me, living is Christ and dying is gain. [22]If I am to live in the flesh, that means fruitful labor for me; and I do not know which I prefer [literally, "choose"]. [23]I am hard pressed between the two: my desire is to depart and be with Christ, for that is far better. (Phil. 1:20-23)

Though it is clear that Paul is struggling with his "preference," either life or death, it is equally clear which fate he considers better for him personally: to die and gain — gain his home in the presence of his Lord.

The intensity of Paul's struggle expressed in this passage (1:18b-26) is heightened when we realize, however, that he is almost certainly wrestling not merely with a preference over which he has no control (such as the outcome of his pending trial), but with an agonizing choice.[65] Indeed, the Greek word rendered "prefer" at the end of v. 22 — "I do not know which I *prefer*" — is really the word "choose."[66] What Paul contemplates, then, is a choice, a decision. That decision is whether to find a way to end his own life — or at least not to try to prevent someone else (such as a Roman official) from ending his life.

It is unbelievable to many that the apostle Paul would ever consider "suicide," or voluntary death, but in this very self-revealing passage, that may be precisely what we see.[67] "Dying is gain" is a commonplace in antiquity's discourse about suicide, when suicide was frequently viewed as a "noble death." Paul's struggle can only be fully appreciated in the context of the ideas expressed by a near contemporary, the Stoic Seneca:

> No general statement can be made, therefore, with regard to the question whether, when a power beyond our control threatens us with death, we should anticipate death, or await it. For there are many arguments to pull us in either direction. If one death is accompanied by torture, and the other is simple and easy, why not snatch the latter? Just as I shall select my ship when I am about to go on a voyage, or my house when I propose to take a residence, so I shall choose my death when I am about to depart from life. Moreover, just as a long-drawn-out life does not necessarily mean a better one, so

65. These verses in Philippians may exemplify, more poignantly than any others, the truth of Richard B. Hays's assertion that Paul is "theologizing as he writes" (*The Moral Vision of the New Testament: A Contemporary Introduction to New Testament Ethics* [San Francisco: HarperCollins, 1996], p. 19). Indeed, here we see Paul vigorously engaging in personal, theological decision making as he writes. That the decision-making process is done in public reflects Paul's honesty and vulnerability; that it is resolved in favor of cruciformity bespeaks his apostolic integrity.

66. Both RSV and NIV render the verb "shall choose." The Greek is the future form of the verb "to choose" *(hairēsomai),* not the present tense of "to want," "to wish" (e.g., *boulomai, thelō*), or a similar verb. "Prefer" (NRSV) is therefore misleading.

67. For similar readings of this passage that stress Paul's having real choice, see C. S. Wansink, *Chained in Christ,* JSNTSup 130 (Sheffield: Sheffield Academic Press, 1996), pp. 97-125, as well as Arthur Droge and J. D. Tabor, *A Noble Death: Suicide and Martyrdom among Christians and Jews in Antiquity* (San Francisco: Harper & Row, 1992), pp. 119-26. It is possible, of course, that Paul considers "a more passive form of voluntary death" (Wansink, *Chained in Christ,* pp. 119-24; Stephen E. Fowl, "Christology and Ethics in Philippians 2:5-11," in Ralph P. Martin and Brian J. Dodd, eds., *Where Christology Began: Essays on Philippians 2* [Louisville: Westminster/John Knox, 1998], p. 147), such as not appealing a death sentence, but even these are still choices for death, not life. For an important analysis of this text and its function for Paul in exhorting others to faithfulness and selfless love, even to the point of death, see Stephen E. Fowl, "Believing Forms Seeing: Formation for Martyrdom in Philippians," forthcoming from Eerdmans in a collection of essays on character ethics and biblical interpretation, edited by William Brown.

a long-drawn-out death necessarily means a worse one. There is no occasion when the soul should be humoured more than at the moment of death. Let the soul depart as it feels itself impelled to go; whether it seeks the sword, or the halter [noose], or some draught that attacks the veins [poison], let it proceed and burst the bonds of its slavery. Every man ought to make his life acceptable to others besides himself, but his death to himself alone. The best form of death is the one we like. . . . Reason, too, advises us to die, if we may, according to our taste; if this cannot be, she advises us to die according to our ability, and to seize upon whatever means shall offer itself for doing violence to ourselves. It is criminal to "live by robbery"; but, on the other hand, it is most noble to "die by robbery" [suicide]. (*Epistle* 70.11-12, 28, Loeb translation)

The idea that a prisoner like Paul would have the means to commit suicide is not at all farfetched. In fact, Seneca's theoretical reflections quoted above are followed by practical advice: examples of how gladiators (and thus prisoners) found creative ways to commit suicide, and not always with a weapon (*Epistle* 70.19-27). Had Paul possessed the desire, he could have found the means.

The passage Paul composes to the Philippians contains many of the themes found in Seneca's epistle. Like Seneca, Paul is tempted to do what is best for himself and most attractive. This temptation may have been to active suicide or, perhaps more likely, what we might call "passive" suicide — a steadfast opposition to anything that might lead to his release from the Roman guard rather than his death as a martyr.[68] Yet at both the beginning and the end of the passage Paul also expresses his absolute conviction that he will not die:

> [19]I know that through your prayers and the help of the Spirit of Jesus Christ this will turn out for my deliverance. . . . [25]Since I am convinced of this, I know that I will remain and continue with all of you for your progress and joy in faith, [26]so that I may share abundantly in your boasting in Christ Jesus when I come to you again. (Phil. 1:19, 25-26)

This certainty does not merely express his faith in Roman justice or divine deliverance, though it does reveal belief in the latter. More importantly, however, it expresses Paul's commitment to apostolic cruciform love, to choosing that which is "more necessary for you" (1:24).

Considerations of "necessity" were also part of the Stoic discourse on suicide, but Paul cannot share Seneca's self-oriented approach to death: "Every

---

68. Wansink (*Chained in Christ*, pp. 119-24) suggests that Paul contemplated imitating Christ by remaining silent before his Roman accusers.

man ought to make his life acceptable to others besides himself, but his death to himself alone. The best form of death is the one we like." No, says Paul, whether in life or death I want "Christ . . . [to be] exalted now as always in my body" (1:20), and that can only happen when he chooses the way of cruciform love, the way of preferring the needs of others (in this case the Philippians) over his own desires. The pattern of cruciform love is clearly expressed, especially in verses 23-26:

[x] Although I prefer to die, for it is far better (v. 23; cf. v. 21),
[y] I will not choose death (v. 25a),
[z] but life, because that is more necessary for you, for your progress and joy in the faith (vv. 24, 25b-26).

In a very real sense, then, "the real sacrifice for Paul was remaining alive."[69] Paul finds a self-controlled death — despite its gains, indeed *because* of its gains — to be a selfish act. In narrating this decision (or perhaps even deciding while narrating), Paul sets himself up as an "imitator" of Christ's self-emptying (2:6-8) and thus as a worthy paradigm for the Philippians, whom he will urge, beginning in 1:27, also to embody cruciform love.[70]

Conclusion: The Story of Paul's Love

Paul was driven by love and wanted his churches to know that his sometimes odd behavior, not to mention his suffering, was motivated by nothing else. He

---

69. Droge and Tabor, *Noble Death,* p. 122. It is important, however, not to follow the flawed logic of Droge and Tabor, who attempt to argue that Paul and other early Christians (before Augustine), following the example of Jesus, did not oppose voluntary death (suicide) and are therefore (they imply) the basis for a reconsideration of the morality of suicide today ("Conclusion," pp. 185-89). Apart from tremendous differences in the nature of and motives for voluntary death among early Christians and among most modern people, the most important lesson from Paul is that suicide is normally, even for ostensibly noble causes, a selfish decision. It is Christ's voluntary death as an example of self-giving and self-sacrificial love for others that compels Paul *not* to choose his own death. He imitates Jesus precisely by *not* imitating him. The conclusion of Droge and Tabor, that "[c]onceivably, for Paul, an individual could kill himself and be 'glorifying God with his body' by doing so" (p. 124), rests on a dubious interpretation of certain images in Pauline texts and on a failure to take the decision of Paul not to take his own life — and the reasons for the decision — as paradigmatic.

70. Wansink believes that Cicero made a similar decision while in prison, and for a similar reason, as revealed in his *Epistulae ad Quintum fratrem (Letter to My Brother Quintus)* 1.3, but of course Cicero was not trying to conform to Christ.

saw his life and ministry as the embodiment of the normative narrative pattern of faithful love found in Christ — the law of Christ. That cruciform love was manifested in his renunciation of apostolic rights, especially the right to the financial support of those to whom he ministered; in his mode of pastoral care; in his constant suffering; and in other dimensions of his apostolic work. Offering himself as a narrative continuation of the Lord's cross, he invited others to look through him to Christ as the ultimate paradigm of God's love, of cruciform love. He saw "the trajectory of his own life as analogous" to Christ's, and he believed that others, too, could "put on Christ" only if they also "put on the story of Christ."[71]

The texts we have examined that stress Paul's call to imitate him naturally raise the question of Paul's motives. Is he trying to control people? Are his self-described loving actions really acts of power? We will address these questions in the chapter on cruciform power. For now, however, we will give Paul the benefit of the doubt. We will read his call to imitate him as he imitates Christ as a serious manifestation of his desire to love as Christ loved, and for the communities he serves also to embody Christ-like love. The specifics of that community life are the focus of the next chapter.

71. Witherington, *Paul's Narrative Thought World*, pp. 234, 238.

CHAPTER 10

CRUCIFORM LOVE (III)

The Narrative Shape of the Faithful Community

In the two previous chapters we have looked carefully at Paul's narratives of cruciform love as he found that love first in the story of Christ and then in his own ministry. Now we turn to the ways in which Paul urged his readers to manifest the same kind of cruciform love within their own lives and communities. The reformer Martin Luther, commenting on the Philippians text that we have called Paul's "master story," eloquently expressed this summons to cruciform love as follows:

> Here [Phil. 2:4] we see clearly that the Apostle has prescribed this rule for the life of Christians, that we should devote all our works to the welfare of others. . . . As an example of such life the Apostle cites Christ [Phil. 2:5-8 follows]. . . . Paul means this: Although Christ was filled with the form of God and rich in all good things, so that he needed no work and no suffering to make him righteous and saved (for he had all this eternally), yet he was not puffed up by them and did not exalt himself above us and assume power over us, although he could rightly have done so. . . . Although the Christian is thus free from all works, he ought in this liberty to empty himself, take upon himself the form of a servant . . . and to serve. . . . He ought to think. . . . "Although I am an unworthy and condemned man, my God has given me in Christ all the riches of righteousness and salvation without any merit on my part. . . . *I will therefore give myself as a Christ to my neighbor, just as Christ offered himself to me.*" . . . Behold from faith thus flow forth love and joy in the Lord. . . .[1]

1. Martin Luther, *The Freedom of a Christian,* in John Dillenberger, ed., *Martin Luther: Selections from His Writings* (Garden City, N.Y.: Doubleday, 1961), pp. 74-75 (emphasis added). When

What did Paul think believers should do in order to give themselves "as a Christ" to their neighbors as Christ gave himself for them? We will begin this chapter with a very brief review of the chief points about cruciform love discussed in the two previous chapters. We will then examine the Pauline letters one by one in order to discover how Paul sees patterns of cruciform love taking shape in each of the particular communities he addresses.[2] This is helpful, even necessary, because love is so central to Paul's spirituality and such a significant dimension of almost all of his letters. We will then conclude with a synthesis of the texts examined in order to understand, as a whole, the experience of love Paul urges his readers to embody.

Christ's and Paul's Cruciform Love

In the previous two chapters we have examined what Paul describes as "the love of Christ" and his attempt to embody the pattern of that love. Love is clearly central to Paul's spirituality and to his understanding both of Christ and of himself. Love, which by the work of the Spirit fulfills the Law, has essentially a two-dimensional character. On the one hand, it does not seek its own interest but is characterized by the renunciation of status and rights. On the other hand, it seeks the good of others and is characterized by regard for them.

For Paul the source of this understanding of love is in the cross, which is the expression of Christ's love. Paul's master story, the hymn of Philippians 2:6-11, is interpreted by the apostle as a story of love, and echoes of that story of love appear throughout the letters: renunciation of status, not seeking his own interest, acting for the good (salvation) of others. Paul expresses his cruciform love in a variety of ways, all of which resemble the master story of Christ's self-giving, suffering love. Christ's love on the cross is thus the paradigmatic act of love that can give rise to analogous acts by any who are in Christ — whether Paul or his communities.

Just as Christ's obedient faithfulness to God was embodied in love for hu-

---

the great Luther scholar Roland H. Bainton cites this text, he calls it the "epitome of Luther's ethic," translating the italicized line as "I will give myself as a sort of Christ to my neighbor as Christ gave himself for me" (*Here I Stand: A Life of Martin Luther* [New York: New American Library, 1950], pp. 178-79).

2. Some justification for this approach, which is different from the format of other chapters, is in order. The experience of cruciform love is at the heart of Paul's spirituality and thus at the center of his pastoral instructions. Because of the centrality of love, and because for Paul adaptability to a particular context is so important to his spirituality of cruciformity, we will look at each letter/community individually.

manity on the cross, so also believers are to express their faith in love. The invitation to be conformed to the narrative of Christ (and his apostle) takes different forms and has different emphases for each community to which Paul writes. As we will see, however, in examining Paul's directives to the Thessalonians, the Galatians, the Corinthians (each letter separately), the Romans, the Philippians, and Philemon, common — and not unexpected — themes exist.[3]

1 Thessalonians: The Essentials of Cruciform Love

Paul's first letter to the Thessalonians is generally considered to be his oldest preserved piece of correspondence. Although the word "love" appears seven times in the letter,[4] there is no extended treatment of the topic. Nevertheless, the essential elements of Paul's understanding of love are present, elements that will be unpacked in other letters. These elements include the following:

1. *Love is inseparable from faith.* From the opening thanksgiving, in which Paul remembers the Thessalonians' "work of faith and labor of love and steadfastness of hope in our Lord Jesus Christ" (1:2), to his positive reaction to Timothy's report of their "faith and love" (3:6), to his exhortation to them to "put on the breastplate of faith and love" (5:8), the apostle makes it clear that love and faith are to be spoken of and experienced together.
2. *Love is also inseparable from, and is the assurance of, hope.* In both the "triad of theological virtues" noted above (1:2) and again in the description of

---

3. In this chapter I have not burdened the reader with many footnotes containing citations of or references to secondary literature supporting my interpretations of these letters. The reason is for economy of space, since we will be dealing, in some measure, with the entire corpus of the undisputed letters of Paul. Readers intrigued by certain issues or claims should consult appropriate commentaries. Helpful suggestions may be found in Raymond E. Brown, *An Introduction to the New Testament* (New York: Doubleday, 1997); Luke Timothy Johnson, with Todd C. Penner, *The New Testament Writings: An Interpretation,* rev. ed. (Minneapolis: Fortress, 1999); and James D. G. Dunn, *The Theology of Paul the Apostle* (Grand Rapids: Eerdmans, 1998). Particularly helpful on the interpretation of "ethics" in general, and love in particular, in Paul's letters are Richard B. Hays, *The Moral Vision of the New Testament: A Contemporary Introduction to New Testament Ethics* (San Francisco: HarperCollins, 1996); Victor Paul Furnish, *Theology and Ethics in Paul* (Nashville: Abingdon, 1968); Victor Paul Furnish, *The Love Command in the New Testament* (Nashville: Abingdon, 1972); and Pheme Perkins, *Love Commands in the New Testament* (New York: Paulist, 1982).

4. *Agapē* (noun) in 1:3; 3:6, 12; 5:8, 13; *agapaō* (verb) in 1:4; 4:9; and the related noun *philadelphia* in 4:9.

the believer's armor, where "the hope of salvation" is the "helmet" that accompanies the breastplate of faith and love (5:8), Paul insists that love is inseparable not only from faith but also from hope. Yet he says even more; growth in love means growth in holiness, which is required for a "blameless" appearance before God at the coming of Jesus (3:13; 5:23-24). Thus love builds hope and certainty about the future:

> [12]And may the Lord make you increase and abound in love for one another and for all, just as we abound in love for you, [13]with the result that [or, "so that"] God strengthens your hearts and makes them blameless in holiness before our God and Father at the coming of our Lord Jesus with all his saints. (1 Thess. 3:12-13)[5]

Without love, then, there is no certain hope.

3. *Love means encouraging and edifying others.* When Paul instructs the Thessalonian community about the future (4:13–5:11), he does so in order to comfort them because some of their number have died (4:13-18), perhaps as martyrs, and to challenge them because some of their number have grown lax in holiness (5:1-11). More specifically, he wants them to encourage one another with the teachings he imparts.[6] This process he refers to also as "build[ing] up each other" (5:11),[7] a term that will become prominent in several of Paul's other letters.[8] That this is one concrete manifestation of love is clear from the specific exhortation to love that precedes the instructions about the future (4:9-10), as well as from the words that follow (5:12-15). The earlier text (printed under number 5 below) speaks of love generally, while the later text counsels loving actions for specific members of the community and for the assembly as a whole:

> [12][W]e appeal to you, brothers and sisters, to respect those who labor among you, and have charge of you in the Lord and admonish you; [13]esteem them very highly in love because of their work. Be at peace among yourselves. [14]And we urge you, beloved, to admonish the idlers,

---

5. I have altered the NRSV text of v. 13 because, unfortunately (and unlike the RSV), it divides 3:12-13 into two grammatically unrelated sentences, whereas the Greek text clearly indicates that v. 13 is dependent (grammatically and materially) on v. 12, as indicated here. The connection may be one of result or of cause (as shown in the bracketed alternative translation).

6. Although Paul uses the same Greek verb — *parakaleō*, meaning "exhort" or "appeal" — at the conclusion of each set of instructions (4:18; 5:11), it is clear from the context that the verb connotes "comfort" in the first instance and "prod" in the second.

7. Greek *oikodomeō*.

8. The verb or its noun form *oikodomē* is found in 1 Cor. 10:23; 14:3-5, 12, 17, 26; 2 Cor. 12:19; 13:10; Rom. 14:19; 15:2.

encourage the fainthearted, help the weak, be patient with all of them. (1 Thess. 5:12-14)

4. *Love is all-inclusive and always means doing good rather than seeking retaliation or other harm.* Included in the final admonitions about community life is the following text:

> See that none of you repays evil for evil, but always seek to do good to one another and to all. (1 Thess. 5:15)

This text means both that love goes beyond the community of believers (as also in 3:12, to "all"), and that it can never be retaliatory. Love seeks the good of the other, no matter who the "other" is.[9]

5. *Love takes place by means of both divine initiative and human responsibility.* This is stated in the following text:

> [9]Now concerning love of the brothers and sisters [Greek *philadelphias*], you do not need to have anyone write to you, for you yourselves have been taught by God to love one another; [10]and indeed you do love all the brothers and sisters throughout Macedonia. But we urge you, beloved, to do so more and more. . . . (1 Thess. 4:9-10)

For Paul there is a cooperative relationship between God's grace in teaching love and the believer's role in practicing it.

6. *Love has been modeled by the apostle and his colleagues in selfless self-giving.* When Paul exhorts the Thessalonians to "increase and abound in love for one another and for all," he adds "just as we abound in love for you" (3:12). The love to which he refers has been described in the previous chapter; for Paul it involves renouncing the right to make demands, laboring night and day, sharing himself fully, and gently treating the Thessalonians as a nursing mother treats her own children (2:1-12). As noted there, this selfless self-giving is rooted in the cross of Christ.

For a letter with no sustained discussion of love, then, 1 Thessalonians contains a remarkable synopsis of Paul's spirituality of love as it will appear, in expanded form, in other letters. Although no direct link between the exhortations to love and the cross appears in 1 Thessalonians, the love to which Paul calls the Thessalonians — the love that he showed them — is clearly cruciform love: selfless, others-centered, edifying, and nonretaliatory.

9. One specific form of this kind of love may be implied in 4:3-8, where Paul forbids believers to "exploit" others through inappropriate sexual activity. The interpretation of the passage is much contested, however, so we cannot be certain as to Paul's precise meaning.

Galatians: Faith-Generated Love as Fruit of the Spirit and Fulfillment of the Law

The word "love," as either a verb or a noun (Greek *agapē, agapaō*), occurs five times in Galatians, all but one of these (2:20) in 5:6-22. Although other words appear more frequently (such as "faith" and "Abraham" and "justification") and have traditionally been associated with the theme and key concerns of Galatians, love is in fact a central focus of the letter.

As we have already seen, at issue in Galatians is whether and how those who have been "baptized into Christ" (3:27) and "received the Spirit" (3:2) must keep the Jewish Law, as some teachers are advocating. Paul seeks to persuade his readers that Gentile believers do not need to be circumcised for two reasons. First, circumcision would then require "doing" (Greek *poieō*) the Law fully, but doing the Law is not the way to justification. Second, baptized believers do in fact "fulfill" (Greek *plēroō*) the Law, the essence of which is love of neighbor, inasmuch as the Spirit produces in them Christ-like love. Thus for Paul the essential issue at Galatia and the crux of his argument is not the presence or meaning of faith itself, but the credibility of his Law-free gospel, and thus of the sufficiency of the Spirit of the faithful Messiah, as a means to embodying the will of God in daily life. That is, Galatians is about the *connection* between faith — as preached by Paul — and love. Ultimately, that means that the letter is about the connection between the cross and the Spirit.[10]

The connection between faith and love is rooted, of course, in Paul's Christology as it is set out in the thesis of the letter, 2:15-21, especially 2:20. In 2:20, as we have seen in earlier chapters, Paul defines Christ's death by crucifixion as an act of faith toward God that issued in love toward others.

> [I]t is no longer I who live, but it is Christ who lives in me. And the life I now live in the flesh I live by the faith(fulness) of the Son of God, who loved me by giving himself for me. (Gal. 2:20, author's translation)

The "faith(fulness)" of the Son (mentioned also in 2:16) was an act of self-giving love. This establishes, for Paul, the inextricable interconnection of faith

---

10. See the earlier discussions of Galatians, plus Richard B. Hays, "Christology and Ethics in Galatians: The Law of Christ," *Catholic Biblical Quarterly* 49 (1987): 268-90; John M. G. Barclay, *Obeying the Truth: Paul's Ethics in Galatians* (Minneapolis: Fortress, 1991); and Charles H. Cosgrove, *The Cross and the Spirit: A Study in the Argument and Theology of Galatians* (Macon, Ga.: Mercer University Press, 1988).

and love, which then becomes the paradigm of believers' existence and thus the centerpiece of his argument to the Galatians.[11]

At this juncture in the letter Paul also contends that the same Christ indwells him and empowers him to live the life he lives. In chapters 3 and 4 of Galatians, Paul makes it clear that this indwelling Christ is to be identified with the Spirit. The Galatians are undisputed recipients of the Spirit, as attested by signs and wonders (3:1-5). This Spirit is a divine gift, sent to the world by God the Father in a fashion parallel to his sending of the Son (4:4-7):

> [4]But when the fullness of time had come, God sent his Son, born of a woman, born under the law, [5]in order to redeem those who were under the law, so that we might receive adoption as children. [6]And because you are children, God has sent the Spirit of his Son into our hearts, crying, "Abba! Father!" [7]So you are no longer a slave but a child, and if a child then also an heir, through God. (Gal. 4:4-7)

Crucial in this text to Paul's overall argument in Galatians is that the Spirit is the Spirit *of the Son*. When Paul later says that believers live or walk by the Spirit (5:16, 25),[12] he is saying that they live by the Spirit *of the Son*. In other words, they live by means of the indwelling Son of God or, as Paul puts it, "by [means of] the faith of the Son of God" (2:20). These phrases in turn cannot be disconnected from Paul's assertion that he and all believers have been crucified *with* Christ and baptized *into* Christ. The Christ in whom believers dwell and who dwells in believers is indeed equated with the Spirit, but this living Christ is also equated with the crucified Christ. Thus the Spirit is the Spirit of the Son, the Son who demonstrated *faith* (toward the Father) by giving himself in *love* (for others).

After 2:20, the next occurrence of "love" is 5:6, in which Paul says that "neither circumcision nor uncircumcision matters but faith expressing itself in love" (author's translation). It is impossible to miss the connection here: what matters to believers — who are God's adopted children (4:7) — is what mattered to the Son, faith issuing in love, or "faith working practically through love."[13] For Paul then, faith expressing itself in love defines the believing com-

---

11. Hays ("Christology and Ethics," p. 281) rightly calls 2:20 the "hermeneutical key" to several otherwise difficult but very important texts in Galatians. I would simply broaden his claim to say that 2:20 unlocks the entire letter.

12. The vivid metaphor of "walking" (Greek *peripateō*) in or by the Spirit is unfortunately rendered as "living" in the NRSV.

13. Bruce W. Longenecker, *The Triumph of Abraham's God: The Transformation of Identity in Galatians* (Nashville: Abingdon, 1998), passim, as noted in chapter seven.

munity of God's adopted children, because it defined the Son, and those children possess the Spirit of the Son.

How does this connection of faith to love relate to the Law? The answer lies in Paul's belief that Christ's faithful, self-giving, loving death on the cross was recognized by God not as a curse but as a blessing. Although the Law pronounced the crucified Christ a curse (3:10-13), God pronounced him the source of blessing (3:13-14). Thus, Paul implies that the cross does not contravene but fulfills the will of God. As such it becomes the full and sufficient expression of God's will and Law. It is *this* love that fulfilled, and now fulfills, the Law.

Therefore the next references in Galatians to love all make sense as an extension of Paul's assertion that Christ's loving death revealed the will of God. The apparently rather common statement "love fulfills the law" now becomes interpreted in a unique way: the love generated by faith fulfills the law. Inasmuch as this faith is the indwelling "faith of the Son of God" (2:20) it is the "fruit of the Spirit" (5:22), that is, the activity of the Spirit of the Son. The loving death of the crucified Messiah has redefined the law of love. It is now the "law of the Messiah," as Paul says in 6:2. It is a law shaped by the faithful, self-giving, loving death of Jesus. It is the law, or pattern, of cruciform faith active in cruciform love.

This new law of love-generating faith is defined more specifically in two ways. First, it is defined metaphorically as slavery to others. Second, it is defined concretely as "burden-bearing."

> [13]For you were called to freedom, brothers and sisters; only do not use your freedom as an opportunity for self-indulgence, but through love to become slaves to one another. [14]For the whole law is summed up in a single commandment, "You shall love your neighbor as yourself." (Gal. 5:13-14)

> Bear one another's burdens, and in this way you will fulfill the law of Christ. (Gal. 6:2)

The metaphor of slavery is hardly surprising in light of the connections between Christ's death and the servanthood or slavery motif in Paul's understanding and experience of Christ (e.g., Phil. 2:6-8). Furthermore, as we have seen, Paul saw himself as a slave not only of Christ but of those to whom he and his colleagues ministered (e.g., 2 Cor. 4:5, "your slaves for Jesus' sake"). To be a slave, then, is to follow in the footsteps of Christ and of his apostle. It is to renounce self-serving for service to others. It is to allow the fruit of the Spirit, whose first, and arguably chief, activity is love (Gal. 5:22), to exhibit kindness and gentleness as goodness to all in the community and outside it (6:10).

221

This kind of slavery allows the power of the Spirit to replace the power of sin and the flesh. To be a slave in Paul's view is to be mastered by love.[14]

One of the tangible manifestations of this kind of love is the bearing of one another's burdens (6:2). Paul does not specify the nature of these burdens, though he does make it clear that bearing them is not an option but a requirement. For Paul, bearing burdens is a form of self-giving. It is parallel to Christ's giving of himself for us and for our sins, its purpose is the benefit of others, and its realization in daily life is not without personal sacrifice and cost. Burden bearing is the opposite of isolation and indifference, on the one hand, and of "bit[ing] and devour[ing] one another" (5:15), on the other.

It is likely, then, that the burdens to be borne would include any need a fellow believer would have: what we today might categorize as financial, emotional, physical, or spiritual hardships.[15] What matters is that the community or individual respond in love generated by faith, and that the response be motivated by and patterned after the self-giving love of the crucified Messiah. When the Spirit of the Son is operative in the community, these burdens will be borne.[16]

1 Corinthians: Love as Edification Not Arrogance

In the minds of many people, "1 Corinthians" and "love" are closely associated because of the well-known and oft-read text in chapter 13. Although 1 Corinthians 13 is a fundamental expression of Paul's understanding and experience of love, as we noted in chapter eight, the word "love" appears only a few times in the letter outside of chapter 13.[17] One of these texts, however, makes it clear that "love" is a fundamental concern of the letter: "Let all that you do be done in love" (16:14) — which is part of Paul's final, summary exhortations as he closes the letter. Indeed, Paul's first (preserved)[18] letter to the Corinthians is a

14. On the paradox of this kind of love, see Barclay, *Obeying the Truth,* p. 109.

15. The general nature of these burdens is affirmed by most commentators; see Barclay, *Obeying the Truth,* pp. 131-32, 158-59.

16. Nonetheless, this principle does not allow individuals to take advantage of their brothers and sisters by failing to "carry their own loads" (6:5).

17. "Love" appears as a verb in 2:9 and 8:3, but both of human love for God. It appears as a noun in 4:21 and 16:24 in reference to Paul's love for the Corinthians, and in 16:14 with reference to the Corinthians' love for one another. In 4:14, 17 Paul refers first to the Corinthians and then to Timothy as his "beloved."

18. It is clear from 5:9 that Paul had previously written at least one other letter to the Corinthian community.

textbook example of "deliberative" rhetoric — the art of persuading people to ponder and then change their behavior.[19] It is Paul's effort to redirect their community life away from behaviors he deems unloving on the part of those who have "been bought with a price" — Christ's death (6:20) — and who now confess the crucified Christ as their Lord (1:18–2:5; 12:1-3). What Paul offers in place of these unloving behaviors is cruciform love that creates and sustains true community.

The Fundamental Character of Love in 1 Corinthians

The nature of the love Paul promotes in 1 Corinthians is described explicitly in two key texts:

> Knowledge puffs up, but **love builds up**. (8:1b [emphasis added])

> [4]Love is patient; love is kind; love is not envious or boastful or arrogant [5]or rude. **It does not insist on its own way**; it is not irritable or resentful; [6]it does not rejoice in wrongdoing, but rejoices in the truth. [7]It bears all things, believes all things, hopes all things, endures all things. Love never ends. (13:4-8a [emphasis added]).

As we saw first in chapter eight and summarized above, the most significant phrase in 1 Corinthians 13 appears in verse 5: love "does not insist on its own way," or "does not seek its own [advantage]." This is the other side of the coin of 8:1b. As in Paul generally, so also in 1 Corinthians specifically, love has an essentially two-dimensional character. *Negatively,* it does not seek its own advantage or edification. *Positively,* it seeks the good, the advantage, the edification of others. These two essential facets of love undergird the many exhortations we find in 1 Corinthians.

To see how Paul connects these two dimensions of love to the needs he perceives in the Corinthian community, we must look carefully at these two central, defining texts. We begin with chapter 13, not only because it is the best-known and fullest statement of Paul on love, but also because a careful analysis demonstrates Paul's method in naming and addressing the problems he sees.

As we saw in chapter eight, the core of 1 Corinthians 13, verses 4-8a, provides a kind of "anti-description" of the Corinthians, listing characteristics of love that

---

19. So, e.g., Ben Witherington III, *Conflict and Community in Corinth: A Socio-Rhetorical Commentary on 1 and 2 Corinthians* (Grand Rapids: Eerdmans, 1995), pp. 46-48.

are antithetical to the Corinthians' behavior.[20] We may now consider the characteristics of love and the traits of the Corinthians side by side. In so doing we must draw immediate attention to the fact that, despite English translations and usage, Paul uses not a single adjective in his description of love; all the "characteristics of love" are expressed as verbs. That is, for Paul love is an action, a story, a narrative.

Love	The Corinthians
is patient (makrothymei)	"When you come together, it is not really to eat the Lord's supper. For when the time comes to eat, each of you goes ahead [Greek prolambanei] with your own supper, and one goes hungry and another becomes drunk. What! Do you not have homes to eat and drink in? Or do you show contempt for the church of God and humiliate [Greek kataischynete] those who have nothing? . . . So then . . . when you come together to eat, wait for [Greek ekdechesthe] one another." (11:20-22, 33)
is kind (chrēsteuetai)	[no direct parallel, but it is possible that Paul intends a play on words with the Greek word for Christ (christos)]
is not envious (ou zēloi)	". . . as long as there is jealousy [Greek zēlos] and quarreling [Greek eris] among you, are you not of the flesh, and behaving according to human inclinations?" (3:3)
is not boastful (ou perpereuetai)	[synonyms for "boasting" used; cf. also "is not arrogant" below]: "What do you have that you did not receive? And if you received it, why do you boast [Greek kauchasai] as if it were not a gift?" (4:7; see also 1:29-31; 3:21; 5:6)

20. In addition to the references in chapter eight, see Carl A. Holladay, "1 Corinthians 13: Paul as Apostolic Paradigm," in D. L. Balch, E. Ferguson, and W. A. Meeks, eds., *Greeks, Romans, and Christians* (Minneapolis: Fortress, 1990), pp. 80-98.

is not arrogant *(ou physioutai)*	"I have applied all this to Apollos and myself for your benefit . . . so that you may learn through us the meaning of the saying, 'Nothing beyond what is written,' so that none of you will be puffed up [*physiousthe*] in favor of one against another." (4:6)
	"[S]ome of you, thinking that I am not coming to you, have become arrogant [Greek *ephysiōsthēsan*]. But I will come to you soon, if the Lord wills, and I will find out not the talk of these arrogant people [Greek *pephysiōmenōn*] but their power." (4:18-19)
	"It is actually reported that there is sexual immorality among you, and of a kind that is not found even among pagans; for a man is living with his father's wife. And you are arrogant [Greek *pephysiōmenoi*]! Should you not rather have mourned, so that he who has done this would have been removed from among you?" (5:1-2)
	"Knowledge puffs up [Greek *physioi*], but love builds up." (8:1b)
not rude *(ouk aschēmonei)*	"If anyone thinks that he is not behaving properly [Greek *aschēmonein*] toward his fiancée, if his passions are strong, and so it has to be, let him marry as he wishes; it is no sin. Let them marry." (7:36; see also 5:1-2; 6:12-20; 11:2-16, 20-22 for additional "shameful" behavior)
does not insist on its own way *(ou zētei ta heautēs)*	"Do not seek your own advantage [Greek *to heautou*], but that of the other." (10:24)

	"not seeking my own advantage [Greek *to emautou symphoron*], but that of many" (10:33)
is not irritable *(ou paroxynetai)*	[no explicit parallel, but probably a reference to divisions and rivalries]
is not resentful *(ou logizetai to kakon)*	[no explicit parallel, but probably a reference to lawsuits]
does not rejoice in wrongdoing *(ou chairei epi tē̦ adikia̦)*	"When any of you has a grievance against another, do you dare to take it to court before the unrighteous [Greek *adikōn*], instead of taking it before the saints? . . . In fact, to have lawsuits at all with one another is already a defeat for you. Why not rather be wronged [Greek *adikeisthe*]? Why not rather be defrauded? But you yourselves wrong [Greek *adikeite*] and defraud — and believers at that. Or do you not know that wrongdoers [Greek *adikoi*] will not inherit the kingdom of God? Do not be deceived!" (6:1, 7-9b)
rejoices in the truth *(synchairei de tē̦ alētheia̦)*	"Therefore, let us celebrate the festival, not with the old yeast, the yeast of malice and evil, but with the unleavened bread of sincerity and truth [Greek *alētheias*]." (5:8)
bears all things *(panta stegei)*	"we [Paul and his colleagues] endure [Greek *stegomen*] anything" (9:12)
believes all things *(panta pisteuei)*, hopes all things *(panta elpizei)*, endures all things *(panta hypomenei)*	[perhaps a reference to Corinthian disbelief in the resurrection of the body as the hope of all and the ground of endurance (ch. 15)]

From this chart, several things become clear. First, Paul does *not* draw a point-by-point connection between every Corinthian (mis)behavior and the

226

true deeds of love. That would be too wooden and artificial. Second, however, there are sufficient exact verbal parallels, as well as similar phrases, in chapter 13 and elsewhere in the letter to suggest beyond any doubt that Paul intends the Corinthians to see themselves — or rather the antithesis to themselves — in the text of 1 Corinthians 13. Love does what the Corinthians do not; that is the point of 1 Corinthians 13:4-8a. As a corrective device, the text urges the Corinthians to reshape their communal narrative such that it more appropriately corresponds to the story of love, which is for Paul, of course, the story of the cross. Third, while Paul acknowledges that love cannot be described fully by the phrase "does not seek its own [advantage]," he clearly places strong emphasis on this phrase, using it twice in texts that have a general, proverbial character to them (10:24, 33) and linking the phrase — unlike any other in 1 Corinthians 13 — directly to the narrative pattern of Christ (11:1). Moreover, it is clearly the case that many of the other narrative qualities of love are, in fact, expressions of "not seeking one's own advantage" — for example, not being envious, boastful, or arrogant; not being irritable or resentful; and not rejoicing in wrongdoing.

The precise opposite of 1 Corinthians 13:5's "does not seek its own [advantage]" — "but seeks the advantage of the other" (author's translation) — does not appear explicitly in chapter 13 as a quality of love. To be sure, such others-centeredness is part of the very character of actions like being patient and kind, or enduring all things. For the explicit statement, however, we must look to 8:1 and its corollary texts in 10:23–11:1:

> Now concerning food sacrificed to idols: we know that "all of us possess knowledge." Knowledge puffs up, but love builds up. (1 Cor. 8:1)

> 23"All things are lawful," but not all things are beneficial. "All things are lawful," but not all things build up. 24Do not seek your own advantage, but that of the other. . . . 32Give no offense to Jews or to Greeks or to the church of God, 33just as I try to please everyone in everything I do, not seeking my own advantage, but that of many, so that they may be saved. 11 1Be imitators of me, as I am of Christ. (1 Cor. 10:23-24; 10:32–11:1)

These two texts frame the entire discussion about meat offered to idols (more on this below) that appears in 8:1–11:1. In each place the apostle appears to quote and then refute Corinthian position statements or "slogans": "All of us possess knowledge" in 8:1 and "All things are lawful" in 10:23. Each of these positions, Paul implies, reflects a self-centered perspective of seeking one's own advantage, and he counters this with a call to consider the other's interest. In 8:1 he speaks of edification ("love builds up"), while in 10:23–11:1 he repeats that language and adds the vocabulary of "seeking" found in chapter 13 and of "benefiting" (*sympherei,* 10:23) and "pleasing" (*areskō,* 10:33) others. Although the word "love" does not appear in 10:23–11:1, it is clear that Paul means to say to the Corinthians that love edifies, benefits, and pleases the other inasmuch as it seeks the welfare of the other rather than of the self. Paul would not object to our adding such a phrase (if done poetically) to the text of 1 Corinthians 13: "Love edifies."

We turn now to look individually at the various issues that Paul addresses in 1 Corinthians and how he urges the Corinthian community to refashion its communal story into a story of cruciform love, of love that edifies and does not seek its own interest; in fact, of love that goes so far as to renounce its rights for the welfare of others and in conformity to the pattern of the crucified Messiah.

Love in 1 Corinthians 1–7

In 1 Corinthians 1–4 Paul deals with a major crisis, from his perspective: divisions in the Corinthian community. Scholars have long debated the precise cause and nature of these divisions, but this much is clear: Paul views these divisions as damaging to, and potentially destructive of, the community. They are so serious that he finds it necessary to warn the troublemakers of judgment — both his and God's — if they do not alter their behavior:

> [16]Do you not know that you [plural, here and throughout the passage] are God's temple and that God's Spirit dwells in you? [17]If anyone destroys God's temple, God will destroy that person. For God's temple is holy, and you [plural] are that temple. (3:16-17)

> [18][S]ome of you, thinking that I am not coming to you, have become arrogant. [19]But I will come to you soon, if the Lord wills. . . . [21]What would you prefer? Am I to come to you with a stick, or with love in a spirit of gentleness? (4:18-19a, 21)

Paul also clearly views these divisions as unloving. Although there is no exhortation to love per se in chapters 1–4, the words of 1 Corinthians 13 noted above describe the activity of love as that which does not create or encourage jealous divisions. The Corinthians' activity, however, fosters such strife and divisions. The irony in their behavior, from Paul's perspective, is that although the Corinthians consider themselves to be very "spiritual" people, their actions prove them to be still "carnal":

> [1].... I could not speak to you as spiritual people, but rather as people of the flesh, as infants in Christ. . . . [3]. . . . [Y]ou are still of the flesh. For as long as there is jealousy and quarreling among you, are you not of the flesh . . . ? (3:1, 3)

As Paul had already written to the Galatians, he attributed to the flesh such works as "enmities, strife, jealousy, anger, quarrels, dissensions, factions, envy" (Gal. 5:20-21), and to the Spirit such "fruit" as "love . . . patience, kindness . . . gentleness, self-control" (Gal. 5:22-23). Those led by this Spirit, whose hallmark is love, do not "become conceited, competing against one another, envying one another" (Gal. 5:26).

By urging the Corinthians to end their divisions, Paul implicitly exhorts them to the love that is the proof of the Spirit's presence and activity in the community. This love does not destroy community but builds it up (8:1).[21] Unfortunately, four chapters will not suffice to deal with this problem at Corinth, for it manifests itself in several ways, and Paul will return to the topic in chapter 6 and especially in addressing the community's liturgical life (chs. 11, 12–14).

In the discussions immediately following chapters 1–4, Paul does not speak explicitly, but only implicitly, of love. In 5:1-13 he rebukes the Corinthians for their arrogance in tolerating a man's living with his "father's wife" (stepmother). Arrogance, according to 1 Corinthians 13, is not the work of love; nor is "rejoicing in wrongdoing," in "sexual immorality . . . of a kind that is not found even among pagans" (5:1). What is unloving about such tolerance is, once again, its community-destructive consequences. Much of the community seems to have a certain kind of "knowledge" (as they see it) that bodily actions such as sex are of no moral or spiritual consequence. That Paul sees such so-called knowledge as destructive and hence unloving is once again evident from his threat of judgment, as well as his concern for the health of the community — and even for the salvation of the errant man:

> [3]For though absent in body, I am present in spirit; and as if present I have already pronounced judgment [4]in the name of the Lord Jesus on the man who has done such a thing. When you are assembled, and my spirit is present with the power of our Lord Jesus, [5]you are to hand this man over to Satan for the destruction of the flesh, so that his spirit may be saved in the day of the Lord. [6]Your boasting is not a good thing. Do you not know that a little yeast leavens the whole batch of dough? (5:3-6)

---

21. Raymond Pickett's very helpful discussion of 1 Corinthians 1–4 (*The Cross in Corinth: The Social Significance of the Death of Jesus*, JSNTSup 143 [Sheffield: Sheffield Academic Press, 1997], pp. 37-84) focuses on Paul's call to imitate his cruciform *weakness* as the solution to divisions, but even Pickett implies that the motive for this weakness is love (e.g., p. 84).

The loving thing for the Corinthians to do is to reverse their arrogant behavior and replace it with the (paradoxically) edifying action of "excommunicating" the man for the sake of both the community and the individual.

In 6:1-11 Paul addresses another kind of division, the phenomenon of lawsuits among believers within the Roman court system. While the first critique Paul makes of this practice plays on the supposed wisdom of the Corinthian community that should permit the settling of disputes without recourse to the courts,[22] the real focus of his concern is on the very existence of lawsuits:

> [7]In fact, to have lawsuits at all with one another is already a defeat for you. Why not rather be wronged? Why not rather be defrauded? [8]But you yourselves wrong and defraud — and believers at that. (6:7-8)

The litigious Corinthians are not now merely *rejoicing* in wrongdoing (5:1-13), they are *committing* it, and thus clearly acting in unloving ways. Those associated with God, the Lord Jesus, and God's Spirit (6:10-11) should know that the loving response, the *cruciform* response, to being wronged is to accept the wrong rather than retaliate. The text itself, like Romans 12:9-21, has echoes of Jesus' teaching on nonretaliation in the so-called Sermon on the Mount/Sermon on the Plain (Matt. 5:39-40; Luke 6:28-30). Though Paul does not name the cross in this passage, it is difficult to believe that it is far from his mind, since for Paul the cross is Christ's act of accepting insults as an act of self-sacrifice and neighborly love (Rom. 15:1-3). Those justified in the name of this Lord (5:11) must live the law of love that he both taught and manifested in death. The behavior Paul urges echoes the pattern of rights-renouncing, others-regarding love that we have seen as one of his key narratives of the cross: although [x], not [y] but [z]. We may summarize his two-stage exhortation as follows:

[x] Although you have the Roman right to sue your fellow believers in a Roman court,

[y] to do so is to prove your community's lack of wisdom, so avoid the Roman courts,

[z] and instead find judges within the community to settle the matter.

This argument can hardly be, and of course is not, Paul's final point, for it does not sufficiently correspond to the narrative of the cross. Thus he continues, saying in effect:

---

22. 6:1-6; cf. the emphasis on wisdom in 1 Corinthians 1–4.

[x] Although you also have the alternative "right" [beyond the right of redress in the Roman courts] to pursue your grievance before the court of the community and its wise leaders,

[y] abandon the pursuit of such grievances altogether *because it is doing wrong to another and thus contradicts the cross,*

[z] and instead be willing to be wronged and defrauded.

Such are the radical implications of the cross in the life of the individual and community.[23]

Paul's treatment of sex and marriage in 1 Corinthians 6:12-20 and 7:1-40 does not focus on love, much to some people's disappointment. The theme of love is not, however, completely absent. Paul emphasizes "conjugal rights" (7:3) — or rather, conjugal responsibilities — that derive at least in part from his concern that all relationships be built on interest in the needs of the other rather than the self. If this is true, then in Paul's view of marriage, mutual concern for the physical needs of the other means that both persons in the marriage have their needs met without being self-indulgent. The Christ pattern again echoes in this text, though perhaps more faintly than in 6:1-11:

[x] Although you have the power to withhold sexual relations from your spouse, even for religious reasons,

[y] do not do so, or do so only for appropriate short, mutually agreed upon times, but normally

[z] give your spouse his or her "conjugal rights."

Paul is also down-to-earth in his acknowledgment that husbands and wives are — and should be — anxious to "please" their spouses (7:33-34), even though such love distracts a person from a singular commitment to the work of the Lord Jesus (7:32-35). Paul's understanding of the believer's calling to love as well as purity in sexual matters also leads him to counsel those who might behave improperly toward a fiancée to marry (7:36). While this may not fit our modern romantic definitions of love, it fits Paul's, for "love is not rude" (13:5, better rendered "does not act shamefully").

23. See also Pickett, *The Cross in Corinth,* pp. 112-14.

Love in 1 Corinthians 8–16

Renouncing Rights

As we noted in the previous chapter, 1 Corinthians 8–10 (actually 8:1–11:1) deals with additional divisions within the Corinthian community over the propriety of eating meat that has been offered to idols. The specific situation is somewhat complex and difficult to decipher (especially as it is partially described in 10:23–11:1). It seems most likely to be a split between those who consider themselves to possess a knowledge that leads to the right to eat meat offered to idols, probably even in a pagan temple (8:10), and those who find such eating offensive and idolatrous but perhaps also tempting. The former apparently argue their case on somewhat sound theological grounds but do so, at least from Paul's perspective, without any regard for the effect of such eating on their neighbors — the fellow believers "for whom Christ died" and who are now at risk of being "destroyed" by this behavior (8:11). Paul responds to this additional threat of destruction in the community with an argument in a chiastic (A-B-A') pattern, in which he deals with the issue in chapters 8 and 10 by sandwiching a description of himself as a paradigm (chapter 9) between the two discussions of the issue.

The language of destruction (8:11) is reminiscent of the discussion in chapters 1–4, while the connection between sinning "against members of your family [literally, 'against the brothers']" and sinning "against Christ" foreshadows the well-known discussion of the one body of Christ in chapter 12. Those who insist on eating — on exercising their legitimate "liberty" or "right"[24] — manifest, according to Paul, an erroneous preference for a life guided by knowledge and rights rather than by love. It is not (at least not according to chapter 8)[25] that the *theology* of the "knowledgeable ones" is incorrect; Paul, in fact, sides with them in affirming the oneness of God, the nonexistence of idols, and the goodness of all God has created (8:4-6). Even more significantly, *Paul does not even deny the existence of the right to eat the meat.* What Paul does deny is the propriety of any behavior that fails to consider the effect of its action on others, particularly actions that could seriously endanger the well-being and even salvation of another. Since love builds up, while knowledge puffs up, Paul

24. Greek *exousia*: "power," "right," "authority," or "liberty."
25. Paul's response to this situation is a kind of "one-two punch," where he deals first with the ethical dimension of the Corinthians' insensitive behavior (8:1-13) and then returns to the theological or spiritual problem of idolatry associated with participating in meals at pagan temples, where fellowship with demons (which stand behind the nonexistent "gods") competes with the community's exclusive fellowship with the Lord Jesus (10:1-22).

urges the believers who *know* to be believers who *love*. They are to follow the apostle's example:

> Therefore, if food is a cause of their falling, I will never eat meat, so that I may not cause one of them to fall. (8:13)

As we saw in the previous two chapters, the following exposition (9:1–11:1) grounds Paul's understanding of love as this kind of forsaking the exercise of legitimate rights for the sake of others in the concrete examples of himself and ultimately of the Lord Jesus. Love does not "make use of" rights (9:15) but willingly forgoes their use for the welfare — specifically the salvation — of others (9:20-23; 10:33). The status-renouncing, others-regarding narrative of the cross is clearly present in this admonition:

[x] Although you possess the right to eat whatever the one true God has created,

[y] do not exercise this right if it might wound the conscience of the weak, or even cause their destruction,

[z] but rather be willing never again to eat meat offered to idols in order to prevent anyone from falling.

This kind of "self-enslavement" (9:19, 27) makes no sense to Paul without its being grounded in the status-renouncing, self-enslaving love of Jesus, of whom Paul, as we have seen repeatedly, has become an imitator (11:1). As noted above, therefore, love means doing that which benefits, that which edifies (10:23), that which seeks the advantage, not of self but of others, both individuals and the community as a whole (10:24, 33). It is this kind of love that brings glory to God in the most mundane activities of life — eating and drinking — and indeed in all of life's many dimensions (10:31). Thus Paul's general admonition to love may be depicted as follows:

[x] Although you as believers possess certain rights or powers that flow from your freedom in Christ, just as apostles possess certain rights as freed persons of the Lord — who himself had certain rights owing to his status,

[y] do not look out for your own interest or try to please yourself by making indiscriminate use of these rights, for neither I as an apostle nor Jesus our Lord selfishly exercise(d) the prerogatives of our status,

[z] but rather always do that which benefits and edifies others, seeking their advantage and good, just as the Lord Jesus did and just as I have done as an imitator of our Lord.

The Cross at the Supper

Chapters 8–10 also prepare the way for a familiar topic — divisions — to be addressed once again in 11:17-34. Paul has little trouble believing that factions exist in yet another arena, and he lets the Corinthians know so with poignant understatement: "I hear that there are divisions among you; and to some extent I believe it" (11:18b).

In 10:14-22 the community's liturgical bread and cup are highlighted as a fellowship meal with the Lord Jesus; in 11:17-34 this event reappears as an experience of unifying fellowship among believers. It is not such in Corinth, however; indeed it has become "not the Lord's supper" (11:20) but a series of individual meals. Now the divisions are explicitly between the haves and the have-nots, between those with sufficient liberty and social status to arrive early at the house of their host (and social equal?) and those whose responsibilities and status cause them to arrive later. In the Roman empire, dinners where rich and poor were both invited, for whatever reason, afforded the rich an opportunity to insult and demean the poor by giving them inferior seating, insufficient food, cheap wine, and "service" by abusive servants.[26] Such could hardly be the supper of the crucified Lord.

In response to the problem at Corinth, the link Paul makes between communion with the Lord and loving communion with others is as creative as it is profound. The Lord's supper is a proclamation of the Lord's death (11:23-26). As such it must reflect the cruciform love of the Lord; otherwise it is a mockery of his death. As we have seen elsewhere in 1 Corinthians, those who fail to embody this love for all members of the community incur the judgment of God (11:27-32), in this case specifically for failing to "discern the body" (11:29) — that is, the one body of Christ present in the wide variety of believers who assemble for the Lord's supper.[27] Concrete concern and consideration — waiting for all to arrive and eating one common meal — is the only loving thing to do. It is, of course, the antithesis of the self-indulgent behavior the Corinthians are currently displaying. The familiar status-renouncing, others-regarding pattern of the cross reemerges:

---

26. See, e.g., Ramsey MacMullen, *Roman Social Relations: 50 B.C. to A.D. 284* (New Haven: Yale University Press, 1974), p. 111.

27. This is the interpretation of most commentators (e.g., Gordon D. Fee, *The First Epistle to the Corinthians,* The New International Commentary on the New Testament [Grand Rapids: Eerdmans, 1987], pp. 562-64; Witherington, *Conflict and Community in Corinth,* pp. 251-52; Richard B. Hays, *First Corinthians,* Interpretation [Louisville: Westminster/John Knox, 1997], p. 200, emphatically). A recent Roman Catholic commentator takes the "body" to mean both the eucharistic body and the community (Raymond F. Collins, *First Corinthians,* Sacra Pagina [Collegeville, Minn.: Liturgical, 1999], p. 439).

[x] Although social status and convention privilege you in your attendance at meals, and you have transferred this honor to the meal associated with the Lord's supper,

[y] do not make selfish use of the (so-called) rights associated with your status, such as (over-)eating and (over-)drinking before all have arrived (which shows contempt for the church of God, humiliates the poor, and fails to discern and express the body of Christ),

[z] but rather wait for one another and eat the Lord's supper together in a worthy manner, as one body.

Again Paul asserts that the narrative of Christ's cross must become the narrative of the community's life together.[28]

The Cruciform Exercise of Gifts

Cruciform concern for the other and for the community as a whole drives the argument of chapters 12–14, of which chapter 13, on love, is clearly the centerpiece in a chiastic structure reminiscent of chapters 8–10. The issue being addressed here, however, is not love per se but the appropriate exercise of valid "spiritual gifts" — including and especially unusual ones like glossolalia ("speaking in tongues") — within the community. Chapter 12 argues for the importance and validity of such gifts, while chapter 14 expresses the apostle's concrete directions on the proper use of the "controversial" gifts in light of the principles enunciated in chapter 12 and, especially, the paradigm of love offered in chapter 13.

Chapter 12 focuses on the unity and diversity of the body of Christ effected by the diversity of spiritual gifts that serve common, overarching goals — the service of the one God and one Lord Jesus and the common good:

> [4]Now there are varieties of gifts, but the same Spirit; [5]and there are varieties of services, but the same Lord; [6]and there are varieties of activities, but it is the same God who activates all of them in everyone. [7]To each is given the manifestation of the Spirit for the common good [Greek *pros to sympheron*]. (12:4-7)

This perspective on the gifts of the Spirit carries with it an implicit appropriate attitude toward the gifts possessed by oneself and by others. On the one hand, one's own spiritual gift is not meant for self-aggrandizement or even

---

28. See also Pickett, *The Cross in Corinth,* pp. 118-25.

self-edification, but rather for the good of others. On the other hand, the spiritual gifts of others are to be recognized, accepted, and affirmed (12:14-26), with special, even exaggerated, consideration given to the "weaker" or less prominent members of the body and their gifts (12:22-26). The purpose of this special attention to the "weaker" (Greek *asthenestera*) and "less honorable" (Greek *atimotera*) members of the body seems to be a thinly veiled allusion to those of a "weak" conscience described in chapter 8, and those who are nothing or have nothing in chapters 1 and 11. The result will be "no dissension" and mutual care within the body (12:25).

Once again, the status-renouncing, others-regarding love of the cruciform community is being urged. Paul's argument is clear, upon careful reading:

[x] Although you have been given certain spiritual gifts, some of which appear more necessary and useful than others,

[y] do not be inflated about these gifts (remembering their source and goal) or despise the gifts of other, especially weaker, members,

[z] but receive and use all gifts — yours and others' — for the common good.

Paul will not, however, leave the issue here, for he clearly finds it, like the weaker members of the body, in need of greater attention; hence the appearance of chapter 13, the "love" chapter. The opening verses of chapter 13 (vv. 1-3) connect it directly to the issue at hand. The purpose of the chapter is not to provide an alternative to spiritual gifts but a "more excellent way" — or at least a more specifically described way — to exercise any and all gifts (12:31). Chapter 13 provides, in other words, the *modus operandi* for the use of spiritual gifts. Without love they are meaningless if not dangerous (vv. 1-3). Unlike the gifts themselves, love — like faith and hope — will endure in God's eschatological future (vv. 8-13); indeed, as the greatest of that triad, love can be said to *define* God's future.[29] Just as the cross manifested the love of God for the world, so too the world redeemed by God experiences and expresses love for all eternity.

This love, as described more fully in the center section (vv. 4-7), is of course cruciform in character, as we have noted at various points. Above all it does not insist on its own way, or interest, or advantage, or rights asserted, or rights regained by redress, but in patience and kindness bears all things, rejoices in the truth, and — in light of 8:1 and the entire context — edifies the other.

---

29. Paul portrays "the provisional character of all the spiritual gifts, juxtaposed to the abiding character of love," but he "does not write about love in order to debunk tongues and other spiritual gifts" (Hays, *First Corinthians*, pp. 221, 222).

Following the heights of such poetry, Paul must return to the valleys of real life at Corinth, where he encounters chaotic worship services in which the uncontrolled exercise of spiritual gifts is creating poor worship and witness (chapter 14). Of particular importance for Paul is the substitution of prophecy for glossolalia, especially "uninterpreted" tongues, as the signature spiritual gift used in Corinthian worship.

Paul does not question the validity of "tongues" as a divinely given gift; on the contrary, he affirms it in the strongest possible language by appealing to his own abundant experience of the gift (14:18). The problem with glossolalia is that it needs translation to function for the common good. Otherwise, it is merely communication with God (14:2) that edifies the speakers themselves but not the whole church (14:4). Untranslated tongues, in the public assembly, fails to meet the fundamental criterion for the exercise of spiritual gifts in public: "that the church may be built up" (14:5). Those who prophesy (addressing the church in Greek, i.e., the common language of the people) do in fact build up the church and are therefore greater than those who speak in tongues:

> ⁴Those who speak in a tongue build up themselves, but those who prophesy build up the church. ⁵Now I would like all of you to speak in tongues, but even more to prophesy. One who prophesies is greater than one who speaks in tongues, unless someone interprets, so that the church may be built up. (1 Cor. 14:4-5)

The community, and its individual members, should therefore strive to obtain and use gifts that build up the church (14:12), including the gift of interpretation for those who speak in tongues (14:13) so that the legitimate gift may profit and edify not merely the gifted but the entire church (14:17, 19): "Let all things be done for building up" (14:26b).

Curiously, not once does the word "love" appear in chapter 14, yet it is the theme of the chapter and of Paul's exhortation. The public use of uninterpreted tongues is, from Paul's vantage point, an exercise in seeking one's own advantage rather than that of others. It is therefore unloving. Possession of the gift is not, of course, wrong or unloving, for it is a gift of divine grace. The loving thing to do, however, is not to use the gift unless it can and will edify others; thus, remaining silent is the loving thing for one who speaks in tongues to do if no interpreter is present (14:28).³⁰ Just as Paul would not eat meat if it might

---

30. Jerome H. Neyrey's claim that "[e]dification . . . becomes Paul's code word for a cosmology of a controlled body" (*Paul, In Other Words: A Cultural Reading of His Letters* [Louisville: Westminster/John Knox, 1990], p. 129) is partially correct but fails to connect Paul's supposed desire for control of the Corinthians with his more fundamental commitment to cruciformity.

cause someone to stumble, so also he would prefer to speak five understand-able, edifying words rather than 10,000 in (uninterpreted) tongues (14:19), and Paul expects the same of the Corinthians. His pattern of cruciformity is again vividly present:

[x] Although you have been given a divine gift that you should use to wor-ship God and edify yourself,

[y] do not selfishly exercise the gift in the public assembly if it will only ed-ify you,

[z] but rather seek the edification of others present by praying for the gift of interpretation, calling on another to interpret, or remaining silent so that everything done in the assembly will edify the body.

Cruciform Love and Resurrection

Unlike chapters 12–14, there is no specific mention of, or even allusion to, love in chapter 15. Nevertheless, chapter 15 is not unrelated to the many exhorta-tions to cruciform love in the letter. Throughout 1 Corinthians, the death of Christ has figured prominently in Paul's argument. The gospel of the crucified Messiah addresses divisions, lawsuits, issues of freedom, sexual conduct, and li-turgical behavior. Chapter 15, though devoted primarily to the resurrection, re-minds the recipients of the letter that they have received and continue to affirm this gospel of the crucified and resurrected Messiah (15:3-11). *Those who affirm the death of Christ in creed must affirm his death in deed.* Whatever "labor" the community performs, knowing that the resurrection guarantees that such labor is not in vain (15:58), must be executed in cruciform love — which is why the final admonition to do all things "in love" appears in 16:14.

1 Corinthians, then, is an appeal for cruciform love at Corinth. This, Paul believes, will create the harmony in the community that the one body of Christ should experience.

2 Corinthians: Suffering Love

Paul's second canonical letter to the Corinthians is more likely his fourth (or possibly even his fourth, fifth, and sixth). As we have already noted, most schol-ars believe that Paul wrote at least one letter between our 1 and 2 Corinthians, and many believe that 2 Corinthians itself is a composite of two or more letters, one of which may even be the intervening letter. Although a good argument can be made for a thematic unity in the letter as we have it, namely, suffering love, that theme is so thoroughly Pauline that it could — and indeed does — appear in all of his letters. Thus by itself, the presence of such a theme does not argue convincingly for the indivisibility of 2 Corinthians.

In fact, whether one letter or more, our 2 Corinthians divides neatly into three major sections, as indicated earlier: an explanation of apostolic ministry (chs. 1–7), a pair of appeals for financial support of Paul's collection for the impoverished Jerusalem church (chs. 8–9), and a stinging critique of his opponents coupled with a vigorous defense of his own form of apostolic ministry (chs. 10–13). As noted in the previous chapter, the difference in tone between chapters 1–7, on the one hand, and chapters 10–13, on the other, suggests at the very least that Paul has addressed different situations, if not written different letters. Nonetheless, what holds these two sections together individually is also what unites them in one spirit: the theme of apostolic cruciform love that suffers for others, a love grounded ultimately in the love of Christ (5:14). We have examined this theme in the previous chapter, where the relative infrequency of the word "love" in 2 Corinthians 1–7 and 10–13 was noted (three times as a verb, four times as a noun), but its centrality nonetheless affirmed. Paul's defense of his ministry rests on his embodiment of Christ's cruciform love (2:4; 11:11). His primary goal in both sections of the letter is to reconcile the Corinthians to himself, his gospel, and his ministry, which will indeed be reconciliation with God (5:20).

It comes as no surprise, therefore, that the letter's admonitions, whether explicit or implicit, about how the Corinthians should treat both Paul as an apostle and fellow believers in general, are exhortations to cruciform love, specifically to reconciliation and to generosity.

Cruciform Love as Reconciliation in 2 Corinthians 1–7 and 10–13

As we have seen in the previous two chapters, reconciliation is the key theological term in 2 Corinthians 1–7, appearing several times in what is certainly the hermeneutical key to the letter, 5:11-21. In this passage Paul grounds his ministry in "the love of Christ" as a sacrificial act for the benefit of others (5:14). Paul's purpose here is not purely theological; despite claims to the contrary in 5:12 (as in 3:1), he is clearly commending himself (as also in 2:17 and 4:2), but he commends himself only inasmuch as he embodies the cruciform, suffering love of Christ that was God's act of reconciling the world (5:18-21):

> [12]We are not commending ourselves to you again, but giving you an opportunity to boast about us, so that you may be able to answer those who boast in

outward appearance and not in the heart. [13]For if we are beside ourselves, it is for God; if we are in our right mind, it is for you. [14]For the love of Christ urges us on, because we are convinced that one has died for all. . . . (2 Cor. 5:12-14a)

This self-commendation is made explicit immediately after 5:11-21:

> [3]We are putting no obstacle in anyone's way, so that no fault may be found with our ministry, [4]but as servants of God we have commended ourselves in every way: through great endurance, in afflictions, hardships, calamities. . . . (2 Cor. 6:3-4)

Since the knowledge and power of God's reconciling act are made available by God through the preaching of Paul's gospel, reconciliation with Paul is no light matter; not to be reconciled to Paul — that is, to Paul's gospel — is to risk losing salvation, to have "accept[ed] the grace of God in vain" (6:1). For this reason Paul urges the Corinthians to love him as he has loved them and, indeed, as God has loved them through him:

> [11]We have spoken frankly to you Corinthians; our heart is wide open to you. [12]There is no restriction in our affections, but only in yours. [13]In return — I speak as to children — open wide your hearts also. . . . [7:2]Make room in your hearts for us; we have wronged no one, we have corrupted no one, we have taken advantage of no one. (2 Cor. 6:11-13; 7:2)

That the Corinthians will do so is Paul's firm conviction (7:16), based on the fact that once before they had done so, as he relates in 7:5-15.

It is crucial for Paul, then, that the Corinthians be reconciled to him, that they once again love him. Is this mere apostolic arrogance and power at work? One might regard Paul's motives with such suspicion, as some have done. Fundamentally, however, Paul's concern is that the Corinthian community respond appropriately to the gospel of the love of God and Christ manifested in the cross. He even implies that this response would be one of obedience (7:12), but only inasmuch, once again, as Paul's exhortation, like all of his ministry, embodies the cruciform love of God to which the proper response is one of "listening" (6:2) or obedience. As an act of reconciliation, that obedient love requires acts of reconciliation on the part of those who embrace it. Such reconciliation can require repentance, as it does in this case and did once before (7:9), and appropriate repentance leads to salvation (7:10). To do otherwise is to risk losing the benefit of the divine reconciling act. Having in some way injured Paul (7:12), the Corinthians are now to be reconciled to him. This would be an act of genuine, indeed cruciform, love.

Yet cruciform love as reconciliation not only means repentance; it also means forgiveness. Part of the second chapter of this letter highlights this dimension. The precise situation to which Paul alludes in 2 Corinthians 2:5-11 is unclear. Someone had "caused pain" to the Corinthians' community and received some form of "punishment by the majority" (2:5-6). Although some interpreters have linked this passage to the account of the man sleeping with his stepmother in 1 Corinthians 5, the connection is unlikely. Rather, the unnamed person and his or her offense remain unknown, but a good case can be made that the offense includes slander against Paul.[31] What we know is that Paul deems the punishment for the pain sufficient, and that now is the time for reconciliation, for forgiving love:

> [6]This punishment by the majority is enough for such a person; [7]so now instead you should forgive and console him, so that he may not be overwhelmed by excessive sorrow. [8]So I urge you to reaffirm your love for him. [9]I wrote for this reason: to test you and to know whether you are obedient in everything. (2 Cor. 2:6-9)

The pattern of cruciform love that we have seen elsewhere also emerges here:

[x] Although this man has caused you pain and you have been wronged,
[y] do not further punish him,
[z] but rather forgive and console him, out of obedient love and for his good.

As in 2 Corinthians 7, Paul again mixes love and obedience. We should not, however, be surprised at this connection. The gospel of divine love that Paul preaches is not merely an option but a divine call, and its requirement of love not an expendable supplement but an integral part of the response. Not to forgive is not to love, and not to love is ultimately to be "outwitted by Satan" (2:11).

---

31. For complete discussion, see Ralph P. Martin, *2 Corinthians*, Word Biblical Commentary 40 (Waco, Tex.: Word, 1986), pp. 31-40, and especially Victor Paul Furnish, *II Corinthians*, Anchor Bible 32A (Garden City, N.Y.: Doubleday, 1984), pp. 163-68, both of whom argue for slander against Paul or an associate as the offense in question.

Cruciform Love as the Grace of
Generosity in 2 Corinthians 8–9

The way of obedient love in chapters 2 and 7 finds additional expression in chapters 8 and 9, where Paul appeals[32] to the Corinthians to contribute to his collection for the Jerusalem church, which was quite poor. This plea, especially chapter 8, is a rhetorical tour de force in which Paul appeals to the example of other believers, himself, Christ, and God to urge the Corinthians to manifest "the genuineness of your love" (2 Cor. 8:8; cf. 8:24).[33] We will focus here on chapter 8, with occasional references to chapter 9.

The rhetorical power of chapter 8 hinges in large measure on a wordplay with the Greek word *charis,* "grace," that leaps out from the Greek text but is almost entirely invisible to readers of the English text. The word appears seven times in chapter 8 (plus three times in chapter 9), in the following verses (the NRSV English translation of *charis* being boldfaced):

> [1]We want you to know, brothers and sisters, about the **grace** of God that has been granted to the churches of Macedonia; [2]for during a severe ordeal of affliction, their abundant joy and their extreme poverty have overflowed in a wealth of generosity on their part. [3]For, as I can testify, they voluntarily gave according to their means, and even beyond their means, [4]begging us earnestly for the **privilege** of sharing in this ministry to the saints — [5]and this, not merely as we expected; they gave themselves first to the Lord and, by the will of God, to us, [6]so that we might urge Titus that, as he had already made a beginning, so he should also complete this **generous undertaking** among you. [7]Now as you excel in everything — in faith, in speech, in knowledge, in utmost eagerness, and in our love for you — so we want you to excel also in this **generous undertaking**. [8]I do not say this as a command, but I am testing the genuineness of your love against the earnestness of others. [9]For you know the **generous act** of our Lord Jesus Christ, that though he was rich, yet for your sakes he became poor, so that by his poverty you might become rich. . . . [16]But **thanks** be to God who put in the heart of Titus the same eagerness for you that I myself have. [17]For he not only accepted our appeal, but since he is more eager than ever, he is going to you of his own accord. [18]With him we are sending the brother who is famous among

---

32. Some scholars, such as Hans Dieter Betz (*2 Corinthians 8 and 9,* Hermeneia [Philadelphia: Fortress, 1985]) believe that each chapter is a separate letter, issued at different times.

33. In so doing the Corinthians will also "glorify God by your obedience to the confession of the gospel of Christ and by the generosity of your sharing with them and with all others" (2 Cor. 9:13). The connection between obedience (= faith) and love should again be noted.

all the churches for his proclaiming the good news; ¹⁹and not only that, but he has also been appointed by the churches to travel with us while we are administering this **generous undertaking** for the glory of the Lord himself and to show our goodwill. . . . ²⁴Therefore openly before the churches, show them the proof of your love and of our reason for boasting about you. (2 Corinthians 8, selected verses)

As verses 8 and 24 clearly indicate, Paul's fundamental exhortation is for the Corinthians to "love" their fellow, poorer believers in Jerusalem. This love is linked directly to the Corinthians' experience of "grace," specifically the "grace of our Lord Jesus Christ" — that is, the love of Jesus (8:9), God's "indescribable gift" (9:15).

As we have seen, the language Paul employs in verse 9 to describe the grace of Jesus is the narrative language of status-renouncing, others-regarding love parallel to Philippians 2:6-8:

[x] [T]hough he was rich,
[y] [he did not remain in his position of wealth],
[z] yet for your sakes he became poor,
    so that by his poverty you might become rich.

Paul, too, makes others rich by continuing the narrative of Christ through his ministry:

[We are treated as] poor, yet making many rich. (2 Cor. 6:10)

Though the wealth to which he refers is "spiritual" wealth in Christ, that wealth includes material support and concern; the Macedonian believers, in fact, says Paul, begged him for the opportunity to participate in his ministry of grace (8:4) by sharing in the financial support of the Jerusalem church.

Astonishingly, the Macedonians also continued the Christ narrative through their generosity, or graciousness, but generosity that emerged from poverty. Their narrative, in fact, would read as follows:

[x] Although the Macedonians were in deep poverty, and in the midst of severe affliction,
[y] [they did not act selfishly and refrain from participating in the collection],
[z] but they overflowed in a wealth of liberality, giving according to and even beyond their means.

243

Those who have truly experienced this grace/love now embody it, continuing the narrative. Paul's message is clear: "[x] although you Corinthians are relatively wealthy and excel in all spiritual gifts, [y] do not keep the grace/blessing of God to yourselves, [z] but share it generously and cheerfully[34] with the Jerusalem saints."

For Paul, then, grace experienced must become grace shared in concrete service (Greek *koinōnia* and *diakonia,* 8:4; 9:12, 13) to others in need. The grace shared must have the same form as the grace experienced — abundant, sacrificial, concerned for the good of the other; that is, it must be cruciform. Those who allow themselves to be instruments of cruciform grace are promised not burden but enrichment in every way (8:14-15; 9:6-12).

Genuine Love in Romans:
Cruciform Nonretaliation and Hospitality

Paul's letter to the Romans is the most systematic and comprehensive of his extant correspondence. The reasons for these features of the letter have been hotly debated. At the very least, we can be sure that Romans is the way it is in part because Paul had not ever evangelized or even visited Rome. Despite the breadth of the letter, however, it has a distinct theme: the impartial righteousness of God for Jew and Gentile.[35] Whether this theme addresses particular circumstances in the Roman church — and what precisely those circumstances were — is also contested.[36] Yet no matter the situation, for Paul the gospel of God's impartial righteousness is the gospel of God's love for "enemies," and those who are reconciled to this God by responding to the gospel in faith must express love to all. This "genuine" love (12:9) has two primary manifestations according to Romans: nonretaliation toward enemies and nonjudgmental hospitality toward fellow believers.

The Gospel of the Love of God in Christ

Romans divides itself into two major sections, the first (chs. 1–11) presenting in detail Paul's gospel and the second (chs. 12–15) suggesting some of the ma-

34. See 2 Cor. 8:6-7.

35. See Jouette Bassler, *Divine Impartiality: Paul and a Theological Axiom,* SBLDS 59 (Chico, Calif.: Scholars Press, 1982).

36. See the introduction to any of the commentaries or A. J. M. Wedderburn, *The Reasons for Romans* (Minneapolis: Fortress, 1988).

jor existential implications of this gospel of God's "mercies" (12:1). Paul announces the theme of the letter in the following way:

> [16]For I am not ashamed of the gospel; it is the power of God for salvation to everyone who has faith, to the Jew first and also to the Greek. [17]For in it the righteousness of God is revealed through faith for faith; as it is written, "The one who is righteous will live by faith." (Rom. 1:16-17)

This gospel is needed by all people, Paul explains, because all — both Gentiles and Jews — have turned from God and find themselves now "under the power of sin" (3:9) and falling short of the glory of God (3:23).

Humanity's turning away from God and failing to keep God's covenant has resulted in a state of enmity between humanity and God, for which reconciliation is needed. Thus God, in covenant faithfulness and despite humanity's idolatry, wickedness, and faithlessness, has proven faithful and impartial by initiating restoration of the appropriate God-humanity relationship. Rather than dealing with estranged humanity as with an enemy — by means of permanent wrath and punishment — God has lovingly and faithfully effected reconciliation through the gift and death of his Son:

> [8]**But God proves his love for us in that while we still were sinners Christ died for us.** [9]Much more surely then, now that we have been justified by his blood, will we be saved through him from the wrath of God. [10]For if **while we were enemies**, we were reconciled to God through the death of his Son, much more surely, having been reconciled, will we be saved by his life. [11]But more than that, we even boast in God through our Lord Jesus Christ, through whom we have now received reconciliation. (Rom. 5:8-11 [emphasis added]; cf. Rom. 3:21-26)

As noted in earlier chapters, Paul understands the love of God manifested on the cross to be also the love of Christ. Indeed, the cross is the guarantee that, in the present, nothing — no power or pain — can separate believers from God's love, which is also Christ's love (8:31-39). The official prosecutor and judge of the sinful human race have acted with love rather than malice and condemnation.

Thus the foundation and motivation of God's salvation, which comes to humans through the gospel, is the love of God for all humans, Gentiles and Jews, while they (we) were God's enemies. As Richard Hays says, in Paul's letters *"the death of Christ is interpreted as God's peace initiative."*[37] It is thus univer-

---

37. Hays, *Moral Vision*, p. 330 (emphasis added).

sally, or impartially, welcoming (15:1-7), and both nonviolent and non-retaliatory, as Paul reminds his readers in the last part of Romans. So also, therefore, is genuine human love. Again, Hays captures the spirit of Paul:

> How does God treat enemies? Rather than killing them, Paul declares, he gives his Son to die for them. This has profound implications for the subsequent behavior of those who are reconciled to God through Jesus' death: to be "saved by his life" [Rom. 5:10] means to enter into a life that recapitulates the pattern of Christ's self-giving. . . . [T]hose whose lives are reshaped in Christ must deal with enemies in the same way that God in Christ dealt with enemies.[38]

This way of love is described in Romans 12–15.

Genuine Love in Romans 12–15: Nonretaliation and Hospitality

It is widely recognized that 1 Corinthians 13 is Paul's "love" chapter, and upon close inspection it is clear that the themes of that chapter echo throughout the entire letter. Similar, but less widely recognized, is the situation with respect to Romans 12:9–13:10. Although not designated a "chapter," these verses — apart perhaps from the infamously difficult discussion of "the state" in 13:1-7 — present a rather comprehensive portrait of love that contains echoes of earlier chapters and that finds extended application to a concrete issue in 14:1–15:13. It has been plausibly suggested, in fact, that Romans 12–15 draws on 1 Corinthians (especially 1 Cor. 8:1–11:1). In these latter chapters of Romans, Paul explains that the nonretaliatory, hospitable, cruciform love of God in Christ is paradigmatic for the Christian community in both its external and its internal affairs.[39]

The overall theme of chapters 12–15 appears at the very beginning of chapter 12, with Paul's exhortation that the Roman believers, in response to the mercies of God, offer themselves to God as "a living sacrifice, holy and accept-

---

38. Hays, *Moral Vision*, p. 330.

39. The apostle, who in Romans 1–11 "focus[es] on God's righteousness being made good through Christ's faithfulness and understands Christ's faithfulness as his generative adaptation to the needs of others, . . . sketches [in chapters 12–15] an ethic of community based on the principle of faithfulness as adaptability to others" (Stanley K. Stowers, *A Rereading of Romans: Justice, Jews and Gentiles* [New Haven: Yale University Press, 1994], p. 318; cf. p. 326). While I do not agree with the totality of Stowers's thesis, nor find the term "adaptability" particularly inviting, I do believe that he has captured an essential element of continuity between Christ, the apostle Paul, and his communities as love expressed in adapting to the needs of others.

able to God," which is their "spiritual worship" (12:1). As such, they are not to "be conformed to this world, but be transformed by the renewing of [their] minds, so that [they] may discern what is the will of God" (12:2). This is faith. Fundamental to this renewing of the mind — though Paul does not say it quite this way — is the adopting of the mind of Christ, a mind of cruciform love. Faith issues in love, here as elsewhere in Paul.

As we have already noted, this love is to be "genuine" (12:9; Greek *anypokritos*). The precise meaning of this word is not clear by itself, but it is perfectly clear in context: the community's love is to correspond to the nonretaliatory, hospitable love of God in Christ. Although Paul begins with and emphasizes love within the community, he does not avoid the subject of nonbelievers — which is where we will begin.

Although the exhortations to "extend hospitality to strangers" (12:13) and "'love your neighbor as yourself'" (13:8-10) could include nonbelievers, they more likely refer to visiting believers, especially perhaps visiting missionaries such as Paul, and to believers generally. The chief exhortations to the Romans clearly regarding nonbelievers have to do with nonretaliation, treating their "enemies" as God had treated them when they were God's "enemies." Writes Paul, echoing (as in 1 Cor. 4:9-13) the tradition of Jesus' teaching:

> [14]Bless those who persecute you; bless and do not curse them. . . . [17]Do not repay anyone evil for evil, but take thought for what is noble in the sight of all. [18]If it is possible, so far as it depends on you, live peaceably with all. [19]Beloved, never avenge yourselves, but leave room for the wrath of God; for it is written, "Vengeance is mine, I will repay, says the Lord." [20]No, "if your enemies are hungry, feed them; if they are thirsty, give them something to drink; for by doing this you will heap burning coals on their heads." [21]Do not be overcome by evil, but overcome evil with good. (Rom. 12:14, 17-21)

One should not assume that all nonbelievers in Rome were "persecuting" the believers, but the environment is clearly assumed to be at least sometimes hostile. It is possible that the Roman church had been affected by Claudius's expulsion of the Jews some years earlier (in 49), and that the Roman believers were still experiencing political or, more likely, social pressures.

Paul's general admonition to live in peace (Greek *eirēneuontes*, v. 18) reflects his conviction that he and the Roman believers have "peace [Greek *eirēnēn*] with God through our Lord Jesus Christ" (5:1). One specific demonstration of this general peaceable posture is nonretaliation, that is, treating their enemies not with wrath and vengeance but with food and drink (v. 20). That this reaction "will heap burning coals on their heads" should be understood in context not as subtle retaliation after all, but as a "wake-up call" that might lead the enemies, or evildoers, to the gospel, thus not merely responding to evil but conquering evil (v. 21).[40] Nonretaliation is thus both a loving and a witness-bearing activity.[41] As Richard Hays notes in commenting on Romans 12, *"There is not a syllable in the Pauline letters that can be cited in support of Christians employing violence."*[42] Indeed, nonviolence, suggests Luke Johnson, is the "test case for this [Pauline] Christian morality based in the work and character and death of Jesus the messiah," because violence and vengeance toward enemies were accepted in both Jewish and non-Jewish moral codes.[43] Nonviolence and nonretaliation are essential marks of cruciform love in Paul's experience and instructions.

It is within this context of nonretaliation toward enemies that Romans 13:1-7, Paul's famous words on political power and taxation, must be interpreted. Without exploring all the dimensions of this complex and long-disputed passage, we may say that the main issue addressed in the text is the payment of taxes (13:6-7). Jewish antipathy toward Rome — its benefactor, yes, but also its enemy — was sometimes expressed in revolt (A.D. 66-70, 135), the beginnings of which could take the form of withholding taxes, among other actions. For Paul to admonish the believers in Rome not to pay taxes to Rome would have been an act of enemy hatred or retaliation that both denied believers' faith in the sovereign God of Israel, who ruled the nations, and contradicted the demands of cruciform love even for enemies.[44]

With respect to fellow believers, according to chapters 12 and 13, love means that the Romans should

> [10]love one another with mutual affection; outdo one another in showing honor. . . . [13]Contribute to the needs of the saints; extend hospitality to strangers. . . . [15]Rejoice with those who rejoice, weep with those who weep. [16]Live in harmony with one another; do not be haughty, but associate with the lowly; do not claim to be wiser than you are. (Rom. 12:10, 13, 15-16)

---

40. The major interpretive options for the "burning coals" text are listed in Joseph A. Fitzmyer, *Romans: A New Translation with Introduction and Commentary,* Anchor Bible 33 (New York: Doubleday, 1993), pp. 657-58. With most interpreters, Fitzmyer argues that the text cannot contradict its context and therefore that heaping the burning coals must somehow be a charitable action for the good of the other.

41. That Paul allows for divine wrath and vengeance does not contradict his gospel of love, since he asserts that divine wrath is real and active in the world (1:18) and will still be the fate of those who do not respond to the gospel of divine love (5:9) — the alternative to wrath.

42. Hays, *Moral Vision,* p. 331 (emphasis added).

43. Luke Timothy Johnson, *Reading Romans: A Literary and Theological Commentary* (New York: Crossroad, 1997), p. 184.

44. See further discussion in chapter thirteen.

Luke Johnson correctly points out that in 12:16 the combination of the Greek terms for "lowly" (or "humble"; *tapeinois*) and "mind" *(phronountes)* (in the idiom "claim to be wiser than you are") echoes the same terms in Philippians 2:5.[45] Indeed, the entire text is similar in structure *(mēde/mēden . . . alla)* and vocabulary to Philippians 2:1-11; this is clear in transliteration even for readers who do not know Greek:

Romans 12:16	Philippians 2:1-11 (excerpts)
to auto eis allēlous phronountes	*to auto phronēte* (v. 2)
	to hen phronountes (v. 2)
	touto phroneite (v. 5)
mē ta hypsēla phronountes	*mēden kat' eritheian* (v. 3)
	mēde kata kenodoxian (v. 3)
alla	*alla . . . alla* (vv. 3, 4, 7)
tois tapeinois synapagomenoi	*tē tapeinophrosynē* (v. 3)
	sympsychoi (v. 2)
	etapeinōsen heauton (v. 8)
mē ginesthe phronimoi par' heautois	*allēlous hēgoumenoi hyperechontas heautōn* (v. 3)
	genomenos (vv. 7, 8)

Once again, then, Paul has drawn on the pattern of Christ to describe the love he expects in the community. He continues:

> [8]Owe no one anything, except to love one another; for the one who loves another has fulfilled the law. [9]The commandments, "You shall not commit adultery; You shall not murder; You shall not steal; You shall not covet"; and any other commandment, are summed up in this word, "Love your neighbor as yourself." [10]Love does no wrong to a neighbor; therefore, love is the fulfilling of the law. (Rom. 13:8-10)

In these two passages the basic virtues of hospitality, humility,[46] and concern for the other ("neighbor") are stressed, with several general — though tangible — examples provided, including both financial and emotional support.

45. Johnson, *Reading Romans*, pp. 183-84.
46. In antiquity, humility was associated with slavery and was not considered a virtue until Christians correlated it with the mind of the slave-Lord Christ.

In 14:1–15:13, Paul further concretizes this understanding of love, linking it more explicitly to the narrative of God in Christ. This section of Romans reflects tension — most likely actual, but possibly only potential — between two main groups within the Roman community. Although the precise nature of this tension has been widely debated, the most convincing scenario is that there were two groups divided roughly along Gentile and Jewish lines. The word "roughly" is key, because each group likely included sympathetic people from the "other" ethnic group. Thus the Roman community of believers was split between those who did or did not eat certain foods, and did or did not observe certain days.[47]

What united the two groups was their conviction that the other group was in grievous error; Paul criticizes this attitude as inappropriately "passing judgment":

> [10]Why do you pass judgment on your brother or sister? Or you, why do you despise your brother or sister? For we will all stand before the judgment seat of God. [11]For it is written, "As I live, says the Lord, every knee shall bow to me, and every tongue shall give praise to God." [12]So then, each of us will be accountable to God. (Rom. 14:10-12)

As "God has welcomed them" (14:3) — both Jew and Gentile, vegetarian and meat eater, observant and nonobservant — so they are to welcome one another. This point is stressed again at the end of this section:

> [7]Welcome one another, therefore, just as Christ has welcomed you, for the glory of God. [8]For I tell you that Christ has become a servant of the circumcised on behalf of the truth of God in order that he might confirm the promises given to the patriarchs, [9]and in order that the Gentiles might glorify God for his mercy. . . . (Rom. 15:7-9a).

A community of Gentiles and Jews (cf. Gal. 3:28) who welcome one another is the goal of Paul's preaching and, at least for now, of God's salvific work. Thus the inhospitable mutual rejection of one another, manifested in the passing of judgment about things that do not matter, is antithetical to the gospel and to love.

Paul's exhortation, however, is not merely "Stop passing judgment!" As in 1 Corinthians 8:1–11:1, he carefully articulates a spirituality of love understood as freedom and responsibility. Eating and calendar observance in themselves

---

47. "In a very real sense, Paul is engaging here the issue that is in the present day referred to as multiculturalism" (Johnson, *Reading Romans*, p. 198).

are of relatively little consequence — what the Stoics called *adiaphora.* However, although these matters are not crucial to the faith, believers' accountability first to their Lord, and then to one another in love, is crucially important:

> [7]We do not live to ourselves, and we do not die to ourselves. [8]If we live, we live to the Lord, and if we die, we die to the Lord; so then, whether we live or whether we die, we are the Lord's. [9]For to this end **Christ died and lived again,** so that he might be Lord of both the dead and the living. . . . [14]I know and am persuaded in the Lord Jesus that nothing is unclean in itself; but it is unclean for anyone who thinks it unclean. [15]If your brother or sister is being injured by what you eat, **you are no longer walking in love.** Do not let what you eat cause the ruin of **one for whom Christ died.** [16]So do not let your good be spoken of as evil. [17]For the kingdom of God is not food and drink but righteousness and peace and joy in the Holy Spirit. [18]The one who thus serves Christ is acceptable to God and has human approval. [19]Let us then pursue what makes for peace and for mutual upbuilding. [20]Do not, for the sake of food, destroy the work of God. Everything is indeed clean, but it is wrong for you to make others fall by what you eat; [21]it is good not to eat meat or drink wine or do anything that makes your brother or sister stumble. (Rom. 14:7-9, 14-21 [emphasis added])

The "debt of love" (13:8) is now being explained and grounded in terms of cruciform love. Those who have experienced the love of Christ expressed on the cross will not exercise their freedom indiscriminately but lovingly, for the peace, unity, and edification of the body (v. 19) and the care of each and every individual *for whom Christ died* (v. 15). As Richard Hays tersely summarizes Paul's message to those without dietary scruples regarding their treatment of those with such scruples:

> Jesus was willing to die for these people, says Paul, and you aren't even willing to modify your diet?[48]

Service to Christ (v. 18) is thus expressed in cruciform love; faith is expressing itself in love (cf. Gal. 5:6).

This grounding in Christ's love on the cross is further stressed in the summary exhortation that appears at the beginning of chapter 15:

> [1]We who are strong ought to put up with the failings of the weak, and not to please ourselves. [2]Each of us must please our neighbor for the good purpose

---

48. Hays, *Moral Vision,* p. 28.

of building up the neighbor. ³For Christ did not please himself; but, as it is written, "The insults of those who insult you have fallen on me." ⁴For whatever was written in former days was written for our instruction, so that by steadfastness and by the encouragement of the scriptures we might have hope. ⁵May the God of steadfastness and encouragement grant you to live in harmony with one another, in accordance with Christ Jesus, ⁶so that together you may with one voice glorify the God and Father of our Lord Jesus Christ. ⁷Welcome one another, therefore, just as Christ has welcomed you, for the glory of God. (Rom. 15:1-7)

As in 1 Corinthians 10:33, Paul here uses the language of "pleasing" (vv. 1-2). In 1 Corinthians he points to himself as a model of Christ's non-self-pleasing love; here he calls the Corinthians to that same love. The narrative pattern of status renunciation that we have seen so often in Paul again reappears:

[x] Although you have the right by faith[49] to eat meat and/or abstain from calendar observance — matters of little consequence,

[y] do not please yourself by exercising your faith in this way if it will cause another to stumble,

[z] but rather please — that is love and build up — your neighbor, your fellow believer.[50]

So essential to the integrity of the gospel and the life of the community is this call to cruciform, hospitable love that Paul concludes this section of Romans (and the argument of the entire letter) with two closely related observations. First, when such a multicultural community of cruciform love exists, and only when it exists, the glory due God from humans is possible (15:7). Second, as noted above, when this kind of loving community exists, the prophetically declared plan of God for humanity is achieved (15:7-13). Only in this sort

---

49. "Faith" in this context seems to mean a conviction (about behavior) that proceeds from faith in the gospel (see 14:1, 22-23).

50. As Brendan Byrne writes, "The exercise of Christian *agapē* is a continuation of the fundamental *agapē* of Christ in giving himself up to death for us all when we were 'weak' (Rom 5:6, 8, 10). Paul appeals to the 'strong' to be ready to display towards their fellow believers 'weak in faith' (14:1) the same kind of self-sacrificing love which they, themselves once 'weak' (5:6), received from Christ" (*Romans*, Sacra Pagina [Collegeville, Minn.: Liturgical, 1996], pp. 416-17). Similarly, Stowers: "God has accepted the weak and the strong alike. Who are they not to accept one another! Christ's acceptance of the ungodly meant adapting himself to their level to meet their needs (for example, in 5:6-8; 8:3-4). The weak and the strong must adapt themselves to one another in the same way" (*Rereading of Romans*, p. 323). It is clearly the case, however, that Paul expects more of the "strong" than he does of the "weak."

of community of love can the faith and hope preached by Paul exist and can the blessing of God rest:

> May the God of hope fill you with all joy and peace in believing, so that you may abound in hope by the power of the Holy Spirit. (Rom. 15:13)

Luke Johnson is right, therefore, to insist that the words of Romans 15:1-13 "represent the climax of Paul's theological argument. He draws together in one place the pattern of edification of the community, the pattern of the messiah Jesus, and the pattern of God's work in the world for Jew and Gentile, so that they appear as *one single pattern of self-giving and self-emptying for the benefit of others.*"[51]

Love as Humble Regard for Others and the Community in Philippians

No letter focuses as explicitly and uniformly on cruciformity as does Philippians. In the last chapter we noted the importance of apostolic cruciformity in chapter 1. We have already explored the significance of Paul's "master story," the Christ hymn in 2:6-11, at several points, as well as briefly noted in chapter eight the deliberate parallels Paul constructs in Philippians between Christ and believers — to which we will give close attention momentarily. Indeed, the hymnic narrative in 2:6-11 is the centerpiece of the letter to the Philippians, the entire letter being a kind of commentary on, or perhaps spiritual exegesis of, this centerpiece. In Philippians, Richard Hays writes,

> Paul offers a metaphorical reading of Christ's self-emptying and death; the power of the metaphor is precisely a function of its daring improbability, inviting the readers to see their own lives and vocations as corresponding to the gracious action of the Lord whom they acclaim in their worship.[52]

---

51. Johnson, *Reading Romans,* p. 203 (emphasis added).

52. Hays, *Moral Vision,* p. 30. (In private conversation, Stephen Fowl has suggested that the term "analogical" is more appropriate than "metaphorical" in the first sentence of this quote from Hays.) For Hays's reading of Philippians in light of 2:6-11, which is similar to that offered here, see *Moral Vision,* pp. 28-31. For other similar, but lengthier, readings, see Gerald F. Hawthorne, "The Imitation of Christ: Discipleship in Philippians," in Richard N. Longenecker, ed., *Patterns of Discipleship in the New Testament* (Grand Rapids: Eerdmans, 1996), pp. 163-79; William S. Kurz, "Kenotic Imitation of Paul and of Christ in Philippians 2 and 3," in Fernando F. Segovia, ed., *Discipleship in the New Testament* (Philadelphia: Fortress, 1985), pp. 103-26; Larry W. Hurtado, "Jesus as Lordly Example in Philippians 2.5-11," in Peter Richardson and

Above all, the content of this "daring improbability" is cruciform love.

As we noted in the previous chapter, the theme of love in Philippians begins with the apostle's autobiographical remarks and wishes in chapter 1. In 1:8 Paul expresses his concern for the Philippians as a yearning for them with the affection of Christ Jesus, pointing ahead to the hymn. He narrates his own decision to demonstrate Christ-like selfless affection for the Philippians over selfish gain for himself (1:20-26). Moreover, Paul says, inasmuch as the Philippians' love overflows they will bring glory (Greek *doxan*) to God on the day of Christ (1:10-11). By connecting "love" and "glory" Paul again anticipates his interpretation of Christ's story of love in action that brings glory to God (cf. 2:1, 11). At the beginning of the letter, then, Paul depicts himself and issues his basic appeal in the language of the self-renouncing slavery paradigm, with the accent falling heavily on its being a paradigm of affection and love.

The apostle begins his parenesis, or exhortation, in earnest in 1:27. In 1:27-30 he calls his readers to be unified (v. 27) and to suffer as he does (vv. 29-30) for the gospel, for to them it has been graciously granted (Greek *echaristhē*) by Christ not only to believe in him (literally, "into," Greek *eis*) but also to suffer for him. This call comes in response to opposition from outside the community. Then, in 2:1-4, the immediate context of the hymn, Paul calls the Philippians to unity in love, perhaps in the face of dissensions within:

> [1]If then there is any encouragement in Christ, any consolation from love, any sharing in the Spirit, any compassion and sympathy, [2]make my joy complete: be of the same mind, having the same love, being in full accord and of one mind. [3]Do nothing from selfish ambition or conceit, but in humility regard others as better than yourselves. [4]Let each of you look not to your own interests, but to the interests of others. (Phil. 2:1-4)

The passage consists of four presuppositions[53] about life in Christ (v. 1), an exhortation to the Philippians to complete Paul's joy by being united in attitude/mind (v. 2a), and a series of phrases that restate and amplify the meaning of the

---

John C. Hurd, eds., *From Jesus to Paul,* Francis W. Beare Festschrift (Waterloo: Wilfred Laurier University Press, 1984); and Stephen E. Fowl, *The Story of Christ in the Ethics of Paul: An Analysis of the Function of the Hymnic Material in the Pauline Corpus,* JSNTSup 36 (Sheffield: JSOT Press, 1990), pp. 77-101.

53. The "if" that introduces the verse, in combination with the series of occurrences of the word "any," should be read rhetorically to imply the actual existence, rather than the possibility, of the conditions (e.g., almost as "since").

unity ("the same mind"; Greek *to auto phronēte*) Paul calls for at the beginning of verse 2 — which is itself an echo of 1:27. In these verses Paul brings together numerous expressions to make one main point: unity in love.[54]

In v. 1 Paul sets out the theological, pastoral, and ecclesiological context for the exhortation to follow. Paul reminds the Philippians that both he and they are "in Christ" and that the church is the province of the Spirit. In Christ the norm is "encouragement" and "love" (Greek *paraklēsis* and *agapē*). The Spirit who operates in the Church produces *koinōnia*, fellowship expressed in affection and compassion. Paul introduces his parenesis, therefore, with a reminder of the way of love, community, and affection that is the norm for life together in Christ. This positive, indicative description of the normal way the Spirit operates in the Church ("in Christ") becomes the content of the specific exhortations in verses 2b-4.

Verses 2b-4 first present three positive affirmations about unity in love (v. 2b) corresponding to the description of life in Christ in 2:1. Then, as we noted in chapter eight, follow two pairs of radically opposed phrases, each disjoined by the word "but" (Greek *alla*):

2:3	2:4
Do nothing from selfish ambition or conceit,	Let each of you look not to your own interests,
but	but
in humility regard others as better than yourselves.	[look] to the interests of others.

Pitted against one another in verse 3 are acting in selfishness, ambition, and conceit (Greek *kenodoxian*), on the one hand, and regarding (Greek *hēgoumenoi*) and therefore treating others as better than oneself, on the other. Opposed in verse 4 are looking out for "your own interests" (*ta heautōn* . . .

---

54. Cf. David Alan Black, "Paul and Christian Unity: A Formal Analysis of Philippians 2:1-4," *Journal of the Evangelical Theological Society* 28 (1985): 299-304. Johnson (*Writings*, pp. 372-73) notes that Paul uses typical Hellenistic "rhetoric of friendship" to make his point. In 1:27, for instance, Paul uses the Greek phrases "in one spirit" and "in one soul." (See further Stanley K. Stowers, "Friends and Enemies in the Politics of Heaven," in Jouette M. Bassler, ed., *Pauline Theology*, vol. 1: *Thessalonians, Philippians, Galatians, Philemon* [Minneapolis: Fortress, 1991], pp. 105-21.) However, even if the language used here is that of friendship, Paul grounds the believers' mutual responsibilities in theological realities and uses the language of friendship not descriptively, but prescriptively. In so doing, does he not alter the meaning of friendship from a relationship that happens quite by accident (perhaps due to common interests) to a relationship that can be mandated because of a preexisting common interest or relationship ("in Christ"), and a common exemplar?

skopountes) and looking out for "the interests of others."[55] In Philippians 2:3-4, then, selfish action is twice opposed to action directed toward and for others. What the Philippians should *not* do is radically contrasted with what they *should* do.

As we noted in chapter eight, 2:3-4 and 2:6-8 have clearly parallel structures. There is a striking similarity between the pair of "not [*y*] but rather [*z*]" imperatives in 2:3-4 and the sequence of "not [*y*] but rather [*z*]" indicative phrases in 2:6-8, where Christ's self-emptying and self-humbling are described using the same pattern. These structural parallels can be seen clearly in the following chart:

Philippians 2:3, 4 (rearranged)	Philippians 2:6-8
	who, though he was in the form of God,
Do nothing from selfish ambition or conceit [Greek *kenodoxian;* literally, "empty glory"] [and] Let each of you look not to your own interests [Greek *ta heautōn*]	did not **regard** [Greek *hēgēsato*] equality with God as something to be exploited,
but [Greek *alla*]	but [Greek *alla*]
in **humility** [Greek *tapeinophrosynē*] **regard** [Greek *hēgoumenoi*] others as better than yourselves [Greek *hyper-echontas heautōn*] [and]	emptied himself [Greek *heauton ekenōsen*], taking the form of a slave, being born in human likeness. And being found in human form, he **humbled himself** [Greek *etapeinōsen heauton*] and became obedient to the point of death — even death on a cross.
[look] to the interests of others.	

55. The word "interests" (Greek *symphora*) is missing but implied. Compare 1 Cor. 10:24; 13:5, where similar phrases do not have the Greek word "interests," and 10:33, where the word does appear. By "interests" Paul means benefit of any kind, but primarily edification in Christ (cf. the application of 1 Corinthians 13 to 1 Corinthians 14). The adversative conjunction *alla* ("but rather") in 1 Cor. 10:24, 33, as here, radically disjoins self-interest and concern for others. The similarity of context (unity and love) and construction ("not self but others") between 1 Corinthians and Philippians further confirms that Paul intends the reader to supply *symphora* after *ta heautōn* and *ta heterōn* ("others").

In both columns the word "but" disjoins radically opposed actions, the first of which is negated and the other(s) affirmed. Moreover, in the phrases disjoined in both the hymn and the exhortation, reflexive constructions are employed to indicate that the acts Christ performed and the acts the Philippians ought to perform involve the self deeply in a choice between radical opposites.[56]

As the chart shows, the similarities between verses 3-4 in the parenesis and verses 6-8 in the hymn are not limited to structure but extend also to vocabulary. These verbal parallels give expression to several fundamental conceptual similarities between the parenesis and the hymn. Because Christ "emptied himself" and later received the exalted status he did not seek or use to his own advantage, the Philippians should do nothing out of "conceit" — literally "empty glory." Just as Christ "humbled himself," the Philippians are instructed to "regard" others better than themselves — in "humility." Just as Christ did not "regard" his position to be something to use for selfish advantage, so also the Philippians are to do nothing out of selfish ambition.[57] In saying "no" to selfishness, they act in love and thereby create the unity Paul finds so essential to the community's life.

The parallels we have noted demonstrate that for Paul the story of Christ must become the story of the community. The pattern of life to be exhibited by those who are in Christ may be summarized not only in terms of moral virtues — "not 'empty glory' but humility" — but also, and more fundamentally, in terms of self-orientation and action — "looking out not for self but for others." Moreover, it is clear that for Paul there is a radical opposition between looking out for self and concern for others. These two opposites could no more be complementary than could Christ's self-emptying and his self-serving utilization of equality with God.[58]

---

56. So too, in 1 Cor. 10:24–11:1, Paul explicitly grounds his "not [y] but rather [z] exhortation" (10:24) immediately in himself (10:33) but ultimately in Christ (11:1). Earlier in Philippians (1:19-26), as we saw at the end of the previous chapter, Paul does the same thing implicitly in the context of Philippians.

57. In addition to these parallels between vv. 3-4 and vv. 6-8, there is a distinct similarity between the Greek phrases *hyperechontas heautōn* (v. 3) and *auton hyperypsōsen* ("highly exalted," v. 9) and between *kenodoxian* (v. 3) and *doxan* ("glory," v. 11). Exalting *oneself* above others is antithetical to exaltation by God; so too, self-glory and the glory of God are mutually exclusive. The "exaltation" pattern from 2:9-11 clearly has no place in Paul's parenesis as something to be sought or self-imposed. Confirming Paul's rejection of the "exaltation" pattern for present existence is the contrast between the duty of suffering given *(echaristhē)* to believers (1:29) and the name and honor given *(echarisato)* to Christ (2:9).

58. It should be noted again that 2:4 does not contain the word "only" (Greek *monon*), though it does in some translations: "not only for your own interests." Nor does the Greek construction *alla kai* imply such an addition, for it would contradict the texts in 1 Corinthians and, more importantly, the sharp contrast here in 2:6-11. The *kai* following *alla* increases rather than

Thus the structure, vocabulary, and essential message of the exhortation to unity in love that is presented in verses 3-4 closely parallel the narrative of Christ's self-humbling in verses 6-8 within the larger narrative of humiliation and glory contained in verses 6-11. Paul intends the exhortation to the Philippians and the narrative of Christ's self-emptying and self-humbling to be understood as two versions of one self-renouncing, others-regarding pattern of slavery, with Christ as the paradigm and the Philippians as the "reincarnation." From Christ, then, the Philippians learn the meaning of love. By abiding in Christ, their living and loving Lord, they naturally will engage in analogous, though new and different, acts of Christ's love.[59]

Following 2:1-11, Paul turns in 2:19-30 to his immediate plans to send Timothy (2:19-24) and Epaphroditus (2:25-30) to the Philippians as he awaits his own fate (2:23-24). Although the form and ostensible subject of these paragraphs are quite different from the preceding parenesis, in reality the same theme is continued: others-oriented rather than self-oriented living. Paul provides three examples of this paradigm of love, of self-renouncing slavery to and interest in others — himself, Timothy, and Epaphroditus — and one example of the opposite — those around him other than Timothy.

Paul says that his own happiness depends on knowing "news" of the Philippians (Greek *ta peri hymōn*, 2:19). Paul does not simply want news for the sake of news; he is deeply concerned about the Philippians. Timothy, like Paul, is also exemplary in that he is "genuinely concerned" about the Philippians'

---

decreases the force of *alla:* "but rather," not "but also." See also p. 160, n. 10; and Markus Bockmuehl, *The Epistle to the Philippians,* Black's New Testament Commntaries (London: A. & C. Black, 1997), pp. 113-14.

59. Similarly also Gerald F. Hawthorne, *Philippians,* Word Biblical Commentary 43 (Waco, Tex.: Word, 1983), p. 89. It must be noted that Paul does not use precisely the same language to describe what the Philippians ought to do and what Christ did. Paul does not seek to minimize the uniqueness of what Christ did and of God's response to that; only Christ became a human being, died on the cross, and was exalted to universal lordship. Those such as Ralph P. Martin who have rejected the "exemplary" interpretation in part because of Christ's uniqueness fail to perceive that Paul clearly wants to ground the Philippians' way of life in Christ's way and that his primary concern is the similarities, not the differences, between these two ways. In fact, Stephen Fowl perceptively suggests that Paul's use of the analogy of Christ and the believing community, with Christ as exemplar, is like analogies and exemplars universally in depending on "similarities-in-difference" (*Story,* pp. 92-95). "It is up to Paul to note the similarities-in-difference between the story of Christ narrated in 2:6-11 and the particular situation of the church and to draw the appropriate analogies" (pp. 94-95). Drawing on a term coined by philosopher John Milbank, Fowl also refers to this kind of analogical imitation as "non-identical repetition" ("Christology and Ethics in Philippians 2:5-11," in Ralph P. Martin and Brian J. Dodd, eds., *Where Christology Began: Essays on Philippians 2* [Louisville: Westminster/John Knox, 1998], p. 148).

"welfare" (2:20; Greek *ta peri hymōn*). He is held up in contrast to those "seeking their own interests" (2:21; Greek *ta heautōn,* as in 2:4). Furthermore, Timothy is exemplary because he has shown himself to be a slave, as indeed was Christ (2:22; *edouleusen;* cf. *doulou* in 2:7), with Paul for the gospel. Now, "seeking their own interests" is contrasted not merely with concern for others but with seeking the interests or concerns of Jesus Christ. By not being concerned about the believers in Philippi, the others simultaneously show themselves unconcerned about the things of Christ. The proof of seeking Christ's interests, for Paul, is loving concern for others rather than for oneself.

Epaphroditus is also an example of the paradigm of cruciform love for others. He is Paul's servant (Greek *leitourgon,* v. 25), completing the Philippians' service (Greek *leitourgias,* v. 30; cf. *leitourgia,* v. 17) to Paul; he is deeply concerned about (Greek *epipothōn,* v. 26) the Philippians; and he had been at the point of dying (Greek *thanatō,* v. 27; *mechri thanatou ēngisen* ["came close to death"], v. 30; cf. *mechri thanatou* ["obedient to the point of death"] of Christ in v. 8). The appeal to Euodia and Syntyche in 4:2 also echoes 2:1-11. Paul repeats both the ground for his exhortation ("in the Lord"; cf. 2:5, 11) and, in shorthand form, its norm of unity in love (Greek *to auto phronein;* cf. 2:2) — that is, the unity that is achieved by embodying the paradigm of self-renouncing regard for others. In these people Paul finds examples of the paradigm, established by Christ, of "not seeking one's own." As is the case in the parenesis, the vocabulary is sometimes the same as and sometimes different from the vocabulary of 2:6-8, but the paradigm is the same.[60]

Finally, in 4:14-20 Paul commends the Philippians for their fellowship with him in suffering (v. 14), specifically their provision of a financial gift, which was a sacrifice pleasing to God. By so doing, Paul implies, the church was conformed to the paradigm that he was urging and that was found in himself and ultimately in Christ. They had acted obediently, like Christ, in cruciform love, toward him. Now, they should do the same toward one another.

Love as Renouncing Power and Receiving a Sibling in Philemon

Paul's briefest letter is also perhaps his most rhetorically masterful. Whatever the precise circumstances of Onesimus's departure, it is likely that the once-unbelieving, now-believing slave owes something to Philemon, his believing

---

60. For similar interpretations, see: Hawthorne, *Philippians,* p. 108, passim; R. A. Culpepper, "Coworkers in Suffering: Philippians 2:19-30," *Review and Expositor* 77 (1980): 349-58; Johnson, *Writings,* pp. 375-77.

owner, after having wronged him (v. 18). Paul's task in this letter is to convince Philemon, in the presence of the church that meets in his house (vv. 1-2), to treat Onesimus as he would treat Paul himself — as a brother in Christ, for so he is.

To accomplish this task, Paul must convince Philemon that he and his slave are now brothers. Paul informs Philemon that Onesimus is now his son (v. 10), clearly a reference to Onesimus's conversion in the prison with Paul. Paul then reminds Philemon that he, too, is Paul's son in the faith, which is certainly the meaning of the phrase "your owing me even your own self" (v. 19). If Paul is the spiritual father of each man, then clearly they are brothers — "sons" of Paul, brothers in Christ. In other words they are both, and equally, "holy ones" or "saints," Paul's common term for believers.

Philemon, Paul says early in the missive in his thanksgiving, has a reputation:

> [4]When I remember you in my prayers, I always thank my God [5]because I hear of your **love for all the saints** and your faith toward the Lord Jesus. (Philem. 4-5 [emphasis added])

Paul himself has been the indirect beneficiary of "your [Philemon's] love" because "the hearts of the saints have been refreshed through you, my brother" (v. 7). Now Paul urges Philemon his partner (vv. 1b, 17) and brother (again in v. 20) to act for Paul's benefit once more (v. 20) by welcoming Onesimus "as you would welcome me" (v. 17). Indeed, Onesimus is Paul's "own heart" (v. 12); he is not only Paul's son but his brother (v. 16).

With that combination of logical and emotional appeal before him, what choice does Philemon have except, once again, to exercise love for the saints by showing love toward Philemon? Yet what concretely would that mean for Philemon and for Onesimus? Paul's answer is direct:

> [15]Perhaps this is the reason he was separated from you for a while, so that you might have him back forever, [16]no longer as a slave but more than a slave, a beloved brother — especially to me but how much more to you, both in the flesh and in the Lord. (vv. 15-16)

Onesimus is no longer Philemon's slave but more than a slave, a brother. There has been a dramatic change in Onesimus's status and thus in the relationship between him and Philemon, a change that affects their relationship both within the Church ("in the Lord") and more generally ("in the flesh"). Any power or rights Philemon once had over Onesimus (including, but not limited to, punishment if Onesimus wronged Philemon) have been abolished, because the slave-master relationship has ended. If Paul is willing to sacrifice himself in a

Christ-like way to pay Onesimus's debt to Philemon (see v. 18 and the discussion in the previous chapter), then Philemon himself can and must respond in kind to Onesimus.

That Paul expects this to happen as an act of Philemon's obedience (v. 21) suggests that the apostle is once again connecting faith, or obedience, with love. If Philemon truly has faith, he will express it in love for a saint, just as he has always done (v. 5). What ultimately matters in this letter is not the supposedly thinly veiled command of Paul but the uncompromising law of Christ. For Philemon, failing to obey Paul here would be failing to show love and therefore also failing to show faith. It would be a denial of his reputation for these virtues (v. 5) and, more importantly, of his very identity. It would be a decision to undo the decision he made at baptism irrevocably to put on the story of Christ and to allow all of his relationships to be governed by the lordship of Christ.[61] For this reason, by letter Paul "engineers a crisis for his fellow worker" — and simultaneously for the entire community.[62]

It is difficult, therefore, to avoid the conclusion that this obedience means forgiving Onesimus for any harm or wrong, refraining from punishment, releasing him from slavery, and welcoming him back permanently as his brother in the Church, not as his slave. Although, according to Roman law, Philemon probably has certain rights over his slave, Paul calls him to model his behavior on Paul himself and not to exercise his power and rights but to demonstrate love. The familiar pattern of "although [x], not [y] but [z]" appears once again.

EXCURSUS: CRUCIFORM LOVE IN EPHESIANS, WITH SPECIAL REFERENCE TO EPHESIANS 5

Although the focus of this book is on the undisputed letters of Paul, and the authorship of Ephesians is disputed, the theme of cruciform love does occur in Ephesians, and it does so in connection with a controversial text on marriage (5:21-33). For this reason, it merits some attention. The text on marriage can only be understood in the larger context of the letter and what it says about the fundamental responsibility of believers to one another: self-sacrificing, mutually submitting love.

61. See the similar interpretation in Norman R. Petersen, *Rediscovering Paul: Philemon and the Sociology of Paul's Narrative World* (Philadelphia: Fortress, 1985), esp. pp. 269-70: "If Philemon slams the door of his house in Onesimus's face in rejection of Paul's 'appeal,' he will be tacitly excluding himself from the house church into which he has retreated" (p. 270).
62. Petersen, *Rediscovering Paul*, p. 269, cf. pp. 99, 288.

The letter to the Ephesians (if it was indeed sent to Ephesus)[63] can be divided rather nearly into two main sections, chapters 1–3 and chapters 4–6, the former dealing primarily with the indicative of salvation ("theology"), the latter primarily with the consequent imperative of salvation ("ethics"; note the "therefore" of 4:1). The second half opens with a general call to "lead a life worthy of the calling to which you have been called" (4:1) that enumerates standard Pauline virtues: humility, gentleness, patience, love, and unity. Life in the body of Christ is then described, with leaders being expected to "equip the saints for the work of ministry" (4:12) and all persons in the community being urged to speak the truth "in love" (4:15) and, once equipped, to foster "the body's growth in building itself up in love" (4:16).

This general description of community life acts as a preface to a more sustained characterization of the necessary contrast between the readers' old way of life and their new way, the way of Christ (4:17–6:20). Central to this way of life is the experience of God's forgiveness, found in the self-sacrificing love of Christ and logically requiring a corresponding life of forgiveness and self-sacrificial love:

> [31]Put away from you all bitterness and wrath and anger and wrangling and slander, together with all malice, [32]and be kind to one another, tenderhearted, forgiving one another, as God in Christ has forgiven you. [5:1]Therefore be imitators of God, as beloved children, [2]and live in love, as Christ loved us and gave himself up for us [Greek *ēgapēsen hēmas kai paredōken heauton hyper hēmōn*],[64] a fragrant offering and sacrifice to God. (Eph. 4:31–5:2)

Following additional discussion and admonitions about the new life over against the old (5:3-16), the section concludes its general exhortations for the entire community with a final call to understand the will of the Lord and to be filled, not with wine, but with the Spirit, which is defined with a series of several communal responsibilities:

> [18]Do not get drunk with wine, for that is debauchery; but be filled with the Spirit, [19]as you sing psalms and hymns and spiritual songs among yourselves, singing and making melody to the Lord in your hearts, [20]giving thanks to

---

63. The absence of "in Ephesus" from the address (1:1) in some manuscripts renders the destination of the letter impossible to ascertain with certainty.

64. This text is parallel to the phrase from Gal. 2:20 that we have translated "who loved me by giving himself for me" *(tou agapēsantos me kai paradontos heauton hyper emou)* and should be translated similarly: "Christ loved us by giving himself up for us."

God the Father at all times and for everything in the name of our Lord Jesus Christ. [21]Be subject to one another out of reverence for Christ. (Eph. 5:18-21)

A more literal rendition of verses 18b-21, in which all the Greek verbs following the injunction to "be filled" are participles, would be as follows:

> [18]. . . [Be] filled with the Spirit, by
> [19]*singing* psalms and hymns and spiritual songs among yourselves,
> *singing and making melody to the Lord* in your hearts,
> [20]*giving thanks to God the Father* at all times and for everything in
> the name of our Lord Jesus Christ,
> [21]*being subject to one another* out of reverence for Christ.

The "filling" of the Spirit, in other words, puts the members of the community into special relationship with God the Father, Jesus Christ, and one another. With respect to God and Christ, this is fundamentally a relationship of joyful, musical praise; with respect to fellow believers, it is one of mutual submission.

Whatever else "mutual submission" or "being subject to one another" means (v. 21), it is here set forth as the hallmark of the entire transformed, believing community. It is the central principle of life together, the nonnegotiable norm of all relationships. It must be understood, therefore, as another way of saying "live in love, as Christ loved us by giving himself up for us" (5:2, author's translation). (This equation of the terms "love" and "being subject" is confirmed by their use in 5:21-33, as we will see.) For that reason, the author does not leave the norm in general terms but attempts to apply it to some of the most complex relationships within the believing community: husband-wife, father-children, even master-slave (5:22–6:9). This cruciform love must somehow penetrate all these relationships.

The husband-wife relationship is addressed first (5:21-33). This text has been interpreted in four main ways, which may be labeled patriarchal, radical, modified radical, and egalitarian. The patriarchal interpretation sees the wife as having a subordinate place to the husband and affirms this role; the radical view agrees that the text makes the wife inferior but then rejects the text as patriarchal and oppressive; the modified radical perspective finds a qualified patriarchy in the text; and the egalitarian reading finds, and affirms, equality given to the husband and wife.

The patriarchal, radical, and modified radical interpretations agree that the woman is given an inferior place. It is argued that she alone is told to "be subject" (vv. 22, 24), and subject "in everything" (v. 24), while the husband is explicitly called "the head of the wife just as Christ is the head of the church"

(v. 23) and the wife (at least implicitly) his body (vv. 28-29), suggesting that the husband alone has the Christ-like role of head and savior.[65]

Although on first reading this interpretation has some obvious points in its favor, it must be fundamentally questioned for four significant reasons. First, the principal verbs used to describe marital responsibility — "be subject" (vv. 22, 24), "respect" (v. 33) and "love [as Christ loved the church by giving himself up for her]" (vv. 25, 28, 33) — are drawn directly from the general, fundamental injunctions to all believers stated in 5:2 and 5:21, as the following parallels (author's translation) indicate:

Wives

5:21   All must be subject to one another in the respect of Christ[66]
          hypotassomenoi allēlois en phobō Christou

5:22, 24   Wives, [being subject] to your husbands as to the Lord. . . . Just as the church is subject to Christ, so also wives [are to be subject] to their husbands in all things.
          hai gynaikes tois idiois andrasin hōs tō kyriō . . . hōs hē ekklēsia
          hypotassetai tō Christō, houtōs kai hai gynaikes tois andrasin en panti

5:33   . . . a wife should respect her husband.
          hē de gynē hina phobētai ton andra

65. For a radical reading of this text, see E. Elizabeth Johnson, "Ephesians," in Carol A. Newsom and Sharon H. Ringe, eds., *The Women's Bible Commentary,* expanded ed. (Louisville: Westminster/John Knox, 1998), pp. 428-32. According to Johnson, this text is a "reassertion of conventional patriarchal morality" that "contradicts" Paul and from which the "patriarchal sting" cannot be removed by appeal to 5:21 (p. 431). Actually, however, most contemporary interpreters find some version of qualified patriarchy in the text. Elisabeth Schüssler Fiorenza (*In Memory of Her: A Feminist Theological Reconstruction of Christian Origins* [New York: Crossroad, 1983], pp. 266-70), often associated with a critique of radical patriarchy, claims that 5:22 "clearly reinforces the patriarchal marriage pattern" but admits that this is "radically questioned" by the references to Christ's "paradigmatic love" (pp. 269-70). J. Paul Sampley (*'And the Two Shall Become One Flesh': A Study of Traditions in Ephesians 5:21-33* [Cambridge: Cambridge University Press, 1971]) admits that 5:21 is supposed to qualify the household code that the writer inherits, but "husbands are nowhere in 5:22-23 exhorted to submission or to anything like submission" (pp. 116-17). Andrew Lincoln (*Ephesians,* Word Biblical Commentary 42 [Waco, Tex.: Word, 1990], pp. 366-74) goes a bit further: he refers to 5:1-2 in his discussion of 5:21-33 but implies that the passage still treats women as unequal to men (p. 374). Nevertheless, Lincoln argues, the passage does challenge the patriarchal status quo by using the verb *agapaō* (not normally part of household codes), by omitting any exhortation to husbands to rule, and by implying that the "exercise of headship . . . will not be through self-assertion but through self-sacrifice" (p. 374).

66. The use of the verb "respect" *(phobeomai)* in v. 33 suggests that the "respect" mentioned in v. 21 refers not only to "reverence for Christ" (NRSV) but also to mutual respect within the community.

Husbands

5:2   All must walk in love, just as Christ also loved us by handing himself
over for us. . . .
*peripateite en agapē, kathōs kai ho Christos ēgapēsen hēmas kai
paredōken heauton hyper hēmōn . . .*

5:25   Husbands, love your wives just as also Christ loved the church by
handing himself over for it.
*hoi andres, agapate tas gynaikas kathōs kai ho Christos ēgapēsen tēn
ekklēsian kai heauton paredōken hyper autēs*

In each case, marital responsibility — whether that of the wife or the husband
— is no different from the responsibilities of all believers. Although the text
grounds the rationale for the separate responsibilities in different aspects of the
Christ-believer relationship, which provides some tension within the text, it is
nonetheless the case that wives and husbands alike are being called to act out in
marriage the same type of self-sacrificing, respectful, submissive love they
would in any and all relationships within the believing community.

Second, this understanding of marital relationships indicated by the vocabulary is reinforced by the structure (syntax) of verse 22. Although most
translations, including the NRSV, begin a new sentence at 5:22, the Greek text
of 5:22 must be seen as a continuation of 5:21. This is absolutely clear because
there is no verb in 5:22; the verbal idea is implied or borrowed from the participial phrase in 5:21, "being subject to one another." In other words, 5:22 is completely dependent on 5:21. The import of this connection may be shown in the
following translation:

> [21]Be filled with the Spirit . . . by being subject to one another in the respect of
> Christ — [22]wives to your husbands. . . .

It is as if the responsibility of wives to their husbands is presented as the first example of the meaning of mutual submission within the believing community;
one expects that more will follow. The wife's marital responsibility may have
particular manifestations, but it is essentially the same obligation that she has
to all members of the community.

Third, the connection between the husband's responsibility and the narrative cruciform paradigm of Christ precludes any interpretation of the text that
would grant the husband some sort of power over his wife that contradicts that
self-giving, altruistic love of Christ. The kindness and tenderheartedness expected of believers because of their experience of God's love in Christ applies to
husbands as to all men in the community. In fact, the love to which husbands

are called in marriage is a death experience, in which the self denies its own will and gives itself to another for the other's good. This responsibility of the husband, then, is no less a form of subjection to his wife than is her subjection to him — despite the fact that different verbs are used for each one's obligation.

Fourth, then, the parallelism of obligations within marriage suggests that the primary purpose of the "head" and "body" language in 5:22-33 is *not* to reinforce hierarchy and stress differences in marital roles. Rather, the language is intended to show the need for mutual care because of the unity of persons that marriage creates (cf. especially v. 31). The language of "submitting to one's head" and "caring for one's own body" does not, then, *express* patriarchal or patronizing values but *challenges* them.

It is beyond the scope of this excursus to deal at length with the remaining topics of fathers and children and of slaves and masters. The principles developed in this excursus apply, however, also to those relationships. While the particulars may vary depending on the circumstances in life, masters and fathers are now called to act in ways that befit their having Jesus as their master and God as their father. That this entails relationships of love, of self-giving, and even of mutual submission is implied by everything in the context.

Conclusion: The Story of Love

Cruciform love is, for Paul, a polyvalent motif. As Richard Hays says, Paul does not provide "a predetermined rule or set of rules for conduct; rather, the right action must be *discerned* on the basis of a christological paradigm, with a view to the need of the community."[67] Believers live within the law, or pattern, of the crucified Messiah's love. Paul's creative term for himself in 1 Corinthians 9:21 — "within the law of the Messiah" — applies to all believers; they are, as James Dunn says, "in-lawed to Christ."[68] We might more specifically say that they are living into the story that has given them life.[69]

---

67. Hays, *Moral Vision*, p. 43 (emphasis his).

68. Dunn, *Theology*, p. 668, and Ben Witherington III, *Paul's Narrative Thought World: The Tapestry of Tragedy and Triumph* (Louisville: Westminster/John Knox, 1994), p. 240.

69. For another approach to Paul that also stresses the pattern of "faith expressing itself in love" as the coherent structure of Paul's experience, letters, and theology, see now Troels Engberg-Pedersen, *Paul and the Stoics* (Louisville: Westminster/John Knox, 2000). Although I do not agree that this structure derives from the Stoics, Engberg-Pedersen rightly contends that central to Paul is the experience of moving from self-centeredness to other-centeredness via identification with Christ.

To paraphrase the apostle's encomium to love in 1 Corinthians 13, we may conclude this chapter in the following words:

Cruciform love is faith in action. It does not seek its own good but the good of others. Indeed, for the good of others it renounces the use of certain rights. Cruciform love edifies others and never harms them, not even enemies. It never retaliates or uses violence. Cruciform love welcomes diversity. It is not judgmental, but neither is it tolerant of values antithetical to the cross, and at times it can be tough.

Cruciform love is hospitable and generous, especially to the poor and weak — those marginalized or rejected by others. If it has worldly status, it becomes downwardly mobile in order to lift others up. It gives of itself and its material possessions. Cruciform love, in a word, continues the story of the cross in new times and places. Cruciform love is imaginative.

CHAPTER 11

CRUCIFORM POWER

The Paradox of Weakness

As we observed in chapter eight, Paul is well known for his suffering as an apostle of Jesus Christ. That he interpreted his suffering as an experience of love — both his love for others and the presence of God's love for him — was the subject of that chapter. In this chapter we consider yet another, though related, paradoxical aspect of the apostle's experience: power in weakness. Indeed, this is undoubtedly the signature paradox of Paul's apostolic existence: that he found in his weakness and suffering the power of God.[1] We may refer to this paradox as Paul's experience of cruciform power, because it shares in the shape and thus the power of the crucified Christ, who is, for Paul, the power of God.

In this chapter we look first briefly at the meaning of power in the ancient world and in Paul's experience apart from Christ. We then proceed to an examination of Christ as the power of God in Paul's life, and to his experience of that power in his ministry. We continue with a brief consideration of the relationship between cruciform power and cruciform love, and conclude with an exploration of the meaning of cruciform power for Paul's readers.

Power in the Ancient World and in Paul's Experience apart from the Power of Christ

Power is a difficult word to define. Today it is frequently understood as a relationship rather than as something one "possesses." Without denying the rela-

---

1. Thomas H. Tobin calls power the "root metaphor" of Paul's life (*The Spirituality of Paul,* Message of Biblical Spirituality 4 [Collegeville, Minn.: Liturgical, 1991], pp. 64-68).

tional character of power, we are primarily interested, in this chapter, in power understood as the ability to exercise significant control or influence, either for good or for ill, over people and/or history. Power, we might say, is the ability to form or to transform.[2]

Some Forms of Greco-Roman Power

In the ancient world, power lay first in the hands of the gods and of other suprahuman entities and forces, and then also in the hands of humans who somehow had a share in these suprahuman powers. Among humans, political authorities had a close connection to the gods: "in the ancient world religious authority was the wellspring and symbol of all social control and political authority and might."[3] In Paul's time, the greatest human power was imperial. The *pax Romana,* or Roman peace, over which the emperor presided was possible only because of the power that he and his subordinates wielded.

The emperor was perceived by his supporters as nearly (or actually) divine even before, but especially after, his death. Out of this there developed a complex system of emperor adulation known as the "imperial cult," an interconnected network of religio-political symbols, buildings, and practices: images, statues, temples, oaths, hymns, games, rhetoric and poetry contests, and other public events in honor of the emperor.[4] This attitude and its corresponding cult were part of a complex ideology that invested the Roman empire with divine authority and blessing; indeed, for many, imperial rule was a divine "golden age," a kind of paradise on earth, the realization of secular and religious hopes. The emperor was not only the god-man who presided over this divine order but also a father figure managing the great imperial household. By many, then, imperial power was perceived to be beneficent, like the power of any good Roman patriarch.

---

2. For a similar, independent definition, see Graham Tomlin, *The Power of the Cross: Theology and the Death of Christ in Paul, Luther, and Pascal* (Carlisle, U.K.: Paternoster, 1999), p. 313: "the capability to influence people or situations and to transform them."

3. Dieter Georgi, *Theocracy in Paul's Praxis and Theology* (Minneapolis, Minn.: Fortress, 1991), p. 54.

4. There is much literature on this topic. For a brief overview, see Klaus Wengst, *Pax Romana and the Peace of Jesus Christ,* trans. John Bowden (Philadelphia: Fortress, 1987), pp. 46-51. For more depth, see also S. R. F. Price, "Rituals and Power," in Richard A. Horsley, ed., *Paul and Empire: Religion and Power in Roman Imperial Society* (Harrisburg, Pa.: Trinity, 1997), pp. 47-71; Paul Zanker, "The Power of Images," in Richard A. Horsley, ed., *Paul and Empire: Religion and Power in Roman Imperial Society* (Harrisburg, Pa.: Trinity, 1997), pp. 72-86; and Alistair Kee, "The Imperial Cult: The Unmasking of an Ideology," *Scottish Journal of Religious Studies* 6 (1985): 112-28.

Yet not by all. The peace over which the emperor presided was, for many others, oppression, nothing less than raw power. Imperial power meant the power to crush opposition, to expand borders, to colonize, to enslave, and to crucify. It is no wonder, then, that enemies of the imperial power developed and sometimes found expression in outright revolt, as in the Jewish war of 66-70 and the revolt of 135.[5]

The emperor was at the top of a ladder of Roman power, with his closest associates just beneath him. Below the most powerful lay a hierarchy of power, "a culture of competition based on meritocracy . . . in which admiration, esteem, and recognition were crucial motivating factors."[6] The higher up the ladder people were, the greater the honor they were due and the closer to the divine realm they were believed to be. Indeed, "there was a slighting of the boundary that separates the human from the divine — in fact the superhuman was taken as the cultural standard."[7]

In this cultural context, "power" and "glory," or "honor," were associated with high culture and status. Among the means of possessing and displaying power and honor were wealth and abundance; political, social, and military achievements and influence; family heritage and status; friends; impressive physical appearance; learning; and eloquent speech.[8] Not to possess, or to lose, these status indicators resulted in shame; people who did so were not powerful but weak. Thus the great Roman orator Cicero asserted, "Rank must be preserved."[9] Though wealth itself was worshipped (the god *Pecunia*, or Money), the cult of money was, according to Roman historian Ramsay MacMullen, "tributary to another, Status *(Philotimia)*"; "[n]o word, understood to its depths, goes farther to explain the Greco-Roman achievement" than *philotimia.*[10] Status meant influence — power.

In addition to gods and humans, power was often thought to lie within the

---

5. See Ramsay MacMullen, *Enemies of the Roman Order* (Cambridge, Mass.: Harvard University Press, 1966).

6. Georgi, *Theocracy*, p. 63.

7. Georgi, *Theocracy*, p. 63.

8. See, e.g., Ramsay MacMullen's classic work, *Roman Social Relations: 50 B.C. to A.D. 284* (New Haven: Yale University Press, 1974), pp. 57-127 (esp. pp. 105-20), and, among many others, Raymond Pickett, *The Cross in Corinth: The Social Significance of the Death of Jesus,* JSNTSup 143 (Sheffield: Sheffield Academic Press, 1997), pp. 45-46, 184. Honor is a claim to worth combined with the acknowledgment of that worth by others (especially peers); see Bruce J. Malina, *The New Testament World: Insights from Cultural Anthropology,* rev. ed. (Louisville: Westminster/John Knox, 1993), pp. 25-35.

9. Cicero, *Pro Plancio (In Defense of Plancius)* 15, cited in MacMullen, *Roman Social Relations,* p. 105.

10. MacMullen, *Roman Social Relations,* pp. 118, 125.

stars and other cosmic entities and forces. Fate was frequently believed to exercise significant control, in concert with a variety of malevolent powers (Greek *daimones*), over individuals and history. For many people in the Greco-Roman world, from the lowest to the highest on the social ladder, such cosmic forces created anxiety and fear. The aim of religious and magical practices was, at least in part, to secure the favor and assistance of these forces.[11]

Power in Judaism

From earliest times, the people of Israel and their religious leaders of course knew about the beliefs and practices of their neighbors, even at times borrowing from and engaging those foreign ways. For them, the gods of the nations and other forces in the world did indeed possess power, but the one true and supreme God, Yahweh, had been victorious over such forces in the past and would again be victorious in the future. The power of the Lord was expressed not only in battle and deliverance (as in the Exodus)[12] but also in creation — which was itself a powerful victory over the forces of chaos — and in the ongoing maintenance of that creation. Since that creation was spoken into existence ("God said, 'Let there be . . .'"),[13] Israel emphatically affirmed the power of God's spoken word:

> [10][A]s the rain and the snow come down from heaven, and do not return there until they have watered the earth, making it bring forth and sprout, giving seed to the sower and bread to the eater, [11]so shall my word be that goes out from my mouth; it shall not return to me empty, but it shall accomplish that which I purpose, and succeed in the thing for which I sent it. (Isa. 55:10-11)

> [4]Now the word of the Lord came to me, saying, [5]"Before I formed you in the womb I knew you, and before you were born I consecrated you; I appointed you a prophet to the nations." . . . [9]Then the Lord put out his hand and touched my mouth; and the Lord said to me, "Now I have put my words in your mouth. [10]See, today I appoint you over nations and over kingdoms, to

---

11. For a full discussion, see Walter Wink's classic *Naming the Powers: The Language of Power in the New Testament* (Philadelphia: Fortress, 1984).

12. For example, Deut. 4:37a: "He brought you out of Egypt with his own presence, by his great power"; Ps. 66:3: "Say to God, 'How awesome are your deeds! Because of your great power, your enemies cringe before you.'"

13. Genesis 1; cf. Ps. 33:6, 9.

pluck up and to pull down, to destroy and to overthrow, to build and to plant." . . . [12]Then the Lord said to me, ". . . I am watching over my word to perform it." (Jer. 1:4-5, 9-10, 12)

Ultimately, God's power, known first by Israel in the Exodus, meant God's saving power, God's salvation: "May God be gracious to us and bless us and make his face to shine upon us, that your way may be known upon earth, your saving power among all nations" (Ps. 67:1-2). The specific meaning of that salvation was understood differently from age to age, but it always meant the deliverance of God's people from oppression as Israel and the Jews retold their story "through exodus memory."[14]

Apocalyptic Judaism, which emerged in the centuries immediately preceding Paul, retained the Hebrew tradition's worship of one powerful God but found the universe to be inhabited by other, lesser powers as well. Assisting God were angels, while opposed to God was (the) Satan, who was in turn assisted by various demons.[15]

Paul and Power(s)

Paul lived within the universe constructed by the Hebrew tradition and first-century apocalyptic Judaism, as well as the various pagan philosophical and religious traditions of his day. As we have noted in earlier chapters, his "cosmos is crowded with . . . personified malevolent figures."[16] Thus Paul affirms the existence and activity of suprahuman evil powers, beginning with "the god of this world" who "has blinded the minds of the unbelievers" (2 Cor. 4:4), and who is certainly to be identified with Satan. It is Satan who sent Paul the "thorn . . . in

14. Walter Brueggemann, *Theology of the Old Testament: Testimony, Dispute, Advocacy* (Minneapolis, Minn.: Fortress, 1997), p. 177. His discussion of Yahweh as the One who delivers, and its continuation with Jesus and Paul, is very insightful (pp. 174-81).

15. See the classic work of Kurt Koch, *The Rediscovery of Apocalyptic* (London: SCM, 1972).

16. Jerome H. Neyrey, *Paul, In Other Words: A Cultural Reading of His Letters* (Louisville: Westminster/John Knox, 1990), p. 162. Neyrey lists the following: death (1 Cor. 15:26; Rom. 5:14, 17), sin (Rom. 5:21; 6:12; 7:11-23), Satan (Rom. 16:20; 1 Cor. 5:5; 7:5; 2 Cor. 2:11; 11:14; 12:7; 1 Thess. 2:18), rule (Greek *archē;* 1 Cor. 15:24; Rom. 8:38), rulers (Greek *archontes;* 1 Cor. 2:6, 8), power (Greek *exousia, dynamis;* 1 Cor. 15:24), the tempter (1 Thess. 3:5), elements (Greek *stoicheia;* Gal. 4:3, 9), spirit of the world (1 Cor. 2:12), demons (1 Cor. 10:20-21), angels (1 Cor. 6:3; 2 Cor. 11:14; 12:7; Gal. 1:8; Rom. 8:38), and the god of this age/world (2 Cor. 4:4). For a brief but helpful discussion, see James D. G. Dunn, *The Theology of Paul the Apostle* (Grand Rapids: Eerdmans, 1998), pp. 104-10.

the flesh" to "torment" him (2 Cor. 12:7), and who attempts to tempt, outwit, and hinder believers.[17] Though Satan has power now, he will "shortly" be crushed by God (Rom. 16:20).

Paul also acknowledges the reality of additional traditional hostile powers in the universe. While others believe in various gods and lords (1 Cor. 8:5), Paul attributes their attraction and influence to "demons" (1 Cor. 10:19-22).[18] He also mentions the "elemental spirits" (Greek *stoicheia*) of the world (Gal. 4:3, 8-9), suggesting a link between certain cosmic powers and false religious beliefs and practices.[19] In his famous list of powers that cannot separate believers from God's love in Christ — though they must certainly make every effort to do so — Paul acknowledges the many hostile forces that could disturb people apart from Christ:

> [38]For I am convinced that neither death, nor life, nor angels, nor rulers, nor things present, nor things to come, nor powers, [39]nor height, nor depth, nor anything else in all creation, will be able to separate us from the love of God in Christ Jesus our Lord. (Rom. 8:38-39)[20]

The list in Romans 8 points to at least two other sets of hostile powers known to Paul, political and — for lack of a better term — anthropological. Regarding the former, the term "rulers" (Greek *archontes*) may be related to "angels" and/or "powers" as political forces are to the cosmic powers behind them. In 1 Corinthians 2:6-8 the rulers are almost certainly political powers, since they "crucified the Lord of glory." They, like Satan, belong to this (evil) age and are, again like Satan, "doomed to perish." That there is cosmic power behind such political power, in Paul's view, is likely.[21]

It is the "anthropological" powers, however, that are of greatest concern to

---

17. 1 Cor. 7:5; 2 Cor. 2:11; 11:14-15; 1 Thess. 2:18.

18. "The gods are not ontically nothing, but in their positive significance they are irrelevant. They are classified as powerless powers . . . as demons who are divinely worshipped but for whom worship is not appropriate" (Jürgen Becker, *Paul: Apostle to the Gentiles*, trans. O. C. Dean, Jr. [Louisville: Westminster/John Knox, 1993], p. 43).

19. The word *stoicheia* may be a reference to the four cosmic substances named by Aristotle (earth, water, air, fire) and routinely invested with quasi-divine power, but Paul seems to broaden the term and make it refer to any hostile cosmic powers contrary to the worship of the true God (similarly Wink, *Naming the Powers*, pp. 67-77; Dunn, *Theology*, pp. 108-9).

20. The Paul of the undisputed letters does not, however, focus on these powers (so also Dunn, *Theology*, p. 109), which become more prominent in Colossians and Ephesians.

21. In *Naming the Powers*, Walter Wink argues persuasively that the language of the "powers" in the New Testament is used "generically for all manifestations of power, seen under the dual aspect of their physical or institutional concretion on the one hand, and their essence or spirituality on the other" (p. 107).

Paul — death, mentioned in Romans 8:38, and sin. They are so fully personified in Paul's writings that they could be considered proper nouns in English and capitalized — Sin and Death.[22] These, too, are cosmic in scope like the other powers, not merely interior to human beings. What they have in common is their focused and profound tyranny over the human race (hence "anthropological"). Sin, writes James Dunn, "is the spider which succeeds in entrapping humankind in the web of death."[23] Sin and death cooperate to "reign" (Rom. 5:14, 17, 21; 6:12, 14) over humanity, creating a desperate situation, a slavery, from which the human race needs not merely forgiveness but liberation and victory.[24] Or, in a word, apocalyptic *power:*

> . . . all, both Jews and Greeks, are under the power of sin. (Rom. 3:9; cf. Gal. 3:22)

> [12]Therefore, just as sin came into the world through one man, and death came through sin, and so death spread to all because all have sinned. . . . [14]. . . [D]eath exercised dominion from Adam to Moses, even over those whose sins were not like the transgression of Adam, who is a type of the one who was to come. . . . [20]But law came in, with the result that the trespass multiplied. . . . [21]. . . [S]in exercised dominion in death. (Rom. 5:12, 14, 20a, 21a)

> [20]When you were slaves of sin, you were free in regard to righteousness. [21]So what advantage did you then get from the things of which you now are ashamed? The end of those things is death. [22]But now that you have been freed from sin and enslaved to God, the advantage you get is sanctification. The end is eternal life. [23]For the wages of sin is death, but the free gift of God is eternal life in Christ Jesus our Lord. (Rom. 6:20-23)

> [13]Did what is good [the law], then, bring death to me? By no means! It was sin, working death in me through what is good, in order that sin might be shown to be sin, and through the commandment might become sinful be-

22. See the excellent discussion in Dunn, *Theology,* pp. 111-26. On the "flesh," which some consider also to be a power, see the note in chapter six, p. 102, n. 23.

23. Dunn, *Theology,* p. 129. Changing (and mixing) metaphors, Dunn says that Paul's ultimate concern here, no matter what name it is given, is "the reality of this dimension of evil, breaking through into individual and social living, entrapping and driving individuals and communities like a pitiless slave owner, entwining its tentacles ever more tightly around persons and circumstances in an embrace of death" (p. 114).

24. Among many discussions, see the excellent article by Martinus C. de Boer, "Paul and Jewish Apocalyptic Eschatology," in Joel Marcus and Marion L. Soards, eds., *Apocalyptic and the New Testament: Essays in Honor of J. Louis Martyn,* JSNTSup 24 (Sheffield: Sheffield Academic Press, 1989), pp. 169-90.

yond measure. [14]For we know that the law is spiritual; but I am of the flesh, sold into slavery under sin. [15]I do not understand my own actions. For I do not do what I want, but I do the very thing I hate. [16]Now if I do what I do not want, I agree that the law is good. [17]But in fact it is no longer I that do it, but sin that dwells within me. [18]For I know that nothing good dwells within me, that is, in my flesh. I can will what is right, but I cannot do it. [19]For I do not do the good I want, but the evil I do not want is what I do. [20]Now if I do what I do not want, it is no longer I that do it, but sin that dwells within me. . . . [24]Wretched man that I am! Who will rescue me from this body of death? (Rom. 7:13-20, 24)

Paul, then, finds himself and the entire human race under attack by hostile powers that belong to this age: Satan, demons, "elemental spirits," rulers and powers, sin, and death. For him — as the conclusion of each of the preceding excerpts indicates — the liberating power needed has been provided by God through the Messiah Jesus. What, then, is Paul's understanding and experience of this liberating power?

Christ Crucified as the Power of God

In the thesis statement of his letter to the Romans, Paul writes that he is not

[16]. . . ashamed of the gospel; it is the power of God for salvation to everyone who has faith, to the Jew first and also to the Greek. [17]For in it the righteousness of God is revealed through [or better, "from"; Greek *ek*] faith for [or, "to"; Greek *eis*] faith; as it is written, "The one who is righteous will live by faith." (Rom. 1:16-17)

Here Paul announces that the gospel, the good news, is more than a mere message; it is a divine word that accomplishes that which it sets out to do, "a performative utterance,"[25] a power — God's power. As in Hebrew Scripture, the gospel as word of God is not just *about* God's saving power, it *is* God's saving power. Certainly Paul means to say that the message he and others preach has caused many Gentiles to turn "to God from idols, to serve a living and true God" (1 Thess. 1:9), and many Jews to realize that in Christ "every one of God's promises is a 'Yes'" (2 Cor. 1:20a). The word has "performed" salvation.

Yet there is more. The transforming, salvific power of which Paul speaks is

---

25. The phrase is Luke Timothy Johnson's (*Reading Romans: A Literary and Theological Commentary* [New York: Crossroad, 1997], p. 25).

a curious one, for the content of Paul's gospel, and thus his experience of its power, is focused on a crucified Messiah, on the cross of Christ. The power of the gospel message depends ultimately on the odd power of the act to which the message bears witness. To be sure, this act is a sacrifice for sins, conveying divine absolution and reconciliation. Yet that does not exhaust the meaning of the power of the cross. As Bultmann wrote many years ago:

> *Christ's death* is not merely a sacrifice which cancels the guilt of sin (i.e. the punishment contracted by sinning), but is also *the means of release from the powers of this age: Law, Sin, and Death.*[26]

Believers are "set free from the law of sin and of death" (Rom. 8:2). Thus Paul declares that the purpose and effect of Christ's death were apocalyptic, effecting the change in eons or ages that meant the inauguration of the new age, and liberating those who respond from the power of the old:

> [18]Therefore just as one man's trespass led to condemnation for all, so one man's act of righteousness leads to justification and life for all. . . . [21]. . . [J]ust as sin exercised dominion in death, so grace might also exercise dominion through justification [righteousness] leading to eternal life through Jesus Christ our Lord. (Rom. 5:18, 21)

> [4][The Lord Jesus Christ] gave himself for our sins **to set us free from the present evil age**, according to the will of our God and Father, [5]to whom be the glory forever and ever. (Gal. 1:4-5 [emphasis added])

Paul here claims that the reason for Christ's self-giving (i.e., loving; cf. Gal. 2:20) death was to rescue people from the hostile, apocalyptic powers of this evil age — sin, death, the "elemental spirits," and any other powers that captivate and enslave.[27] Believers now live under the power of grace (Rom. 5:12-21; 6:15), the grace manifested in the cross, the grace that has inaugurated the new creation "where the love of Christ is the operative power and princi-

---

26. Rudolf Bultmann, *Theology of the New Testament,* trans. Kendrick Grobel (New York: Charles Scribner's Sons, 1951), 1:297-98 (emphasis in the original).

27. In Galatians, Paul specifically names sin (3:22), the elemental spirits (4:3, 8-9), and the flesh-death (6:8) as powers that oppress the human race. Victor Furnish rightly stresses that although in Gal. 1:4 Paul quotes a traditional text about Christ's self-offering as an atonement for sins, he interprets this tradition to mean "release from sin's power" and liberation from "the tyrannical forces which, under sin's rule, hold the world in thrall" ("'He Gave Himself [Was Given] Up . . .': Paul's Use of a Christological Assertion," in Abraham J. Malherbe and Wayne A. Meeks, eds., *The Future of Christology: Essays in Honor of Leander E. Keck* [Minneapolis: Fortress, 1993], p. 113).

ple"[28] (2 Cor. 5:14, 17). The text in Galatians 1:4 constitutes a preliminary statement of Paul's thesis in Galatians, which is then unfolded in 2:15-21, where the indwelling power of Christ is connected explicitly to the love of Christ demonstrated on the cross.

As we observed in chapter six, the first chapter on faith, Paul probably alludes to this salvific aspect of divine power also in the thesis statement of Romans, in 1:17: "For in it [the gospel] the righteousness of God is revealed through faith for faith" (NRSV). As we argued in that chapter (see pp. 117-18), the more literal translation, "from faith toward faith," corresponds to what is likely a reference to the faithful death of Jesus and to the resulting faith among those who obey the gospel summons: "God's fidelity revealed in Christ's fidelity to engender our fidelity." Thus the saving power of God and the death of Jesus are very closely connected not only in the basic claim of Galatians but also, implicitly, in the theme statement of Romans.

The connections in Galatians and Romans are made explicit again, in more detail, in the thesis statement of 1 Corinthians, in which the word "power" also occurs — three times — along with a form of the word "strength" (cf. the bold-faced words):

> [17]For Christ did not send me to baptize but to proclaim the gospel, and not with eloquent wisdom, so that the cross of Christ might not be emptied of its **power**. [18]For the message about the cross is foolishness to those who are perishing, but to us who are being saved it is the **power** of God. . . . [21]For since, in the wisdom of God, the world did not know God through wisdom, God decided, through the foolishness of our proclamation, to save those who believe. [22]For Jews demand signs and Greeks desire wisdom, [23]but we proclaim Christ crucified, a stumbling block to Jews and foolishness to Gentiles, [24]but to those who are the called, both Jews and Greeks, Christ the **power** of God and the wisdom of God. [25]For God's foolishness is wiser than human wisdom, and God's weakness is **stronger** than human strength. (1 Cor. 1:17-18, 21-25)

As in Romans, proclamation and salvation are again connected (v. 21), only now the substance of the proclamation is specified as "the message about the cross" (v. 18). In verse 18 Paul identifies this message of the cross as the power of God. In the same breath he can say that the cross itself has power (v. 17) and that Christ himself is the power of God (v. 24). This overlapping of meanings does not suggest cloudy thinking on Paul's part. Rather, Paul means that Christ as the crucified Messiah — and *only* as the crucified Messiah — is the power of

---

28. Pickett, *The Cross in Corinth*, p. 153.

God, a power unleashed in the proclamation of the Messiah — but only in the proclamation of the *crucified* Messiah.

It is absolutely crucial to note here that Paul never denies the weakness of the crucified Messiah. God's decisive act in Jesus stands all forms of power and authority on their heads.[29] Indeed, it is in and as weakness — as humans normally understand weakness — that Christ is God's power. Christ is thus the locus and revelation of divine power only as the weak, the crucified one. *Christ is, for Paul, God's power-in-weakness.* Paul's experience of Jesus as "the Lord of glory" (1 Cor. 2:8) leads him to insist that the crucifixion of Jesus is "the decisive demonstration of God's glory and rulership" — God's power.[30] This understanding and experience of divine power become for Paul the interpretive key to his own experience of power-in-weakness, as well as the key to his desires for the use of power within his communities. The first two chapters of 1 Corinthians show that

> God gets things done not by a conventional human use of power, by displays of force, impressive signs or sophisticated wisdom. He achieves salvation through an act of what to human eyes is powerlessness on the cross; he chooses to dwell in Corinth in a group of "nothings" in the eyes of Corinthian society; he creates these new communities through the preaching of an unimpressive artisan tentmaker.[31]

What the Greco-Roman world views as weakness, and therefore folly, is for Paul God's power and wisdom.[32]

The centrality of Paul's understanding and experience of the cross as God's power is reinforced for us by a brief return to Paul's "master narrative," Philippians 2:6-11. Although the word "power" (like the word "love") does not appear in this text, recent interpreters have stressed the quantity and significance of political vocabulary in the letter to the Philippians.[33] Power is, of course, a political notion, and it seems to have been close to the mind of Paul in composing Philippians from jail, under the thumb of imperial power. David Seeley convincingly argues that the hymn text in Philippians 2:6-11 "appropriates for Jesus some of the most important claims for the emperor and for Is-

---

29. Georgi, *Theocracy,* p. 54.

30. See Georgi, *Theocracy,* p. 56.

31. Tomlin, *The Power of the Cross,* pp. 99-100.

32. See Pickett, *The Cross in Corinth,* pp. 68-72, for the logical connections between weakness and folly.

33. See any of the recent commentaries and, e.g., David Seeley, "The Background of the Philippians Hymn," *Journal of Higher Criticism* 1 (1994): 49-72.

rael's supreme ruler, the lord God."[34] Christ is portrayed as the opposite, Seeley argues, of the power-seeking emperor Caligula (ruled 37-41). Whether or not the hymn has Caligula specifically in mind, in the context of the politically charged language of Philippians, the experience of imperial power cannot be far from the mind of either the author or readers of the letter.[35]

This suggestion is borne out by the likelihood that Philippians 2:6-11, as a reinterpretation of Isaiah's fourth servant hymn, implicitly — and perhaps in its use by Paul even explicitly — contrasts two antithetical understandings of power. In the hymn, Christ is narrated in exemplary form as one who embodies a "radical reversal of honor values"[36] by humbling himself rather than honoring himself. The expected pursuit of honor and power has become a quest for dishonor and powerlessness. No honorable Greco-Roman person, no man worthy of the name, certainly no "Lord" or emperor would redefine power in this way (self-enslavement), yet the Christ of the hymn that Paul cites is the powerful, life-giving force of the Philippian community, embodying the power of powerlessness as humans measure it. Jesus, like Isaiah's servant and like other suffering righteous among the Jewish people, obediently served God to the point of death, and thus became Lord by receiving rather than inflicting the violent power of Rome.[37]

Christ is also narrated in the Philippians hymn as the preexistent one who expresses deity and divine power by self-emptying rather than self-aggrandizing. He does not glorify, or bring honor to, himself, but rather is honored by his Father because of this act of *kenosis*. Inhabitants of the Greco-Roman world would see this as both the fulfillment and the opposite of Roman deity and imperial

34. Seeley, "Background," p. 52.

35. Most commentators find the "background" of the hymn in either Isaiah's suffering-servant hymn or in the story of Adam, or both. Seeley ("Background"), however, is not particularly impressed by either of these theories. While acknowledging a possible multiplicity of backgrounds, he stresses the traditions of Judaism's suffering righteous ones, Greco-Roman ruler worship, and the royal monotheism of Isaiah 45. He argues (pp. 61-68) that the ideal Greco-Roman ruler was not self-aggrandizing but would, in fact, have looked out for the best interests of his people, like a slave. Caligula, however, was known and described as the opposite of this ideal. The hymn, Seeley argues, describes the ideal ruler, over against the despicable Caligula, and thereby claims that Jesus is in fact the ideal lord, similar to what everyone expects from a good emperor and dissimilar from Caligula. While it is true that our written sources depict the "ideal" ruler as beneficent and self-giving, it is crucial to remember that the hymn's perspective is primarily contrast. Normal expectations of how to exercise power and divinity — whether by the emperor or Adam or anyone else — are undermined by the hymnic narrative.

36. S. Scott Bartchy, "Undermining Ancient Patriarchy: The Apostle Paul's Vision of a Society of Siblings," *Biblical Theology Bulletin* 29 (1999): 71.

37. See Seeley, "Background," pp. 56-61.

power. On the one hand, they believed that good rulers should be beneficent and even self-giving, rather than merely self-aggrandizing. On the other hand, they believed that gods and emperors (who shared in the power of the gods) possessed omnipotence and deserved all its corollary benefits, such as honor and glory. Many had living proof in their own experience that imperial power could be vicious. Paul's narrative of Christ undermines any understanding of deity and divine power as self-aggrandizing or violent. The cross of Christ shows that divine power consists of weakness and suffering and love.

Paul's reinterpretation of divine power is, therefore, startling, and it should not be underestimated.[38] In it, however, he does not completely deny more traditional understandings of divine power. The power of God is displayed in the creation (Rom. 1:20). The power of God was the source of Jesus' resurrection and will be the source of believers' resurrection (1 Cor. 6:14; cf. Rom. 1:4). The power of God is displayed in the extraordinary manifestations of the Spirit both in Paul's ministry (1 Thess. 1:5; 1 Cor. 2:4; 2 Cor. 12:12; Rom. 15:19) and in the life of his communities (Gal. 3:5; 1 Cor. 12:10, 28-29). However, as we discovered in chapter three on Paul's experience of the Spirit, and as we will again see below, Paul never divorces these experiences of God's power from the experience of the cross as the center of divine power. The life-giving power of God is most fully experienced by Paul in the cross of Christ and in the life of cruciform power that shares in that cross.

This emphasis on the cross as divine power, then, does not for Paul undermine or undervalue the resurrection as the power of God. Indeed, Paul (with Abraham, he asserts) experiences God as the one "who gives life to the dead and calls into existence the things that do not exist" (Rom. 4:17):

God raised the Lord and will also raise us by his power. (1 Cor. 6:14)

For he was crucified in weakness, but lives by the power of God. (2 Cor. 13:4a)

Paul's great desire is, in fact, to know the power of Christ's resurrection (Phil. 3:10). The question for Paul is not *whether* the life-creating, resurrection power of God is real and can be experienced in the present, but *how* that power is encountered now. For Paul, the *how* of that power is by means of cruciformity. Moreover, "the power demonstrated in the resurrection is not pure, undefined power. The cross gives it specificity as 'the power of *love.*'"[39] Thus, the power of God found in the cross is the life-giving, liberating power of divine love. This is

---

38. See also chapter one.

39. Charles B. Cousar, *A Theology of the Cross* (Minneapolis: Fortress, 1990), p. 104.

the kind of love that is vulnerable; it is power in weakness.[40] That experience of power is Paul's, and he wants it also to be the experience of all believers. We now look at these two experiences of power.

Paul's Experience of God's Power in Weakness

"Whenever I am weak, then I am strong" writes the apostle in 2 Corinthians 12:10. What precisely does he mean by such a sweeping generalization, such a paradoxical claim? At least three specific questions present themselves: (1) In what way(s) did Paul consider himself to be weak? (2) Why did he think weakness was so vital to his apostolic ministry? and (3) In what sense(s) did Paul find power in his weakness? We will consider one by one the several ways in which Paul understands himself to be weak. After examining each of these, we will turn to a synthesis of Paul's experience and to the last two questions. Throughout the discussion, special attention will be given to 2 Corinthians, especially chapters 10–13. In these chapters Paul attends most fully and systematically to the question of weakness and power, and they constitute the interpretive key to the narratives of Paul's apostolic ministry across his correspondence.

As we consider Paul's letters, we find that from the apostle's own perspective, weakness (Greek *astheneia*) was a fundamental characteristic of his ministry; indeed, it was his *modus operandi*. Clearly Paul's ministry did not depend on a sense of affirmation and welcome from his audience, for his success was sometimes amid much persecution (e.g., 1 Thess. 2:2). Nor did it depend on his physical or even psychological strength and power, for he ministered to the Galatians while physically ill and weak (Gal. 4:13),[41] and to the Corinthians while, by his own admission, an emotional wreck (1 Cor. 2:3).[42]

We may discern five principal ways in which Paul understood his apostolic ministry as weakness: his personal presence and rhetorical skill; his constant suffering; his mysterious "thorn in the flesh" (2 Cor. 12:7); his refusal of finan-

---

40. Paul (most forcefully in 2 Corinthians) emphasizes that "'the normal' structures of reality based on demonstration and imposition of power run counter to reality and are in fact destructive. . . . Only what is weak deserves to be called strong. Only powerlessness is power" (Georgi, *Theocracy*, p. 63).

41. NRSV "because of a physical infirmity"; literally "because of [a] weakness of the flesh" (Greek *astheneian tēs sarkos*). The phrase "because of" may be intended to convey the notion that Paul embraced his weakness as strength rather than pass up the opportunity to preach in Galatia while ill.

42. NRSV "in weakness and in fear and in much trembling"; Greek *en astheneią kai en phobǭ kai en tromǭ pollǭ.*

cial support and his performance of manual labor; and his attitude of humility and meekness. Although two of these topics (suffering and self-support) appeared in chapter nine, in this chapter we relate them to power rather than love.

Weakness in Personal Presence and Rhetorical Skill

That Paul had a rather feeble, uncharismatic personal presence, coupled with a lack of rhetorical polish in the arena of both public and one-on-one speech, seems to have been a commonly held view during his lifetime.[43] The Corinthians, who greatly admired a good speaker, seem to have been particularly repelled by this apostolic trait:

> [9]I do not want to seem as though I am trying to frighten you with my letters. [10]For they say, "His letters are weighty and strong, but his bodily presence is weak, and his speech contemptible." (2 Cor. 10:9-10)

Although Paul is quick to defend his apostleship, as well as the continuity in intention and message between his presence and his letters (see, e.g., 2 Cor. 10:11), he never denies the essential charge of weakness made by his critics:

> [1]I myself, Paul, appeal to you by the meekness and gentleness of Christ — I who am humble when face to face with you, but bold toward you when I am away! — [2]I ask that when I am present I need not show boldness by daring to oppose those who think we are acting according to human standards. (2 Cor. 10:1-2)

> [5]I think that I am not in the least inferior to these super-apostles. [6]I may be untrained in speech, but not in knowledge; certainly in every way and in all things we have made this evident to you. (2 Cor. 11:5-6)

In fact, he had earlier written to the Corinthians that his ministry among them was precisely and *deliberately* one of weakness and lack of eloquence:

> [1]When I came to you, brothers and sisters, I did not come proclaiming the mystery of God to you in lofty words or wisdom. [2]For I decided to know

---

43. And also afterwards, if the apocryphal tales are indicative. See, for example, the second-century *Acts of Paul and Thecla* 3, in which Paul is described as "a man small of stature, with a bald head and crooked legs, in a good state of body, with eyebrows meeting and nose somewhat hooked" (Wilhelm Schneemelcher, ed., *New Testament Apocrypha*, trans. R. McL. Wilson [Philadelphia: Westminster, 1965], 2:353-54).

nothing among you except Jesus Christ, and him crucified. ³And I came to you in weakness and in fear and in much trembling. ⁴My speech and my proclamation were not with plausible words of wisdom, but with a demonstration of the Spirit and of power, ⁵so that your faith might rest not on human wisdom but on the power of God. (1 Cor. 2:1-5)

For Christ did not send me to baptize but to proclaim the gospel, and not with eloquent wisdom, so that the cross of Christ might not be emptied of its power. (1 Cor. 1:17)

Paul, in other words, is not a "charismatic" public speaker; he does not view his speaking ministry as a place to showcase rhetorical skill or, even less, artificial ornamentation — as rhetorical competitors who were commonly found in Corinth might do. Paul explicitly avers that his lack of rhetorical polish and ornamentation insure that the Corinthians' response to his preaching is the work of divine power, the power of the cross, not human intellect or emotional, rhetorical manipulation. Just as important, however, is Paul's implicit claim that his style of ministry not only allows the power of the cross to function but also corresponds to the cross.

Having defined the wisdom and power of God in terms of the crucified Christ (1 Cor. 1:17-25), Paul presents as witnesses to this strange redefinition two realities: the socioeconomic makeup of the Corinthian community (1 Cor. 1:26-31) and the mode of his own ministry (1 Cor. 2:1-5). God's power in weakness, in other words, is revealed on the cross and confirmed by the overall weakness (1 Cor. 1:26-28), or low status, of the Corinthians, and by the weakness (1 Cor. 2:3) of Paul.

One might accuse Paul here of finding a theological rationale for his personal failures or lack of certain skills. Even if that is partially true, for Paul what matters is that *his* weakness allows *God's* power to be manifested. Cruciform power means that no one can attribute the effects of Paul's preaching and teaching to successful marketing techniques — ancient or modern — but only to the inherent power of the cross as the revelation of God.

The Weakness of Suffering

We have seen that Paul finds God's power at work in the weakness of his particular style of ministry. It is also at work in Paul's many experiences of pain and suffering for the gospel and for the communities he founded. These experiences are weaknesses in that they have the air of defeat rather than victory, of tragedy rather than triumph. Yet for Paul not only the love but also the power of God is revealed in the midst of affliction.

As we saw in the chapter on apostolic cruciform love, Paul catalogs these sufferings several times: 1 Corinthians 4:8-13; 2 Corinthians 1:3-11; 4:7-12; 6:3-10; 11:23-33; 12:10; Romans 8:35. The kinds of pain and suffering he enumerates include, as we have seen, public disgrace and psychological pain, physical deprivation and pain, fatigue from physical labor, and political punishment and torture. We may summarize these experiences by means of the chart on pp. 286-87.

The variety and intensity of these catalogs of Paul's suffering are astounding. The intense social and even political character of many of the items in the catalogs should not be overlooked.[44] Yet two generalizations about Paul's attitude toward (or spirituality of) suffering emerge from the various lists. First, Paul characterizes himself as "weak" (1 Cor. 4:10), and he considers each and every specific kind of suffering as a "weakness," which paradoxically, mysteriously, makes Christ's power present:

> [8]Three times I appealed to the Lord about this [his "thorn in the flesh"], that it would leave me, [9]but he said to me, "My grace is sufficient for you, for power is made perfect in **weakness**." So, I will boast all the more gladly of my **weaknesses**, so that the power of Christ may dwell in me. [10]Therefore I am content with **weaknesses**, insults, hardships, persecutions, and calamities for the sake of Christ; for whenever I am weak, then I am strong. (2 Cor. 12:8-10 [emphasis added])[45]

Second, more specifically, Paul considers himself to be sentenced to death, carrying about in his body the dying of Jesus:

> For I think that God has exhibited us apostles as last of all, as though sentenced to death, because we have become a spectacle to the world, to angels and to mortals. (1 Cor. 4:9)

> [7]But we have this treasure in clay jars, so that it may be made clear that this extraordinary power belongs to God and does not come from us. [8]We are af-

---

44. In addition to the afflictions enumerated in these catalogs, we may add the "great opposition" cited in 1 Thess. 2:2; the unspecified "physical infirmity" or "weakness of the flesh" mentioned in Gal. 4:13; the terrible "affliction" described in 2 Cor. 1:8-10; and, perhaps, the fighting "with wild animals" mentioned in 1 Cor. 15:32. Klaus Wengst (in *Pax Romana*, pp. 73-75) argues that the texts we are considering suggest that Paul had frequent problems with Rome.

45. See also Rom. 5:3: "we also boast in our sufferings."

flicted in every way, but not crushed; perplexed, but not driven to despair; [9]persecuted, but not forsaken; struck down, but not destroyed; [10]always carrying in the body the death [or "dying"] of Jesus, so that the life of Jesus may also be made visible in our bodies. [11]For while we live, we are always being given up to death for Jesus' sake, so that the life of Jesus may be made visible in our mortal flesh. [12]So death is at work in us, but life in you. (2 Cor. 4:7-12)

Although on one occasion the reference to a "sentence of death" is specifically to the threat of physical death (2 Cor. 1:8-9), Paul's metaphors of "being sentenced to death" and "carrying around the dying of Jesus" are much more comprehensive and polyvalent than allusions to actual dying. Rather, the metaphor of being in a constant process of dying articulates Paul's fundamental self-understanding as an apostle; "I die every day," he claims (1 Cor. 15:31). The "existential significance of the death of Jesus is nowhere set forth more explicitly than in Paul's reference . . . to 'carrying in the body the death of Jesus.'"[46] The language of this metaphor, especially as it appears in 2 Corinthians 4:11, echoes the narrative pattern of the crucified Christ in passages like Galatians 2:20:

For while we live, we are always being given up to death [Greek *paradidometha*] for Jesus' sake. . . . (2 Cor. 4:11)

. . . the faith in [of] the Son of God, who loved me and gave himself [Greek *paradontos heauton*] for me. (Gal. 2:20)

This constant weakness and suffering is, then, a sharing in the sufferings of Christ, a "co-suffering" with him, as Paul describes it in Romans:

. . . and if children, then heirs, heirs of God and joint heirs with Christ — if, in fact, we suffer with him [literally, "co-suffer"; Greek *sympaschomen*] so that we may also be glorified with him. (Rom. 8:17)

The same idea is present elsewhere, using the language of sharing in Christ's sufferings (2 Corinthians and Philippians), or of being "co-formed" to his death (Philippians):

---

46. Pickett, *The Cross in Corinth*, p. 126. Pickett's entire discussion of this passage is valuable (pp. 129-42). As noted in chapter five, the meaning of the word translated "death" or "dying" of Jesus *(nekrōsis)* has been debated. However, whether the sense is "dying" as a process, "death" as an event, or "deadness" as the state that death brings on, the meaning for Paul is the same: a permanent existential participation in the crucifixion of Jesus.

Catalog of Paul's Sufferings	Generalized Pain and Suffering	Public Disgrace and Psychological Pain	Physical Deprivation and Pain	Fatigue from Physical Labor	Political Punishment and Torture
1 Corinthians 4:8-13	last of all; as though sentenced to death; weak; like the rubbish of the world, the dregs of all things	spectacle to the world; fools for the sake of Christ; held in disrepute; reviled; slandered	hungry and thirsty; poorly clothed; homeless	weary from the work of our own hands	beaten; persecuted
2 Corinthians 1:3-11	affliction; sufferings of Christ in abundance; felt that we had received the sentence of death	so utterly, unbearably crushed; despaired of life itself	so deadly a peril		
2 Corinthians 4:7-12	afflicted; always carrying in the body the death of Jesus; always being given up to death for Jesus' sake	perplexed			persecuted; struck down
2 Corinthians 6:3-10	afflictions; hardships; calamities; as dying	riots; dishonor; ill repute; treated as impostors; as unknown; sorrowful	imprisonments; sleepless nights; hunger; poor; having nothing	labors	beatings; punished

2 Corinthians 11:23-33	weak/weakness	daily pressure because of my anxiety for all the churches; indignant (offended?)	five times forty lashes minus one; once a stoning; three times shipwrecked; a night and a day adrift at sea; in danger from rivers, bandits, Jews, Gentiles, in the city, in the wilderness, at sea, from false brothers and sisters; many a sleepless night; hungry and thirsty; often without food; cold; naked	(far greater) labors [than the "superapostles"]; frequent journeys; toil and hardship	(far more) imprisonments [than the "superapostles"]; countless floggings; often near death; three times beaten with rods; near-arrest
2 Corinthians 12:10	weaknesses; calamities	insults	hardships		persecutions
Romans 8:35	hardship; distress; peril		famine; nakedness		persecution; [sword]*

*The sword (v. 35) likely refers to the Roman practice of beheading with the sword (John S. Pobee, *Persecution and Martyrdom in the Theology of Paul*, JSNTsup 6 [Sheffield: JSOT Press, 1985], p. 5), with which Paul would have been familiar but had obviously not yet experienced. (The list in Rom. 8:35 is a list of threats to believers, most experienced but some perhaps only potential, and thus differs slightly from the other lists presented here.)

[J]ust as the sufferings of Christ [Greek *ta pathēmata tou Christou*] are abundant for us, so also our consolation is abundant through Christ. (2 Cor. 1:5)

[10]I want to know Christ and the power of his resurrection and the sharing of his sufferings [Greek *koinōnian pathēmatōn autou*] by becoming like him in his death [Greek *symmorphizomenos tō thanatō autou*], [11]if somehow I may attain the resurrection from the dead. (Phil. 3:10-11)

These texts are significant because they demonstrate that for Paul, cruciformity — though it cannot be restricted to physical suffering — certainly includes all kinds of physical afflictions, at least for apostles. The metaphor of dying with Christ is not merely meant to refer to self-giving love, or the termination of selfish desires. It includes — especially when the word suffer/suffering appears — a variety of concrete, physical pains suffered for the sake of the gospel of the crucified Christ. Paul does not allow the metaphor to lose its grounding — and continued manifestation — in real pain. Whereas the Corinthians "had been persuaded that the gospel of glory and power was incongruous with an apostolic ministry which exhibited the frailties of mortal existence,"[47] Paul knew from experience that in his pain was revealed the power of God. As J. Louis Martyn writes, commenting on Paul's scars, which are mentioned in Galatians 6:17:

> Paul's physical body is thus a place in which one finds a sign of the present activity of the redeemer in the world. . . . The glad tiding of Jesus' redemptive death is preached by the one who inevitably participates in that death, and whose apostolic sufferings are paradoxically the locus of God's gift of life, *being the present form of Jesus's own death-life pattern.*[48]

The Weakness of Paul's "Thorn in the Flesh"

A third form of Paul's weakness may be closely related to his experiences of pain: the infamous "thorn in the flesh" of 2 Corinthians 12.

[1]It is necessary to boast; nothing is to be gained by it, but I will go on to visions and revelations of the Lord. . . . [6]But if I wish to boast, I will not be a fool, for I will be speaking the truth. But I refrain from it, so that no one may

---

47. Pickett, *The Cross in Corinth*, p. 130.

48. J. Louis Martyn, *Galatians: A New Translation with Introduction and Commentary,* Anchor Bible 33A (New York: Doubleday, 1997), p. 569 (emphasis added).

think better of me than what is seen in me or heard from me, [7]even consider-ing the exceptional character of the revelations. Therefore, **to keep me from being too elated**, a thorn was given me in the flesh, a messenger of Satan to torment me, **to keep me from being too elated**. [8]Three times I appealed to the Lord about this, that it would leave me, [9]but he said to me, "My grace is sufficient for you, for power is made perfect in weakness." So, I will boast all the more gladly of my weaknesses, so that the power of Christ may dwell in me. [10]Therefore I am content with weaknesses, insults, hardships, persecu-tions, and calamities for the sake of Christ; for **whenever I am weak, then I am strong**. (2 Cor. 12:1, 6-10 [emphasis added])

Although this text has already been mentioned several times, its uniqueness merits at least some brief, direct attention.

Speculation about Paul's "thorn" has gone on for centuries.[49] It has usually been associated with some disease, deformity, or other physical ailment. This interpretation fits well with the context, in which the general category of "weaknesses" includes "insults, hardships, persecutions, and calamities for the sake of Christ" (12:10). Some interpreters, however, have often found the solu-tion to the conundrum in Paul's opponents: *they,* it is argued, constitute Paul's thorn in the flesh.[50] This might be an apt solution in light of Paul's calling the thorn a "messenger of Satan" (12:7). More recently, however, it has been sug-gested that the thorn is an angelic opponent common in the *merkabah* mystical tradition, whose job it was to attack or destroy unworthy participants in the as-cent to heaven.[51] No matter what the solution to this elusive term, what matters to Paul is not its identity but its significance, which is rich.

For one thing, Paul experiences the thorn as a check on his pride (v. 7). It re-minds him that God, not he, is the source of his spiritual experiences, and that these experiences neither supplant the cross nor have ultimate significance. For another, the thorn has a pedagogical function, teaching Paul that God's grace suffices and that God's power appears in the midst of human weakness. Indeed, this is the most important part of the experience for Paul: power in weakness. God's power is activated by and most fully present in Paul's weakness. Paul knows this only because he knows the cross as God's power in weakness.

49. For an overview, see Ralph P. Martin, *Second Corinthians,* Word Biblical Commentary 40 (Waco, Tex.: Word, 1986), pp. 410-23.

50. E.g., Michael L. Barré, "Qumran and the Weakness of Paul," *Catholic Biblical Quarterly* 42 (1980): 216-27.

51. E.g., C. R. A. Morray-Jones, "Paradise Revisited (2 Cor 12:1-12): The Jewish Mystical Background of Paul's Apostolate, Part 2: Paul's Heavenly Ascent and Its Significance," *Harvard Theological Review* 86 (1993): 280-83. Paul narrates such an ascent in 2 Cor. 12:2-5.

The Weakness of Refusing Support and Performing Manual Labor

In the first century, philosophical and religious services normally carried a charge; "you get what you pay for" would have rung true with many folks. A teacher who did not charge would appear to have nothing much to offer. Furthermore, as we saw in chapter nine, manual labor was deemed, at least by the upper class, to be the degrading work of the lower class and slaves.[52] A true philosopher or religious leader would not stoop to such a position of self-support by manual work but would charge for services rendered. Paul, however, did not charge — though he expected his churches to support his work in other communities — and he did work with his hands. He did this deliberately, taking a significant reduction in social status, and he even boasted about his stance. In terms of Greco-Roman values, his decision was not honorable but shameful. He paid a price for the decision but maintained his position steadfastly in the face of criticism and mockery (see, e.g., 1 Thess. 2:5-9; 1 Cor. 9:15-18; 2 Cor. 11:7-12).

As we noted in chapter nine on apostolic cruciform love, Paul finds in his own personal narrative of refusing financial help and descending the social ladder an embodiment of the story of Jesus. It is a story of self-giving love (1 Thess. 2:8; 2 Cor. 11:11), of renouncing rights and even enslaving oneself so as not to burden others (1 Thess. 2:9; 1 Cor. 9:12, 15, 18-19; 2 Cor. 11:7-11; 12:13). It is also a story of power in weakness.

The seriousness with which Paul takes this matter is brought home especially in 2 Corinthians 11. Those who are his rivals at Corinth — the "superapostles" (2 Cor. 11:5) or "pseudo-apostles" (2 Cor. 11:13; NRSV "false apostles") — apparently claim equality with (if not superiority to) Paul in part because they, unlike Paul, do demand remuneration for their preaching. This establishes a relationship of patronage and power between these preachers and the Corinthians that is totally unacceptable to Paul:

> [20]For you put up with it when someone makes slaves of you, or preys upon you, or takes advantage of you, or puts on airs, or gives you a slap in the face. [21]To my shame, I must say, we were too weak for that! (2 Cor. 11:20-21)

Paul's dripping sarcasm ("to my shame") is mixed with his ironic acceptance of the label "weak" — whether given by his opponents, the Corinthians, or him-

---

52. Ronald F. Hock, *The Social Context of Paul's Ministry: Tentmaking and Apostleship* (Philadelphia: Fortress, 1980); Dale B. Martin, *Slavery as Salvation: The Metaphor of Slavery in Pauline Christianity* (New Haven and London: Yale University Press, 1990), pp. 69-70, 123-24, and passim, stressing the different attitudes held by the lower and upper class.

self. The rest of 2 Corinthians 11 lists the other weaknesses (the sufferings noted above) about which Paul boasts, but none receives the extended treatment that his refusal of financial support receives. This is clearly a very sore spot in the relations between Paul and the Corinthians, yet he refuses to budge. The only reason for this obstinacy is Paul's absolute commitment to living out the story of Christ's power in weakness — the power of cruciform love. The parody of Paul's opponents' self-praise, in the form of a list of weaknesses, is Paul's "serious attempt" to define the criteria of true apostolicity.[53]

Weakness in Attitude: Humility and Meekness

It would be a grave mistake to think that Paul's weakness refers only to his lack of charisma and his various physical weaknesses. Paul, in conformity to Christ, has also cultivated a general attitude of humility and meekness toward both God and other humans. This attitude is another dimension of his power in weakness.

Humility (Greek *tapeinophrosynē*) was not a Greek or Roman virtue, though it is certainly a biblical and Jewish one.[54] Paul has become convinced in Christ that the pride that characterizes all human beings needs an appropriate focus, not on oneself but on, or "in," the Lord: "Let the one who boasts, boast in the Lord" (1 Cor. 1:31; 2 Cor. 10:17). Because justification is a gift, it offers no occasion for boasting in oneself (Rom. 3:27). Paul does boast in the "hope of sharing the glory of God" and therefore also in his sufferings (Rom. 5:2-3), though he does not understand these as his accomplishments but as a paradoxical experience of both humility and pride, weakness and power.

While it is also true that Paul can boast of his evangelistic accomplishments and his exemplary churches,[55] and even of his refusal to burden his potential converts (1 Cor. 9:15; 2 Cor. 11:10), ultimately his boasting is not in himself but in the power of God working through him (e.g., 1 Cor. 3:5-9: "neither the one who plants nor the one who waters is anything, but only God who gives the growth" [v. 7]). Even his "visions and revelations of the Lord" are meant to cultivate in him an attitude of humility and, indeed, as we have seen, of weakness (2 Corinthians 12). Thus Paul's attitude toward God is one of humble dependence and pride in his weakness.

---

53. Pickett, *The Cross in Corinth,* p. 179.
54. See the comments in the next chapter.
55. Rom. 15:17; 1 Cor. 15:31; 2 Cor. 1:14; 7:4; 8:24; 10:12-18; Phil. 2:16; 4:1; 1 Thess. 2:19-20.

So, too, Paul approaches others, he claims, with "the meekness and gentleness of Christ" (2 Cor. 10:1). This should not be taken as Paul's absolute refusal to exercise his apostolic authority, which he will do if necessary (as 2 Cor. 10:2-11 indicates), but rather as Paul's preferred way of dealing with his wayward flocks: "What would you prefer? Am I to come to you with a stick, or with love in a spirit of gentleness?" (1 Cor. 4:21). In fact, it appears that the only reason Paul will forsake humility is to avoid being humiliated by God for having failed to convince his readers to change their ways (see 2 Cor. 12:21). Thus, as we have seen in the chapter on apostolic cruciform love, Paul urges the Thessalonians and Philemon toward lives in conformity with the gospel, not by throwing his apostolic weight around but by operating in the Spirit of gentleness (Gal. 5:23) — even if that gentleness is at times quite firm.

To pursue meekness and humility, no matter how rhetorically powerful, is in the eyes of Greco-Roman culture to cultivate attitudes and practices of weakness.[56] These Paul is both prepared and (paradoxically) proud to practice, for they correspond to the humility and weakness of the cross.

Synthesis: Apostolic Power in Weakness

The weaknesses Paul experiences demonstrate, for him, the power of Christ. These weaknesses are both physical and social, or cultural (status-related), and attitudinal.[57] Some are chosen, some are not. However, as Paul writes in a text already cited above, in apt summary of all the weaknesses he has experienced:

> [9] . . . [The Lord] said to me, "My grace is sufficient for you, for power is made perfect in weakness." So, I will boast all the more gladly of my weaknesses, so that the power of Christ may dwell in me. [10]Therefore I am content with weaknesses, insults, hardships, persecutions, and calamities for the sake of Christ; for whenever I am weak, then I am strong. (2 Cor. 12:9-10)

"*Whenever* I am weak, then I am strong" — such is the central paradoxical claim of Paul's life. It is only then, Paul believes with all his heart, that the resur-

---

56. André Resner aptly refers to Paul's defense of his weaknesses as the ironic but necessary "reverse *ēthos*," or appeal to personal character, that was exactly the opposite of Roman social and rhetorical expectations and conventions (André Resner, Jr., *Preacher and Cross: Person and Message in Theology and Rhetoric* [Grand Rapids: Eerdmans, 1999], pp. 83-131).

57. In an appropriate effort to stress the social significance and paradigmatic character of Paul's freely chosen social or status-related weakness, Pickett *(The Cross in Corinth)* underestimates the import of physical weaknesses and experiences for Paul.

rection, life-creating power of Christ is at work in and through him (cf. Phil. 4:13). Indeed, since the apocalyptic, liberating, life-creating act of God in Christ was power manifested in weakness, so too apostolic power in weakness both permits and ensures the continuation of this apocalyptic action:

> [11]For while we live, we are always being given up to death for Jesus' sake, so that the life of Jesus may be made visible in our mortal flesh. [12]So death is at work in us, but life in you. (2 Cor. 4:11-12)

Thus whenever Paul explains or defends himself, he is explaining and defending his weakness as the necessary corollary of the gospel of Christ crucified as the power of God. This necessary paradox is the essence of his very existence. The apostolic way is the way of "carrying the dying of Jesus" in daily, bodily existence, of "being given up to death," so that the life of Jesus may be paradoxically present in that dying. For that is precisely what happened on the cross: the life of Jesus was being manifested in his death, for the good of the entire world. Human weakness was met with a powerful divine weakness, the shadow of death with a life-giving death. So also now the fellowship of the cross continues to communicate the resurrection power of God in the ministry of weakness and death. Lives are transformed, human needs met, communities of cruciformity created. Such is the power of God in Paul's ministry, the apostle testifies. Like the cross of Christ, Paul's power in weakness is, for the apostle, an expression of love: "everything is for your sake" (2 Cor. 4:15).

Power and Love: Does the Apostle Betray His Lord?

It has sometimes been suggested that Paul is on what is colloquially called "a power trip," that his attitude is "my way or the highway." For example, some interpreters of 1 Corinthians 13, Paul's essay on love, take it to be nothing more than a manipulative call for obedient imitation of Paul's way.[58] Elizabeth Castelli has devoted an entire book to the thesis of Paul as power seeker.[59] Is this interpretation correct?

Castelli's work argues both that Paul's "notion of mimesis [imitation]

---

58. See Elizabeth Stuart, "Love Is . . . Paul," *The Expository Times* 102 (1991): 264-66. Stuart asserts that "[u]nder the guise of a hymn of love Paul seeks to assert his authority over the Corinthians" (p. 264) and that "under the mask of sublimity" Paul is "at his most manipulative" in 1 Corinthians 13 (p. 265).

59. Elizabeth Castelli, *Imitating Paul: A Discourse of Power*, Literary Currents in Biblical Interpretation (Louisville: Westminster/John Knox, 1991).

functions in Paul's letters as a strategy of power" and that the goal and effect of this strategy is to produce "sameness" in the communities by imposing a repressive form of hierarchical power. To begin with the charge of seeking sameness, we have seen in examining Galatians and especially 1 Corinthians and Romans that "sameness" is not a fair description of what Paul seeks. Sameness, at the expense of appropriate diversity, is actually antithetical to Paul and his message. With respect to imitation as power, we argued in chapter nine, concerning apostolic cruciform love, that Paul's call to imitation was a call to embody the pattern of Christ-like, status-renouncing love. Is imitation language meant to express love or power? Can it possibly do both?

Fully to engage Castelli is beyond the scope of this chapter. However, our analysis of Paul's texts about love and power does suggest that, in the mind and experience of the apostle, his exercise of power is an expression of Christ's love, and his exercise of love is an expression of Christ's power. In other words, Paul's desire to order community life according to his standards is, for him, an expression of the will of God and specifically of God's desire to form cruciform communities faithful to the story of Christ.[60] These communities are similar to one another, but not the same; nor are all the individuals the same as Paul or Christ even as imitators of them. What marks Pauline spirituality is its ability to affirm diverse expressions of God's power in weakness.

Nonetheless, that Paul is consciously willing to exercise power is clear from texts such as the following:

> [14]I am not writing this to make you ashamed, but to admonish you as my beloved children. [15]For though you might have ten thousand guardians in Christ, you do not have many fathers. Indeed, in Christ Jesus I became your father through the gospel. [16]I appeal to you, then, be imitators of me. [17]For this reason I sent you Timothy, who is my beloved and faithful child in the Lord, to remind you of my ways in Christ Jesus, as I teach them everywhere in every church. [18]But some of you, thinking that I am not coming to you, have become arrogant. [19]But I will come to you soon, if the Lord wills, and I will find out not the talk of these arrogant people but their power. [20]For the kingdom of God depends not on talk but on power. [21]What would you prefer? Am I to come to you with a stick, or with love in a spirit of gentleness? (1 Cor. 4:14-21)

60. For a treatment of Paul's response to problems at Corinth as "an *alternative* understanding of power" as love, see Tomlin, *The Power of the Cross*, pp. 11-107, which includes a brief response to Castelli in his summary (pp. 98-101). See also Pickett, *The Cross in Corinth*, pp. 192-208.

Though Paul here uses the language of power, it is language that must be understood in light of his definition of divine power as cruciform power, as in fact Christ crucified (1 Cor. 1:18–2:5, esp. 1:24). What Paul contests is arrogant, human power that boasts in particular and irrelevant human accomplishments and status indicators rather than in the cross of Christ. That kind of power destroys the community that Christ died to create, and as an apostle Paul is commissioned to engage in a kind of preliminary "second coming" so that the community and its leaders will survive the real judgment day (1 Cor. 3:12-17). That is, ultimately, an act of love.

Similarly, Paul expresses loving concern for both the integrity of the community and the eschatological survival of the offender in the episode involving a man sleeping with his father's wife:

> [3]For though absent in body, I am present in spirit; and as if present I have already pronounced judgment [4]in the name of the Lord Jesus on the man who has done such a thing. When you are assembled, and my spirit is present with the power of our Lord Jesus, [5]you are to hand this man over to Satan for the destruction of the flesh, so that his spirit may be saved in the day of the Lord. [6]Your boasting is not a good thing. Do you not know that a little yeast leavens the whole batch of dough? [7]Clean out the old yeast so that you may be a new batch, as you really are unleavened. For our paschal lamb, Christ, has been sacrificed. [8]Therefore, let us celebrate the festival, not with the old yeast, the yeast of malice and evil, but with the unleavened bread of sincerity and truth. (1 Cor. 5:3-8)

In this passage, not only does Paul express concern for individual and group alike,[61] but he derives this concern from the two foci of his gospel, the past event of the cross and the future event of the parousia.

Finally, similar themes emerge in 2 Corinthians 13:

> [1]This is the third time I am coming to you. "Any charge must be sustained by the evidence of two or three witnesses." [2]I warned those who sinned previously and all the others, and I warn them now while absent, as I did when present on my second visit, that if I come again, I will not be lenient — [3]since you desire proof that Christ is speaking in me. He is not weak in dealing with you, but is powerful in you. [4]For he was crucified in weakness, but lives by the power of God. For we are weak in him, but in dealing with you we will live

---

61. Westerners, as advocates of tolerance sympathetic to the individual, may have difficulty identifying with Paul's assumption that sin is corruption and disease that mortally threatens the community and thus requires intolerance. See Neyrey, *Paul, In Other Words*, pp. 151-56.

with him by the power of God. ⁵Examine yourselves to see whether you are living⁶² in the faith. . . . ⁸For we cannot do anything against the truth, but only for the truth. ⁹For we rejoice when we are weak and you are strong. This is what we pray for, that you may become perfect. (2 Cor. 13:1-5a, 8-9)

In this passage Paul almost seems to contradict his own notion of his, Christ's, and God's power as cruciform. Is he planning to come and deal with the Corinthians in power (v. 4) or weakness (v. 9)?

The answer is both. He cannot literally "whip them into shape." What he can do is to come and once again express in word and deed the resurrection power of God in Christ through the apostolic power of cruciform weakness (vv. 4, 9).⁶³ Anything less, or different, would be "against the truth" (v. 8). Paul's desire, his prayer, is that the Corinthians will experience the strength of God's resurrection power by living lives of cruciformity — unlike the false, superapostles described in 2 Corinthians 10–12, and like the apostle Paul and his colleagues.

What is at stake in these texts, from Paul's vantage point, is nothing less than the integrity and thus the salvation of the community for which Christ died and for which Paul has labored. Failure to do what is needed to bring the community back into conformity with Paul's divinely given gospel of the cross would be, for the apostle, a betrayal of his apostolic commission and a failure of love. It would also be a failure to recognize that the gospel of Christ crucified has been unleashed as God's apocalyptic weapon against all the powers that enslave the human race (Gal. 1:4). Paul therefore sees himself as God's co-warrior, though his armor is faith, hope, and love (1 Thess. 5:8) and the weapons of his warfare are "not fleshly [NRSV 'merely human']" (2 Cor. 10:4):

> ³Indeed, we live as human beings, but we do not wage war according to human standards; ⁴for the weapons of our warfare are not merely human, but they have divine power to destroy strongholds. We destroy arguments ⁵and every proud obstacle raised up against the knowledge of God, and we take every thought captive to obey Christ. ⁶We are ready to punish every disobedience when your obedience is complete. (2 Cor. 10:3-6)

Paul's desire to "control" community life is, for him, no more or less than an acknowledgment that his gospel is not his but God's, that it is God who is at work

---

62. The verb "living" does not appear in the Greek text. The verse should be translated "Examine yourselves to see whether you [plural] are in the faith," whether they are a believing community at all — which of course they are because Christ lives within their community (v. 5b), unless they fail the test — the test of cruciform strength.

63. Georgi aptly notes that Paul's "threats to demonstrate strength" in 2 Corinthians "are not without dialectical irony" (*Theocracy,* p. 62).

both in him and in the various communities, and that the suffering he endures is worthwhile if — and only if — his gospel is indeed the weapon of victory in the apocalyptic war and thus "the word of life":

> [12]Therefore, my beloved, just as you have always obeyed me, not only in my presence, but much more now in my absence, work out your own salvation with fear and trembling; [13]for it is God who is at work in you, enabling you both to will and to work for his good pleasure. [14]Do all things without murmuring and arguing, [15]so that you may be blameless and innocent, children of God without blemish in the midst of a crooked and perverse generation, in which you shine like stars in the world. [16]It is by your holding fast to the word of life that I can boast on the day of Christ that I did not run in vain or labor in vain. [17]But even if I am being poured out as a libation over the sacrifice and the offering of your faith, I am glad and rejoice with all of you — [18]and in the same way you also must be glad and rejoice with me. (Phil. 2:12-18)

If the gospel of the exalted crucified Christ is indeed the gospel of God, Paul is willing to sacrifice himself "to the nth degree" for that gospel and its communities. What Paul is completely unwilling to do, however — or to allow in the communities for which he has responsibility — is to "control" that about which he is unsure or that which does not matter. For instance, he has little more than good, thoughtful pastoral advice about the subject of marriage (1 Corinthians 7), even though he *thinks* he has the Spirit of God on the matter (1 Cor. 7:40). He steadfastly refuses, on profound theological grounds, to control the expression of cultural differences about food and calendar in order artificially to unite a divided community (Romans 14–15). In that situation, indeed, it is the very refusal to control the community that is both the loving and the powerful thing to do: loving because it expresses divine love, and powerful because it expresses, and will hopefully effect, the divine will known in the gospel within the Roman community.[64]

So, does Paul attempt to control and "homogenize" his communities? To impose the pattern of his life on them? Yes, but only in this way: with the goal that they will be imaginatively conformed to the exalted crucified Messiah Jesus. That they will be communities of unity in diversity, of love and humility and vulnerability — and thus of divine power. This is, for Paul, the ministry of powerful love and loving power to which he has been called.[65]

---

64. On the connection in Paul between love, power, and edification, see Pickett, *The Cross in Corinth*, pp. 192-208.

65. See also Martin, *Slavery*, p. 141.

In the final analysis, Paul's primary intent was not to "throw his weight around" or even to vindicate his apostleship and win admirers. Rather, in the words of Raymond Pickett, people's "perception of his apostleship was a concern of secondary importance to their behavioural compliance with the christological pattern that integrates weakness and power."[66] He consistently claimed to use his "weight," his status as apostle, with a power motivated only by love and shaped by Christ's power in weakness.[67]

Ordinary Believers and the Power of God

If for Paul the cross of Christ is Christ's downwardly mobile power in love, then what he seeks to "pass on" to the Corinthians and others is in fact a form of power, but power redefined. Although Paul does not say much about this explicitly, we can infer a number of things about the experience of power he wishes his communities to have, in part because of his (deliberately?) ambiguous use of the pronoun "we" when talking about power, particularly in 2 Corinthians.

It will be recalled that for our purposes power is defined as the "ability to exercise significant control or influence, either for good or for ill, over people and/or history." Luke Johnson has suggested that the texts of the New Testament relate early Christian experiences of power; the early Christians "considered themselves caught up by, defined by, a power not in their control but rather controlling them, a power that derived from the crucified and raised Messiah Jesus."[68] How does this power of the cross, of the exalted crucified Messiah Jesus, work its influence in the life of everyday believers according to Paul? It occurs in several ways.

Power as Moral Transformation (Holiness)

For Paul the first experience of believers, as we have seen, is cruciform faith. As the appropriate response to the gospel of the cruciform power of God, this faith transfers the believer into the realm of God's dominion or power. The power of the new age, which the cross inaugurates, thereby becomes available to the believer. Sin no longer dominates and indwells; rather, a new power — Christ himself, or the Spirit — governs and guides (see especially Romans 6–8).

---

66. Pickett, *The Cross in Corinth*, p. 203.

67. See also Pickett, *The Cross in Corinth*, pp. 204-8.

68. Luke Timothy Johnson, *Religious Experience in Earliest Christianity: A Missing Dimension of New Testament Studies* (Minneapolis: Fortress, 1998), p. 184.

The result of this transfer of dominions and powers is transformation. Power effects change. The power of the Spirit undoes the consequences of the power of sin. Thus Paul writes to the Corinthians:

> [9]Do you not know that wrongdoers will not inherit the kingdom of God? Do not be deceived! Fornicators, idolaters, adulterers, male prostitutes, sodomites, [10]thieves, the greedy, drunkards, revilers, robbers — none of these will inherit the kingdom of God. [11]And this is what some of you used to be. But you were washed, you were sanctified, you were justified in the name of our Lord Jesus Christ and in the Spirit of our God. (1 Cor. 6:9-11)

The apostle clearly assumes — and expresses with understatement ("And this is what 'some of you' used to be") — that radical moral transformation is the norm for those who embrace God in Christ. Or, more precisely, it is the norm for those embraced and set apart by God, as the three passive verbs in the second half of verse 11 stress.

This power from outside the self enables believers to control themselves on a daily basis, not just in a dramatic initial transformation:

> [3]For this is the will of God, your sanctification: that you abstain from fornication; [4]that each one of you know how to control your own body in holiness and honor, [5]not with lustful passion, like the Gentiles who do not know God. . . . [7]For God did not call us to impurity but holiness. [8]Therefore whoever rejects this rejects not human authority but God, who also gives his Holy Spirit to you. (1 Thess. 4:3-5, 7-8)

According to Galatians 5:23, one dimension of the "fruit" of the Spirit is self-control. Antiquity's search for a power able to influence the human self and the human community for good is realized, for Paul, in the Spirit of God's Son.

Power as Status Transcendence and Reversal

As we have repeatedly seen, the Spirit of God's Son is, in Paul's experience, the Spirit of the cross, the cruciform Spirit. This means that the power of sanctification and self-control are ultimately measured by cruciformity. In antiquity — as in many times — control or power was measured by social rank. For believers within Paul's communities, however, the normal measurements of power are reversed. God's power to transform human life is experienced primarily not by the socially superior but by the socially inferior. Paul writes to the Corinthians:

299

[26]Consider your own call, brothers and sisters: not many of you were wise by human standards, not many were powerful, not many were of noble birth. [27]But God chose what is foolish in the world to shame the wise; God chose what is weak in the world to shame the strong; [28]God chose what is low and despised in the world, things that are not, to reduce to nothing things that are, [29]so that no one might boast in the presence of God. [30]He is the source of your life in Christ Jesus. . . . (1 Cor. 1:26-30a)

Here Paul echoes but radically transforms the exhortation of Jeremiah 9:23-24 that the wise, mighty, and/or wealthy should not boast in their wisdom, might, and/or wealth but in their knowledge of the Lord. For Paul, God chooses the opposite of power so that those who are chosen know that "the source of [their] life" — the power of their existence and the reason for their privileged status — has absolutely nothing to do with their "power" measured in human terms. Indeed, God's power makes "somebodies" out of "nobodies." Inferiority, graced by God in Christ, becomes power.

All other claims to or attempts at power are thereby rendered impotent. Hellenistic society, like perhaps all societies, was based on success. Yet Paul

> asserts that since Jesus, humankind is not intrinsically controlled by competition and success, superiority and inferiority, superordination and subordination. Rather, humanity is controlled by the mutual solidarity of a life born out of a common death.[69]

It is for this reason that Paul's communities transcend gender, class, and racial barriers (Gal. 3:28): life in Christ is grounded in a power that makes somebodies out of nobodies and renders so-called somebodies no more or less significant than their "inferiors." Power in the Pauline communities is not to be found in social *power* but in social *weakness,* in those who are weak and despised, just as this power is grounded in the one who manifested God's power as a weak and cursed "nobody" on a Roman cross. The cross "reveals the way God works now, not just the way he achieved salvation in the past. . . . He works *now* in conformity with the pattern seen *then* on the cross: it is the God of the cross with whom the Corinthians [and all believers] now have to deal."[70]

Furthermore, this shared power is expressed in the Pauline communities in the possession and exercise of spiritual gifts, or gifts of grace (Greek *charismata*). Although there is a hierarchy to the gifts, based on their perceived ability to benefit the community (1 Cor. 12:28; ch. 14), everyone possesses a gift, and

69. Georgi, *Theocracy,* p. 71.
70. Tomlin, *The Power of the Cross,* p. 100.

300

each gift — and therefore each member of the community — is important and valued. Indeed, the socially inferior are the communally superior; status is not only transcended but reversed:

> [7]To each is given the manifestation of the Spirit for the common good. . . . [22]. . . [T]he members of the body that seem to be weaker are indispensable, [23]and those members of the body that we think less honorable we clothe with greater honor, and our less respectable members are treated with greater respect; [24]whereas our more respectable members do not need this. But God has so arranged the body, giving the greater honor to the inferior member, [25]that there may be no dissension within the body, but the members may have the same care for one another. (1 Cor. 12:7, 22-25)

While social distinctions remain in the Pauline communities (slaves — at least the slaves of nonbelievers — are still slaves), the strongest forces experienced in these communities are not those that distinguish the socially inferior from the socially superior. Rather, these communities experience a power that transcends and reverses social status, a power known only in the cross and in communities shaped by it.

Power as Boasting and Victory in Suffering

Paul is no masochist, but he does expect that all believers will likely endure suffering. It is not merely for the apostles and their team. The "we" of "we boast also in our sufferings" (Rom. 5:3) is clearly inclusive, as Romans 8:17 requires (only those who suffer are truly heirs with Christ) and Philippians 1:29 demonstrates (the Philippians are graced not only to believe but also to suffer).[71] Suffering is somehow part of the grace of believing existence.

We will return to this topic of suffering again in more depth in the next chapter (on hope). For now we simply stress that inasmuch as Paul expects believers to suffer, he also expects them "in all these things [afflictions]" to be, like the apostles, "more than conquerors" (Rom. 8:37). The experience of suffering is not one of defeat, but of victory, of power. This can be true only because God's love has been shown and experienced in the cross of Christ, and because death and all other powers have been conquered in the resurrection of Christ. Walter Wink writes concerning the various afflictions Paul lists in Romans 8:35:

---

71. See also 2 Cor. 1:6.

In short, every sanction that the state, religion, the economic system, the courts, police, the army, public opinion, mob action, or peer pressure can bring to bear to enforce our complicity in the great defection from God has been robbed of its power. They can kill us all day long, as Ps. 44:22 says, but they cannot separate us from Christ, and so they can no longer compel us to comply (v. 36).[72]

The love of God, in other words, is the power of God in daily life, even the life of suffering, as the conclusion to Romans 8 summarizes the believer's situation:

> [38]For I am convinced that neither death, nor life, nor angels, nor rulers, nor things present, nor things to come, nor powers, [39]nor height, nor depth, nor anything else in all creation, will be able to separate us from the love of God in Christ Jesus our Lord. (Rom. 8:38-39)

Once again, the "we" — here actually the "us" — is inclusive (cf. Phil. 4:13).

Power as Cruciform Care for Others, Especially the Poor and "Weak"

Finally, and perhaps most importantly, for Paul the cruciform power he wishes to pass on to his communities is the power of cruciform care, the power of suffering love. Without repeating what has been said at length about love in earlier chapters, we need simply here to stress that cruciform love is powerful because it is effective — it alters human life for the good.

We have seen, for example, that Paul calls the Corinthians to share their material resources with other believers (e.g., 2 Corinthians 8–9). For him, this is the evidence and activity of the grace of God, which transforms the (spiritually) poor into the (spiritually) rich. So too, if the Corinthians allow the powerful grace of God to have sway in their community, their "present abundance" will change the situation of the less fortunate believers in Jerusalem, and, in the reciprocity of cruciform grace and power, their own situation will be dramatically affected for the better (2 Cor. 8:13-15).

In similar fashion, throughout his letters Paul connects sacrificial love with positive, powerful activity, especially the power to create unity and harmony. Since the creation of unity is the primary goal of some letters (e.g., 1 Corinthians) and one of the goals of every letter, Paul's correspondence promotes cruciform love as the power that must be unleashed in each community.

---

72. Wink, *Naming the Powers*, p. 48.

This is not the power of influence as it is normally understood — the power of self-interested control — but the power of *kenosis,* of self-humbling and self-giving, the very kinds of activities that the cross of Christ reveals. These activities express the power of God. Indeed, when social prerogatives and power are allowed to define and control the community, the community falls apart, as it was doing in Corinth, where there existed not one unified assembly eating "the Lord's supper" but in effect cliques of people eating a series of meals with different guests, foods, and tables, based largely on social class (1 Cor. 11:17-34). In this situation and in others at Corinth that manifested neglect of the poorer or weaker members of the community, Paul's strategy of creating unity is to take sides — not with those who agree with him or are like him, but with those whom the more powerful members have forsaken. He does this because his experience of the cross tells him that God has taken, and does take, sides with the poor and weak.[73]

For Paul, any claims to being the body of Christ in communion with him are rendered null and void when the members of the community fail to express their power as love, especially for the weak. In the concluding words of Graham Tomlin's study of the power of the cross in Paul:

> The cross operates as a counter-ideology to the uses of power current within the church, fostering a regard for love rather than knowledge, the poor rather than the wealthy . . . mutual upbuilding rather than spiritual showing-off. Theology that begins at the cross is for Paul the radical antidote to any religion that is a thinly veiled copy of a power-seeking culture.[74]

Conclusion: God's Power in Weakness

In the story of Christ, Paul sees power defined and manifested in the most radical *kenosis* or powerlessness. His own experience is an attempt to continue that narrative by reembodying it and then passing it on to the communities to which he writes. They, in turn, the apostle hopes, will become communities of power, marked not by their culture's understanding of honor, respect, and control, but by the sign of the cross, the power of suffering love, God's power in weakness. This paradoxical kind of power gives both life and hope to these communities. Thus, we turn now to the future of cruciformity.

---

73. See also Tomlin, *The Power of the Cross,* p. 96. In contemporary theological ethics, this kind of "taking sides" is sometimes known as a "preferential option for the poor."

74. Tomlin, *The Power of the Cross,* p. 101. See also Pickett, *The Cross in Corinth.*

CHAPTER 12

CRUCIFORM HOPE

The Future of Cruciformity

Thus far we have examined Paul's experience of faith, love, and power. Hope is also a fundamental dimension of Paul's spirituality, "one of the primary blessings of the Spirit"[1] for the apostle. The word "hope" appears in his letters at key junctures and is one of the three so-called "theological virtues" (the others, of course, being faith and love) enunciated by Paul. Indeed, it has been argued — with only some exaggeration — that the theme of Paul's most comprehensive and systematic letter, Romans, is hope.[2] The content of this hope is expressed in various ways, including eternal life, righteousness, salvation, escaping the coming wrath, resurrection, the redemption of our bodies, being in the presence of the Lord, being heirs of God and co-heirs with Christ, and glory.[3]

However, one of the most significant — but also disconcerting — texts in Paul's letters appears in his discussion of believers' hope-filled experience of the Spirit, Romans 8:17:

> [15]. . . When we cry, "Abba! Father!" [16]it is that very Spirit bearing witness with our spirit that we are children of God, [17]and if children, then heirs, heirs of

---

1. James D. G. Dunn, *The Theology of Paul the Apostle* (Grand Rapids: Eerdmans, 1998), p. 438.

2. John Paul Heil, *Romans — Paul's Letter of Hope*, Analecta Biblica 112 (Rome: Biblical Institute Press, 1987).

3. E.g., Rom. 6:23 (eternal life); Gal. 5:5 (righteousness); 1 Thess. 5:8 (salvation); 1 Thess. 1:10 (escaping the coming wrath); Phil. 3:11, 14 (resurrection); Rom. 8:23 (the redemption of our bodies); Phil. 1:23 (being in the presence of the Lord); and Rom. 8:17 (heirs of God and co-heirs with Christ, and glory [also 2 Cor. 4:17]).

God and joint heirs with Christ — **if, in fact, we suffer with him so that we may also be glorified with him.** (Rom. 8:15b-17 [emphasis added])

In this text Paul infers the absolute necessity of suffering on the part of those who live in Christ and hope to share in his glory in the future. Does this make Paul into a sadist or masochist? Sadly, some have come, and might still come, to this conclusion.

For Paul, however, suffering is intimately connected to hope, which is in fact the theme of the second half of Romans 8 that is introduced by the text quoted above. Suffering leads not to despair but to the assurance of future salvation and glory. This, for Paul, is not wishful thinking or some other sophisticated psychological device to deal with his life of persecution and other difficulties. Rather, both the inevitability of suffering and the certainty of future glory are for him *theological and spiritual necessities.* For Paul, hope is fundamentally the certainty that the ultimate fate of the humiliated, crucified Messiah will also be the ultimate fate of himself and of all others who are co-crucified with Christ. That is, hope is the conviction that the future of cruciformity is resurrection and exaltation, or, in a word, glory — the completion of the process of conformity to the narrative pattern of the Messiah.

In this chapter we first consider the roots of Paul's cruciform hope in his appropriation of Scripture and Jewish tradition, in his gospel, and in his experience of the exalted crucified Messiah Jesus. Several polyvalent patterns of death and life, of humiliation and exaltation, will emerge. We may refer to these as patterns of reversal, even though we will find — ironically — that for Paul that reversal is also the culmination of a continuous process. We will also examine four dimensions of this cruciform hope expressed in Paul's letters — personal, communal, universal, and cosmic — and the role of cruciform hope in daily life as Paul understands and experiences it.

Patterns of Reversal in Scripture and Jewish Tradition

Paul's Jewish background provided him with at least four distinct but not dissimilar traditions in which suffering and hope were connected in a narrative pattern of reversal: God's exaltation of the humble, God's vindication of the persecuted and of righteous sufferers, God's ultimate resolution of messianic "birth pangs" in the new age, and God's raising of the dead.

God Exalts the Humble

In the first place, the wisdom and prophetic traditions provided a fundamental Jewish insight: God will bring down the arrogant and the self-important powerful but will honor and exalt the humble and the poor who rely not on themselves but on God:

> Toward the scorners he is scornful, but to the humble he shows favor. (Prov. 3:34)[4]

> 2[17]Those who fear the Lord prepare their hearts, and humble themselves before him. . . . 3[17]My child, perform your tasks with humility; then you will be loved by those whom God accepts. [18]The greater you are, the more you must humble yourself; so you will find favor in the sight of the Lord. [[19]Many are lofty and renowned, but to the humble he reveals his secrets.] [20]For great is the might of the Lord; but by the humble he is glorified. (Sir. 2:17; 3:17-20)[5]

> [12]The beginning of human pride is to forsake the Lord; the heart has withdrawn from its Maker. [13]For the beginning of pride is sin, and the one who clings to it pours out abominations. Therefore the Lord brings upon them unheard-of calamities, and destroys them completely. [14]The Lord overthrows the thrones of rulers, and enthrones the lowly in their place. [15]The Lord plucks up the roots of the nations, and plants the humble in their place. (Sir. 10:12-15)

> 18[27]For you deliver a humble people, but the haughty eyes you bring down. . . . 25[9]He leads the humble in what is right, and teaches the humble his way. (Ps. 18:27; 25:9)

> [4]For the LORD takes pleasure in his people; he adorns the humble with victory. [5]Let the faithful exult in glory; let them sing for joy on their couches. (Ps. 149:4-5).

---

4. Quoted with modifications in 1 Pet. 5:5: "God opposes the proud, but gives grace to the humble." Cf. also Matt. 23:12: "All who exalt themselves will be humbled, and all who humble themselves will be exalted."

5. Sirach, also known as The Wisdom of Jesus Son of Sirach, or Ecclesiasticus, was written in Jerusalem in about 200 B.C. or slightly later. Verse 19 of chapter 3 is enclosed in brackets because it does not appear in all manuscripts.

God Vindicates the Persecuted Righteous

Second, and similarly, many of the Psalms contain pleas for, and (usually) affirmations of, deliverance for those who are persecuted for God's sake. A few of many examples will suffice:

> [24]Vindicate me, O LORD, my God, according to your righteousness, and do not let them rejoice over me. Do not let them say to themselves, "Aha, we have our heart's desire." [25]Do not let them say, "We have swallowed you up." [26]Let all those who rejoice at my calamity be put to shame and confusion; let those who exalt themselves against me be clothed with shame and dishonor. [27]Let those who desire my vindication shout for joy and be glad, and say evermore, "Great is the Lord, who delights in the welfare of his servant." [28]Then my tongue shall tell of your righteousness and of your praise all day long. (Ps. 35:24-28)

> Vindicate me, O God, and defend my cause against an ungodly people; from those who are deceitful and unjust deliver me! (Ps. 43:1)

Somewhat less optimistic and quite angry, but not lacking in hope, is Psalm 44, to which Paul will be drawn (Rom. 8:36):

> [8]In God we have boasted continually, and we will give thanks to your name forever. [9]Yet you have rejected us and abased us, and have not gone out with our armies. [10]You made us turn back from the foe, and our enemies have gotten spoil. [11]You have made us like sheep for slaughter, and have scattered us among the nations. . . . [17]All this has come upon us, yet we have not forgotten you, or been false to your covenant. [18]Our heart has not turned back, nor have our steps departed from your way. . . . [22]Because of you we are being killed all day long, and accounted as sheep for the slaughter. [23]Rouse yourself! Why do you sleep, O Lord? Awake, do not cast us off forever. . . . [26]Rise up, come to our help. Redeem us for the sake of your steadfast love. (Ps. 44:8-11, 17-18, 22-23, 26)[6]

In a significant development of this theme of hope for the faithful in the midst of suffering, 2 Maccabees 7 reveals the Jewish hope for vindication and resurrection for those who at the time of Antiochus IV Epiphanes (reigned 175-164 B.C.) died for their refusal to compromise their faith. Seven brothers and their mother die as martyrs, addressing Antiochus as they are tortured in preparation for death:

---

6. According to Wisd. of Sol. 2:12-20 the unrighteous mock this hope, in a text apparently based on Isa. 52:13–53:12.

[9]... "You accursed wretch, you dismiss us from this present life, but the King of the universe will raise us up to an everlasting renewal of life, because we have died for his laws." ... [14]... "One cannot but choose to die at the hands of mortals and to cherish the hope God gives of being raised again by him. But for you there will be no resurrection to life!" ... [20]The mother was especially admirable and worthy of honorable memory. Although she saw her seven sons perish within a single day, she bore it with good courage because of her hope in the Lord. ... [40]So he [the last son] died in his integrity, putting his whole trust in the Lord. (2 Macc. 7:9, 14, 20, 40)[7]

These two closely related themes of vindication and exaltation come together in the Hebrew Bible nowhere as vividly as they do in the fourth servant hymn of Isaiah 52:13–53:12. We have already noted the influence of this text on Paul's Christ hymn (Phil. 2:6-11), and we will return to that subject below. For the moment, we briefly consider the entire servant hymn and the main image its text and structure embody. That image is one of the servant's innocent but divinely willed vicarious suffering and consequent divine exaltation. The text is marked in the following way to highlight the literary skill with which this image appears in the text:

- key phrases of the text that have to do with suffering and humiliation are underlined;
- key phrases that have to do with exaltation are **boldfaced**;
- key phrases that suggest the servant's innocence are *italicized*;
- key phrases that convey salvific effect on others are in all CAPITAL LETTERS; and
- key words that show the connection between humiliation and exaltation are set in UNDERLINED CAPITAL LETTERS.

[13]See, my servant **shall prosper;**
he **shall be exalted and lifted up,**
and **shall be very high.**
[14]Just as there were many who were astonished at him
— so marred was his appearance, beyond human semblance,
and his form beyond that of mortals —
[15]so **he shall startle many nations;**
kings shall shut their mouths because of him;
for that which had not been told them they shall see,

<hr />

7. For the development of eschatological hope for the righteous martyrs in Judaism, see John S. Pobee, *Persecution and Martyrdom in the Theology of Paul*, JSNTSup 6 (Sheffield: JSOT Press, 1985), pp. 41-45.

and that which they had not heard they shall contemplate.
[1]Who has believed what we have heard?
And to whom has the arm of the Lord been revealed?
[2]For he grew up before him like a young plant,
and like a root out of dry ground;
he had no form or majesty that we should look at him,
nothing in his appearance that we should desire him.
[3]He was despised and rejected by others;
a man of suffering and acquainted with infirmity;
and as one from whom others hide their faces
he was despised, and we held him of no account.
[4]Surely he has BORNE OUR INFIRMITIES
and CARRIED OUR DISEASES;
yet we accounted him stricken,
struck down by God, and afflicted.
[5]But he was wounded FOR OUR TRANSGRESSIONS,
crushed FOR OUR INIQUITIES;
upon him was the punishment that MADE US WHOLE,
and by his bruises WE ARE HEALED.
[6]All we like sheep have gone astray;
we have all turned to our own way,
and THE LORD HAS LAID ON HIM
THE INIQUITY OF US ALL.
[7]He was oppressed, and he was afflicted,
yet he *did not open his mouth;*
like a lamb that is led to the slaughter,
and like a sheep that before its shearers is silent,
so he did not open his mouth.
[8]*By a perversion of justice he was taken away.*
Who could have imagined his future?
For he was cut off from the land of the living,
stricken FOR THE TRANSGRESSION OF MY PEOPLE.
[9]They made his grave with the wicked
and his tomb with the rich,
although he had done no violence,
and there was no deceit in his mouth.
[10]Yet it was the WILL OF THE LORD to crush him with pain.
When you MAKE HIS LIFE AN OFFERING FOR SIN
he shall see his offspring, and shall prolong his days;
THROUGH HIM THE WILL OF THE LORD SHALL PROSPER.

> [11]Out of his <u>anguish</u> he shall see light;
> he shall **find satisfaction** through his knowledge.
> *The righteous one,* my <u>servant</u>, SHALL MAKE MANY RIGHTEOUS,
> and he shall BEAR THEIR INIQUITIES.
> [12]<u>THEREFORE</u> I will **allot him a portion with the great,**
> and **he shall divide the spoil with the strong;**
> <u>BECAUSE</u> he poured out himself to death,
> and was <u>numbered with the transgressors;</u>
> yet he BORE THE SIN OF MANY
> AND MADE INTERCESSION FOR THE TRANSGRESSORS.

What is central to this hymn are the literary structure that corresponds to the image and the theological reality to which it is intended to witness. The opening lines (52:13-15) serve as a kind of announcement of the main theme of exaltation. This text, the opening words proclaim, is ultimately a hymn of victory, even though much of the text depicts humiliation and suffering. The main portion of the text (53:1-12) is then divided into a portrait of the servant's innocent, salvific suffering (53:1-9) and God's affirmative response of exaltation (53:10-12). The divine reward is repeatedly and explicitly portrayed as a consequence of the vicarious suffering,[8] such that the humiliation is never forgotten even as the exaltation is announced. Here, truly, the humble and persecuted one — no matter what his original identity (Israel, the prophet or another individual, etc.) — is vindicated by God because he has carried out God's will.

This figure, it should be noted, would almost certainly not have been seen by any Jew as a Messiah. He is more like a martyr or other hero who dies in some way for God's cause and God's people. The image of the righteous martyr, as noted above, becomes important within Judaism (and, later, within early Christianity). The image of a suffering messiah, however, is developed only by the early followers and interpreters of Jesus in response to his self-understanding and with repeated reference to Isaiah 52:13–53:12.

God Concludes the Messianic Woes

In fact, when Paul (among others) reads Jesus' mission in light of the fourth servant hymn, he does so also in the context of yet a third Jewish motif of suffering and hope, that of "messianic woes." The development of apocalyptic

---

8. See the excellent discussion in Richard Bauckham, *God Crucified: Monotheism and Christology in the New Testament* (Grand Rapids: Eerdmans, 1998), pp. 47-51, 59-61.

thought — in which the imminent inbreaking of God to end this evil age and establish the new age of peace and righteousness was the central tenet — added this theme to Jewish contemplation of suffering. There arose a conviction that preceding the arrival of the glorious future kingdom of God — when the righteous dead would be raised to life and the evildoers punished — would come a period of intense suffering and pain for God's people:

> ¹"At that time Michael, the great prince, the protector of your people, shall arise. There shall be a time of anguish, such as has never occurred since nations first came into existence. But at that time your people shall be delivered, everyone who is found written in the book. ²Many of those who sleep in the dust of the earth shall awake, some to everlasting life, and some to shame and everlasting contempt. ³Those who are wise shall shine like the brightness of the sky, and those who lead many to righteousness, like the stars forever and ever. ⁴But you, Daniel, keep the words secret and the book sealed until the time of the end. Many shall be running back and forth, and evil shall increase." (Dan. 12:1-4)

God Raises the Dead

The previous two sections have each contained texts that speak of resurrection: Daniel 12:2-3, cited immediately above, and part of 2 Maccabees:

> "One cannot but choose to die at the hands of mortals and to cherish the hope God gives of being raised again by him. But for you there will be no resurrection to life!" (2 Macc. 7:14; cf. 7:23)

These texts date from the second century B.C. and appear to represent developments later than most of the prophets. Scholars debate whether or not the subject of resurrection exists in the Old Testament, but, even if it does, resurrection does not appear to have been a prominent theme in Israel's life.

In addition to Daniel 12:2-3, there is also Isaiah 26:19 — the dating of which is itself debated:

> Your dead shall live, their corpses shall rise. O dwellers in the dust, awake and sing for joy! For your dew is as radiant dew, and the earth will give birth to those long dead.

Whatever the precise beliefs in ancient Israel, the raw material for belief in resurrection was present in the hope that God would keep the faithful from the grave and especially Sheol (e.g., Ps. 6:4-5; 16:10) and in the hope that God would deliver Israel from exile and thus resurrect the nation from the dead (Ezekiel 37, especially v. 12).

By the time of Paul, these hopes had become more specific but certainly not monolithic. There existed a variety of hopes for personal immortality in early Judaism (immortality of the soul as well as resurrection of the body), as witnessed by such documents as the Wisdom of Solomon, 2 Baruch, and 1 Enoch. In the century of Jesus and Paul, the Pharisees distinguished themselves from the Sadducees, in part, by their affirmation of the resurrection of the dead, as both the New Testament and Josephus attest.[9] The Gospels also attest to the reality that the question of the resurrection of the dead was "in the air" of the first century.

Paul, as a Pharisee, was heir to this conviction about the resurrection, and heir also to the other motifs that relate suffering to hope and that we have briefly considered. His creative genius was, in part, his ability to synthesize these traditions and to reconfigure them in light of his experience of the crucified, raised, and exalted Messiah Jesus.[10]

The Messianic Pattern of Reversal

Unlike faith, love, and even power, hope is a trait that Paul does not explicitly attribute to Christ. There is not, for example, a clear text in Paul like Hebrews 12:2, which says that "for the sake of the joy that was set before him [Jesus] endured the cross, disregarding its shame." There is, however, throughout Paul's correspondence — and in the rest of the New Testament, including Hebrews — a consistent Christological narrative pattern of reversal — of death followed by resurrection, of humiliation followed by exaltation.[11] That is, although Paul does not find the "virtue" of hope per se in the narrative of Christ, he does find the *substance* of hope in the pattern of Christ's humiliation-exaltation.

---

9. E.g., Acts 23:6-8 (cf. Mark 12:18 and parallels); Josephus *Jewish War* 2.163-66; *Antiquities* 18.12-17.

10. Dale B. Martin (*Slavery as Salvation: The Metaphor of Slavery in Pauline Christianity* [New Haven and London: Yale University Press, 1990], p. 130) points out that the humiliation-exaltation pattern appears also in some depictions of ancient slavery in which slaves move up the social ladder or into freedom. While offering parallels to Paul's experience and thought, these are likely not as central to Paul's self-understanding as the traditions discussed here.

11. Heb. 12:2, in fact, concludes the text cited above with the words "and has taken his seat at the right hand of the throne of God." The pattern seems to have been constitutive of early Christian preaching and experience. The "joy" of 1 Thess. 1:6 *might* refer to Jesus.

It is more precise and helpful to consider this narrative pattern of reversal as two closely related patterns, one of death followed by resurrection, the other of humiliation followed by exaltation. Both patterns clearly preceded Paul and also survived after him, but few early Christians exploited them as fully as did Paul.

Death-Resurrection

Early, pre-Pauline traditions, which Paul frequently quotes, had already quite naturally brought together the death and resurrection of Jesus in creedal statements. For example, in Romans 4:24-25 Paul cites and interprets a simple death-resurrection narrative that is thought by most scholars to predate him:

> [24]. . . It [righteousness] will be reckoned to us who believe in him who raised Jesus our Lord from the dead, [25]who was handed over [Greek *paredothē*] to death for our trespasses and was raised for our justification. (Rom. 4:24-25)

Of special importance in this text is the absolutely passive role played by Jesus; he was "handed over" and "he was raised." The agent of the latter is clearly God.[12] By whom Jesus was "handed over," however, is not clear, at least for the citation itself without reference to Paul's broader interpretation of it. The agent could have been Judas, or humans in general, or God. In light of the rest of the letter (especially Rom. 3:21-26; 5:6-8; 8:3-4, 32), Paul almost certainly intends the hearer to assume that God also did the handing over to death.[13] Thus it is God's will and power that effect both the death and the resurrection of Christ. The will of God is inseparably expressed in both events, and human salvation is inextricably linked to both.[14]

---

12. Paul normally speaks of Jesus being raised by God, though he makes Jesus the subject of an active verb for resurrection in Rom. 14:9 ("Christ lived again") and 1 Thess. 4:14 ("Jesus . . . rose again").

13. In each of these texts, Paul asserts that God takes the initiative in Christ's death. Especially telling is Paul's language in Rom. 8:32, where the verb *(paradidōmi)* that appears in the passive voice in 4:25 occurs in the active voice: "He who did not withhold his own Son, but gave him up for all of us [Greek *hyper hēmōn pantōn paredōken auton*], will he not with him also give us everything else?" See also 3:24-25 ("Christ Jesus, whom God put forward as a sacrifice of atonement by his blood"); 5:8 ("But God proves his love for us in that while we still were sinners Christ died for us"); and 8:3 ("sending his own Son in the likeness of sinful flesh, and to deal with sin"). These texts, it has often been noted, are echoes of the story of Abraham's willingness to sacrifice his only son Isaac (Gen. 22:1-19).

14. An apparent contradiction of this unity of death and resurrection is Rom. 10:9, which says, "if you confess with your lips that Jesus is Lord and believe in your heart that God raised

313

Similarly, Paul's argument to the Corinthians about the necessity and meaning of bodily resurrection (1 Corinthians 15) is premised on his and their shared affirmations about Christ's death and resurrection:

> [3]For I handed on to you as of first importance what I in turn had received: that Christ **died** for our sins in accordance with the scriptures, [4]and that he **was buried**, and that he **was raised** on the third day in accordance with the scriptures, [5]and that he **appeared** to Cephas, then to the twelve. [6]Then he appeared to more than five hundred brothers and sisters at one time, most of whom are still alive, though some have died. (1 Cor. 15:3-6 [emphasis added])

This excerpt from a very ancient Christian creed has four key "articles," or affirmations, corresponding to the main verbs "died," "was buried," "was raised," and "appeared."[15] The two main verbs are split between those associated with Jesus' death (died, was buried) and those linked to his resurrection (was raised, appeared), creating an expanded but still symmetrical narrative pattern of death-resurrection. As in Romans 4:25, God raises Jesus, though here the tradition baldly states "he died" without reference to the agent of the dying (though the purpose, "for our sins," is the same as in Rom. 4:25). That resurrection is absolutely crucial, not only to the narrative of Jesus but also to the Corinthians' salvation and thus to their hope, is made explicit in 1 Corinthians 15:12-19, as the following verses illustrate:

> [17]If Christ has not been raised, your faith is futile and you are still in your sins. . . . [19]If for this life only we have hoped in Christ, we are of all people most to be pitied. (1 Cor. 15:17, 19)

For Paul, then, the death of Christ without the resurrection is meaningless. The raising of Christ is God's vindication of his death and, as noted above, the beginning of the resurrection of believers, "the first fruits of those who have died" (1 Cor. 15:20).[16]

------

him from the dead, you will be saved," with no mention of Jesus' death. Yet the discrepancy is indeed only superficial, for in Romans 10 Paul also refers to the need for a response to the entirety of his gospel (10:8, "the word of faith that we proclaim"). Similarly, the assignment in Rom. 4:25 of Christ's death and resurrection to apparently different aspects of salvation is more for poetic or rhetorical effect than for theological casuistry.

15. The fourth "article," "appeared," is expanded through the repetition of the verb and the enlargement of the list of witnesses in vv. 6-8.

16. The death-resurrection motif also appears in the pre-Pauline formula in Rom. 1:4 ("resurrection from the dead").

The close connection between Christ's death and his resurrection was also made in the common early Christian experience of baptism, as Paul reminds his readers in Romans 6 (about which we will have more to say). In the opening verses of that chapter, as we have already seen, Paul describes the baptismal experience as one of co-dying, co-burial, and co-resurrection with Christ (Rom. 6:3-10). The specific affirmations about Christ are not unlike those found in 1 Corinthians 15:

> [3]. . . death? [4]. . . buried . . . death . . . raised from the dead by the glory of the Father. . . . [5]. . . death . . . resurrection. . . . [6]. . . crucified. . . . [8]. . . died . . . live. . . . [9]. . . being raised from the dead will never die again; death no longer has dominion over him. [10]The death he died, he died to sin, once for all; but the life he lives, he lives to God.

The clear emphasis in this text (see especially v. 10) is on the *finality* of Christ's death both as a defeat of sin ("[with respect] to sin") and as a victory over death itself, such that Christ lives now and forever. As we have already noted and will consider once again below, these two aspects of the finality of Christ's death provide Paul with two corresponding patterns for believers: metaphorical dying as the termination of sin, and literal, physical dying as the prelude to resurrection.

Similarly, in Philippians 3 (about which more will also be said below), Paul expresses his desire to

> know Christ and the power of his resurrection and the sharing of his sufferings by becoming like him in his death, if somehow I may attain the resurrection from the dead. (Phil. 3:10-11)

What is different and striking in this text, however, is the occurrence of one of only two Pauline references to the sufferings (Greek *pathēmatōn*) of Christ. The other instance is in 2 Corinthians 1:5 ("the sufferings of Christ are abundant for us"). In both cases the sufferings of Christ are connected to the suffering of apostles and other believers.[17] The focus of the Philippians text is still resurrection as the consequence of Christ's (suffering and) death.

---

17. 2 Cor. 1:6 speaks of the Corinthians "patiently endur[ing] the same sufferings that we are also suffering," while the letter to the Philippians has already noted the "privilege" of suffering for Christ (1:29).

Humiliation-Exaltation

That Paul's experience of Jesus was paradoxical has been noted in several earlier chapters. The crucified one is now Lord, which means both that Jesus has been exalted by God as Lord and that he remains the crucified one whose cruciform life continues in the community. Yet in terms of Christological narratives, Paul stresses the sequential nature of the events narrated, which thus constitute a pattern of reversal. In addition to the basic pattern of death followed by resurrection, Paul also has the Christological pattern of humiliation followed by exaltation. Indeed, this is the pattern of his "master story," Philippians 2:6-11.

In previous chapters we have highlighted the narrative patterns in the first half of this hymn (vv. 6-8), patterns that express Paul's conviction that the death of Jesus was his embodiment of faithful status-renouncing love for others. As a whole, however, the hymn's narrative pattern is one of reversal, with the self-emptying obedience of Jesus to death (vv. 6-8) answered by God's reversal, God's exaltation of Jesus (vv. 9-11):

Philippians 2:6-8 (NRSV)	Philippians 2:9-11 (NRSV)
[6]. . . [T]hough he [Christ Jesus] was in the form of God, [he] did not regard equality with God as something to be exploited,	[9]Therefore God also highly exalted him and gave him the name that is above every name,
[7]but emptied himself, taking the form of a slave, being born in human likeness. And being found in human form,	[10]so that at the name of Jesus every knee should bend, in heaven and on earth and under the earth,
[8]he humbled himself and became obedient to the point of death — even death on a cross.	[11]and every tongue should confess that Jesus Christ is Lord, to the glory of God the Father.

Much has been written about the possible couplets and stanzas (or "strophes") in this hymn. It is clear, however, that a major division — *the* major division — in the hymn occurs with the shift in grammatical subject from "Christ Jesus" in vv. 6-8 to God in v. 9. As the subject changes, the sequence of verbs of humiliation and lowliness in the first half of the hymn gives way to the one main verb of the second half — "highly exalted" (Greek *hyperypsōsen*). The narrative pattern is remarkably parallel to that of the fourth servant hymn of Isaiah (Isa. 52:13–53:12) discussed above, in which the servant's humiliation is followed by God's exaltation.[13] The fate of the Isaianic servant, however, is told in the hymn's opening line, in advance of the full narrative:

> See, my servant shall prosper; he shall be exalted and lifted up, and shall be very high. (Isa. 52:13)[19]

In the narrative of the hymn itself, this exaltation occurs in Isaiah 53:10-12. The language there suggests that the exaltation is some kind of resurrection, but whatever its precise meaning, the exaltation is clearly a *consequence of and reward for the humiliation and death:*[20]

> [12]**Therefore** I will allot him a portion with the great, and he shall divide the spoil with the strong; **because** he poured out himself to death, and was numbered with the transgressors; yet he bore the sin of many and made intercession for the transgressors. (Isa. 53:12 [emphasis added])

The exalted language of the hymnic preface (Isa. 52:13), mixed with the narrative conclusion (53:12), becomes for Paul (or the earlier Christian hymn writer) the conclusion expressed in Philippians 2:9: Jesus is exalted by God because of his obedient death. This action of superexaltation on God's part, expressed in a verb used nowhere else in the New Testament, is clearly conferred upon him —

18. So also, e.g., Stephen E. Fowl, *The Story of Christ in the Ethics of Paul: An Analysis of the Function of the Hymnic Material in the Pauline Corpus,* JSNTSup 36 (Sheffield: JSOT Press, 1990), pp. 73-75. Fowl is perhaps too critical of those who find explicit verbal parallels and thus literary dependence, but he is correct to emphasize the "general pattern" of humiliation-exaltation expressed in the Isaianic hymn (and in the early chapters of Wisdom) as the "conceptual background" of Philippians 2. In an effort to prove that Paul's understanding of Christ's death has no connection to the Isaianic servant passages, David Seeley (*The Noble Death: Graeco-Roman Martyrology and Paul's Concept of Salvation* [Sheffield: JSOT Press, 1989], pp. 50-57, esp. p. 55) looks too closely at the Greek and Hebrew words translated "therefore," rather than at the overall structure of the fourth servant hymn and Phil. 2:6-11, and their corresponding theologies. Throughout his book, Seeley is right in what he affirms (that Christ's vicarious death is appropriated by imitating or reenacting it) but wrong in what he denies (that there is no association in Paul between Christ's death and the temple sacrifices, the suffering servant, or the story of Abraham's offering of Isaac).

19. The Septuagint (Greek) version of this text uses the verbs *hypsoō* ("exalt") and *doxazō* ("glorify"), both of which are echoed in Philippians 2 (*hyperypsōsen* [from *hyper* plus *hypsoō*] in 2:9 and *doxan* in 2:11), though the specific glory mentioned in 2:11 is given to God the Father, not to Christ the servant.

20. Pobee (*Persecution*, p. 81), arguing against any connection between Philippians 2 and Isa. 52:13–53:12, incorrectly asserts that "unlike Phil. 2, Is. 52.13 does not say that the exaltation is the result of the humiliation."

as upon the Isaianic servant — *as a consequence* ("Therefore," Phil. 2:9) of his humiliation.

The universal worship and acclamation of Jesus as Lord mentioned in Philippians 2:10-11 do not add to but only recognize Jesus' God-given status. These verses have no direct parallel in the Isaianic servant hymn, but they are also drawn from chapters 40–55 of the book of Isaiah. Isaiah 45 contains an impassioned exposition of the oneness of God and the appropriateness of true worship of this one true God. Within that context, the following is said:

> [22]Turn to me and be saved, all the ends of the earth!
> For I am God, and there is no other.
> [23]By myself I have sworn, from my mouth has gone forth in righteousness
> a word that shall not return:
> "To me every knee shall bow, every tongue shall swear." (Isa. 45:22-23)

The conclusion of Philippians 2:6-11, "in language that sounds blasphemous,"[21] transfers to Christ as Lord that which Isaiah 45 — and any Jew — would leave to God alone: recognition as sovereign Lord. As James Dunn has said, "[o]n any count that is an astounding transfer for any Jew to make or appropriate."[22] Nonetheless, Paul's hymn retains the ultimate honor for God the Father, who both wills the exaltation and is in fact glorified by it and by the acclamation of Jesus as Lord (Phil. 2:11).[23]

This narrative sequence must impress upon us once again the significance of the term "Lord" for Paul, especially as it is associated with the crucified Jesus. Implicit in every occurrence of "the Lord Jesus" — nearly 200 in the undisputed Pauline letters — is Paul's conviction that the crucified Jesus has been raised and exalted by God. To affirm and experience this Lord is therefore to be

---

21. Dieter Georgi, *Theocracy in Paul's Praxis and Theology* (Minneapolis: Fortress, 1991), p. 23, who adds, "When Paul and his associates understand their christological experience as demanding a reversal of the concept of God, they do so compelled by their interpretation of the biblical-Jewish experiential heritage. . . . Therefore, this conception is not to be seen as a theory Paul is advancing but as the reflected praxis of both Paul and his forebears."

22. Dunn, *Theology,* p. 251. See also N. T. Wright, "Jesus Christ Is Lord: Philippians 2:5-11," in his *The Climax of the Covenant: Christ and the Law in Pauline Theology* (Edinburgh: T. & T. Clark, 1991; Minneapolis: Fortress, 1993), pp. 56-98, esp. p. 94; and Richard J. Bauckham, "The Worship of Jesus in Philippians 2:9-11," in Ralph P. Martin and Brian J. Dodd, eds., *Where Christology Began: Essays on Philippians 2* (Louisville: Westminster/John Knox, 1993), pp. 128-39.

23. For a study that focuses on the "eschatological" rather than the "ethical" meaning of the hymn, see Larry Kreitzer, "When He at Last Is First: Philippians 2:5-11 and the Exaltation of the Lord," in Ralph P. Martin and Brian J. Dodd, eds., *Where Christology Began: Essays on Philippians 2* (Louisville: Westminster/John Knox, 1993), pp. 111-27.

privileged to participate in a similar narrative of death followed by resurrection, of humiliation followed by exaltation.[24]

Paul's Experience and the Narrative Patterns of Reversal

Paul finds the narrative death-resurrection and humiliation-exaltation patterns of Christ to be paradigmatic for his own life and that of his communities. His basic conviction may be summarized as follows: to the extent that people (himself included) share in the death of Jesus, so they will also share in his life. Christ's narrative pattern of reversal, from humiliation and death to resurrection and exaltation, is also theirs. His death and subsequent exaltation by God have created a "new map of time" in the believer's symbolic universe, a map that must be "replicated in the *map of life time* of each follower."[25] Hope, therefore, is inextricably tied up with humiliation and suffering.

Before looking at the texts in which this conviction, and its underlying experience, appear, we should first explore the question, Why does Paul see the need for hope, that is, for future salvation? Why do Jesus' death and resurrection not mean that salvation is fully experienced *now*, in the present? Why, in other words, is Paul's eschatology — his belief about the future of human experience with God — not a fully "realized" (present) eschatology?

As noted above, Jews with apocalyptic hopes expected the imminent coming of God to reverse history's fortunes and exalt the now humiliated and persecuted Jews. They divided history into "this [evil] age" and "the [righteous] age to come." Paul's experience of the exalted crucified Messiah led him to reinterpret this conviction and to rearrange its corollary timetable of history. For him, the intervention of God in the crucified and resurrected Messiah means that the age to come has arrived in part, but only in part; its fulfillment awaits, according to Paul, the *parousia* or return of Christ. The intervening time — the "overlap of the ages" (1 Cor. 10:11, author's translation) — is characterized by the presence of the future but also the relics of the past, including the powers of sin and death. Those powers have been attacked and defeated, but not yet fi-

---

24. Phil. 2:6-11 provides a "normative account of the humiliation and vindication of the founder of [the Philippians'] community, Christ" (Fowl, *Story*, p. 91), "providing an account of Christ's own activity to which the Philippians should conform . . . [and] a precedent for how God responds to the suffering of the righteous servant of God from which the Philippians, as those in Christ, can draw an analogy to their own situation" (pp. 90-91).

25. Jerome H. Neyrey (*Paul, In Other Words: A Cultural Reading of His Letters* [Louisville: Westminster/John Knox, 1990], p. 49), who refers only to Christ's *death* as the new map to be replicated, whereas Paul clearly would want us also to include the resurrection/exaltation.

nally destroyed. This belief in an overlapping of the ages stems from Paul's experience with, and interpretation of, Jesus' death and resurrection.[26]

Paul, it seems, believed that the death of Christ inaugurated the period of messianic woes, the period of severe suffering that many Jews expected before the coming of the Messiah. Christ's resurrection, however, also inaugurated the age of resurrection, his resurrection being the "first fruits" (1 Corinthians 15) of the great resurrection harvest. For Christ, these two events were "back-to-back," for the resurrection happened "on the third day" (1 Cor. 15:4). For believers, however, the twin realities of Jesus' death and God's vindication of him in resurrection create an experiential tension. By identifying with his death, they experience his humiliation; by identifying with his resurrection, they experience the joy of exaltation — but only in part, only in process, and only in paradoxical connection with an ongoing death.

Thus, as we saw in Romans 6, believers' (bodily) resurrection is future (Rom. 6:5), even though they are now raised, existentially, to new life (Rom. 6:4). Ironically, however, the new life to which they are raised is a life of dying, of being co-crucified, of cruciformity. Paul says this not only to the Romans, but perhaps most poignantly to the Philippians:

> [8]. . . For his [Christ's] sake I have suffered the loss of all things, and I regard them as rubbish, in order that I may gain Christ . . . ; [10]I want to know Christ and the power of his resurrection and the sharing of his sufferings by becoming like him in his death. (Phil. 3:8b, 10)

To live in the "overlap of the ages" is simultaneously both to live in the period of messianic woes and to live — proleptically and partially, not fully — in the period of resurrection and glory. To collapse the future into the present — as Paul may have believed some of the leading Corinthians had done — would be for Paul a fundamental error:

> [8]Already you have all you want! Already you have become rich! Quite apart from us you have become kings! Indeed, I wish that you had become kings, so that we might be kings with you! [9]For I think that God has exhibited us apostles as last of all, as though sentenced to death, because we have become a spectacle to the world, to angels and to mortals. (1 Cor. 4:8-9)[27]

---

26. For helpful "timelines" presenting non-Pauline Jewish and Pauline belief in the two ages (including, for Paul, their overlapping), see Dunn, *Theology*, pp. 464-65.

27. The trend in recent scholarship is to find in this text an allusion to the influence of Cynic or Stoic thinking on the most elite Corinthians, generating in them an inappropriate pride based in social status (see, e.g., Richard B. Hays, *First Corinthians*, Interpretation [Louis-

On the other hand, to deny a foretaste of glory in the present would be no less an error, for the Spirit is a "guarantee" or "down payment" (Greek *arrabōn*, 2 Cor. 5:5) of the future reality of salvation. Writing later to the same community, Paul reminds the Corinthians:

> all of us, with unveiled faces, seeing the glory of the Lord as though reflected in a mirror, are being transformed into the same image from one degree of glory to another; for this comes from the Lord, the Spirit. (2 Cor. 3:18)[28]

For Paul, then, life in the present is one of hope, the "hope of sharing the glory of God" (Rom. 5:2),[29] the fruit of the cruciform life in the present age. It is the expectation that the current metamorphosis does not end at death but is at that point completed.

To the texts that reveal this hope more fully, we now turn, examining the following aspects: dying and rising; the present conditions for future hope; and the theme of conformity, which unifies for Paul present and future experience. What we will find throughout these texts is significant continuity, as well as discontinuity and reversal, in the apostle's experience of the present and his anticipated experience of the future.[30]

---

ville: Westminster/John Knox, 1997], pp. 70-71). However, the older opinion that the Corinthian elite felt that their experience was a kind of "heaven on earth" that denied the necessity of future resurrection does not necessarily contradict, and in fact may support, Cynic influence, as Ben Witherington III seems still to think (*Conflict and Community in Corinth: A Socio-Rhetorical Commentary on 1 and 2 Corinthians* [Grand Rapids: Eerdmans, 1995], pp. 141-43, but see p. 301, n. 43). Hays (*First Corinthians*, p. 259) and others argue that the Corinthian elite had no such "collapsed" (or "realized") eschatology but very simply denied resurrection. I am not convinced. For a recent defense of the realized eschatology interpretation, see Christopher M. Tuckett, "The Corinthians Who Say There Is No Resurrection of the Dead (1 Cor 15,12)," in R. Bieringer, ed., *The Corinthian Correspondence*, Bibliotheca Ephemeridum Theologicarum Lovaniensium 125 (Leuven: University Press, 1996), pp. 247-75.

28. The potential "triumphalism" of such texts — which are based on "reflection and looking — in good Greek-Hellenistic fashion" — is put in its "proper place through the latter's context of the theology of the cross" (Jürgen Becker, *Paul: Apostle to the Gentiles*, trans. O. C. Dean, Jr. [Louisville: Westminster/John Knox, 1993], p. 419).

29. More literally, "hope of [or, 'for'] the glory of God." Similar phrases appear in Col. 1:27 ("the hope of glory") and Titus 2:13 ("the blessed hope and the manifestation of the glory of our great God and Savior, Jesus Christ" [or, "and our Savior, Jesus Christ"]).

30. The texts that bear witness to Paul's hope for glory do not divide neatly into those about resurrection and those about exaltation, unlike the Christological narratives.

Dying and Rising

Twice in Romans 6 Paul mentions the hope of future resurrection, even though the main concern of the chapter is resurrection to "newness of life" (Rom. 6:4).[31] As we saw in chapter seven on faith, the subject of Romans 6 is the correspondence between Christ and believers in the experience of dying and rising:

> [3]Do you not know that all of us who have been baptized into Christ Jesus were baptized into his death? [4]Therefore we have been buried with him by baptism into death, so that, just as Christ was raised from the dead by the glory of the Father, **so we too might walk in newness of life.** [5]For if we have been united with him in a death like his, **we will certainly be united with him in a resurrection like his.** [6]We know that our old self was crucified with him so that the body of sin might be destroyed, and we might no longer be enslaved to sin. [7]For whoever has died is freed from sin. [8]But if we have died with Christ, **we believe that we will also live with him.** (Rom. 6:3-8 [emphasis added])

In the three phrases emphasized above, the first (v. 4) clearly refers to the present, while the second and third (vv. 5, 8), employing the future tense, most likely refer to a future reality.[32] Thus for Paul, dying with Christ is followed by a kind of two-stage resurrection: first, resurrection to new life in Christ, and second, resurrection to eternal life in Christ — as the chapter's conclusion reminds the reader:

> [22]But now that you have been freed from sin and enslaved to God, the advantage you get is sanctification. The end is eternal life. [23]For the wages of sin is death, but the free gift of God is eternal life in Christ Jesus our Lord. (Rom. 6:22-23)

Paul's hope, then, is that the experience of resurrection to newness of life now will find its logical conclusion in the experience of resurrection to eternal life in the future. This reveals a certain paradox in Paul's hope: the reversal he anticipates, from death to life, also has continuity with present existence. As we will

31. That Paul's main concern in Romans 6 is life in the present, not future, is indicated by the questions and exhortations about sin that govern the chapter (vv. 1-2, 11-22). It is therefore odd indeed that some interpreters of Paul find no room in his theology or spirituality for a resurrection in the present. See the note on this text in chapter two (p. 34, n. 34) and especially A. J. M. Wedderburn, *Baptism and Resurrection: Studies in Pauline Theology against Its Graeco-Roman Background* (Tübingen: J. C. B. Mohr [Paul Siebeck], 1987).

32. Although it is technically possible that the future-tense verbs in these phrases are "logical" rather than "chronological" uses of the future, it is more likely that Paul envisions a future resurrection.

see below, this corresponds to Paul's conviction that the present life of cruciformity is a process of transformation that culminates in the final goal of conformity to the already-glorified Christ.

The pattern of reversal in dying and rising comes to expression at length in Paul's treatise on the resurrection in 1 Corinthians 15. In that chapter, which both culminates and underlies all of 1 Corinthians, Paul seeks to connect the death and resurrection of believers with those of Christ, and thereby to correct misunderstandings he perceives on the part of the Corinthians. As always, Paul is convinced that experience and theology are closely connected to each other.

As noted above, Paul begins the chapter by quoting from an early creed that corresponds to the gospel he had preached to the Corinthians (15:3-7). This creedal statement highlights four gospel facts: that Christ died, was buried, was raised, and was seen. Paul then takes on those Corinthians who disavow resurrection — and specifically, it appears, the future, bodily resurrection of believers — which would be a disavowal of Christ's resurrection. He then proceeds to list the consequences if Christ has not been raised (15:13-19) as well as the consequences of the reality of his resurrection (15:20-23). Christ, Paul asserts, both constitutes the beginning ("first fruits") of the general resurrection and establishes the pattern of reversal for believers:

> [20]But in fact Christ has been raised from the dead, the first fruits of those who have died. [21]For since death came through a human being, the resurrection of the dead has also come through a human being; [22]for as all die in Adam, so all will be made alive in Christ. [23]But each in his own order: Christ the first fruits, then at his coming those who belong to Christ. (1 Cor. 15:20-23)

Death is reversed by resurrection; the dead are liberated by being raised, by "be[ing] made alive" (15:22). Christ's experience is no anomaly; it is the paradigm, the pattern for others. What happened to Christ — being raised by God — is precisely what will happen also to all who "belong to" or are "in" Christ.

Neither Christ nor believers, however, rise on their own power. Paul specifies God as the one who raises the dead. Paul does so either by constructing sentences with God as the subject or, more often, by using the passive voice: Christ has been raised (vv. 15:4, 12-17, 20), and others will be raised or will be made alive (vv. 22, 35, 42-44, 52). The active agent throughout 1 Corinthians 15, and in nearly every case in Paul's letters, is God, not Christ or believers.[33]

---

33. The exceptions, as noted above, are Rom. 14:9 ("Christ died and lived again") and 1 Thess. 4:14, 16 ("Jesus died and rose again.... [T]he dead in Christ will rise first"). Most commentators believe that in 1 Thess. 4:14 Paul is quoting an earlier tradition (e.g., F. F. Bruce, *1 & 2 Thessalonians,* Word Biblical Commentary 45 [Waco, Tex.: Word, 1982], p. 97).

Paul's comments give rise to questions: How? With what sort of body? Paul also addresses these concerns, stressing both the reversal, or discontinuity, and also the continuity of the believers' bodily experiences:

> [42]. . . What is sown [the body] is perishable, what is raised is imperishable. [43]It is sown in dishonor, it is raised in glory. It is sown in weakness, it is raised in power. [44]It is sown a physical body, it is raised a spiritual body. (1 Cor. 15:42b-44a)

The reversal from death to life has the necessary corollary of transformation:

> [50]What I am saying, brothers and sisters, is this: flesh and blood cannot inherit the kingdom of God, nor does the perishable inherit the imperishable. [51]Listen, I will tell you a mystery! We will not all die, but **we will all be changed,** [52]in a moment, in the twinkling of an eye, at the last trumpet. For the trumpet will sound, and the dead will be raised imperishable, and **we will be changed.** [53]For this perishable body must put on imperishability, and this mortal body must put on immortality. (1 Cor. 15:50-53 [emphasis added])

The result will be transformation into the likeness of the resurrected Christ:

> [47]The first man was from the earth, a man of dust; the second man is from heaven. [48]As was the man of dust, so are those who are of the dust; and as is the man of heaven, so are those who are of heaven. [49]Just as we have borne the image of the man of dust, **we will also bear the image** [Greek *eikona*] **of the man of heaven.** (1 Cor. 15:47-49 [emphasis added])

It would be a critical mistake to think that Paul is here writing about ideas or "theology," if by theology one means convictions that do not bear on daily life. The passion — even the sense of relief — of Paul's writing reveals quite the contrary. These are literally life-or-death matters for him; his hope of resurrection means that the enemy that is death does not have the final word in the future, and that therefore the believing community's efforts to serve its Lord in the present are not in vain.

> [54]When this perishable body puts on imperishability, and this mortal body puts on immortality, then the saying that is written will be fulfilled: "Death has been swallowed up in victory." [55]"Where, O death, is your victory? Where, O death, is your sting?" [56]The sting of death is sin, and the power of sin is the law. [57]But thanks be to God, who gives us the victory through our Lord Jesus Christ. [58]Therefore, my beloved, be steadfast, immovable, always

324

excelling in the work of the Lord, because you know that in the Lord your labor is not in vain. (1 Cor. 15:54-58)

We will see the word "victory" again when we consider Romans 8 in the next section.

Conditional Hope

Romans 8 contains Paul's most comprehensive account of the nature of believing, cruciform existence as God's children who live in Christ according to the Spirit. It merges themes from earlier parts of Romans and from other letters, particularly Galatians. Among the many motifs that appear in Romans 8, hope is predominant. This hope is clearly cruciform in character, and it is conditional.

As Richard Hays notes, the first half of Romans 8 (vv. 1-17a) paints a picture of "glorious fulfillment" in which "the community in Christ experiences freedom from the power of the flesh and, through the presence of the Holy Spirit, participates already with Christ in the promised inheritance." "Suddenly, however," continues Hays, "Paul's account of life in Christ takes a sharp turn" by qualifying the claim of "joint heirs with Christ" with the conditional clause "if in fact we suffer with him so that we may also be glorified with him" (8:17b). This clause "introduces the 'eschatological reservation' that constantly qualifies Paul's understanding of Christian existence on this side of the parousia."[34]

As we observed in chapter three on Paul and the Spirit, Romans 8 promises — subject to certain conditions — a future experience of the glory of God as the climax and culmination of life in Christ, life in the Spirit. This conditional promise for the future is especially clear and emphatic in the second half of the chapter (vv. 18-39), a chapter that divides itself into two main sections at the fulcrum text of 8:17:

> [16]it is that very Spirit bearing witness with our spirit that we are children of God, [17]and if children, then heirs, heirs of God and joint-heirs with Christ — **if, in fact**, we suffer with him [Christ] so that we may also be glorified with him. (Rom. 8:16-17 [emphasis added])

---

34. Richard B. Hays, *The Moral Vision of the New Testament: A Contemporary Introduction to New Testament Ethics* (San Francisco: HarperCollins, 1996), p. 25. Cf. J. Christiaan Beker's characterization of the change from the first half to the second half as a shift in focus from "present triumph to future hope" (*Paul the Apostle: The Triumph of God in Life and Thought* [Philadelphia: Fortress, 1980], p. 364).

The promise of a future "inheritance" with Christ as God's children — the promise of "glorification" — is subject to a condition: "if, in fact, we suffer with him so that we may also be glorified with him." The word translated "if, in fact" is better translated "provided that."[35] The grammar of the sentence clearly conveys Paul's conviction that suffering is the necessary condition for glory.[36]

Yet the conditional character of this hope is also already mentioned in the first half of Romans 8:

> [12]So then, brothers and sisters, we are debtors, not to the flesh, to live according to the flesh — [13]for if you live according to the flesh, you will die; but if by the Spirit you put to death the deeds of the body [i.e., the body dominated by the flesh], you will live. (Rom. 8:12-13 [emphasis added])

The promise "you will live" is subject to the condition "if by the Spirit you put to death the deeds of the body." Thus, according to Paul in Romans 8, there are two conditions to resurrection (or life, or glorification): dying to the flesh and suffering with Christ.[37]

As we observed in chapter three, in Paul's experience the Spirit links believers to the cross. More specifically, the hope engendered by the Spirit is cruciform in that it is the promise of resurrection following suffering and death. This cruciformity includes both "conditions" that we have observed: ongoing death to the flesh (Rom. 8:1-17) plus suffering (Rom. 8:18-39). Before looking at these two dimensions of cruciformity in Romans 8, and their connection to hope, we must first raise the question "Why?" Why does resurrection require cruciformity?

Paul's most basic answer to this question is given in his description of the narrative shape and goal of believers' experience:

35. So, e.g., Beker, *Paul the Apostle*, pp. 293, 364; Brendan Byrne, *Romans*, Sacra Pagina (Collegeville, Minn.: Liturgical, 1996), pp. 253-54; James D. G. Dunn, *Romans*, Word Biblical Commentary 38A, 38B, 2 vols. (Waco, Tex.: Word, 1988), 1:456.

36. According to Dunn (*Romans*, 1:456), the Greek word *eiper*, "provided that," "denotes a condition not yet fulfilled and therefore a consequence dependent on the fulfillment of the condition." Furthermore, the Greek word *hina*, "so that," "should not be weakened" because the "implication is again clear: that suffering with Christ is not an optional extra or a decline or a lapse from the saving purpose of God . . . [but] a necessary and indispensable part of that purpose."

37. There is an interesting parallel to Romans 6 here. As we have seen in previous chapters, Romans 6 speaks of two kinds of cruciformity, death to the old self and ongoing "slavery" to God, and death to sin, through self-offering to him. Similarly, Romans 8 speaks of cruciform death to the flesh and ongoing suffering. The details differ, but the pattern is very similar (hence our language of "initial" and "ongoing" cruciformity [chapter seven] and Wedderburn's references to "life through death" and "life in death" [*Baptism and Resurrection*, pp. 381-92]).

²⁸We know that all things work together for good for those who love God, who are called according to his purpose. ²⁹For those whom he foreknew he also predestined to be **conformed to the image of his Son**, in order that he might be the firstborn within a large family. ³⁰And those whom he predestined he also called; and those whom he called he also justified; and those whom he justified he also glorified. (Rom. 8:28-30 [emphasis added])

God's goal, writes Paul, is to call a people, to create a family of persons "conformed to the image of his Son" (v. 29). That conformity, for Paul, is narrative in character, a two-part drama of suffering/death followed by resurrection/exaltation. Thus the narrative of the community in Christ must correspond to the narrative of its Lord. The "conditional promise" to which we referred above simply means that the two parts of the narrative — death and resurrection — are inseparable. Conformity to Christ — "to the image of [God's] Son" — in resurrection is the logical and guaranteed sequel to a life of death to self and of suffering for the gospel that corresponds to the narrative of Christ's dying and rising (see further discussion in the next section).

The first half of Romans 8, then, narrates the first dimension of cruciform hope, "put[ting] to death the deeds of the body" (v. 13) — what Paul calls elsewhere "crucify[ing] the flesh" (Gal. 5:24), "dying to sin" (Rom. 6:2), and "crucify[ing] the old self with Christ" (Rom. 6:6). Paul is clearly not disparaging the body per se, nor the activities of the body, as texts like Romans 6:13 ("present yourselves . . . present your members to God"), Romans 12:1-2 ("present your bodies as a living sacrifice"), and 1 Corinthians 6:19-20 ("your body is a temple of the Holy Spirit. . . . Therefore glorify God in your body") make plain.

The real issue for Paul is not the body but the "flesh" — the human person considered apart from and in opposition to God — and the mind yielded to sin. When the mind is under the power of sin and attentive to the flesh, rather than the Spirit, the body becomes the place where anti-God behaviors are expressed, which is why Paul stresses the role of the mind in both Romans 8 and Romans 12. In such conditions, the body is a "body of death" (Rom. 7:24) whose end is death rather than eternal life (Rom. 6:21-23).

The second half of Romans 8 (vv. 18-39) narrates the second dimension of cruciform hope, suffering. From his background and experience, Paul had at least four major options for the interpretation of suffering. The first was the apocalyptic option, in which suffering was understood as something to be *endured* during the time immediately preceding the coming of the kingdom of God, the period of the "messianic woes." The second option was to understand his experience as that of unjust suffering by the righteous (see discussion earlier in this chapter). The third option was to accept suffering as character education or divine discipline.[38] The fourth option was the Stoic approach to suffering, in which suffering was ignored, because it did not affect the true, inner self, and was thus "conquered" [Greek *nikaō*].[39]

None of these interpretations of his sufferings fully satisfied Paul. Suffering was not merely to be apocalyptically or faithfully or pedagogically endured, and especially not stoically "conquered." Rather, it was to be *overwhelmingly conquered.* Believers are "more than conquerors" (Rom. 8:37; Greek *hypernikōmen,* from *hyper* and *nikaō*).

On the one hand, whereas Paul did understand suffering with and for Christ as an experience of the messianic woes, as unjust suffering for the sake of God, and as education in character, he knew that there was meaning inherent in the suffering itself. The suffering of Christ was, after all, the demonstration of God's love, of God's being *pro nobis* — emphatically for us.

> [31]What then are we to say about these things? If God is for us, who is against us? [32]He who did not withhold his own Son, but gave him up for all of us, will he not with him also give us everything else? [33]Who will bring any charge against God's elect? It is God who justifies. [34]Who is to condemn? It is Christ Jesus, who died, yes, who was raised, who is at the right hand of God, who indeed intercedes for us. [35]Who will separate us from the love of Christ? Will hardship, or distress, or persecution, or famine, or nakedness, or peril, or sword? [36]As it is written, "For your sake we are being killed all day long; we are accounted as sheep to be slaughtered." [37]No, in all these things we are more than conquerors through him who loved us. [38]For I am convinced that neither death, nor life, nor angels, nor rulers, nor things present, nor things to come, nor powers, [39]nor height, nor depth, nor anything else in all creation, will be able to separate us from the love of God in Christ Jesus our Lord. (Rom. 8:31-39)

In quoting Psalm 44 (Rom. 8:36), Paul reveals that he "discerns in Scripture a foreshadowing of the church,"[40] and particularly of his faithful, cruciform apostolic mission. Paul is equally certain that if "we" now suffer for Christ, Christ has suffered first for us. Suffering therefore has redemptive value, as believers experience the presence of God's Spirit in prayerful anticipation of the future

38. See Charles H. Talbert, *Learning through Suffering: The Educational Value of Suffering in the New Testament and Its Milieu* (Collegeville, Minn.: Liturgical, 1991).

39. See, e.g., Epictetus *Discourses* 1.18.22. The "invincible" person is the one unaffected by external experiences, whether positive or negative (as most people judge): reputation, abuse, praise, or death. The Stoic is able to overcome or conquer them all *(dynatai tauta panta nikēsai).*

40. Richard B. Hays, *Echoes of Scripture in the Letters of Paul* (New Haven: Yale University Press, 1989), p. 58. His entire discussion (pp. 57-63) of this text is very insightful.

glory (Rom. 8:26-27) and suffer with Christ (8:17) as a continuation of the narrative of divine love. Thus Paul's experience of suffering was more *positive in the present* than that of Jewish apocalypticists.[41]

On the other hand, Paul's experience of suffering was more *hopeful about the future* than that of the Stoics. The use or creation of the verb "more-than-conquer" (Greek *hypernikaō*, v. 37) indicates that Paul deliberately contrasts his experience and understanding of suffering with that of the Stoics. Believers do not ignore suffering because it has no effect on the true self, but rather they see in the suffering of Christ the full involvement of the self of God and of Christ in and for the world. God, after all, had "sent *his own* Son" (Rom. 8:3 [emphasis added]), not sparing him (Rom. 8:32).

Simultaneously, believers see in the midst of suffering, because of God's gift, a divine guarantee that suffering is not the last word; that death gives way to resurrection, suffering to glory; and that "all things" — God's final redemption of all creation — are sure. *This* is victory for Paul. It is *excessive* victory, not the mere "conquering" of suffering experienced by the Stoics. As Walter Wink says in commenting on Romans 8, "neither human (vv. 31-37) nor cosmic (vv. 38-39) powers, nor time and space itself, can undermine the victory believers share in Christ."[42] The sure hope of future glory does not eliminate suffering, but it does relativize it because it will in fact be reversed:

> I consider that the sufferings of this present time are not worth comparing with the glory about to be revealed to us. (Rom. 8:18)

Paul expresses the same fundamental hope of a reversal of fortunes in even more powerful contrasting terms in 2 Corinthians:

> [16]So we do not lose heart. Even though our outer nature is wasting away, our inner nature is being renewed day by day. [17]For this **slight momentary affliction** is preparing us for an **eternal weight of glory beyond all measure**, [18]because we look not at what can be seen but at what cannot be seen; for what can be seen is temporary, but what cannot be seen is eternal. (2 Cor. 4:16-18 [emphasis added])

Paul, then, experiences hope in the midst of suffering, but he understands his suffering not merely as something to be endured or conquered because it enables him to participate in the sufferings of Christ, the final end of which is

---

41. For a similar interpretation, see Beker, *Paul the Apostle*, p. 302.

42. Walter Wink, *Naming the Powers: The Language of Power in the New Testament* (Philadelphia: Fortress, 1984), p. 50.

glory. This is cruciform hope: conformity to the image of God's Son (Rom. 8:29) in suffering and glory, in the present and the future.

Conformity Present and Future

Language about the experience of conformity to Christ's narrative pattern of humiliation and exaltation appears also, and in an even more pronounced way, in Philippians 3. In that chapter, Paul tells his own story as a kind of imitation of Christ's story narrated in the hymn found in Philippians 2:6-11. The hymn provides Paul's metaphor of salvation as slavery, for himself and for all believers: "[b]y following Christ down, [the Philippians] will also eventually follow him up."[43]

Philippians 3 is autobiographical in character. Unlike other texts in which Paul's autobiographical narratives refer primarily to his cruciform love, Philippians 3 depicts his profound cruciform hope. The emphasis is not on his self-enslavement but on his suffering as the prelude to exaltation. To be sure, the paradigm of status-renouncing slavery reappears in chapter 3, but in a slightly different form and only in connection with the larger humiliation-exaltation theme.

In 3:4-11 Paul presents his own life as an example of these interconnected patterns. The familiar status-renouncing pattern of "although [x] not [y] but [z]" has the predictable elements of status, decision, and self-humbling, even to death: Paul's status as a righteous Pharisee (vv. 4-6); his decision to regard (vv. 7-8; cf. 2:6)[44] that status as loss and dung; and his loss of all things (i.e., his status, v. 9) in order to gain Christ, share his sufferings, and be conformed to his death.

Paul's great desire now that he is in Christ is expressed as follows:

> [10]I want to know Christ and [or, "that is"][45] the power of his resurrection and the sharing of his sufferings by becoming like him in his death, [11]if somehow I may attain the resurrection from the dead. (Phil. 3:10-11)

---

43. Martin, *Slavery,* p. 131.

44. Greek *hēgēmai, hēgoumai* [twice]; cf. *hēgēsato* of Christ in 2:6.

45. What knowing Christ means is "spelt out in the following clauses" (G. B. Caird, *Paul's Letters from Prison in the Revised Standard Version,* NCB [Oxford: Oxford University Press, 1976], p. 139). So also Gordon D. Fee (*God's Empowering Presence: The Holy Spirit in the Letters of Paul* [Peabody, Mass.: Hendrickson, 1994], p. 825; *Paul's Letter to the Philippians,* The New International Commentary on the New Testament [Grand Rapids: Eerdmans, 1995], p. 328), and many commentators. The Greek word *kai* ("and," "that is") does not coordinate but is explanatory or epexegetic.

The text of these verses, with its language about conformity to Christ's death (Greek *symmorphizomenos tō thanatō autou*), clearly echoes the first half of the master story/hymn preserved in 2:6-8 (Greek *morphē, morphēn* ["form"], and *thanatou* ["death"]). Paul here defines what "knowing Christ" means for him, and only careful attention to the grammar and structure of the sentence reveals that precise definition. Paul *does not* list three things he wishes to know, but rather explains that "knowing Christ" has a twofold meaning, knowing *both* "the power of his resurrection" *and* "the fellowship of his sufferings."[46]

How this happens is then explained: "by being conformed to his death," "so that if possible [Greek *ei pōs*] I may attain the resurrection from the dead." The "power of the resurrection," at least in this text, is not primarily a present experience but a future hope, the hoped-for consequence of the cruciform life of participation (Greek *koinōnia*) in Christ's sufferings. Paul unpacks throughout the entire letter the meaning of this experience of fellowship with Christ in suffering,[47] but in this text it is connected immediately with the hope of resurrection. Sharing in Christ's sufferings is Paul's hope for sharing in the future power of the resurrection from the dead. As Christ was vindicated by God after his obedience to the point of death, so also will the suffering Philippians be vindicated.[48]

Yet what of Paul's desire to "know Christ — that is, the power of his resurrection"? How is Christ known in the present? Is the resurrection experienced now in any way? If so, is this something other than the sharing of Christ's sufferings and becoming like him in his death?

46. The words "to know him [Christ]" are followed first by the Greek word *kai*, which should not be translated "and" here but "that is," and then by two distinct elements, each mentioned twice within an a-b-b'-a' structure:

power of his resurrection . . .	a
sharing of his sufferings . . .	b
becoming like him in his death . . .	b'
attain the resurrection from the dead	a'

This chiastic structure is noted also by Fee (*Philippians,* pp. 312-13, 329), who rightly stresses the close grammatical and rhetorical connection between power and suffering (pp. 311, 329-37)

47. Wayne A. Meeks has aptly said that the book of Philippians' "most comprehensive purpose is the shaping of a Christian *phronēsis,* a practical moral reasoning that is 'conformed to [Christ's] death' in hope of his resurrection" ("The Man from Heaven in Paul's Letter to the Philippians," in Birger Pearson, ed., *The Future of Early Christianity: Essays in Honor of Helmut Koester* [Minneapolis: Fortress, 1991], p. 333). We might, however, replace the phrase "practical moral reasoning" with "spirituality."

48. F. Gregory Bloomquist goes so far (probably too far) as to conclude that the "main point of 2.6-11 is its underscoring the fact that vindication follows suffering" (*The Function of Suffering in Philippians,* JSNTSup 78 [Sheffield: JSOT Press, 1993], p. 195). However, this is clearly a very central dimension of the text — the creation of hope.

Paul's answers to these questions are supplied both by the immediate context in Philippians and the wider context of his letters. For Paul, the resurrection ("to newness of life" in Rom. 6:4) is experienced not by seeking power or powerful experiences but by embracing the cross, by living as "friends," rather than enemies (see Phil. 3:18), of the cross. This is the way to "press on toward the goal for the prize of the heavenly call of God in Christ Jesus" (Phil. 3:14). *The power of the resurrection operates in the present as the power of conformity to the death of Christ, which in turn guarantees a place in the future resurrection.*

The humiliation-exaltation pattern of reversal appears not once but twice in Philippians 3. All who imitate Paul (3:17) in befriending and conforming to the cross are offered the hope of future resurrection when the Lord Jesus returns:

> He will transform [Greek *metaschēmatisei*] the body of our humiliation [Greek *tapeinōseōs*] that it may be conformed [Greek *symmorphon*] to the body of his glory [Greek *doxēs*], by the power that also enables him to make all things subject to himself. (Phil. 3:21)

The language of this text once again echoes the two-part pattern of the hymn in chapter 2: humility gives way to glory by the power of God. The hope of all believers who share in the sufferings of Christ, in his self-renouncing death for others, is conformity to his resurrected, exalted body of glory — "the redemption of our bodies" (Rom. 8:23). As we will see in the next section, this future hope of transformation is not limited to human beings, and it is not even limited completely to the future.

The Focal Point and Scope of Glory

For Paul, hope, as we have seen, is the conviction, based on the past narrative of Christ and the present narrative of believers' experience, that the future of cruciformity is glory.[49] In examining the basic texts expressing the pattern of this cruciform hope, we have noted especially the coming transformation of believers that Paul expects, the change from present suffering and death to future glory. Yet the future transformation of believers is not all Paul expects. He also sees transformation into glory beginning now, and his vision of the future

---

49. Cf. the more general definition of hope offered by John Paul Heil and applied to Paul: It is the "act or the attitude of confident expectation for God's salvific activity that arises from faith in what God has promised and/or already accomplished on our behalf" (*Romans — Paul's Letter of Hope,* Analecta Biblica 112 [Rome: Biblical Institute Press, 1987], p. 6).

glory is broad rather than narrow. In this section we examine the *when* and the comprehensive *what* of Paul's hope.

When: The Focal Point of Paul's Hope

The ultimate fate of the crucified Messiah was resurrection and exaltation. This is for Paul the basis and substance of his hope. However, in good apocalyptic fashion, Paul's hope is not merely a vague assurance of eternal life; it is focused on the future of the world and on the unfolding of specific apocalyptic events. Although Paul does not appear to be overly concerned about the details of a timetable for these events, he is convinced that something dramatic is going to happen.[50]

It has often been said that Paul experiences life in Christ as an existence "between the times,"[51] that is, between the old age and the age to come, between the first and second comings of Jesus. More precisely, as we have seen, Paul perceives the current time in which believers live as the "overlap of the ages" (1 Cor. 10:11), a period that began with the death and resurrection of Jesus and will end with his return. This future coming of the Lord, then, is the focal point of Paul's hope. It will bring about the resurrection of the dead, end the current evil age, and begin the age to come in its fullness. The return of Jesus triggers the fulfillment of all of Paul's hopes.

The language Paul uses to refer to the "return" of Jesus is significant. On the one hand, he frequently borrows the language of the Hebrew prophets, referring to "the Day of the Lord," Israel's hope for (and warning about) God's judgment for the wicked and salvation for the righteous (Amos 5:18-20; Isa. 2:12-22; Joel; Ezek. 30:1-4; Zeph. 1:14–2:3; 3:8-13; Zechariah 12–14).[52] That the day of Yahweh has become the day of Jesus is clear from Paul's using explicitly Christocentric phrases such as "the Day of (Jesus) Christ" and "the Day of the Lord Jesus" as well as "the Day of the Lord."[53] Thus Paul's Jewish hopes in the

---

50. To be sure, there are some Pauline texts that resemble apocalyptic timetables (e.g., 1 Thess. 4:15-17; 1 Cor. 15:51-52), but these do not take center stage in Paul's experience of hope. Moreover, like other Jewish apocalyptic writings, the timetables in the Pauline corpus are diverse with respect to detail and schematization. See L. Joseph Kreitzer, *Jesus and God in Paul's Eschatology*, JSNTSup 19 (Sheffield: Sheffield Academic Press, 1987).

51. E.g., J. Paul Sampley, *Walking Between the Times: Paul's Moral Reasoning* (Minneapolis: Fortress, 1991).

52. The specifics of "the day of the Lord" vary from prophet to prophet.

53. 1 Thess. 5:2; 1 Cor. 5:5 ("the day of the Lord"). 1 Cor. 1:8; 2 Cor. 1:14 ("the day of the Lord Jesus"). Phil. 1:6 ("the day of Jesus Christ"). Phil. 1:10; 2:16 ("the day of Christ"), abbreviated occasionally also to "the day" (1 Cor. 3:13; Rom. 13:12). See Kreitzer, *Jesus and God,* esp. pp. 93-129.

day of Yahweh have been transferred to, and transformed by, his experience of Jesus as Lord. Nonetheless, Paul also believes that the final act of Christ's lordship is the transferal of the kingdom to the Father (1 Cor. 15:24-28).

On the other hand, Paul also borrows the language of Roman military and imperial visits to refer to Jesus' return. The term he uses is *parousia,* meaning "presence" or "arrival." It was often applied to the arrival of the emperor or of a significant military general and to the "saving" benefits of his arrival or the cause of his coming (e.g., victory in war). Although in literature on Paul the term *parousia* has become the standard way of referring to Paul's belief in Jesus' imminent return, the apostle actually uses the term only five times of Jesus' return (1 Thess. 2:19; 3:13; 4:15; 5:23; 1 Cor. 15:23).[54] Nonetheless, Paul's hope in the *parousia* of Jesus is implicitly a rejection of hope in other *parousias,* be they imperial or military, to enhance or transform human existence. Roman hopes especially in any imperial *parousia* are transferred to, and transformed by, Paul's experience of Jesus, not the emperor, as the true Savior and Lord.

Thus the day of Christ, his *parousia,* is for Paul the focal point of his hope. His mission is to form communities of cruciform faith, love, power, and hope that anticipate the fullness of God's coming kingdom — God's universal "empire."[55] Yet the return of Jesus does not *exhaust* Paul's hope, for his hope is broad in scope, and the point of Jesus' coming is to actualize the full scope of this hope.

What: The Scope of Glory

In Paul's experience, hope in the future glory of God has at least four major expressions: personal, communal, universal, and cosmic. These emerge from his conviction that his experience of God in the exalted crucified Messiah is part of God's larger work of eschatological reconciliation and re-creation. The beneficiaries or objects of this hope for glory, in other words, are Paul as individual believer (and thus each believer), beginning already in the present; the community of believers; the world of both Gentiles and Jews; and even the entire created order.[56] Before considering each of these in turn, we must first consider

---

54. It appears also in 2 Thess. 2:1, 8, and Paul uses the term five times to refer to apostolic comings.

55. We shall return to this topic in the next chapter.

56. These four "beneficiaries" of glory correspond to the four partners of Yahweh — Israel (the community), the individual, the nations (Gentiles and Jews), and the creation — noted by Walter Brueggemann (*Theology of the Old Testament: Testimony, Dispute, Advocacy* [Minneapolis: Fortress, 1997], pp. 408-12) and mentioned in the first note in chapter one.

Paul's understanding of glory, for though it summarizes the pattern of reversal from suffering and death, it is something of an uncommon and elusive term.

The words "glory" and "glorify" have two different but related uses in Paul's writings. One meaning is "honor" or "praise," as in bringing God glory through the spread of the gospel and through lives and communities shaped appropriately in response to that gospel.[57] The second and more important meaning for our purposes is the "splendor" of God and the sharing of that splendor with others. Paul associates this splendor or glory of God with the "image of God." Human beings, by failing to glorify God (Rom. 1:21, 23), lack or fall short of the glory of God (Rom. 3:23). That is, they fail to experience their divinely intended relationship to God as creature to creator, as bearer of the divine image (Gen. 1:27).

Christ, however, is the "image" of God, such that Paul's gospel is "the gospel of the glory of Christ, who is the image of God" (2 Cor. 4:4). That is, "the glory of God" is found "in the face of Jesus Christ" (2 Cor. 4:6). The image or glory of God in Christ is completed by virtue of the resurrection, in which Christ's body is now a body of "glory" (Phil. 3:21). Those who belong to Christ now share partially, and will share fully, in this glory.

Although this shared "glory" is most frequently associated with the future experience of believers that has been prepared for them (1 Cor. 2:7), Paul's vision of the glorification of believers widens to include the whole creation. Thus the term "glory of God" becomes for Paul a catch-all term to refer to the future reality of salvation in all its splendor, the renewal of all things so that God's original intentions for humanity and all creation are fulfilled.[58]

The Hope of Glory and the Individual

On the personal level, Paul is absolutely convinced that his sufferings are not the end of his story. Were they the end, he writes passionately to the Corinthians, he would be first among many fools who believe in resurrection:

> [30]And why are we putting ourselves in danger every hour? [31]I die every day! That is as certain, brothers and sisters, as my boasting of you — a boast that I make in Christ Jesus our Lord. [32]If with merely human hopes I fought with wild animals at Ephesus, what would I have gained by it? If the dead are not raised, "Let us eat and drink, for tomorrow we die." (1 Cor. 15:30-32)

57. See, e.g., Rom. 15:7; Phil. 1:11; 1 Cor. 6:20; 10:31; 2 Cor. 8:19; 9:13.

58. According to Beker *(Paul the Apostle),* for Paul the glory of God is the "destiny of creation" (p. 200), the "actualization of the redemption of God's created order in his kingdom" (p. 363).

Rather, Paul finds comfort and joy in the knowledge that the end of his life will be the beginning of a new life, a new experience of God. His grave will not read like that of many in antiquity: "I was not; I was; I am not; I care not."[59] When Paul dies, he will be "with" the Lord, whereas now he is absent from him; he will be "home," whereas now he is away:

> [21]For to me, living is Christ and dying is gain. [22]If I am to live in the flesh, that means fruitful labor for me; and I do not know which I prefer ["will choose"]. [23]I am hard pressed between the two: **my desire is to depart and be with Christ, for that is far better.** (Phil. 1:21-23 [emphasis added])

> [1][W]e know that if the earthly tent we live in is destroyed, we have a building from God, a house not made with hands, eternal in the heavens. [2]For in this tent we groan, longing to be clothed with our heavenly dwelling — [3]if indeed, when we have taken it off we will not be found naked. [4]For while we are still in this tent, we groan under our burden, because we wish not to be unclothed but to be further clothed, so that what is mortal may be swallowed up by life. [5]He who has prepared us for this very thing is God, who has given us the Spirit as a guarantee. [6]So we are always confident; even though we know that **while we are at home in the body we are away from the Lord** — [7]for we walk by faith, not by sight. [8]Yes, we do have confidence, and we would rather be **away from the body and at home with the Lord.** (2 Cor. 5:1-8 [emphasis added])

This hope, of course, is not Paul's alone; it belongs to all in Christ. Paul says "we" here (and elsewhere), referring to himself, his fellow apostles, the Corinthian believers, and — implicitly — all who call Jesus Lord, all who have experienced the outpouring of God's love by the Holy Spirit and the hope that that experience generates (Rom. 5:1-5).

As we noted at the very beginning of this chapter, Paul's hope is expressed in a variety of images, some general and others more specific: eternal life (Rom. 6:23), righteousness (Gal. 5:5), salvation (1 Thess. 5:8), escaping the coming wrath (1 Thess. 1:10; 5:9), resurrection from the dead (Phil. 3:11, 14), the re-

---

59. Dale B. Martin, *The Corinthian Body* (New Haven: Yale University Press, 1995), p. 109, citing Richard Lattimore, *Themes in Greek and Latin Epitaphs*, Illinois Studies in Language and Literature, vol. 28, nos. 1-2 (Urbana, Ill.: University of Illinois Press, 1942), p. 84. The shorter form of this epitaph, "I was not, I am not, I care not" (Latin *non fui, non sum, non curo*), was so popular that it was abbreviated to *n.f.n.s.n.c.* Martin concludes that Greek and Latin epitaphs reveal that although some people had a belief in the afterlife, most were agnostic or apathetic about it and did not expect the gods to provide it (p. 109). Philosophers, of course, were more interested in the topic, but not necessarily less skeptical (pp. 112-17).

demption of our bodies (Rom. 8:23), being in the presence of the Lord (Phil. 1:23), being heirs of God and co-heirs with Christ (Rom. 8:17), and glory (Rom. 8:17; 2 Cor. 4:17).[60] Of supreme importance to Paul in his experience of hope is the anticipation of reversal and transformation, just as Christ experienced the reversal of death and the transformation of his body. Suffering will give way to glory; death will lead to resurrection; mortality and corruptibility will become immortality and incorruptibility. In short, *cruciformity becomes glory.*

The great irony in Paul's experience, however, is that this process of transformation begins in the present, as he writes to the Corinthians (2 Cor. 3:7-18), concluding as follows:

> And all of us, with unveiled faces, seeing the glory of the Lord as though reflected in a mirror, are being transformed into the same image from one degree of glory to another; for this comes from the Lord, the Spirit. (2 Cor. 3:18)

The contemplation of the Lord — specifically of the Lord's reflected glory — begins the process of glorification in this life. Indeed, the purpose of God's calling Gentiles and Jews alike is to transform them into the image of the Son:

> For those whom he foreknew he also predestined to be conformed to the image of his Son, in order that he might be the firstborn within a large family. (Rom. 8:29)

As we have already noted, this is fundamentally a two-part process. Transformation into the image of Christ in the present is the ongoing experience of cruciformity; transformation into the image of Christ in the future is the bodily resurrection and the completion of Christlikeness. Each part is a necessary component of growing into the image of Christ — of being glorified and restored to the original, divinely intended image of and relation to God.

The Hope of Glory and the Community

The hope of resurrection is not limited to a merely personal assurance, whether that of the apostle or of the ordinary believer. Hope is a communal experience for Paul. He includes himself with all Corinthian believers when he writes as follows:

60. The references are not intended to be exhaustive.

[17]If Christ has not been raised, your faith is futile and you are still in your sins. [18]Then those also who have died in Christ have perished. [19]If for this life only we have hoped in Christ, **we** are of all people most to be pitied.[20]But in fact Christ has been raised from the dead, the first fruits of those who have died. (1 Cor. 15:17-20)[61]

Writing to the Thessalonians, who had experienced the death of fellow believers (by martyrdom?) when they had probably assumed that they would all be alive for the return of their Lord, Paul urges them to comfort one another in the hope of resurrection:

[13]But we do not want you to be uninformed, brothers and sisters, about those who have died, **so that you may not grieve as others do who have no hope.** [14]For since we believe that Jesus died and rose again, even so, through Jesus, God will bring with him those who have died. [15]For this we declare to you by the word of the Lord, that we who are alive, who are left until the coming of the Lord, will by no means precede those who have died. [16]For the Lord himself, with a cry of command, with the archangel's call and with the sound of God's trumpet, will descend from heaven, and the dead in Christ will rise first. [17]Then we who are alive, who are left, will be caught up in the clouds together with them to meet the Lord in the air; and so we will be with the Lord forever. [18]**Therefore encourage one another with these words.** (1 Thess. 4:13-18 [emphasis added])

The note of eschatological hope is a pastoral one that permeates the entire letter. Paul reminds the Thessalonians that they had "turned to God from idols, to serve a living and true God, and to *wait* . . ." (1 Thess. 1:9-10 [emphasis added]). The Pauline triad of "theological virtues" — faith, hope, and love (e.g., 1 Cor. 13:13) — is ordered with hope emphatically placed last in 1 Thessalonians (1:3; 5:8). Hope, then, is a communal experience, both as lived reality and as ground for mutual exhortation. Hope is something that needs to be nourished, to be constantly renewed, especially in the face of experiences such as death that seem to undermine it. Those who have died have done so in hope, and those remaining must live in hope and continue the waiting process for which they were converted.

---

61. Paul above all continues the theme of communal hope in those otherwise perplexing words about "baptism for the dead": "Otherwise, what will those people do who receive baptism on behalf of the dead? If the dead are not raised at all, why are people baptized on their behalf?" (1 Cor. 15:29).

The Hope of Glory and Gentiles and Jews

If hope is not merely personal but also communal, it is not only communal, either. Paul's eschatological hope, though thoroughly Christocentric, is shaped by the vision of hope in God's future articulated by the Hebrew poetic and prophetic writings. The vision is one of the nations honoring the one true God:

> All the nations you have made shall come and bow down before you, O Lord, and shall glorify your name. (Ps. 86:9)

This vision often has the nations flocking to Zion, or Jerusalem (e.g., Isa. 2:2-4; 11:10; 42:6-7; 49:5-7; Mic. 4:1-4; Zech. 8:20-23).[62] Thus Paul, who thinks of the world as consisting of Jews and Gentiles, hopes in a future that includes both Gentiles and Jews. Indeed, it includes all people:

> [9]Therefore God also highly exalted him and gave him the name that is above every name, [10]so that at the name of Jesus **every knee should bend**, in heaven and on earth and under the earth, [11]and **every tongue should confess** that Jesus Christ is Lord, to the glory of God the Father. (Phil. 2:9-11)

The most poignant revelation of Paul's hope in the future of his fellow Jews is the extended essay in Romans 9–11. Despite the many ambiguities of this disputed and variously interpreted text, a few points are absolutely clear.[63] Prominent among these is that God has neither rejected nor given up on the covenant people. They remain the object of divine faithfulness and love, such that Paul is absolutely certain that, in the end, "all Israel will be saved" (Rom. 11:26). In the context of Romans 9–11 as a literary unit, this "Israel" must be closely connected to ethnic Israel, Paul's fellow Jews, for whom he would sacrifice his own salvation for theirs (9:2-3). Paul is absolutely certain that this self-sacrifice would be worthwhile, but even more certain that it will be unnecessary, for God's covenant faithfulness — indeed God's integrity — has been demonstrated in the death of Christ, through whom salvation is now open to all nations and guaranteed to hardhearted, rebellious Israel.

Was Paul, then, a universalist? Hardly, if one defines universalist as one convinced that all will be saved, no matter what. The gospel message to which

---

62. See also Tob. 14:5-7. For an excellent overview of Israel's hope before and during the time of Paul, see N. T. Wright, *The New Testament and the People of God* (Minneapolis: Fortress, 1992), pp. 280-338.

63. For a discussion of these chapters that includes the history of interpretation and extensive bibliography, see Joseph A. Fitzmyer, *Romans: A New Translation with Introduction and Commentary*, Anchor Bible 33 (New York: Doubleday, 1993), pp. 539-636.

he devoted his life required faith, an appropriate — as we have seen, a cruciform — response. Yet Paul could not believe that the very gospel of God was anything less than the hope of the *world,* for in Christ "God was reconciling the world to himself" (2 Cor. 5:19). Thus the general and persistent disbelief of his fellow Jews meant for Paul a time for the reconciliation of the Gentile world — or at least "the full number of the Gentiles" (Rom. 11:25). Paul's universalism is his hope — in the sense of absolute assurance — that the one God of Gentiles and Jews has so provided for their salvation that its success is assured. While the response of faith is required, it is in some sense guaranteed — not that all will believe, but that the word of the Lord cannot fail, has not failed, and will not fail. The gospel, as the gospel of the one God, can be nothing less than universal in scope. Paul's hope is therefore universal in the sense that those who know the God of all mercies must be "radically open to the incalculable, uncontrollable and limitless future salvation of God."[64]

The Hope of Glory and the Entire Creation

Once again, however, Paul's hope is not restricted even to a universal vision. It is, ultimately, a cosmic hope. This dimension of Paul's experience of hope comes through most clearly — and not surprisingly — in Romans 8:

> [19]For the creation waits with eager longing for the revealing of the children of God; [20]for the creation was subjected to futility, not of its own will but by the will of the one who subjected it, **in hope** [21]**that the creation itself will be set free from its bondage to decay** and will obtain the freedom of the glory of the children of God. [22]We know that the whole creation has been groaning in labor pains until now. . . . (Rom. 8:19-22 [emphasis added])

J. Christiaan Beker's comments on this theme in Paul demonstrate its centrality to the apostle's spirituality:

> According to Paul, Christians can never surrender the universal-cosmic future horizon of the Christ-event, and the imminence of God's kingdom, if they consider the resurrection of Christ to be of fundamental importance to

---

64. Heil, *Romans,* p. 81. A definitive universalism in Paul is sometimes traced to his theology of Adam and Christ, in whom all died and all will be made alive, respectively (Romans 5; 1 Corinthians 15). This argument fails, however, to recognize a crucial difference between Paul's "in Adam" and "in Christ" language. For the apostle, all are in Adam by virtue of being human, but not all are in Christ. The "penalties" associated with Adam's disobedience apply to all, but the "benefits" associated with Christ's obedience (death) apply only to those who respond in faith.

their faith. Indeed, the resurrection prompts Christians to an apocalyptic self-understanding in the world. For in their own bodies Christians live existentially the tension of their present incompleted existence in solidarity with an unredeemed creation, and they must therefore yearn for the consummation of the resurrection, which is nothing but God's triumph over the power of death that poisons his creation.[65]

The cosmic emphasis in Paul is found also in his conviction that the resurrection of Christ and then of believers is part of the divine strategy of defeating all the hostile powers, including political powers, namely, those of Rome and Satan,[66] and, especially, the ultimate power in the universe, death:

> [24]Then comes the end, when he hands over the kingdom to God the Father, after he has destroyed every ruler and every authority and power. [25]For he must reign until he has put all his enemies under his feet. [26]The last enemy to be destroyed is death. (1 Cor. 15:24-26)

Personal, communal, and even universal resurrection and exaltation, then, are meaningful for Paul only as stages or dimensions of a grand apocalyptic vision in which suffering and death are no more. Again, Beker notes:

> In Paul hope has an apocalyptic specificity. It centers on a happening in time and space that is the object of the yearning and sighing of the Christian, that is the victory over evil and death in the *parousia* of Christ or the kingdom of God (1 Cor. 15:24). Paul's apocalyptic dualism is not a Gnostic dualism of contempt for this world, or otherworldliness. It is determined by the event of Christ, an event that not only negated the old order but also initiated the hope for the transformation of the creation that has gone astray and is in travail because it longs for its redemption from decay (Rom. 8:20). Although the glory of God will break into our fallen world, it will not annihilate the world but only break off its present structure of death, because it aims to transform the cosmos rather than to confirm its ontological nothingness.[67]

This, then, is the hope of Paul for the "glory" of God. It is hope, expressed in language borrowed from the Law and the Prophets, for a "new creation" (Gal. 6:15; 2 Cor. 5:17). It is a hope that will be fulfilled when Christ returns and

---

65. Beker, *Paul the Apostle*, p. 179.

66. On the defeat of the political powers, see Klaus Wengst, *Pax Romana and the Peace of Jesus Christ*, trans. John Bowden (Philadelphia: Fortress, 1987), pp. 78-79. On Satan, see Rom. 16:20a: "The God of peace will shortly crush Satan under your feet."

67. Beker, *Paul the Apostle*, p. 149.

completes the experience of God's glorious future made possible by his death and resurrection. In the meantime, believers live as people of faith and love, looking backward to the cross, and as people of hope, looking ahead to the glory of God in resurrection, exaltation, and final redemption. The experience of this hope in the daily life of believers must now be explored.

Cruciform Hope in Daily Life

As we have clearly seen, for Paul suffering and hope are inextricably intertwined in both experience and conviction. Among the existential realities of cruciform hope in Paul's daily life are the formation of character, including hope and trust; solidarity with Christ, other believers, and the creation; the rejection of imperial eschatology; and sober yet joyful recognition of the reality but incompleteness of salvation in the present — all blended together with a yearning for the completion of that salvation.

Hope, Suffering, and Character

It was a commonplace in antiquity that suffering could serve as a kind of school for character building.[68] Paul at first seems to echo this perspective:

> [1]Therefore, since we are justified by faith, we have peace with God through our Lord Jesus Christ, [2]through whom we have obtained access to this grace in which we stand; and we boast in our hope of sharing the glory of God. [3]And not only that, but we also boast in our sufferings, knowing that suffering produces endurance, [4]and endurance produces character, and character produces hope, [5]and hope does not disappoint us, because God's love has been poured into our hearts through the Holy Spirit that has been given to us. (Rom. 5:1-5)

Paul's point here, however, is not merely that suffering produces character. It is rather, ultimately, that suffering produces hope. Suffering is, in essence, the guarantor of hope. Believers "boast" in suffering for the same reason they boast in the hope of glory. Having known God's love in Christ as a past and present reality (Rom. 5:5; cf. 5:6-8), they are confident of God's love in the future.[69]

---

68. See Talbert, *Learning Through Suffering.*

69. This is, of course, the theme of Romans 8, which develops the language and themes of Romans 5.

Thus their learning from suffering is rooted not merely in their own experience and frail search for meaning and hope in the midst of pain, but also in the experience of Christ and the victory of God. Thus believers do not merely endure or conquer the daily suffering they experience, much less shun it. Rather, they boast in it, because in fact they will one day be more than victorious (Rom. 8:37), even as Christ suffered and yet conquered death by God's power. Believers are being prepared even now for that ultimate victory.

In the meantime, however, believers do in fact learn from their suffering. Specifically, they learn not to depend on themselves but on God. Paul finds purpose and meaning in suffering as the inevitable source of trust or faith:

> [8]We do not want you to be unaware, brothers and sisters, of the affliction we experienced in Asia; for we were so utterly, unbearably crushed that we despaired of life itself. [9]Indeed, we felt that we had received the sentence of death so that we would rely not on ourselves but on God who raises the dead. [10]He who rescued us from so deadly a peril will continue to rescue us; on him we have set our hope that he will rescue us again. (2 Cor. 1:8-10)

As in Romans 5, so also here — but perhaps with a more pragmatic twist — Paul espouses suffering as both tutor and guarantor of hope. Implicit in this text is also the foundational biblical conviction that God will exalt the humble, those who "trust in the Lord with all their heart."

So, too, those who live with hope will order their lives in preparation for the fulfillment of that hope. In Paul's experience, the sufferings of this present age continually present a temptation to abandon hope and thus character. For this reason he reminds the Thessalonians — who knew the cost of their commitments[70] — to live in ways appropriate to their hope:

> [1]Now concerning the times and the seasons, brothers and sisters, you do not need to have anything written to you. [2]For you yourselves know very well that the day of the Lord will come like a thief in the night. [3]When they say, "There is peace and security," then sudden destruction will come upon them, as labor pains come upon a pregnant woman, and there will be no escape! [4]But you, beloved, are not in darkness, for that day to surprise you like a thief; [5]for you are all children of light and children of the day; we are

---

70. "For you, brothers and sisters, became imitators of the churches of God in Christ Jesus that are in Judea, for you suffered the same things from your own compatriots as they did from the Jews, who killed both the Lord Jesus and the prophets, and drove us out; they displease God and oppose everyone . . ." (1 Thess. 2:14-16). Though this text has often been understood as a later (and even "anti-Semitic") interpolation, its theme of imitation is thoroughly Pauline, and it fits the immediate and larger contexts of 1 Thessalonians quite well.

not of the night or of darkness. [6]So then let us not fall asleep as others do, but let us keep awake and be sober; [7]for those who sleep sleep at night, and those who are drunk get drunk at night. [8]But since we belong to the day, let us be sober, and put on the breastplate of faith and love, and for a helmet the hope of salvation. [9]For God has destined us not for wrath but for obtaining salvation through our Lord Jesus Christ, [10]who died for us, so that whether we are awake or asleep we may live with him. [11]Therefore encourage one another and build up each other, as indeed you are doing. (1 Thess. 5:1-11)

Similarly, Paul admonishes the Romans and the Corinthians:

[11]Besides this, you know what time it is, how it is now the moment for you to wake from sleep. For salvation is nearer to us now than when we became believers; [12]the night is far gone, the day is near. Let us then lay aside the works of darkness and put on the armor of light; [13]let us live honorably as in the day, not in reveling and drunkenness, not in debauchery and licentiousness, not in quarreling and jealousy. [14]Instead, put on the Lord Jesus Christ, and make no provision for the flesh, to gratify its desires. (Rom. 13:11-14)

[13]. . . [T]the body is meant not for fornication but for the Lord, and the Lord for the body. [14]And God raised the Lord and will also raise us by his power. (1 Cor. 6:13b-14)

In this last text Paul draws the obvious conclusion that many Corinthians apparently could not understand on their own: that the truth of future bodily resurrection means that what one does with and in the body now is of crucial importance. Embodied life in the present (life in the body now) is to be life lived "for" the Lord in the hope of a future, embodied existence "with" the Lord.[71]

Solidarity with Christ, Other Believers, and the Creation

As we have seen, Paul can describe suffering and its corollary of hope as an experience of fellowship or solidarity. It is first of all solidarity with Christ: "the fellowship [Greek *koinōnia*] of his sufferings" in the anticipation of resurrec-

---

71. Cf. Rom. 14:9: "For to this end Christ died and lived again, so that he might be Lord of both the dead and the living."

tion (Phil. 3:10). The believing community's hope calls the community, and each member of it, to an ongoing life of transformation through cruciformity.[72]

As an experience of communal solidarity with Christ, cruciform hope is also, therefore, solidarity with others, such that

> [4]. . . we may be able to console those who are in any affliction with the consolation with which we ourselves are consoled by God. [5]For just as the sufferings of Christ are abundant for us, so also our consolation is abundant through Christ. (2 Cor. 1:4b-5)

Indeed, Paul expects his communities to be communities of solidarity in simultaneous suffering and hope:

> [12]Rejoice in hope, be patient in suffering, persevere in prayer. [13]Contribute to the needs of the saints; extend hospitality to strangers. [14]Bless those who persecute you; bless and do not curse them. [15]Rejoice with those who rejoice, weep with those who weep. (Rom. 12:12-15)

For Paul, it is only in the context of cruciform hope that nonretaliation makes theological and experiential sense. Furthermore, it is in the context of unrequited persecution and other forms of suffering that reciprocal sharing of joy and sorrow (v. 15) is both humanly needed and spiritually required. While Paul focuses his remarks about such reciprocal care on the community, his requirement that the community do good to all people (Gal. 6:10) suggests that the solidarity of cruciform hope must be extended beyond the community.

Indeed, Paul's experience of solidarity with the entire creation demands precisely that kind of extension of hope beyond the community. His experience of simultaneous suffering and hope, according to Romans 8, is predicated upon, and is a subset of, the hopeful groaning of the entire creation (Rom. 8:22-23). This means that the believing community identifies with, and suffers with, the whole of creation — people in pain, the world in crisis, the environment at risk, and so on. In other words, cruciform hope implies a mission, not an eschatological daydream.[73]

---

72. For a creative and compelling interpretation of the necessity (for Paul) of community for cruciform transformation, see Richard Hays's discussion of the Corinthian community as a "letter from Christ" (2 Cor. 3:1–4:6) in *Echoes,* pp. 122-53.

73. As Beker emphasizes, without mission, Paul's words about his grand hope for the liberation of creation at the revelation of the children of God are reduced to a "faint ecclesial whimper" (*Paul the Apostle,* p. 327).

The Rejection of Imperial Eschatology

Hope is a unifying human experience, one that can bring people together for good (as in the civil rights movement under Rev. Dr. Martin Luther King, Jr.) or for ill (as in Nazi Germany under Adolf Hitler's leadership). The Roman empire sought not only to give people hope but also to proclaim the presence of the "golden age" in the rule of Rome and its emperors. Imperial propaganda was, essentially, a message of realized eschatology inaugurated by the military and cultural successes of the emperors, beginning with Augustus. The rule of "peace" and the subjugation of nations accomplished by the empire seemed to many (though not all, we noted in the previous chapter) to be the realization of the best intentions of the gods.[74]

Escaping this omnipresent belief, and the structures that honored and furthered it, would have been no easy task. For early believers the temptation to continue acknowledging Caesar, rather than Jesus, as Savior (cf. Phil. 3:20) would have been great indeed, with social, economic, and other forms of pressure pushing them in that direction. Paul, however, urges his readers from Thessalonica to Corinth to Philippi and to Rome to accept an alternative hope, one grounded in love and cruciform power rather than violence, one offering true peace and security (cf. 1 Thess. 5:3) through loyalty to God in Jesus rather than to the emperor. This, for Paul, is a certain hope, a confidence that the sufferings of the present are mysteriously the firstfruits and guarantor of the true glory to come, the glory not of Rome, but of God.

"Now but Not Yet": Sober but Joyful

Paul's experience of cruciform existence in Christ should not be understood as depressing or moribund. His letter to the Philippians, arguably the most focused on the cruciform life, is also known as his most joyful letter.[75] He is completely serious, moreover, when he claims to rejoice in sufferings because of the coming glory of God. And suffer he did, so rejoice he did as well.

Paul's joy stems from three main sources: his communities (though they could cause him pain and sorrow, too), his present experience, and his future hope of glory. For our purposes we focus only on the last two, and especially on how they work together.

---

74. Of the many discussions of imperial eschatology and propaganda, the brief overview in Witherington, *Conflict and Community,* pp. 295-98, is an excellent starting point.

75. Words for "joy" and "rejoice" appear more than fifteen times.

Almost all interpreters of Paul stress his so-called "eschatological reservation" — the second half of his experience of "already but not yet": the final resurrection has not occurred (*contra* the elitists or enthusiasts at Corinth), the Spirit is a down payment — real but only partial — of the future, and so on. Paul is indeed aware that

> now we see in a mirror, dimly, but then we will see face to face. Now I know only in part; then I will know fully, even as I have been fully known. (1 Cor. 13:12)

Yet what drives Paul's life and mission is not merely a far-off hope. Rather, it is the certainty that the future is already beginning now, that the transformation into glory has begun (2 Cor. 3:18), and that "salvation is nearer to us now than when we became believers; the night is far gone, the day is near" (Rom. 13:11-12). *This, indeed, may be Paul's most radical interpretation of the experience of those in Christ: cruciform hope means that the very thing (suffering) that suggests that glory is distant is, in fact, the proof of its proximity.* That assurance means that joy and rejoicing characterize believing existence now. Cruciform hope does not mean resignation to present circumstances in the hope of a better though distant future, but rather confidence that the Day and the glory have already begun in the experience of cruciformity. Only those who have as their ultimate telos "conformity to the image of God's Son" (Rom. 8:29) can and do rejoice in the process of getting to that telos, which is in fact the experience of that telos already in the present.

Conclusion: Cruciform Hope

For Paul, hope is grounded in divine actions of reversal revealed in Scripture and known most fully in the death-resurrection, humiliation-exaltation experience of Jesus. This means, therefore, that hope is inherently cruciform.

Paul's experience and advocacy of cruciform hope may be a bitter pill to swallow; conditional hope, predicated on the necessity of suffering, may sound not only difficult, but even sadistic. For Paul, however, suffering is neither the main plot line of the story nor the conclusion to it. Rather, it is the necessary but temporary reality of those who identify with the suffering — and exalted! — Messiah. For this reason, Paul is able to write with joy and confidence that the future of believers and of the universe is glorious indeed:

> What no eye has seen, nor ear heard, nor the human heart conceived, what God has prepared for those who love him. (1 Cor. 2:9)

For this slight momentary affliction is preparing us for an eternal weight of glory beyond all measure. (2 Cor. 4:17)

[18]I consider that the sufferings of this present time are not worth comparing with the glory about to be revealed to us. [19]For the creation waits with eager longing for the revealing of the children of God . . . [21][for then] the creation itself will be set free from its bondage to decay and will obtain the freedom of the glory of the children of God. (Rom. 8:18-19, 21)

CHAPTER 13

COMMUNITIES OF CRUCIFORMITY

Paul's Experience and Vision of the Church

I n the preceding chapters we have explored Paul's cross-centered encounter with God, Christ, the Spirit, and the Trinity, as well as his corresponding experience of cruciform faith, love, power, and hope. We have characterized this comprehensive yet focused experience as a "narrative spirituality," and we have seen how Paul finds in himself, and desires for those to whom he writes, patterns of living that tell once again the story of Christ's cruciform existence.

Despite the fact that Paul, of course, was an individual, and despite the fact that he naturally expected each and every believer to embody the story of Christ, his spirituality of cruciformity is fundamentally *communal* in character. That is to say, Paul's mission was not merely to preach a message that produced individuals who lived new lives of cruciformity. Rather, his mission was to announce the gospel of Jesus Christ as the true Lord of all — in continuity with the God of Israel and in contrast to the counterfeit lord, the Roman emperor — and to form visible alternative communities of cruciformity animated and governed by this true Lord. These communities, then, were to exist in connection with Israel and in contradistinction to the empire and culture of Rome.

Thus, as previous chapters have suggested, cruciformity is inherently a corporate and even political spirituality. It challenges, for example, Roman ideologies and realities of power and hope. In this concluding chapter of our study of Paul per se, we consider the communal character of cruciformity. We will briefly recall the corporate character of Paul's experience, consider the theo-political nature of Paul's gospel, and then focus on the resulting political reality of the churches as communities, even "colonies," of cruciformity.

349

The Corporate Character of Cruciformity

Early in this book (chapter two), we discovered the corporate character of Paul's experience of being "in Christ." This relationship, though personal, is not private. To be "in Christ" is to live within a community that is shaped by his story, not merely to have a "personal relationship" with Christ.

This corporate character of being in Christ corresponds to the inherently relational character of cruciformity. Cruciform faith is not complete until it issues in cruciform love for others. Cruciform love and power are ways of being for others, expressions of commitment to the weak, to a larger body, and to enemies. Even cruciform hope requires a vision of the future much broader than the fate of the self alone.

The communal nature of Paul's spirituality is expressed in the way he composes his pastoral correspondence. Paul writes his letters — at least the ones that have been preserved — to communities, not individuals.[1] This is the case even in the so-called letter to Philemon, which is actually addressed to "Philemon our dear friend and coworker, to Apphia our sister, to Archippus our fellow soldier, *and to the church in your house*" (Philem. 1:1b-2 [emphasis added]). Although Paul directs his specific request to Philemon, he does so only by sandwiching the request between words spoken to the church as a whole.[2] Paul clearly intended his letters to be heard and heeded in a communal context.

Readers of Paul's letters in English translation are at a distinct disadvantage because English does not distinguish between the singular and plural forms of "you" (i.e., "you" versus "you all"), or between singular and plural verb forms that are associated with these two pronouns. Yet nearly all of Paul's descriptions of and prescriptions for believers are couched in the plural "you," in second-person-plural language. Some English-translation readers have therefore found it helpful to substitute "you all" for "you," although this does not work in translating the many second-person-plural imperative verbs ("walk," "consider," "be," etc.) that pepper Paul's letters but do not use pronouns in English.

Thus in both substance and grammatical expression, Paul's spirituality is irreducibly communal or corporate in character. Modern individualists must keep that in mind.

---

1. We are here considering only the undisputed letters of Paul. Paul could very well, of course, have written letters to individuals.

2. In addition to vv. 1b-2 of Philemon, vv. 3, 22b, and 25 contain plural pronouns to indicate plural addressees.

The Theo-Political Character of Paul's Gospel

Paul was convinced that the communities he and other apostles were founding constituted a part of the eschatological Israel of God (Gal. 6:16), communities of the "new covenant" promised by the prophets (Jer. 31:31-34; Ezek. 11:14-21; 36:22-32; 1 Cor. 11:25; 2 Cor. 3:6) and anticipated especially by all apocalyptically minded Jews.[3] The Church for Paul was "the dawning of the new age," "the blueprint and beachhead of the kingdom of God," "the interim eschatological community that looks forward to the future of the coming reign of God."[4] Like Israel from its inception, this community of the new age was called by God to be a distinct, peculiar minority presence in the world, set off from the rest of its culture and age by virtue of its consecration to God, its holiness and internal unity.[5] For Paul, it is cruciformity that manifests all these features; cruciformity constitutes the distinctiveness of the community and its dedication to God, even as it creates the requisite unity within the community.[6]

The vocabulary of Paul's spirituality derives, therefore, from the language of Israel. Words like "covenant," "Lord," "salvation," "faith," "gospel," "servant," and "church" or "assembly," for example, are biblical terms, full of meaning for all Jews. However, Paul's Greek vocabulary also reflects the broader Greco-Roman environment in which Hellenistic Judaism existed. Indeed, many key elements of Paul's vocabulary echo not so much the non-Jewish *religious* vo-

---

3. It seems clear that Paul experienced the Church, consisting of Christ-believing Jews and Gentiles, as assemblies of true Israelites (see, e.g., Rom. 2:28-29; 9:6-8; Gal. 3:6-9, 28-29; 6:16) and thus as *part* — but not necessarily the whole — of the eschatological "Israel of God." If we take Galatians and Romans together (which some, however, would not want to do), the "Israel of God" would have meant for Paul: (1) in the present, (a) all Christ-believing Jews ("the remnant of [ethnic] Israel," according to Rom. 11:1-6) and (b) all Christ-believing Gentiles (the "branches" that are "grafted on" to "the olive tree," Rom. 11:11-24), plus, (2) in the future, "all [ethnic] Israel" (Rom. 11:26), whose salvation is guaranteed by the covenant faithfulness of God manifested in the faithful death of Jesus. Unless Paul contradicts himself, this future salvation of all Israel will occur as it now does for all people, by confession of Jesus as God's Messiah (Romans 10).

4. J. Christiaan Beker, *Paul the Apostle: The Triumph of God in Life and Thought* (Philadelphia: Fortress, 1980), pp. 303, 326.

5. See Wayne A. Meeks, *The Moral World of the First Christians* (Philadelphia: Westminster, 1986), p. 130, and T. J. Deidun, *New Covenant Morality in Paul* (Rome: Biblical Institute Press, 1981), p. 16.

6. In summarizing Paul's purpose in 1 Corinthians, to create unity in the community, Raymond Pickett (*The Cross in Corinth: The Social Significance of the Death of Jesus,* JSNTSup 143 [Sheffield: Sheffield Academic Press, 1997], pp. 68-69) aptly notes that the Corinthians' "social harmony . . . is dependent on a unanimous commitment to values which befit a community that has been called into existence through the 'word of the cross.'"

351

cabulary of the various cults of his day as the _political_ vocabulary of the age. That is, much of Paul's language reverberates from the spheres of governance, of empire. However, because ancient peoples, Jewish and otherwise, did not separate religion and politics as we do (or at least claim to do) in the postmodern West, this distinction between religious and political is perhaps misleading. A better term for the Jewish and Greco-Roman language Paul uses is *theo-political* — that which is inextricably both religious (theological) and political.

The chart on p. 353 provides a very brief overview of some items from Paul's vocabulary, indicating what basic meaning(s) the words would have had when spoken to a Greco-Roman audience originating from or connected to Judaism and its Scriptures.[7] The political, as well as religious, character of these terms — and the list could be expanded — is self-evident. Paul's gospel and spirituality are as irreducibly political as they are corporate. What Paul experiences in the Church is a corporate reality that so challenges the political order of the day that it can only be expressed in political, or theo-political, language.

Communities of Cruciformity

We have contended that Paul did not set out merely to save or convert individuals to the gospel but to form communities shaped by the gospel into cruciform, and thereby alternative, theo-political entities. These communities took the ostensibly innocuous form of "house churches," groups that assembled in apartments and larger homes for a variety of purposes, including prayer, Scripture reading, receiving apostolic reports and letters, instruction and encouragement, participating in "the Lord's Supper," eating, collecting money for the poor, and related activities. The key terms that Paul uses to describe this communal experience are therefore not only religious but also social and even political in nature, as were the terms used in his gospel message itself. Of particular importance for Paul is the experience of the Church as a "new creation," as a

---

7. This chart is not meant to be complete. For helpful discussion of these and other terms, see the following chapters of Richard A. Horsley, ed., *Paul and Empire: Religion and Power in Roman Imperial Society* (Harrisburg, Pa.: Trinity Press International, 1997): Richard A. Horsley, "Paul's Counter-Imperial Gospel: Introduction," pp. 140-47; Dieter Georgi, "God Turned Upside Down," pp. 148-57; Helmut Koester, "Imperial Ideology and Paul's Eschatology in 1 Thessalonians," pp. 158-66; and Karl P. Donfried, "The Imperial Cults of Thessalonica and Political Conflict in 1 Thessalonians," pp. 215-23. See also now Richard A. Horsley, ed., *Paul and Politics: Ekklesia, Israel, Imperium, Interpretation* (Harrisburg, Pa.: Trinity Press International, 2000).

Greek Term(s) Used by Paul	Common English Translation(s)	Meaning in Jewish Context	Meaning in Broader Greco-Roman Context
euangelion; euangelizomai	good news/gospel; proclaim good news	good news of God's salvation; announce the good news of God's salvation	good news of military victory or of an emperor's birth/reign; announce the emperor's beneficence
kyrios	Lord	YHWH (God)	master; ruler, emperor (imperial title)
sōtēr; sōtēria	savior; salvation	God as deliverer/savior; God's deliverance/salvation	emperor as political savior; imperial age or results of military victory
basileia	kingdom, reign	God's kingdom, reign	kingdom; empire; imperial rule, age
eirēnē	peace	right relations among humans and between humans and God	imperial rule and cessation of internal and external conflict; Latin *pax* (*pax Romana*)
pistis	faith	covenant faithfulness, fidelity	loyalty (reciprocal between Rome and its citizenry); Latin *fides*
dikaios; dikaiosynē	just, righteous; justice, justification, righteousness	covenant faithfulness and righteousness	just; (Roman) justice
ekklēsia	church	the assembly of God's people	the local assembly of citizens in a city (*polis*)
parousia	[second] coming		imperial or other official arrival, visit, presence

confessing and worshipping community, as *ekklēsia* (assembly) and *polis* (city),[8] as a "body," and as a "family."

New Creation

We begin with "new creation," not because of the prominence of the precise term, but because it suggests Paul's fundamental experience of something *new*. In Christ God has broken into history in a momentous way, such that Paul and his fellow believers live during the "juncture" or "overlap" of the ages, this age and the age to come (1 Cor. 10:11). A new covenant has been established, and God's people of old are now renewed by it when they respond in faith to the faithfulness of God manifested in the faithfulness of Jesus. The same privileges are extended to Gentiles, which in fact marks the time as the beginning of the end, when Gentiles will come to knowledge of the true God. Indeed,

> ... if anyone is in Christ, there is a new creation; everything old has passed away; see everything has become new! (2 Cor. 5:17)

This is the language of prophetic fulfillment.[9] As forgiven and justified people, such Gentiles and Jews form "the Israel of God" (Gal. 6:16), the "embodiment of the new creation."[10] What God intended from the beginning (creation), what humans marred, and what God will complete in the future (new creation) has already broken into human history and life.

Because it is now already the time of the new creation, the old creation as marred by humans — "this world/age" — stands under the judgment of God. It is passing away (1 Cor. 7:31). Those who belong to the new covenant are therefore a people who, in a fundamental sense, do not belong to the age in which they reside (Rom. 12:1-2). Their identity, values, and practices come from the future, which is already present. To live in the old realm, the realm of the flesh, instead of in the new realm, the realm of the Spirit (Galatians 5; Romans 8), is to live a reverse anachronism. It is to allow the old to live, out of place, within the new. Paul's experience and vision of the Church are grounded in this eschatological or apocalyptic reality: the future is present; everything must be viewed in that perspective. Furthermore, because the event that started this new reality

---

8. The Greek terms are deliberately placed before the translations offered because English terms do not easily convey Paul's meaning.

9. See the "new creation" language of Isa. 43:18-19; 65:17; 66:22.

10. The term is from J. Louis Martyn, "Apocalyptic Antinomies," in his *Theological Issues in the Letters of Paul* (Nashville: Abingdon, 1997), p. 122.

is the cross (Gal. 1:4; 2 Cor. 5:11-21), to live in the world as the embodiment of the new creation is to live in the world as the embodiment of the cross. This is the starting point for Paul's experience of the Church, which confesses and worships the one God who is revealed in the cross of Christ.

Confessing and Worshipping Community

Paul knew well that in the ancient world there were "many gods and lords" (1 Cor. 8:5). These gods and lords were satisfied to share their place in the cosmos, and in the lives of mortals, with one another. However, this was of course not true of the one God of Israel, and Paul's monotheistic Judaism is to be shared by his converts from the Gentile world: "[W]e know that 'no idol in the world really exists,' and that 'there is no God but one'" (1 Cor. 8:4). Because, however, this God has been revealed in the crucified Messiah, Paul and his communities, with all early Christians, confess that "Jesus is Lord" (e.g., 1 Cor. 12:3; Rom. 10:9; Phil. 2:11). "For us," writes Paul,

> there is one God, the Father, from whom are all things and for whom we exist, and one Lord, Jesus Christ, through whom are all things and through whom we exist. (1 Cor. 8:6)

N. T. Wright has aptly described this as "christological monotheism."[11] As we saw in chapter four, Paul's experience of the Spirit means that this Christological monotheism is infused by a power that could lead him to describe it only in "Trinitarian" language. The power at work in the cults of other gods and lords, on the other hand, is demonic (1 Cor. 10:20-21).

According to Paul's most thorough description of early Christian worship (1 Corinthians 8–14), the community assembles to express and experience its own unity, which is grounded in the oneness of their God and Lord, in the oneness of the Spirit at work among them, and especially in the one meal of bread and wine they share (1 Cor. 10:14-22; 11:17-34). Ultimately this unity is generated by the cross, the sign of God's love for all: Gentile and Jew, male and female, slave and free, rich and poor, strong and weak. The meal of bread and the cup, "the Lord's Supper" (1 Cor. 11:20), functions in several ways. It is both a commemoration and a proclamation of the Lord's self-offering on the cross as the community's foundational, defining, and unifying event (1 Cor. 11:23-26).

---

11. N. T. Wright, "Monotheism, Christology, and Ethics: 1 Corinthians 8," in his *The Climax of the Covenant: Christ and the Law in Pauline Theology* (Edinburgh: T. & T. Clark, 1991; Minneapolis: Fortress, 1993), p. 129.

It is therefore an expression of unity that transcends all divisions based on status (1 Cor. 11:17-22, 27-34). As an act of worship, it is an experience of participation (Greek *koinōnia*, 1 Cor. 10:16) in Christ and his death.

Thus participation in this community has to be exclusive; those "in Christ" can acknowledge no other god or lord, whether by verbal confession or by participation in a cultic meal dedicated to some other deity:

> You cannot drink the cup of the Lord and the cup of demons. You cannot partake of the table of the Lord and the table of demons. (1 Cor. 10:21)

In a culture where "inclusivity" — participation in multiple cults — was the norm, this exclusivity was provokingly countercultural. The Pauline "church" is not like other religious bodies. When it assembles, therefore, it does so not only to celebrate the Lord's Supper, not only to sing, pray, and offer praise (1 Cor. 14:15-17, 26), but especially to hear prophecy (the primary topic of 1 Corinthians 14) — words of edification, encouragement, and consolation offered in the spirit of cruciform love. In other words, the assembly meets to *unlearn* the ancient culture of honor and status and to *learn* what it means to exist as an exclusive alternative community, worshipping the one God, grounded in the cross of Christ, and infused by the cruciform Spirit. They meet, in other words, as God's "called-out community," God's *ekklēsia*.[12]

Ekklēsia and Polis

The word *ekklēsia*, which most Bible translations render as "church," is the word Paul uses to refer to the assembly of God's people who confess and worship Jesus as God's exalted, crucified Messiah. As noted in the chart above, however, the word *ekklēsia* has not only Jewish roots but also Greco-Roman political connotations. To be sure, for Paul the Church is the "assembly of the Lord," the "assembly of God" (see, e.g., Gal. 1:13; 1 Cor. 1:2; 2 Cor. 1:1), just as the people of Israel met as "the assembly [Hebrew *qahal*] of God" or the "assembly of Israel." This assembly, however, takes place in the context of the Ro-

---

12. Ironically, this *exclusivist* community with respect to gods was thoroughly *inclusivist* with respect to human beings: Gentile and Jew, male and female, slave and free. A note about the etymology and "meaning" of *ekklēsia* is in order. Formed from the Greek preposition *ek* ("out/out of") and the verb *kaleō* ("call"), the noun *ekklēsia* is popularly said to mean something like "those called out." Although critics of this perspective rightly point out that etymology (word origin and development) does not determine meaning, in this case the etymology and the meaning do, in fact, correspond significantly.

man empire, especially in the diaspora, or Jewish dispersion throughout Gentile lands, where assemblies of Jews and Christ-believers alike are peculiar entities.

While the assemblies Paul founded can be compared and contrasted with several social bodies of his day,[13] his preference for the term *ekklēsia* suggests that he experienced the assembly as "the political assembly of the people 'in Christ' in pointed juxtaposition and 'competition' with the official city assembly."[14] Like the city assembly, the *ekklēsia* meets to provide a public forum for its citizens, including a place for acclamation ("prophecy," "lesson," "interpretation," "revelation": 1 Corinthians 14), discussion, and appropriate "judicial" activity apart from the Roman courts.[15] As noted above, the "citizens" of this *ekklēsia* are from every race, gender, and socioeconomic state.

These communities Paul founded, the *ekklēsiai* (plural), are, individually, alternative assemblies to the local *polis*, and, corporately, an international network of communities constituting an alternative empire to that of Rome. Whether the *ekklēsia* is experienced only at the local level, or at the intercity and international level, this community exists in contrast both to the local *polis* and to the empire itself, to which every *polis* paid allegiance. For the *ekklēsiai*, Caesar is not Lord, because the exalted crucified Jesus is. In continuity with Israel's affirmation of its one Sovereign Lord over all political pretenders to the divine throne, the *ekklēsiai* acknowledge Jesus alone as the Lord, appointed by the God of Israel and thus the displacer of "Lord" Caesar.[15] As David Seeley writes, commenting on Paul's master story (Phil. 2:6-11):

---

13. E.g., synagogue and guild/voluntary association. See Wayne A. Meeks, *The First Urban Christians: The Social World of the Apostle Paul* (New Haven: Yale University Press, 1983), pp. 77-81, 108. Some clubs called their meetings *ekklēsiai* (p. 108), but Paul's usage seems more closely related to the larger political and religious symbols of Rome and Israel.

14. Richard A. Horsley, "Introduction: Building an Alternative Society," in Richard A. Horsley, ed., *Paul and Empire: Religion and Power in Roman Imperial Society* (Harrisburg, Pa.: Trinity Press International, 1997), p. 209. For similar interpretations, see Meeks, *First Urban Christians*, p. 108, and Dieter Georgi, *Theocracy in Paul's Praxis and Theology* (Minneapolis: Fortress, 1991), p. 57.

15. See 1 Cor. 6:1-8 as well as the extensive use of judicial language in the entire letter; also Beker, *Paul the Apostle*, pp. 317, 320.

16. See also, e.g., Horsley, "Introduction: Building an Alternative Society," and John L. White, *The Apostle of God: Paul and the Promise of Abraham* (Peabody, Mass.: Hendrickson, 1999), pp. 173-208, 237-45. There is no need, with James D. G. Dunn (*The Theology of Paul the Apostle* [Grand Rapids: Eerdmans, 1998], pp. 537-43, esp. p. 537), to choose between "assembly of God," in continuity with Israel, and "assembly of the citizenry," in contrast to the Roman assembly. It is precisely in the distinctiveness of the synagogue's, and thus the Church's, assembly that it is both God's assembly and *not* the city's or the emperor's assembly.

357

The hymn places this leader [Jesus] in a position of clear superiority vis-à-vis the emperor, and describes God as transferring to him the epithet "lord," previously reserved for God alone. The emperor presided over a very real political entity. So, too, had the God of Israel. . . . Though the hymn proclaimed Jesus' lordship over all, it must have been painfully obvious that his realm could not yet match such reality. Even so, his rule was becoming manifest in small cells forming within the Empire. These were not plagued by the Empire's corruption or limited by the ethnic constraints of Israel.[17]

It is not surprising, therefore, that in the letter to the Philippians, Paul's political vision of the *ekklēsia* comes perhaps to its fullest expression in the language of *polis*, or city. Not only does Paul narrate Christ in counter-imperial terms (2:6-11), but he specifically describes the Philippians in the language of a counter-*polis*, a counter-city. He informs the citizens that their "commonwealth" (Greek *politeuma*, from *polis*) is "in heaven" (3:20; NRSV margin), not (it is therefore implied) in Rome.[18] This image would especially impress itself on the church of Philippi, since their city was a proud colony of Rome. However, because the Philippian believers' seat of power and allegiance is in heaven rather than in Rome, they constitute a colony within the colony — a colony of heaven — from which they "are expecting" their "savior," who is not an earthly emperor but the true Lord, Jesus. G. B. Caird comments:

> Each local church is a colony of heaven, its members enjoying full citizenship of the heavenly city . . . but charged with the responsibility of bringing the world to acknowledge the sovereignty of Christ.[19]

17. David Seeley, "The Background of the Philippians Hymn," *Journal of Higher Criticism* 1 (1994): 72.

18. On the term *politeuma*, see, e.g., Klaus Wengst, *Pax Romana and the Peace of Jesus Christ*, trans. John Bowden (Philadelphia: Fortress, 1987), p. 79, and the commentaries, especially Peter O'Brien, *The Epistle to the Philippians* (Grand Rapids: Eerdmans, 1991), pp. 459-61. The term had a range of meanings, including "community" or "state," "citizenship," and "commonwealth." The NRSV rendering, "citizenship," is rejected by most commentators here. O'Brien (p. 460) finds the term to be parallel to "kingdom" or "reign" (Greek *basileia*) in the Synoptic Gospels, with a dynamic sense. Meeks (*First Urban Christians*, pp. 35-36) observes that the term was sometimes used by Jewish communities to refer to themselves as a "virtual city within the city."

19. G. B. Caird, *Paul's Letters from Prison in the Revised Standard Version*, NCB (Oxford: Oxford University Press, 1976), p. 148. A similar interpretation may be found, e.g., in Gordon D. Fee, *Paul's Letter to the Philippians*, The New International Commentary on the New Testament (Grand Rapids: Eerdmans, 1995), p. 379. Fee uses the language of "colony" and "outpost" of heaven and stresses the "cruciform" character of life in this colony.

That is to say, then, that the source of the Church's political identity is in heaven, not in Rome, as the "average Philippian on the streets" would say. The "commonwealth" or "imperial reign" believers experience is that of the crucified and cruciform Lord Jesus. Their city charter is his story (2:6-11), and they are called to "live their lives as citizens" (author's translation; Greek *politeuesthe,* from *polis*) in a manner worthy of this story, which is the good news about Christ (1:27).[20] They fulfill the obligations of heavenly citizenship, not by avoiding the world, but by continuing the countercultural and counter-imperial story of cruciform humility and love in the world (1:27-30; 2:12-16) as well as in the Church (2:1-4). In so doing, they prove that their names are written, not on the rosters of Philippi's citizens, but in the "book of life" (4:3), the rollbook of the heavenly commonwealth.[21] The message of Philippians, with all its political language, can be summarized as follows:

> Live faithfully now as a colony of citizens of that heavenly imperial city, in the midst of this colony of Rome. Your Lord and Savior — your "Emperor" — is Jesus, whose cruciform pattern of faith, love, power, and hope is the city charter of your colony. And as you live by this charter, do so in unity, for you must be one as you face persecution together for the sake of Christ, just as I, Paul, am imprisoned — though the gospel we sing, preach, and live is not.

If this is the message of Philippians, and if this message is delivered elsewhere by Paul, as we have suggested, what are we to make of the famous passage in Romans 13? The text of Romans 13:1-7, in which Paul admonishes the Roman assembly to pay their taxes to Rome, might at first seem to undermine the radical anti-imperial quality of Paul's vision. It does not. Romans 13:1-7 has, of course, been the subject of much investigation and consternation. In essence, however, it affirms, in good Hellenistic fashion, the sovereignty of God over all political powers, even enemy powers. It thus denies, over against first-century

20. Unfortunately, the NRSV does not capture the political language and symbolism of the text ("live your life in a manner worthy of the gospel of Christ"). Paul does not use his more common word for "live" (i.e., *peripateō,* "walk").

21. It is crucial to note the countercultural dimension of this citizenship. Paul is not appealing to the Philippians' "dual citizenship" in the empire and in heaven, as Fee suggests (*Philippians,* pp. 161-62, 378-79), but to their true citizenship in contrast with the city's status as a Roman colony. This is both historically and theologically significant, since many members of the Church would likely not have been citizens, and since the claims of each empire on its citizens are at odds. See the brief but insightful discussion of Marcus Bockmuehl, *The Epistle to the Philippians,* Black's New Testament Commentaries (London: A. & C. Black, 1997), pp. 97-98.

Jewish tendencies toward revolution, any sense in which the Church is politically revolutionary; after all, in context (Romans 12–13), peace, love, and good — rather than vengeance — are the appropriate responses to *all* outsiders, whether enemies or authorities. Paul wants to make it clear that the conflict with the *pax Romana* lies not in the paying of taxes but in inappropriate culturally approved values, whether Jewish or pagan, that might infiltrate the community. For Paul, as we noted in chapter ten, refusing to pay taxes to Rome in the larger historical context of Jewish antipathy and revolts would have been an act of vengeance toward Rome, on the one hand, and of disobedience toward the sovereign God, on the other. Thus refusing to pay taxes in that context contradicts, rather than embodies, Paul's countercultural message of cruciform enemy love. Paul's vision was not to oppose, remove, and replace Rome but to create an alternative to Rome, even if Rome demanded back the very money it had minted. The chief concern of believers should not be who receives their money but who receives their honor (Rom. 13:7). In the context of Romans 12–13, this means that they are to "outdo one another in showing honor [to one another]" (Rom. 12:10). This is the "debt" of cruciform love (Rom. 13:8-10) owed to one another in the assembly that is the "body," not of the emperor, but of the heavenly Lord Christ (Rom. 12:5).[22]

Body

Paul, then, further experiences and describes the assembly as the "body" of Christ (Rom. 12:4-8; 1 Cor. 11:29; 1 Corinthians 12), the presence in the world of the exalted crucified Lord. "Body" imagery was commonly used in antiquity, even as today, to describe political and social entities.[23] As the body of Christ, the *(ekklēsia)* exists as a public, corporate reminder of its master story, its foundational narrative, in continuity with the story of Israel and in contrast to the story, the ideology, and the values of Rome and its body politic. The citizens of this body know that their assemblies are designed not to foster allegiance to Rome and its cultural values, but to Jesus and to the values of cruciform faith, love, power, and hope.

22. However, by stressing Paul's specific historical context of possible Jewish revolution, one could conclude that the admonition to pay taxes might not be a universal Christian moral imperative.

23. See, for example, Margaret M. Mitchell, *Paul and the Rhetoric of Reconciliation* (Tübingen: J. C. B. Mohr [Paul Siebeck], 1991), pp. 157-64, and Robert Banks, *Paul's Idea of Community: The Early House Churches in Their Historical Setting,* 2nd ed. (Peabody, Mass.: Hendrickson, 1994).

Like Rome, the Church knows (truly) that its destiny is glory. However, because the Church awaits its resurrection and glorification in the future, its primary purpose in the present is to retell the *cruciform* half of the master story. Because its exalted Lord is the crucified Jesus,

> Christ's exaltation . . . makes the church the means whereby his earthly fate cannot be forgotten. Pauline ecclesiology is part of the apostle's theology of the cross and to that degree can only be understood in the light of his Christology. . . . [T]he body is destined for service and only participates in the glory of the exalted Lord in so far as it remains his instrument in earthly lowliness. For it is this which gives the church its unique character and eschatological significance.[24]

The first hallmark of the Church as the body of Christ is interdependent edification (Greek *oikodomē*) and cooperation "guided by a vision of community that bears the stamp of the crucified *and* risen Lord."[25] As the community of the *risen* Lord, the Church experiences the Lord's power, but as the community of the *risen crucified* Lord, that power is experienced only as power in weakness, as the power of love. The uniqueness of this sort of political body is that there is a reversal of values demanded by the cross; honor and attention are not lavished on the rich and strong but on the weak:

> [22]. . . [T]he members of the body that seem to be weaker are indispensable, [23]and those members of the body that we think less honorable we clothe with greater honor, and our less respectable members are treated with greater respect; [24]whereas our more respectable members do not need this. But God has so arranged the body, giving the greater honor to the inferior member, [25]that there may be no dissension within the body, but the members may have the same care for one another. [26]If one member suffers, all suffer together with it; if one member is honored, all rejoice together with it. (1 Cor. 12:22-26)[26]

As the German scholar Gerd Theissen has said, Paul's use of the body imagery, encapsulated in these verses, is so contrary to its normal use in antiquity that it

---

24. Ernst Käsemann, "The Theological Problem Presented by the Motif of the Body of Christ," in his *Perspectives on Paul*, trans. Margaret Kohl (Philadelphia: Fortress, 1971; reprinted Mifflintown, Pa.: Sigler, 1996), pp. 113-14, 117.

25. Pickett, *The Cross in Corinth*, p. 205 (emphasis in the original).

26. For Paul, as the subsequent verses (1 Cor. 12:27-31) demonstrate, this preferential option for the weak does not negate a kind of "hierarchy" of gifts, but the value of the gifts is in fact a function of their ability to edify.

would require a "cognitive restructuring" of the social environment of those who heard it.[27]

As colonies of cruciformity, Paul's communities both constitute and experience a radical alternative to Roman culture at large. The power of weakness and love subverts a culture based on status, or "love of honor" (philotimia). "Participation without distinction," a "discipleship of equals," is the second hallmark of the Pauline churches — or at least of Paul's experience and vision.[28] This radical experience of community created problems — as 1 Corinthians especially attests — in a culture that naturally practiced "social and occupational selectivity" in its assemblies.[29] Yet the ekklēsia opened its doors to all who had faith in the gospel of God, experienced the Spirit, and were baptized into Christ, thereby granting all who came equal status before God and one another — in the body of Christ (1 Cor. 12:13; Gal. 3:28).

Family

This experience of equality and mutual concern, in contrast to the culture of rank and pursuit of honor, Paul narrates also in the language of family. He experienced community life in Christ as family life, encouraging his fellow believers to understand the ekklēsia as a surrogate or alternative family, a "society of siblings."[30] The term "brother(s)," referring to Paul's fellow believer(s), both male and female, occurs more than 100 times in the undisputed letters of Paul.[31]

Within Greco-Roman culture, interaction among nonfamily members was infused with the pursuit of honor and with challenges to honor, especially among the males who were the heads of households. Within the blood family,

27. Gerd Theissen, *Psychological Aspects of Pauline Theology* (Philadelphia: Fortress, 1987), pp. 326-30.

28. The first quote is from Jürgen Becker, *Paul: Apostle to the Gentiles,* trans. O. C. Dean, Jr. (Louisville: Westminster/John Knox, 1993), p. 245; the second, from Elisabeth Schüssler Fiorenza, *Discipleship of Equals: A Critical Feminist Ekklesia-logy of Liberation* (New York: Crossroad, 1993).

29. The term is from Becker, *Paul,* p. 244.

30. See S. Scott Bartchy, "Undermining Ancient Patriarchy: The Apostle Paul's Vision of a Society of Siblings," *Biblical Theology Bulletin* 29 (1999): 68-78. The terms "surrogate family" and especially "alternative family" are preferable to the label "fictive family" that is often used by social scientists.

31. The word "brother," *adelphos,* occurs in the singular twenty-nine times and in the plural eighty-three times, the latter certainly meant to be a generic word that includes female believers, or sisters, as the NRSV usually indicates (rendering the plural *adelphoi* as "brothers and sisters"). The singular form of the feminine *adelphē,* "sister," appears five times.

however, ties were extremely close, and brothers gave honor to all siblings without fear of competition and dishonor. For Paul, the Church is a family of nonblood siblings, siblings by "personal commitment."[32] They are called to treat one another as blood family by outdoing one another in showing honor (Rom. 12:10). Within this family there are people from all socioeconomic classes, but they now constitute one family. As such, they contradict cultural expectations for people from differing strata by practicing "generalized reciprocity," or "sharing without keeping score" — which was the norm for behavior within the blood family, but not for life in the society at large.[33] As family members, believers would experience the "intense loyalty and mutual honoring at the core of sibling values."[34] Shaped by the cross, these expectations are even further intensified and clarified. The siblings, in other words, practice cruciformity.

These dimensions of the apostle's experience of the Church — new creation, confessing and worshipping community, *ekklēsia* and *polis*, body of Christ, and family — are clearly inextricably interrelated. Each aspect stresses the inevitably social, political, and countercultural nature of the Church. In large measure, the Pauline Church is a community of outcasts — "social deviants," but not individualists.[35] It is a community of cruciformity in a culture where the cross, together with all that it symbolizes, is repudiated.

The Missionary Character of the Colony

Unfortunately, the characterization of Paul's communities as "colonies" can create the impression that Paul's experience and vision of the *ekklēsiai* are that they are ghetto-like or "sectarian" — communities withdrawn from their world. Yet for Paul the Church is not "a sequestered cloister, barricaded against the onslaughts of the world."[36] Not only is that form of corporate spirituality rejected by Paul (despite the existence of models that he could have imitated, such as the Qumran community that produced the Dead Sea Scrolls), but the apostle envisions himself and his communities as embodying Israel's mission as a light to the nations (Gentiles).

32. Bartchy, "Undermining Ancient Patriarchy," p. 70.

33. Bartchy, "Undermining Ancient Patriarchy." The phrases "generalized reciprocity" and "sharing without keeping score" are from pp. 69-70.

34. Bartchy, "Undermining Ancient Patriarchy," p. 72.

35. This way of describing the Church comes from Ben Witherington III, *The Paul Quest: The Renewed Search for the Jew of Tarsus* (Downers Grove, Ill.: InterVarsity, 1998), p. 33.

36. Beker, *Paul the Apostle*, p. 318.

In 2 Corinthians, Paul characterizes himself and his colleagues as "ambassadors for Christ" (2 Cor. 5:18-20). Apart from the political context and character of Paul's message, one might hear this term merely as a vivid metaphor for "apostles," meaning "authorized representatives." It is more. Paul and the other apostles are indeed Christ's authorized representatives, but they are so as delegates of the one, true Lord in a world ruled by a counterfeit lord and other illegitimate powers. The ambassadorial language is not, therefore, metaphorical or reducible to a common semantic element between two different kinds of agents (apostles and ambassadors). Paul sees his mission as one means of extending the reign of Jesus the universal Lord into the enemy-occupied and enemy-governed world. His letters and "pastoral visits" demonstrate his sense of responsibility "for seeing those assemblies of a society alternative to the Roman imperial order remain intact until the *parousia* of their true *Sōtēr* [Savior] and the establishment of the kingdom of God."[37]

Furthermore, this ambassadorial function is not limited to Paul and his colleagues. Paul's letter to the Philippians is full of political language, including the references discussed above to the Philippian *ekklēsia* as the Lord's colony (1:27; 3:20). Following the recitation of the master story, the apostle describes the Church's mission as being "children of God without blemish in the midst of a crooked and perverse generation, in which you shine like stars in the world" (2:15). It is impossible to resist the conclusion that inasmuch as the Philippians constitute an alternative community of cruciformity they bear witness to the servant-Lord in whom they live, just as Israel, God's servant, bore witness to the Gentiles:

> I am the Lord, I have called you in righteousness, I have taken you by the hand and kept you; I have given you as a covenant to the people, a light to the nations. . . . (Isa. 42:6)

> I will give you as a light to the nations, that my salvation may reach to the end of the earth. (Isa. 49:6b)[38]

These verses appear in the first and second of the so-called "servant songs" in Isaiah 40–55. In context, the servant is clearly identified as Israel (41:8-10; 44:1-2, 21). The people of Israel's role is to be God's witnesses (Isa. 43:10; 44:8), testifying among the nations that the Lord alone is the one true God and king (Isa. 42:3; 43:10-13; 44:6-8; ch. 45, etc.). The former text indicates Israel's original mission, at which it has failed and for which it is being punished by exile. The

---

37. Horsley, "Introduction: Building an Alternative Society," p. 214.
38. See also Isa. 51:4.

latter text indicates that God will redeem Israel and restore its original mission to the nations.

For Paul, of course, the light to the nations is now the *ekklēsia*, the people who recognize Jesus as God's anointed Christ and appointed Lord, who have been redeemed from slavery, and who bear witness to a "perverse generation." They are now the Lord's servant because they constitute the body and continue the narrative of God's obedient servant, Jesus.

As the living embodiment of the light to the nations, the *ekklēsia* now offers to the world the promises of the God of Israel: salvation, justice, peace, and safety, as the prophets envisioned them. This offer of God's salvation to the nations stands in stark contrast to the counterfeit offers of "peace and security" (1 Thess. 5:3) from the Roman empire. It is within the colonies of the heavenly Lord Jesus that real peace and security can be experienced now and guaranteed for the eschatological future. Paradoxically, the experience of this peace and security turns the community into a band of soldiers — not the emperors' soldiers, but warriors of the true king, whose power comes from the armor of faith, hope, and love (1 Thess. 5:8).

This soldier imagery is appropriate to an apocalyptic figure like Paul. Yet the battle Paul imagines is already won, guaranteed by God's resurrection of the crucified Messiah. The soldiers' battle, therefore, is to spread the message of certain and coming victory, and to stand as a sign to the world, and indeed the cosmos (Rom. 8:18-25), of that final triumph. As such, the battle consists of the Church's act of daily "worship," a life of liturgy understood not as ritual but as right living in and for this world, this age, though not conformed to it (Rom. 12:1-2). Otherwise, as noted in the previous chapter, "the sighing of the Christian for the redemption of the world . . . is simply reduced to a faint ecclesial whimper."[39]

For this reason, Paul's admonition to do good, not only to fellow believers, but "to all" (1 Thess. 5:15; Gal. 6:10), matches his conviction that the Church neither can nor should withdraw from the world (1 Cor. 5:10), even though "the present form of this world" is already passing away (1 Cor. 7:31). The colony, then, has a mission, a mission that clearly is not limited to "evangelism," though it just as clearly includes that. Although Paul's letters primarily address internal issues within the *ekklēsiai*, with special emphasis on group solidarity and cohesion, this situation presupposes a set of conditions in which the Church interacts with the world and is often persecuted by that world (e.g., 1 Thess. 2:14-16; 3:1-5; Phil. 1:27-30). As a colony of cruciformity, the Church first tells its story to itself in liturgy and prophetic edification, so that it can live

---

39. Beker, *Paul the Apostle*, p. 327.

the story of cruciform faith, love, hope, and power within itself. It is then equipped to tell and live the story — the gospel message — in the world, summoning people to faith by the power of the Spirit, and living by love and hope even in the face of opposition from enemies of the cross.

The danger of this mission is not sufficiently recognized by most readers of Paul's letters. Though "official persecution" may have been rare in the first Christian century (although Nero should not be forgotten), the *ekklēsiai* and their members posed various kinds of threats. The Roman social order and imperial claims were not subverted without cost and penalty; families, guilds and other clubs, the army, the imperial service, the networks of the elite, and much more were all impacted by the gospel. Perhaps the only thing that kept the danger to a relative minimum was the tiny size of the house churches. Even a very large house would probably have accommodated, at most, only between fifty and seventy-five. Such houses may have been used for occasional meetings of even smaller house churches, which may have numbered ten to twenty, depending on the size of the urban house or even apartment.

Yet no matter how dangerous the mission, how frequent or intense the persecution, the Church Paul knows practices only nonretaliation (e.g., 1 Thess. 5:15; 1 Cor. 4:12; Rom. 12:14-21). The community of the crucified is, in the words of Klaus Wengst, a "sphere of interrupted violence in the midst of a violent world."[40] Its peace-filled, cruciform life constitutes its message to the world.

Conclusion: The Church as Living Exegesis of the Master Story

For Paul, the experience of dying with Christ, though intensely personal, can never be private. Fundamentally, cruciformity means community, and community means cruciformity. Paul, we have seen, did not come merely to "save" individuals but to form communities, specifically what we might call "exclusivist-inclusivist" alternative communities of cruciform faith, love, power, and hope. These communities exclude allegiance to every other so-called lord or god, but include people of all stations in life who confess and live Jesus as Lord, thus challenging the values of the day by their very existence. They are communities formed by and into the countercultural story of their countercultural Lord.

As such, Paul's communities become living commentaries on their master story, the story that is told most fully in Philippians 2:6-11. Not surprisingly,

40. Wengst, *Pax Romana*, p. 88.

then, the letter to the Philippians most perfectly illustrates the connection between the master story and the community's story as an exegesis of it. Yet the connection is made throughout all of Paul's letters, as we have seen in every chapter of this book. For Paul the most faithful interpretation of the Messiah's story is not a letter or an argument but a living body, one whose life unfolds step-by-step in ways analogous to Messiah Jesus. Such a body will bear — literally, or metaphorically, or both — "the marks of Jesus" branded on its body (Gal. 6:17). To use the language of art, rather than story and exegesis, the Church is a living icon of the cross, of the crucified Messiah. Or again, in the language of drama, the Church is God's spectacle (Greek *theatron*, 1 Cor. 4:9), God's "theatrical performance" of the cross as the life-giving power of God. The Church performs the gospel as a living commentary on it.[41]

The *ekklēsia*, then, is not for Paul an optional supplement to a private spirituality of dying and rising with Christ. Rather, the *ekklēsia* is what God is up to in the world: re-creating a people whose corporate life tells the world what the death and resurrection of the Messiah is all about. This people, the "Church," lives the story, embodies the story, tells the story. It is the living exegesis of God's master story of faith, love, power, and hope.[42]

---

41. Basil S. Davis ("The Meaning of *proegraphē* in the Context of Galatians 3:1," *New Testament Studies* 45 [1999]: 210-11) makes the connection between Paul's ministry and God's "theater"; I have expanded it to include the life of the entire Church. On the "performance" of Scripture, see, for example, Nicholas Lash, "Performing the Scriptures," in his *Theology on the Way to Emmaus* (London: S.C.M., 1986), pp. 37-46.

42. For the notion of living exegesis, see Michael J. Gorman, *Elements of Biblical Exegesis: A Basic Guide for Students and Ministers* (Peabody, Mass.: Hendrickson, 2001), pp. 128, 131-33.

CHAPTER 14

CRUCIFORMITY TODAY

Challenges to, and the Challenges of, the Cross

Throughout this book we have seen that Paul's spirituality of the cross was a challenge both to the religious and even to the political and social status quo of his day, as well as to advocates of "alternative spiritualities" within the communities to which he wrote that took the cross less seriously or understood it differently. Moreover, Paul's cruciformity was not always universally welcomed, especially not in its application to the apostle himself, and probably not in its understanding of Christ or in its interpretation of believers' experience and obligations.

In this final chapter we will consider cruciformity today. We will look at some challenges to it from various quarters, as well as some challenges it poses both to the cultural status quo, especially as that status quo expresses itself in the Church, and to alternative spiritualities within the Church. I write as an American Christian, and specifically as a Protestant (United Methodist), so my thoughts will be directed toward, and reflect, that social and religious location. (It is probably helpful for the reader to know also that I have spent a decade teaching in both components of a theological school that has a Roman Catholic as well as an ecumenical division.)

We begin by considering the centrality of cruciformity to Paul, not as a review or synthesis of the previous chapters but as a conclusion to them and as a way of suggesting the importance of the topic for contemporary reflection.

Cruciformity at the Center

Interpreters of Paul throughout the last century or so have conducted a (sometimes fierce) debate about the most important dimension of Paul's theology. This is often described as the "center" of Paul's theology, though some have sought other language to describe the "heart," so to speak, of the apostle's thought. One prominent interpreter, Paul Achtemeier, speaks of a "generative center."[1]

Some of the most serious contenders for this place of honor have been justification by faith, participation in (especially dying and rising with) Christ, Christ himself, the cross, the resurrection, reconciliation, covenant, and the apocalyptic triumph of God. While some interpreters of Paul argue steadfastly for one or another as the true center, others would make room for several near the center, attempting to show the inner-connectedness of a set of central themes or images. Many in this latter group have sought — rightly, in my estimation — to show that "justification by faith" and "participation in Christ" or "dying and rising with Christ" are not mutually exclusive options but complementary realities, even two sides of the same coin. As such, these two inseparable themes can be placed within an apocalyptic *and* covenantal framework or narrative that focuses on (the now resurrected) Christ and his cross, as I have attempted to do.

Readers of this book might expect its author — if push came to shove — to side with those who find "dying and rising with Christ" to be the best way to articulate the center of Paul's theology. "Cruciformity," after all, is about conformity to the crucified Christ, expressed as faith, love, power, and hope. Although the emphasis of this book has been on the "dying" side of the "dying and rising" formula, the theme of resurrection to new life was treated in the discussion of faith, and the theme of resurrection of the body in the chapter on hope. Cruciformity is indeed central to the apostle, but it is a comprehensive rather than a narrow experience, encompassing even resurrection.

Despite its centrality to Paul, however, cruciformity should not be described fundamentally as "the center of Paul's theology." In the first place, this book has deliberately chosen not to speak of Paul's theology but of his spirituality. Cruciformity is indeed essential to Paul's spirituality — to his experience and to the experience he desires for his readers. While it is true that, throughout the book, I have made reference both to Paul's thought and to his experience,

---

1. Paul J. Achtemeier, "The Continuing Quest for Coherence in St. Paul: An Experiment in Thought," in Eugene H. Lovering and Jerry L. Sumney, eds., *Theology and Ethics in Paul and His Interpreters* (Nashville: Abingdon, 1996), pp. 132-45. For Achtemeier this generative center is Paul's conviction that "God raised Jesus from the dead" (pp. 138-40).

abstracting his thought or theology from that experience is fraught with problems. Paul did not primarily *think* about cruciformity, he *lived* it: "I die every day!" (1 Cor. 15:31). Having said this, however, I admit that, if one insisted on identifying the center of Paul's theology, cruciformity would be the most appropriate nominee for that role.

A second and more fundamental problem with the description of cruciformity (or anything else) as the "center" of Paul's theology, or even his spirituality, is the weakness of the metaphor of a center.[2] The notion of a center suggests one of two images. One is that of a wheel consisting of a hub and spokes, in which the spokes proceed from and are all independently related to the hub. The other image is that of a solar system, in which the planets all revolve around the center at various distances, some closer and some more peripheral to the center of the system. In each of these two images, the center does not function to relate the parts to one another and therefore does not truly integrate the system.

Finally, and perhaps most importantly, the recent emphasis on Paul's narrative theology, ethics, and (in this book) spirituality calls into question the appropriateness of the language of a theological "center." Stories have plots and patterns and even midpoints, but not centers. A narrative suggests action and movement not merely around an immovable central feature but *within* the central phenomena of the story.[3]

2. One aspect of the image of a "center" that some see as a weakness — that it suggests stability rather than development — is rather, in my reading of Paul, a strength. Although Paul is not inflexible or even 100 percent consistent, there is an overall consistency to his life and thought, even as it manifests itself differently in various situations. On this matter, the important formulation of J. Christiaan Beker is significant. Beker found in Paul a pattern of "coherence and contingency," that is, of a gospel defined by an apocalyptic interpretation of the death and resurrection of Christ reinterpreted for a variety of contingent circumstances (in *Paul the Apostle: The Triumph of God in Life and Thought* [Philadelphia: Fortress, 1980], as well as subsequent books and articles). I would, however, place more emphasis on the polyvalent experience of cruciformity as that which constitutes the coherent and contingent pattern of Paul's spirituality (and theology).

3. James D. G. Dunn's approach to Paul's theology (*The Theology of Paul the Apostle* [Grand Rapids: Eerdmans, 1998], pp. 713-37) attempts to sort out some of these concerns and balance the various elements of Paul's thought and experience. Dunn depicts Paul's theology as an ongoing dialogue, especially an interaction between two stories, the story of Israel and the story of Christ (p. 726). The former is the "stable foundation" (p. 716) of Paul's theology, while Christ is the all-embracing "focal and pivotal point" or "fulcrum" of it (pp. 722-28). Of central importance to this fulcrum are the cross and resurrection (p. 727), and especially the "process of salvation as a growing conformity to Christ, and not least to his death," a concept that "evokes a kind of mysticism" (p. 728). Dunn, in other words, is close to articulating what we have called "cruciformity."

We need, therefore, a better way to express the centrality of cruciformity to the apostle Paul.

An approach that might be more accurate and more beneficial for our understanding of Paul is to describe cruciformity as the "integrative narrative experience" of his life and thought. The word "experience," of course, is meant as a reminder that cruciformity is fundamentally about living rather than conceptualizing. The word "integrative" is intended to convey the truth that Paul's experience of conformity to the exalted crucified Messiah *defined* his entire experience and *permeated* every dimension of it. Cruciformity united what might have otherwise been unrelated or even conflicting experiences, such as wanting to die and not wanting to die, or insisting on the right to be paid for his ministry and working with his own hands so as not to be a financial burden. Thus cruciformity is not merely for Paul a "generative" conviction or experience, one that gives rise to other beliefs or experiences, but a unitive one.[4] The word "narrative" is a reminder that Paul's experience always manifests a story, one with predictable patterns but always new particulars. In brief, Paul wanted his life to tell a story — *the* story, and he wanted the lives of individual believers and believing communities to tell the same story wherever they were.

The all-pervasive character of cruciformity for Paul — the narrative experience by which he understands and interprets himself and his mission — has emerged in this book as various crucial dimensions of the apostle's experience and reflections have been treated: God, Christ, the Spirit, and the Trinity, as well as faith, love, power, and hope. One could also look at Paul's experience of cruciform wisdom, cruciform freedom, and perhaps other aspects of his "theological vocabulary" as manifested in his spiritual experience. Paul wanted his communities to have an all-embracing "cruciform mind" formed by his master story.[5]

What matters most, however, is that we stress the *omnipresence* of cruciformity in Paul's experience, or spirituality, and therefore also in his writings and "theology." *Cruciformity is the all-encompassing, integrating narrative reality of Paul's life and thought, expressed and experienced in every dimension of his being, bringing together the diverse and potentially divergent aspects of that existence.* Cruciformity is, in sum, what Paul is all about, and what the communities of the Messiah that he founded and/or nurtured were also all about.

---

4. Similarly, Dunn suggests that if we accept the notion of some "coherence" in Paul, "then Christ (the experience of Christ and the christology which is in symbiotic relationship with that experience) has to be seen as that which gave Paul's whole enterprise as theologian, missionary, and pastor its coherence" (*Theology*, p. 730)

5. The term "cruciform mind" is from Alexandra R. Brown, *The Cross and Human Transformation: Paul's Apocalyptic World in 1 Corinthians* (Minneapolis: Fortress, 1995), pp. 145, 168.

Cruciformity is, therefore, to paraphrase a Lutheran formula,[6] the experience by which the church — at least according to Paul — stands or falls.

Challenges to Cruciformity

Cruciformity is obviously a spirituality of the cross. Increasingly in recent years the cross has come under attack, first as a theological item — the centerpiece of traditional understandings of the atonement — and then, by extension, as a matter of spirituality. In fact, the theological critique of the cross has often been motivated by spiritual and pastoral concerns. Theologies of the cross/atonement that stress suffering, it has been argued, encourage others either to inflict or to accept unjust suffering. The conclusion of some, writes James F. Kay, is that "[r]esponsible preachers no longer bear the word of the cross; they must become its enemies (cf. Phil 3:18)."[7]

In a recent article, theologian William Placher reviews three criticisms of traditional understandings of the atonement, especially those that stress Christ's death as, in some sense, a substitutionary death. Placher summarizes the three criticisms of this theology as follows: it fosters human suffering by glorifying it; it posits a vindictive God; and it assumes that vicarious punishment makes moral sense.[8] More generally, the cross has been challenged (1) as Placher indicates, *in itself, that is, as a means of atonement;* (2) *in association with, and as justification for, violence;* and (3) *as an ethical and spiritual paradigm of self-sacrifice.*

Some of these challenges are old, some new. Critics of atonement by means of the cross have sometimes referred to the cross as bloody divine vengeance or even "divine child abuse."[9] The many who see the cross connected to violence rightly point out the crusades (from the Latin *crux,* "cross"), anti-Semitism, the joint colonial and missionary movements, slavery, suppression of women, the Holocaust, the hate-filled burning of crosses by the Ku Klux Klan, and too many other horrific episodes from the history of Christianity, and of the cultures and subcultures it has influenced. In these atrocities the Church's chief

---

6. Referring to justification by faith as the ultimately essential and foundational doctrine.

7. James F. Kay, "The Word of the Cross at the Turn of the Ages," *Interpretation* 53 (1999): 45.

8. William C. Placher, "Christ Takes Our Place: Rethinking the Atonement," *Interpretation* 53 (1999): 5-20.

9. For example, Joanne Carlson Brown and Rebecca Parker, "For God So Loved the World?" in Joanne Carlson Brown and Carole R. Bohn, eds., *Christianity, Patriarchy and Abuse* (New York: Pilgrim, 1989), p. 2.

brings abuse to θ & closer God

symbol has not only been a visible presence among the violent oppressors but also an explicit justification for the violence.[10] As Jürgen Moltmann wrote in his classic *The Crucified God*, the church "has much abused the theology of the cross and the mysticism [spirituality] of the passion in the interest of those who cause the suffering."[11] Partly as a result of some of these horrors, any spirituality or ethic that smacks of cross, sacrifice, or self-denial may be described as oppressive, whether of women, of African-Americans, of the poor in the southern hemisphere, and so on.

These three dimensions of the cross that are challenged (atonement, violence, self-sacrifice) are of course closely interrelated. For example, Joanne Carlson Brown and Rebecca Parker, writing angrily from their pastoral experience of being told by abused women that suffering domestic abuse brought them closer to Jesus and should be endured out of love, focus on the patriarchal abuse of atonement theology as it is expressed in violence toward women.[12] They find, however, the roots of all kinds of violence in atonement theology. Lying behind the notion of sacrificial atonement, they contend, is the assumption that some life is expendable.[13] That women should accept such violence, in "Christ-like fashion," is one possible ethical corollary of the theology.

In a similar vein, Delores S. Williams, a womanist (female liberationist of color) theologian, argues that humanity is redeemed not through Jesus' death but through his "ministerial vision of life." She cannot forget the cross, but neither can she "glorify" it, for to do so is to glorify suffering and sacralize the oppression and exploitation of African-American women.[14] Many feminist and womanist theologians have drawn the conclusion that because the doctrine of atonement and the corollary call to "take up one's cross" have been used against women, these remnants of an oppressive, patriarchal Christianity need to be abandoned.

Some African-American liberationist theologians, however, have a more nuanced attitude toward the cross, even while critical of its role in oppression.

10. For example, that "the Jews" supposedly committed deicide by crucifying Jesus was used to justify violence against Jews.

11. Jürgen Moltmann, *The Crucified God: The Cross of Christ as the Foundation and Criticism of Christian Theology*, trans. R. A. Wilson and John Bowden (New York: Harper & Row, 1974), p. 49.

12. Brown and Parker, "For God So Loved the World?" In a personal conversation (January 11, 1999), Rebecca Parker relayed to me the pastoral context and concerns — as well as the understandable anger — that motivated the article.

13. Personal conversation with Rebecca Parker, January 11, 1999.

14. Delores S. Williams, *Sisters in the Wilderness: The Challenge of Womanist God-Talk* (Maryknoll, N.Y.: Orbis, 1993), pp. 164-67.

For instance, James Cone recognizes the positive power that the cross had for black slaves, as reflected in their spirituals:

> In Jesus' death poor blacks saw themselves, and they unleashed their imagination [in spirituals]. . . . The death of Jesus meant that he died on the cross for black slaves. His death was a symbol of their suffering, their trials and tribulations in an unjust world. Because black slaves knew the significance of the pain and shame of Jesus' death on the cross, they found themselves by his side.[15]

According to Cone, Martin Luther King integrated (1) the American tradition of freedom with (2) the prophetic tradition of justice and liberation and (3) the New Testament tradition of Jesus' cross as both love and suffering. For King and those who follow in his footsteps, the suffering love of God in Jesus becomes the norm for and means to liberation from oppression. This will always involve suffering, since Jesus suffered on the cross, but of course it does not justify suffering.[16]

Looking with similar eyes but more globally, many theologians have drawn attention to the ongoing "scandal of a crucified world,"[17] a world of incredible poverty, oppression, and suffering, the causes of which are, at least in part, the result of colonial expansion in the name of the cross.

Clearly one of the most important sources of criticism of the cross has been the Holocaust, a horror of oppression and annihilation perpetrated by the Nazis, whose symbol was a perverted cross, the swastika. One of the many stories that could testify to the reasons for antipathy toward the cross is the experience of a Jewish friend who survived the Nazi takeover of Belgium. Raised in Antwerp among Catholic and Protestant children who often called her "dirty Jewess," in 1943 my friend was summoned, with her elder sister, to "go to work" for the Germans in Germany. Suspicious but clueless as to the full reality of what would happen, the teens' mother was able to delay the departure of the younger girl. When the family discovered that the elder sister had been shipped directly to Auschwitz and gassed, they split up and fled into hiding. Taken in as a "Protestant orphan" by kind Sisters at a convent and boarding school, my friend climbed into bed her first night in hiding and noticed a crucifix on the

---

15. James H. Cone, "An African-American Perspective on the Cross and Suffering," in Yacob Tesfai, ed., *The Scandal of a Crucified World: Perspectives on the Cross and Suffering* (Maryknoll, N.Y.: Orbis, 1994), p. 52.

16. Cone, "An African-American Perspective," p. 53.

17. The phrase is taken from the title of the collection of essays edited by Tesfai, *The Scandal of a Crucified World: Perspectives on the Cross and Suffering.*

wall. Angrily she yelled at the crucified Jesus, "It's all your fault that I'm in this trouble!" She pulled the crucifix off the wall and hid it under her bed.

Rabbi Leon Klenicki begins an essay in the following words:

> I see it every time I leave the synagogue. On Saturday morning after services, while going home, it is there, waiting for me, challenging me. It is the cross of a nearby church. Why does it disturb me? The sanctity of the day is marred by an image projecting memories of the past, memories transmitted by generations, my parents. They are images of contempt for my people. I am overwhelmed despite my own religious feelings of fellowship and commitment to an ongoing dialogue with Christians. The cross is there, a challenge to my own belief.[18]

Responses to these kinds of charges are varied. While some may dismiss the charges, others, as noted above, are ready to dismiss the cross. Still others attempt to "rescue" or "redeem" the cross by reinterpreting it. Neither of the first two options — dismissing the charges or the cross — is theologically defensible, in my view. Yet although reinterpretation is always needed in the Church, it must always be done very carefully.[19] It is all too easy to "throw out the baby with the bath water." In my own view, cruciformity, as experienced and articulated by Paul, does not so much need reinterpretation in the hope of redeeming it in a new and different form as it needs careful unpacking in its original context for appropriation in our own context. *In my view, then, cruciformity is not the problem; misunderstanding it is.*

Responding to the Challenges

It is beyond the scope of this book, and this writer's expertise, to deal with all of the charges noted above, as well as others that may be voiced — not to mention all the reinterpretations of the cross and cruciformity. My goal in this brief response to such criticisms is to focus on the issue of glorifying and justifying suffering and violence, arguing that Paul's spirituality of the cross does not demand what people like Parker, Brown, and Williams have found, and, in fact, that cruciformity stands staunchly against such suffering and violence.

18. Leon Klenicki, "Toward a Process of Healing: Understanding the Other as a Person of God," in Leon Klenicki, ed., *Toward a Theological Encounter: Jewish Understandings of Christianity* (Mahwah, N.J.: Paulist, 1991), p. 1.

19. For an excellent treatment ("redemption") of the meaning of the cross in light of "Christian" mistreatment of Jews, see Mary C. Boys, "The Cross: Should a Symbol Betrayed Be Reclaimed?" *Cross Currents* 44 (1994): 5-27.

1. *Paul's understanding of the cross does not focus on substitution demanded by a vindictive God but on the love and freedom of both God and Christ that liberates humans from oppressive powers.* While it is true that Paul inherits and accepts a sacrificial and even substitutionary understanding of the death of Christ, he places his own emphasis elsewhere. In particular, Paul is concerned to show that Christ's death is an act of God's love and of Christ's love, and that Christ accepted his death voluntarily — even if obediently. He was not the passive recipient of punishment but the initiator of an act of love. Placher reminds us that Christ is not a passive victim but "actively accepts suffering for the sake of transforming the world" and that Christ suffers, not as a scapegoat, but as a "volunteer in the battle against evil."[20] God's sending of Christ was not experienced by Paul fundamentally as an act of violence but as a gift of love for enemies and willful sinners who were simultaneously victims of the evil they embraced.

Paul, then, is not concerned about the details of how atonement occurs, but about the *motivation* of love behind and in the death, and about the *effects* of that act of love. It reconciles people to God as it defeats the powers of sin and death, thereby inaugurating a new age — *the* new age — in which hate and violence have no place.[21]

2. *Christ's death represents not God's justification for suffering but God's identification with those who suffer.* In the cross we know first and foremost "Deus pro nobis," God for us. In Christ we know God as the One who has not only heard

---

20. Placher, "Christ Takes Our Place," p. 16.

21. I want to make it clear that I in no way wish to *eliminate* or even *minimize* the function of the cross as God's means of atonement. My concern is to stress that Paul does not know a vindictive God but a loving one. I therefore find inadequate, and somewhat misguided, the attempt of Elisabeth Moltmann-Wendel to liberate the cross from Paul and from what she sees as the patriarchal emphasis on the forgiveness of sins rooted in him ("Is There a Feminist Theology of the Cross?" in Yacob Tesfai, ed., *The Scandal of a Crucified World: Perspectives on the Cross and Suffering* [Maryknoll, N.Y.: Orbis, 1994], pp. 87-98). With empathy for but also critique of other feminists who want to dispense with the cross, she finds "three feminist dimensions of the cross that do not reduce the cross to the principle of the forgiveness of sins and in which women can involve themselves existentially" (p. 94): the cross as solidarity in suffering, as suffering from structural sin, and as paradoxical symbol of life (pp. 95-98). Although these aspects of the cross are legitimate, and although Moltmann-Wendel claims not to completely dismiss the cross as the means of forgiveness of sins, she certainly shies away from the cross as atonement. Furthermore, ironically, she blames Paul for winning out over the Synoptic tradition and causing the patriarchal errors with his emphasis on the cross as forgiveness of sins. However, as we have seen throughout the book and will spell out more clearly in this chapter, Paul actually shares some of what Moltmann-Wendel affirms without being guilty of that for which she blames him.

the cries of suffering people and come down (Exod. 3:7-8) but also suffered as we have and more. This God does not inflict suffering on people or justify it, but *feels* their anguish, promising to be present and loving to them in the intensity of their anguish. As feminist theologian Nancy Duff writes, stressing that Christ's suffering death is a unique act of atonement:

> [T]he logic of the cross is not that we are able to become victims consistent with Christ hanging on the cross, but that Christ became a victim to release us from the powers of sin and death. The abused wife does not "represent Christ" through exemplary self-sacrificial love. She is not the incarnate God suffering on behalf of sinful humanity. Rather, Christ on the cross represents her, reveals God's presence with her, and uncovers the sin of those who abuse or neglect her. Christ makes known to her and the world that her suffering represents *the opposite* of God's will.[22]

3. *By redefining the meaning of power, the cross of Paul's gospel undermines the very power structures that make the abuse of the cross possible.* Feminist theologian Sally Purvis argues that the cross "can only be used to harm and suppress within certain shared assumptions about power," but "[p]roperly understood, the 'power of the cross' subverts its own nature as harmful and oppressive."[23] Patriarchal power, whether first-century Roman or twenty-first-century American, is built on certain foundational principles about the male self and its relation to God and others. The cross causes those foundations to crumble by displaying a naked, powerless man as the power of God. In the cross, power has become life-giving love; it is the power to be weak, the power to serve, the power not to be in power.

The cross undermines other forms of power, too, and these are not all patriarchal. The abuse of power is not limited to males on the basis of their maleness. Elitism, love of status, and the pursuit of power over others manifest themselves in all communities, even those in which women are in control. If it is possible for the oppressed to become the oppressor, it is possible even for oppressed females to become female oppressors.

The cross of Paul's gospel allows for none of this kind of power; it does not require that the power be patriarchal before it can undergo critique. What the gospel does require, no matter what form the power takes, is for power to be conformed to the cross. In every instance, this means that power structures

22. Nancy J. Duff, "Atonement and the Christian Life: Reformed Doctrine from a Feminist Perspective," *Interpretation* 53 (1999): 27.

23. Sally Purvis, *The Power of the Cross: Foundations for a Christian Feminist Ethic of Community* (Nashville: Abingdon, 1993), p. 14.

must first be destabilized and deconstructed under the shadow of the cross, so that they may be rebuilt on new foundations that are appropriate to the gospel and that are life-giving to the communities that embody them.

4. *The God who justifies by means of the cross does so to liberate people from the violence that enslaves them, not to endorse it.* We have seen throughout this book that there is no room in Paul's spirituality of the cross for violence or any other form of unloving behavior. Clearly Paul himself did not move from cross to violence, but rather from cross to nonviolence. Identifying with the cross, in fact, means that one dies to all the forms of injustice and ungodliness that characterize the old eon and the old person. Inflicting suffering on others is replaced by willingness to accept suffering — not because suffering is inherently good, but because it can be a means to the good of another.

This does not mean that people should endure violence that they can escape; the Christian faith has generally discouraged people from pursuing martyrdom. When an abused wife endures violence at the hand of her husband as an "act of love," she is unwittingly allowing her husband to betray his own commitment to love and thus to live out the evil desires of the old age and old self. Accepting this violence is not an act of suffering love but — again, unwittingly — complicity with the powers of the old age. In this, however, the woman has no blame, because her violent husband and situation have gained control and dominion of her through deception and other evils. The God revealed on the cross does not endorse the husband's violence but desires his liberation from it and, of course, the woman's protection from it.

For the God of the cross of Christ, no life is expendable; even the enemy is loved by God, who willed and wills the reconciliation of the world through the cross. Indeed, no life is expendable.

5. *Self-giving, self-sacrificial, and even suffering love is a necessary corollary to the gospel of Christ and an expression of the most profound freedom.* Paul's understanding and experience of love never led him to impose a cruciform existence on anyone, for such a life must be freely chosen. To be sure, he advocated it passionately because such was Christ's life, but he never forced it on anyone. This was because Paul believed with all his heart that voluntarily chosen cruciform love — even involving self-sacrifice and suffering — was the ultimate experience of freedom.

Furthermore, because cruciformity must be freely chosen and because it is intended to benefit others, especially the poor and weak, it can never be imposed "top-down." That is, the weak can never be forced by the powerful into relinquishing the small amount of freedom and power they possess. They, above all, must be shown cruciform love, yet they too may experience the joy and freedom of Christ by choosing, as they are able, to give themselves in love to others. Indeed, it is only in doing so that any of us, rich or poor, "strong" or "weak," fully experience the freedom for which Christ has set us free.

The abuse of the cross by some cannot become an excuse for watered-down versions of Christianity in which there is no place for suffering love. Following Christ, as Paul knew, was not an easy path. "Triumphalism" can come in many forms; it contends that the Christian life is all "victory" and "freedom" without cost, without obedience to One whose own freedom was manifested in death for others. Placher comments on the need for what we have called cruciformity in the Church today:

> I hear and understand the protests of feminist theologians and others that women and other oppressed groups have been called too often by the Christian faith to endure suffering. But as I look at our typical congregations, I think one could also make a contrary case: that we have created the kind of comfortable "Christendom" Kierkegaard decried and often do not ask enough by way of suffering.[24]

Writing more broadly about the basic pattern of Christian existence, Luke Timothy Johnson contends that

> nowhere in the New Testament [do we find] an understanding of Christian discipleship compatible with a life devoted to one's own success, pleasure, comfort, freedom from suffering, or power at the expense of others. . . . The basic pattern of faithful obedience to God and loving service to others is the image of Christ that the Spirit replicates in the freedom of those who belong to Christ.[25]

This pattern, Johnson rightly contends, is nonnegotiable for Christians. Even though openness to the Spirit makes ambiguity an inherent part of the Christian life,

> there is no ambiguity to be found in this basic pattern. . . . The imitation of Christ in his life of suffering and service — not as an act of masochism for the sake of suppressing one's own life but as an act of love for the enhancement of others' life — is not an optional version of Christian identity. It is the very *essence* of Christian identity. It is the pattern by which every other

24. Placher, "Christ Takes Our Place," p. 16.
25. Luke Timothy Johnson, *Living Jesus: Learning the Heart of the Gospel* (New York: HarperSanFrancisco, 1999), p. 200.

claim about the spiritual life must be measured if it is to be considered Christian. It is what is learned from Jesus. It is what learning Jesus means.[26]

6. *Without the cross, there is no Pauline gospel, no Christian gospel.* No matter how often or how much the cross has been misinterpreted, misused, abused, and misapplied, it stands at the heart of the Pauline and the historic Christian gospel. It is a word of life, not death; of hope, not despair; of love, not hate. As James Kay puts it,

> without a saving cross, would the Christian message still be Christian? Granting that negative consequences have resulted from church proclamation, is the criterion of consequence the only one for assessing faithfulness to Jesus Christ? Appeals to scripture, tradition, and worship show the cross as woven throughout the fabric of the faith: Paul preached a cross-resurrection kerygma; this kerygma was subsequently stretched into a passion narrative at the heart of our canonical gospels; and this narrative is ritually signified in the Christian sacraments of initiation and communion. *For these reasons, the elimination of the cross from Christian proclamation may well indicate a kind of anti-gospel of which Paul warned* (Gal 1:8-9).[27]

He continues:

> The test . . . of all our earthly God-talk is not whether it demonstrates itself in ecstatic spirituality, but whether, by passing through the cross, it proclaims God's power to extinguish in us all that prevents us from discerning and serving "the neighbor who is in need." . . .

> For this reason, *any preaching of the cross that denies our cross-won freedom to love our neighbor is to be rejected. Likewise, any taking up of the cross as an ornamental symbol or rhetorical device whereby we can further promote our own status or stature is unworthy of the gospel.* The cross is not a talisman and its word is not a mantra. Insofar as attacks on doctrines of the atonement by contemporary pastors and theologians are attacks on the *kata-sarka* ["according to the flesh"] construals of the cross, these attacks are faithful to the word of the cross. But insofar as these attacks are a call, whether in the name of the Spirit or of Easter, to bypass the cross, then they too must be rejected as belonging to the old age. The Spirit of God is the Spirit of the Crucified. Easter follows Good Friday but never replaces it.[28]

26. Johnson, *Living Jesus,* p. 201 (emphasis in the original).
27. Kay, "Word of the Cross," p. 45 (emphasis added).
28. Kay, "Word of the Cross," p. 47 (emphasis added).

This is to say, quite simply, that without the cross, there is no Christian faith.

This brief response to the criticisms, implicit or explicit, of cruciformity today has only touched on some of the most salient points at issue. Nevertheless, it should be clear that a "violent" interpretation of the cross is neither advocated by Paul nor necessary for those who understand and experience its spirituality in a Pauline fashion. Cruciformity is not dangerous to the Church, or to certain people and groups. Those who say that it is may be well-meaning, but their conclusions are at best unnecessary, and at worst more dangerous than the evils they attempt to identify.

The Challenge of Cruciformity

Having briefly considered some of the current challenges to the cross and thus to a spirituality of the cross, we may now attempt to examine some of the implications of cruciformity for our day on the assumption that most of the criticisms of the cross are either misinformed or misguided, or are directed against interpretations of the cross that themselves are misinformed, misguided, or both. I write now, then, as an advocate of Paul's cruciform spirituality, for I am persuaded, with Graham Tomlin, that "[t]he cross acts as God's signature, the mark of his action in the present," and with the late John Howard Yoder that "people who bear crosses are working with the grain of the universe."[29] Moreover, I am equally persuaded, with Susan Wood, that

> [w]omen [and men!] reject images of service and *kenosis* [self-emptying] only with great peril. Either the entire Christian community follows the model that Jesus sets for us, or we are doomed to struggle for positions of honor and elitism, domination and power. We cannot have it both ways. We serve one another or we dominate one another. There is no middle ground.[30]

In our context, where the cross has been both abused and annulled, we must hear again the words of Ernst Käsemann, who argued that "the catchword about the 'theology of the cross' loses its original meaning if used non-polemically," for it was "always a critical attack on the dominating traditional interpretation of

29. Graham Tomlin, *The Power of the Cross: Theology and the Death of Christ in Paul, Luther and Pascal* (Carlisle, U.K.: Paternoster, 1999), p. 279; John Howard Yoder, "Armaments and Eschatology," *Studies in Christian Ethics* 1 (1988): 58. On various occasions Stanley Hauerwas has cited Yoder's claim with approval.

30. Susan Wood, "Is Philippians 2:5-11 Incompatible with Feminist Concerns?" *Pro Ecclesia* 6 (1997): 183 (the article's closing paragraph).

the Christian message."[31] For us, then, cruciformity is a polemical spirituality, for it is critical of any and all traditional abuses of the cross, on the one hand, even as it is no less critical of the currently reigning attempts to eliminate the cross from Christianity, on the other.

We will begin with five general statements about cruciformity, and then proceed to reflect on cruciform faith, love, power, and hope.

1. *Cruciformity is a comprehensive and imaginative spirituality.* In this book we have seen that for Paul the cross has touched, and must touch, every dimension of his experience and understanding. There is no area of his "theology" or of his life that is not shaped by the cross. The cross required for him a complete re-arrangement of his values and priorities. Despite the consistency — and relative simplicity — in his understanding of the cross as a symbol of status-renunciation, self-giving, and so on, its incarnation in his life and in the life of his communities was anything but static.

We often prefer both to compartmentalize and to routinize our lives, not only in terms of inconsequential habits but also in terms of our spirituality. It is not uncommon for people, though perhaps not consciously or deliberately, to separate their "spiritual" or religious beliefs and practices from their behavior. It is tempting to apply our spirituality, say, to our family life but not to our job, or to our views about a topic of "personal morality" but not to our politics. Once "applied," it is easier to leave our understandings in place rather than con-stantly to rethink the shape of our life in light of our spiritual commitments.

Cruciformity does not permit any of this. It requires a constantly active and creative imagination to discern how it is to be embodied in every dimen-sion of our existence and in ever-new situations. This is no less the case for Christian communities than it is for individuals. The critical questions before us are always: *In what part of our life story is the story of the cross not being, or not being faithfully, told?* and *How can the story of the cross be told in new ways in this or that situation of our life together?*

Cruciformity is both predictable and unpredictable in its comprehensive-ness. It is predictable in that it always excludes certain options, such as ven-geance; it is unpredictable in that it is the work of the Spirit of the living Christ, whose faithful act of self-giving on the cross can never be replicated but is al-ways being reactualized. By its very nature — its inability to be repeated — the cross must always be new and different even as it is consistent with the un-

---

31. Ernst Käsemann, "The Saving Significance of the Death of Jesus in Paul," in his *Perspectives on Paul,* trans. Margaret Kohl (Philadelphia: Fortress, 1971; reprinted Mifflintown, Pa.: Sigler, 1996), p. 35; he calls the cross "the signature of the one who is risen" (p. 56).

repeatable act of the Son of God. Thus cruciformity cannot be inscribed or legislated; it cannot be codified or routinized. It can only be remembered and recited, hymned and prayed, and then lived by the power of the Spirit and the work of inspired individual and corporate imagination.

It is not accidental, in my view, that Paul's "master story" — Philippians 2:6-11 — took the form of a *hymn that said nothing explicit* about faith, love, power, or hope, and yet it defined and constantly redefined those four dimensions of Paul's spirituality. Such is the power of this story to mold our spiritual imaginations.

2. *Cruciformity is a charismatic and prophetic spirituality.* For Paul, of course, the cross stood normal religious, philosophical, socioeconomic, and political conventions on their heads. The status quo was rocked. That Paul understood himself to be a prophet like Jeremiah (Gal. 1:15-16) is appropriate, for his spirituality is indeed odd and strange. It challenges every "given," every accepted practice, and every norm, and, for that reason, it is not always welcome. It is the work of God's Spirit, who is behind and within all prophetic activity in the biblical tradition. The story of the cross is an alternative word, an alternative master story or "metanarrative."[32]

The cross, like all prophetic and charismatic acts, is a creative event; indeed, it creates a new horizon, a new world. For Paul, "[t]he world created by the cross is characterized by strange reversals; it is a world in which wisdom is characterized as folly, the least become the greatest, strength resides in weakness, and fullness of being arises from emptiness."[33] This new world is created for us, as it was for Paul's hearers, primarily by the spoken and the embodied word of the cross. The power of this divine yet Pauline word is captured by Alexandra Brown: "wielding the Word of the Cross, [Paul] invades the percep-

---

32. The term "metanarrative" has been variously defined. Walter Brueggemann (*Theology of the Old Testament: Testimony, Dispute, Advocacy* [Minneapolis: Fortress, 1997], p. 558) uses it to mean "a more-or-less coherent perspective on reality." We might call it an implicit or explicit story of how the world does and should operate, with roles outlined for various participants. Brueggemann convincingly suggests that the dominant metanarrative in the West is "military consumerism" (or "commodity militarism," p. 486), in which individuals authorize themselves, "in unfettered freedom," to seek "well-being, security, and happiness as they choose," with "force, coercion, or violence" at their (supposedly) legitimate disposal "either to secure or to maintain a disproportion" of whatever is necessary to achieve those ends (p. 718). He proposes that Israel's testimony in the Old Testament offers an alternative way of construing reality and being human, stressing holiness and neighbor love, that is not, in my view, unlike the way of cruciformity (pp. 485-86, 558-64, 719-20, passim). The biblical story is always a "'sub-version' of reality that means to subvert other, more dominant versions" (p. 126).

33. Brown, *The Cross and Human Transformation*, p. 93.

tual landscape of his hearers, cutting across their accustomed (and, he believes, false) ways of knowing with the sharp expression of a new reality."[34]

Twenty centuries later the cross has become so familiar to us, and perhaps so sanitized of its stark reality as a tool of political and social control, that we often fail to perceive the inherently radical nature of a spirituality of the cross. Our distance from the meaning of crucifixion in the first century means our connection to it is bound to be skewed. Embracing the cross requires, therefore, another act of the imagination, this time of the historical imagination.[35]

We must realize indeed that the cross was folly and weakness to anyone in the first century, and that its becoming for Paul the definition and embodiment of wisdom and power meant that all notions of wisdom, power, and everything else are now up for grabs. Every convention, every value, every virtue — they are all at risk. Scrutiny of everything becomes the order of the day.

Yet not simply for the sake of criticism. The kind of prophetic critique that cruciformity demands is motivated solely by an interest in someone's good and the ultimate good that God wills. The cross, after all, is God for us — *pro nobis*. Base motives are not acceptable. The cross examines not only the values of the status quo but also the motives of those who criticize the status quo. Pride and self-righteousness have no place in a spirituality of the cross.

Nevertheless, cruciformity requires us to have the courage to think about and perhaps even to speak about *everything* in light of the cross. It becomes the lens through which we see, perceive, and evaluate everything, especially claims about faith, love, power, and hope. Indeed, spirituality itself is cruciformity's first object of scrutiny.

3. *Cruciformity is a communal spirituality.* Much of Western Christianity, as many have lamented, is decidedly private and individualistic. We find a spirituality that is narrowly focused on "me and Jesus," and the corollary convictions that the Church is optional and that salvation is a private, "spiritual" matter.

Paul's intimate experience of co-crucifixion with Christ, who lives in him and in whom he lives, was very different from this Western privatism. Cruciformity, while personal, is not private. In the first place, it can be known and experienced only in the body of Christ, for that is the presence of the exalted Christ in the world. The Church is the place where believers dwell in Christ, and the place where they receive the same Christ who dwells within.

34. Brown, *The Cross and Human Transformation,* p. xvii.
35. For me, a recent trip to the Louvre in Paris, where a first-century sculpture of a naked, helpless, crucified man is on exhibit, reminded me vividly of the shame and foolishness of the cross in human terms.

Moreover, a cruciform existence is inevitably relational. One cannot experience the Christ-like union of faith and love without offering oneself to others, both inside and outside of the Church.

The call to cruciformity is, therefore, a call that no one can fulfill in isolation. It requires others to remind us, inspire us, encourage us, work with us, and count the cost with us. Cruciformity requires that people be able to give to and receive from one another. Finally, cruciformity requires a community in which the story of Christ crucified can be learned, nurtured, contemplated, and performed.

4. *Cruciformity is a narrative spirituality.* The characterization of cruciformity as "narrative" is, of course, fundamental to this book, as expressed in its subtitle. By narrative spirituality, as the introduction suggests, I mean a spirituality that is both grounded in a narrative and expressed as a narrative. It is an ongoing, dynamic life-story, a community's creative "nonidentical repetition" of its master story.[36] The community becomes a living exegesis of the story.

In this kind of community, "the narrative of the cross provides the dynamic to enable the 'will to love' not the 'will to power' to drive its relationships and life."[37] The story of Christ crucified is sung, preached, and reenacted, not simply in words and not merely as the means to personal salvation, but as the *modus operandi* of daily life in this world.[38]

5. *Cruciformity is a costly spirituality.* Dietrich Bonhoeffer's classic work, *The Cost of Discipleship*, is an exposition of the call of Jesus, the Sermon on the Mount, and, not surprisingly, some key texts from the Pauline writings. The book is about cruciformity, although the term itself does not appear. One of the classic lines (in the 1950s translation) from the early chapters is: "When Christ bids a man, he bids him come and die."[39] Another is: "Cheap grace is the deadly

36. The term "non-identical repetition," as noted earlier, is from philosopher John Milbank and has been popularized in biblical studies by Stephen Fowl.

37. Tomlin, *Power of the Cross*, p. 314.

38. For the importance of cruciformity for preaching, see André Resner, Jr., *Preacher and Cross: Person and Message in Theology and Rhetoric* (Grand Rapids: Eerdmans, 1999). Resner suggests, for example, regarding personal "witness" through stories in the pulpit, that "viewed from the perspective of the cross-event-proclaimed, most personal stories ought to point out the frailty and failure of the preacher even in the face of an action of God which turned the event around redemptively" (p. 179). Resner offers this suggestion in the context (pp. 168-72, passim) of contrasting ways of using *ēthos*, or personal character, rhetorically: either (1) for personal gain (*kata sarka*, according to the flesh), serving one's financial ends, or status, or political agenda, or (2) for the sake of the gospel (*kata stauron*, according to the cross).

39. Dietrich Bonhoeffer, *The Cost of Discipleship*, rev. ed., trans. R. H. Fuller (New York: Macmillan, 1959), p. 99. See the entire chapter, "Discipleship and the Cross," pp. 95-114.

enemy of our Church. We are fighting today for costly grace."[40] "Such grace," Bonhoeffer continues, "is *costly* because it calls us to follow, and it is *grace* because it calls us to follow *Jesus Christ*."[41]

Cheap grace, however, is grace "without price . . . without cost."[42] It "means the justification of sin without the justification of the sinner."[43] It is

> *the grace we bestow on ourselves.* Cheap grace is the preaching of forgiveness without requiring repentance, baptism without church discipline, Communion without confession, absolution without personal confession. Cheap grace is grace without discipleship, *grace without the cross*, grace without Jesus Christ, living and incarnate.[44]

Bonhoeffer was writing for and about his beloved Lutheran (Evangelical) church in Germany during the rise of the Nazi regime. In the following quotation, we may substitute, I would suggest, our own denomination or our own era:

> We Lutherans have gathered like eagles round the carcase of cheap grace, and there we have drunk of the poison which has killed the life of following Christ. . . . Cheap grace has turned out to be utterly merciless to our Evangelical Church. This cheap grace has been no less disastrous to our own spiritual lives. Instead of opening up the way to Christ it has closed it. . . . The word of cheap grace has been the ruin of more Christians than any commandment of works.[45]

Cruciformity is the embodiment of the costly grace of which Jesus spoke and both Paul and Bonhoeffer wrote. Only God can ever know precisely what form that discipleship should and could take in each person's life, in each church, in each moment in time. Yet the basic story each believing community and person is to tell is clear; it is a story of faith, love, power, and hope that bears a credible similarity to the story of Jesus, and that is predictably and inevitably costly.

Building on these general affirmations about cruciformity, we turn now to consider more specifically cruciform faith, love, power, and hope.

---

40. Bonhoeffer, *Cost of Discipleship*, p. 46.
41. Bonhoeffer, *Cost of Discipleship*, p. 47 (emphasis his).
42. Bonhoeffer, *Cost of Discipleship*, p. 45.
43. Bonhoeffer, *Cost of Discipleship*, p. 46.
44. Bonhoeffer, *Cost of Discipleship*, p. 47 (emphasis added).
45. Bonhoeffer, *Cost of Discipleship*, pp. 57-59.

Cruciform Faith

"Faith" is one of those religious words that is susceptible to constant redefinition and thus "watering down." It is sometimes used interchangeably with "positive thinking." As we have seen, however, the faith of which Paul spoke is well-defined, and it is certainly costly. What does such faith mean today?

1. *Cruciform faith refers to a dynamic initial and ongoing narrative posture before God.* Cruciform faith is not merely assent to certain affirmations, though it has a cognitive dimension and requires intellectual conversion. Neither is cruciform faith merely trust, though it has an emotive dimension and requires child-like confidence in a personal God. Cruciform faith is both of these and more. It is a "posture," for lack of a better word, in which the believer abandons all ultimate commitments save one, thus putting his or her complete trust in the God revealed in Christ's cross and giving him- or herself completely to the plan and mission of that same God.

As such, cruciform faith can never be "once-for-all" faith. It must both initiate the believer's faith journey as a whole and also frame it day by day. Cruciform faith finds in each new challenge an opportunity to reimagine itself and to discover new ways of both trust in and self-giving to God.

2. *Cruciform faith means obedience.* In many circles, faith is "in," while obedience is "out." "Obedience" is a nasty word in such quarters, associated (interestingly) with blind, unquestioning faith and with a bygone era in which authority or "legalism" was the dominant mode of Christian piety. Yet obedience is just another word for cruciform faith. Cruciform faith means obedience à la Christ; it means a life story that is unflinchingly oriented toward God in a way somehow similar to the way in which Christ was totally focused on God and God's will, even to the point of having to die for that commitment.

When faith is "in" but obedience "out," the God whom believers worship is transformed into a foreign deity whose primary goal is to satisfy the needs of individuals rather than to transform the world. The chief activity of this God is not to create a distinctive people characterized as "holy" (obedient, conformed) and sent out to announce a different kind of lord and empire, but to bless with happiness and success a people who can easily meld their gods and lords together with any and all — including the Christian god — who will send good fortune their way. Cruciform faith, however, knows that the God from whom all blessings flow is also the God to whom all allegiance is owed.[46]

46. For a defense of obedience as a theological category and a spiritual discipline, within a

3. *Cruciform faith expresses itself in cruciform love.* Perhaps the cruelest form of spirituality, Christian or otherwise, is the kind that claims to know, love, or serve God but neglects — or even hates — the neighbor. Cruciform faith does not allow — cannot even imagine — the separation of faith toward God and love toward neighbor. Indeed, because Christ's act for the redemption of the world was simultaneously an act of both faith and love, henceforth all legitimate spiritual deeds must express both faith and love. No good deed is truly an act of love without being an expression of faith, while no claim to faith is credible or verifiable apart from an act of Christ-like love for another.

It is truly a shame, if not a crime, that the relationship between faith and love (or, more generally, "good works") has preoccupied the Church for so long. Fortunately, the 1999 *Joint Declaration on the Doctrine of Justification,* signed by Roman Catholics and Lutherans, rightly affirms both the priority of grace and the inseparability of faith and love. Luther already knew this a half-millennium ago. In his "Preface to the Epistle of St. Paul to the Romans," Luther writes about the connection between what we have called cruciform faith and cruciform love:

> Faith . . . is something God effects in us. It changes us and we are reborn from God. . . . Faith puts the old Adam to death and makes us quite different men in heart, in mind, and in all our powers. . . . O, when it comes to faith, what a living, creative, active, powerful thing it is. It cannot do other than good at all times. . . . That is what the Holy Spirit effects through faith. Hence, the man of faith, without being driven, willingly and gladly seeks to do good to everyone, serve everyone, suffer all kinds of hardships, for the sake of the love and glory of the God who has shown such grace. It is impossible, indeed, to separate works from faith, just as it is impossible to separate heat and light from fire.[47]

---

covenantal framework, over against "a Christian tradition tempted to antinomianism" and "a modern tradition tempted by an illusion of autonomous freedom," see Brueggemann, *Theology,* pp. 198-201, passim (quotations from p. 200), as well as his *The Covenanted Self: Explorations in Law and Covenant,* ed. Patrick D. Miller (Minneapolis: Fortress, 1999) and other writings.

47. Martin Luther, "Preface to the Epistle of St. Paul to the Romans," in John Dillenberger, ed., *Martin Luther: Selections from His Writings* (Garden City, N.Y.: Doubleday, 1961), pp. 23-34. The cruciform character of Luther's understanding of both faith ("puts the old Adam to death") and love ("seeks to do good . . . serve . . . suffer all kinds of hardships") is evident.

Cruciform Love

If cruciform faith always expresses itself in cruciform love, what does such love look like? We may identify several key characteristics.

1. *Cruciform love is others-centered and community-driven.* Much of Western culture for many years has been infected with two related, deadly social diseases, which together breed all kinds of destruction: individualism and self-centeredness. The former says that the "I" is the all-important social entity, while the latter specifies this "I" — me — as the most important of the all-important individuals.

Cruciform love takes its cue from the cross; Christ's death was the ultimate act of selflessness that focused not only on others as individuals ("Christ died for me") but on others as corporate bodies, as communities in need of reconciliation and harmony ("God was in Christ reconciling the world to himself"). Cruciform love resists the temptation to make myself the focus of everything, even of my spirituality. Cruciform love refuses to exercise rights, powers, privileges, spiritual gifts, and so forth, if their use will do me good but someone else, or a community of which I am a part, harm. It liberates me from myself and for the other.

2. *Cruciform love is enduring.* Sadly, ours is a culture of short-lived loves: husbands and wives who come and go; parents, employees, and professional athletes who renege on commitments; governments that fail to fulfill promises of greater justice. Often victims of the drive to satisfy the self above all, the practitioners of ephemeral love can even sometimes (often?) justify their behavior in "spiritual" language: "it makes me happier"; "I am at peace about it"; "God would not want anyone to put up with that situation"; and so on.

Cruciform love, however, is "in it for the long haul." It is not surprised by difficulty or even rejection but finds joy in the challenge of lasting through difficult circumstances. For this reason it is tied inextricably not only to faith but also to hope. Cruciform love knows that the normal response to love is sometimes just as likely to be indifference or opposition as it is acceptance. Yet it endures. It is modeled not on the uncertainties of soap-opera romance but on the stability of covenant love, like Hosea's love for his unfaithful wife Gomer and God's love for us while we were yet sinners.

3. *Cruciform love motivates people with status, privilege, power, and/or money to be downwardly mobile.* Every culture defines for itself its "status indicators" — its marks of success that bestow respect and privilege on those who possess the status indicators.

Despite the fact that few of the members of Paul's communities were wealthy and powerful, or possessed other status indicators in significant measure, a substantial amount of his instruction in cruciform love focuses on the responsibility of such people to others. The fundamental word to them is not merely to be others-centered or community-minded, but to do so in a way that relinquishes or redistributes their status, privilege, power, wealth, and so on. In a word, they are to become "downwardly mobile," to move not up but down the social ladder.

Cruciform love does not motivate people to make decisions or take action based on how the decision or action will impress those of like or higher socio-economic status. Rather, it motivates people to decide and to act on the basis of the needs of others with less socioeconomic status. This is not a form of arrogant, self-conscious condescension or *noblesse oblige*, but a fundamental abandonment of the privileges of power. Like Christ, the one in a place of honor must recognize that insisting on maintaining that place and its privileges will inevitably mean that others will be negatively affected. Cruciform love persistently and imaginatively asks two questions: first, How might the exercise of my privileges or rights be harming others? and second, How might I reconfigure or even renounce the spiritual and material benefits of my status for the good of others?

This does not mean, for example, that Christians of means will become homeless. Equality of some sort was Paul's goal, and it has much to commend to us.[48] What it does mean, however, is that no Christian of means (or power or other status) has the right to retain that which may harm, or benefit, another. Cruciform love puts whatever we have at the disposal of God and others.

Thus, while cruciform love is especially demanding for those of means, it excludes no one in its call to abandon privilege. Power and privilege are relative social commodities, and even the most downtrodden individual or community has something to offer, some blessing to share, that could be easily hoarded. The gift of the self to others is invaluable, no matter how materially poor or socially insignificant that self may be. The gift of self always involves the loss of something, with the promise of gaining much more in return.

4. *Cruciform love attends to people's emotional and physical needs as well as their spiritual needs.* If God's act in Christ for the redemption of the world was simultaneously an act of faith and love that sought (and seeks) to elicit a response of faith and love, it suggests that the fundamental human needs for faith and love are inseparable. Human beings need to experience, and to share, an intimate relationship with God and intimate relationships with others. Cruci-

---

48. 2 Cor. 8:14; Greek *isotēs*; NRSV, "fair balance."

form love attempts to be part of the process that makes such relationships possible and real.

Cruciform love also recognizes that people are whole, unified beings consisting of "body and soul," whose physical reality and needs cannot be neglected. One of Paul's most poignant appeals to the cross is his call to the Corinthians to give of themselves and their earthly possessions as Christ became poor for us. In contemporary idiom, we might say that evangelism, pastoral care, holistic health, and spiritual direction must go hand in hand with deeds of compassion and justice. For wealthy Christians and churches, that will involve voluntary redistribution of some of their wealth, in addition to other creative means of sharing their blessings with others in order to move ever so slightly toward the Pauline goal of equality among the saints.

Saying that the spiritual and material needs of people must both be met is easy, self-evident to most, and by now almost a cliché. The difficulty is converting it from cliché to concrete practice. Yet cruciform love would have it no other way.

5. *Cruciform love is inclusive.* Cruciform love, continuing the story of God's love in Christ for all the world, includes all: believer and nonbeliever, Gentile and Jew, woman and man, friend and enemy. It is a love characterized not by "exclusion" but by "embrace."[49]

This does not mean, however, that it is love without direction. Inclusive, cruciform love requires imaginative discernment so that a person's (or people's) needs may be known (as much as possible) and then addressed. A wayward teenage daughter, a terminally ill grandfather of ninety years, and the marginalized ethnic poor in a particular urban neighborhood all need cruciform love, but hardly the same concrete manifestation of it. As it was for Paul, so it is for us: our consistency is, in part, in our adaptability. How can we make the self-giving, others-centered, nonretaliatory love of Christ known here and now? Such a daring question is best asked, and answered, in the first-person plural, that is, in community. Cruciform love, like the Ten Commandments, is difficult to embody alone.[50]

49. See Miroslav Volf, *Exclusion and Embrace: A Theological Exploration of Identity, Otherness, and Reconciliation* (Nashville: Abingdon, 1996). This emphasis on inclusion is not meant to suggest that there are no grounds for exclusion from the believing, Christian community, for there were for Paul and must still be for us. My point is rather that cruciform love is first of all inclusive, not exclusive.

50. See Stanley M. Hauerwas and William H. Willimon, *The Truth About God: The Ten Commandments in Christian Life* (Nashville: Abingdon, 1999), p. 19: "Apart from this community [the Church], the commands of God appear heroic, impossible, idealistic, or just odd. Church,

6. *Cruciform love liberates people from violence and vengeance.* It takes very little experience of the world to resonate with Pope John Paul II's characterization of our civilization as a "culture of death."[51] There are the rumors and realities of wars with their peculiar modern corollaries like "ethnic cleansing" and economic sanctions that starve children to death. There are the increasing numbers of killing sprees in office buildings and even schools, of cases of domestic violence and sexual abuse, and of every imaginable and unimaginable sort of violence and revenge. There appears to be little decline in the number of abortions, growing acceptance of euthanasia, and, in some circles, a kind of glee at the use of the death penalty. The list could go on and on.

It is true that many acts of violence and vengeance are instigated or defended on religious grounds, often Christian grounds. Supposedly Christian pilots pray for the success of their bombing campaigns. Supposedly Christian husbands defend their use of emotional or physical force to control their wives or children as the head of the household. Supposedly Christian theologians, pastors, and lay people defend — even quoting the Bible — abortion, physician-assisted suicide, the death penalty, the right to have a hand gun and use it in self-defense, and weapons of mass destruction.

Cruciformity, the spirituality of the cross, sanctions none of this. Rather, it liberates people from the need and the desire for violence and vengeance. It recognizes, as we have said before, that no life is expendable.

The story of the cross that we receive from Paul is first of all a story of how God treats enemies. Those who have come to know the love of God in Christ have experienced the love of One who has responded to enemies, not with vengeance or violence, but with unmerited love. To have faith in this God is thus to be embraced by such love; to pass such love on to others is the only proof of having received it. The story of God's love in Christ is continued in a new "incarnation."

As we noted earlier, some today would wish to deemphasize the cross in part to curb Christians' use and defense of violence. What is really needed, however, is just the opposite: more emphasis on the cross, specifically on the cross as God's manifestation of nonretaliatory, self-giving love. Only then will the contemporary Church become what the Pauline church was, a "sphere of interrupted violence in the midst of a violent world."[52]

---

a community of the forgiven, a people who keep coming together to worship God, makes the commandments intelligible. In fact we might put on the Decalogue a warning: *Don't try to obey any of these commandments alone.*"

51. The term was made popular by Pope John Paul II in his encyclical *The Gospel of Life* [*Evangelium Vitae*] (New York: Random House, 1995), para. 28 (pp. 50-51).

52. Klaus Wengst, *Pax Romana and the Peace of Jesus Christ*, trans. John Bowden (Philadelphia: Fortress, 1987), p. 88.

One further point must be made. There can be no lasting spirituality of nonviolence as a way of life without the realization that all of us are capable of violence. As theologian Karl Barth wrote, there is in each of us a caged wolf waiting to spring out and attack at the first opportunity, at the first moment the cage is opened ever so slightly.[53] We cannot realize in full the nonviolent love of God for us as enemies until we admit that we ourselves are at enmity with God, and that in part because we have the capacity, and even occasionally the desire, for violence and vengeance. Not to admit this, on the one hand, is folly, and even spiritual death. To admit it, on the other hand, is to open ourselves first to receive, and then to relive, this love of God known in the death of Christ for us.

7. *Cruciform love seeks mercy and justice for "crucified people."* One of the most significant theological developments of the last generation has been the rise of theological perspectives that fuse Christian faith and the pursuit of justice for the oppressed. Cruciformity is a spirituality that demands such a fusion, for it understands love and faith as inextricably intertwined, and it perceives that much of the world is founded on forms of power that, by oppressing the poor, oppose the character of God revealed in the gospel.

In a provocative book, Latin American theologian Jon Sobrino writes about *The Principle of Mercy: Taking the Crucified People from the Cross.* In this collection of his essays, Sobrino contends that "the sign of the times, . . . par excellence, is 'the existence of a crucified people'" and that the primary human and Christian duty is that we "take them down from the cross," that "the crucified peoples be shown mercy."[54] Sobrino calls the Church and the world to "awaken from the sleep of inhumanity" and to face both the reality that "this world is one gigantic cross for millions of innocent people" and the truth that somehow we are in part responsible.[55] For Sobrino,

> [t]he cross on which God is placed is the most eloquent proclamation that God loves the victimized of this world. On that cross, God's love is impotent

53. Karl Barth, *Church Dogmatics* III/4, trans. A. T. Mackay et al. (Edinburgh: T. & T. Clark, 1961), p. 413. I am grateful to Professor Daniel Migliore of Princeton Theological Seminary for helping me locate this reference.

54. Jon Sobrino, *The Principle of Mercy: Taking the Crucified People from the Cross* (Maryknoll, N.Y.: Orbis, 1994), p. vii. The phrase in quotations within Sobrino's quote is taken from a Salvadoran priest-martyr, Fr. Ignacio Ellacuría. For Sobrino, the crucified peoples of the world are Yahweh's suffering servant today, "the actualization of Christ crucified" (p. 51; see the chapter, "The Crucified Peoples: Yahweh's Suffering Servant Today," pp. 49-57).

55. See Sobrino, "Introduction: Awakening from the Sleep of Inhumanity," in *Principle of Mercy,* pp. 1-11, esp. pp. 4-5 (first published in *The Christian Century,* April 1992).

yet believable. And it is from that perspective that the mystery of God must be reformulated.[56]

Into a world of crucified peoples, the Church is sent as an instrument of mercy and love, which means working for justice, which is "the name love acquires when it comes to entire majorities of people unjustly oppressed."[57] The Church may debate how this principle of mercy — cruciform mercy — is to take shape as a living exegesis of the cross, and it may debate what name to give this form of spirituality ("liberationist" or simply "cruciform"), but it cannot debate its appropriateness, its necessity, for those who identify with the crucified one.[58]

Cruciform Power

Power is one of those words and realities, it seems, to which people are either drawn or which they studiously avoid. It is enigmatic and mysterious. For Christians, it must be rightly understood and used. Cruciform power is by nature paradoxical.

1. *Cruciform power is measured not by human or worldly standards but by the standards of the gospel of Christ crucified and resurrected.* If power may be defined as the ability to exercise influence and even control over people and events, then its moral status may appear at first to be neutral. That Christians associate power with the cross — with powerlessness and defeat rather than domination and victory — means, however, that power as it is normally understood and experienced must be approached with great suspicion.

The cross does not deny the possibility that power can be good, but it does stress that power as it is commonly exercised is often evil, and it completely reverses the criteria for what good, or true, power is. True power is not "imperial" in nature; it is not the ability to influence or control people against their will with the possibility or threat of enforcing one's will should others not comply.

---

56. Sobrino, *Principle of Mercy,* p. 9.

57. Sobrino, *Principle of Mercy,* p. 10.

58. For a moving narrative account of a Christian community that embodied cruciform love for both enemies and the crucified people (in this case Jews in France in the 1940s), see Philip Hallie, *Lest Innocent Blood Be Shed: The Story of the Village of Le Chambon and How Goodness Happened There* (New York: Harper, 1979, 1994). This small Huguenot village, under the leadership of its pacifist pastors, hid and thereby rescued thousands of Jews from the Gestapo and Vichy police. A documentary made by one of the survivors, *Weapons of the Spirit,* tells the story on film.

True power is cruciform, exercised only to serve the needs and good of others. We may examine each of these, the positive and the negative, a bit more closely.

2. *Cruciform power is not imperial power; it is not domineering or violent.* Paul seems to have known or otherwise intuited the gospel tradition's word from Jesus that the "the kings of the Gentiles lord it over [others] . . . but not so with you" (Luke 22:25-26), for the story of the Son of Man is not about "lording it over" people but about being their servant. The gospel of Christ crucified above all opposes power that makes use of domination, including the threat or reality of violence. In any form whatsoever, such "power" is contrary to the gospel of Christ crucified.

The cross, an instrument of Roman political control and lethal punishment, was the symbol of Roman power in its ability to inflict suffering and death. For Christians, however, the cross is the symbol of power because it is where Christ *endured* suffering and death rather than inflicting it. The cross of Christ therefore judges all Roman cross-like forms of power and begins a new age of power modeled on his cross.

It is sad but obviously true that Christians have too often been prone to bear the imperial cross rather than Christ's. Throughout history, people who bore the name of Christ have betrayed their Lord's cross by using it, implicitly or explicitly, to justify their own or their government's violence. There are no misreadings of the gospel that have produced worse individual or community life stories than those that find a basis for violence in the cross. For this the Church has, sometimes and in some places, repented. I suspect, however, that careful self-examination would lead to more repentance and greater conversion. As Graham Tomlin notes, the Church must take "with the utmost seriousness" a vision of power informed by the cross:

> The theology of the cross insists that whatever power or authority is exercised over others, whether recognised or not, is power *for* others, rather than power *over* others.[59]

With respect to the power of violence, the Church has had, and unfortunately continues to have, at best a mixed record. Our inconsistency — so-called liberals opposing nuclear armament and the death penalty but supporting the "right" to abortion, so-called conservatives opposing abortion but supporting every other form of state-sanctioned violence and the "right" of private citizens to bear and use arms — is as damaging to our public witness as any other form of disunity (see John 17).

59. Tomlin, *Power of the Cross,* p. 313 (emphasis added).

3. Cruciform power, therefore, requires disarmament. In a discussion of turning power relations into a "covenantal fabric of neighborliness" as the means to peace, Walter Brueggemann reflects on theologian Raimon Pannikar's claim that the human race and the Church need not only military but also cultural disarmament.[60] This is a kind of disarmament of the spirit, and Brueggemann finds its paradigmatic mandate in the cross and in Paul's master story. The cross, he provocatively suggests, is the "ultimate disarmament," because Christ did not "take equality with God a thing to be grasped, but emptied himself." Baptism, therefore, is "our decision to live and risk in the name of the Crucified who is utterly disarmed."[61]

Space does not permit a full treatment of the implications of Paul's master story for disarmament on the part of individual Christians as well as churches. I have already briefly indicated, in the discussion of love, the necessity of non-violence for the Church that would be cruciform. It is a fact of Christian experience, both past and present, however, that the Church has too easily embraced and married the various seductive forms of armament our world has created. As I have argued elsewhere, the marriage of the Church and the military, for example, needs finally to end in divorce.[62] Cruciform power and military power are mutually exclusive. Even when all believers and the Church as a whole forsake military violence forever, the violence of the human heart will persist. The only solution to this reality is ongoing cruciform conversion, a constant turning to the cross, to the powerful master story of the powerlessness of the Crucified.

4. Cruciform power is influence at work for the good of others and is therefore an act of love. If true power is cruciform, exercised for the good of others, and if power is truly servanthood, then the exercise of true power is an act of love. To put it the other way around — and perhaps more appropriately — an act of love is an exercise of power:

> The deepest forms of transformation take place not through force, but through love, the surrender of power and privilege; not in a negation of Life, as Nietzsche feared, but in a radical affirmation of the life of another.[63]

---

60. Brueggemann, *Covenanted Self,* p. 80.

61. Brueggemann, *Covenanted Self,* p. 89.

62. Michael J. Gorman, "Irreconcilable Differences: The Church Should Divorce the Military," *Christianity Today,* March 6, 2000, pp. 77-78.

63. Tomlin, *Power of the Cross,* p. 314. See his critique of Nietzsche's fear that because of the cross Christianity is a passive "No to Life" (pp. 303-7).

The fundamental problem with wealth, status, and power for Paul is that they are all "goods" desired and used by human beings in order to further their own interests. The appropriate way to handle these goods is either to abandon them or to transform them into goods for others. Otherwise they embody the antithesis of the gospel and create a personal or communal life story that is not faithful to the cross, and with which God, according to Paul, does not identify. Like cruciform love, cruciform power is expressed by moving down, not up. It is the "downward moving power of the cross."[64]

5. *Cruciform power is available to all believers, even — indeed especially — to the weak, for cruciform power is power in weakness.* Perhaps even more remarkable than the redefinition of power brought about by the cross is the effect that has in daily life. For it means now that power is experienced in and as "weakness" and is therefore available to all who identify with the cross, especially to the weak.

This has three paradoxical consequences: (1) the experience of power is no longer limited to the powerful; (2) "normal" experiences of power prove to be something else; and (3) experiences of weakness can be, in fact, experiences of God's power.

This is indeed a strange sort of power.

Cruciform Hope

The final dimension of cruciformity we have been considering is hope. It, like faith, love, and power, is reconfigured by the cross.

1. *Cruciform hope is confident in the triumph of God because of God's victory, not only on the cross but also in the resurrection.* Cruciformity, including cruciform hope, is founded on God's defeat of the hostile powers that dominate human life — especially sin and death — in the cross and resurrection of Christ. Although Paul was drawn to the cross as the center of his life, he was so moved only because he was certain of Christ's resurrection as the guarantee of his. So, too, we can place the cross at the center only if we are sure that Christ's resurrection is also ours. Otherwise, "let us eat, drink, and be merry, for tomorrow we die" (see 1 Cor. 15:32).

Hope — like faith — is not confidence in *spite* of the facts but confidence in *light* of the facts. The resurrection of Christ is the certain victory that allows

---

64. Brown, *The Cross and Human Transformation*, p. 137.

believers to endure the momentary afflictions of this life — whether for the sake of the gospel or because life brings suffering — and to endure the pain and suffering of others and of the creation.

2. *Nevertheless, cruciform hope is not triumphalist but expects and accepts suffering for the gospel, thereby relativizing all spiritual experience and ecstasy.* In Christ, then, there is certainty about the future. This does not, however, translate into a sense of complete victory *now.* Those who experience the deep purpose in living or the ecstasy in worship that Christ gives to individuals and communities cannot pretend that their spiritual experiences, no matter how enriching and enlivening, preclude suffering or substitute for God's future.

In fact, those who overemphasize the ecstasy of life in Christ will be in for great disappointment. Christians must always bear in mind that, without the cross, Christ had no glory. So too, despite our desires to the contrary, suffering of one sort or another must and will precede our glory.

3. *Cruciform hope relates all suffering to the death of Christ and to the "groaning" of the entire creation, thus making it possible to experience the presence of God in the midst of the suffering.* The Bible is not always clear or consistent on the sources of human pain and suffering. What Paul stresses, however, is that those who adhere to the pattern of Christ will suffer — probably unjustly — and that all of us will also experience the normal sufferings of human life.

The former, for Paul, reveals not the absence of God but the presence of God, who brings hope as the One who raises the dead, who brings life out of death. The latter, it seems, must be placed in the larger context of God's overall plan for creation. In that plan, suffering is still painful and horrible, but it is not the final word. Christians do not deny their pain and suffering but know that they are not the first to suffer. They look, not to the impossible avoidance of suffering, but to the promise of the redemption of all creation in the future and to the mysterious presence of God — the God who is *pro nobis* in Christ — in the present.

4. *Cruciform hope is inclusive of the human body and the entire creation.* American Christians (and perhaps others, too) generally have a very noncorporeal, individualistic belief in the resurrection. Many people really affirm the immortality of the soul, not the resurrection of the dead, or of the body, in spite of Paul's argument in 1 Corinthians 15 and the clear affirmations in the historic Christian creeds.[65]

65. The common remarks heard at funeral homes — such as, "That's just her body; her

Recent Christian theology and spirituality, however, have rightly stressed the biblical experience of being human as *embodiment*. There is no human person without a body, not now, and not in the future. We are embodied by nature, and our bodies are the place in which our relationship with God and with others takes place, both now and in God's future.

This leads us also to American individualism. Overly concerned with the "salvation of the soul" and with "going to heaven," American Christians have forgotten the prophetic and Pauline emphasis on the renewal of creation as the hope of the Christian Church. It is the entire creation, not merely the individual or even the Church, that is the long-term concern of God in Christ. The promise of the gospel is not the immortality of disembodied spirits in some ethereal heaven. It is, rather, participation in the resurrection and transformation of all the dead, which in turn is part of a greater transformation of the universe from a place of suffering and want to a place of joy and abundance.

American Christians need, therefore, to broaden their horizons and reappropriate the concreteness and breadth of cruciform hope. Otherwise, they risk joining the Corinthians in denying the future, bodily resurrection and therefore finding their life's joy only in the private spiritual experiences of the present and in the hope of going to heaven as an invisible soul to continue their private affair with God. Nothing could be further from the hope of the apostle.

5. *Cruciform hope leads to joy in all circumstances.* One of the most remarkable features of Paul's life was his experience of joy in the midst of very difficult circumstances. The letter to the Philippians, for instance, is often noted for its vocabulary of joy, despite the fact that Paul wrote it as a prisoner. Paul's experience of cruciformity was hardly moribund; neither was it gleeful. Rather, it was soberly joyful, the result of confidence in the future that allowed the present — even when painful — to provide deep satisfaction and contentment.

Those who live as heirs to Paul and practice cruciformity today can know similar joy. Joy is not found by seeking it; joy is the byproduct of a life that knows that self-giving, even suffering love, is the most fulfilling type of existence because it possesses the character of the master story.

---

soul is with the Lord" — may betray a pre-Christian belief in the insignificance of the body. However, others display an unhealthy concern for the appearance of the body itself, which is in fact a corpse and which will in fact be transformed in ways that are beyond our imagination. The tension between continuity and discontinuity, both theologically and emotionally, is admittedly a difficult one.

Conclusion: The Impossible Possibility

In the introduction to this book, the term "narrative spirituality" was defined as a spirituality that tells a story, a dynamic life with God that corresponds in some way to the divine "story." Throughout the ensuing chapters, we have seen that Paul wanted his life and ministry to tell a story, a story that corresponded to the master story of Christ's self-emptying, self-giving faith, love, power, and hope. That master story provided patterns for life that created constant occasions for a wide variety of analogous acts of faith, love, power, and hope. The apostle's mission was to approximate a faithful retelling, in his life, of that story, and to create a series of communities that, together and individually, would be a living exegesis of the same story. Paul's cruciform mission continues today.[66]

Cruciformity, then, is Paul's spirituality, and it can be ours. It unites love and faith, reinterprets power in terms of love, and makes hope conditioned upon a faithful, cruciform life, even while maintaining that justification is a gift of God's grace. Cruciformity summons people to adopt a posture before God of radical self-offering (faith), to become a sort of Christ for others (love), to accept weakness as strength (power), and to yearn confidently for their own bodily resurrection and for the transformation of the entire creation (hope).

Such a comprehensive, counter-intuitive summons seems impossible to fulfill, and it would be — no, it is — on a person's or community's own strength. Cruciformity misunderstood as the human imitation of Christ is indeed an impossibility. However, cruciformity is the initial and ongoing work of Christ himself — by his Spirit sent by God — who dwells within each believer and believing community, shaping them to carry on the story (Phil. 4:13). The possibility — the only possibility — of cruciformity lies in that reality, that experience. Cruciformity is, in every sense, the impossible possibility.[67]

Nevertheless, of course, the cruciform Church will fail, and each of us who aspire to cruciformity will also fail — again and again. Even here, however, the cross is the answer. When we fail, we return to the cross, the symbol and means of forgiveness and reconciliation. There we find revealed the faithful God, who does not abandon or reject us, but "whose property is always to have mercy."[68]

66. Similarly, Luke Johnson concludes his book *Living Jesus* (p. 203) reflecting on the prayer of all Christians, who are called to be "saints," that "we might become living texts speaking Jesus in the world."

67. In his book *Paul the Apostle,* Beker uses the term "impossible possibility" to refer to sin on the part of those who have died with Christ and thus also to sin. My usage of the term is obviously different.

68. This beautiful phrase is from the communion prayer of the 1549 *Edwardian Prayer*

The debate about the center of Paul's theology rages on in academic circles. There is no doubt, however, about the integrating, narrative experience of his life, his spirituality. For Paul experienced nothing but the exalted, living *crucified* Christ. Whether by intention, by accident, or by grace, Paul *was* his gospel, his story; and his legacy is to call the Church in every age, especially this age, also to be a community of the cross whose cruciform life lovingly challenges every status quo by bearing witness to an alternative Lord — the true Lord — whose story of faith, love, power, and hope transforms the world.

Book and is still preserved in a few liturgies, including one of the communion liturgies that appears in the hymnal of my own United Methodist denomination.

BIBLIOGRAPHY

Achtemeier, Paul J. "The Continuing Quest for Coherence in St. Paul: An Experiment in Thought." Pp. 132-45 in Eugene H. Lovering and Jerry L. Sumney, eds., *Theology and Ethics in Paul and His Interpreters.* Nashville: Abingdon, 1996.

———. *Romans.* Interpretation. Atlanta: John Knox, 1985.

Ashton, John. *The Religion of Paul the Apostle.* New Haven and London: Yale University Press, 2000.

Bainton, Roland H. *Here I Stand: A Life of Martin Luther.* New York: New American Library, 1950.

Baird, William. "Visions, Revelation, and Ministry: Reflections on 2 Cor 12:1-5 and Gal 1:11-17." *Journal of Biblical Literature* 104 (1985): 651-62.

Banks, Robert. *Paul's Idea of Community: The Early House Churches in Their Historical Setting.* 2nd ed. Peabody, Mass.: Hendrickson, 1994.

Barclay, John M. G. "Conflict in Thessalonica." *Catholic Biblical Quarterly* 55 (1993): 512-30.

———. *Obeying the Truth: Paul's Ethics in Galatians.* Minneapolis: Fortress, 1991.

Barré, Michael L. "Qumran and the Weakness of Paul." *Catholic Biblical Quarterly* 42 (1980): 216-27.

Bartchy, S. Scott. "Undermining Ancient Patriarchy: The Apostle Paul's Vision of a Society of Siblings." *Biblical Theology Bulletin* 29 (1999): 68-78.

Barth, Karl. *Church Dogmatics.* Vol. III/4. Trans. A. T. Mackay et al. Edinburgh: T. & T. Clark, 1961.

Bassler, Jouette. *Divine Impartiality: Paul and a Theological Axiom.* SBLDS 59. Chico, Calif.: Scholars Press, 1982.

Bauckham, Richard. *God Crucified: Monotheism and Christology in the New Testament.* Grand Rapids: Eerdmans, 1998.

———. "The Worship of Jesus in Philippians 2:9-11." Pp. 128-39 in Ralph P. Martin and Brian J. Dodd, eds., *Where Christology Began: Essays on Philippians 2.* Louisville: Westminster/John Knox, 1998.

Becker, Jürgen. *Paul: Apostle to the Gentiles.* Trans. O. C. Dean, Jr. Louisville: Westminster/John Knox, 1993.

Beker, J. Christiaan. *Paul the Apostle: The Triumph of God in Life and Thought.* Philadelphia: Fortress, 1980.

Betz, Hans Dieter. *Galatians.* Hermeneia. Philadelphia: Fortress, 1979.

————. *2 Corinthians 8 and 9.* Hermeneia. Philadelphia: Fortress, 1985.

Black, David Alan. "Paul and Christian Unity: A Formal Analysis of Philippians 2:1-4." *Journal of the Evangelical Theological Society* 28 (1985): 299-304.

Bloomquist, F. Gregory. *The Function of Suffering in Philippians.* JSNTSup 78. Sheffield: JSOT Press, 1993.

Bockmuehl, Markus. *The Epistle to the Philippians.* Black's New Testament Commentaries. London: A. & C. Black, 1997.

Bonhoeffer, Dietrich. *The Cost of Discipleship.* Rev. ed. Trans. R. H. Fuller. New York: Macmillan, 1959.

Boys, Mary C. "The Cross: Should a Symbol Betrayed Be Reclaimed?" *Cross Currents* 44 (1994): 5-27.

Brown, Alexandra R. *The Cross and Human Transformation: Paul's Apocalyptic World in 1 Corinthians.* Minneapolis: Fortress, 1995.

Brown, Joanne Carlson, and Carole R. Bohn, eds., *Christianity, Patriarchy and Abuse.* New York: Pilgrim, 1989.

Brown, Joanne Carlson, and Rebecca Parker. "For God So Loved the World?" Pp. 1-30 in Joanne Carlson Brown and Carole R. Bohn, eds. *Christianity, Patriarchy and Abuse.* New York: Pilgrim, 1989.

Brown, Raymond E. *An Introduction to the New Testament.* New York: Doubleday, 1997.

Bruce, F. F. *1 & 2 Thessalonians.* Word Biblical Commentary 45. Waco, Tex.: Word, 1982.

Brueggemann, Walter. *The Covenanted Self: Explorations in Law and Covenant.* Ed. Patrick D. Miller. Minneapolis: Fortress, 1999.

————. *Theology of the Old Testament: Testimony, Dispute, Advocacy.* Minneapolis: Fortress, 1997.

Bultmann, Rudolf. *Theology of the New Testament.* 2 vols. Trans. Kendrick Grobel. New York: Charles Scribner's Sons, 1951, 1955.

Byrne, Brendan. *Romans.* Sacra Pagina. Collegeville, Minn.: Liturgical, 1996.

Caird, G. B. *New Testament Theology.* Completed and edited by L. D. Hurst. Oxford: Clarendon Press, 1994.

————. *Paul's Letters from Prison in the Revised Standard Version.* NCB. Oxford: Oxford University Press, 1976.

Carroll, John T., and Joel B. Green. "'Nothing but Christ and Him Crucified': Paul's Theology of the Cross." Pp. 113-32 in *The Death of Jesus in Early Christianity.* Peabody, Mass.: Hendrickson, 1995.

Castelli, Elizabeth. *Imitating Paul: A Discourse of Power.* Louisville: Westminster/John Knox, 1991.

Chadwick, Henry. "'All Things to All Men' (1 Cor. 9.22)." *New Testament Studies* 1 (1954-55): 261-75.

Collins, Raymond F. *First Corinthians.* Sacra Pagina. Collegeville, Minn.: Liturgical, 1999.

Cone, James H. "An African-American Perspective on the Cross and Suffering." Pp. 48-60 in Yacob Tesfai, ed., *The Scandal of a Crucified World: Perspectives on the Cross and Suffering.* Maryknoll, N.Y.: Orbis, 1994.

Conzelmann, Hans. *1 Corinthians.* Hermeneia. Philadelphia: Fortress, 1975.

Cosgrove, Charles H. *The Cross and the Spirit: A Study in the Argument and Theology of Galatians.* Macon, Ga.: Mercer University Press, 1988.

Cousar, Charles B. *A Theology of the Cross: The Death of Jesus in the Pauline Letters.* Minneapolis: Fortress, 1990.

Culpepper, R. A. "Coworkers in Suffering: Philippians 2:19-30." *Review and Expositor* 77 (1980): 349-58.

Davis, Basil S. "The Meaning of *proegraphē* in the Context of Galatians 3.1." *New Testament Studies* 45 (1999): 194-212.

de Boer, Martinus C. "Paul and Jewish Apocalyptic Eschatology." Pp. 169-90 in Joel Marcus and Marion L. Soards, eds., *Apocalyptic and the New Testament: Essays in Honor of J. Louis Martyn.* JSNTSup 24. Sheffield: Sheffield Academic Press, 1989.

Deidun, T. J. *New Covenant Morality in Paul.* Rome: Biblical Institute Press, 1981.

Deissmann, Adolf. *Paul: A Study in Social and Religious History.* New York: Harper, 1957; orig. 1912, rev. 1926.

Donaldson, Terence L. *Paul and the Gentiles: Remapping the Apostle's Convictional World.* Minneapolis: Fortress, 1997.

Donfried, Karl P. "The Imperial Cults of Thessalonica and Political Conflict in 1 Thessalonians." Pp. 215-23 in Richard A. Horsley, ed. *Paul and Empire: Religion and Power in Roman Imperial Society.* Harrisburg, Pa.: Trinity Press International, 1997.

Droge, Arthur, and J. D. Tabor. *A Noble Death: Suicide and Martyrdom among Christians and Jews in Antiquity.* San Francisco: Harper & Row, 1992.

Duff, Nancy J. "Atonement and the Christian Life: Reformed Doctrine from a Feminist Perspective." *Interpretation* 53 (1999): 21-33.

Dunn, James D. G. *A Commentary on the Epistle to the Galatians.* Black's New Testament Commentaries. London: A. & C. Black, 1993.

————. *The Epistles to the Colossians and Philemon: A Commentary on the Greek Text.* Grand Rapids: Eerdmans, 1996.

————. *Jesus and the Spirit: A Study of the Religious and Charismatic Experience of Jesus and the First Christians as Reflected in the New Testament.* London: S.C.M., 1975. Reprinted Grand Rapids: Eerdmans, 1997.

————. "Once More, *PISTIS CHRISTOU.*" Pp. 61-81 in E. Elizabeth Johnson and David B. Hay, eds., *Pauline Theology,* vol. 4: *Looking Back, Pressing On.* Atlanta: Scholars Press, 1997.

————. *Romans.* Word Biblical Commentary 38A, 38B. 2 vols. Waco, Tex.: Word, 1988.

————. *The Theology of Paul the Apostle.* Grand Rapids: Eerdmans, 1998.

Edwards, James R. *Romans.* NIBC. Peabody, Mass.: Hendrickson, 1992.

Ehrman, Bart D. *The New Testament: A Historical Introduction to the Early Christian Writings.* 2nd ed. New York: Oxford University Press, 2000.

Elliott, Neil. *Liberating Paul: The Justice of God and the Politics of the Apostle.* Maryknoll, N.Y.: Orbis, 1994.

Engberg-Pedersen, Troels. *Paul and the Stoics.* Louisville: Westminster/John Knox, 2000.

Fee, Gordon D. *The First Epistle to the Corinthians.* The New International Commentary on the New Testament. Grand Rapids: Eerdmans, 1987.

————. *God's Empowering Presence: The Holy Spirit in the Letters of Paul.* Peabody, Mass.: Hendrickson, 1994.

————. *Paul, the Spirit, and the People of God.* Peabody, Mass.: Hendrickson, 1996.

————. *Paul's Letter to the Philippians.* The New International Commentary on the New Testament. Grand Rapids: Eerdmans, 1995.

Fitzmyer, Joseph A. *Paul and His Theology: A Brief Sketch.* 2nd ed. Englewood Cliffs, N.J.: Prentice Hall, 1989.

————. *Romans: A New Translation with Introduction and Commentary.* Anchor Bible 33. New York: Doubleday, 1993.

Fowl, Stephen E. "Believing Forms Seeing: Formation for Martyrdom in Philippians." Unpublished manuscript (forthcoming from Eerdmans in a collection of essays on character ethics and biblical interpretation, edited by William Brown).

————. "Christology and Ethics in Philippians 2:5-11." Pp. 140-53 in Ralph P. Martin and Brian J. Dodd, eds., *Where Christology Began: Essays on Philippians 2.* Louisville: Westminster/John Knox, 1998.

————. *The Story of Christ in the Ethics of Paul: An Analysis of the Function of the Hymnic Material in the Pauline Corpus.* JSNTSup 36. Sheffield: JSOT Press, 1990.

Frilingos, Chris. "'For My Child, Onesimus': Paul and Domestic Power in Philemon." *Journal of Biblical Literature* 119 (2000): 91-104.

Fuchs, Joseph. "Basic Freedom and Morality." Pp. 187-98 in Ronald P. Hamel and Kenneth R. Himes, eds., *Introduction to Christian Ethics: A Reader.* New York: Paulist, 1989.

Furnish, Victor Paul. "'He Gave Himself [Was Given] Up . . .': Paul's Use of a Christological Assertion." Pp. 109-21 in Abraham J. Malherbe and Wayne A. Meeks, eds., *The Future of Christology: Essays in Honor of Leander E. Keck.* Minneapolis: Fortress, 1993.

————. *The Love Command in the New Testament.* Nashville: Abingdon, 1972.

————. *II Corinthians.* Anchor Bible 32A. Garden City, N.Y.: Doubleday, 1984.

————. *Theology and Ethics in Paul.* Nashville: Abingdon, 1968.

Georgi, Dieter. "God Turned Upside Down." Pp. 148-57 in Richard A. Horsley, ed., *Paul and Empire: Religion and Power in Roman Imperial Society.* Harrisburg, Pa.: Trinity Press International, 1997.

————. *Theocracy in Paul's Praxis and Theology.* Minneapolis: Fortress, 1991.

Gorman, Michael J. *Elements of Biblical Exegesis: A Basic Guide for Students and Ministers.* Peabody, Mass.: Hendrickson, 2001.

————. "Irreconcilable Differences: The Church Should Divorce the Military." *Christianity Today,* March 6, 2000, pp. 77-78.

————. "The Self, the Lord, and the Other: The Significance of Reflexive Pronoun Constructions in the Letters of Paul, with a Comparison to the 'Discourses' of Epictetus." Ph.D. diss. Princeton Theological Seminary, 1989.

Grant, Robert M., with David Tracy. *A Short History of the Interpretation of the Bible.* 2nd ed. Philadelphia: Fortress, 1984.

Green, Joel B. "Death of Christ." Pp. 146-63 in Gerald F. Hawthorne et al., eds., *Dictionary of Paul and His Letters.* Downers Grove, Ill.: InterVarsity, 1992.

Gritsch, Eric W. "The Church as Institution: From Doctrinal Pluriformity to Magisterial Mutuality." *Journal of Ecumenical Studies* 16 (1979): 448-56.

————. "Defenders of Cruciformity — Detectors of Idolatry: The Case of Sixteenth-Century Restitutionists." *Katallagete* 6 (1977): 10-14.

Grossouw, W. K. *Spirituality of the New Testament.* Trans. Martin W. Schoenberg. St. Louis/London: Herder, 1961.

Hallie, Philip. *Lest Innocent Blood Be Shed: The Story of the Village of Le Chambon and How Goodness Happened There*. New York: Harper, 1979, 1994.

Hanson, Anthony Tyrell. *The Paradox of the Cross in the Thought of St. Paul*. JSNTSup 17. Sheffield: JSOT Press, 1987.

Hauerwas, Stanley M., and William H. Willimon. *The Truth About God: The Ten Commandments in Christian Life*. Nashville: Abingdon, 1999.

Hawthorne, Gerald F. "The Imitation of Christ: Discipleship in Philippians." Pp. 163-79 in Richard N. Longenecker, ed., *Patterns of Discipleship in the New Testament*. Grand Rapids: Eerdmans, 1996.

————. *Philippians*. Word Biblical Commentary 43. Waco, Tex.: Word, 1983.

Hays, Richard B. "Christology and Ethics in Galatians: The Law of Christ." *Catholic Biblical Quarterly* 49 (1987): 268-90.

————. "Crucified with Christ: A Synthesis of the Theology of 1 and 2 Thessalonians, Philemon, Philippians, and Galatians." Pp. 227-46 in Jouette M. Bassler, ed., *Pauline Theology*, vol 1: *Thessalonians, Philippians, Galatians, Philemon*. Minneapolis: Fortress, 1991.

————. *Echoes of Scripture in the Letters of Paul*. New Haven: Yale University Press, 1989.

————. *The Faith of Jesus Christ: An Investigation of the Narrative Substructure of Galatians 3:1–4:11*. SBLDS 56. Chico, Calif.: Scholars Press, 1983.

————. *First Corinthians*. Interpretation. Louisville: Westminster/John Knox: 1997.

————. "Justification." Pp. 1129-33 in David Noel Freedman, ed., *Anchor Bible Dictionary*, vol. 3. New York: Doubleday, 1992.

————. *The Moral Vision of the New Testament: A Contemporary Introduction to New Testament Ethics*. San Francisco: HarperCollins, 1996.

————. "*PISTIS CHRISTOU* and Pauline Theology: What Is at Stake?" Pp. 35-60 in E. Elizabeth Johnson and David B. Hay, eds., *Pauline Theology,*. vol. 4: *Looking Back, Pressing On*. Atlanta: Scholars Press, 1997.

————. "'The Righteous One' as Eschatological Deliverer: A Case Study in Paul's Apocalyptic Hermeneutics." Pp. 191-216 in Joel Marcus and Marion L. Soards, eds., *Apocalyptic and the New Testament: Essays in Honor of J. Louis Martyn*. JSNTSup 24. Sheffield: Sheffield Academic Press, 1989.

Heil, John Paul. *Romans — Paul's Letter of Hope*. Analecta Biblica 112. Rome: Biblical Institute Press, 1987.

Hengel, Martin. *Crucifixion*. Trans. John Bowden. London: S.C.M., 1977.

Hock, Ronald F. *The Social Context of Paul's Ministry: Tentmaking and Apostleship*. Philadelphia: Fortress, 1980.

Holladay, Carl A. "1 Corinthians 13: Paul as Apostolic Paradigm." Pp. 80-98 in D. L. Balch, E. Ferguson, and W. A. Meeks, eds., *Greeks, Romans, and Christians*. Minneapolis: Fortress, 1990.

Hooker, Morna D. "Interchange and Atonement." Pp. 26-41 in *From Adam to Christ: Essays on Paul*. New York/Cambridge: Cambridge University Press, 1990.

————. "Interchange in Christ." Pp. 13-25 in *From Adam to Christ: Essays on Paul*. New York/Cambridge: Cambridge University Press, 1990.

————. "*PISTIS CHRISTOU*." Pp. 165-86 in *From Adam to Christ: Essays on Paul*. New York/Cambridge: Cambridge University Press, 1990.

Hoover, Roy W. "The *Harpagmos* Enigma: A Philological Solution." *Harvard Theological Review* 56 (1971): 95-119.

Horsley, Richard A., ed. *Paul and Empire: Religion and Power in Roman Imperial Society.* Harrisburg, Pa.: Trinity Press International, 1997.

————, ed. *Paul and Politics: Ekklesia, Israel, Imperium, Interpretation.* Harrisburg, Pa.: Trinity Press International, 2000.

————. "Paul's Counter-Imperial Gospel: Introduction." Pp. 140-47 in Richard A. Horsley, ed., *Paul and Empire: Religion and Power in Roman Imperial Society.* Harrisburg, Pa.: Trinity Press International, 1997.

Howard, G. "The Faith of Christ." *Expository Times* 85 (1974): 212-15.

————. "On the Faith of Christ." *Harvard Theological Review* 60 (1967): 459-65.

Hurst, L. D. "Christ, Adam, and Preexistence Revisited." Pp. 84-95 in Ralph P. Martin and Brian J. Dodd, eds., *Where Christology Began: Essays on Philippians 2.* Louisville: Westminster/John Knox, 1998.

Hurtado, Larry W. "Jesus as Lordly Example in Philippians 2.5-11." Pp. 113-26 in Peter Richardson and John C. Hurd, eds., *From Jesus to Paul.* Francis W. Beare Festschrift. Waterloo: Wilfred Laurier University Press, 1984.

John Paul II. *The Gospel of Life* [*Evangelium Vitae*]. New York: Random House, 1995.

Johnson, E. Elizabeth. "Ephesians." Pp. 428-32 in Carol A. Newsom and Sharon H. Ringe, eds., *The Women's Bible Commentary.* Expanded ed. Louisville: Westminster/John Knox, 1998.

Johnson, Luke Timothy. *Living Jesus: Learning the Heart of the Gospel.* New York: HarperSanFrancisco, 1999.

————. *Reading Romans: A Literary and Theological Commentary.* New York: Crossroad, 1997.

————. *Religious Experience in Earliest Christianity: A Missing Dimension of New Testament Studies.* Minneapolis: Fortress, 1998.

————. "Romans 3:21-26 and the Faith of Jesus." *Catholic Biblical Quarterly* 44 (1982): 77-90.

Johnson, Luke Timothy, with Todd C. Penner. *The New Testament Writings: An Interpretation.* Rev. ed. Minneapolis: Fortress, 1999.

Jones, L. Gregory. "A Thirst for God or Consumer Spirituality? Cultivating Disciplined Practices of Being Engaged by God." *Modern Theology* 13 (1997): 3-28.

Käsemann, Ernst. "The Saving Significance of the Death of Jesus in Paul." Pp. 32-59 in *Perspectives on Paul.* Trans. Margaret Kohl. Philadelphia: Fortress, 1971. Reprinted Mifflintown, Pa.: Sigler, 1996.

————. "The Theological Problem Presented by the Motif of the Body of Christ." Pp. 102-21 in *Perspectives on Paul.* Trans. Margaret Kohl. Philadelphia: Fortress, 1971. Reprinted Mifflintown, Pa.: Sigler, 1996.

————. "Worship in Everyday Life: A Note on Romans 12." Pp. 188-95 in *New Testament Questions of Today.* London: S.C.M., 1969.

Kay, James F. "The Word of the Cross at the Turn of the Ages." *Interpretation* 53 (1999): 44-56.

Keck, Leander E. "Biblical Preaching as Divine Wisdom." Pp. 137-56 in John Burke, ed., *A New Look at Preaching.* Wilmington, Del.: Michael Glazier, 1983.

————. "'Jesus' in Romans." *Journal of Biblical Literature* 108 (1989): 443-60.

Kee, Alistair. "The Imperial Cult: The Unmasking of an Ideology." *Scottish Journal of Religious Studies* 6 (1985): 112-28.

Klenicki, Leon. "Toward a Process of Healing: Understanding the Other as a Person of

God." Pp. 1-15 in Leon Klenicki, ed., *Toward a Theological Encounter: Jewish Under-standings of Christianity*. Mahwah, N.J.: Paulist, 1991.

Koch, Kurt. *The Rediscovery of Apocalyptic*. London: S.C.M., 1972.

Koester, Helmut. "Imperial Ideology and Paul's Eschatology in 1 Thessalonians." Pp. 158-66 in Richard A. Horsley, ed., *Paul and Empire: Religion and Power in Roman Imperial Society*. Harrisburg, Pa.: Trinity Press International, 1997.

Kreitzer, L. Joseph. *Jesus and God in Paul's Eschatology*. JSNTSup 19. Sheffield: Sheffield Academic Press, 1987.

————— [Kreitzer, Larry]. "When He at Last Is First: Philippians 2:5-11 and the Exaltation of the Lord." Pp. 111-27 in Ralph P. Martin and Brian J. Dodd, eds., *Where Christology Began: Essays on Philippians 2*. Louisville: Westminster/John Knox, 1998.

Küng, Hans. *On Being a Christian*. Garden City, N.Y.: Doubleday, 1976.

Kurz, William S. "Kenotic Imitation of Paul and of Christ in Philippians 2 and 3." Pp. 103-26 in Fernando F. Segovia, ed., *Discipleship in the New Testament*. Philadelphia: Fortress, 1985.

Lash, Nicholas. "Performing the Scriptures." Pp. 37-46 in *Theology on the Way to Emmaus*. London: S.C.M., 1986.

Lincoln, Andrew. *Ephesians*. Word Biblical Commentary 42. Waco, Tex.: Word, 1990.

Longenecker, Bruce W. "Contours of Covenant Theology in the Post-Conversion Paul." Pp. 125-46 in Richard W. Longenecker, ed., *The Road from Damascus: The Impact of Paul's Conversion on His Life, Thought, and Ministry*. Grand Rapids: Eerdmans, 1997.

—————. *The Triumph of Abraham's God: The Transformation of Identity in Galatians*. Nashville: Abingdon, 1998.

Longenecker, Richard N., ed. *The Road from Damascus: The Impact of Paul's Conversion on His Life, Thought, and Ministry*. Grand Rapids: Eerdmans, 1997.

Lubac, Henri de. *Medieval Exegesis*, vol. 1: *The Four Senses of Scripture*. Trans. Mark Sebanc. Grand Rapids: Eerdmans, 1998.

Luther, Martin. *The Freedom of a Christian*. Pp. 42-85 in John Dillenberger, ed., *Martin Luther: Selections from His Writings*. Garden City, N.Y.: Doubleday, 1961.

—————. "Preface to the Epistle of St. Paul to the Romans." Pp. 19-34 in John Dillenberger, ed., *Martin Luther: Selections from His Writings*. Garden City, N.Y.: Doubleday, 1961.

McGinn, Bernard, and John Meyendorff, eds. *Christian Spirituality: Origins to the Twelfth Century*. New York: Crossroad, 1985.

MacMullen, Ramsay. *Enemies of the Roman Order*. Cambridge, Mass.: Harvard University Press, 1966.

—————. *Roman Social Relations: 50 B.C. to A.D. 284*. New Haven: Yale University Press, 1974.

Malherbe, Abraham. "Gentle as a Nurse." Pp. 35-48 in *Paul and the Popular Philosophers*. Minneapolis: Fortress, 1989.

Malina, Bruce J. *The New Testament World: Insights from Cultural Anthropology*. Rev. ed. Louisville: Westminster/John Knox, 1993.

Martin, Dale B. *The Corinthian Body*. New Haven: Yale University Press, 1995.

—————. *Slavery as Salvation: The Metaphor of Slavery in Pauline Christianity*. New Haven and London: Yale University Press, 1990.

Martin, Ralph P. *A Hymn of Christ: Philippians 2:5-11 in Recent Interpretation and in the Setting of Early Christian Worship*. 3rd ed. Downers Grove, Ill.: InterVarsity, 1997. Earlier editions (1967, 1983) were titled *Carmen Christi*.

————. *Second Corinthians*. Word Biblical Commentary 40. Waco, Tex.: Word, 1986.

Martyn, J. Louis. "Apocalyptic Antinomies." Pp. 111-23 in *Theological Issues in the Letters of Paul*. Edinburgh: T. & T. Clark; Nashville: Abingdon, 1997.

————. "Epistemology at the Turn of the Ages." Pp. 89-110 in *Theological Issues in the Letters of Paul*. Edinburgh: T. & T. Clark; Nashville: Abingdon, 1997.

————. *Galatians: A New Translation with Introduction and Commentary*. Anchor Bible 33A. New York: Doubleday, 1997.

Matera, Frank J. *Galatians*. Sacra Pagina. Collegeville, Minn.: Liturgical, 1992.

————. *New Testament Christology*. Louisville: Westminster/John Knox, 1999.

Mauser, Ulrich. "One God and Trinitarian Language in the Letters of Paul." *Horizons in Biblical Theology* 20 (1998): 99-108.

Meeks, Wayne A. *The First Urban Christians: The Social World of the Apostle Paul*. New Haven: Yale University Press, 1983.

————. "The Man from Heaven in Paul's Letter to the Philippians." Pp. 329-36 in Birger Pearson, ed., *The Future of Early Christianity: Essays in Honor of Helmut Koester*. Minneapolis: Fortress, 1991.

————. *The Moral World of the First Christians*. Philadelphia: Westminster, 1986.

Meyer, Paul W. "The Holy Spirit in the Pauline Letters." *Interpretation* 33 (1979): 3-18.

Mitchell, Margaret M. *Paul and the Rhetoric of Reconciliation*. Tübingen: J. C. B. Mohr (Paul Siebeck), 1991.

Moltmann, Jürgen. *The Crucified God: The Cross of Christ as the Foundation and Criticism of Christian Theology*. Trans. R. A. Wilson and John Bowden. New York: Harper & Row, 1974.

Moltmann-Wendel, Elisabeth. "Is There a Feminist Theology of the Cross?" Pp. 87-98 in Yacob Tesfai, ed., *The Scandal of a Crucified World: Perspectives on the Cross and Suffering*. Maryknoll, N.Y.: Orbis, 1994.

Morray-Jones, C. R. A. "Paradise Revisited (2 Cor 12:1-12): The Jewish Mystical Background of Paul's Apostolate, Part 1: The Jewish Sources." *Harvard Theological Review* 86 (1993): 177-217.

————. "Paradise Revisited (2 Cor 12:1-12): The Jewish Mystical Background of Paul's Apostolate, Part 2: Paul's Heavenly Ascent and Its Significance." *Harvard Theological Review* 86 (1993): 265-92.

Moule, C. F. D. "Further Reflexions on Philippians 2:5-11." Pp. 264-76 in W. W. Gasque and R. P. Martin, eds. *Apostolic History and the Gospel: Biblical and Historical Essays Presented to F. F. Bruce on His 60th Birthday*. Exeter: Paternoster, 1970.

Murphy O'Connor, Jerome. *Paul: A Critical Life*. Oxford/New York: Oxford University Press, 1997.

Neyrey, Jerome H. *Paul, In Other Words: A Cultural Reading of His Letters*. Louisville: Westminster/John Knox, 1990.

O'Brien, Peter. *The Epistle to the Philippians*. Grand Rapids: Eerdmans, 1991.

Penna, Romano. "Problems and Nature of Pauline Mysticism." Pp. 235-73 in *Paul the Apostle: Wisdom and Folly of the Cross*. Trans. Thomas P. Wahl. Collegeville, Minn.: Liturgical, 1996.

Perkins, Pheme. *Love Commands in the New Testament*. New York: Paulist, 1982.

Petersen, Norman R. *Rediscovering Paul: Philemon and the Sociology of Paul's Narrative World*. Philadelphia: Fortress, 1985.

Pickett, Raymond. *The Cross in Corinth: The Social Significance of the Death of Jesus.* JSNTSup 143. Sheffield: Sheffield Academic Press, 1997.

Placher, William C. "Christ Takes Our Place: Rethinking the Atonement." *Interpretation* 53 (1999): 5-20.

Pobee, John S. *Persecution and Martyrdom in the Theology of Paul.* JSNTSup 6. Sheffield: JSOT Press, 1985.

Price, S. R. F. "Rituals and Power." Pp. 47-71 in Richard A. Horsley, ed., *Paul and Empire: Religion and Power in Roman Imperial Society.* Harrisburg, Pa.: Trinity Press International, 1997.

Purvis, Sally. *The Power of the Cross: Foundations for a Christian Feminist Ethic of Community.* Nashville: Abingdon, 1993.

Ramsey, A. M. *God, Christ, and the World.* London: S.C.M., 1969.

Resner, André, Jr. *Preacher and Cross: Person and Message in Theology and Rhetoric.* Grand Rapids: Eerdmans, 1999.

Richardson, Neil. *Paul's Language about God.* JSNTSup 99. Sheffield: Sheffield Academic Press, 1994.

Rowland, Christopher. *The Open Heaven.* New York: Crossroad, 1982.

Sampley, J. Paul. *'And the Two Shall Become One Flesh': A Study of Traditions in Ephesians 5:21-33.* Cambridge: Cambridge University Press, 1971.

———. *Walking Between the Times: Paul's Moral Reasoning.* Minneapolis: Fortress, 1991.

Sanders, E. P. *Paul and Palestinian Judaism.* Philadelphia: Fortress, 1977.

Schneemelcher, Wilhelm, ed. *New Testament Apocrypha.* Trans. R. McL. Wilson. Vol. 2. Philadelphia: Westminster, 1965.

Schüssler Fiorenza, Elisabeth. *Discipleship of Equals: A Critical Feminist Ekklesia-logy of Liberation.* New York: Crossroad, 1993.

———. *In Memory of Her: A Feminist Theological Reconstruction of Christian Origins.* New York: Crossroad, 1983.

Schweitzer, Albert. *The Mysticism of the Apostle Paul.* London: Black, 1931.

Seeley, David. "The Background of the Philippians Hymn." *Journal of Higher Criticism* 1 (1994): 49-72.

———. *The Noble Death: Graeco-Roman Martyrology and Paul's Concept of Salvation.* Sheffield: JSOT Press, 1989.

Segal, Alan. *Paul the Convert: The Apostolate and Apostasy of Saul the Pharisee.* New Haven: Yale University Press, 1990.

Sobrino, Jon. *The Principle of Mercy: Taking the Crucified People from the Cross.* Maryknoll, N.Y.: Orbis, 1994.

Stendahl, Krister. *Paul Among Jews and Gentiles.* Philadelphia: Fortress, 1976.

Stowers, Stanley K. "Friends and Enemies in the Politics of Heaven." Pp. 105-21 in Jouette M. Bassler, ed., *Pauline Theology,* vol. 1: *Thessalonians, Philippians, Galatians, Philemon.* Minneapolis: Fortress, 1991.

———. *A Rereading of Romans: Justice, Jews and Gentiles.* New Haven: Yale University Press, 1994.

Stuart, Elizabeth. "Love Is . . . Paul." *The Expository Times* 102 (1991): 264-66.

Sumney, Jerry L. "Paul's 'Weakness': An Integral Part of His Conception of Apostleship." *Journal for the Study of the New Testament* 52 (1993): 71-91.

Talbert, Charles. *Learning through Suffering: The Educational Value of Suffering in the New Testament and Its Milieu.* Collegeville, Minn.: Liturgical, 1991.

————. *Reading John: A Literary and Theological Commentary on the Fourth Gospel and the Johannine Epistles.* New York: Crossroad, 1992.

Tannehill, Robert C. *Dying and Rising with Christ: A Study in Pauline Theology.* Berlin: Alfred Töpelmann, 1966.

Tesfai, Yacob, ed. *The Scandal of a Crucified World: Perspectives on the Cross and Suffering.* Maryknoll, N.Y.: Orbis, 1994.

Theissen, Gerd. *Psychological Aspects of Pauline Theology.* Philadelphia: Fortress, 1987.

Thompson, Marianne Meye. *The Promise of the Father: Jesus and God in the New Testament.* Louisville: Westminster/John Knox, 2000.

Tobin, Thomas H. *The Spirituality of Paul.* Message of Biblical Spirituality 4. Collegeville, Minn.: Liturgical, 1991.

Tomlin, Graham. *The Power of the Cross: Theology and the Death of Christ in Paul, Luther and Pascal.* Carlisle, U.K.: Paternoster, 1999.

Tuckett, Christopher M. "The Corinthians Who Say There Is No Resurrection of the Dead (1 Cor 15,12)." Pp. 247-75 in R. Bieringer, ed., *The Corinthian Correspondence.* Bibliotheca Ephemeridum Theologicarum Lovaniensium 125. Leuven: University Press, 1996.

Volf, Miroslav. *Exclusion and Embrace: A Theological Exploration of Identity, Otherness, and Reconciliation.* Nashville: Abingdon, 1996.

Wansink, C. S. *Chained in Christ.* JSNTSup 130. Sheffield: Sheffield Academic Press, 1996.

Wedderburn, A. J. M. *Baptism and Resurrection: Studies in Pauline Theology against Its Graeco-Roman Background.* Tübingen: J. C. B. Mohr (Paul Siebeck), 1987.

————. *The Reasons for Romans.* Minneapolis: Fortress, 1988.

Wengst, Klaus. *Pax Romana and the Peace of Jesus Christ.* Trans. John Bowden. Philadelphia: Fortress, 1987.

White, John L. *The Apostle of God: Paul and the Promise of Abraham.* Peabody, Mass.: Hendrickson, 1999.

Williams, David J. *Paul's Metaphors: Their Context and Character.* Peabody, Mass.: Hendrickson, 1999.

Williams, Delores S. *Sisters in the Wilderness: The Challenge of Womanist God-Talk.* Maryknoll, N.Y.: Orbis, 1993.

Williams, Sam K. "Again *Pistis Christou.*" *Catholic Biblical Quarterly* 49 (1987): 431-47.

————. *Galatians.* Abingdon New Testament Commentaries. Nashville: Abingdon, 1997.

————. *Jesus' Death as Saving Event.* HDR 2. Missoula, Mont.: Scholars Press, 1975.

Willis, W. L. "Apostolic Apologia? The Form and Function of 1 Corinthians 9." *Journal for the Study of the New Testament* 24 (1985): 33-48.

Wink, Walter. *Naming the Powers: The Language of Power in the New Testament.* Philadelphia: Fortress, 1984.

Witherington III, Ben. *Conflict and Community in Corinth: A Socio-Rhetorical Commentary on 1 and 2 Corinthians.* Grand Rapids: Eerdmans, 1995.

————. *Grace in Galatia: A Commentary on Paul's Letter to the Galatians.* Grand Rapids: Eerdmans, 1998.

————. *The Paul Quest: The Renewed Search for the Jew of Tarsus.* Downers Grove, Ill.: InterVarsity, 1998.

————. *Paul's Narrative Thought World: The Tapestry of Tragedy and Triumph.* Louisville: Westminster/John Knox, 1994.

Wood, Susan. "Is Philippians 2:5-11 Incompatible with Feminist Concerns?" *Pro Ecclesia* 6 (1997): 172-83.

Wright, N. T. *The Climax of the Covenant: Christ and the Law in Pauline Theology.* Edinburgh: T. & T. Clark, 1991; Minneapolis: Fortress, 1993.

————. *Jesus and the Victory of God.* Minneapolis: Fortress, 1996.

————. "Monotheism, Christology, and Ethics: 1 Corinthians 8." Pp. 120-36 in *The Climax of the Covenant: Christ and the Law in Pauline Theology.* Edinburgh: T. & T. Clark, 1991; Minneapolis: Fortress, 1993.

————. *The New Testament and the People of God.* Minneapolis: Fortress, 1992.

————. *What Saint Paul Really Said: Was Paul of Tarsus the Real Founder of Christianity?* Grand Rapids: Eerdmans, 1997.

Yoder, John Howard. "Armaments and Eschatology." *Studies in Christian Ethics* 1 (1988): 43-61.

Zanker, Paul. "The Power of Images." Pp. 72-86 in Richard A. Horsley, ed., *Religion and Power in Roman Imperial Society.* Harrisburg, Pa.: Trinity Press International, 1997.

Ziesler, J. A. *The Meaning of Righteousness in Paul: A Linguistic and Theological Enquiry.* SNTSMS 20. Cambridge: Cambridge University Press, 1972.

INDEX OF MODERN AUTHORS

INDEX OF SCRIPTURE REFERENCES
AND OTHER ANCIENT SOURCES

417